CHICANA
MOVIDAS

CHICANA MOVIDAS

NEW NARRATIVES of ACTIVISM and FEMINISM in the MOVEMENT ERA

edited by
Dionne Espinoza
María Eugenia Cotera
Maylei Blackwell

University of Texas Press ✦ Austin

Copyright © 2018 by the University of Texas Press
All rights reserved
Printed in the United States of America
First edition, 2018
Second paperback printing, 2019

Requests for permission to reproduce material from this work should be sent to:
    Permissions
    University of Texas Press
    P.O. Box 7819
    Austin, TX 78713–7819
    utpress.utexas.edu/rp-form

♾ The paper used in this book meets the minimum requirements of ANSI/NISO Z39.48–1992 (R1997) (Permanence of Paper).

Library of Congress Cataloging-in-Publication Data

Names: Espinoza, Dionne, editor. | Cotera, María Eugenia, editor. | Blackwell, Maylei, editor.
Title: Chicana movidas : new narratives of activism and feminism in the movement era / edited by Dionne Espinoza, María Eugenia Cotera, and Maylei Blackwell.
Description: First edition. | Austin : University of Texas Press, 2018. | Includes bibliographical references and index.
Identifiers: LCCN 2017048975
    ISBN 978-1-4773-1559-0 (pbk. : alk. paper)
    ISBN 978-1-4773-1682-5 (library e-book)
    ISBN 978-1-4773-1683-2 (nonlibrary e-book)
Subjects: LCSH: Mexican American women. | Women political activists—United States—History—20th century. | Feminism—United States—History—20th century.
Classification: LCC E184.M5 C395 2018 | DDC 305.48/86872073—dc23
LC record available at https://lccn.loc.gov/2017048975

doi:10.7560/315583

CONTENTS

ACKNOWLEDGMENTS

This book represents both a long journey and a labor of love. It is the product of over five years of collaboration, shared vision, and dialogue among three scholars who have devoted their careers to visibilizing women of color, indigenous, and Chicana/Latina lives and stories. The numerous virtual and in-person meetings—often wedged into conferences or research trips—where we willed this project into existence have become part of the *ritmo de nuestras vidas*. We stole time from our individual research projects and institutional demands for daylong work sessions, editorial meetings, and many phone conferences in places like Oakland, Los Angeles, San Diego, Ann Arbor, and Denver. In the years that it took to bring this volume into being, each of us also experienced a number of personal life changes, births, and deaths, but we still stayed with the vision of seeing this collaboration through to the book you have in your hands. In the process we made community. This community includes the authors who contributed to this volume and many more who assisted in its creation. Linda Garcia-Merchant was an early collaborator on the project. We reluctantly let her off the hook to begin a doctoral program in English at the University of Nebraska.

When we first sat down to brainstorm our vision for the anthology, one of our goals was to create an intergenerational dialogue among those who lived the stories—the activists who made this history possible—and the scholars who have dedicated themselves to documenting and analyzing those histories. We wanted to include community researchers and scholars at all levels of their journeys from graduate students to new faculty and mid-career colleagues. We realized this goal and feel our lives and the book itself are richer for it. We want to thank all of our contributors for staying with us on this long path toward publication and especially for their passion, dedication, and excellent work.

We want to offer a special thank you to the individuals who provided much-needed assistance with the technical and logistical dimensions of this project, especially Isabel Millán, who was our first graduate assistant and is now a tenure-track professor; Hannah Noel, who helped with communication between the editors and contributors early on in the process; and Audrey Silvestre, who is also involved in her own editorial and publication projects with Third Woman Press while pursuing her doctorate in Chicana and Chicano studies at UCLA. We especially wish to thank senior editor Kerry Webb as well as Lynne Chapman and Angelica Lopez-Torres at the University of Texas Press for their dedication to seeing this volume through to completion. We also wish to acknowledge funding and support from the following sources: the Chicana por mi Raza Digital Memory Collective, the UCLA Chicano Studies Research Center, the UCLA Institute of American Cultures, and the California State University, Los Angeles, College of Arts and Letters, Office of the Dean.

Finally, we offer our gratitude and never-ending respect to the many women at the heart of this volume, whose intellectual labor, commitment, and insight have shaped our understanding of what it means to do this work. They are our *comadres* in struggle. We offer this volume as a testament to their enduring impact on our lives.

CHICANA
MOVIDAS

MOVEMENTS, MOVIMIENTOS, AND MOVIDAS

MARÍA COTERA, MAYLEI BLACKWELL,
AND DIONNE ESPINOZA

We have not one movement but many. Our political, literary, and artistic movements are discarding the patriarchal model of the hero/leader leading the rank and file. Ours are individual and small group movidas, *unpublicized* movimientos—*movements not of media stars or popular authors but of small groups or single mujeres, many of whom have not written books or spoken at national conferences.*

—GLORIA ANZALDÚA, *MAKING FACE/MAKING SOUL*

The 1960s and 1970s were times of great political upheaval and social transformation across the globe. During this period, Mexican American youth in the United States developed a new and powerful form of political consciousness they called "Chicanismo." Part of a worldwide youth revolt in the 1960s, their calls for "Chicano liberation" responded to economic inequality, everyday and institutional racism, and the increasingly militant struggle to end the Vietnam War. Within mass-based organizations, through murals and artistic practices, in community-based organizations or small consciousness-raising groups, Chicanas were on the front lines of forging these new cultures of rebellion. Women played significant roles in the major mobilizations and organizations that coalesced into what is now understood historiographically as the Chicano movement era, including both well-known movement formations—like the United Farm Workers, the Crusade for Justice, the land grant movement, and La Raza Unida Party—and numerous regional and national initiatives. Moving within and between multiple sites of struggle, they challenged conventional notions of oppositional subjectivity and created their own, specifically Chicana, praxis of resistance. As Chicanas built on what they learned in multiple movement spaces, they also forged a liberation practice that was shaped by an emergent analysis of the multivalent nature of oppression. Enacting a new kind of *política* (politics) at the intersection of race, class, gender, and sexuality, they developed innovative concepts, tactics, and methodologies that in turn generated new theories, art forms, organizational spaces, and strategies of alliance. This is the praxis documented in *Chicana Movidas: New Narratives of Activism and Feminism in the Movement Era*.

In her introduction to *Making Face/Making Soul*, Gloria Anzaldúa articulates the difference between the praxis (theory/practice) of women of color and the grand narratives of "movement" and *movimiento* that have structured both popular and scholarly conceptions of social change. Anzaldúa's attentiveness to the minor and the provisional, to the small acts of *rebeldía* that reshape movement discourses and practices from the inside out—and especially her articulation of the shifting grounds upon which women of color stage their strategies for social change—offers a fruitful critical frame for scholars who wish to uncover the central yet still largely unexplored terrain of Chicana feminist *movidas* during the movement years.[1]

In conventional understandings, a *movida* can describe multiple kinds of "moves," from those undertaken in games and on dance floors to those that take more subversive forms like forbidden social encounters, underground economies, and political maneuvers. For this reason *movida* often carries with it connotations of not only the strategic and tactical but also the undercover, the dissident, the illicit—that which is not part of approved and publicly acknowledged political strategies, histories, and economic and social relations. When understood as a mode of submerged and undercover activity, a *movida* operates as both the generative "other" of what is visible, accredited, and sanctioned and as a strategy of subversion. Within this constellation of meanings, *movidas* are outside of the specular range of large-scale political and social relations. Enacted in backrooms and bedrooms, hallways and kitchens, they are collective and individual maneuvers, undertaken in a context of social mobilization, that seek to work within, around, and between the positionings, ideologies, and practices of publicly visible social relations. Taking up Anzaldúa's conceptual thread in her book *Methodology of the Oppressed*, Chela Sandoval identifies *movidas* as a repertoire of "revolutionary maneuvers" and "technologies" that "grasp meaning—transforming and moving it on both sides [. . .], a political site for the third meaning, that obtuse shimmering of signification that glances through every binary opposition."[2] The essays in this anthology track an archive of resistance to reveal a broader women of color praxis articulated and mobilized in and between the movements, actions, and organizations that have come to define in retrospect the political narratives of the 1960s and 1970s.

Our focus on *movidas* as a submerged technology of struggle is not meant to suggest that Chicana activists were not key participants in the major events, planning meetings, and organizational spaces of the Chicano movement. Rather, centering Chicana *movidas* illuminates a multimodal engagement with movement politics that included acts of everyday labor and support as well as strategic and sometimes subversive interventions within movement spaces. As political actors who were multiply constituted by intersecting social, economic, and political forces, Chicanas developed and deployed their own political and cultural technologies to navigate the multiple fronts of struggle in which they were engaged. Through these tactical *movidas*, they named oppressions that had been ignored, subordinated, or not perceived, and they ultimately identified and challenged the marginalization of their communities by outlining the ways in which gender, race, class, and sexuality were mutually constituted. They also opened up spaces for different approaches to organizing with other women and created new counterpublics in which they could further develop their aesthetic, theoretical, and political practices. This volume excavates the complex history of *movidas* that collectively form a Chicana political, aesthetic, and theoretical praxis in the movement years—a praxis that gave rise to a field of knowledge that crossed the boundaries of Chicano studies, feminist theory, and queer theory to generate a new way of thinking about oppression and resistance: Chicana feminist studies.

Much like the "gear shifting" of Chela Sandoval's "differential subject," the subversive, transitory, and transactional movement of Chicana *movidas* destabilizes normative practices and ideologies insofar as these practices and ideologies enact relations of subordination, inequality, or invisibilization. As "minor" strategies and tactics embedded within and between larger movements, Chicana *movidas* are rarely included in conventional histories of social movements, which all too often structure their accounts of the past on "major" figures, events, and political organizations. For this reason, shifting the critical optic from "movements" to *movidas* is itself a theoretical *movida*, one that uncovers and makes manifest the varying strategies through which Chicanas worked to shape multiple social movements from the margins. Notwithstanding their impact on movement organizing and their continued relevance to theories of social change, these deeply consequential *movidas* have remained at the margins of movement historiography for far too long. Our critical and curatorial *movida* is to move these theoretical insights, tactical interventions, and political activities from the margin to the center of analysis so that we may gain a richer and more complete understanding of the everyday actors and unrecognized leaders who shaped the political landscape of the movement years.

Projects of historical recovery like the one enacted in the pages of this book present scholars with multiple methodological, conceptual, and interpretive challenges. How does one move historical subjects and their technologies of resistance from the margins to the center, especially when their stories are mostly absent from both the archive and the secondary literature? What operations, techniques, and narrative *movidas* are required to excavate this history and to mine its insights? Taking our inspiration from the methodological and conceptual innovations—the *movidas*—of the Chicanas documented in this volume, we propose that such an effort necessitates a shift from a linear vision of movement trajectories to one that maps the heterogeneity and networked connectivities of Chicana praxis in the movement years.[3]

Mapping *movidas* is a technique for reading against the grain of dominant historiography in order to examine the array of political, social, analytic, and aesthetic strategies that Chicanas mobilized to imagine and enact collective social change.[4] It requires us to question commonsense ideas about social movements and to work within (and against) conventional historical accounts of the movement years to upend the logics of remembrance that exile women of color to the historical margins. It means generating our own strategies for reading beyond the usual suspects, spaces, events, and organizational narratives that have shaped our understanding of the past and looking to the interstices and margins, the places where Chicana *movidas* made social change in small and big ways.

While we are invested in understanding broader movement histories and critical genealogies of participation, conflict, and collaboration, we have focused this collection less on building a comprehensive account of Chicana participation in movement activities than on excavating the stunning heterogeneity of collective forms of praxis generated within, between, and outside of various movements for social change. These experiences and tactics shaped the emergence of Chicana feminism as a *field of resistance* constituted by alternative networks, counterpublics, and countermemories. While capturing the entire breadth and depth of these activities and strategic deployments would be impossible, in *Chicana Movidas* we offer scholars, teachers, and students a glimpse into the complexities of Chicana activism in the movement era and at the same time open up a much-needed conversation about contemporary Chicana feminist thought and its relation to the activities and interventions of an earlier generation of Chicana thinkers.

This is a collection of essays that each of us, at one point or another, wished existed: one that destabilizes conventional narratives of what happened in the Chicano movement and women's movement and pushes against the conceptual silos that keep accounts of these movements (and other New Left movements) separated into discrete historical trajectories. The essays collected in this volume document a series of tactics, spaces, and ideological interventions emblematic of the vast array of Chicana *movidas* for social transformation. Collectively, they provide an interdisciplinary and transgenerational perspective on Chicana feminist praxis in multiple movement spaces. For example, while the volume includes essays by established and emerging scholars from a variety of disciplinary fields (history, religious studies, anthropology, media studies, creative writing), added to this mix are new essays by an earlier generation of Chicana feminists like Anna NietoGomez, Olga Talamante, Inés Hernández-Ávila, Osa Hidalgo de la Riva, and Martha Cotera, who offer not only critical firsthand perspectives on the organizations, individuals, and events that shaped Chicana *movidas* in the 1960s and 1970s but also their own historical analyses of the events and organizations in which they were involved. In many ways, this collection brings to the surface a diffuse yet networked alternative archive that has been exiled, until now, to spaces of extrainstitutional memory.

This alternative archive and the essays through which it speaks challenge the ways in which social movement spaces and histories have been conceptualized, from the wave model that has shaped historiography on feminist mobilizations to the focus on only male-dominated organizations in Chicano movement scholarship—a focus that generates and sustains multiple gender, temporal, and regional exclusions. Indeed, many of the essays included in this volume press productively against the long-standing conceptual boundaries of more traditional frames for understanding the period. For example, in their focus on Chicana mobilizations outside of the US Southwest, several contributors to our collection challenge the spatial logic through which the Chicano movement has been conceptualized in conventional historical accounts. By including essays on women in the Chicano movement in the Pacific Northwest and the Midwest, we aim to expose readers to important emerging scholarship on the network of activists, organizations, conferences, and publications that constituted Chicana feminism on a national scale while also remaining attentive to the particular regional *movidas* that Chicanas undertook in response to a movement in which they were doubly marginalized as women and as political subjects who did not fit in the spatial logics of the Aztlán imaginary.[5]

This respatialization of the Chicano movement also expands the temporal frame that has been based on a historiographic consensus that the Chicano movement started in the late 1960s and ended by 1975. Several essays in this volume depart from that chronology altogether, exploring linkages between early articulations of Chicana feminism and the theoretical and political insights of the generation of feminists that rose to prominence in the 1980s with the publication of books like *This Bridge Called My Back* and *Borderlands/La Frontera*.[6] Such transgenerational networks illustrate how dominant organizing logics in social movement historiography may obscure the complex and shifting ways in which identities intersect and thereby erase the strategic identifications of activists who foregrounded one identity over others at different points in their activist trajectories. For example, Chicana lesbians, many of whom were cultural and political leaders who often organized under the banner of Chicana or women's rights in the 1970s, would later produce creative scholarship that would define Chicana lesbian feminist theory in the 1980s and 1990s.

Uncovering Chicanas' strategic mobilizations of identity—and the ways in which they shifted between identifications with women's liberation, Chicano liberation, "Third World" liberation, sexual liberation, and workers rights movements—requires that scholars look beyond the apparent absence of "out" lesbian voices in the archive of the 1960s and 1970s and develop a broader understanding of how lesbians of color were often multiply insurgent subjects who transferred their knowledge from one movement space—the UFW, for example—into other movement spaces such as women's art collectives. Indeed, many gays and lesbians were active in Chicano movement organizations, sometimes even in leadership positions, but these spaces were not always conducive to outward self-identification, forcing some activists to negotiate their identities with comrades inside movement spaces. While some Chicana lesbians simply chose not to center sexuality as a prominent issue at certain points in their organizing, for others the marginalization and even demonization of lesbian identity within some political spaces prompted their distancing from the movement, but these underground *movidas* nevertheless shaped movement practices and cultures. Without understanding the tactical nature of the strategically shifting identity and consciousness deployed by Chicanas, one could assume that the "lesbian" referenced in archival documents—primarily as an anti-feminist disciplining mechanism used against Chicana feminists—meant that there were no lesbians in the Chicano movement. In this collection we challenge that narrative to show that Chicana feminist lesbians were activists who participated in a number of the major efforts of the movement, from the farmworkers movement to La Raza Unida Party and beyond, often as bridging figures to the next phase in the Chicana feminist movement. Chicana lesbian acts of transfer and translation across multiple movement spaces and temporal generations drew from a living archive of embodied knowledge developed on various fronts of struggle. The "repertoire of resistance" they developed to address overlapping oppressions ultimately shaped the foundational praxis of what we now call "intersectionality."[7]

These examples demonstrate how something as simple as an established historical chronology such as locating the "movement years" from the late 1960s to 1975 can frame how we understand a period and its implications, not to mention the historical actors who properly belong to it. While we understand and appreciate the need for a cut-off point for the movement era—Without such conceptual bracketing how do scholars engage the distinctiveness of a particular historical moment?—as women of color scholars we also understand how conceptual boundaries like periodization are generated and perpetuated in the focus on some stories over others. Scholarship on the long civil rights movement has demonstrated that the radicalism of the 1960s and '70s has direct organizational and ideological links to organizing in the Chicano context in the 1940s, and we carry this conversation forward in this collection. Here, we shift the center of our stories about the movement years and demonstrate how such a shift necessarily transforms the conceptual boundaries and explanatory logics that have generated a significant and continuing pattern of exclusion. By mapping the *movidas* of Chicana feminism across a broad constellation of activities, interventions, and social spaces, this volume not only complicates our understanding of the key organizations and activities of the movement years, it also reveals the conceptual limitations of conventional movement historiography.

HISTORIOGRAPHIC MOVIDAS

Notwithstanding contemporary reevaluations of the movement years, there can be little doubt that the historiography of the Chicano movement, with few exceptions, has been characterized by the absence of Chicana activist visibility.[8] While *Chicana Movidas* is part of a larger and ongoing scholarly reconsideration of the

Chicano movement period,[9] its genealogy can be traced to a decades-long effort to document Chicana history. This volume would not have been possible without the pathbreaking work of women of color historians and critics who have excavated the terrain before us and opened up a space for the articulation and critical examination of Chicana feminist praxis in the 1960s and 1970s.[10] Among the key markers that suggested a major shift in the historiography of the Chicano movement was the 1990 essay by Alma M. García titled "The Development of Chicana Feminist Discourse, 1970–1980."[11] García followed that groundbreaking essay with a 1997 text that might be considered a companion volume, *Chicana Feminist Thought: The Basic Historical Writings*, a compendium of published writing and speeches by Chicanas in the 1960s and 1970s.[12] The importance of García's historiographic *movida* in *Chicana Feminist Thought* cannot be overstated. In making accessible a collection of women's writing from the Chicano movement era, García's book demonstrated the incredible range of articulations, debates, analyses, and positions of Chicana activists during the period; it represented a proliferation of discourse that had been largely ignored in earlier books on the Chicano movement that in most cases offered only token mentions of women. No longer would scholars and teachers have to search institutional archives to track down the writings referenced here and there in the few published essays on Chicana feminism and movement activism. We now had a volume of works that spoke to the rich and dynamic *voces* and *movidas* of Chicana activists.

Following on García's important intervention, encounters with the Chicana archive have broken many silences and disrupted consensus narratives of the his/herstoriography, not only through the methods of oral history, archival recovery, and visual culture analysis but also through interpretive practices that reclaim those spaces that single-identity narratives have left out—spaces that speak to Chicana identities at the intersection of multiple oppressions. The works of critical feminist thinkers like Chela Sandoval, Norma Alarcón, Dolores Delgado Bernal, Yolanda Broyles-González, and Maylei Blackwell have challenged the hegemonic narratives that have structured our understandings of the past, whether they be narratives of the women's movement like the wave model, the "great man" narratives of the Chicano movement, or narratives of feminist theory that reduce and appropriate the key insights of women of color praxis.[13] Their analyses call for careful examination of how consensus and hegemonic narratives are constructed and what they leave out—even as they teach us to be wary of constructing yet another hegemonic narrative within/about Chicana feminism or Chicana activism in the movement years.

A number of Chicana scholars have also proposed a variety of routes of Chicana activist involvement in the Chicano movement era. Historian Vicki Ruiz integrated a chapter on women in the Chicano movement entitled "La Nueva Chicana" into her sweeping historical account of 100 years, *From Out of the Shadows: Mexican Women in Twentieth-Century America* (1998), which begins with the migratory journeys of the 1900s and ends with the community organizing of the

1990s.[14] By centering the participation of Chicanas within the Chicano movement and making their work essential to understanding Chicana/o history, *From Out of the Shadows* opened up a space for other examinations of Chicana activism in the movement years. For example, in her scholarship on women who worked within the Centro de Acción Social Autonomo (CASA) in Los Angeles, the historian Marisela R. Chávez put forward the stories of Chicana activists who worked within a Marxist organization and whose notions of social change were global in scope.[15] Dionne Espinoza also engaged the organizational case study approach in her article on the participation of women in the East Los Angeles Brown Beret chapter, a narrative that challenged the existing stereotype that only men had been members of this organization.[16] She followed this analysis with another incisive organizational study of Chicanas in the Texas Raza Unida Party (RUP) that explored the ways in which women helped build the party despite a top-down leadership structure.[17] Both Chávez and Espinoza highlighted women's contributions to these organizations as well as the ways in which women created solidarities that empowered them within these groups. Contributing to this wave of reassessment, scholars like Dolores Delgado Bernal, in her study of women in the East Los Angeles blowouts, and Yolanda Broyles-González, in her 1994 study of women involved in Teatro Campesino, argued that to accurately understand Chicanas in movement history we must shift the paradigms of leadership and challenge the discursive frameworks that have relegated women to the margins.[18] Lorena Oropeza and Dionne Espinoza enacted precisely this kind of shift in their edited compendium of the journalism of Enriqueta Vásquez, a Colorado- and New Mexico–based activist. Vásquez had started her activism with Los Voluntarios and the Crusade for Justice and then moved to northern New Mexico, where she wrote a column, "Despierten Hermanos," for *El Grito del Norte*, the newspaper that Elizabeth "Betita" Martínez cofounded with Beverly Axelrod to document the land-grant struggles in northern New Mexico. Oropeza and Espinoza's edited volume of Vásquez's writings centered themes of Chicana identity in relation to indigenous identities, land rights, anticommercialism, peace, and international and Third World spheres.

Vásquez and Martínez were not the only Chicanas who contributed to the development of a vibrant (and frequently feminist) print culture during the Chicano movement. In her 2005 book on Chicana/o resistance to the Vietnam War, *¡Raza Si! ¡Guerra No!*, Lorena Oropeza documented how two Chicanas, Lea Ybarra and Nina Genera, used print media to actively organize their communities in "one of the [Chicano] movement's longest running anti-draft efforts."[19] The bilingual pamphlet Ybarra and Genera wrote, printed, and distributed to young Chicanos in front of Selective Service offices, "La Batalla Está Aquí! Chicanos and the War" (1972), stands as an example of Chicanas' strategic uses of print media in their organizing work. Likewise, Maylei Blackwell has excavated and theorized Chicana journalism and the formation of a "Chicana counterpublic" as a key *movida* that was not confined to the movement era.[20] In Los Angeles,

Chicana print culture built on the extensive, long-running vision and work of Francisca Flores, cofounder of the League of Mexican American Women and editor of the journals *Carta Editorial* and *Regeneración*. Chicana writers and activists like Anna NietoGomez, who has an essay on Francisca Flores in this volume, and Corinne Sánchez, among others, followed Flores's example and published their own newspaper (*Las Hijas de Cuauhtémoc*) and, later, a nationally recognized Chicana feminist journal, *Encuentro Femenil*.

Blackwell's *¡Chicana Power! Contested Histories of Feminism in the Chicano Movement*, the only published monograph to date that focuses entirely on Chicana activism during the 1960s and 1970s, proposes a new methodology of historical storytelling that she terms "retrofitted memory." Blackwell tells the story of Las Hijas de Cuauhtémoc: from their difficult experiences on the campus at Long Beach State University, to their community organizing in Los Angeles, to their struggles to make sense of the political conflicts at the first national Chicana conference, held in Houston in 1971. She demonstrates how the print culture that they created to theorize these experiences called attention to women's historic role in social change and flipped the movement script that relegated Chicanas to the margins, or framed them as traitors for trying to organize women. Through this narrative, Blackwell explores a practice of countermemory that reaches back to examine the Mexican and transnational roots of Chicana feminisms and strategically redeploys "fragments of older histories that have been disjunctured by colonial practices of organizing historical knowledge or by masculine renderings of history that disappear women's political involvement."[21] Because such historical practices fail to engage an intersectional understanding of power and oppression, they cannot apprehend the nature of "multiple feminist insurgencies"— the tactics through which Chicanas, as multiply constituted subjects, work in and between movements even as they engage various fronts of struggle in one movement, such as struggles around gender and sexuality. Nor can they see the exclusions from other movement spaces that often produce the kinds of Chicana *movidas* that are documented in this volume. Blackwell proposes her own *movida* to challenge these logics of exclusion and uncover the Chicana counterpublics they erase. Borrowing from the DJ tactics of mixing and spinning the historical record, *¡Chicana Power!* offers a nonlinear and anticolonial approach to Chicana her/story/telling that lays the groundwork for more effectively tracing Chicana *movidas* and their counterpublics.[22]

Ongoing research projects have enriched and expanded this field of inquiry. For example, Dionne Espinoza's multisited examination of women's participation in three major Chicano movement organizations—the Crusade for Justice, La Raza Unida Party, and El Movimiento Estudiantil Chicano de Aztlán—spans various regions and diverse political and ideological formations and has increased the breadth and comparative knowledge of women's activism within many of the Chicano movement's major organizations as well as less well-known formations in which activists developed new, innovative forms of Chicana consciousness.

Espinoza's work contributes important analytics to other ongoing research initiatives that are also building the field, like María Cotera and Linda Garcia Merchant's Chicana por mi Raza Digital Memory Collective, an online collection of Chicana oral histories and personal archives that not only offers scholars, students, and community organizations access to new archival sources but also proposes a new way of thinking about Chicana archival praxis. Cotera and Garcia Merchant enact their own archival *movida* in cyberspace, deploying the democratizing possibilities enabled by "the digital turn" to expand on Blackwell's DJ tactics and encourage a new generation of scholarship on Chicanas in the movement era.

These monographs and research projects respond to one of the challenges of writing Chicanas into the historiography of the Chicano movement: the fact that they were all too often the invisible subjects of the collective, a conceptualization of community organizing intended to democratize the labor of movement building by not listing an individual name next to an article, photograph, or agenda item. In the context of the patriarchal relations governing many movement structures and labor relations, such collectivizing impulses often erased women's strategic, philosophical, and organizational contributions to movement activities. Indeed, the famous feminist slogan "Anonymous was a woman" is borne out in our many conversations with women who made contributions as activists, editors, journalists, and photographers but whose names have been left out of the archive. This may explain why historians tend not to interview women and continue to claim that there were no women leaders in the Chicano movement.

Pushing against this assumption, scholars of Chicana activism have shown that Chicana contributions to *movimiento* initiatives did not just involve the labor of organizing, mobilizing, and building community but also the intellectual labor of writing and producing Chicano newspapers and the aesthetic labor of imagining new subjectivities. We know from many interviews with women who worked on movement publications that even though they often wrote several stories or produced photojournalism, they were seldom given bylines or photo credits. This lack of recognition under the guise of collectivism structured an absence into the Chicano print culture of the day as well as in the archival record to which contemporary scholars turn in writing their accounts of the Chicano movement. Such absences in the record replicate the invisibilization of Chicana labor in the 1960s and 1970s and reinforce the need for oral historians and researchers to talk directly to movement activists, explore extrainstitutional archives, and perhaps more importantly, ask the right questions of their sources. More often than not, excavations of Chicana memory have been undertaken from the ground up, with scholars tracking down sources, sifting through personal archives, and conducting lengthy interviews and oral histories.

In many ways the present collection is an enactment of these kinds of archival *movidas*, one that expands the notion of "archive" to include not only documents (newspapers, letters, reports, and photographs) but also the embodied knowledges offered in firsthand accounts of participants in social movements. While other modes of producing historical knowledge use oral history, this Chicana methodological *movida* relies on a deep interpersonal engagement with the archive of embodied knowledge—an engagement that often involves long-term collaboration with primary subjects. Spending time in kitchens and living rooms and other spaces outside the institutional locations that otherwise shape our scholarly work, the contributors to this volume have in many cases developed personal relationships with their sources. As participants entrust materials and memories to them that are not available in institutional settings, a different kind of relationship between scholars and their objects of study take shape, and a different archival landscape emerges. Even as the contents of a recuperated archive challenge conventional knowledge about the movement years, the very process of its recovery demands a different set of scholarly commitments, practices, and accountabilities from those who would excavate its meanings. Doing this work, in other words, has required us to generate our own *movidas* and to rethink conventional scholarly scripts, both methodological and theoretical. It has moved us into an unknown but not entirely uncharted territory. This collection should therefore be understood as both a corrective to the feminist and Chicano historical imaginaries that have largely structured our knowledge about the movement era and an invitation to reimagine the archive, its meanings, and our scholarly relation to it.

MAPPING MOVIDAS

New approaches to understanding the past and new conceptual frames of analysis shift our historiographic gaze to the insurgencies weaving below the surface of multiple movements and attune us to the minor and interstitial acts that comprised Chicana technologies of resistance in the movement years. Mapping *movidas* is a mode of historical analysis that allows us to chart the small scale, intimate political moves, gestures, and collaborations that reflect the tactics women used to negotiate the internalities of power within broader social movements. It identifies how they tracked and negotiated multiple scales of power within their homes, communities, organizations, social movements, and dominant society. It recuperates both silenced memories and their documentary evidence to tell a story of the intimacies of struggle, challenging the knowledge/power system of traditional archival spaces and methodologies. It looks not only to marches, meetings, and conferences but also to alternative sites of collective action: the kitchens, hallways, and living rooms where Chicanas forged a praxis at the intersection of their identities.

Mapping *movidas* alters the process of deciding what counts and who matters, offering a different way of seeing the Chicano movement, one that brings to light the organizing that happened both on the side and within major movement formations. It illuminates the flexible strategies of coalition and compromise that shaped Chicana technologies of resistance and brings into greater focus the independent organizations that Chicanas formed to address their own lived realities. Finally, mapping *movidas* shows us how Chicanas deployed tactics of remembrance in an effort to recuperate the hidden genealogies of struggle—the *movidas* that came before them. Collectively, these *movidas* and the many others that are explored in this book trace a genealogy of Chicana political, theoretical, practical, and analytical approaches born out of their rich and varied experiences. They map a field of resistance, innovation, and transformation that continues to inform Chicana feminist theory today.

In the sections that follow, we map these *movidas* into four interconnected and overlapping sites of struggle and resistance—"Hallway Movidas" (the hidden insurgencies within and at the margins of political and institutional spaces), "Home-Making Movidas" (making a space for Chicana feminism to live and develop), "Movidas of Crossing" (crossing borders and forging coalitions), and "Memory Movidas" (strategic recuperations of countermemory). The cartography we propose is neither comprehensive nor directive. In fact, unlike most maps, it is meant to *disorient*—to shift our collective center of gravity so that we may better see and feel the technologies of resistance that have shaped Chicana praxis. Weaving the Chicana *movidas* documented in this volume into our own (admittedly limited) account of these practices, we offer a map of both the collection and the hidden history of *movidas* that it documents.

HALLWAY MOVIDAS: WORKING WITHIN, THROUGH, AND AROUND MOVEMENT-ERA HEGEMONIES

Hallways, passages, kitchens—places in between or outside of the main events— these are the spaces of transit and possibility where Chicanas mobilized strategies to challenge the internalities of power and form new networks of resistance. As a spatial metaphor, the "hallway" locates *movidas* undertaken within and between movements that did not always address the full array of issues impacting women of color. Hallway *movidas* index the strategic ways activists met each other in the hallways of meetings, conferences, and political gatherings to address the ways they were excluded, to expand the agenda of the Chicano movement and the women's movement, or to multiply the social subject enlisted by monolithic visions of social change. Undertaken in interstitial spaces where Chicanas trafficked and exchanged ideas, discourses, and experiences from one movement into another to generate a more complete revolutionary praxis, hallway *movidas* expanded what Sonia Alvarez, writing in the context of Latin America, has referred to as the "spaces and places" in which feminist consciousness was found, discussed, and deployed.[23] Uncovering these hallway *movidas* requires not only focusing on unorthodox sites of political formation, but also shifting our analytical lens away from leaders of social movements and toward the day-to-day activities and experiences that shaped Chicana feminist praxis within, between, and outside of movements.

Scholars of the period as well as Chicana feminists themselves have noted that even though women were often the organizational backbone of movements, their labor was just as often devalued. While others have called attention to this gendered division of political labor or called for seeing leadership in a different way to account for the power base of women, what has not yet been explored is how encountering each other in devalued spaces like the kitchen and the hallway—often between sessions, meetings, or conference panels—offered Chicanas a critical opportunity to collaborate, name their frustrations, and devise strategies to address them. Some hallway *movidas* include "hidden gender insurgencies," those formal and informal spaces used by Chicanas to expand the impact of the Chicano movement to the whole community, and more particularly to the lives of women and their families.[24]

Critically, hidden gender insurgencies are not always visible to those outside the movement and do not necessarily lead to the formation of Chicana organizations and spaces. Indeed, hallway *movidas* may also include those instances when women meet and there is no public eruption or (documented) challenge, but the critiques generated are nevertheless advanced in the groundswell of organizing that eventually leads to change. One of the most infamous statements on women's participation in the Chicano movement came at the 1969 Denver Youth Liberation Conference when it was reported that the Chicana caucus declared that "the Chicana does not want to be liberated." Notwithstanding this seeming disavowal of feminist goals, we must not overlook the fact that women actively created the space to have a separate Chicana *plática* (discussion) when they arrived at the Denver conference and found no formal space to address women's issues. Moreover, Chicanas who participated in the caucus reported that the discussion of the role of women in the Chicano movement led many to eventually engage in a *movida* of *doble militancia* (multiple militancy) that involved initiating Chicana study groups, organizations, newspapers, and coalitions while continuing their work within the Chicano movement.[25]

This book demonstrates that Chicana hallway *movidas* have a genealogy that predates the movement years. In the first chapter in this volume, "Francisca Flores, the League of Mexican American Women, and the Comisión Femenil Mexicana Nacional, 1958–1975," Anna NietoGomez backfills the genealogy of Chicana activism to remind us that the history of Chicana/Mexican American women's organizing for social change does not begin in the late 1960s. Offering an account of Flores's efforts to visibilize women and build power for social change in Mexican American organizations of the 1950s, NietoGomez details the early history of this longtime Chicana spokesperson and advocate, widely acknowledged as one of the godmothers of Chicana feminism. As NietoGomez demonstrates, Flores's hallway *movidas* ensured Chicana visibility while they also led to the formation of several important organizations including the League of Mexican American Women, established in the early 1960s as a vehicle for recognizing women's leadership in civic affairs. Recuperating this prehistory,

NietoGomez reveals the genealogical connections between Chicana efforts to establish a number of organizations, service centers, and research initiatives in the 1970s and the work of an earlier generation of activists like Francisca Flores. As evidence of this connection, she offers the Comisión Femenil Mexicana Nacional (National Mexican Women's Commission), which was founded in 1970s by Flores and became a national organization supporting Chicana achievement in higher education and employment through its Chicana Service Action Center (CSAC) initiative.

The productive nature of these hallway *movidas* is illuminated in different contexts by Martha Cotera and Leticia Wiggins. Pioneering Chicana feminist Martha Cotera demonstrates in her contribution to this volume that hallway *movidas* were not exclusive to the Chicano movement. Cotera's essay, "Mujeres Bravas: How Chicanas Shaped the Feminist Agenda at the National IWY Conference in Houston, 1977," offers a detailed excavation of the ways in which Chicanas organized before and during the 1977 International Women's Year (IWY) conference in Houston. The Houston conference was organized to generate a national action plan for US women as a follow-up to the United Nations-sponsored IWY conference held in Mexico City in 1975. In a riveting account based on personal archive and her own recollections of participation in this effort, Cotera documents how Chicanas met in hallways, hotel rooms, nearby restaurants, and other off-site locations to orchestrate the strategies that would ensure that their agenda would be heard within the official space of this groundbreaking national conference. In a similar vein, Wiggins's essay, "'Women Need to Find Their Voice': Latinas Speak Out in the Midwest, 1972," focuses on the actions of Jane Gonzalez and some fifty other women who challenged their confinement to the kitchen during the agenda-setting process at the 1972 Mi Raza Primero conference in Muskegon, Michigan. Wiggins shows how Chicanas responded to their exclusion by unanimously adopting resolutions to push for gender equality. Led by Gonzalez and Olga Villa Parra, they went on to organize their own conference, Adelante Mujer, in South Bend, Indiana, in 1972, the first of its kind in the Midwest.

Hallway *movidas* can also work to create new sites for Chicana feminism within unexpected or even hostile spaces, such as the Catholic Church. Though the Church has historically been a place of women's organizing, it is associated for many with women's oppression because of the way doctrine is used to justify heteropatriarchy and colonialism. However, close examination of Chicana activism in the Church shows how women crafted realms of freedom inside dominant institutions that are hierarchically organized to exclude women and are therefore not free or safe spaces. As Lara Medina has documented, one of these "realms of freedom" was Las Hermanas, a collective of Mexican American Catholic nuns and laywomen who came together in Texas in the early 1970s to reform the Catholic Church by calling for more cultural awareness, greater commitment to working with the people, and more integration and visibility for women in the Church.[26]

Susana Gallardo's essay in this volume, "'It's Not a Natural Order': Religion and the Emergence of Chicana Feminism in the Cursillo Movement in San Jose," shifts attention from nuns to laywomen who participated in the Catholic Cursillo movement (a series of short courses in Christian teaching for laypeople), examining the ways they mobilized existing structures in the Church to develop a greater sense of their own agency and power. The women Gallardo interviewed reflected on how their participation in the Church-sanctioned activity of the Cursillos gave them an opportunity to read and share their experiences as women. In showing how these laywomen drew upon their own experiences in both secular (activist) and religious spheres to challenge the abstractions of church doctrine, Gallardo reveals how they appropriated priestly privilege/status to transform the Cursillo into a radical spiritual vehicle.

The hallway is a spatial metaphor that signals the interstitial locations through which and in which Chicanas articulated a flexible oppositional consciousness that refused monocausal understandings of oppression and power as well as conventional ideological scripts. As Chela Sandoval has argued, theorizing from her own embodied experiences in feminist, third world,[27] and Chicano movement spaces, this "flexible consciousness" is a key technology of resistance that arises from the necessary identity negotiations that women of color must make as they work within and between multiple movements to combat oppression.[28] Gloria Anzaldúa's *testimonio*, "Many Roads, One Path," reveals not only the complex identity negotiations of a Chicana lesbian moving through different political and cultural spaces (many of which excluded her) but also the ways in which the act of "moving" itself produced not only dissident political positionings but also an understanding of how "difference" could be central to the coalitional praxis of women of color. Anzaldúa's testimony demonstrates that shifting our focus to the strategic operations of hallway *movidas* complicates simplistic ideological and tactical divides—between "conservative," "liberal," and "radical" approaches toward social change—that too often render invisible the ways in which Chicanas crafted spaces of liberation within and beyond the conceptual limitations of existing organizations. Whether in the Church, the university, the political party system, or other established organizations that set the terms of participation, through their hallway *movidas* Chicanas aptly negotiated those terms or expanded them in ways that inevitably moved them toward alliance building that bridged difference in the interest of collective social change.

HOME-MAKING MOVIDAS: BUILDING CHICANA AESTHETICS, SPACES, PROJECTS, AND INSTITUTIONS

Focusing on the complex interplay between multiple movements and political spaces also reveals the tensions and differences within movement institutions that motivated Chicanas to envision alternative spaces, projects, and institutional formations. While sometimes a source of division, these tensions were also generative of new Chicana postures, aesthetics, and organizations through which activists sought to express their political commitments and address their multiple and intersecting identities holistically. Indeed, it was this necessity for Chicanas to make a home even in spaces that excluded them that engendered some of the most powerful practices of coalition, community, and movement building to emerge from the era. A focus on Chicana home-making *movidas*—which we define as both their organizing work within existing Chicano movement projects and their efforts to create separate and independent Chicana institutions—not only illuminates the invisible labor that Chicanas often undertook to ensure the success of various movement initiatives (community service, popular education, political organizing, print media), it also reveals the rich history of Chicana-led social spaces, cultural initiatives, and institutions.[29]

While Chicanas worked within many of the political, artistic, and service institutions of the Chicano movement era, they also created alternative spaces that could better address their visions of social change. Within movement organizations, Chicanas often created safe spaces for young women who felt alienated by the masculinist ethos and patriarchal power structures of revolutionary politics. For example, Chicanas who were active in El Movimiento Estudiantil Chicano de Aztlán (MEChA) and other student organizations frequently formed separate women's groups to discuss gender issues and develop strategies for interrupting sexist organizational dynamics. Groups like Hijas de Cuauhtémoc in Long Beach as well as Las Chicanas, a San Diego–based group, figured out that they would have to meet separately from MEChA organizations on their campuses in order to be heard and to have the issues that were important to them validated and acted upon. In their meetings they focused on topics that were relevant to their lives as young, first-generation college-going women, such as sexual health, male dominance, and economic issues. In these groups and others like them (the Mujeres Caucus of the Raza Unida Party, for example), Chicanas designed workshops, led meetings and consciousness-raising groups, and organized regional and national conferences focused on social, economic, and cultural issues impacting Chicanas.[30]

A widespread movement practice was to form study groups in which participants discussed influential readings or "rap groups" to discuss the nature of oppression and how to combat it. Chicanas participating in these informal groups frequently formed counterstudy groups to directly address Chicana experiences or break patriarchal forms of female competition (a dynamic that often played out in movement spaces) that stood in the way of solidarity, community, and radical consciousness raising. These spaces of intellectual exchange allowed Chicanas to tackle revolutionary texts and build their confidence with political theory while also forging a sense of community and what Las Hijas de Cuauhtémoc called *hermanidad* (sisterhood), a feminist counter to the exclusively male *carnalismo* (brotherhood). Chicanas at San Diego State College established a separate reading group where they read a foundational feminist text, *The Woman Question* by Edward Aveling and Eleanor Marx.[31] Hilda Rodriguez recalled that by studying books like this one and relating them back to concrete examples from her life experiences, she was able to better understand her "struggle for self-identity."[32] Such texts opened the door to an understanding of women's subordination for the circle of Chicana student activists with whom Rodriguez organized. At Long Beach State University, Anna NietoGomez and others also turned to a key feminist text in the Chicana reading group they established. Noticing that many of the Chicana freshmen she helped as an Educational Opportunity Program counselor had to give up their dreams of a college education because they ended up pregnant, NietoGomez picked *Our Bodies, Ourselves*, a foundational text in the women's health movement, as one of the first books to read in her Chicana group.[33]

Chicanas also created new homes in the Chicano movement and society at large through aesthetic *movidas* like *teatro*, creative and expository writing, art making, altar making, filmmaking, performing, and singing. Through these creative home-making *movidas*, Chicanas imagined their communities and cultures from a woman-centered perspective even as they made their presence known in movement social and political spaces. Groups like Teatro Chicana and Teatro Las Cucarachas and spoken-word performers like Dorinda Moreno engaged in forms of cultural critique that called out the gender politics of movement classics like Corky Gonzales's epic poem "Yo soy Joaquín" and reimagined Chicano history as a sweeping Chicana herstory from La Llorona (the Mexican legend of the weeping woman) to the female labor organizers featured in the film *Salt of the Earth*.[34]

For the filmmaker and poet Osa Hidalgo de la Riva, this home-making *movida* takes the form of "*mujerista* aesthetics," a woman-identified, nonhierarchical, politically oriented, and *rasquache* (homemade, vernacular, and repurposed aesthetic forms) practice that rewrites epic Chicano histories and memories of the movement to create blueprints for a better world. In the *testimonio* she shared with Maylei Blackwell in this volume, "Visions of Utopia while Living in Occupied Aztlán," Hidalgo de la Riva contemplates her own genealogy of matrilineal, lesbian kinship and her affective connections to the untold *lesbiana* undercurrents of the Chicano movement. Her *testimonio* illustrates how lesbians created a home in Chicano culture through art, literature, film, and community-building initiatives. As Hidalgo de la Riva's *testimonio* suggests, feminist and lesbian movement spaces required no small amount of negotiation and skillful *movidas*. Reimagining and rewriting the ways in which women have been made to feel like outsiders in their own homes and movements, Chicana artists, muralists, filmmakers, and writers have used culture to create spaces where they can holistically exist and be at home within their multiple selves, within the Chicano movement and within society at large.

In her exploration of artist Ester Hernández's body of work, Maylei Blackwell explores a different kind of personal and political narrative, one that is refracted through Hernandez's primary communicative tool—visual art. Drawing on interviews with Hernández, Blackwell demonstrates how Hernández's visual vocabulary emerged from her childhood experience in the fields of the

San Joaquin Valley, and how her varied political commitments (to the Chicano movement, the farmworkers, queer politics, and solidarity efforts with Central America) shaped the thematic and formal concerns of her body of work. Blackwell's essay reveals how Hernández made a home for her multiple selves, as a Chicana, an artist, and a lesbian, through a practice of social and political critique birthed from a female-centered world and told from the point of view of the worker, the migrant, the musician, the weaver. The new aesthetic home Hernández crafts incorporates the spiritual realm as well, syncretically fusing a warrior diosa with the Statue of Liberty, La Muerte with the Sun Maid Raisin Girl, and La Virgen with a terrorist. These hybrid female icons constitute a Chicana feminist cosmology that implicitly critiques oppressive relations: an aesthetic movida that liberates signs, symbols, and icons from their home cultures to challenge the patriarchal and colonial logics embedded within them. Through this home-making aesthetic *movida*, Hernández shows that what has been relegated to an indigenous past endures in the present, and even opens the way for new possible futures. Hernández's art, like her life, cannot be easily compartmentalized into any single political, aesthetic, formal, or even temporal box. Instead, as Blackwell argues, her multiply situated *obras* offer a visual analog for her experience—a theory in the flesh (and paint)—and a way home.

Hernández answered the revolutionary call to create new spaces and organizations that would serve the interests of the community, crafting livable homes for their work within Chicano, third world, and women's liberation projects. Indeed, "service to the people" was a core principle of radical social movements led by people of color. Collectively they created new institutions or commandeered existing institutions (hospitals, health centers, schools, churches, radio stations) that were not serving the communities in which they were located. These initiatives included the breakfast programs of the Black Panther Party, the medical testing and medical services of the Young Lords Party, the Barrio Free Clinic established by the East Los Angeles Brown Berets, and the employment service of the Chicana Service Action Center. While such efforts were usually focused on service provision to communities in need, they also functioned as spaces for consciousness raising and community mobilization. Not surprisingly, given the crucial importance of such initiatives within movement cultures, conflicts over administrative control, ideological direction, and media attention frequently arose, and the conflicts often had a gendered dimension. While women often led these institution-building projects, they occasionally broke off to form their own organizations due to the unequally gendered division of labor that working within existing organizations often entailed. This dynamic is richly illustrated in Dionne Espinoza's study of the women Brown Beret members in Los Angeles, in which she reveals that Gloria Arellanes—who was charged by Brown Beret Prime Minister David Sánchez to lead the Barrio Free Clinic—eventually called the male leadership out on the unequal gendered division of labor. When their behavior did not change, she, along with other

Chicana Brown Berets who comprised the core of clinic workers, formed a separate organization, Las Adelitas de Aztlán.[35]

A focus on Chicana institution-building *movidas* reveals how their labor inside movement spaces was frequently invisibilized in the tendency to devalue women's contributions as "volunteer work." This framing of women's labor as voluntary (a labor of love) continues to structure absences in the historical record. As Dolores Delgado Bernal has demonstrated, traditional notions of leadership (who stands in front of the mic) can erase the grassroots, organizational backbone of social movements, the hidden labor most often undertaken by women that enables successful movements.[36] In his chapter on Seattle's El Centro de La Raza, Michael Aguirre responds to the historical erasure of women's labor in movement initiatives by demonstrating that much of the organizational and administrative work of getting the Centro up and running and keeping it running fell on the shoulders of women. Nevertheless their involvement and contributions have not been sufficiently recognized. Aguirre's chapter in this volume, "Excavating the Chicano Movement: Chicana Feminism, Mobilization, and Leadership at El Centro de la Raza, 1972–1979," documents the participation of women at the heart of this community resource and demonstrates that in order to have a more complete understanding of one of the cornerstones of Seattle's Chicano movement, we must first understand Chicanas' foundational contributions to its success. Likewise, Monica De La Torre recuperates the work that Chicanas did to build a key community resource in the Pacific Northwest: Radio KDNA, the nation's first full-time Spanish language noncommercial radio station. In her chapter in this volume, "Feminista Frequencies: Chicana Radio Activism in the Pacific Northwest," De La Torre theorizes how the Chicana leadership of Radio KDNA fundamentally transformed the aims and structure of the station's radio activism by ensuring that Chicanas held positions of leadership. Chicanas at KDNA trained women as radio producers, created content and radio programming unique to the Chicana experience, and implemented antisexist practices within the radio station.

In yet another example of a home-making movida, Alicia Escalante founded the East Los Angeles Welfare Rights Organization—one of the earliest Chicana advocacy organizations of the period—to challenge public policies (like the Talmadge Amendment of 1971) and address their negative impact on women who, like Escalante, experienced racialized and gendered class exploitation. Rosie Bermudez offers a revealing political biography of Escalante in her contribution to this volume, "La Causa de los Pobres: Alicia Escalante's Lived Experiences of Poverty and the Struggle for Economic Justice," an essay that documents how Escalante's understanding of Chicana feminism developed from a struggle against women's economic marginalization, poverty, and a class-based politics. Drawing from her personal interviews with Alicia Escalante as well as the collection of Escalante materials in the Chicana por mi Raza Digital Memory Collective, Bermudez demonstrates that from the start, Escalante approached her social justice work from an intersectional analysis based largely on her own experiences of poverty and marginalization as a woman of color—experiences that differed from both the dominant paradigms of the Chicano movement and those of the emergent welfare rights movement. While movement narratives have illustrated rural poverty and the hardships of farmwork, albeit with less attention to the experiences of women, Escalante's biography gives us both a powerful personal narrative about multigenerational urban poverty and a framework for the analysis of racialized, gendered, class exploitation long before there was an understanding of the feminization of poverty.

By the mid-1970s, a burgeoning network of organizations and programs led by Chicanas and focused on their needs developed across the Southwest, Pacific Northwest, and Midwest. These efforts were spurred on by the increase in funding made available through federal initiatives like the Women's Educational Equity Act of 1974, which included a focus on women who experienced "multiple discrimination based on gender and on race, ethnicity, national origin, disability, or age."[37] Some organizations and initiatives were outgrowths of the various Chicana conferences and meetings that were held in the early 1970s to address the particular social and economic needs of women. Organizations like Chicago's Mujeres Latinas en Acción, still active today, and Mujeres Unidas de Michigan, which had branches in Flint, Detroit, and Lansing in the 1970s and 1980s, were a direct result of the call to action issued in 1972 at Adelante Mujer, the first national Chicana conference to be held in the Midwest (documented in Leticia Wiggins's chapter 3 in this volume). Chicanas established other organizations by forming "women's caucuses" within Chicano-led political organizations such as the Raza Unida Party. One institutional outgrowth of this strategy of caucus formation was the Chicana Research and Learning Center (CRLC), founded in Austin, Texas, in 1974 by Raza Unida Party members Martha P. Cotera and Evey Chapa. As a clearinghouse for educational materials on Chicanas and women of color, the CRLC sponsored independent research and writing and was intended to serve both community education projects and the curricular needs of newly established Chicano studies and women's studies programs.

In her contribution to this volume, "The Space in Between: Exploring the Development of Chicana Feminist Thought in Central Texas," Brenda Sendejo draws from personal interviews and archival research to tell the story of the Chicana Research and Learning Center as a critical site for knowledge production by and about Chicanas and women of color in the 1970s. Sendejo demonstrates how the CRLC functioned as an important bridge between the university and the community that ensured that early Chicana scholarship and teaching would remain relevant and accountable to the community. Extending the "bridge" metaphor from institutional space and applying it to the genealogy of Chicana feminism, Sendejo observes that the establishment of the Chicana Research and Learning Center marked a key and, until now, unrecognized bridge between the early work of Chicana feminists in on-the-ground political struggles and the rise of Chicana feminist studies within the academy.

MOVIDAS OF CROSSING: BORDERS, COALITION, SOLIDARITIES

Chicanas often moved between, beyond, and across multiple borders, including those of nationalisms, cultures, social movements, nation-states, histories, languages, and group identities, to make common cause with others who shared their social justice goals. These movements enabled new kinds of relationships, transforming existing approaches to social justice particularly when top-down approaches did not take into account the multiple and intersecting nature of oppression. In and through these *movidas* of crossing, Chicanas developed a set of methodologies and technologies of resistance that have become central to women of color feminism today.[38] Understanding the strategic importance of difference in successful organizing work, learning to shift the center in order to illuminate the ways in which oppressions impact communities differently, working through the delicate negotiations between self and other, understanding the self *in* the other—all of these tactics destabilized conventional notions of identity and power and shaped what Chela Sandoval has called a new "hermeneutics of social change."[39]

In her essay in this volume, "Forging a Brown-Black Movement: Chicana and African American Women Organizing for Welfare Rights in Los Angeles," Alejandra Marchevsky documents the delicate negotiations between the specificities of identity, race, and language as they relate to a sense of collective identity for Chicanas and African American women on welfare. Challenging "silo" narratives that set up conceptual borders that separate racialized ethnic groups and their organizational histories—as if they exist without interaction—and/or that assume only tensions between the groups, Marchevsky maps the landscape of women of color welfare rights organizing in Los Angeles around cross-racial dialogue. In doing so, she illuminates the ways in which Chicana welfare rights activist Alicia Escalante navigated the points of coalition (and difference) in the experiences of welfare for black women and Chicanas. In a quite different context of organizing—the mainstream women's movement and the campaign for the Equal Rights Amendment—Martha Cotera's contribution to this volume, "Mujeres Bravas," reveals how Chicana feminists brought together a group of women who had felt left out of the proceedings, including self-described "low-income women" and lesbians, across perceived borders of difference to forge a strategic coalition that challenged classism, racism, and heterosexism in the construction of a "women's agenda" in the 1977 International Women's Year follow-up conference in Houston.

Such Chicana border-crossing *movidas* were not limited to social movements in the United States. Indeed, many Chicanas developed a sense of their own identities as marginalized subjects through experiences of organizing with international and third world liberation struggles. In her essay in this volume, "'Tu Reata Es Mi Espada': Elizabeth Sutherland's Chicana Formation," Annemarie Perez traces the ways in which the journalist and social justice warrior Elizabeth "Betita" Martínez shifted her self-identification as she documented anticolonial struggles around the world including the black civil rights movement and the Cuban Revolution. Perez argues that it was these experiences, along with her growing identification as a Chicana and as a third world woman, that led Martínez to shed the pen name she had adopted in her early career as a journalist, "Elizabeth Sutherland." In effect, Elizabeth Sutherland became Elizabeth "Betita" Martínez, a transformation that ultimately led Martínez to move to New Mexico, where she articulated a Third-Worldist perspective on Chicano liberation through her work as a journalist and editor of *El Grito del Norte* newspaper.

Like Elizabeth "Betita" Martínez, many other Chicanas framed their struggles within a global context and identified key points of connection between their experiences and those of women across the world who were also struggling against "the many headed demon of oppression."[40] They built these connections through journalism, consciousness raising, and travel. Chicanas like María Elena Martínez (state party chair for the RUP) and Hijas de Cuauhtémoc member Sylvia Castillo were instrumentally involved in organizing trips to Cuba for the Venceremos Brigade. Chicanas also traveled to Vancouver, Canada, for the Indochinese Women's Conference in April 1971 and to Mexico City for the first UN-sponsored World Conference on Women (International Women's Year 1975), both of which were reported widely in articles and at meetings. In other instances such border crossing involved writing and publishing to raise consciousness about issues impacting women beyond the US nation-state. Chicana writers for the radical press (Elizabeth "Betita" Martínez, Enriqueta Vásquez, and scores of others) regularly reported on liberation struggles in the United States and beyond (Cuba, Puerto Rico, Chile, Palestine, Africa). Working with a group of students within San Francisco State University's fledgling Raza studies program, the poet Dorinda Moreno edited the anthology *La mujer: En pie de lucha* (1973), that put Filipinas, Puerto Rican women, Mexican women, Chicanas, and African American women into dialogue.[41] Dionne Espinoza's essay in the present volume, "'La Raza en Canada': San Diego Chicana Activists, the Indochinese Women's Conference of 1971, and Third World Womanism," opens a much-needed conversation about the complexities of Chicana/third world woman identification by focusing on the meanings of third world solidarity for Chicana activists who participated in coalitional transnational spaces or who published reflective pieces about how the third world concept reframed Chicanas' understandings of oppression, both globally and locally. Espinoza's essay makes an important two-pronged intervention, first in demonstrating that many Chicanas in the 1970s were aware and active in global decolonial politics (before their engagement with Central American solidarity struggles in the 1980s) and second by inserting Chicana feminists into a narrative of the emergence of global feminism in the 1970s that has rarely included them.

Recuperating the transnational *movidas* of Chicana feminism is key to disrupting a too-narrow contextual frame that figures the development of Chicana and women-of-color feminism as something that can be isolated to the borders of the United States. Too often the emergence of Chicana and women-of-color feminism is exclusively attributed to a feminist critique of nationalism or an antiracist critique of hegemonic feminism. These third world coalitional *movidas* illuminate the various roots and routes Chicana activists took in expressing their feminism, including the third world solidarity and internationalist impulses that allowed them to form new coalitions globally and within their own local organizing contexts. Testimonial narratives such as Olga Talamante's contribution to this volume, "De Campesina a Internacionalista: A Journey of Encuentros y Desencuentros," reveal the complex activist routes that Chicana feminists and *lesbianas* have taken through internationalism, leftist party politics, and many other movements and formations. Talamante's *testimonio* calls into question the scholarly tendency to reduce the complexities of the movement years to a singular movement narrative, even as she demonstrates how that approach fails to accurately capture the holistic way Chicana activists have engaged politics as their experiences and insights traverse multiple movements at one time and over time.

The arc of Talamante's trajectory, as well as her ability to tell it and make meaning out of it, introduces new ways of writing histories that move across several different movements, documenting what Chela Sandoval has termed "differential consciousness" through an account of lived experience.[42] This *movida* of crossing reveals the stories of those who crossed movements and borders to build new solidarities and insights that are key to development of Chicana feminism. Building on this *movida* of crossing in its method and its content, "María Jiménez: Reflexiones on Traversing Multiple Fronteras in the South," the essay coauthored by Samantha Rodriguez and Stalina Emmanuelle Villarreal (María Jiménez's daughter), represents a collaborative crossing of generations. Rodriguez and Villarreal's essay draws from oral history and other interviews to tell the story of María Jiménez, one of the most respected Chicana *activistas* in the Houston Chicano movement and a woman who has remained active in labor, immigration, and transnational Latina/o political movements. Part biographical account of Jiménez's life and part extended analysis of a mode of feminism that crossed the borders of race, class, gender, and nationality in the interest of social justice, the essay draws equally from Jiménez's memories of her life as an activist and her critical perspectives on those experiences, illuminating the complexities and contradictions of feminism in the borderlands.

MEMORY MOVIDAS: COUNTERMEMORY, GENEALOGY, TESTIMONIO

Often submerged and untold—or discounted as a purely "personal" or "private" epistemology—the practice and deployment of critical memory has been a central technology in the repertoire of Chicana social movement strategies. Chicana memory *movidas* vary widely and include practices of writing (historiography, poetry, testimonio), collecting (bibliographies, sourcebooks, personal libraries and archives), aesthetic production (film, theater, visual art, slideshows), and even modes of organizing. Chicanas in the movement used collective memory to forge new political spaces and identities for themselves, mobilizing practices of countermemory (either collective or personal) to highlight the unique perspective of subjects at the intersection of multiple oppressions. Chicana memory *movidas* recovered and reworked submerged and fractured historical narratives of women in the Mexican Revolution, first-wave Mexican feminist activism, and the iconography of the *soldaderas*. Chicanas retrofitted *revolucionaria* identities and discourses to enter into the discursive terrain of struggle on which the Chicano movement was staged, shifting that terrain away from the mythic role of women in Aztec cosmology to the historical and material experiences of women's activism leading up to and during the Mexican Revolution at the turn of the twentieth century.

Chicana historiography produced during the movement years, like Martha Cotera's self-published *Diosa y Hembra* (a touchstone for early Chicana feminists and widely considered to be the first comprehensive historical analysis of Mexican women in the United States written from a Chicana perspective) departed from the norms of traditional historiography to draw genealogical connections between the lived experiences of indigenous women of the precolonial period and contemporary Chicanas.[43] The book included meditations on the *diosas* of Mesoamerica, recuperations of historical figures like borderlands feminist Sara Estela Ramírez, and a list of contemporary Chicana organizations. As if visualizing this Chicana historiographic *movida*, Anna NietoGomez's slideshow *La Chicana* (1976), which was later transformed into a groundbreaking documentary in collaboration with Chicana filmmaker Sylvia Morales, offered its own visual remix of history compiled from archival and contemporary photographs, visual art, and indigenous codices.[44] Proposing something more than a countermemory or a contestatory account of what happened, such Chicana memory *movidas* figure history itself as an active site of meaning and contestation, of recuperation and revolution. We see such an approach to history in the labors of Adelaida del Castillo and Norma Alarcón to recuperate the image of La Malinche, in Gloria Anzaldúa's weaving of poetry, memory (auto)ethnography, and history into an account of borderlands subjectivity that is both deeply personal and collective, in the "theory in the flesh" of Cherríe Moraga, and in the efforts of contemporary Chicanas to make a place for *testimonio* in their scholarly work.[45]

Storytelling, through *testimonio*, oral history, or biography, is central to this practice of historical recuperation and its political deployment of memory. More than a simple or transparent narration of what happened, storytelling implies an act of intentional construction that fuses personal narrative with collective experience to shape a story and its meaning. It is a key Chicana memory *movida* that gets to the heart of the politics of telling—whether it be telling personal stories, recovering collective memories, or upending traditional movement histories. Is it enough that a story is told, or do we need to attend to the ways in which the story is told? What material conditions produce the story? What are the relations of power that obscure it or make it possible to be heard? Drawing from Chicana feminist movement practices such as rap sessions, workshops, and women's caucuses that allowed women to speak about their experiences of oppression—sometimes for the first time—and inspired by third world movements for national liberation, Chicanas developed a feminist practice of speaking out and "speaking bitterness" to name and begin to analyze the sources and conditions of oppression they were confronting. They also drew from Latin American revolutionary traditions of bearing witness to the collective history of a people, mobilizing story as a memory *movida* that helped to raise political consciousness in its understanding of lived experiences within a collective frame of struggle. This is particularly important for women of color activists whose multiple oppressions were either hidden by the public/private dichotomy or obscured by the "primary oppression" mandate of single-issue movements and identities.

The personal narratives included in this collection are experiential and geared toward collective empowerment and healing for self and others. Similar to the way Rosie Castro, the San Antonio–based Raza Unida Party activist, described Chicana leadership as one that empowers others, many Chicana feminists deploy a narrative strategy of telling that empowers others to tell their stories, to add their voices, and to add to the collective reflection and theorization of shared oppressions and modes of resistance.[46] These calls to "voice" invite a practice of multivocality that echoes the multigenre, multiformat practices of Chicana print communities of the movement era as well as the anthologizing practices that women of color mobilized to create political community and liberatory pedagogies across diverse political sectors. In this volume the call to voice encompasses different modes of storytelling (manifesto and *testimonio*) and various genres and narrative frames such as biography and oral history. What sets these narratives apart from other traditional forms of *testimonio* and biography is that the narrators here foreground analysis over pure narration, to make meaning and explore the historical significance of their own history, and to contribute their own modes of analysis to the historiographic record. While much *testimonio* has relied on an interlocutor from the outside to come and give voice to the subaltern—to those with little access to institutional modes of knowledge production—this collection marks how bearing witness to a movement and writing from the individual "I" can be a key *movida* that inspires others to voice and incites other strategies for social change.

The multivocal storytelling strategies in this collection also invite different historical imaginaries and different modes of telling that are based in the ways that Chicana and Latina feminists have used the personal and the intimate to speak truth to power and to situate and ground their own "theories in the flesh."[47]

Deanna Romero's memoir in this volume, "My Deliberate Pursuit of Freedom," narrates her early formation as a child of the movement born to parents who were committed activists in Denver's Chicano movement. While honoring her parents and the Chicano movement generation, Romero also speaks to the lived experience of the individual who is negotiating between the self and the collective and seeking her own path to freedom as a deliberate pursuit. Romero sees herself in the cycle of generations of women who, over time, are breaking from the scripted narrative of Chicana womanhood. From her grandmother to her mother to her own decision to leave her marriage and come out as queer, Romero's reflective self-analysis offers a gentle weave of insights and observations along with an account of her spiritual journey as a trained health care professional who incorporated non-Western spiritual practices in her holistic approach to community health. Romero's brief memoir illustrates that it is only through an individual act of self-narration that we can grasp a sense of the complex nature of lived experience in the context of political, personal, and social transformation.

The narratives of Olga Talamante, Gloria Anzaldúa, Deanna Romero, Ester Hernández, and Osa Hidalgo de la Riva in this volume are particularly illuminating in terms of understanding the complex routes of political identity in relation to gender and sexuality. In these accounts, we find no singular coming-out narrative like those emplotted by white lesbian and gay activists onto a gay liberation imaginary. Like many women of this era, their sexuality was woven into their Chicanidad and part of their emerging feminism. Indeed, these narratives of experience demand modes of analysis that do not dissect one element of who Chicana lesbians are from the other parts of themselves. Some women-loving women did/do not identify as lesbian, while others contributed to the formation of distinct lesbian political communities in the United States in the 1970s and 1980s. Many Chicana *lesbianas* dedicated most of their artistic and organizing energies to the Chicano movement, and found ways to express their sexuality within their Chicanidad, as is richly illustrated by Ester Hernandez's painting *La Ofrenda*, which not only illustrates the strength of Mexicanas and Chicanas but also the female-centered erotic power of everyday life. Others, like Gloria Anzaldúa, embraced alternative spaces and coalitional gestures to articulate a fluid, borderlands sexuality. Still others, like Olga Talamante, found ways of coming out after decades of political work while staying in their communities and organizations. The diverse sexual routes of movement work that are illuminated in the narratives of Talamante, Anzaldúa, and Hernández suggest the myriad *movidas* that Chicanas deployed to navigate the demonization of feminism via lesbian baiting in the Chicano movement. Their efforts to build women-centered Chicana cultural, political, and healing practices are illustrative of the complex negotiations of sexuality in the movement years.

This is not to romanticize or minimize the violence many lesbian and bisexual women experienced in Chicano movement spaces and within the women's movement. While sexuality has come to be recognized as an integral part of Chicana identity and struggle, for many years Chicana lesbians were among the most talented leaders of organizations but often suffered the invisibilization of their sexuality at the risk of expulsion from movement spaces. Even emergent Chicana lesbian feminist cultures of the late 1970s and 1980s tended to shun those who challenged normative gender scripts (such as masculine-identified women and other gender "deviants") as being dupes of the patriarchy or examples of the excesses of capitalist individualism. This is true of community leaders and activists like Diane Felix, who because of her butch presentation was consistently excluded from feminist and lesbian formations. She ultimately felt more comfortable organizing with gay Chicano men, and in 1975 they founded Gay Latino Alliance (GALA), an organization that brought together Chicano power with the gay liberation sentiments of Chicana/o gays and lesbians, many of whom had participated in the United Farm Workers and other Chicano movement organizations in the San Francisco Bay Area and San Jose, California.[48] Diane Felix became a major political and organizing force within GALA in San Francisco. She went on to start Proyecto contra SIDA por Vida (PCPV) in response to the HIV/AIDS crisis and has built political and affective communities through her skills as DJ Chili D, organizing women's *bailes* and spinning for queer events nationally and internationally since the 1970s.

While the Chicana lesbian storytelling *movidas* in this collection give us an intimate understanding of how women navigated the complicating difference of sexuality within and outside their communities, for other women included in this volume, memory *movidas* involve experimentation with the form of *testimonio* itself. In her essay, "Manifestos de Memoria: (Re)Living the Movement without Blinking," Chicana/Nez Perce scholar Inés Hernández-Ávila creates a dialogue between her published poetry, meant to be performed for audiences, and her personal reflections on identity, creativity, and feminism to offer a multigenre narrative of her childhood in Houston, her involvement in the Chicano student movement at the University of Houston, her early years as a poet and academic at the University of Texas at Austin (where she and Gloria Anzaldúa developed the first classes on La Chicana and she published the short-lived Chicana feminist journal *HEMBRA*), and her organizing work with the Texas Farm Workers and the Raza Unida Party. In its border-crossing form—which draws equally from prose and poetry, recollection and archive, public performance and private reflection—Hernández-Ávila's chapter maps the borders she has regularly crossed in her own life as a woman who moved within and between Chicano and indigenous communities. It also gives readers a vivid sense of the political landscape of Austin and Houston in the mid-1970s, a context that puts her essay into productive dialogue with Brenda Sendejo's essay on the Chicana Research and Learning Center, Gloria Anzaldúa's *testimonio*, and Rodriguez and Villarreal's account of the life of Houston-area María Jiménez. Reading across this collection will no doubt incite other such interconnections and overlaps, which suggests the political and affective commitments to movement women that our contributors share as well as their commitment to work in collaboration to document and interpret their collective experience and to be accountable to each other for those theories and research practices.

The practice of feminist oral history has been essential to the recovery of women's involvement in the Chicano movement and many other resistance cultures of the 1960s, especially in terms of looking to the intimacy of memory to uncover what has, until very recently, been overlooked by researchers. The same can be said of the painstaking recuperation of a long-ignored Chicana archive. Where other researchers have overlooked the small stories about women sometimes buried in or completely absent from institutional archives, the contributors to this volume have hunted down women's stories from multiple sources—institutional and community-based archives, materials in personal collections, oral histories and interviews—developing research relationships in the process that are built over many, many years. These collaborations are themselves a kind of memory *movida*, one that builds a shared archive of remembrance and a lived/living repository for multigenerational feminist dialogue and scholarship. Projects like the Chicana por mi Raza Digital Memory Collective embody these collaborative and cross-generational relations of production through the deployment of new technologies that enable an even broader community of scholars, students, teachers, and organizers to share their stories. Indeed, as María Cotera discusses in her contribution to this volume, "Unpacking Our Mothers' Libraries: Practices of Chicana Memory before and after the Digital Turn," it is through practices of memory that Chicanas make key connections between history, genealogy, and personal experience and forge linkages across different generations, geopolitical borders, and political traditions or ideologies. Cotera argues that Chicana acts of memory and memorialization have allowed for the development of new political subjectivities and vocabularies of struggle that draw on prior generations and connect individual experiences of oppression to historical and contemporary collectivities. In and through its efforts to preserve Chicana memory via the collection of oral histories and the digitization of archives in personal collections, the Chicana por mi Raza project enacts and preserves the memory *movidas* of an earlier generation of Chicanas. As Cotera argues, such recovery projects, which work to recuperate and preserve memory, and in the process "relate new constituencies into coalitions of resistance," suggest new possibilities for memory *movidas* in the digital age.[49]

Moreover, in their potential to generate new scholarship on Chicanas, recovery projects contribute to the crafting of new genealogies of struggle. Several of the essays included in this volume (Bermudez, Wiggins, Rodriguez and Villarreal, Chávez) draw from the Chicana por mi Raza digital archive. The project has also spawned numerous partner projects like Tess Arenas's Wisconsin-based digital oral history initiative Somos Latinas and Elena Gutiérrez's Chicana Chicago project, both of which have made substantial contributions to previous efforts to document Chicana and Latina activism in the Great Lakes region.[50] Elena

Gutiérrez and Virginia Martínez's contribution to this volume, "La Mariposa de Oro: The Journey of an Advocate," is a first-person account of her development as legal voice for Latina issues. This *testimonio* was part of Elena Gutierrez's Chicana Chicago project and is an excellent example of how such projects can expand the scope of our understanding of the spaces and places of Chicana activism. Martínez's *testimonio* also vividly demonstrates the importance of local as well as national Chicana networks to the development of social justice agendas well into the 1990s.

The memories documented in the Chicana por mi Raza digital archive have also generated new memory *movidas* like Marisela R. Chávez's essay in this volume, "Refocusing Chicana International Feminism: Photographs, Postmemory, and Political Trauma," which centers on the workings of memory and the "silences of the archive." Chávez's essay draws inspiration from photographs of Chicanas at the International Women's Year conference in Mexico City in 1975. The photographs, taken by Nancy De Los Santos, who attended the conference as part of a delegation of Chicanas from Chicago, were uncovered during an oral history interview in 2013 conducted by the Chicana por mi Raza project.[51] De Los Santos's photographs incite Chávez's reflection on the research process and the frustration she frequently felt when participants' vague memories and the lack of archival evidence made it difficult for her to tell the story of Chicana participation in the Mexico City conference.[52] Returning to the historic event via these recovered photos, Chávez admits that while the photos fail to answer all of the questions she originally had regarding Chicanas' participation in the conference, they do remind her that uncovering Chicana history often requires us to listen to the silences in the archive and find meaning in the absences and gaps of the official record. As Chávez notes, recovering meaning that others may miss means reading between the lines of the archive and engaging stories and lived experiences as a critical site of theory. This signature *movida* of Chicana feminist memory practice aims to generate political analyses from personal lived experience as a way to create a collective reference of struggle—what Cherríe Moraga calls "theories in the flesh." Through such memory *movidas* Chicana feminists theorize from their own experiences and common frames of reference to make sense of the world around them and to name the power relations that structure inequality and produce violence, frequently through processes of invisibilization.

The diverse array of memory *movidas*—from the act of storytelling and *testimonio*, to the dialogical and collaborative preservation of memory, to the theories in the flesh that shape our praxis—constitute a key genealogical link between the work we do in this volume and the Chicana *movidas* it traces. Indeed, we were formed as women of color feminists and scholars in an intellectual and political genealogy that includes organizations like the Third World Women's Alliance and Hijas de Cuauhtémoc, collectives like Combahee River and Kitchen Table, scholar-poets like Audre Lorde, Cherríe Moraga, Barbara Smith, Merle Woo, Chrystos, and Gloria Anzaldúa, among many others. This is the grounding and the hidden history that inspired us to trace the genealogies of Linda Burnham, Frances Beale, Anna NietoGomez, Gloria Arellanes, Martha Cotera, Dorinda Moreno, Alicia Escalante, Enriqueta Vásquez, Elizabeth Martínez, and many others. As a "middle" or "bridge" generation, we understand that these memory *movidas* are not just about constructing women of color feminist genealogies or even learning from previous activist strategies. They are also—as they were for the generations before us—about creating an analytic from which to understand power and build a theory that centers subjects who experience multiple and intersecting oppressions, in order to better understand and, more importantly, *undo* relations of domination and subordination in and through our scholarship. More important still, this collection—our own memory *movida*—represents a pedagogical commitment to root the next generation within a genealogy of US third world feminist and queer theory. For as much as *memoria* is a political tradition and a poetic tradition, it is also a pedagogical tradition.

Like most practices of collection (archives, oral histories, libraries), our effort to gather these essays together is a profoundly theoretical and political act. As women of color scholars who have labored to uncover a genealogy of feminist praxis that has been ignored, marginalized, and sometimes actively silenced, we understand that the stories and artifacts we choose to preserve and the ways in which we organize these stories and artifacts into narratives shape the field of knowledge and even the kinds of questions we can ask about the past. We have approached the tasks of collecting and organizing from a theoretical perspective birthed in and through the very Chicana feminist praxis we seek to document in this volume. We offer it in the spirit of a Chicana praxis of *memoria* and (re)collecting that is invested not only in the lessons of the past but also in what those lessons teach us about the present and how they might offer us the technologies of resistance that can guide us to a blueprint for the future. It is our hope that in bridging these temporalities we can engage in an act of recovery—spiritual and archival—that is also a space of healing: our very own Chicana *movida*.

PART I

HALLWAY MOVIDAS

1 FRANCISCA FLORES, THE LEAGUE OF MEXICAN AMERICAN WOMEN, AND THE COMISIÓN FEMENIL MEXICANA NACIONAL, 1958–1975

ANNA NIETOGOMEZ

The history of the League of Mexican American Women and its evolution into the Comisión Femenil Mexicana Nacional is an example of how the external struggle for civil rights inevitably engendered the Chicana feminist movement. Sexism within the movement radicalized women activists to adopt civil rights strategies to organize themselves into a separate political Chicana organization. This all began with the women's assertion that women played an important role in the Mexican American movement; the progression was spurred on by the dissatisfaction with gender inequities in the arbitrary heteropatriarchal social hierarchy inside the Mexican American and Chicano movement; and it was crystalized when Chicanas decided to take action to improve the socioeconomic conditions of Mexican American women.

In the Mexican American movement's struggle to gain civil rights and attain socioeconomic equality, racism was condemned but sexism was preserved. The movement challenged the belief system of power and dominance that underlies racism, and it rejected the myth that white people were superior and predestined by God to dominate Mexican Americans. Nonetheless, the movement did not reject the parallel sophistry that propagated sexism. Conservative patriarchal traditionalists who held power and influence or had a stake in the subordination of women in the movement resisted applying the democratic idea that women should have equal rights and equal representation. They did not find it morally wrong that men benefited from gender inequality in the social hierarchy of the social justice movement. Perhaps this moral contradiction was not self-evident to those who narrowly envisioned a system of racial equality where only Mexican

American men achieved equality with white men. If so, their main complaint was that in the social hierarchy of a patriarchal racist society, socioeconomic benefits were only available to the dominant white males and denied to the perceived inferior subordinate nonwhite males. Following this line of thinking, nonwhite males could only claim superiority and dominance over the lesser, subordinate nonwhite women. For those who accepted this social dominant ideology, gender equality was unacceptable because it would be an admission that men were as inferior as Mexican American women and that they were not worthy or capable of becoming equal to white men. In addition, it meant surrendering the patriarchal customs that automatically granted men authority over women. Men would have to compete with women for leadership and social status. Merit rather than one's sex would be the primary determinant of who did what in the organization.[1]

Nevertheless, the Mexican American civil rights movement needed women to join its ranks, and it called for women to become politically aware and to participate in tearing down all sociopolitical-economic barriers of racial inequality. On one hand, the movement recognized the need for women's participation. At the same time it also devalued women's work. Once women joined the movement, they were usually steered into subservient roles performing only lower-level decision-making duties and doing the grunt work in the organizations. In good faith, women activists volunteered their time, knowledge, and skills to pursue social justice; in return, patriarchs treated them as unpaid servants. They expected women to be seen but not heard. In most cases, heteropatriarchal practices attempted to confine this vital workforce of women to traditional gender roles and kept them outside of the sphere of power and influence in the organization. The male chiefs rarely had any desire to include women in the planning, decision making, or leadership.

In contrast to the patriarchal traditions that permeated many Mexican American civil rights organizations, Chicana feminist organizations cultivated a safe place where women were able to freely share ideas, collaborate, solve problems, plan, and make decisions. Early Chicana feminist organizations recognized women as equal human beings and provided a primary social and political space that acknowledged the value of women's work in the movement. These organizations created settings where women worked together to overcome oppression and seek equality, social justice, and human rights for both women and men. They were stimulating environments and served as experimental laboratories and think tanks where Chicanas gained confidence to take risks, challenge the traditional thinking about their role in society, and take political action. Here, women could develop a collective identity in alignment with the values of the civil rights movement; such spaces allowed women to practice public speaking and leadership skills that prepared them to challenge and grow the movement.

In Los Angeles, California, from the late 1930s to the 1990s, Francisca Flores was a civil rights activist in the Mexican American movement who evolved into a Chicana feminist organizer and leader. Flores and other Mexican American women committed to civil rights values found themselves up against a two-sided front, one that fought for racial equality and another that sought gender equality within the Mexican American movement.

Flores's feminist activities were a political reaction to the heteropatriarchal practices in some of the early civil rights organizations she helped found. Flores played a key role in inspiring women to join together to create four Chicana feminist organizations that arose during the post–World War II era in Los Angeles. They were the League of Mexican American Women (referred to as the League hereafter) in 1958, Comisión Femenil Mexicana (CFM) in 1970, Chicana Service Action Center (CSAC) in 1972, and Centro de Niños in 1973. These were all products of the League's determination to provide women with the social and political capital necessary to elicit social change. This story is also a brief history of how these Chicana feminist organizations emerged.

Flores was born in Los Angeles on December 3, 1913, six years before women won the right to vote in the United States. The child of a poor working family, she lived through the Depression, when racial and gender prejudice made it even more difficult for Mexican men and women to earn a decent living.[2] Flores's feminism was a logical outcome of her experience as a child and her activism. She was a passionate and determined civil rights activist. She strongly believed in equal rights and equal representation. Flores saw politics as a necessary means to make the community a better place.[3] She was progressive in her politics. She opposed racial segregation; she advocated for labor unions, national health insurance, public works jobs, and women's equality. She was an activist in the California Independent Progressive Party and the National Progressive Party.[4] She was also a member of Mexican American civil rights organizations such as the Sleepy Lagoon Barrio Defense Committee in 1942; Asociación Nacional México Americana, founded in 1949;[5] the Community Service Organization (CSO), formed in 1947;[6] and the Mexican American Political Association (MAPA), created in 1960.[7]

Equally important, in July of 1963, Flores and Delfino Varela became the publishers and associate editors of a bimonthly opinion and informational newsletter, *Carta Editorial*. In general its focus was Mexican American politics. The purpose of the newsletter was to present a point of view absent in the mainstream press.[8] Flores and Varela wrote op-ed and informational pieces. In so doing, Flores created a public voice and critique that reflected her views concerning politics, civil rights, and gender discrimination. In addition, she recognized the accomplishments of Mexican American women.

Flores considered the national civil rights campaign a necessary platform for affirming Mexican American rights. Shortly after President Kennedy proposed civil rights legislation in June 1963, Flores and Varela expressed their support for civil rights in *Carta Editorial*. They reminded their readers that the US Declaration of Independence was also a part of the heritage of the Mexican American people.[9] In August 1963, while thousands of Americans prepared to march on Washington, DC, to support the enactment of civil rights legislation, Flores took to her typewriter and rallied the Mexican American community to support the civil rights movement. She believed that the fight for equality would bring about social and political changes that would produce a renaissance of development and growth not seen in the United States in many decades.[10]

In the same June issue of *Carta Editorial*, Flores exposed the hypocrisy of Mexican American leaders who condemned racism and yet practiced sexism. In August 1963, Vice President Lyndon Johnson, the chairman of the President's Committee on Equal Employment Opportunity, agreed to meet with Mexican American leaders in Los Angeles to discuss the unequal employment hiring practices faced by Mexican Americans and the status of Mexican Americans in the Democratic Party. MAPA sponsored a luncheon honoring Johnson and expected 1,000 guests. During a planning meeting for the luncheon, Congressman Edward Roybal and other MAPA leaders voted against having women represented at the head table during the event. Soon after the vote, the men were embarrassed when the women members, who were also present at the meeting, explained to the "brave bulls" that the vote to exclude women meant Lady Bird Johnson could not sit with her husband at the head table. It was then that the men realized that they would have to vote again to correct this omission. Flores publicly shamed the MAPA leaders for their provincial sexist behavior. In *Carta Editorial*, Flores wrote, "Women and Dogs not allowed. In some areas, Mexicans and dogs are not allowed. . . . This way of thinking is rapidly being relegated to the trashcan where it belongs. But not so where women are concerned for the MACHOS who met in Congressman Roybal's office."[11]

In late 1958, Flores and Ramona Tijerina Morín organized an alternative political space where Mexican American women activists could circumvent these types of heteropatriarchal practices. Ramona Morín was born in Kansas City, Missouri, in 1919, one year before women won the right to vote. Her family moved to Los Angeles in search of employment. By the eighth grade, Morín dropped out of school and went to work to augment their parents' earnings. Her husband, Raul Morín, was a World War II Bronze Medal and Purple Heart recipient and author of *Among the Valiant: Mexican-Americans in WW II and Korea*.[12] During the late 1940s, Ramona Morín and her husband encountered racist practices that blocked their socioeconomic opportunities. Eventually, racial discrimination and exclusion led them to join CSO, and they also helped organize the American G.I. Forum (AGIF) and American G.I. Forum Ladies Auxiliary (AGIFLA) in California.[13]

Francisca Flores and Ramona Morín were founding members of the CSO Los Angeles chapter (CSOLA) and MAPA.[14] Even so, they were dissatisfied that these organizations had not recognized the significant role women played in electing candidates. The work women did such as typing, stuffing envelopes, making telephone calls, registering people to vote, and taking them to the voting polls was undervalued. It went unnoticed because the work was viewed as an extension of men's work and a natural part of what women do to serve men.

Similarly, Flores and Morín were frustrated that although women in MAPA and CSO had the right to vote, there was resistance to electing women to executive elected positions. For example, CSO was established in 1947, and by 1958, there were more than thirty CSO chapters in California and Arizona. Women were at least 50 percent of its membership, and yet only a few chapters elected only a handful of women to the office of president or vice president.[15] CSOLA had never elected a woman president, and Henrietta Villaescusa, a founding CSO member, believed it never would. Consequently, Villaescusa left the CSOLA chapter, organized a new chapter in the Los Angeles neighborhood of Lincoln Heights, and was elected its first president.[16] Likewise, MAPA was founded in 1960; however, MAPA did not elect a woman president until 1973.[17]

In contrast, Mexican American women experienced upward mobility in the Democratic Party. Morín was the chairperson of the Democratic Women Committee of the East Los Angeles (ELA)-Belvedere club. Elected officials appointed Villaescusa and Morín to the Democratic Party State Central Committee, and Governor Edmund "Pat" Brown appointed Villaescusa to one of California's state commissions.[18] Under these circumstances, Flores and Morín decided to create an alternative place for women to get involved in politics. A Mexican American women's political organization was appealing because it was independent, encouraged women to fulfill their potential, recognized women's accomplishments, empowered women to be decision makers, grew its own leaders, and thereby acquired various levels of political influence and power.

The Young Women's Christian Association (YWCA) was an example of a leading national woman's organization, and it was one of the most powerful and influential in the country. In addition, it was inclusive. In 1956, the YWCA pledged to utilize its influence and resources to eliminate racism, empower women, and include minority women in the YWCA boards of directors. And in 1962 Morín became a member of the YWCA board of directors.[19]

Morín knew from personal experience that Mexican American women had more success acquiring leadership positions in women's organizations such as the YWCA and AGIFLA. In addition to her experience with the YWCA, Morín had also been the chairwoman of the California AGIFLA from 1956 to 1957 and of the Los Angeles AGIFLA chapter from 1956 to 1962.[20]

In the past, other Mexican American women had also formed their own independent activist organizations in reaction to being disenfranchised by male-dominated Mexican American political organizations. The League of United Latin American Citizens (LULAC) was founded in 1929 and the American G.I. Forum was created in 1948. Membership in the organizations was open to Mexican American men only. Nonetheless, the whole family participated in these organizations. Even though they did not have a vote, the wives were considered extensions of the husbands and were enlisted to assist in planning and implementing the organization's activities. The wives eventually enfranchised themselves when they established the League of United Latin American Citizens Ladies Auxiliary (LULACLA) in 1933 and AGIFLA in 1956. AGIFLA and LULACLA were interested in gaining equality for all Mexican Americans and did not start out advancing a feminist agenda. Nevertheless, the auxiliaries were independent women's activist organizations. Their activities included voter registration and campaigns to desegregate schools. What is more, they recognized women's accomplishments, empowered women to be decision makers, and grew their own leaders.[21]

In similar fashion, in 1958 Flores and Morín decided to create their own women's political organization, the League of Mexican American Women. From 1958 to 1964, Morín was the League's president and Flores was its secretary. Most of the women who joined the League were seasoned activists from CSO, MAPA, and the Democratic Party.

The goals of the League were to provide a safe place where a "band of women" could share ideas and vent frustrations resulting from the limitations imposed on women in the male-dominated movement and society. The League offered Mexican American women opportunities to collaborate and improve problem solving, decision making, and leadership skills. The League organized political educational forums where they would discuss issues affecting their communities. The League's aim was to prepare women to unite people to work for peace, eliminate racism, and achieve equal socioeconomic opportunities for their communities and for Mexican American women.[22]

In addition, the League organized an annual achievement award banquet from 1960 to 1969 to publicly acknowledge the value and significance of women's contributions to the movement.[23] Each year the League solicited names and information about women who were leaders in Mexican American communities. At each event, two women received the League's Outstanding Achievement Award, and twenty-five women received the Honor Roll Award for making a difference in their communities. These recognition awards served an important role because they contradicted the prevailing racial and gender myths that existed at the time. Blatant segregation and racial and gender prejudice was the norm, and there was hostile resistance to changing the status quo. Wherever Mexican Americans resided, Anglo society considered them a lesser race, incapable of achievements comparable to those of Anglo-Americans. What is more, society in general was also incredulous that Mexican American women were capable and qualified to perform leadership roles. The League's recognition of women's accomplishments shattered the common sexist stereotype that Mexican American women were generally subordinate, ignorant, barefoot, and pregnant. Therefore, it was a significant accomplishment that political and community leaders who attended the women's achievement award banquets walked away aware that there were Mexican American women who made a difference in politics and in social change.

The League's banquets did more than recognize women. The League gained recognition as a women's political organization. The League orchestrated the women's achievement awards banquets to occur just before the primary elections. Local, state, and national political and community leaders attended these events to win support and votes. The public acknowledgement served as a political strategy to draw attention to the League's political importance to the Democratic Party and Mexican American politics. The League endorsed candidates and organized social events where candidates campaigned for the Mexican American vote. Movers and shakers in the Democratic Party and in the Mexican American movement attended these banquets.[24]

The time had come when politicians saw the value of gaining the Mexican American vote. In 1962, candidates sought the Mexican American vote thanks in large part to the Viva Kennedy campaign that helped elect John Kennedy as president of the United States in 1960. In 1962, Governor Edmund Brown was running for reelection, and George Brown Jr. was running for Congress. In addition, for the first time in the twentieth century, Mexican Americans were running for California Assembly and Congress. Los Angeles City Councilman Edward Roybal was running for Congress. John Moreno and Phil Soto were running for the California State Assembly.[25]

Flores and Morín decided the time was right to put a spotlight on the role Mexican American women played in the electoral process. Since the women in the League belonged to the ELA Belvedere Democratic Club, the League organized the achievement awards banquet under the auspices of the Democratic Women of the ELA Belvedere Democratic Club. The League scheduled the event just before the 1962 primary election. The purpose of the event was to recruit women from the Democratic party to campaign for George Brown and Edward Roybal. The theme was "Outstanding Women in Politics." The awards banquet had a dual purpose, to support candidates running for election and to publicly recognize what the League referred to as the "unsung heroines" who worked side by side with men building Mexican American political power and organizations in the movement. The League appreciated that: "Some of these women are dynamos, while others are followers, but all of them are doers. Unfortunately, for many reasons, the Mexican American woman's work, contributions and/or activity, has not been properly recognized."[26]

Flores and Morín wrote,

> This banquet and its presentation of women active in our community is but a brief view of what actually is a way of life for many others who quietly come forward when work needs to be done. It is hoped that in singling out those presented, all will share in the honor, which is given today in recognition of the vitality women lend [to] the political campaigns. Let the roster grow so that next year, twice or three times as many will be presented.[27]

Flores and Morín were in charge of publicity. Flores was the acting secretary of the ELA Belvedere Democratic Club and sent out a letter, inviting club members to the event. In her usual brusque manner, she bluntly stated that men would have a minor role in the event. She said, "This banquet will be strictly a women's affair. The only men who will speak will be some of the candidates."[28] In contrast,

Morín, the president of ELA Democratic Club, sent out a more diplomatic press release that had a more inclusive message regarding the role of men. She said, "Although the banquet is dedicated to women, a very special most cordial invitation is extended to the men to attend, after all, without the men where would the women be."[29]

The event was the talk of the town, and the list of attendees included all the candidates running for election from the Democratic Party as well as MAPA and CSO leaders. The Outstanding Women in Politics Achievement Award Banquet was so successful that the League continued holding the banquets until 1969. During that time, the League recognized more than 100 community and professional Mexican American women from California, Colorado, and Arizona. Some of the League's honorees were self-educated, and others were college-educated. All the same, the League knew it had only tapped the surface of wealth in the human resources that women represented.[30]

For the League's 1966 achievement awards banquet, Morín and Flores wrote, "Each woman who to date received an Achievement Award or who has answered the Honor Roll Call, is a history of devotion and hard work. And the sum total of all of these women is a firm foundation for a history of Mexican American women in the Southwest—USA."[31] In *Carta Editorial*, Flores also noted that these annual banquets offered an important opportunity for "Mexican American feminists" to "assess the female contributions to the community."[32]

Over the years, the outstanding achievement awards went to Mexican American women activists who would influence public policy and would have a positive impact on the lives of future generations. In addition, many of them played significant roles in pushing forward the early Chicana feminist agenda in the 1970s. For example, at least two of the Outstanding Achievement Award (OAA) recipients, Graciela Olivarez and María Urquides, organized a chapter of the League in Phoenix and Tucson, Arizona, respectively. They also spoke at the first national Chicana conference, in Houston in 1971.[33] Today, most of these women have received national recognition for their leadership and lifetime achievements to improve society. Be that as it may, in the 1960s these women were an open secret to most in the movement. Hence, it is important to give examples of some of the recipients of the League's Outstanding Achievement Award between 1962 and 1966 and to appreciate their accomplishments at the time of the award.

The 1962 recipients of the Outstanding Women in Politics award went to Judge Vaino H. Spencer and Lucille Beserra Roybal.[34] Judge Spencer, an African American lawyer, was a leader in the civil rights movement and the first woman of color to become a California municipal court judge.[35] Lucille Beserra Roybal, the wife of Edward Roybal, was a founding member of CSO in 1947 and of MAPA in 1960. She led a "Get out the Vote" campaign that resulted in the election of Edward Roybal to the Los Angeles City Council in 1949. She was the first Latina voter registrar in Los Angeles County. She deputized 125 CSO members as voter registrars, and under her leadership, they registered 12,000 new voters. At the banquet, Beserra

Roybal thanked the League for recognizing her work and said it <u>was the first time in twelve years</u> of service that she had received public recognition for her achievements in politics.[36]

The 1963 OAAs went to Bertha Solorio and Graciela Olivarez.[37] Latin music and dances such as the mambo and the cha-cha were very popular at this time, and Bertha Solorio was the marketing manager for RCA Records Latin Department in Los Angeles. The League appreciated Solorio's success given that it was rare at that time for a woman, much less a Mexican American woman, to represent a national record company.[38]

Graciela Olivarez was a thirty-five-year-old high school dropout and single parent who in the 1950s began her vocation in civil rights in Phoenix, Arizona. By the time she received the League's award, she had received a grant from the Ford Foundation to study the impact of racial discrimination on the living conditions of Mexican Americans in the five southwestern states and had reported her findings at the 1963 hearing of the US Commission of Economic Opportunity in Arizona.[39]

The 1964 OAAs went to Audrey Rojas Kaslow and Lena Lovato Archuleta. Audrey Rojas Kaslow was a licensed clinical social worker and a probation officer for the California Department of Corrections. She was the first director of community relations in Los Angeles for the California Fair Employment Practices Commission for the California Department of Industrial Relations.[40] During that year, Rojas Kaslow waged an unsuccessful campaign against the real estate industry–sponsored Proposition 14. When Proposition 14 was passed in 1964, it repealed the 1963 Rumford Fair Housing Act and amended the California constitution to allow discrimination in the sale or rental of housing; fortunately, in 1967 the Supreme Court ruled that Proposition 14 was unconstitutional and overturned it.[41]

Lena Lovato Archuleta, forty-four at the time, was an elementary school teacher and librarian who fought for desegregation in education and assisted in the implementation of bilingual bicultural curriculum in Denver, Colorado. In 1964, Lovato Archuleta was also one of three community activists who cofounded the Latin American Research and Service Agency (LARASA) in Denver. The purpose of LARASA was to address the needs of Latinos in education, youth motivation, job development, training and employment, health and welfare, housing, and community resources.[42]

The 1965 OAAs went to Faustina Solis, forty-two, and Maria Urquides, fifty-five.[43] Faustina Solis had become the assistant director of the California Department of Community Services and Development and oversaw the California War on Poverty programs such as VISTA (Volunteers in Service to America) and Job Corps for Youth. Before this appointment, she had been a medical social worker for the California State Department of Health Services, where she pioneered education, day care, housing, and health care programs for migrant workers.[44]

In 1965, Maria Urquides, an elementary school teacher in Tucson, was the chair and the only woman on the Arizona Board of Public Welfare. In 1950, she initiated campaigns to desegregate Tucson schools. In addition, she played a pivotal role in the passage of federal legislation for bilingual education.[45]

The 1966 OAAs went to Dolores Huerta and Lilia Acuna Aceves.[46] The League recognized Dolores Huerta's accomplishments as the first woman in the United States to become a vice president of a union. In 1966, Huerta negotiated the first United Farm Workers Organizing Committee (UFWOC) contract with the Schenley Vineyard Company. This was the first time in US history that farmworkers negotiated a collective bargaining agreement with an agricultural corporation. In 1965, Huerta became the lead organizer of the grape boycott in New York. As a lobbyist for CSO, she was instrumental in garnering votes to pass a variety of legislation for the farmworkers and the poor, including the 1961 Noncitizen Old Age Pension for California residents.

It was difficult being a female union organizer. In the beginning, farmworkers did not accept Huerta because she was an independent woman traveling alone. The men would often cancel house meetings or walk out of meetings when they saw that the union organizer was a woman. Nevertheless, she organized hiring halls, administered union contracts, and conducted grievance procedures on behalf of farmworkers.[47]

Lilia Aceves said she was uncomfortable receiving the 1966 OAA. She felt her community activism paled when compared to Dolores Huerta's. The League nonetheless believed her activism in the child care movement and with the Los Angeles Board of Education was noteworthy. The League recognized that without child care, few women would have become activists.[48] Aceves had been the president of a parent group with the Heights Nursery Cooperative, a child care center serving children living in the Ramona Gardens public housing. The League recognized Aceves for her leadership role in getting parents involved in their children's education.[49]

Aceves had also excelled in the Mexican-American Education Ad Hoc Committee. This was a subcommittee of the Los Angeles Board of Education Ad Hoc Committee. In 1964, four years before the East Los Angeles student walkouts, the Mexican-American Education Ad Hoc Committee recommended that the board implement a bilingual and bicultural curriculum and hire bilingual and bicultural teachers and administrators. According to Aceves, the Los Angeles Board of Education accepted their recommendations but said that it could only implement them if the Mexican American community supported a measure to increase taxes. Aceves and other members of the Mexican-American Education Ad Hoc Committee countered with the argument that to date, taxes paid by the Mexican American community had been used to improve schools outside of the community. It asserted that it was time that the Board of Education change this practice and redirect funds from these taxes back into the schools in ELA. The net result was that these recommendations were never implemented, and in 1968, high school students walked out to protest the failure to provide adequate and relevant education.[50]

The League believed the OAA events demonstrated that there was more than an adequate supply of competent, trained, and experienced Mexican American women who were leaders in the community. Therefore, Flores was aghast when governmental and national women's antipoverty programs continued to exclude Mexican American women from governmental advisory and decision-making positions. In 1964, Flores noted that Los Angeles Mayor Sam Yorty had failed to appoint Mexican American women to the Los Angeles City Commission on the Status of Women.[51] Also the following year, Mexican American women were again not represented in the newly funded antipoverty Job Corp programs. In 1965, the newly established Women in Community Service Inc. (WICS) antipoverty agency from Washington, DC, received funding to administer a Job Corps employment-training program to train low-income women in Los Angeles. WICS was the product of the coalition of the Church Women United, National Council of Catholic Women, National Council of Jewish Women, and the National Council of Negro Women. The purpose of WICS was to expand the focus of the Job Corp program to include low-income minority women as well as men. Their mission was to fight racism and to improve poor women's socioeconomic status.[52] And yet, Flores doubted their sincerity and ability to serve Mexican American women because WICS had not included Mexican American women in executive and administrative levels of the organization, and its Los Angeles employment-training program did not target Mexican American women as a service group. Frustrated but determined, Flores and the League set out to change things.[53]

First, the League had to attract national political attention. The League's strategy was to ally with the AGIFLA and exert political pressure on the leaders of the antipoverty federal programs to include Mexican American women in the planning, development, and implementation of antipoverty programs for women. The first step was to make a political statement on behalf of Mexican American women at the national level. The opportunity came at the 1967 annual conference of Women in the War on Poverty, in Washington, DC. It was sponsored by a coalition of women's organizations intent on ensuring that antipoverty programs served poor women as well as men.[54] Francisca Flores, Graciela Olivarez, and Maria Urquides, along with Dominga G. Coronado, president of the Austin, Texas, AGIFLA, and Clotilde García, a physician and founder of AGIFLA, all spoke at the conference. When Flores spoke, she pressed the conference leaders to include Mexican American women when planning future conferences. Ultimately, her message was heard and Graciela Olivarez was appointed to the national coordinating committee of women volunteers that would plan the next conference of Women in the War on Poverty.[55]

Next, the League allied with AGIFLA to address WICS exclusion of Mexican American women in its organization and its programs. During the week of October 26, 1967, four of the fifty-one Mexican American presenters at President Johnson's Cabinet Hearings on Mexican American Affairs in El Paso, Texas, were women. Both Flores and Morín attended the conference. Morín represented the

League and the California AGIFLA. Dominga G. Coronado, then the chair of the national AGIFLA, made the case against WICS. She said that WICS was not quali- fied to serve Mexican American women because it had excluded them from its organizational structure and it had failed to deliver services to them. The League supported Coronado's recommendation that WICS include Mexican American women in positions of authority and planning and that its employment proposals detail how it would serve Mexican American women.[56] WICS accepted AGIFLA's recommendations and invited AGIFLA to join the WICS Executive Committee in 1971; it was the only nonreligious organization on the committee.[57]

It may not have been lost on Flores that AGIFLA and not the League had achieved national political recognition. The problem was that the League was not a national organization and did not have the human resources to operate on a national basis. Her vision to build a national Chicana feminist political organiza- tion may have crystalized at that time. Flores and other members of the League such as Simmie Romero Goldsmith, Josephine Valdez Banda, Evelyn Velarde Ben- son, and Irene Mendes were all seasoned activists who had helped found MAPA and other Mexican American organizations. Now they were ready to embark on creating their own national Chicana feminist organization.

The opportunity to organize a national Chicana feminist organization came in 1970. Manuel Banda, Josephine Valdez Banda's husband and chairperson of the planning committee for the first Annual Mexican American National Issues Conference (AMANIC), asked Flores and the League to organize a Chicana work- shop for the conference.[58] Since the early 1960s, Flores had been conducting Chi- cana workshops to discuss why women should have equality in male-dominated Mexican American movement organizations. The workshops were open to men, but only a few attended. Instead, the workshops became consciousness-raising forums where recommendations for change were submitted, but few if any changes occurred.[59] This time, Flores and the League decided to use the 1970 Chicana workshop to inspire women to create their own organization.

AN ORGANIZATION OF OUR OWN: THE 1970 CHICANA WORKSHOP AND THE FOUNDING OF COMISIÓN FEMENIL

First, Flores had to determine if Chicanas were ready to start their own organiza- tion. Flores and Romero Goldsmith developed a list of preliminary ideas to dis- cuss at the workshop in the form of a survey to identify what Chicanas believed were the major issues confronting them including what they thought about women's rights and the women's movement. Valdez Banda, Velarde Benson, and Mendes distributed the survey statewide to women who were members of MAPA, AGIFLA, the Association of Mexican American Educators (AMAE), and Chicano college student organizations.

The survey asked Chicanas what they thought about the new women's rights legislation such as the 1963 Equal Pay Act, the removal of protective legislation for women in the workplace, and new provisions requiring maternity leave with pay. It also asked what feminism meant to them and what direction they saw the Chicana going.[60]

By 1970, the first two minority women had been elected to Congress. Patsy Takemoto Mink, a Japanese American woman, was elected in 1965, and Shirley Chisholm, an African American woman, was elected in 1968.[61] However, a Chicana had yet to be elected to in the United States Congress. The survey asked Chicanas what they thought about women running for public office. The 1965 Economic Opportunity Act provided funding for child care for low-income families through Head Start programs.[62] Survey respondents were asked if they supported sending their children to child care centers. In 1965, the Supreme Court in *Griswold v. Connecticut* gave married couples the right to use birth control. In 1970, Title X of the Public Health Service Act made contraceptives available regardless of income, and yet it was still illegal for single women to use birth control in twenty-six states and abortion was still illegal in all states.[63] The survey asked whether Chicanas supported birth control and abortion. During the Vietnam War, General Lewis B. Hershey, the US Selective Service director, announced that should the government have an inadequate number of men to serve in the army, there were plans to draft women into the military.[64] Therefore, the survey asked whether women should be drafted.

In general, Chicanas did not respond to any specific questions about women's civil rights. And yet, the respondents appeared ready to entertain the idea of starting a Chicana organization. Among the topics that they suggested be discussed at the workshop were these: Why were Mexican American women suppressed, and what could be done to liberate them? How were the objectives of the Chicana movement different from the Chicano movement? Why did Chicanas have to separate from the Chicano movement? What would be the objectives of a Chicana organization? What were the differences between Mexican American women's movement and other women's movements? What were the irreconcilable effects of machismo and Chicana liberation in the home, business, and movement and on interpersonal relationships? And what did Chicana liberation mean for homemakers and housewives?[65]

The responses to the survey reflected the increasing discontent with the growing pervasiveness of "macho" attitudes toward women in the movement since the 1969 National Chicano Youth Liberation Conference was held in Denver. At the youth conference, cultural nationalism was formally adopted as the ideology of the Chicano movement. Cultural nationalism appeared to promote orthodox Mexican traditional family values and signaled a shift further to the right regarding women's roles in the movement and the family. At the conference, a group of Chicanas organized a Chicana Caucus to discuss equality for women and the role of women in the movement. During the caucus, a debate developed between Chicana traditionalists who held that women's role was to support the men in the movement and the feminists who insisted that their struggle was to achieve equality and self-determination for both Chicanos and Chicanas. The majority of the participants supported the feminist position and approved a resolution that in general asserted that the women in the movement were repressed; women should adopt a new, revolutionary consciousness that defined Chicanas as equal human beings; and Chicanas should be encouraged to participate in all levels of the struggle according to their capabilities. In addition, they stipulated that men and women were jointly responsible for the care of the home, family, and education of the children. They resolved that Chicanas should organize and educate other Chicanas to strive for self-determination and equality for women as well as men.

Regrettably, this resolution was never given to the general assembly. Instead, the assembly heard the resolution that was written by the minority point of view, the Chicana traditionalists. It said, "It was the consensus of the group that the Chicana woman does not want to be liberated."[66] Although this statement represented the minority point of view held in the caucus, it has been echoed for decades as the only point of view.[67] Rather than having a chilling effect, the 1969 Chicana Caucus resolution motivated feminists to act, and it launched a perfect environment to consider initiating a Chicana political organization.

Flores was pleased with the survey's results. She saw the larger picture. She recognized that the passage of the new civil rights legislation gave rise to powerful women's political organizations that lobbied for laws and social policy without input from Mexican American women. In addition, Flores believed that the only way to deal with the opposition to gender equity in the movement was to do the unthinkable: organize a separate Chicana political organization.

The momentous Chicana workshop occurred on October 10, 1970, in Sacramento, California. It was different from previous Chicana workshops in that it was scheduled for six hours, enough time to create a new organization. Flores asked eight women, Irene Tovar, Frances Bojórquez, Josefa Sanchez, Lillian Aceves, Polly Baca, Cecilia Suarez, Marion Ojeda, and Bernice Rincon, to present three-minute issue papers to open the discussion and set the tone.[68] The discourse that followed was tape-recorded and transcribed by Arturo Cabrera. More than forty people attended the workshop and made history. Flores started the workshop by suggesting that the women consider discussing the need for creating a women's political organization. She said she hoped that the outcome of the workshop would be to establish a committee to create a Mexican American women's political organization.

The workshop began with a discussion about the stereotypical myth that Chicanas did not need an education because married women did not work. Bernice Rincon, thirty-nine, a member of MAPA and AMAE and a director of a Fresno Head Start program, passed out the paper she prepared for the workshop. The title of the paper was "La Chicana, Her Role in the Past, and Her Search for a New Role in the Future."[69] Rincon said that women need an education just as much as men do. She contended that seven out of ten married Chicanas worked after they got married. They worked when husbands were low-wage earners or became disabled and were unable to work. What is more, many married women became single heads of households before the age of forty. Rincon knew from personal experience how true this picture was. First, both her mother and father worked all their married life, and second, Rincon was a single parent and had to work to support her family. In 1944, she graduated from Fresno High School and joined the Women's Army Corps because she did not have the financial means to go to college. Unfortunately, the military discharged her after she married and became pregnant. Shortly thereafter, she became a single parent and had to find a job immediately. She worked full time as a barber and went to college part-time until she graduated and became an elementary school teacher. As her education increased, so did her earning power.[70]

Another topic of discussion centered around the failure to recognize the contributions of Mexican American women. The 1965 OAA recipient, Maria Urquides, proudly reported that the League had spent the last ten years acknowledging outstanding Mexican American women. And yet, she was dismayed that a recently published study guide, *A Mexican American Source Book* by Feliciano Ribera, was about outstanding Mexican Americans but failed to include any pictures of or information about outstanding Mexican American women.[71]

Flores joined in to say that the accomplishments of women in CSO also went unrecognized until the League took action. She said,

> We had women registrars for years, but no one knew about it. We felt we had many women who were doing as much if not more than the men. The only problem was that no one knew about it. The work women did in campaigns went unnoticed. Lucille Roybal was very active in all of Edward Roybal's campaigns, but no one knew about it until the League of Mexican American Women recognized her.[72]

The conversation shifted to equal representation of women in leadership positions. Women testified that there was intense resistance against electing women to the office of president in MAPA and Chicano college student organizations such as Movimiento Estudiantil Chicano de Aztlán (MEChA). Flores observed, "As long as women participated in organizations controlled by men, the women would continue to find themselves stuck in the kitchen or at the registration table while men made decisions in the dining room or inside the conference room."[73] Most of the women agreed that it was unlikely that they would achieve equal status in male-dominated organizations. They concluded that although they did not want to become separatists, they reluctantly agreed there was no other choice but to form their own women's organization.

The women envisioned a commission of Mexican/Chicana women that would "terminate the exclusion of female leadership in the Chicano/Mexican movement" as well as advocate on their behalf.[74] The workshop named the commission the Comisión Femenil Mexicana (CFM). It would prepare Mexican American women to assume leadership positions and nominate them to local, state, and federal Commissions on the Status of Women and other policy-making entities. In so doing, it would lobby for legislation such as access to birth control and the legalization of abortion as well as for other measures that improved the socioeconomic status of Mexican American women.

There were so many things that CFM would accomplish. It would create bilingual/bicultural, twenty-four-hour child care centers to facilitate women's ability to complete their education, enter the labor market, and work without having the burden of leaving their children home and unattended. CFM would disseminate news and information regarding the work and achievement of Mexican/Chicana women. What is more, it would open up communication and ally with other women's organizations on issues facing women in the world.

The women at the workshop elected Flores as chairwoman and Simmie Romero Goldsmith as secretary of the CFM steering committee charged with the responsibility of building CFM into an organization.[75] Following the conference, Flores and Goldsmith created the newsletter *Comisión Femenil Mexicana Report*, also called the CFM *Report*. The newsletter would give an account of the CFM steering committee's activities and impart news as to what other Chicanas were doing to advance equal rights and equal representation as well as recruit Chicanas to participate in legislative forums regarding social policy that had a direct impact on Mexican American women such as child care legislation and employment.[76]

A year later, it was time for Flores to give a formal account of the steering committee's activities. Since CFM was born at the 1970 Chicana workshop held at the first annual Mexican American National Issues Conference and the workshop's resolutions dictated CFM's original platform of issues, Flores saw it as her duty to give a progress report at the next conference to the 1971 Chicana workshop participants.[77] Be that as it may, the women at the 1971 Chicana workshop did not see themselves as being CFM's constituent body. They recommended that CFM organize a separate annual conference, establish a governing body, and set its own goals. About six months later, CFM held its first conference on March 12, 1972, and Josephine Valdez Banda was elected the second CFM president. Valdez Banda was a teacher and one of the founders of AMAE. Under Valdez Banda's leadership, CFM established Comisión Femenil Mexicana Nacional (CFMN) as the umbrella organization of individual CFM chapters. In order to secure funding to start up future Chicana programs, CFMN became a nonprofit corporation.[78]

Building a new organization required a full-time effort to organize chapters and provide leadership training. Regardless, the members of CFMN's executive committee worked full-time jobs and did not have the financial means that would allow them to quit their day jobs. Instead, CFMN recruited new members and provided leadership training at its annual statewide conferences and at local Chicana conferences; in turn, it encouraged its members to bring together ten women to form local CFM chapters.

New CFM chapters gradually came into being. For example, soon after the 1970 Chicana workshop, Flores worked with Frances Bojórquez and a group of

Chicana students at California State College in Los Angeles (CSCLA) to form the first CFM campus chapter. On January 19, 1971, CFM was recognized as a new student organization at CSULA. La Comisión Femenil De Arizona, and CFM Los Angeles, were founded in 1972.[79]

In its early years, CFMN reluctantly put aside organization building because it was busy starting up programs that were consistent with its program goals. For example, in March 1972, Flores attended a US Department of Labor women's conference and came back with an agreement to fund a Chicana self-help and advocacy center for women's rights. They called it the Chicana Service Action Center (CSAC).

At the 1971 Chicana workshop, CFM made a resolution to establish a women's center that would provide information, training, and social services.[80] CFMN fulfilled that commitment when CSAC opened its doors on July 15, 1972. It was housed at the International Institute, a branch of the YWCA, in the Boyle Heights neighborhood of East Los Angeles. Initially, Lilia Aceves was the CSAC director. When Aceves resigned in 1973, Flores became the CSAC executive director.[81]

Flores had minimal training to be an executive director. She was self-educated. She had worked as a journalist and in public relations; however, she had worked primarily as a secretary and clerk, with some administrative and management experience. Assuming the duties of the executive director entailed a substantial learning curve; still, she was up for the challenge and exceeded all expectations.[82] The CFMN executive committee was also inexperienced in administering a government contract. In their eagerness to get the job done, the CFMN board members appointed themselves to the CSAC board of directors, rather than recruit new blood for the job. Consequently, CFMN became consumed with the tasks of starting up the CSAC. Instead of focusing on building a community organization, they had to learn how to operate as a contracting agent and sustain funding as well as oversee a new employment program.

Over time, the members of the CFMN executive board became concerned that it was losing its identity as a community organization and becoming more an agent for CSAC. Valdez Banda believed CFMN needed to create a new CFM chapter that could take the lead in expanding the CFMN network. Under Valdez Banda's direction, Evelyn Velarde Benson organized a committee to establish the Los Angeles CFM (CFMLA) chapter. In November 1972, eighty women attended the founding of the CFMLA chapter and elected Gloria Molina its first president. For better or worse, CFMLA also became enmeshed in CSAC. According to one CFMN board member, Flores, the CSAC director, had more influence on the role of the CFMLA than the CFMN board.[83] Instead of focusing on building new chapters or building its own membership, it soon became consumed with starting up two child care centers, Centro de Niños in East Los Angeles and Echo Park, funded by the state Department of Education in 1973.[84]

By 1975, both CFMN and CSAC had expanded. CFMN had five new chapters (three in Los Angeles, one in Fresno, and one in Oakland) and an effective

got sucked into CSAC

advocacy program. Furthermore, CSAC had grown from a $50,000 self-referral program to a $500,000 employment program with two employment centers in Los Angeles, and it had plans to create more centers and programs. CSAC had expanded faster than the CFMN/CSAC Board could manage. It is not surprising that the board had difficulty keeping up with its duties as CSAC's contracting agent and eventually relinquished all CSAC board responsibilities. As a result, CSAC became incorporated and created its own independent CSAC board of directors.[85] Initially, this was a painful growing experience, but in the long run it was good for both organizations. CFMN was then able to refocus on growing its organization, and CSAC's leadership would continue to devote its total attention to expanding its own programs.

CONCLUSION

Francisca Flores played a pivotal role in creating a political space where Chicanas came together to form three Chicana feminist organizations in Los Angeles. This all began with the establishment of the League of Mexican American Women and its campaign to recognize the achievements of women in politics. At the 1970 Chicana workshop, Flores facilitated a consensus for Chicanas to establish their own political organization.

Flores brought together seasoned women activists, and they established the League, CFMN, and CSAC. These organizations gave more women the opportunity to gain executive, organizational, and leadership experience than did traditional organizations. In so doing, they circumvented the heteropatriarchal bottleneck that existed in male-dominated organizations and achieved equal status with these organizations in the community. In so doing, they helped launch the early Chicana feminist movement.

2 MUJERES BRAVAS

HOW CHICANAS SHAPED THE FEMINIST AGENDA AT THE NATIONAL IWY CONFERENCE IN HOUSTON, 1977

MARTHA P. COTERA

In 1976, as Chicana feminists in Texas we could hardly believe that magical moment for women. After decades advocating for the Equal Rights Amendment (ERA), it was ratified in thirty-four states including Texas by coalitions of women of color and mainstream feminists. A supportive federal government, energized by enthusiastic US representatives attending the 1975 UN International Women's Year (IWY) conference in Mexico City on the status of women worldwide, proposed a follow-up IWY National Women's Conference in Houston, Texas, in 1977. The IWY National Women's Conference would be preceded by preparatory state IWY meetings in 1976–1977, and our Texas Women's Meeting was scheduled for June 24–26, 1977, in Austin. For Chicanas active in the Chicano movement's Raza Unida Party (RUP) and in the Democratic and Republican Parties, these meetings were opportunities for final ratification of the ERA and instituting essential pro-women policies. This essay recounts the sequence of events and organizing by Texas Chicanas with our national networks to achieve a pro-ERA, pro-woman Texas Women's Meeting and to ensure the success of the 1977 IWY National Women's Conference in Houston despite documented obstructionist actions by prominent white feminists.

Initially, Chicanas were encouraged by the federal government's mandate on participation of women of color in the IWY state and national conferences. Incredulous, Chicana networks strategized our inclusion in state meetings, a once-in-a-lifetime opportunity to expand mainstream feminism, strengthen powerful coalitions with diverse communities through funded meetings, and develop leadership, possibly leading women of color to the national policy arena!

We envisioned preparatory state meetings in 1976–1977 easily approving the federal government's proposed pro-women resolutions including ratification of the ERA and approval of critical welfare rights and reproductive health resolutions for presentation to the 1977 IWY National Women's Conference. Far from it, the state preparatory meetings and even the 1977 IWY National Women's Conference in Houston became the site of Chicanas' last hurrah in the feminist movement. Sadly, our experience in 1976–1977, similar to the 1920s suffrage movement, revealed that white women leaders' passion for preserving the privilege of their race, class, and heterosexual preferences outweighed liberation for "every woman," actions I have previously experienced, researched, and documented.[1] After 1976–1977, as a veteran feminist, I considered that absent the passion, substance, skill, and everlasting activism of women of color, the mainstream feminist movement would be hollow, ineffectual, meaningless, and marginalized.

In 1976–1977 the Chicana community was in the throes of the Chicano movement (*el movimiento*), with all its moving parts, and passionately involved in RUP, a powerful third party in Texas chaired by María Elena Martínez and inclusive of strong Chicana feminists, equally at home in mainstream feminism.[2] Beyond Texas, RUP had ardent feminist supporters throughout the Southwest and Midwest who advocated for women's liberation and ratification of the ERA nationwide; prior to 1968 and by the time of RUP's founding in 1972, we had coalesced with progressive legislators, socialists, lesbian feminists, and progressive women on women's issues. Feminists in the Chicano movement were particularly concerned with addressing sexism, racism, and classism simultaneously.[3] Despite challenges within the Chicano movement, the emergent women's caucus of RUP in 1972 coalesced with other parties to lobby minority and progressive legislators, and it led in ratifying the ERA in Texas on June 22, 1972, leading to endorsement of the ERA in the Texas Raza Unida Party platform of 1972.

> Raza Unida Party resolves that: 1. The amendment to the US Constitution providing equal protection under the law for women be endorsed and supported.[4]

Similar ERA leadership was provided by Chicanas in California, Colorado, New Mexico, Illinois, Michigan, Wisconsin, Nevada, and other states with RUP partisans and Chicana feminists. The influential Comisión Femenil Mexicana Nacional of California enthusiastically championed the ERA.

> The Comisión worked with feminist organizations across the country to advocate for equal rights. The organization publicly endorsed the Equal Rights Amendment (ERA), and members participated in the Los Angeles Coalition for the ERA march in May 1976. Members also attended a rally to show solidarity with the national lobbying efforts in Springfield, Illinois. . . . An October 1976 quarterly report noted that CFMN was "aggressively" supporting passage of the ERA nationally, especially "in Arizona, Nevada and Illinois where Chicana organizations exist."

CFMN also joined NOW, the National Organization for Women, for a national march in support of the ERA in Washington, DC, in July 1978.[5]

So why support the ERA in the midst of a vigorous cultural nationalist Chicano movement? Feminists passionate about self-determination have been part of every decolonization and liberation movement of the Mexican and Mexican American community since the Spanish invasion in 1492. Further, from Texas's annexation to the United States in 1845 and since the United States appropriated half of Mexico's territory in 1848, US Chicana feminists have advocated decolonization and women's liberation and historically have been part of liberation movements for race, class, gender, labor, and environmental justice.[6]

Feminists Pauline Martínez, Maria Cardenas, María Elena Martínez, Pauline Jacobo, and I, with large numbers of Chicanas, were founders of the Texas Women's Political Caucus (TWPC) and also joined leaders Ruth "Rhea" Mojica Hammer, Gracia Molina de Pick, Lupe Anguiano, and other Chicanas nationwide in founding the National Women's Political Caucus (NWPC), focused on ERA ratification.[7] Unwittingly we became the conscience and voice for race, class, and sexual orientation in mainstream feminism. As a founding member of TWPC, at the first statewide meeting in Mesquite, Texas, March 11, 1972, I advocated addressing racism as well as sexism in the liberation struggle.[8]

The RUP Women's Caucus was incorporated into NWPC, equally ranked with caucuses representing the Democratic and Republican Parties; however, from the beginning, obstructionist actions by white feminist leaders hindered equality and leadership status for women of color. Affirmative votes for independent caucuses for women of color were undemocratically overturned by officials in NWPC in Washington, DC. Ruth "Rhea" Mojica Hammer, Pauline Martínez, and other women of color in leadership positions were marginalized, as shown in writings of Texas feminist Evey Chapa and chronicled in my book *Diosa y Hembra* and in Linda Garcia Merchant's groundbreaking video, *Las mujeres de la Caucus Chicana*.[9] Also very disturbing was the position of NWPC's leadership on the ERA. In 1977, with the ERA's approval pending in fifteen states and just three states short of ratification, Chicanas networked nationally with Ruth "Rhea" Mojica Hammer, Cecilia Burciaga, Pauline Martínez, Evey Chapa, Anita Cuarón, Olga Solíz, Jane Gonzalez, Enriqueta Vásquez, and Elizabeth "Betita" Martínez, plus leaders of the Comisión Femenil Mexicana Nacional, on coalitions with white feminists advocating ratification. In Texas, California, Colorado, Arizona, and New Mexico the ERA was ratified through lobbying efforts by women of color who provided support from grassroots communities for legislators voting for the amendment. Mindful of this, Chicanas from the Mexican American Business and Professional Women of Austin (MABPWA) and RUP met with national feminist leaders Liz Carpenter, Sarah Weddington, and Ann Richards,[10] engaged in ERA ratification to propose coalitions with minority communities in unratified states, since as prominent, well-funded leaders, they could potentially succeed in southern and Midwestern states with large minority constituencies. Unconvinced, the white leaders continued ineffectual top-down ERA lobbying while complaining that minorities were not ready for liberation! MABPWA members worried that these feminist leaders would sacrifice the ERA rather than legitimize and empower every woman.

By 1976, concerned with the real possibility of the ERA's eventual failure, Chicanas enacted piecemeal policy and programs in Austin, San Antonio, Los Angeles, El Paso, Denver, and other major cities through RUP, Brown Berets, non-profits like the Chicana Research and Learning Center, the Hispanic and women's chambers of commerce, the National Welfare Rights Organization, MABPWA's Texas chapters, and Comisión Femenil Mexicana Nacional's chapters nationally. Typical programs included Austin's Medical Assistance Program (including reproductive services), Center for Battered Women and Rape Crisis Center, arts institutions, and safe spaces for gays and lesbians. Chicana and Chicano studies programs were instituted nationwide, and for civil rights advocacy, the Mexican American Legal Defense and Education Fund (MALDEF) was established.

Chicana feminists in the Midwest were Ruth "Rhea" Mojica Hammer (*El Clarín* newspaper, Chicago), María Mangual (Mujeres Latinas en Acción, Chicago), Olga Villa (Midwest Council of la Raza, Indiana), and Janie Gonzalez (city council-woman, Muskegon, Michigan). Excellent documentation now exists in oral histories and institutional records being digitized by the Chicana por mi Raza Digital Memory Collective.[11] Also, Maylei Blackwell's work *¡Chicana Power! Contested Histories of Feminism in the Chicano Movement*, documents Chicana feminist institution building in the period.

> Throughout the 1970s US women of color built coalitions around key issues such as prisoners' rights and violence against women of color. . . . Other shared political interests that forged a women of color political project included a call to end forced sterilization and the articulation of a broader reproductive health agenda for women of color. . . . Various organizations started third world women's child-care centers and collectives to address the need for childcare that was attentive to linguistic and cultural differences. Other convergences occurred around labor rights, welfare rights, and access to education and affirmative action.[12]

In this context, and vastly experienced in policy and institution building, Chicanas embarked on the IWY National Women's Conference process, providing a second life for ERA ratification.

PROMISES, PROMISES: UNITED NATIONS IWY CONFERENCE IN MEXICO CITY, 1975

Another backstory and inspiration was Chicanas' presence at the UN IWY conference in Mexico City on June 19, 1975. Lupe Anguiano, María Rodriguez, and other Raza Unida Party delegates joined the "IWY Tribune" (unofficial counterpart to the government-representatives' conference), voicing dissatisfaction with the lack of minorities in the official US delegation and supporting the World Plan of Action to Improve the Conditions of Women. The "Presentation by Chicanas of RUP" identified our goal to work for "the liberation of all world women . . . from a premise of mutual respect for language and cultural variations."[13] It outlined the political ideals of a grassroots political party as a tool for Chicana/o liberation, and for liberation, not development, to be the vehicle for women's equality in this country. Yolanda M. López, representing California and reporting on the IWY Tribune conference, skeptically considered the IWY Plan of Action approved in Mexico City in 1975, saying that despite its "sincere sounding rhetoric," it would end up in the UN basement. She critiqued the official representation from the United States and other nations as representing their countries' national policies and not as chosen women's representatives. López contended, "The benefit of these conferences comes from the exchange of ideas and addresses the lower echelon participants. It is these women who paid their own way who are vitally concerned without benefit of official status who are the fundamental materials of change."[14]

Basically, Yolanda López expressed Chicana expectations for the IWY Mexico City conference to provide an internationally sanctioned policy agenda on women's issues for our use. As she stated, what ultimately mattered were our community collaborations, political growth, and grassroots work. Although the most vocal feminists in RUP were not selected to attend the unofficial conference, nevertheless, the international focus on women's liberation intensified our desire to ratify the ERA, which we considered pivotal to achieve color-blind liberation for US women.[15]

MORE PROMISES: IWY NATIONAL WOMEN'S CONFERENCE OF 1977

The international and national fervor also inspired the IWY National Women's Conference of 1977 and the related IWY Texas Women's Conference. US Congresswoman Bella Abzug, dismayed by the lack of "voice and no consensus among American women" following the United Nations IWY Conference in Mexico City of 1975, proposed Public Law 94–16, providing that state and regional meetings were to be held in 1976–1977, culminating in a National Women's Conference on November 18–21, 1977, in Houston. The primary purposes of state meetings and the national conference were to advocate for ERA ratification and celebrate International Women's Year. They were also to identify women's policies and programs in the United States for the next decade and to place "special emphasis on the representation of low-income women, members of diverse racial, ethnic, and religious groups, and women of all ages."[16]

Nationwide, RUP Chicanas and other networks monitored the call for a national IWY conference in 1977 administered by a newly expanded National

Commission on the Observance of International Women's Year (IWY) headed by Congresswoman Bella Abzug. The purpose was "to promote equality between men and women" and provide an appropriation of $5 million for state or regional meetings and for the national conference in 1977. The women's meeting in Texas would receive $100,000.[17]

Though initially Chicanas lacked representation on the expanded National Commission on the Observance of International Women's Year (IWY), our informal networks prioritized participation in our respective state IWY coordinating committees. By September 1976, feminist champions Cecilia Burciaga and Gracia Molina de Pick (California), Ruth "Rhea" Mojica Hammer (Illinois), Anita Cuarón (Colorado), and others set Chicana delegate goals for their states and personally challenged me to match them in Texas. Because of past political setbacks within NWPC and TWPC, Chicanas were loath to engage white feminists ever again; nevertheless, for our *hermanas* (sisters) and for the ERA we accepted. From September 1976 to early December 1976 we submitted to IWY national offices in Washington, DC, 100-plus pro-ERA Chicana nominees to serve on the Texas IWY Coordinating Committee. Still, by late December 1976, with a state meeting pending and a national conference to host in Texas by November 1977, Chicanas had no response on nominees or on instituting the IWY Coordinating Committee! Rumors that white feminists held closed-door meetings reached us, as did a leaked list of appointees to the Texas IWY Coordinating Committee, without Chicana feminists, lesbians, radical women, or progressive religious women. From Washington, DC, more leaked reports detailed closed meetings in Austin on December 28–29, 1976, involving leaders Liz Carpenter, Jane Hickie, and Cathy Bonner. Still no official communication with Chicanas (figures 2.1–2.4).[18]

Furious, Texas Chicanas lobbied IWY offices in Washington, DC, and our political representatives, demanding Texas's compliance with federal guidelines on race, ethnicity, religion, age, and income. We demanded inclusion on the Texas IWY Coordinating Committee and appointment of Chicanas to the National Commission of IWY. Information blackouts convinced us that white feminists intentionally excluded us and jeopardized the success of Texas's IWY conference, which depended on a diverse and politicized IWY Coordinating Committee. That meant Chicanas and our feminist allies, as the record shows, were the most experienced, organized, and seasoned pro-ERA advocates, therefore the most conversant with women's needs. Our passionate motivation sprang from our underprivileged, vulnerable, and marginalized condition, heightened by the need to resolve reproductive health and sexual orientation issues. Without Chicanas, lesbians, and progressive religious women, Texas, the host state for the national IWY conference, would not deliver a pro-ERA, pro-woman conference.[19]

Finally, in March 1977 Ruth "Rhea" Mojica Hammer (Illinois), Cecilia Burciaga (California), and Puerto Rican Carmen Delgado-Votaw (Maryland), strong feminists, were appointed to the National Commission for IWY. At-large delegate Gracia Molina de Pick (California) and the Comisión Femenil Mexicana Nacional

Ms. Pat Vasquez
Mexican American Education and Legal Defense Fund
Chicana Rights Project
501 Petroleum Commerce Building
201 North St. Marys Street
San Antonio, Texas   78205

Estimada Pat:

Here are some of my thoughts on the IWY experience. Unfortunately, I
still get incoherently angry when I think of it all. I don't trust
myself to talk to some Committee Members, yet. I guess in time.

I have it in writing from Owanah Anderson, the presiding officer,
"Had the Chicanas not come- - the Anti's would have taken the delegates". This was written begrudgingly.

But the question has to be asked, which group was placing the hurdles
before us, making racist - classist statements. Was it the Anti's?
No! It was the "white liberal women". The new world saviors.
However, in spite of the white feminists, chicanas made their mark.

Nos vemos,

Diana

Diana Camacho

FIGURE 2.1 Diana Camacho to Pat Vasquez, letter of transmittal.

Chicanas Change Course of Texas IWY

This statement is not too bold. It is not strong enough, it requires elaboration, realization, full discussion. Yes, we changed the course of Texas IWY. Chicanas have been monitoring IWY for years - since Mexico City, even. We were there, not officially but with our own money we made the trip. Then recently, like September, 1976 we sent over 100 nominations , just from Austin, for Texas Coordinating Committee membership to National IWY Commission. We stay on top of the nomination process. We wrote our congresspersons, called friends in Washington, held meetings, threatened and demanded representation, and we got <u>some</u>.

Through all this, Mexico City meeting to present, remember the name Martha Cotera; the energy, anger, stamina. If anyone deserves an award for the one who put it together, kept it together, encouraged the disillusioned-- give it to her. It's true one person did not do it all, but she was the constant current, the force. She tapped chicana talent, chicana resources, chicana energy and chicana anger. She pushed her activities across chicana party lines, across income levels, education levels, and organizational jealousies. While doing this, she wrote a book! "Chicana Feminism" What more can I say about her? Plenty.

Martha was not a member of Texas IWY Coordinating Committee - well, not officially anyway. The day before the Texas IWY Conference, one gringa said it was not fair that Martha seemed to be given the opportunity to speak her opinion more than most Committee Members. We pointed out that Martha attended more Coordinating Committee Meetings than more of its members; and so it went.

In January, 1977, the newly appointed Texas IWY Coordinating Committee members recieved word we were to meet in two weeks. We were (get this) to bring copies of proposals for the Texas IWY Conference, but federal regs were not available except for one copy at the State Library in Austin and copies committee members had. In two weeks we were to prepare conference proposals and bring 40 copies. Imagine. (Please read first attachment for fuller story) Then we found out about a meeting held in Austin, 6 to 8 weeks before, attended by Liz Carpenter, Jane Hickie, and Cathy Bonner. They discussed and decided what proposal Cathy Bonner would submit and strategies for awarding it to her. She had a copy of the regs. As you see she had 6 to 8 weeks, while we had less than two.

Chicanas who found out were pissed, we were mad!! How can I put it, "era rabia". We bootlegged a copy of names of Chicanas on the newly appointed committee. Using watts lines and other forms of communication, Chicanas in Austin invited them to meet us at Villa Capri Restaurant for a pre-meeting meeting the morning of the first Texas IWY Coordinating Committee Meeting, February, 1977. At the Villa Capri Chicana Meeting (photos of meeting available) we strategized, decided on motions, and resolutions.

At the Coordinating Committee Meeting, two hours later, all hell broke loose. Yes, we blew their "ladies tea party meeting", but from then on their respect for us was firmly established. Not that the rest of the months were easy, but they always knew we were not to be bought off, we had nothing to loose. Let me tell you, they knew and shall <u>not</u> now forget our presence.

FIGURE 2.2 Camacho report, "Chicanas Change Course of Texas IWY," page 1.

From IWY process and conference (September 1976 to June 1977), I gathered some interesting and pursuable relections. These reflections are outlined not in chronological narrative form, but by groups of people - no stereotyping intended. These are my observations of four different groups of women as seen by one Chicana on their interactions with Chicanas.

1. <u>Chicanas</u>: Energetic; open; up front; angry; heritage proud; sometimes viewing negotiations with other groups as sign of weakness; needing more experiences as to political processes; weak in task oriented meeting participation; apparently large numbers of us interact with only those of our own philosophy; seriously lacking in the speaking, persuasive, oratorical skills - those that sway groups; few have a chicana state perspective; unprepared for the in-vogue "assertive" tricks used on us; know our needs and issues; <u>not</u> requiring or wanting Chicana "Big Mamas."

2. <u>Radical Women</u>: Seeking allies; committed; least classist traits of any group there; flexible to the ethnic minority women's requests; able to deal with monstrous insults hurled at them; initial unawareness of diversity among chicanas, but quick to pick that up.

3. <u>White Liberal Women</u>: (The elected and those on organizations such as Caucus, WEAL, NOW, Women in Communications League, etc.) Back room decision making; patronizing; assuming they are leaders of mixed group coalitions; clumsy with ethnic minorities, not interacting naturally with chicanas; settling for minority coalition as best of two evils - felt option was chicanas or anti-ERA; using newly acquired assertiveness skills against ethnic minorities. (to quote a chicana - they were "mother-foggers"); while confident they speak for and represent us, they feel chicanas never represent them; righting a wrong still means hiring a Black - electing a Black; not involved in entire IWY process while blatant exclusion of certain groups evident; but scared into involvement when the anti-ERA became a real IWY force in their minds (two weeks before conference) i.e., still unwilling to coalesce with us when we are under attack but demanding coalition building and eloquent on its merits when they are threatened. Relying on their "Big Mamas."

4. <u>Other Ethnic Minorities</u>: Not entirely sure how to deal with a group they were not well acquainted with. They were familiar with the chicano but here were the women.

(2)

FIGURE 2.3 Camacho report, page 2.

I could elaborate on countless events to further substantiate evidence of the threat they felt. If I am asked, "Was that necessary?". Then I would realize how little, you reader, know of Chicana Herstory at hands of the "white feminist". (Please see attached memos and letters.) Be aware and try to mentally tabulate amount of money we spent out of out pockets. For the Texas Conference in June, Chicanas had a huge organization. We had Housing Committee, Resolutions Committee, Media and PR Committee, Chicana Caucus Meetings Committee, Food and Entertainment Committee, Chicana Reception Booth Committee. How many participated you ask. I need more time to gather the info. The organizing Chicanas in Austin met every Monday for three months.

Recommendation: Funding sought for a state Chicana conference, yes, we need to get together again, and again. Do you recall Chicanas across every line such as geography, party lines, education, income ever coming together? No. We need to learn skills together, share information, experiences, get angry, laugh, and cry together. It is long overdue. We did it in June, 1977, we can do it again. Call it a Chicana Congress.

(3)

FIGURE 2.4 Camacho report, page 3.

served as national resources. Chicanas totally understood the politics of their late appointment, seven months after launching plans for the state/regional and national conferences. One state meeting had been held, and four months remained to convene the rest prior to November 1977. Chicanas shared speculations that though late, the national commission appointments were to quiet our anger, provide token visibility, and through limited timing, to undermine the effectiveness of women of color and Chicana and Latina national commissioners. On March 18, 1977, Cecilia Burciaga expressed her concerns to me: "By a process that remains fairly mysterious to me—I've been appointed as a Commissioner on the National Commission on IWY. Ruth "Rhea" Mojica Hammer and I are two Chicanas thus far. I am very concerned about Texas and the politics in that state that Jimmy Carter is so indebted to."[20]

IWY Commissioner Ruth "Rhea" Mojica Hammer, passionate feminist and lifelong friend, in conversations shared fears that Chicana commissioners' late appointment would set them up as scapegoats since Chicanas and other Latinas, presumed to be uninformed, were expected to be severely underrepresented in the state meetings and national conference.

"No contaban con nuestra astucia" (They underestimated our ingenuity/movidas).[21] Cecilia Burciaga, Ruth "Rhea" Mojica Hammer, and Gracia Molina de Pick, as I've mentioned, had coordinated with Chicana/Latina networks that launched recruitment in Texas, California, New Mexico, Colorado, and the Midwest in September 1976. Although appointed late, they were current on our actions and from March 1977 were invaluable in helping Chicanas navigate the remaining process until November 1977.

Alarmingly, on other fronts were reports that in Texas, disillusioned lesbians, radical feminists, and progressive religious women threatened to boycott and possibly protest the state and national conferences over their exclusion from meetings and appointments to the Texas IWY Coordinating Committee. By working through our coalitions and mutual trust (as a result of ongoing work with the Center for Battered Women, Womenspace, labor organizing, ERA ratification, and many other efforts), I convinced them otherwise. Leaders Janna Zumbrun, Glen Scott, Martha Boethel, Rita Starpattern, and others joined Chicanas in the IWY struggle. United, we resolved to prevent privileged white feminists from derailing pro-women policies. Even today, Texas Chicanas and our radical feminist friends wonder about white feminist leaders' rejection, given our involvement, commitment, political skill, and labor with NWPC, TWPC, and other feminist institutions. For us ERA ratification was a do-or-die issue. Privileged white feminists had choices then and have them now. Marginalized women of color, radical women, and other low-income women did not and still don't.

Four decades later, reviewing the 1977 meeting report of the Texas IWY Coordinating Committee,[22] I've tried to understand the IWY Coordinating Committee's strategy. Perhaps white feminist leaders interpreted "uninvolved women" indicated in federal guidelines as women not involved in pro-women's issues;

therefore women involved in anti-choice, anti-women, or anti-ERA activities qualified for the "uninvolved" category. But then, why actively recruit anti-women participants to a conference focused on ERA and pro-women policies? Also, the report does not include the deliberate strategies to exclude low-income women, radical women, and lesbians, strategies that were justified by the IWY Coordinating Committee as a practical effort to avoid jeopardizing the success of the state conference and prevent disruptive agendas. To them, women's issues were disruptive! Yet the above-mentioned report proudly boasts that LaNeil Wright, the head of the anti-ERA forces in Texas, was recommended by the Nominating Committee of the IWY Texas Coordinating Committee as a national delegate nominee; to the relief of many, she was not elected at the Texas Women's Meeting.[23] Talk about jeopardizing success! Obviously, Chicana feminists, radical women, and lesbians totally disagreed with the majority of IWY Coordinating Committee members' interpretation of the federal mandate regarding fundamentals of a successful pro-women state meeting and national conference.

SPRING INTO ACTION: CHICANA ADVISORY COMMITTEE FOR IWY

In December 1976, frustrated and still without a Texas IWY Coordinating Committee or word on our 100 nominees for committee service, I made a bold recommendation to Chicana leadership and allies in Austin, Houston, Dallas, San Antonio, and South Texas: to organize a Chicana Advisory Committee (CAC) for IWY and initiate recruitment of excluded women as well as to prepare for Chicanas' appointment to the Texas IWY Coordinating Committee. I volunteered to coordinate, finance, and house the organization in Austin. CAC organizers included Chicana Democrats, Republicans, and RUP members, Brown Berets, University of Texas Mexican American Student Organization (MASO), MEChA, and MABPWA chapters in Austin, San Antonio, Dallas, and El Paso. CAC leaders were María Elena Martínez, Diana Camacho, Linda del Toro, Amalia Rodríguez, Belinda Herrera, Cynthia Pérez, Rosa María González, Nora González Dodson, Alma Pérez, Angelita Mendoza, Juanita Luera, Consuelo Avila, Lydia Espinosa, Lydia Serrata, Diana Zuñiga, Norma Carreón, Annabelle Valle, Frances Rizzo, Marta Sotomayor, Ino Álvarez, Orelia Hisbrook Cole, and other Chicanas statewide. My responsibilities included outreach to lesbian, radical, and progressive religious women. Diana Camacho, in her detailed report to Pat Vasquez, director of MALDEF's Chicana Rights Project, wrote that CAC met every Monday for six months and before and during every meeting of the official IWY Coordinating Committee, which held four regular meetings, and numerous subcommittee meetings.[24]

CAC Chicanas predicted pitifully low numbers of pro-ERA and pro-women participants at the Texas Women's Meeting, given the recruitment strategies of the IWY Coordinating Committee. Potential feminist participants numbered approximately 240 mostly TWPC members, which included some Chicanas and a few African American women. According to our sources, to overcome these low numbers, instead of recruiting feminists of color, IWY organizers targeted university women, mainstream religious women's networks, and rural white women, who even today are very conservative on women's issues. In fact, Texas resolutions in the final Texas Women's Meeting report clearly show the racist, classist, and misogynist leanings of the workshop leaders recruited and appointed by the majority of the Texas IWY Coordinating Committee.

CAC in Texas prioritized demands that the national IWY commission in Washington, DC, appoint a representative Texas IWY Coordinating Committee to replace the one whose membership was leaked in December 1976. Sadly, our advocacy and success at recruitment created terrible problems for our loyal friend and supporter Rose Marie Roybal, a hardworking staffer in the DC office who was removed from activity in Texas and as I understand it from the entire Southwest. Eventually she was terminated from the office of the national commission through machinations of Liz Carpenter and Janie Hickie, according to information shared by feminist leader Olga Solíz, who also complained about Nikki Van Hightower's feigned ignorance about this and other IWY issues.[25] Rose Marie's account is available in digital archives of Chicana por mi Raza Digital Memory Collective.

Victory at last! In January 1977, a revised representative list for the Texas IWY Coordinating Committee was leaked to us, and it now included Owanah Anderson, a Native American, and State Representative Irma Rangel as co-chairs. Although this resulted from CAC's relentless lobbying, in the final Texas report, white leaders assumed credit for having women of color co-chairs. Predictably, no Raza Unida Party feminists, lesbians, or radical women were appointed to the committee. The revised, improved final list included Chicana activists Hermila Anzaldúa, Mary Castillo, Diana Escobedo, Jessie Flores, Lupe Anguiano, Guadalupe Quintanilla, and Diana Camacho, a CAC member and MABPWA officer. One last effort to add Janna Zumbrun representing lesbian women failed during the March 25, 1977, meeting of the official committee.[26] Although Chicana feminists like Diana Camacho and Hermila Anzaldúa were now on the Texas IWY Coordinating Committee, Chicanas were still outnumbered and outvoted.

CAC set about incorporating Chicanas newly appointed to the IWY Coordinating Committee into CAC for coordinated recruitment, workshop and resolution planning, and conference logistics. By February 7, 1977, immediately following their appointment, Chicana committee members received a congratulatory memo from CAC outlining IWY Texas Women's Meeting planning processes and introducing CAC as a feminist coalition, including our origins and relevance to the IWY process. Diplomatically, CAC drew them in, offering a vision and mission: "Please take it in the spirit of cooperation and advocacy in which it is provided. We feel that your role, your ability to share with others, and your voice will help determine our place as women's issues are brought up in the State Conference. These issues will be carried to the national conference and, hopefully, will be incorporated into policy-making and legislative activities."[27]

We briefed them on IWY processes, the state meeting on June 24–27, 1977, and on the national conference on November 18–21, 1977, in Houston, so they were as informed as others on the IWY Coordinating Committee. We shared CAC's values, detailing strategies and support:

> Chicanas do not want to come into the Conference as "observers," "subsidized women," etc. We are taxpayers, the largest ethnic group in Texas, as citizens and taxpayers, we want full consideration and participation; every session and every workshop is to have a Chicana component, which is why we are concerned about the type of staff that coordinates the Conference. . . . We would like to say that we are with you every step of the way, and that this entire effort will demonstrate how "together" we are in seeking fair and equitable presentation of Chicana concerns in our state.[28]

We outlined our wish list to add lesbian and radical women to the official committee, transparency from the IWY Coordinating Committee regarding irregularities in contracting and hiring, recommendations for free registration or for fees not exceeding $1, and rejection of intimidating or humiliating "fee waivers" for low-income women and/or women of color.[29] CAC member Diana Camacho, an appointee to the National IWY Coordinating Committee, was invaluable in convincing other Chicana members to join CAC, and all except Lupe Anguiano joined CAC and agreed to meet with us prior to each of the four regular monthly meetings of the IWY Coordinating Committee. Subsequently, CAC volunteers met on the same dates and places as the IWY Coordinating Committee and coordinated with Chicana members of the IWY Coordinating Committee, anticipated needs, complemented and supplemented their duties, and independently of the IWY Coordinating Committee worked with them through subcommittees of the IWY Coordinating Committee on workshops and resolutions for the state meeting. CAC was a wraparound support system for them. On meeting days of the IWY Coordinating Committee in Austin, we met independently with Chicana members of the IWY Coordinating Committee and with our allies, reporting progress, strategizing on official agenda items, and joining them at the official meeting of the IWY Coordinating Committee. The close relations between CAC and Chicana members of the IWY Coordinating Committee helped our volunteers secure some voting privileges in the official subcommittees (workshops, resolutions, logistics, and so forth) of the IWY Coordinating Committee. Besides attending meetings of the IWY Coordinating Committee, CAC members met every Monday in Austin from January 1977 until the state conference in June 1977.

Incorporation of CAC members like myself into the IWY Coordinating Committee's planning process greatly annoyed some of its members, and one, according to Diana Camacho, complained that "it was not fair that Martha [Cotera] seemed to be given the opportunity to speak her opinion more than most Committee members. We pointed out that Martha [Cotera] attended more Coordinating Committee meetings than more of its members; and so it went."[30]

EN LA UNIÓN ESTÁ LA FUERZA: FORGING FEMINIST COALITIONS FOR IWY

Since the IWY Coordinating Committee was considering proposals for management of the state meeting, CAC members active in the Austin Coalition on Battered Women recruited other coalition members from the lesbian, radical, and progressive religious communities to join in submitting a coalition proposal. We committed to recruit at least 500 Chicanas and 200–300 progressive women for the Texas conference, whether or not our proposal was funded. We submitted our proposal on February 5, 1977, at the first meeting of Texas IWY State Coordinating Committee, although as indicated in our transmittal, we were unsure about guidelines, which the temporary convener Sarah Weddington failed to provide. In the coalition proposal, my submittal was through my consulting company, Information Systems Development; Megan Seaholm and Lois Ahrens submitted as Womenspace YWCA; Ginger Jarmon, as United Campus Ministry; Martha Boethel, as individual consultant; and Mary Sanger, also as an individual consultant to recruit progressive women statewide.[31]

My submittal was titled "Services to Provide for Outreach and Programming for the Participation of Texas Chicanas at the IWY State Conference (Period March 1, 1977–July 10, 1977)"; the proposed $10,915 would provide CAC outreach (mail-outs and media) for 500-plus Chicanas, workshop content, resource women, cultural events, displays, logistics, in-kind volunteers, and overall coordination. My rationale:

> Chicanas have become experts at setting goals and objectives for eliminating barriers, and welcome the opportunity to share this information. . . . Mexican American women can both provide valuable information on international exploitation and at the same time perhaps acquire new and powerful allies in our fight for human rights. Chicanas are born and raised with the specter of inhuman and cruel immigration policies which tear families apart and which have deprived the community of valuable leadership. These policies in 1977 continue to violate the constitutional rights of women and children in Texas.[32]

YWCA Womenspace's title was "The Radical Feminist Perspective at the Texas International Women's year Conference," and its aim was "to insure that the radical feminist perspective is sufficiently represented. . . . [P]oor or working-class women are outside the privileges of class, money, education, leisure time, and even experience in dealing with political processes in order to affect change in their lives. Lesbians live outside the cultural sanctions of heterosexual institutions, i.e., marriage and the traditional family." The proposal included workshop content, resource women, volunteers, displays, events, and a powerful plea for disenfranchised women of all races and ethnicities, $8,081.63.[33] Ginger Brittain Jarman, co-coordinator of the Texas NOW Task Force on Women and Religion and director of United Campus Ministry of Austin, proposed "Recruitment of 'Unorganized Women,'" as characterized in the federal guidelines. It involved older women, rural women, young women, local churches and organizations, campus ministries statewide reaching women excluded from public policy, collaboration of the progressive ecumenical Campus Ministry of Austin and the ecumenical movement's Church Women United in Texas, $8,000.[34]

I describe our coalition and proposal contents in this cautionary tale to dissuade contemporary feminist scholars from the idea that white mainstream feminists inspired and mentored Chicana feminism, lesbian feminists, and radical feminists (actually, it was probably the reverse) and to dissuade our own third-wave Chicana feminists from the idea that second-wave Chicana feminists failed because as cultural nationalists we disavowed our lesbian sisters and radical women, did not attempt coalition building, and didn't try hard enough to join mainstream feminism.

We were totally ignored; our coalition proposal was never acknowledged, nor were contracting transactions or management of the Texas Women's Meeting ever disclosed. White middle-class participants were recruited with paid staff, while Chicanas and the rest were on our own. The $100,000 federal grant was spent without transparency, and while I had a verbal commitment for reimbursable CAC expenses, when submitting my payment request for the $10,000-plus spent, I was callously told that all the "leftover" money (basically, our money) had been sent back to the National Commission for IWY in Washington, DC. In today's dollars I spent $41,000 in addition to generous donations from my husband, Juan Cotera, chair of the Hispanic Chamber of Commerce, and from our volunteers and Chicano businesses.

Despite pleas for equity in hiring, only white women were employed by the IWY Coordinating Committee in professional positions from March 15 to July 15, 1977. Barbara Langham was executive director; Valerie Bristol and Jill Fain were assistants, and Alessandra Bybee, volunteer coordinator. To fulfill federal guidelines on diversity, its final report cluelessly states, "María Alma Pérez provided skilled secretarial services and filled a prerequisite of the Committee that there be a Spanish Speaking staffer."[35] Again, "No contaban con nuestra astucia." We anticipated this, but ironically, and in blissful ignorance, they hired María Alma, feminist Brown Beret, RUP activist, and joyous CAC volunteer, who covertly strategized with us.

On March 25, 1977, at the second meeting of IWY Coordinating Committee, our Chicana appointees were outvoted in attempts to add lesbian representation in a "request by Janna Zumbrun to reconsider lesbian representation on the

Texas Coordinating Committee. . . . After lengthy discussion, motion that Janna Zumbrun be added to the Coordinating Committee in direct defiance of National IWY Commission policy. . . . Motion failed."[36] The statement in "direct defiance" meant that federal guidelines would have permitted adding Janna to the IWY Coordinating Committee.

CHICANAS RESPOND: SINSABORES Y TRIUNFOS

By the IWY Coordinating Committee's first meeting, CAC's mailing list was 3,000 and soon became 5,000 through input by CAC volunteers and Chicana members of the IWY Coordinating Committee. CAC monitored diversity, identified scholarship and travel benefits for candidates, identified potential workshop leaders and participants (for carefully crafted workshop topics and resolutions), and identified delegate nominees to vote at the national conference. Everything was coordinated with Chicana members of the IWY Coordinating Committee, Hermila Anzaldúa, McAllen, Texas; Jesse Flores, El Paso; State Representative Irma Rangel, Corpus Christi; and Mary Castillo, Houston, who distributed and collected CAC information in community meetings.[37] Despite requests by Hermila Anzaldúa, outreach chair for IWY Coordinating Committee, Lupe Anguiano and Jane Macon (members of the IWY Coordinating Committee) did not volunteer to recruit in San Antonio and never collaborated with CAC.[38] Consequently, Pat Vasquez of the Chicana Rights Project, a Mexican American Education and Legal Defense Fund (MALDEF) initiative in San Antonio, questioned the transparency of the process. This became a sensitive issue since no one, least of all me, wanted CAC involved in conflicts between Pat Vasquez and these two influential feminists; nevertheless, when Pat requested an informal report from the CAC, we provided it to her.[39] In a letter to Owanah Anderson on May 19, I detailed how CAC without any funds was complying with federal guidelines, while the IWY Coordinating Committee with $100,000 in funding refused to recruit low-income, minority, and other vulnerable women, and I also discussed attempts to restrict voting at the state meeting.[40]

By March 15, 1977, CAC had identified approximately 500 committed participants and dozens of workshop leaders, in contrast to the IWY Coordinating Committee, which anxiously sought African American participants as late as May 2, 1977, for mail-in preregistration forms due May 16, 1977.[41] By June 24–27, 1977, Chicanas were registered in record numbers, surpassing all groups and foretelling high delegate representation at the IWY National Women's Conference in Houston. CAC's collaborations with lesbian and other progressive women increased participation and delegate strength, averting some of the failures of the IWY Coordinating Committee—such as the abysmally low registration of African American women—that later required crisis interventions.

Reflecting our participation rates, Chicanas, lesbian leaders, and progressives received the most votes as delegates to the national IWY conference at the Texas conference in June 1977. Irma Rangel, Sylvia Garcia, Irene Rodriguez, Estela Salinas, Margie Flores, Patricia Vasquez, Janna Zumbrun, I, and others received the most votes, in the 898–947 range, up to 200 more votes than prominent leaders Sarah Weddington, Ann Richards, Nikki Van Hightower, and Jane Macon.[42]

HOLY MOLE! MANO A MANO FOR A PRO-ERA, PRO-WOMAN CONFERENCE

In the conference planning process, when Chicana members of the IWY Coordinating Committee were outvoted on race and class issues like outreach, registration fees, resolutions, and workshop leader appointments, CAC aggressively fought to eliminate barriers. Writing to Owanah Anderson, committee chair, I requested lowering fees from $5 to $2 (approved by the Coordinating Committee, then undemocratically rescinded). I wrote, "First $5.00 is a high fee for poorly paid, non-income, or welfare women in Texas of all races, . . . [and] there are real morale problems with the Committee if individuals cannot trust the fact that clear decisions have been made at meetings."[43] Our request for a "check-off" fee waiver was denied, forcing low-income women into visible "free fee" lines, which we called classist and disgusting but which we resolved by having all CAC participants and our allies use the free-fee registration line.

On the critical issue of the resolutions promoting a women's agenda to be presented, voted, and advanced to the national conference, the National IWY Coordinating Committee had the option of approving them in-house and advancing them to the national conference. Predictably, it chose the more conservative option of allowing individual states to take control of the process. The Texas IWY Coordinating Committee voted to present the pro-women agenda resolutions at the state meeting itself for approval by statewide participants. "Holy, moly," as we say in Texas! The federal government's pro-woman resolutions were at the mercy of the participants recruited by the IWY Coordinating Committee, whose early registrants were primarily anti-ERA women, organizations, and men.

"No contaban con nuestra astucia." Anticipating this, CAC developed a plan that included a parallel Chicana component for every session and every workshop that would include the federally mandated topics and resolutions, in addition to our own progressive resolutions. During recruitment we designed workshops and strategies and identified about ninety workshop leaders and hundreds of participants for potential workshops. Every Chicana and progressive vote was necessary to pass pro-women resolutions and defeat anti-women agendas and resolutions. Leaders would be knowledgeable, assertive, and courageous presenters, skillful in getting affirmative votes.

Workshops and resolutions were negotiated in subcommittees of the IWY Coordinating Committee, and since CAC had some voting privileges, Lydia Espinosa and other courageous CAC members successfully overcame obstacles to include our CAC Chicana components in 95 percent of the workshops. Fierce fights within the subcommittee of the IWY Coordinating Committee pitted Lydia and others against Ann Richards's and Liz Carpenter's conservative positions. Later, during Ann Richards's campaign for Texas governor, Lydia Espinosa would recall how Richards had fiercely opposed Chicana and progressive resolutions during those subcommittee meetings.

The majority membership of the IWY Coordinating Committee, protective of conservative sensibilities and to overrule CAC, imposed a workshop process with morning and afternoon sessions for the state meeting in which the same or different resolutions and votes were to be taken as desired or allowed by workshop leaders. Therefore, one workshop session might pass pro-women resolutions, while its second session (generally those with low Chicana and progressive participation) might pass anti-women or anti-minority resolutions. Strategically, we placed CAC's strongest activists and our feminist allies as leaders in key workshops to introduce and pass vital pro-women resolutions and to defeat anti-women, classist, and racist resolutions. Evey Chapa, Chelo Avila, Melba Vasquez, Margaret Gomez, Bec Runte, Emma Lou Linn, and I were responsible for workshops with the most difficult and controversial resolutions. Nevertheless, every single CAC workshop leader was prepared to challenge anti-woman resolutions in their workshops. Nothing was left to chance. Long before the state meeting, CAC prepared resolutions, and strategies for passing them. Besides workshop leaders, we also recruited massive numbers of participants for targeted workshops. For example, 400 Chicanas and allies attended my workshop on sexism, classism, and racism; likewise, large numbers participated in Margaret Gomez's key workshop on alternative lifestyles with awesome outcomes. Further, we encouraged CAC participants to attend workshops where anti-women's-rights factions might attempt passing anti-choice, anti-ERA, anti-voting-rights, and anti-lesbian resolutions.

A review of the deconstruction of workshops, leaders, and CAC resolutions passed at the Texas Women's Meeting reveals CAC's successful strategies as detailed here: Evey Chapa's "Where Am I Now That I Need Me?" workshop on sex-role stereotyping in education passed affirmative action resolutions.[44] Diana Camacho's "Women's Health Care: As It Is and Should Be" passed resolutions on Medicaid funding for health care including abortions and one against selling Norform contraceptives in foreign countries. Participants also defeated the anti-abortion resolution, 57–36.[45] Margaret Gomez's workshop "Alternative Life Styles" included topics on Chicana activist mothers and lifestyles of single career women, traditional homemakers, lesbians, and low-income and welfare-recipient mothers; the workshop passed progressive resolutions in Margaret Gomez's morning session. The afternoon session with another leader passed resolutions that were pro-Christian women, pro-family, pro-marriage, and pro-motherhood, and another prohibiting teaching of alternative lifestyles in public schools.[46]

Grace Garcia, a brilliant strategist and feminist, led a "How to Plan a Political Campaign" workshop, which passed progressive resolutions on public campaign financing and tax credits for campaign contributions. Defeated were conservative resolutions on restricting voting rights.[47] Rita Gomez, who was not part of CAC, led the "Mothers and Children" resolution on parenthood and on utilizing parent resources in the schools.[48] Dynamic leader Melba Vasquez's workshop "Life Planning—Or How to Get Where You Want to Be" was selected by right-to-life proponents for passage of their resolution, but it failed.[49] Tina Navarro led the "Violence against Women" workshop that passed wide-ranging resolutions on progressive, pro-women legislation.[50] The workshop "Sexism, Classism, and Racism," co-led by Nina Wouk, Loretta Shaw, and me, covered race and sex, child care, lesbian rights, and progressive education issues. Although intentionally repetitive of other workshops, its goal was to do any heavy lifting on resolutions that might fail in other workshops. About 400 participants attended the morning and afternoon sessions of this workshop, and thirty-four progressive resolutions were passed. According to the state report, the "Anti-ERA people were there, but they only asked questions."[51]

Chelo Avila, a feminist-activist veteran, led "How to Start a Women's Center," addressing the need for multipurpose women's centers and describing our Chicana Research and Learning Center in Austin. Here, the critical resolution in support of the ERA passed, along with a commendation of the Texas legislature for its early ratification of the ERA, in June 1972, and for blocking the rescission of the ERA.[52] On international issues, Lupe Anguiano and María de la Paz Becerril (not CAC) presented "World Women: A Call for Peace, Understanding and Cooperation; IWY World Plan of Action." No resolutions were reported for this workshop.[53] In other workshops, Lucille Garza (not CAC) led "Rural Women: The Overlooked Minority," which passed anti-welfare and anti-small farmer resolutions,[54] and our social work leaders, Marta Sotomayor and Carmen Zapata, led "Maturing Woman," which passed resolutions on programs for elderly women. Here an attempt was made to pass the anti-abortion resolution, but it failed since the chairs challenged its pertinence to the workshop topic.[55] Lupe Anguiano, Deluvina Hernandez, and Elena Romero (not CAC) presented "Low Income Women: Quality of Life for Them and Their Families," but no resolutions or report were submitted from that workshop.[56]

EXAMPLE OF A CONSERVATIVE WORKSHOP

The "Women and Power" workshop with physicians Norma Selvidge and Hortense Dixon, along with Margaret Keys, is a good example of how the moderate conservatives recruited by white women on the official committee would have torpedoed the conference if they had controlled it. In this session, since we were denied a Chicana facilitator, all pro-women of color resolutions failed; fortunately, since we had covered our key resolutions in other workshops, we did not target this one workshop, and with only 10 Chicanas attending among 200-plus attendees, the outcome is revealing. Defeated resolutions were Chicana rights and affirmative action, 111 against and 95 for; that IWY women boycott corporations that do not hire women in the United States and oppress women in third world countries; that we deplore US support of the dictatorship in Chile; and that we support increased appointment of Chicanas to Texas state commissions and state employment.[57]

CAC progressive resolutions advanced to the IWY National Women's Conference in November 1977. In fact, the Texas Women's Meeting reported a pro-ERA, pro-lesbian-rights, pro-choice, and overall pro-women agenda state conference despite our sad beginnings. CAC accomplished this through coalitions, recruitment, preparation, and strategically advancing resolutions. Predictably, our efforts were summarily dismissed. A final resolution by the IWY Coordinating Committee stated, "Whereas, without their help and contributions the Texas Women's Meeting would have gone wanting, BE IT RESOLVED that the Texas Women's Meeting offer its thanks and appreciation to"—there follows a long list of organizations including our Mexican American Business and Professional Women; there is no mention here or in the official report of the Texas Women's Meeting of the Chicana Advisory Committee for IWY (CAC) or of its 500 Chicana and more than 300 lesbian and progressive participants and our contribution. Importantly for the national agenda and conference goals, our votes were pro-ERA and pro-women, and our workshops maximized our voting strength at the state meeting and in the national conference. We met the federal mandate governing state IWY meetings.[58]

Delegate nominations for the national conference in November 1977 were based on registrations, and Chicanas were allotted 17 of 58 delegates, the same as California's numbers. We had met IWY Commissioner Cecilia Burciaga's friendly challenge and made IWY Commissioner Ruth "Rhea" Mojica Hammer very happy. Delegate representation to the IWY National Women's Conference was based on race, ethnicity, class, and other categories. Ann Richards, chair of delegate nominations, called me late one night urging me to be a delegate in the low-income category and to get other Chicanas to do the same, so more white women could be delegates, since they were overrepresented in the higher-income categories! All of us refused. At 900-vote levels, Chicanas were the highest vote getters as delegates to the national conference. Significantly, of the 58 Texas delegates, 52 were pro-women and only 6 were anti-women votes.

Through CAC activism and the challenges and motivation we presented to reluctant white leaders, the Texas Women's Meeting was a resounding success. As we predicted, women from the Texas Women's Political Caucus numbered approximately 200; Chicana participants recruited by CAC numbered more than 500, although the Texas Women's Meeting report concedes us only 321, and progressive women had more than 300 participants.[59]

The final Texas Women's Meeting report excludes all documentation of Chicanas' role in salvaging the ERA, handing to white feminist leaders a pro-ERA, pro-women state meeting, and securing for all time feminist credibility for Ann

Richards, Sarah Weddington, Liz Carpenter, Jane Hickie, Cathy Bonner, Jane Macon, Nikki Van Hightower, and others. Nevertheless, Co-Chair Owanah Anderson did give us credit. Diana Camacho, one of our IWY Coordinating Committee members wrote in a letter to Pat Vazquez, "I have it in writing from Owanah Anderson, the presiding officer, 'Had the Chicanas not come—the Anti's would have taken the delegates.' This was written begrudgingly."[60] Likewise, a week after the state conference, Martha E. Smiley of Austin, a fellow founder of the Texas Women's Political Caucus and a Coordinating Committee member, invited me to Scholz Garten, a local political hangout, to tell me how much she appreciated our work. She said, "Martha, I know that no one will ever say this to you, so I am saying it now. . . . You and the Chicanas of the Chicana Advisory Committee gave us a pro-ERA conference. And I want you to know, that if you all had not done what you did, it would have been mightily embarrassing for Texas women, since Texas was the host state for the national IWY conference and we would not have had a pro-ERA conference and delegation."[61] Over the years, I have repeated this conversation to many people, along with my appreciation for Martha Smiley's friendship and honesty.

MINORITY WOMEN'S POWER AT THE 1977 NATIONAL IWY CONFERENCE IN HOUSTON

At the national IWY conference, Chicana delegate numbers were important since women of color would ensure approval of ERA and pro-woman resolutions to advance the national agenda. In fact, at the national conference Chicanas from Texas, California, and New Mexico led the Hispanic Women's Caucus, which in turn inspired the Minority Caucus, as acknowledged in the *Spirit of Houston* report: "The Hispanic women inspired unity by coming up with an umbrella statement representing Chicana, Puerto Rican, Cuban and other Latina delegates, the first time such a national coalition had ever been made."[62] The Minority Caucus, which we worked hard to organize at the national conference, included Hispanics, African Americans, Asian Pacific women, and Native American women. This Minority Caucus worked to replace the three-paragraph minority women resolution originally suggested by the IWY National Commission with a wide-ranging, representative, and very progressive resolution supported by most minority delegates present. Again, stereotypes about minorities not being able to coalesce were overturned.[63] The extreme importance of the Minority Women Resolution approved by the entire conference was that it unequivocally advanced the pro-ERA, pro-choice, pro-immigrant, pro-civil rights and equity for all, and generally pro-women agenda that the IWY National Women's Conference was supposed to achieve.

It was such a strong statement of purpose for all women in the United States that even anti-choice women found themselves voting in favor of it, and in every report, including *Spirit of Houston: The First National Women's Conference*, this resolution is credited for the success of the national conference.

> When the resulting statement was finally read on the Conference floor by members of each major caucus (see narrative), many felt it to be the most significant event of Houston and of all that had preceded it. For the first time minority women—many of whom had been in the leadership of the women's movement precisely because of their greater political understanding of discrimination—were present in such a critical mass that they were able to define their own needs as well as to declare their state in each women's issue. They were also able to make the media aware of their importance and to forge their own internal networks and coalitions in a way that was far reaching, inclusive, and an historic "first" for their communities, for women and men.[64]

In this context as well, Chicanas from Texas are credited: "The Texas 'host' delegation included more Chicanas than any other state did, whose co-chairs were both minority women."[65]

Most Hispanic women at the national conference disagreed with the decision of some Minority Caucus members to bring in National IWY Commissioner Gloria Steinem to help with the coalition language. Having had firsthand experience with what we considered Gloria Steinem's patronizing and classist treatment of Hispanic women at National Women's Political Caucus meetings, Tejanas especially were disappointed. Actually, it made little sense that someone who had torpedoed the idea of a coalition model for the National Women's Political Caucus was now helping "hammer out coalition language" for us. Worse still, according to the *Spirit of Houston* report, some minority women then "cheerfully" referred to her as "the token," which everyone seemed to think was really cute, apparently, including Gloria Steinem, or she would not have "cheerfully" accepted the epithet.[66] Not so much for minority women victimized as "tokens" and by "tokens" in real life. This whole episode was totally demeaning and cast a pall on an otherwise exhilarating experience.

MUJERES BRAVAS AND DECONSTRUCTING THE TEXAS REPORT ON IWY

The final report of the IWY Coordinating Committee, *Texas Women's Meeting, Women at the Grass Roots: Growing toward Unity, June 24–26, 1977*, is an example of historical erasure, and deconstructing it is instructive. The staff and the IWY Coordinating Committee assumed undeserved credit for a successful pro-ERA, pro-women Texas IWY conference when they failed to acknowledge their obstruction in fulfilling the stated federal mandates regarding the participation of minority women and of the promotion of the ERA and pro-women resolutions and agenda. Further, there is no acknowledgment of CAC and the hundreds of volunteer hours, of obstructions through lack of official status, transparency, funding, staffing, or control of the process, and in general, the hostile environment of management and of the majority of the IWY Coordinating Committee. Omissions and erasures are plentiful in the report, so a few examples suffice. The report calls attention to the Spanish-speaking outreach and fails to mention that CAC took care of 90 percent of outreach to Chicanas and other vast networks with our own funds and labor.[67] More humiliating, since the IWY Coordinating Committee controlled the information and proportionate delegate appointments, Chicanas are credited with only 321 participants, as opposed to the 500-plus we recorded and as evidenced by the 900-plus votes our Chicana delegate nominees received at the Texas meeting. Erased also is the critical participation of Texas's lesbian and radical communities.

In particular, the report expresses pride in how equitable the IWY Coordinating Committee was in its efforts to attract institutions and participants representing an anti-woman agenda. Yes, the white leadership certainly did that, and thankfully the anti-woman agenda failed. At great financial cost and hard work, Chicanas and our allies successfully fulfilled the pro-women objectives of the state meeting and overcame the money and paid labor white leaders spent recruiting anti-women Texans.[68] Cynically, in the same report the leadership rejoices that the "one bloc of key feminist resolutions—including commendation to Texas legislature for its early ratification of ERA—passed by 140 votes," but the report fails to mention that it was a CAC volunteer, Chelo Avila, whose "Women's Centers" workshop passed this resolution, and so on.[69]

Predictably, with this latest incursion into the mainstream of the women's movement, Chicanas in Texas had had enough. The bitterness Chicanas felt after this experience of working within the mainstream feminist movement is reflected in the frank report that IWY Texas Coordinating Committee member Diana Camacho wrote for Pat Vasquez's Chicana Rights Project, "Chicanas Change Course of Texas IWY."[70] Camacho reveals the ways in which white women leaders of the mainstream feminist movement appropriated the successes of the conference without giving credit to the work that Chicanas had done to make it successful. Another excellent summary of the dynamics between women of color feminists and the mainstream feminist movement on a national scale is provided by Cecilia Preciado [Burciaga], an IWY national commissioner, in her work "The 1977 National Women's Conference in Houston."[71]

Unfortunately for Chicanas, no conference resolution will change national agendas toward women when empowered women willfully discriminate against other women based on class, race, religion, or sexual orientation, as many of the white feminist leaders in Texas and in Washington, DC, did. Our prediction held, that often powerful white feminists lacked commitment to the Chicana ideal of women's liberation as universal liberation. Apparently liberation meant empowerment of the privileged who would on their own terms decide whether to empower women different from themselves. Chicanas had previous experience with Chicanos in the Chicano movement similarly committed to liberation empowering men, who also on their own terms chose which women and other human beings to empower. In fact, given the current powerlessness of Chicanas and other minority women at the national level, perhaps the victory on the national scene in 1977—largely owed to the vast numbers of activist women of color attending—hardened white women's determination to strengthen their power by closing ranks even more, locally and nationally, to marginalize women of color. An effective strategy for consolidating white power, as many Chicanas mentioned in the 1970s, is to keep minority communities in a permanent state of underdevelopment. Perhaps we showed our hand too efficiently, and our success might have sealed our national fate politically until our numbers become too powerful for subjugation.

Still, readers might ask why Chicanas did it all. Chicanas oppressed by race and gender were the most motivated to move the Chicano movement toward a concept of universal liberation to include gender. Likewise, we were the most motivated to move the mainstream women's liberation movement toward the same concept of universal liberation to include race, class, and other human beings. For an elegant scholarly statement of the ideal, Maylei Blackwell has an excellent explanation of third-space feminism:

> While understanding the racial or class oppression that was named by both nationalists and Marxists in the movimiento, Chicana feminists began using what would later be called an intersectional analysis, one of the touchstones of women of color feminist theory. Like other sister formations, early Chicana feminists called attention to the ways that their experience of economic exploitation was both racial and gendered and, similarly, how racial hatred and discrimination were constructed along class, gender and sexual dimensions. Chicana feminists began to point out how they experienced class exploitation vis-à-vis the marginalization of women's role in production and their exploitation in the reproduction of labor. While both white women and Chicano men faced labor market segmentation and economic discrimination, Chicanas showed how patriarchy, capitalism, and racism came together as overlapping systems of power to marginalize them.[72]

As Mujeres Bravas, we fought courageously for our liberation ideal even when we knew better, but then Chicanas have always been and will always be *MUJERES BRAVAS*.

3 "WOMEN NEED TO FIND THEIR VOICE"

LATINAS SPEAK OUT IN THE MIDWEST, 1972

LETICIA WIGGINS

Martha Cotera [the keynote speaker] told us we were not just wives or girl-friends or sisters or mothers, that we were human beings. . . . What she was trying to tell us in that opening session was that we had no self-worth unless we put it there. Nobody else can put it there for us. If we were everything to somebody else, then we were nothing to ourselves. And she talked about the national [activism], like what women were doing in California and what women were doing in other places like Chicago. And I thought, "Wow."

—OLGA VILLA, 2011

Olga Villa's eyes widened as she recounted the keynote speech given at the Adelante Mujer (Onward, woman) conference in South Bend, Indiana, in the spring of 1972. The keynote speaker, Texas-based Chicana activist Martha Cotera, reminded Villa, then secretary of the Midwest Council of La Raza (MWCLR), and the nearly 100 other La Raza women sitting in the United Auto Workers Hall of their self-worth.[1] For many in that room, the message not only affirmed their dignity, but also urged them to reconsider common perceptions of both Chicana and Latina womanhood. The Adelante Mujer conference provided the spark behind a *revolución verdadera* (real revolution, coined by Chicana activist Anna NietoGomez) where women joined men as equals to advance *el movimiento*, the movement.[2] NietoGomez's "revolución verdadera" did not assume the same form for each individual in what we understand as the larger Chicana/o movement; indeed, it took a very particular form for Chicana and Latina women in the Midwest. In this essay, I explore the complex relations between Villa and other women attending the Adelante Mujer conference and the organizations and institutions at the center of the Chicano movement in the Midwest to offer an analysis of what this *revolución* meant for La Raza women in the Midwest.

Adelante Mujer arose from a group of women who self-identified as "Chicana," "Latina," "La Raza," and "Mexican American." While the exact number of Chicana, Puerto Rican, and Latin American women is unknown, this conference was not purely Chicana, especially in the Midwest, which boasted a smaller but more diverse Latina/o population. When the MWCLR, which hosted Adelante Mujer, defined itself as "La Raza," for example, it not only referred to a "Chicano" identity but to "the millions of Americans who trace their origin from Mexico, Puerto Rico, Cuba, and South America."[3] This is the definition of "La Raza" that Villa understood as she referred to those who attended Adelante Mujer often as "La Raza" women.[4] When using "La Raza" in this chapter, I employ the broader definition understood by Villa and the MWCLR. Therefore, I use the terms "Chicana" and "Latina" reservedly. In order to respect these women, I use these identification terms as they appear in the historical sources.

Villa's memory of Cotera's speech emphasizes many factors informing discussions of being Chicana/o or Latina/o in the late 1960s and early 1970s. Embracing ethnic identity became a central tenet of the Chicano movement that emerged in the mid-1960s, when Chicanas/os in the United States championed an imagined and mythical community of Aztlán—the ancestral home of the Nahua people—and called for "the independence of our mestizo nation. . . . Before the world, before all of North America, before all our brothers in the brown continent, we are a union of free pueblos, we are Aztlán."[5] The culture of Aztlán and its rhetorical significance within the Chicano movement, however, tended to reinforce patriarchal nationalism. It therefore created a "subaltern masculinity" in which machismo endowed Chicanos with strength and superiority to combat the oppressive forces of a dominant white male narrative.[6] Chicanas united, most notably in the early 1970s, to take a stand against the sexism promoted by masculinist visions of Chicano liberation. In a 1971 article for the Los Angeles–based Chicana/o magazine *Regeneración*, Francisca Flores, a founding editor, wrote that what Chicanas wanted was "the opportunity to assume organizational, political leadership and responsibility in the movement of La Causa (The Cause)."[7] By 1972, when the Adelante Mujer conference was organized and Olga Villa was introduced to a new, specifically Chicana identity, discussions of sexuality and gender within the Chicano movement extended throughout the nation, from California to Chicago.

Recently scholars including Maylei Blackwell, Laura Pulido, Dionne Espinoza, and Lorena Oropeza have offered important recuperations of this neglected and underrepresented Chicana history.[8] While such scholarship has undoubtedly reshaped how we view the Chicano movement, it has also focused on women in the Southwest, leaving the geographical heart of the country untreated, specifically the midwestern states such as Illinois, Indiana, Michigan, Ohio, and Wisconsin.[9] Midwestern Chicana feminist Olga Villa's voice is only one of many echoing the Chicana critiques of patriarchy heard during the tumultuous decades of the 1960s and 1970s.[10] Her remembrances reflect a particular time, geography, and institutional context—one that is essential to include in the greater discussions of Chicana feminism and activism during that period. As I hope to demonstrate in this essay, the Midwest Latina or La Raza population constituted an important part of the larger Chicana movement for equality and rights in the 1970s. In introducing midwestern Latina voices to this rich activist history and analyzing the geopolitical particularities of their activism, I seek to answer two important questions: How do La Raza women in the Midwest expand our understanding of strategies employed by the Chicana and Chicano movement? And what dynamics, institutional support, and limitations circumscribed La Raza activism in the Midwest?

INSIDE THE COUNTRY, OUTSIDE OF AZTLÁN

There can be little doubt that by the 1960s, the experience of Latinas/os in the Midwest differed from that of Chicanas in the Southwest. First, the northern geographical region was not historically part of Mexico, nor did it come into being in the post-1848 moment. Upon settling in the Midwest, Chicanos could not claim that the border crossed them, nor could they capitalize on the Chicano movement's critique of US empire from their vantage point. The Midwest as a region did not have the same ancestral connection to Aztlán. Rather, existing indigenous communities, the French Empire, and subsequent Anglo expansion shaped the Midwest's history. In addition to these historical complexities, the Midwest's demographic concentration of Chicanas/os was much smaller than that of the Southwest and its history of migration distinct.

Latinas/os came to the Midwest as the result of a push-and-pull cycle driven by labor and instability, as exemplified by Puerto Rican and Mexican migration to the region.[11] The Mexican Revolution of the 1920s triggered the first wave of Mexican immigration to Southwestern states. The influx of migrant workers to the Southwest created a surplus of labor in the region, while World War I expanded the number of available jobs in the Midwest. Midwestern recruiters, *enganchistas*, enticed Mexican workers to agricultural, railroad, and manufacturing industries in states such as Illinois, Indiana, Michigan, and Ohio.[12] Puerto Ricans experienced a similar migratory pattern as Operation Bootstrap (1942–1960) attempted to ameliorate Puerto Rico's economic woes by introducing US companies to the island and reducing "overpopulation" by transporting laborers to take up factory and agrarian work in states including those in the Midwest.[13] This fluid migratory movement from South to North fostered strong and lasting ties between families and communities. The connections are evident especially when considering Southwestern representation in Midwest conferences like Mi Raza Primero, hosted in Muskegon, Michigan, in January 1972, which featured Bert Corona and José Ángel Gutiérrez as keynote speakers.[14]

By 1970, South Bend, Indiana, the site of Adelante Mujer, boasted around 3,000 Spanish speakers, while Houston, Texas, claimed over one million primarily

Mexican American Spanish speakers. From 1970 to 1980, approximately 62.5 percent of the Midwest's Latina/o population was of Mexican American descent, 19 percent was Puerto Rican, and the remaining 16 percent had come from South America, Central America, and the Caribbean.[15] The multicultural mix promoted a distinct community formation among both Chicana/o and Latina/o actors in the region who experienced cultural, linguistic, and economic marginalization from an established Anglo presence. Finally, institutional support, though prevalent throughout the Chicano movement, was a particularly important component of Midwest activism. Indeed, activism in South Bend was organized and guided by a prominent local educational institution—the University of Notre Dame, which provided funding through the Institute of Urban Studies for the creation of the Midwest Council of La Raza.[16]

Before the Midwest Council, various forms of activism took hold in the Midwest region; one such organization was La Raza Unida Party. The Southwest iteration of La Raza Unida Party (RUP) resulted from a meeting of more than 300 Mexican Americans in Crystal City, Texas, on January 17, 1970. Intent on "achieving greater political representation in local and national politics," formation of La Raza Unida Party began a sort of "Chicano third-party movement."[17] The Midwest La Raza Unida Party was not a primary vehicle for political organizing, as the smaller Chicana/o population did not provide as large a basis for electoral power.[18] It served more as a "pressure organization" than a political party.[19] Additionally, RUP was regionally divided on a state-by-state basis. The need arose for a central organization to broadly address the plight of Latinas/os in the Midwest.

The Midwest Council of La Raza came into existence in 1970, after the first Midwest Mexican American Conference, a gathering of Latinas/os and Chicanas/os throughout the Midwest, held by Notre Dame's Institute for Urban Studies on April 17–18, 1970.[20] Three major actors from Notre Dame coordinated this very first meeting—sociology professor Julian Samora, law professor Thomas Broden, and Notre Dame's first Latina law student, Graciela Olivarez. Of all three actors, Olivarez in particular rallied support for the conference within the immediate community. According to Gilberto Cárdenas, one of Julian Samora's graduate students at the time, "It wouldn't have happened without her."[21] Olga Villa was also part of the MWCLR from its inception. She drove from Muskegon, Michigan, as one of more than 200 other attendees from throughout the Midwest drawn to South Bend with the hopes of alleviating the social and political ills plaguing midwestern Mexican American communities.[22] The conference ended with the establishment of the MWCLR, and the various leaders present recruited Villa to act as secretary.[23] Her appointment gave a title to Villa's activism as she became an integral part of the council.

According to Gilberto Cárdenas, though the director, Ricardo Parra, headed the Midwest Council, Olga Villa was "the muscle of the whole organization."[24] Villa, a young woman at the time, forewent dresses and heels for a trademark ensemble of *pantalones* (pants) and tennis shoes, a practical outfit for a practical woman.[25] She developed her activist tendencies in the house of a dear friend, Jane Gonzalez, the woman who would later lead a "revolt of Raza women" during the MWCLR's first major conference, Mi Raza Primero, in 1972. Living with Gonzalez (known as "Janie" to friends), Villa witnessed firsthand the challenges women faced while attempting to act in their own self-interest in a male-dominated world. Gonzalez firmly felt that women had an essential—if often overlooked—role in the movement, a sentiment her husband did not share. Though he subscribed to the tenets of machismo and demanded that Jane act as mother and worker in the domestic realm, her husband's patriarchal notions did not impede Gonzalez's passion for gender equality. In fact, Villa attended the first meeting of Chicanas/os in South Bend per Gonzalez's urging.[26]

As part of the Midwest Council, Villa recognized the need to look beyond the academic stage to the larger community even after she married the council director, Ricardo Parra, in 1979. Her ties with Jane Gonzalez and other women in the community taught her the importance of networks of family and friends. Historians like Vicki Ruiz and Dionne Espinoza, among others, have demonstrated how Chicanas' and Latinas' women's abilities to establish strong connections within their larger ethnic communities proves essential to organizing social movements.[27] A belief in the centrality of women to successful organizing was no doubt in play when Villa, Gonzalez, and other women challenged the male leadership of the MWCLR during its first major event, the Mi Raza Primero conference in Muskegon. The conference hosted more than 1,000 Chicano/as and other Latino/as from throughout the Midwest. Representatives from communities discussed methods of educating their respective Spanish-speaking members on issues related to immigration, student activism, farmworker resolutions, and anti–Vietnam War activism, among other topics.[28] The setting marked what scholar Ricardo Parra considered "a new independent political movement in the Midwest" and a writer for *Race Relations Reporter* called a promulgator of political awareness and self-identity.[29] While such statements paint a rosy hue of awareness and coalescence, not all found the conference edifying.

What was described as "a revolt of sorts by the women of La Raza Unida" resulted as conference attendees, led by Chicana community activist Jane Gonzalez, decried the lack of female voices, macho attitudes, and general inattention to women's issues.[30] They formed the first Women's Caucus in the organization, presenting a number of formal demands and declaring, "Up until now the men have been coordinating the meetings and the women the kitchen."[31] Women who came forward wanted more than just acceptance within the organization; they wanted to "be recognized by Latino men as competent, effective leaders in all spheres of the Latino struggle for justice."[32]

Approximately fifty women unanimously adopted resolutions to push for gender equality as well as bicultural and bilingual representation in all agencies of the federal and state governments. They also formed an organization, the Mid-West Mujeres de la Raza. To continue their discussions of Latina representation—in the greater movement, government, and household—the women planned to hold a conference they named Adelante Mujer. Their discussions and the conference would allow "the Mexican American woman . . . to plan, participate, speak and take equal part in all Raza activities."[33] MWCLR leader Ricardo Parra recognized these demands. In the follow-up message to conference attendees he wrote, "Currently, there is a tentative idea of holding a Raza Woman's Conference early this summer or late spring. Let us know your ideas."[34] The "revolt of women" during the Mi Raza Primero conference thus provided the impetus for the Adelante Mujer conference in June 1972.

Adelante Mujer was both a response to Mi Raza Primero and an example of a growing national Chicana and Latina consciousness. The Conferencia de Mujeres por La Raza was held May 28–30, 1971, in Houston, approximately a year before Adelante Mujer. As the first national Chicana conference, it was a "watershed moment for emerging Chicana feminism."[35] Also based in a religious organization, the YWCA at Magnolia Park, the Houston conference was an important site of comparison for Adelante Mujer. Further documenting the experience of women at Adelante Mujer expands the scope of Chicana feminist herstory beyond the Southwest to the Midwest.

"THE REVOLT OF THE WOMEN": A MIDWEST RISING

So, there I am at Chicano Mental Health Training Program and John says, "You need to go to a conference. We've been asked to send a representative to a conference in South Bend, Indiana." I'm thinking, "Where the f@!# is South Bend, Indiana?! I'm not a native here."

—MARIA MANGUAL, 2003

In the wake of a successful Mi Raza Primero conference, Olga Villa dispersed announcements printed on MWCLR stationery throughout the Midwest inviting Chicana and Latina women to a conference in South Bend "for Raza Women in the Mid-West."[36] One of these invitations reached the desk of an administrator at El Centro de la Causa in Chicago, who passed it along to Chicana staff member Maria Mangual. For Mangual, South Bend did not resonate as the most obvious location for a Latina conference.[37] Mangual's initial reaction likely echoed the thoughts of many women receiving the invitation. South Bend's Spanish-speaking population, while present, was not as large as that of Chicago or larger Michigan cities that may have been more obvious choices for the conference. Yet the outreach effort still enticed many Chicanas and Latinas from throughout the region to travel to South Bend in June 1972 for the conference.

Indeed, Villa's strong connections to community and other women in various organizations helped her get assistance and attendees for Adelante Mujer. Responses arrived from men and women intent on attending the conference or supporting the women's efforts. Villa targeted many governmental organizations, contacting friends in those institutions to locate speakers and request financial support and educational information. She selected an impressive panel of speakers: Lupe Anguiano, a civil rights activist working to support the Equal Rights Amendment who traveled back and forth to Washington, DC; Ruth "Rhea" Mojica Hammer, the first Latina to run for Congress from Chicago; and Martha Cotera, from the prior year's Conferencia de Mujeres por La Raza in Houston.[38]

Cotera by the late 1960s and 1970s knew well the characteristics of the Mexican and Latin American migrant stream. As a librarian who worked in various Texas locations, moving from El Paso to Austin to Crystal City, she kept her finger on the pulse of a growing current of Latina/o scholarship. Cotera's work on scholarly acquisitions for the library introduced her to Julian Samora and his graduate students' work on the migrant stream. This would be her first brush with the Midwest and Midwest Council of La Raza. From her Southwest-based vantage point, Cotera saw the MWCLR as an essential part of organizing Latinas/os in the Midwest. This proved especially true for the migrants she saw leaving the Southwest, drawn by the promise of midwestern employment opportunities: "I can't even imagine how the [Chicano] movement in the Midwest would have fared without the Midwest Council. . . . I would call this [South Bend, Indiana] a hot spot. . . . And when I think about the reach and their influence academically in the area of migrant and ethnic studies, women, and Chicanos, I don't think there would be this field in the Midwest academically without Samora and the council."[39]

Cotera, at the time, saw the council as an organization whose work primed the Midwest ground for members of the migrant stream to put down roots. The MWCLR's existence comforted Cotera; it meant migrants heading north from the Southwest were not "heading into the dark," as there were institutions to welcome them.[40] Her early ties with Samora's academic work contributed to Cotera's later involvement in Adelante Mujer, acquainting her with Julian Samora personally, the Midwest Council, and in turn Olga Villa. This is merely one example of the strong social relationships connecting the Southwest with the Midwest Chicana/o activism.

While women throughout the nation supported Villa's work on Adelante Mujer, archived correspondence shows that she also faced major challenges. In particular, she struggled with the institutional racism of one of the conference's major sponsors, the University of Notre Dame. Though the university generally supported the idea of a woman's conference, it was less enthusiastic when it came to Chicanas' quest for greater representation and leadership within the institutional formations supporting the movement. Considering the complex relations between the nascent Midwest Chicano movement and powerful regional institutions like Notre Dame, Chicanas who worked within (and outside) these institutions made intentional decisions regarding the spaces they chose as venues to discuss their potential activism.

ORGANIZING LAS MUJERES

The organization of the Adelante Mujer conference confronted certain challenges, demonstrating the difficulty of Chicana organizing in the region. Initially, since Notre Dame sponsored the MWCLR, Villa asked the university to secure a space to hold the conference. This request did not elicit the response she had hoped. On April 26, 1972, Villa sent a letter to Thomas Bergin, the dean of Notre Dame's Continuing Education Center. The letter reads as a follow-up to her earlier request to Mancis L. Foss for the use of the college's facilities for Adelante Mujer in May. She wrote to Bergin, "Mr. Foss treated us most cordially and was most hospitable, but in the process revealed his prejudicial attitude."[41] Foss's attitude of racial intolerance left Villa speechless, as she wrote,

> The following comments were offered to us, unsolicited by Mr. Foss:
>
> (1) He stated that the term Chicano should not be used because it is a dirty word.
>
> (2) He said that he hoped that the people coming to this conference would not be like the people who attended a previous conference at Continuing Education Center, because they were mean people, who marched on the Church, asked for free food and tried to oust Rev. Hesburgh.
>
> (3) He made reference to people in Mexico who are friendly not like those who came to the conference.
>
> (4) He stated further that the Blacks had retarded things for themselves through their activism.[42]

The copy of the letter ends there, but the racist biases of this particular administrator are evident. Foss's language presents a documented instance of racism from the collaborating institution. Declaring "Chicano" a dirty word politicized an ethnic group that many in US society considered unsanitary, inferior, and unfit citizens.[43] Foss's reference to "the people who attended a previous conference at the Continuing Education Center" was regarding the first Mexican American meeting in April 1970 that founded the MWCLR. During that conference, a group of around fifty students from the Chicano Coalition stormed the Sacred Heart Church on campus with a list of points calling for the dismissal of the University of Notre Dame president, Father Theodore Hesburgh.[44] Foss read the Chicano Coalition's actions as disrespectful and indicative of action taken by larger civil rights movements that it seems he found threatening, a point that can be interpreted from his comment regarding black activism.

Foss's attitude, as evidenced in Villa's written account of her interaction with him, suggests that the university's attempts to engage with the community did not override individual racism. Indeed, Villa's letter detailing his prejudice elucidates the particular challenges of working within the institutional structure of Notre Dame, which then claimed to be an ally to the Latina/o community. It demonstrates how the institution helped and hindered the development of the Chicano movement in the Midwest.

Notre Dame's reputation as a Catholic institution heavily influenced its decisions to engage in civil rights struggles as well as the Midwest Council of La Raza during the 1960s and 1970s. The MWCLR and other Latinas/os on campus used a new and more liberal version of Catholicism that demanded equal treatment and aid from the university and larger church. This language included an understanding of Gustavo Gutiérrez's liberation theology, which shifted the Church's focus to helping impoverished Latina Americans, Vatican II's teachings of a more inclusive church, and a general consideration of social justice and the commitment to surrounding populations in immediate need. Despite these promises, conflicts still arose due to discriminatory practices on the part of the university and its staff. This is also indicative of the historically fraught relationship between the Catholic Church and Latinas/os in the United States.[45]

Foss's response also shows how the institution as an actor shaped early attempts to build a Chicana feminist movement. Women had limited access to space for their South Bend meeting. Perhaps Foss's letter deterred Villa from holding the conference on campus, as she eventually found a location for the women to meet on Saturday, June 17—South Bend's United Auto Workers (UAW) Hall.[46] Connections with the UAW in South Bend likely enabled Villa to reserve the hall, a space that would be filled with more than 100 women from throughout the Midwest along with speakers from Texas and Washington, DC.[47]

VAMOS A HACER COMADRE: LET'S CREATE A SPACE OF WOMEN'S COMMUNITY

"Qué pasó, tú preguntas?" (What happened, you ask?), Villa laughingly responded when asked about the conference. She remembered there being a lecture, then not enough food for lunch, and then as suddenly as it began, "se acabó," it was over.[48] She offered few definite details but recalled a general sense of camaraderie and empowerment. Yet, a few existing newspaper articles, along with Villa's own recollections, provide important insights into this historical meeting of Raza women in the Midwest. The memories and reports coalesce to give us a clearer understanding of the first Midwest Latina meeting. Villa's reflections also complicate notions of the call for a meeting of Latinas. The pointed nature of the conference challenged her belief in inclusivity and a broader definition of the "new woman" of gender equality.

During the revolt of women at Mi Raza Primero in Muskegon, what confused Olga Villa most was the antagonism some women expressed toward men.[49] She could not understand how one could discredit and denounce the same person they married.[50] As a respected member of the Midwest Council, Villa felt treated as an equal among men. The racial exclusivity of the conference confused her as well, as she explained: "I thought to myself, why do they have to have just Latinas [at the conference]? Isn't that moving it from the universal to the particular? . . . That's going backwards!"[51] She remembered even expressing to her activist friends at one point, "If we Latina women are going to be new women tomorrow, we have to be new women for everyone, not just Latinas."[52] Villa initially questioned the need for a conference planned solely for Latinas, but once the conversation shifted to discussions of self-worth that were particular to the Latina condition, she experienced that "wow" moment.[53] Villa explained the resonance and novelty of Cotera's explanation of Chicana labor's economic value, of how Latinas' work often went unrecognized and undervalued both in public and domestic realms.

The topics at Adelante Mujer varied, much like those in the Chicana conference in Houston the year before.[54] Another facet of women's work in the home was their role as primary child care providers. Of the issues raised at the conference, one of the most important concerned La Raza children. "We oppose the damaging classification of our children as culturally deprived and retarded because fortunately they do not fit the model of the monolingual Anglo-Saxons," women wrote in a resolution.[55] Latinas wanted to be a part of their children's lives, and to stand up against the discriminatory practices their children experienced in educational and child care settings, yet they felt excluded by schools and the day care system.

As historian Nora Salas details, Chicanas/os from Michigan especially found their children labeled "'migrants' and therefore 'foreign.'"[56] The labels justified the separation and exclusion of migrant children from public schooling, especially during the 1950s and 1960s.[57] By the late 1960s and early 1970s, programs for migrant children expanded; as the La Raza Citizens Advisory Committee based in Michigan reported, twenty school districts in the state qualified for migrant program funding but did not create summer programs for these students.[58] Jesse Soriano, a bilingual-education worker, member of the Midwest Council of La Raza from 1971 to 1976, and chair of the Mi Raza Primero conference, said, "It's not uncommon to hear that 'we can't have a summer school program for the Mexican kids because recreation program funds were cut for our kids.' The townspeople would be very upset if we had a program for the Mexican kids."[59] As Jesse Soriano continued to explain, a smaller Latina/o population made the Midwest even more alienating for Spanish-speaking children than the Southwest.[60] Latinas in the Midwest, excluded from the predominantly Anglo-led educational systems, decided on methods of providing for their children such as pushing for programming that valued their children's culture and language. Bilingual education became a particular concern for these women.

Conference attendees also considered Latina roles in society and women's rights on a national level, speaking to issues like domestic violence and health insurance.[61] Speaker Lupe Anguiano stressed the importance of rallying around the Equal Rights Amendment, reminding women how recently they had gained the right to vote, a fact that shocked some women in attendance. Representatives of the Socialist Workers Party, Linda Jenness and Andrew Pulley, distributed campaign literature that "drew an enthusiastic response from the women."[62] Representatives from the Women's National Abortion Action Coalition also attended, distributed coalition literature, and discussed their upcoming national conference in New York.[63] The various themes considered women's agency in their homes, surrounding institutions, and political systems.

THE CHURCH AND WOMEN'S LIBERATION

While it is not clear how participants responded to the Women's National Abortion Action Coalition, the coalition's presence at Adelante Mujer points to the significance of the Church and Catholicism in the attendees' lives. Most women at Adelante Mujer were involved in the Catholic Church in some capacity. Yet Villa noted with some surprise, "We didn't pray at that conference! Not a single blessing."[64] Religion, unlike at the conference in Houston, did not impede unity of the women; they moved beyond the idea of belonging to the Church. Even the nuns in attendance found themselves moved by these moments of self-appreciation, becoming a part of the hugging and crying and recognition that "it was just who we are right then at that moment."[65] Cotera's keynote speech also advanced the women's self-worth by giving it a dollar amount, calling on them to consider how much their labor might cost if their husbands paid for it.[66] She gave women a new conception of their economic worth. Many of the attendees could barely afford the cost of gas, and Cotera's words finally gave their unpaid labor a price. As a result, Olga Villa recalled Cotera's speech as a powerful message that urged women to understand "if we were everything to somebody else, then we were nothing to ourselves."[67]

Attendees felt a new sense of self-awareness, but whether it can be characterized as purely feminist is uncertain. One of the few newspaper accounts of the conference reported that it was "to be a consciousness raising session to give Chicano women a clearer understanding of their feminism."[68] As Villa's reflections show, however, not all women agreed with the total denouncement of men or even ideas about gender oppression. Their ambivalence was about more than just the frequent characterization of feminism as man-hating. Not all women shared the same feelings regarding female equality and the recognition of an oppressive patriarchy.

Despite theoretical disagreements, conference-goers attempted to fashion their own safe space for Latinas. Women who attended wanted the press barred from the conference "because they did not feel free talking in front of people with cameras and notebooks." In creating this Latina-focused environment, the racial component of the movement's solidarity also came into question. The tension became especially prevalent when "two women [from the] Kansas delegation proposed excluding a few non-Chicana women present at the workshops."[69] One was a Black woman from Ohio who reportedly left her home at 2 a.m. to reach the conference on time, and another was a woman of Asian descent who left her home at 5 a.m.[70] Perhaps the women were expecting a conference that fostered solidarity among women of color in a seemingly homogeneously white region.

Yet some Chicanas felt they needed a racially exclusive space for themselves. While the motion to exclude non-Chicanas never came to an official vote, those who opposed their attendance expressed concern that their presence might deter Chicanas from feeling comfortable and speaking candidly during workshops.[71] They also feared that non-Latina women were biased by the media's misconstrued notions of what it meant to be Latina. Those who opposed the motion to exclude non-Latinas claimed the decision would make them guilty of the very discrimination they were fighting to eradicate.[72] After a break for lunch, the motion was dropped.

Villa's memory of the lunch break provides an important view into the sense of community among the women at the conference. With humor, Villa recounted that the Mexican food donated for lunch only provided enough to feed a maximum of forty people. To ensure that everyone was fed, women offered up apples and other snacks they had packed for their car rides, donating what they could to the communal hodgepodge spread.[73] These moments of improvisation characterize the resourcefulness and solidarity exhibited by the Midwest *mujeres*. As a greater testament to this solidarity, by the end of the conference, the women cleaned the UAW's floor, scrubbed the bathrooms, and refilled the toilet paper, causing a worker at the hall to remark that he had never seen it so clean.[74] When asked why the women decided to clean the place, Villa responded, "I think it's because, that's what we do normally, it's in the back of our heads."[75] The women's postconference cleaning hints at the domestic roles many women considered their duty. This was the very work that Villa realized had economic value, a dollar amount. Putting a monetary value on women's work opened many Latinas' eyes to the importance of their actions.

The conference ended with the election of board members for each state—in Indiana, Delfina Landeros from South Bend, Joyce Juarez from Fort Wayne, and Ricarda Bidella from East Chicago. Michigan members were Maria Elena Castellanos, from Saginaw, and Linda Caballero, from Flint.[76] Their election reflected the importance of regional representation. Adelante Mujer sent them and other women back to their communities, tasking them with promoting lessons from the conference in their communities. One of the women was Maria Mangual, who later helped found the influential Mujeres Latinas en Acción in Chicago.[77] Political inspiration thus traveled from the small town of South Bend to larger cities throughout the Midwest. Adelante Mujer organizers sought to extend the activism outside of the UAW Hall; members from each of the midwestern states were called also to head their own Adelante Mujer conferences within the following six months.[78] In addition to calls for organization, Villa noted that the conference demanded moments of self-reflection in asking, "What am I doing? What am I learning? I can type, I can say <u>thank you</u> and I can do this and that. I think a key thing for a lot of *mujeres* at that time was 'What did I learn?'"[79] Not only did female attendees of the conference learn from the experience, but men within the movement also recognized the oppressive forces these women faced. Though men were not allowed to attend the conference, they offered support in other ways.

News of the Adelante Mujer conference spread widely throughout the Midwest. Domingo Rosas of the organization Chicanos Organizados Rebeldes de Aztlán (CORA, Chicano Rebel Organizers of Aztlán) sent congratulations and a letter of support to the women of MWCLR in August 1972:

> La Raza Women are to be highly congratulated on the success of the Conference. Although as males, we are not always able to "feel" the humiliation which La Raza Women have endured as a matter of course for many decades, we gain a pretty good insight into their plight from such Conferences as the "Adelante Mujer" Conference.
>
> Our hearts go out to you courageous ladies whose determination to live as dignified La Raza women often puts us males to shame.[80]

Letters from male heads of organizations signify recognition of the changing roles of Chicana and Latina women. This recognition within the larger movement also manifested in the MWCLR's newsletter, *Los Desarraigados* (The Uprooted Ones).[81] Ricardo Parra, the director, would often devote space in the newsletter to topics concerning *mujeres*, notifying its readers of future conference organizing and feminist literature.[82] In this way, women carved out a place in the greater Chicana/o midwestern struggle; they found their voice. Beyond the organizational response, it is difficult to say if other male reactions were as positive as CORA's. Villa remarked, for example, that the day of the conference, Jane Gonzalez had to rush home and get to bed before her husband realized she had driven to South Bend. Women who pursued feminist organizing did not always have support at home.

"JUST PART OF THE STORY"

Villa astutely noted that the difficulty women faced in balancing friends and family was "just part of the story (our story) here in the Midwest, it could be California, San Francisco, it could be New York, Miami. Because women need to find their voice."[83] Jane Gonzalez, as one of the main leaders and organizers helping Villa with advancing women's voices in the movement, sacrificed her relationship with her children and husband. Missing her presence in the home, Gonzalez's children only later appreciated their mother's activism, while her husband never understood the cause she championed.[84]

The domestic and political realities of these Latinas called for pragmatic decisions. According to Villa, those who chose not to strongly identify as "feminist" or "Chicana" were often seen as "selling out." Villa discussed this phrase in the interview, noting, "I use the word 'sell out' loosely, because some people have to survive. . . . I often feel sorry for people who have to live a whole different life as not themselves." She became most aware of the difficulties surrounding women while working with the MWCLR. Villa recognized the importance of moving beyond intellectual ideas "just flying in the air" to have a balance of theories of liberation and direct action in the community.[85] In this region, where passing as something other than Latina was in certain ways easier, the women's activism becomes more courageous.

After the council disbanded in 1979, Villa married the director of the MWCLR, Ricardo Parra, and likely experienced her fair share of the theoretical discussions surrounding the plight of Latina/os. Parra was an intellectual who quoted from others who wrote on oppression such as Karl Marx, Kahlil Gibran, and Paolo Freire.[86] In trying to situate her activism, Villa understood the importance of moving beyond theories to connecting with others on an emotional level. In order to be the most effective agent of change, one had to achieve a balance of emotion and intelligence. In an interview years later Villa admitted, "I'm post being a woman, I'm post being a lot of things, and now's my time to think about it, to reflect on it."[87] In being "post woman" Villa provided an interesting assessment of her role in the movement. Her assertion provides another layer of complexity in understanding how the women understood their activism.

As Maylei Blackwell has noted, the dominant narrative of second-wave feminism placed limits on articulations of feminism that diverged from the concerns of mainstream white feminist organizing as well as "the diversity of struggles from which they emerge, and the breadth of agendas they produced."[88] Villa's self-identification as "post woman" challenges the idea that the women's liberation movement was the sole producer of real feminism. In identifying outside the monolithic vision of oppression of the women's movement, even if during a retrospective moment, Villa demonstrated an understanding of the complexity of Latinas' social location by refusing to adhere to a single notion of womanhood or feminism. The expressions of feminism are incredibly diverse and influenced by the intersection of class, education, ethnicity, generation, and relation to the larger understanding of Anglo-feminism at the time. It is difficult to define a single expression of feminism among participants in the Adelante Mujer conference, but each of the women identified as La Raza women who faced unique forms of oppression based on gender and race.[89]

Broadening our view of the greater women's liberation movement in the 1970s leads to a more expansive understanding of the intersecting oppressions facing women like Olga Villa. Her complicated experience as one of the primary organizers of the Adelante Mujer conference also opens up questions of Chicana and Latina identification with the greater Chicana movement, adding depth and breadth to our historical understandings of feminism as part of a Latina experience.

IN THE END, IT WAS A STARTING POINT

Olga Villa explained that the Adelante Mujer conference "was a starting point for a lot of our lives" in that it brought together Latinas from throughout the

Midwest to organize and define their activism.[90] This sentiment echoes a statement broadcast by Elma Barrera during her *Chicanas and Chicanos* radio show that the Conferencia de Mujeres in Houston "was anger, sisterhood, disunity; it was organizing for the future."[91] The two conferences presented Latinas with the chance to organize and advance their calls for equality and recognition within the greater movement. With the help of the MWCLR, midwestern women found it possible to meet and discuss many issues of concern and claim a voice within the Chicano movement as it developed in the Midwest. Latinas faced their share of difficulties and successes in planning and executing a meeting of women in the Midwest.

Midwest activism as represented in the Adelante Mujer conference redefines our understanding of La Raza feminism in action. The women's activism was not entirely grassroots; it drew on resources from Notre Dame and support from the Midwest Council of La Raza. Nor was it entirely institutional. Indeed, it seems the institution was reluctant to make a space for their organizing. That their actions were pragmatic does not make any less impressive their determination to produce "new forms of racial consciousness, gender awareness and political identities," though in a different setting and with a diverse cast of actors.[92]

Adelante Mujer presents us with an opportunity to analyze unexplored articulations of regionalism, feminism, and activism within the Chicano movement. This foundational manifestation of Chicana and Latina activism in the Midwest demonstrates how ideas that are feminist are not only filtered through the lens of a Chicana experience, but a very particular Midwest La Raza experience. Throughout the 1970s, the Midwest Council of La Raza played a central role in advocating for the social, political, and religious rights of Latinas/os in the Midwest. Given its position as an activist organization affiliated with a powerful educational institution, analysis of the MWCLR complicates and broadens our understanding of the nature of movement politics in the 1970. From this microhistory of a conference we can begin to expand the geographical scope of Chicana and Latina feminism to consider the experience of women in the Midwest and their claims to a place in the greater Chicana/Chicano movement.

4 "IT'S NOT A NATURAL ORDER"

RELIGION AND THE EMERGENCE OF CHICANA FEMINISM IN THE CURSILLO MOVEMENT IN SAN JOSE

SUSANA L. GALLARDO

Chicana feminists have long lamented the various ways in which Catholicism underpins the subordination of women and human sexuality within Mexican American culture. The intertwining of patriarchal and heterosexual privilege in religion and culture seem to offer little space for Chicana feminist intervention. In this essay I explore the complexity of Chicana Catholic religious practices and how one group of women in San Jose, California, successfully navigated that difficult terrain. I offer a case study of a series of Chicana Catholic *movidas* in which a group of women recognized themselves as multiply marginalized within the Catholic religious institution and actively transformed that knowledge into a strategy of creating new organizational spaces and unexpected alliances. Seizing upon a gender-segregated retreat space of the Catholic Cursillo as a site to share common experiences and ask difficult questions, these women forged a place for themselves in the Catholic tradition that reflected their unique location in the *movimiento* of the 1960s and 1970s.[1]

In these pages I share the spiritual narratives of three Chicana Catholics—Maria Oropesa, Jessie Garibaldi, and Phyllis Soto—active in the Chicano *movimiento* in San Jose in the 1960s and 1970s and within their working-class Catholic parish. In the context of a gender-segregated Catholic Cursillo retreat, they nurtured an emergent Chicana feminist sensibility that enabled them to engage *movimiento* discourse in a religious context and allowed them to share and affirm new conceptions of self. Just as among Chicanas within the *movimiento*, I show how Chicana Catholics—empowered by the Catholic Cursillos and by their own life experiences—managed to contest the patriarchal church while maintaining an insistent belonging to a beloved religious institution.

CATHOLICISM AND THE MOVIMIENTO

The link between Catholicism, religiosity, and the Chicano movement permeated movement discourses; elements of Christian spirituality suffused almost every aspect of the Chicano *movimiento*. The place of the Virgen de Guadalupe at the head of United Farm Workers (UFW) labor marches is well known, as is Cesar Chavez's personal Catholic piety. In New Mexico, Reies López Tijerina fused Pentecostal and social justice worldviews in his leadership of the Alianza movement.[2] Other Chicanos across the Southwest sought out and reclaimed indigenous spiritualities like *curanderismo* and Aztec dancing. Chicana/o writers and poets channeled incredible bursts of spiritual creativity into poetry and prose, from the Aztlán creation story and "El Plan Espiritual de Aztlán" to Anzaldúa's later vision of a queer borderlands.

Yet the most common characterization of religion in the *movimiento* was a biting nationalist critique that denounced the colonial history and presence of the institutional Church.[3] Also prominent was a specifically *Chicana feminist* critique that focused on patriarchal religious norms restricting women's sexuality and reproductive rights.[4] Chicano activism included several different approaches from within and beyond the Church. Chicano Catholic activists in California would articulate demands upon the hierarchy to directly support *movimiento* goals. Catholic activists would protest the million-dollar budgets of new cathedrals in Los Angeles and San Francisco and call upon local dioceses to intervene in union organizing or fund Chicano community projects.[5] Within the Catholic hierarchy itself, Chicana/o and Latina/o priests and nuns would engage with local communities, join protest marches, and work to more directly address institutional discrimination and long-term change.[6] By the 1980s, an abundance of theological work questioned doctrinal frameworks by addressing issues of gender, race, and class, such as Ada María Isasi Díaz's *Mujerista Theology* and Anthony Stevens-Arroyo's *Prophets Denied Honor*.[7] Finally, many Chicanas and Latinas would leave the Church altogether to explore new fusions of indigenous and feminist spiritualities.[8]

As substantive as these critiques and movements were, it was still impossible to ignore the persistence of the Catholic tradition among Mexican Americans. In the 1960s, between 80 and 90 percent of Mexican Americans identified as Catholic. Catholic religious ideas and symbols permeated the culture despite a rapidly growing Protestant minority. Even those activists who launched the most stinging analyses and rejection of the institutional Catholic Church belied an intimate relationship with its symbols and rituals. Ana Castillo notes two of the most common attitudes of Chicano activists toward the church: either rejecting it altogether as an oppressive institution in a secular Marxist-influenced agenda for social change, or compartmentalizing religious "traditions" as part of Chicano culture.[9] In either case, she suggests,

The church continued to influence their personal lives in myriad ways, activistas went on living their lives. . . . They worked in government-funded jobs in their barrios in Chicago and on Christmas Eve made tamales with mothers and tías and went to Midnight Mass. They started bilingual pre-schools in San Francisco and stood up as the Maid of Honor at their best friend's wedding. They painted socially relevant murals in San Diego and sponsored a niece for her *quinceañera*.[10]

Important moments of life transition were marked by Catholic sacraments like baptism, communion, marriage, and funerals that regularly called families together. Domestic rituals like prayer, *bendiciones*, reciting the rosary, and keeping home altars solidified family relationships and reinforced the reach of the Church in everyday life.

At the local level, the religious experience of Chicana/o parishioners ranged widely, depending on geographic location, demographics, pastoral leadership, and diocesan resources.[11] Though Mexican Americans constituted two-thirds of the Catholic community in five southwestern states, Chicanas/os and Latinas/os remained drastically underrepresented in the clerical hierarchy, so that most Latina/o parishes were pastored by white priests, or if they were lucky, foreign priests from Spanish-speaking countries.[12] At the same time, individual churches and pastors offered great resources: physical space for community interaction, familiar social networks, and the exchange of ideas in dynamic political contexts that would in some cases birth and support local activism.

TRANSFORMING THE CURSILLO IN SAN JOSE

In San Jose, the Chicana/o Catholic community centered around a new parish, Our Lady of Guadalupe, in the Eastside neighborhood of Mayfair, also known as Sal Si Puedes (Get out if you can), the birthplace of Cesar Chavez. The community itself was being reshaped in a time of tremendous change in California and the country in general. The convergence of the Vatican II meetings in Rome, the African American civil rights movement and national civil rights legislation, the emerging Chicano *movimiento*, and the United Farm Workers labor movement made the late '60s a unique historical moment for Guadalupe parishioners. The movements gave rise to a new era of activism in which Mexican Americans increasingly "began to name anti-Mexican racism as a primary cause of local and national patterns of inequality."[13] The GI Bill gave young men of color entry into higher education in significant numbers for the first time, and San Jose began seeing new forms of Mexican American youth activism at San Jose State College and San Jose City College as well as in local community groups. As in other Mexican American communities throughout the US Southwest, San Jose activists began analyzing parallels with African Americans as a US minority group and drawing on new "Chicano" discourses of self-determination emerging in Chicano activist circles across many cities in the Southwest. Historian Steve Pitti notes that many young people in the San Jose area began designating themselves as "Chicano" to signify a uniquely Mexican *and* American identity or to "express the fact that they were Mexican Americans who 'did not have an Anglo view of themselves.'"[14]

This was the local political context in which groups of Chicanas from Guadalupe would organize and gather for the retreat, a formulaic weekend of self-reflection and religious engagement aimed at renewing the spiritual life of lapsed Catholics and drawing them into the church community. First developed in Spain in the 1950s, the Catholic Cursillo was transplanted to Texas among Spanish-speaking Catholics and spread quickly throughout the Southwest, with English Cursillos launched in the mid-1960s.[15] The Catholic Cursillo was somewhat different from most retreats because it was developed and led by laypeople in a series of talks known as *rollos*. A priest gave several of the key *rollos*, but most (twelve out of fifteen) were given by laypersons who had previously completed their own Cursillos. Catholic historian Debra Campbell argues that the Cursillo fostered "a level of community and spiritual intensity unavailable in most parishes . . . [that represented] a viable alternative to the clerical vision of Catholic spirituality traditionally nurtured within the parish system."[16]

The women who share their stories here are longtime participants in the Guadalupe Cursillo. Phyllis made her Cursillo in the mid-1960s, Jessie in the early 1970s, and Maria in 1976. Originally the Cursillos were restricted to married women who went only after their husbands had completed their retreats, so that "he would maintain spiritual leadership of the home."[17] The lay-led format was quite malleable, however, depending on the priest's oversight. So when Chicano Franciscan priest Anthony Soto at the Guadalupe church gave free rein to the lay leadership in the late '60s, the Cursillo scripts expanded to address issues specific to Guadalupe's working-class Mexican American community. The retreats were gender-segregated, so Phyllis and other women in the group were free to continually modify the experience. The women's Cursillos first expanded beyond married women to include single women, then divorced women. They used the Cursillo script to explore their spiritual lives, but they also began gradually adding elements of Chicano art, music, and tradition as they shared their stories.

The spiritual scripts—the actual typewritten or handwritten scripts—of the various talks given by laypeople were literally handed down, copied, modified, and rewritten by successive leaders, and over time they became repositories of Chicana spiritual experience, told and retold. The curricular content of the cursillo inevitably began to shift, reflecting women's lives and experiences and some of the Chicano discourse circulating at the time. Talks included the expected spiritual themes but also expressed family worries, marriage issues, painful stories of discrimination and abuse in schools, internalized racism, and various coping strategies. The meeting space functioned as a consciousness-raising group of sorts, and women often left the experience affirmed by the group in their individual struggles.

By the late 1970s, the women and men had significantly modified both the content and structure of the original Cursillo to reflect their growth and experience. Table 4.1 shows the reduction of material on traditional theologies of grace and piety and a corresponding increase in material grounding the church in Chicana/o history and culture, including a section on "La Mujer." This shift would eventually lead its participants away from institutional Catholicism into an independent liturgical structure that continues to meet today.[18]

TABLE 4.1 From Catholic to Chicana Cursillo

Original Cursillo structure, 1965
Lead meditations are given by priests, followed by series of *rollos* given by laypeople

Revised Chicana/o structure, ~1978
All talks given by laypersons

FRIDAY	**FRIDAY**
Meditation: Know Yourself, Prodigal Son	Meditation: Know Yourself, Prodigal Son
1. Ideal	1. Ideal
2. Habitual Grace	
3. Lay Vows in the Church	**SATURDAY**
4. Actual Grace	Meditation: Tres Miradas de Cristo
5. Piety	2. Presence of God
	3. Iglesia
SATURDAY	4. Historia y Cultura
Meditation: The Figure of Christ	5. Espiritualidad Chicana
6. Study	
7. Sacraments	**SUNDAY**
8. Action	Meditation: Misión del Cristiano
9. Obstacles	6. Sacramentos
10. Direction	7. Ambiente
	8. La Mujer
SUNDAY	9. Chicana/o más Allá
Meditation: Friends of Jesus	
11. Environment	
12. A Life of Grace	
13. Christianity in Action	
14. Total Security	
15. Beyond the Cursillo	

A FINAL NOTE ON METHOD

My analysis here draws on "lived religion" theory from my home discipline of religious studies, as it is relevant for an understanding of Chicanas in the Catholic Church. Lived religion is an approach that focuses on religion as a human experience lived out in daily life, as opposed to strictly doctrinal or institutionally oriented analyses. As Marie Griffiths and Barbara Dianne Savage define it, lived religion focuses on

> negotiations of power and identity in ordinary life, within ecclesial structures (church, synagogue, mosque, etc.) and outside them in domestic life and in a wide variety of so-called public spheres (voluntary organizations, the media, or self-help groups, for instance) . . . how diverse peoples have strategically utilized religious practices to maneuver in everyday encounters and thereby have reshaped their own participation in society and culture.[19]

Lived religion theory lends itself well here because a significant component—if not the heart—of Chicana/o Catholicism lies outside the institutional realm of the local parish and priest. Mexican American Catholic practices constitute a distinctive autonomous Catholic culture that overlaps mainstream Catholicism yet has served historically as a central node of Chicana/o cultures, for better or worse. Analyzing Catholicism as a set of cultural practices, what Jay Dolan calls "a Catholic ethos,"[20] helps decenter the institutional sphere of the church to better understand its place in the hearts and lives of its believers. Texas historian Roberto Treviño uses the term "ethno-Catholicism" to reflect a unique Mexican Catholic identity and way of life that combines medieval and Indian roots along with faith healing, saint veneration, home altar worship, and "other practices deemed superstitious by clergy" as well as community-centered religious celebrations that "tended simultaneously to selectively participate in the institutional Catholic Church yet hold it at arm's length."[21]

The autonomous nature of Mexican American Catholicism is particularly important for understanding women's involvement because it better enables us to acknowledge the various roles women play in living out a Catholic spirituality—as midwives, *curanderas*, lay leaders, *altaristas*, and mothers, among others—as well as laypersons. The concept of "lived religion" allows us to reframe our understanding of religious beliefs and practices through the everyday practices of Maria, Jessie, and Phyllis, who were involved in the leadership of the Guadalupe cursillos while raising their families in San Jose from the late 1960s through 1980s.

MARIA, JESSIE, AND PHYLLIS

Maria is a retired social worker, mother of one, and a writer and poet. Jessie is a divorced mother of five who continued to serve various functions in her parish. Phyllis is a retired educational counselor, a widow, and a former foster mother, with the longest history of leadership in the Guadalupe community. Their profiles are based on a series of interviews, ethnographic fieldwork, and archival research I conducted between the mid-1990s and early 2000s. The women discuss how the institution's rituals structured their childhood, but their religious lives emerge in a series of ongoing negotiations with the institutional Catholic Church and their own subjectivity as Mexican American women in a predominantly white institution. Within their stories, the Catholic institution remains an unmarked point of reference for these women; being Catholic is less about something one *does* and more about who one *is*. The experiences of Maria, Jessie, and Phyllis represent some of the many ways in which a Chicana Catholic subjectivity is lived within local Mexican American communities and was shaped during the late 1960s to 1980s in ways that have created a space for Chicana leadership and agency within Catholicism.

Maria: "Priests Don't Know Everything"

For Maria, the cursillo spirituality fit like a glove. Despite initial misgivings, she found that the ideas and spirituality of the cursillo meshed well with her own critical take on Catholicism:

> I know that when I came to the *clausura* [closing], when I made my cursillo in 1976, and we came to the end, and I stood there and at the ending you say how you feel, what feelings you have about what has happened that weekend—and I remember saying, 'I feel like I'm home. Like this is where I'm supposed to be, and this is what I'm searching for."[22]

She worked on the cursillos every year after that, first behind the scenes, then later writing and giving her own *rollos*.

When I met her, Maria was a sixty-something retired social worker, mother of a thirty-something daughter. A petite, agile woman of average height with light brown skin and a crop of short silver hair, she had long identified as Chicana and participated in various local Chicana/o organizations, including a Florisong Writers Group and "el Comite," a group of Chicana/o social workers who sought to reform the city's social services system to better serve Chicana/o communities. She was the only person in her family to identify as Chicana; the rest identified as Mexicanos. "They dislike the word 'Chicano' because they see it as lower class. I am a Chicana," she said once.[23]

Maria spoke with some ambivalence about her Catholic background. She was the youngest of five children, and her childhood was disrupted by immigration and family separation that led to her being raised by various relatives in Noriega, Chihuahua. In an oral history interview in the mid-1980s, she shared how her earliest years were structured by traditional Catholicism. The small Mexican town had no church or priest, but Maria recalled various unofficial practices: baptisms, reciting rosaries at her aunt's house, attending in-home *velorios* (wakes), the

Ave Maria and Padre Nuestro prayers in front of her grandmother's home altar, and occasional visits to Santa Barbara, Chihuahua, five hours away, for Sunday Mass.[24] Many of the town's religious events were handled by townspeople themselves. She recalled, "My paternal grandparents had santos at home; they went to church when they went into town where there was a church and priest. . . . Whenever anyone died in Noriega, there was a certain lady who was called and she said the rosary for the velorio. Relatives were assigned the task of dressing the body and making the casket. Our funerals were without a priest."[25]

As an adult, Maria differentiated herself from her family's traditional Catholicism: "I am the only one who is not traditional."[26] She seemed slightly amused to define herself as Catholic, commenting, "What is Catholic? I'm catholic. With a small c."[27]

After going to live with her older sister in California, she made a rough transition into an all-white school in Cupertino where "there were five or six Mexicans," she recalled. She went on to tell me about being tested in high school and assessed with an IQ of 69.[28] The experience was buffered somewhat by an astute white male teacher who assured her the low score was attributable to vocabulary rather than ability. Maria recalled,

> Well, I had only been in the United States five years. But I had a very understanding history teacher—he was my home teacher. He was very understanding. He looked at me and said, "This doesn't mean anything, because I know that you're intelligent, and look, you're getting very good grades in my class. You just weren't born here; you don't know any of the stuff they ask you. So of course you're gonna have a low score. . . ." But anyway, that's what I wanted. I remember him telling me that, "Don't worry about it, don't worry about it."[29]

Maria nevertheless remembered the incident with clarity some fifty years later. The early mislabeling was particularly ironic, given that Maria was a voracious bibliophile, reading everything from Dorothy Parker to Bill Moyers. She was always up to date on the latest news locally, nationally, globally, and frequently cited various TV news shows and the latest PBS specials. The first time I visited her home, her living room looked like an office space, filled with bookshelves, every table, chair, and free space stacked with journals, newspapers, and more books. She saved editorials from the local paper—articles on politics, domestic violence, spirituality, affirmative action, Mexicans, La Raza, Asian communities, and multiculturalism—always meaning to sort and file them away but usually just creating another pile. She told me a funny story once about a comment her grandchildren made while out somewhere observing a messy environment. "They said it looked like Grandma's house!" Maria said with a laugh. "That's when I thought, I'd better clean things up."

As a young girl and teen in Cupertino, she attended the usual rituals with her family at St. Joseph's Church and at age sixteen even considered becoming a nun after reading St. Francis de Sales's *Introduction to the Devout Life*. But her interests broadened after reading the mystics, she recalled: "The message I got was that there was one God, but there's many different religions." By age twenty-one, Maria balked at going to church and rejected her older sister's interpretation that "the devil was talking to me, and that's why I didn't want to go to church." Maria rejected this interpretation. "I'd say no," said Maria, "I had a lot of things to do—and I can pray while I'm ironing my clothes!"[30]

It wasn't until almost ten years later, as Maria sought a divorce from her five-year-old marriage, that her unease with the Catholic doctrine became explicit. Returning to California with her four-year-old daughter, resituating her life after divorcing an abusive husband, she returned to church, where she was surprised and disappointed to find that her priest expected her to do a substantial penance for the sin of divorce. "I went to confession, and the priest gave me a whole rosary to do, and I don't know how many Our Fathers and [*pauses*] I got real upset because he said that [*pauses*] it was a sin to be divorced."[31] Though this part of Church doctrine could hardly have been news to her, the direct implications for her life elicited an intuitive defense of her decision. She went on to question the priest's assessment:

> I thought, "Gee, I don't think getting a divorce is such a big deal." I said, "Why are you giving me a rosary?" I did ask him! He says, "Well you know it's a sin to be separated." . . . And so then I asked him, "Why?" And then he said, "Because it's a sin to separate from your husband." But I didn't agree with that, and I decided I wasn't going to do the rosary, and that nothing was going to happen to me. This was in 1971, when I was thirty.[32]

As she told me this story in one of our early interviews, I was impressed yet not surprised that Maria would question her priest's judgment. Rather than internalize the priest's judgment, Maria drew instead on her own experience and rejected his assessment of her life. She said, "I decided nothing was going to happen to me if I didn't say the rosary. And that I felt that divorce was not a sin, regardless of what the priest said, and that's really when I made the break, that priests don't know everything and that I was going to . . . attempt to do God's will."[33] With that, Maria essentially rejected the authority of the priest to assess her decision to divorce. She carefully distinguished, however, between the rejection of her faith and the rejection of the priest's judgment, concluding, "It wasn't that I was against God; I was just against the priest."

The rejection of the priest's authority also invoked the more difficult task of depending on her own ability to define sin: "I was going to . . . attempt to do God's will." Her decision affirmed her own assessment of the circumstances and the impact of her divorce upon her young daughter and herself. She also continued to attend church and receive communion, although doctrinally, her failure to do the penance rendered her ineligible for the latter.

I continued going to church. And I continued getting up there and receiving communion, even though I didn't go to confession anymore. I haven't gone to confession since then, so that would be twenty years. . . . But every time I go to church, I go up there and get communion. I can confess my sins direct to God—in fact I don't need to confess—he knows whether I confess or don't confess.[34]

So for Maria, the consequences of her divorce included a new, more complex relationship to the institution, of claiming a belonging but insisting on a just interpretation of her own subjectivity as a single Chicana divorced mother.

Bringing this experience to the cursillo, then, Maria found her sense of home, as she put it, "like this is where I'm supposed to be, and this is what I'm searching for."[35] The cursillo affirmed her relationship to an institutional church she respected but also mediated church doctrine based on the religious experience in the lives of this working-class Mexican American population. The idea of Chicano self-determination taken from nationalist discourse took on new meanings in this context. A central tenet of the cursillo culture was an insistence on spiritual equality and the "priesthood of believers," meaning that every believer was inherently valuable and capable of spiritual power.[36] This egalitarian ethic fostered a sense of competence and agency that would cross religious and secular lines.

For Maria, the sense of spiritual democracy brought a new understanding of her job as a social worker for child protective services. Her work with white coworkers and administrators on one hand and Chicano parents and children on the other required her to navigate carefully through various processes of assessment:[37]

I feel very empowered. I feel that I . . . I *do* ministry in the work that I do, even though we may not call it that. I ask for the spirit to guide me in some of my decisions, and I ask for the spirit to guide me when I need to be very clear and direct with some of the parents when they're being abusive. And to do it in such a way that I'm educating them instead of punishing them, or that I want—let me see, I don't necessarily want their approval of me—but I want them to have insight into their behavior, so that they'll be capable of changing. And that I see as a ministry, because to tell a parent that they're not being good parents—and to say it in such a way that *they* see it—that's ministry. So I feel empowered because I have a community that guides me, that I learn from, each time that I come.[38]

Maria's use of the word "empowered" here signifies several things. First and foremost, it presumes her belonging to the Catholic Church; she identifies as an active, practicing Catholic. Second, it interprets her occupation as a ministry to parents and families, a site of spiritual authority as well as occupational. And finally, it grounds that ministry, a ministry based on her experience and judgment, in the cursillo community of other Chicana Catholics. Her interaction with the cursillo community offered her an opportunity to engage, reflecting on her ministry in a supportive community.

The cursillo community, then, gave Maria a community of peers who affirmed both the political and spiritual value of her work in support of San Jose's families. Maria's faith was thus something that is practiced not only on Sundays but rather is implicated in every moment of her life. It grounded her social work in a Catholic framework, even as she held the institution at a distance. Years later, she would write poetry in English and Spanish that reflected her own assessment of her personal growth.[39]

> *La mujer que fui*
> *Ya no puedo ser*
> *Y en cambio soy la misma*
> *Que fui ayer*
>
> *Del que hacer de casa*
> *No quería saber*
> *Eso yo lo hacía*
> *Con rabia*
>
> *Todavia siento miedo*
> *De volver a ser*
> *La mujer que fui ayer*
> **—MARIA, NOVEMBER 26, 1982**
>
> *The woman I was*
> *I can no longer be*
> *Yet I am still the same*
> *As I was before*
>
> *The one who stayed at home*
> *Didn't want to know*
> *I did this*
> *So angry*
>
> *Still I fear*
> *I will return to be*
> *The woman I was before*
> **—TRANSLATION BY GABRIELA GUTIERREZ Y MUHS**

Jessie: "We Just Go Ahead and Do the Job"

Jessie is a Catholic workhorse, the kind of laywoman that keeps Catholic parishes everywhere running smoothly and efficiently. At the time of our 2011 interview, she served her local parish as translator, trainer, tutor, liturgist, and

Eucharistic minister. Jessie worked with the priest to establish a regular Spanish Mass, tutored him in the Spanish language, trained sacristans and altar boys in Spanish, ran a lunch program, and participated in several other parish organizations. Yet during the 1970s at Guadalupe, she served as *rectora* leading the women's *cursillos*, trained as a permanent deacon (a position restricted to men only), gained certification in ministry from a nondenominational, independent Christian organization, and performed a number of unofficially Catholic baptisms and marriages for family and friends. Jessie told me once, laughing, that her daughter liked to tell people that "her mother was a Catholic priest."

Jessie offers a complicated set of reflections on her relationship to the Church. Born in Salinas, California, she was one of eight children raised by a resourceful single mother. She left school in eighth grade after a fight with a girl who called her "a dirty Mexican." Jessie's mother kept a home altar but rarely attended church "because they didn't have Spanish-speaking churches." Later Jessie's mom found out about the Guadalupe parish and had a friend drive her to attend Mass. Somehow, their mother ensured that Jessie and her siblings fulfilled the usual Catholic rituals of baptism, communion, and confirmation. Jessie's own children have all had the usual sacraments because, she says, "I wanted my kids to have the traditional basic training because someday they might want to get married in the church."[40]

When she attends Mass, however, as she recites the ritual prayers she modifies the language to make it more inclusive, personal, and reflective of her own subjectivity. She changes words as she recites them so that she'll say "men and women" instead of "men." She also personalizes the standard Catholic prayers in Spanish, using the informal *tu* form of "you" in Spanish to personalize them. Despite her own unusual ministry, she told me she loves the ritual of the Mass. "I just love being there. Just like praying. I love to pray and I like to be part of the mass and I just feel there's that connection. The more I seek him the more I know him and feel it. It becomes alive to me, becomes present to me—and I cry in church a lot," she said with a laugh.[41]

Jessie didn't recall a particular sense of spirituality until well into her twenties. She described picking prunes with her family in Burbank. The family camped overnight in the fields, where one night Jessie had a vision of Jesus descending a stairway "in bright white glowing tunic like coming down the stairs to where I was sleeping." She also recalled being unaffected after hearing a speaker on the Virgin of Guadalupe: "I never had any connection with the Virgin de Guadalupe. I just didn't have that knowledge."[42]

Jessie's lack of connection with the Virgin, however, would change quite dramatically many years later when she had a frightening car accident with her children. Jessie had left the car in the driveway while she ran back into the house for a forgotten item. With three young children in the car and her older daughter holding the baby next to the car door, the car slipped out of gear and began to roll back out of the driveway. Jessie heard screaming and looked out the window to see the car rolling. She recalled, "I call[ed] out to the Virgen—I cry every time I say it—you'd think I'd learned by now—I cried 'my babies! Don't let nothing happen to my kids!' The children were fine except for the oldest whose foot was run over. But that was my belief in the Virgen. I said you saved my babies!"[43]

In some ways, Jessie was a traditional mother of five children. She married a man with "Mexican ways" who insisted that the family attend Mass regularly. This drew Jessie closer into parish life at the only local Spanish Mass at Guadalupe, and she did her *cursillo* after her husband, Manuel, did his. She called the cursillo "very enlightening," awakening in her a sense of appreciation for "the relationship you can build with God." She said it was the first time she understood how "nuns could live in a convent with just a bunch of women [*laughs*] because to me it was important to get married and have kids. Ever since I was little, I knew that's what I wanted." The cursillo enhanced her spiritual life, Jessie said, because she felt "all that praying just kind of gives you a lift and makes you feel so content, at peace, it was beautiful."[44] She would go on to assume regular leadership roles in the women's *cursillos* and the Guadalupe parish.

In 1970, Jessie returned to school at a local community college. Despite having only an eighth-grade education, Jessie thrived in her classes and transferred to Santa Clara University, where she received her bachelor's degree in 1972 and a master's degree in counseling psychology in 1977; she then began doctoral work in education at a satellite campus of a San Diego university. Her relationship with her husband had been gradually deteriorating, however, and they divorced in 1983, with Jessie staying in Campbell, and her husband living at a ranch in a more rural town south of San Jose. She noted wryly that her husband had not wanted her to continue with her education, attributing his resistance to "his Mexican ways." She told me, "I always say my Chicano mind and his Mexican ways—we clashed, we really did!"

Jessie has long been active in the institutional parish at the same time that she has actively questioned its conventions. She observed Guadalupe's Father Anthony Soto eschewing Catholic norms for his working-class parish long before it was accepted practice for priests to do so. He did not require elaborate dress, veil, or gloves for children's first communion, delayed and/or resisted paying church dues to the bishop, and included women in roles previously denied them, such as the ordained position of the permanent diaconate. Jessie would be one of six women and thirty-nine men nominated by the priest for the diaconate in 1971. The nomination of Spanish-speaking, working-class candidates was controversial and the nomination of women even more so. Jessie was flattered to be nominated:

> They started the deacon program for Guadalupe church, and I don't know if that was Spanish-speaking only or what. Anyway Father said these are the people that have been nominated to go into the deacon program, and lo and behold Paz, Adela, and myself were on that list. We started going to the classes and then we

chuckled and say "well la la la." We didn't really expect to stay—we knew that they wouldn't allow us to stay—but we went along with it. Because we figured well, at least we can say we didn't back out of it.

Her use of "well la la la" reflected Jessie's pragmatic expectations of the institution. Father Anthony was Chicano, but the rest of the priestly hierarchy was overwhelmingly white males. It was almost impossible for her to imagine herself among them; for her, it was "putting on airs" ("well la la la"). She was not surprised, then, when the women were rejected. The male candidates briefly considered refusing to continue without the women, but the women encouraged the men to continue.

Oh yeah, well it was one of the meetings he [Soto] brought up that he got word from the bishop and it was a no go for the women. He said, "Should we go ahead?" and of course we said, "Oh yeah. We don't want you to stop because of us." Anyway my thing was, we don't need titles anyway really, we just go ahead and do the job, we get the job done, that's all. That's always been my contention that, you know, titles don't mean anything. It's what you do that counts.

Jessie and Luz would remain active in the parish, but they also went on to gain certification in ministry from a nondenominational independent Christian organization.

Jessie reflected critically on her own growth since her early years as a young parent. She related her interaction with doctors when her daughter was born with cerebral palsy. With hindsight, she described for me how she questioned the doctors on the baby's progress but was ignored. "We're stupid, you know," she commented sarcastically. "Well, what do you know—eighth grade education— you rely on doctors and priests and everybody to tell you what to do."

Jessie's experiences as *rectora* of the cursillo, along with her education and labor activism, buttressed her own growing sense of authority. In our last interview, she distinguished between the basic Ten Commandments and what she called "the manmade rules" of the Church. She most strenuously resisted the valuing of Mass attendance as model Catholic behavior. "I don't believe it's a sin," said Jessie. "I think there's good reason why people don't go to church sometimes. Especially in my mother's time they didn't have cars. It was hard for them to go with all the kids to church so it can't be a sin when you want to and it's an impossibility."[45]

Jessie's experience with religious authority runs the gamut from typical parishioner to heretical female priest. She was able to support Catholic doctrine and ritual, but she was also cognizant of social inequalities that would preclude others conforming to normative practices. She has moved between various positions of service seamlessly, based on her own understanding of ministry and Chicana Catholic subjectivity.

Phyllis: "I've Never Left the Church"

Phyllis was both the most traditional and the most unconventional member of the cursillos. More than any of my other informants, Phyllis conveyed a comprehensive critique of the institutional church and her own fully developed theology based on the idea that individual believers were ultimately responsible for their own faith. Her critique was rooted in an astute assessment of the lack of Chicana/o representation she observed in the various institutions of San Jose, California, in the 1970s—educational and political as well as religious. In one of our first interviews, she lamented the elite structure of the institutional church:

> Of course, the church, its hierarchical structure, all male clerics, and [*lowers her voice*] the classism, and the—can't say whitism [*laughs*]—the racism. I feel very empowered knowing my own spirituality, my parents' spirituality. How could you give somebody else the power of your spirit? What a horrible thing. You're part of a divine energy, God, a flame, whatever, and you can sense that power within you. When you know that, you don't allow someone else to control you, to make decisions for you.[46]

From the very beginning of my interviews with her, Phyllis maintained a pragmatic critique of a predominantly white male hierarchy alongside a keen sense of her own spiritual authority.

One of three women most influential in the cursillos, Phyllis was a lifelong Catholic. As a widow who lived near the church raising her two children, she traced her membership back to the mid-1950s when the church was only a mission site for traveling Catholic priests. But she had long been active in a string of women's groups, actively networking among women and men to foster friendship, support, and spirituality. She lived a half mile from the church and, at the priest's suggestion, began providing foster care to a series of children over the years. She also worked later, after getting married a second time, as a counselor in a local high school, offering myriad forms of assistance to predominantly Chicana/o and Latina/o youth and their families. She became a well-known and respected person in local communities.

Grounded in her experiences as a Chicana daughter, mother, widow, wife, and educator, her own sense of spirituality allowed her to work confidently within the institution while holding a significant part of its doctrine at arm's length. She identified de facto segregation in the church and in the local community and was dispirited by the double disenfranchisement of herself and her colleagues as women and as Mexican Americans.

> All these things came together for us as women, a few of the Mexican American women, Chicanas, all from this area—from all over, actually. We even met with some from Central America. They're very progressive in many places, the women; some of us are very institutional, others are more creative, but they still believe

that we are the Church, and no one can take that away from us. They can say that we are separatist or whatever, but the Catholic beliefs are very much a part of us. We came together as women and realized that we were very much secondary in the church, as Chicanas, más. You know?[47]

Even as she drew on Catholic beliefs as "part of us," she specifically rejected the ritual validity of the Eucharist, the central symbol of the Catholic Mass, because it could only be celebrated by a male priest:

> In the church ritual, women are not included, and it's not . . . the reality of our life. Symbolically, . . . what it says to me is that a man is so sacred, and a woman cannot enter into that sacredness to be before God, to lead the people. I feel that the ritual that's going on now . . . does not reflect a true picture of humanity, a picture of men and women, co-created, and building a life and world and family. Men and women have to be involved in this creativity, this making a better world.[48]

As a woman, as a Chicana, Phyllis demanded to see her identity and experience affirmed in the church, in material ways that would counter hegemonic white culture and male supremacy in the broader world. To see a white male priest presiding over most parishes, but especially predominantly Chicana/o parishes, was simply unacceptable to her. "It's not a natural order!" she told me in one interview. Her concern was mirrored by efforts at Guadalupe to train a group of Chicana and Chicano parishioners to be ordained as permanent deacons (including Jessie) so that at least some of the parish's spiritual leadership would be more inclusive of the local population.

Phyllis's critique not only insisted on seeing gender and racial identity but also problematized the very nature of the priesthood. She questioned the sacredness of the male priest and instead offered human relationships as a more meaningful source of spiritual power:

> If your child died, I think the mother would take that child and give it its blessing, you would give it its love, say something over this child. Isn't that one of the most sacred things that could happen? Does that mother have less power than a man who you don't know coming in from an institution? You have to think of it as magical, that you have no power.

Phyllis questioned the institution and identified the ways in which she saw it actively hurting women and Chicanas in particular. Women who used contraception or needed to terminate pregnancies were "wounded Catholics" who stood on the margins on the Church. "If you practice birth control, or you're a woman in a tight spot and you know you need an abortion . . . you're not in the church. . . . You're kind of a wounded Catholic. No one is perfectly within that whole Catholic spectrum. . . . So who is?"

Many of these ideas are introduced in a talk that Phyllis wrote and delivered on the opening day of many of the women's cursillos. The talk drew directly on her own experience with the treatment of Mexican Americans in public education in the 1960s and 1970s. She specifically named white (Anglo) racism and opened a discussion of internalized racism and other common coping strategies. The faded typescript copy she shared with me read,

> We play a role in front of priests, teachers, in the presence of Anglos, our parents, etc. As Chicanos we had a special problem; it was bad to be mexican and we were a minority; we could not express our real feelings in front of majority society; sometimes we were deeply hurt by the treatment we received or the remarks that were made about us . . .
>
> They sent us to school. There they also put a mask on us and we began to play a role. Because they couldn't pronounce our Mexican names they changed us from Concepcion to "Connie," and from Margarita to "Margie." And if we perhaps had a light complexion we called ourselves "Spanish." They put you in a lower track because they thought you were inferior in intelligence. AND YOU BEGAN TO PLAY THE ROLE OF THE DUMB ONE. They gave you a second-class role and you played it well.[49]

Phyllis's talk addresses some weighty and well-documented issues affecting Chicanas in the 1960s and 1970s: Americanization norms that Anglicized Spanish names, the phenomenon of passing for white among light-skinned women of color, educational issues of biased standardized testing and educators, and the power of social conformity.

To specifically name these kinds of experiences in a Catholic religious environment was to make a connection between personal experience and structural location. In later work, Gloria Anzaldúa would write about the use of spirituality as resource for people of color to mitigate the difficulties of everyday life—not just the major sins but rather the "small acts of *desconocimientos*: ignorance, frustrations, tendencies toward self-destructiveness, feelings of betrayal and powerlessness, and poverty of spirit and imagination."[50] The cursillo gave these women the space to identify such *desconocimientos*. The identification of a common social pressure shifted the discussion from the personal sphere to the communal, making it public. In sharing such personal stories, women could make the connection between personal problems and a general social norms. As Amy Kesselman noted, women realized that these were not just individual problems but rather "social problems that must become social issues and fought together rather than with personal solutions."[51] So when Phyllis raised these issues, to be ashamed of a Mexican name was no longer a personal failing but a group experience named and shared that could now be addressed with religious and ethical support and analysis. This was a powerful shift. As another *cursillo* participant recalled simply,

"I learned something about myself, that I was a good person. They said it was not okay to beat yourself up."[52]

Phyllis's theology also evoked the creative expression of a Chicana Catholic subjectivity in ritual. She performed various marriages and baptisms for friends and family in the San Jose area and eventually wrote out a complete script for a Chicana/o baptism liturgy that was published in a national nondenominational Christian newsletter.[53] The liturgy described her own role as a moderator who supported the parents and godparents as they performed the ritual to baptize the baby. Similarly, she described for me a spontaneous ritual she performed with the cursillo community at her mother's deathbed. The ritual was similar to the Catholic sacrament of last rites.

> So we did everything that ordinarily a priest would do. Our community came; they gave her the blessing, they gave her the affirmation at her death; they did it when she was still able to know. I blessed her hands; I thanked her for using her hands with me as a little girl, I said all these things to her so she could understand the beauty she had given us in her life. Sometimes we don't do that for each other. So we had the opportunity in our home to practice the spirituality that we were talking about. We do that with our children, the blessings, affirmations that we gave our daughter. Life has become much more meaningful, much more meaningful.[54]

Phyllis's theology was particularly inclusive; she ministered easily and successfully to others, from typical churchgoers to lapsed or otherwise marginal Catholics. With no formal institutional affiliation herself, Phyllis's theology affirmed people "wherever they are" as children of a loving Catholic God. The Catholic Church she envisioned looked quite different from the institution she saw, but she refused to relinquish her place within it. Early in my fieldwork I once asked if she would ever come back to the Church. She looked at me quizzically and said, "I've never left the Church."

CONCLUSION

Chicana Catholics practice a diversity of beliefs and behaviors that range within and beyond the institutional framework of the Church. These women work within the Church at the same time that they understand and critique its role in a society of inequality. Their beliefs and practices are not simply bound by doctrinal limits but rather continuously interpreted by the women themselves in the contexts of their lives.

Despite holding a position of little or no power within the hierarchical church, Maria, Jessie, and Phyllis made their own *movidas* to construct powerful, creative religious spaces for themselves and their local communities. Exemplifying the dynamic complexity of Chicana/o Catholicism, they practiced a fluid spirituality that destabilizes key issues of doctrine by drawing directly on a Chicana subjectivity grounded in both religious and secular activist spheres. Jessie showed us a contrast between her traditional churchgoing Mexican husband and her own broader quest for spiritual meaning, rooted in church work, labor organizing, education, and family life. She continued to productively engage the institution at various levels without threatening her own sense of Catholic spirituality and belonging.

Maria continued to find her way in the Church, negotiating amid theologies of female subordination. She rejected her priest's assessment of her newly divorced status and would refocus her religious practices based on her own experiences and her Catholic background. Secure in her decision to raise her daughter alone, she sought to do God's will, eventually reenvisioning her social work as ministry to the families of San Jose's Chicana/o and broader community.

And finally, Phyllis directly engaged the gendered, racialized context of a working-class Chicana/o parish in an urban setting by redefining the church as a community that could challenge its own homogeneous institutional power. As she insisted, "It's not a natural order!" At the same time, she and the others drew on that institutional power to affirm and empower each other as spiritual agents. Their examples demonstrate the need for scholars of religion to push past conventional definitions of religious participation and engage some of the specific issues that continue to emerge for Latina/o Catholics and other people of color. From the margins of power, Chicanas act to hold the institution accountable to their diverse subjectivities and experiences. The analysis of Catholic lived experience is always located in the racialized context of American inequality.

5 MANY ROADS, ONE PATH

A TESTIMONIO OF GLORIA E. ANZALDÚA

MAYLEI BLACKWELL

MAYLEI: This *testimonio* is an except from a series of oral history interviews I conducted with Gloria Anzaldúa in Santa Cruz, California, in 1999. In the 1990s, we had become friends, meeting in cafes to write, discussing how to finish dissertations, and taking long walks along the ocean on West Cliff. As I worked on this collection with Dionne and María, I kept thinking back to our interviews and the way Gloria practiced many of the Chicana *movidas* and technologies of resistance we were theorizing together.[1] I asked Gloria when she became a Chicana.

GLORIA: I became a Chicana early on, probably '68 or '69. I remember first being criticized for calling myself Chicana 'cause Chicanos, that was a word for the lower class, for *la gente, no era una palabra* for *gente decente*, this is what I was told. *Gente decente*, decent people didn't use this word, but I was reading "Yo soy Joaquín" and I was reading Alurista.[2] I was reading some of the early Chicano movement texts that had to do with land rights, with language. I may have gotten these texts from the authors directly; maybe I got it from Alurista. The local people *de allí en* South Texas called themselves Mexicanos, [so] maybe I got it from the younger generation. You know, like the ones around my age, who were doing the more activist kind of stuff—who started to call themselves Chicanos—but it was still a term that their parents, our parents, did not use. I wrote an essay on growing up Chicana, and I think that was probably the first time that I had used it. I had used it in my journal writing but this was a paper I turned in to a professor who critiqued it, who thought it was great, who gave it back to me. It was the only paper that I'd ever written for anyone in a university class that the professor thought the writing was good. I wrote very much the way I write in *Borderlands*.[3]

When I was in Austin, I moved there in '74 after being in Indiana with the migrants [farmworkers] acting as a liaison between the migrant camps and the school officials for the state of Indiana. I came back and I continued on with my interest in farmworkers and went to some of the meetings in Austin and also some of the Raza Unida meetings, a conference, and different marches on the capital. At that time, I was friends with Inés Hernández Tovar [now Hernández Ávila], we were studying Chicanas, but I was also interested in a wider perspective . . . my interests included women of color and white women. I think that tendency goes way back to my early university days. Inés and I would get together. We were originally going to do an anthology on Tejanas. So she and I started gathering material about Chicanas who were putting their theories out about the *movimiento*, about feminism, and all that was happening in '74, '75, '76. I was doing this work and teaching the Chicana, the Mujer Chicana course, and taking some courses. One of which was Homosexuality East and West, and there is where I started including a wide variety of cultures. I started trying to find other women besides Chicanas who were interested in social justice for women and who were articulating points of view that were missing from the movement at that time. So I read Judy Granh and I read this woman named Veronica Cunningham, a Chicana poet, and I think that is where I got the idea of someday having a book that included the voices of women of color. I think it came of out my working with Inés Tovar, on a Chicana feminist anthology.

Anna NietoGomez had that essay that was very important.[4] I was teaching a Mujer Chicana [course] and I was bringing in some of the feminists, like Martha Cotera who came to my class and talked. I brought in some artists and brought in Santa Barraza, who was active in the city and doing strong women-featured art, and focusing on La Virgen de Guadalupe at a time when La Virgen had not become this artistic icon. So, this is when I first ran into some of the queer stuff. I met Frieda Werden and I met Ruthe Winegarten. I met other women who were connected to feminism and lesbianism events going on in the city [Austin]. So, this was like my first inclusion of women from different cultures in my life all together at the same time.

MAYLEI: *Did you use the lesbiana writings in La Mujer Chicana class?*

GLORIA: Yes, I did, but there was very little that I could [find]. I used Veronica Cunningham's poetry. I used the *Day of the Swallows* that [Estela] Portillo [Trambley] had written,[5] which is a play that deals with Chicana lesbianism written from the perspective of a straight woman.

MAYLEI: *What was the response on campus?*

GLORIA: Well, my bringing in the queer stuff and bringing in a very strong feminist perspective in this very traditional Chicano studies [space that] was very conservative at UT Austin, I think it was a little bit of a shock. At the time, they were very suspicious, and then after *This Bridge* came out, when I went back to Austin to do a gig, Chicano Studies [now Center for Mexican American Studies, CMAS] would not sign up as a co-sponsor, would not chip in for an honorarium. They turned their whole backs on me. When I was [a student] there, a lot of the Chicanos were not in Chicano studies, like Ramon Saldívar was my professor, he was out of the English Department. The newer ones, the younger generation had sort of come in, but there were still vestiges of the old guard there. I think the young ones, because they respected my work, it made the other ones, the older ones, pay kind of lip service.

But with the students, I found out recently that they were happy that they had known me and been part of this course because they feel like they were part of history at that time. Austin did a complete reversal of my time there in the city. Instead of keeping me out and not supporting my being there, they instead made a Gloria Anzaldúa Day and gave me, well, the mayor sent his representative to give me the key to the city. All these people came to this reception, and my former students from '74, '75, '76 came. They were saying how a lot of what they found in my other writing like in *Borderlands* and *Haciendo Caras* had its roots beginning in that class.[6] What they said made me think that there is a continuity and expansion of certain things that I have been preoccupied with—themes and issues and debates at that time there—still happening in my work, but they unraveled and expanded and [have] gone off onto tangents. That experience gave me a feeling of a different kind of identity that had this continuity.

What I'm saying is that the time in Austin was like the time for me to get a sense that there [were] these movements going on with Chicanas, with women of color, with . . . white feminism, with . . . lesbian and gay rights, and with the artistic community—an artistic community that was queer. And learn that we had these allies—Inés was an ally—and there were others, there were straight white women and straight Chicanas who were allies.

 I felt—see, I still feel that very strongly—that I've always been kind of a diplomat at heart. I thought, okay, they need to hear my voice and for them to hear my voice I need to hear them. So, I was receptive to them, and then I would just try to jump in and just open my heart to them. When you do it enough—when the groups are smaller, you do it on a one-on-one basis—they'll open their hearts to you. I think it was because I didn't get into an adversary stance with them even though sometimes I would get really pissed off. I would go home and vent about the Chicanos and the Chicanas and the academy and the straights, but I knew that I had this little support group that was mixed, you know mixed race, that I could go to and vent. My friend Randy was very supportive, and he was very instrumental in opening the door to other elements of feminism even though he was a white gay guy. As well as Yolanda Leyva, we were close at that time and she and I we were roommates at one point. To me, it was also a time of cracking open because not only was all this going on, but I was also experimenting with drugs, which I'm not happy to say. But I did. I think it was important for me, and it also opened up the dark and the frightening experiences. I was mugged, I had some really bad frights with the spirit worlds, with things that weren't of this reality. So everything happening then was like . . . *un perecimiento* [a wreck] for my psyche. It was also very hard because I was trying to keep it together: to take these graduate courses, to teach in Chicano Studies, you know, to be part of the consciousness-raising movement that was happening in Austin and still stay connected to my ethnic community through the farmworkers and the Chicanos in Austin. That time opened me up to the lesbian/gay movement, which was, you know, something that was new for me because I hadn't done this before, consciously, in a kind of public way. I was doing public readings, I was doing workshops around sexuality, especially my writing, you know, reading my poems. I had written an essay which is probably the beginning of *Borderlands* and it was called "Growing up Xicana," and I spelled Chicana with an X, this was before the X, the only other person doing it with an X was Alurista, but now it's like everywhere. I turned in the paper to this guy named James Sudac, who was kind of a maverick professor. He was the only one that ever supported all these radical things coming from me, you know, everybody else was so conservative.

I returned [to Texas] from Indiana. I had gone from South Texas working, teaching in public schools with migrant kids, followed the migrants to Indiana and started working for the state of Indiana. Then I decided that I was going to quit public school teaching, so I took all my savings, my teacher retirement out, and started going to the University [of Texas] in comparative literature. I was the only Chicana except for Mary Margaret Navar, the only two Chicanas in comp. lit., so everything was white. I was having trouble. Oh! At this time, I wanted to make feminism and women's studies [a] focus for the studies and for my dissertation. I was told no, I could not do that because it wasn't a legitimate area of study. At the same time, I wanted Chicano literature to be my focus, and I got the same thing, that it wasn't a legitimate literature. The third focus was Spanish literature and they okayed that.

So, what I'm trying to tell you is that my Chicana activist, the feminist and the queer activism, they kind of had a shared genesis, at the same time, even though I had been doing Chicano movement work before. You know, my high school students would do sit-ins. I was finishing my BA in '68, '69, when the students in South Texas, the high school students, were refusing to continue with a curriculum at the high schools, and that was happening all over South Texas. At the same time, the farmworkers were very active. So, this was the whole time that I was trying to get my BA [that] this was happening. After I came back from Indiana I focused on working on a PhD because I wanted to become a writer to commit myself to writing, but I was ignorant that I hadn't gotten a sufficient education, and so I was taking all these different courses, the arts and education, you know, kind of trying to fill in all the gaps. I had already come in with a sense of the

Chicano movement, but I did not have a sense of the women's movement and the gay and lesbian movement, so all three kind of came together in the early 1970s.

MAYLEI: *When did you come out? What was that like?*

GLORIA: Let's see. I think that I didn't come out until San Francisco. I was doing gay and lesbian studies, sort of exploring everything. I must have had an inkling that I was one [a dyke], because I didn't know [then]. Politically I was a lesbian, but it wasn't until San Francisco that I started calling myself a lesbian or I started calling myself queer and a dyke. The lesbian part was just a handy word to use. Yeah, sí, that's how it happened. I was teaching lesbian stuff in the Chicano classes, I was taking queer classes; my friends were queer but I didn't know what [was what with] sex. My identity has always [felt] ambiguous. Probably, if I had any term for it I would have called myself bisexual then, without having had any major relationships or, you know, [without] the whole thing, whatever it is that makes you a lesbian. I was a lesbian in my head.

In developing what to teach in class, I think that was the same way that I decided [to do] the readers. Like creating *This Bridge Called My Back*, creating *Hacienda Caras*, and now working with *This Bridge* twenty years later. It is what I need to communicate to people, [what it is] that I need to learn about the world, me, myself, that I can then share with people and teach them. So it was this vision of where we come from different cultures, different races, but we are in the same terrain, the United States, and we have to work with the same kinds of issues . . . even though our realities are different. How can we bring these multiple voices to bear? Even though I was teaching Chicano studies I was still quoting some of the white feminists that I had studied. I was bringing in things from the Black writers and from Native American authors, even though it was Chicano studies. I felt that Chicano studies should be . . . and this is one of the things that I am going to say at the Latino/Latina studies conference and also in women's studies—that focusing only on race or gender, we need to broaden that. I've always believed that. There [are] links to all these issues that we were studying in Chicano studies. There were links to these other movements, other groups of people, these other experiences. I think that there are certain Chicanas that have always criticized me for that—that I am too inclusive, that I'm letting other non-Chicanas come into a Chicana terrain and letting them have certain space. I think that is one of the things that I've been criticized for. Yeah. But I don't know why I did this. It could be that the reason is because of the fact that I like to read. I would read about other peoples, other cultures, all kinds of literatures. I knew that there were some very basic differences, but there are also some very basic similarities among all people and that the more input we had, the better we could do with our local reality.

MAYLEI: *So how long did you stay in Texas?*

GLORIA: I left Texas summer of '77, all but dissertation.

MAYLEI: *It is our perpetual state.*

GLORIA: Perpetually. Again. *Este,* the spiritual stuff also started happening then because as I told you, there was a Buddhist center there and I would go do meditations. I did my first reading at the Buddhist center. My experiences with ghosts and spirits and the other world, the mythic world, that I am writing about now. I told you I was working on the jaguar, my journals, and my writings were full of things that I wrote then and about these encounters, little snippets.

When I got to Brooklyn in '81 or '82, I started writing my autobiography, and in it I had everything that had happened to me in Austin, that had made an impact. For *Borderlands* I took some of those things from the autobiography and put it in *Borderlands,* but a lot of the stuff from that autobiography are now in the *Prieta* stories fictionalized.[7] I took some autobiographical incidents and I have been fictionalizing them for the last fifteen years. Some of those things are about the experiences that I had with the spirit. I was resisting being taken over. I had an out-of-body experience. I had another experience dealing with angel dust and mushrooms and the mugging that I went through, some sexual encounters. In the autobiography, they were just kind of outlined and described in something that was a paragraph or half a page, but as I developed them, they became like a fifteen-page story flushed out. So a lot of the Austin stuff has been re-created. I'm kinda sort of behind the times because I haven't gotten through fictionalizing what happened to me in San Francisco or in Brooklyn. I guess [it] is a time lapse or a time lag. Yeah, so the spirit thing, the political stuff, the gay and lesbian stuff, the multicultural coalitions, working with Inés. She and I were trying to finish up PhDs but she was much further along. Her PhD was from Houston and she was in Austin teaching the Mujer Chicana course. I took it from her one semester, and then the next semester I was teaching it at her recommendation. She was like my mentor but also my colleague because we were helping each other. We did an interview, one of her interviews is in my book. I guess it was '96 here in my house, and we got to catch up with a lot of stuff. It is strange how our lives have gone, but in some ways they are very similar.

MAYLEI: *So how did you leave Texas? You just up and left?*

GLORIA: I got fed up with the conflict because they wouldn't let me do what I wanted. So I said I can do this dissertation anywhere, ha ha. I'm going to San Francisco because the gay stuff was happening over here. You know how California has always been the forerunner of what is happening in the nation in terms of art, politics, science, *todo.* So I wanted to be here, where the things were happening, so I packed everything . . . that I could get into my car, and I just took off and I drove. Stopped in San Diego to stay with a friend for a couple of days and then drove up the coast, checked into the Mission [District]. The first thing I did was I went straight to the park, and they had an aquarium there. I wanted to see the fish. I'd go to the coffeehouses and the women's cafes and look at their bulletin boards for housing. I made a list of communes and called them up and they'd set up appointments to interview me. That's what I did. After a week and a half I found the San Jose House, which was a commune of fifteen people of all races and all ages. The youngest was seven and the oldest was fifty-seven. There was [a] Black guy and an Asian guy, there were some bisexuals, there were some homosexuals, a couple of lesbians, straights, so it was also multicultural. It was right there on 24th [Street] about a half a block from the [Dolores] Mission. I would roll out of bed and I would just go to coffeehouses and do my writing, but I had to get a job because I didn't have very much money. So I started doing temp jobs, and that is how I supported myself. I went to the Women's Building. This is where I first saw the . . . flyer saying that Merlin Stone is going to do a workshop on the Goddess at Willow [a women's retreat center].[8] It cost so many hundreds [of dollars] but they had two scholarships for low-income or women of color, whoever couldn't afford the registration. So I applied and I got it. I went to Willow, and this where the idea to do *This Bridge Called My Back* came. I was the only Chicana, I was the only person of color. Everybody else was white. There were very few working-class women—me, Merlin Stone, and maybe one other person—everyone else was white, middle-class, mostly dykes, called themselves lesbians. The first day or two they treated me kind of, you know, I was pretty much invisible or ignored, but they didn't treat me disrespectfully. But then the two women that ran Willow found out I was the scholarship girl. I had been given a room, but they took me out of my little private room and they put me in this kind of like a barracks where there were bunk beds, even though they had plenty of space. The first meal that we had after that, I noticed that they were watching what I ate. I got really upset and I couldn't sleep so I got up that night, the night that all this was happening. I was in the kitchen and there was Merlin smoking and drinking tea. It was really quiet. Everybody else was in bed. I started venting my frustration and she could really identify. She was straight but open to gay stuff, she was working class, but really spiritual and was very receptive. I just told her all the frustrations ever since I had been in . . . undergraduate and graduate school and the stuff with the PhD and Austin. All of my frustrations with the white women's movement, *y todo*. It was all coming out.

MAYLEI: *Must have been a long conversation.*

GLORIA: Yeah, all night, *casi*. She encouraged me. She was the one who came up with the idea of collecting all these writings. I said I had been thinking about it, but it was Merlin [who encouraged me]. Before I went to bed that morning, I wrote the first call for papers. The first thing when I got back to the city, I typed it out and made copies, and I started circulating it. I think then I was calling it

"Third World Woman," but when Cherríe and I got to working on it we said—the two of us decided—that we would start using the phrase "woman of color." What I felt [was] that by calling us third world women, we were doing disservice to women who were actually from the third world. Because a lot of us were dark. We were treated as alien, marginalized. The other rationale was that we wanted to be in solidarity with those of us who were targets, you know, like Blacks, the Asians with their features, the Indians. Some of us Chicanas could pass. I mean, I can't pass, I don't think, but some of us could, so we used the term "women of color." At one point, when I did *Haciendo Caras*, I wanted "feminist of color," and when I saw the galleys or whatever, they had "women of color," which then I had them change to "feminist of color."

MAYLEI: *Were you involved in activism in San Francisco?*

GLORIA: I was active. I was active in in three organizations: Radical Women, the Feminist Writers Guild, and Small Press Traffic, which was a little center of the literary movement in San Francisco, the radical alternative literary movement. There I had instigated two things. One was a reading series that I called "El Mundo Surdo," where I had people of color, white people, as well as men come and read.[9] I went to a reading with an open mic, and I read my stuff and Bob Gluck, who was directing Small Press Traffic then, liked it, and we became friends. I would go every week and then he said, "You can use the premises if you want to conduct a writing workshop." So, I started my first writing workshop in the city and it was also mixed, whites and of color. And I started the reading series, and in the reading series I started with people of color and the white faggots and white dykes. There were readings every week.

MAYLEI: *When did you consider yourself a writer?*

GLORIA: When I was in Indiana in '73 I took some classes and I started writing, and that is when I decided that. I've always wanted to be an artist. I've always sketched and wrote in my journal, but I had never done real writing, so I did that. I did a story, I did a poem, I started a novel, and the teacher was so encouraging, she really thought I'd have promise. So, in '73, that was the time for me to commit to that—because I had already committed to an artistic lifestyle, but I wanted to support this lifestyle—so I got a teaching degree. I had taught in the public schools because I knew I was going to need money in order to live this kind of life, but I hadn't committed to writing until then. So in '74 I left Indiana, I took out my teacher retirement money and started graduate school with the purpose of learning more. I took some writing courses but very few because most of those courses were taught by these white guys who were blind—race blind, class blind, and of course gay blind, *también* . . . but I learned some techniques, so I would say, well, I want to be a writer. In '77 when I moved to San Francisco, I started saying "I'm a writer." Writing occupies my priority, and these other things are to support the writing. So I jumped right into what was going on in the Women's Building, what was going on in the Mission [District], what was going on in the literary movement with the gay community . . . the spiritual stuff *también*. I met this woman named Luisah Teish and she gave me my *orishas*. She and this Cuban woman did a psychic reading for me and said "You're my eyes for me," and Oya [the orisha of winds, lightning, storms, death, and rebirth] is like my second mama. I was exploring the spiritual stuff, taking classes, [but] after my operation, my near death, I started really exploring the spiritual. I was taking classes as well as psychic development training. I was learning how to do psychic readings and I would do tarot reading—so everything was, *también*, at the same time. Most people could not tolerate all these different aspects, you know, like when I was with the gay and lesbians, they were very critical of the spiritual and the race stuff, *tú sabes*. . . . When I was in La Misión with the Latinas on that that kind of terrain, they were suspicions of the gay stuff and as well as the spiritual stuff. So parts of me never did fit into all my communities, and I wanted to create a book, a place, where all these different aspects of personality that everybody has could be included and none of them excluded.

So the book was my first effort, but I had to really push hard to get the Native American voice in *Bridge* . . . because they were more invisible. . . . I got some submissions from Asians because Asians had a very strong community there [in San Francisco]. I would go to Ginny Lim's readings. Nellie Wong was in Radical Women with me. From these two different groups, the Radical Women and the Feminist Writers Guild, I got the word out about the book and got some of these voices in. But I had to hustle with the Native American writers. . . . What I did was that I would actually meet with some of the community leaders, like Barbara Cameron. We would have weekly meetings where she would show me her two or three paragraphs. I would give her feedback, and she'd go and rewrite stuff. With Crystos, it was all by mail. She would write to me, then I would take her letters and I would extrapolate things, and kind of re-create an essay for her. I did the same thing in *Haciendo Caras* with her. I felt very strongly that the Native American movement was the closest that I felt to the Chicano movement just because we shared the same history of colonization, attempted genocide, and basically the same blood, because Chicanos are primarily Indian but they've just forgotten it. So, I was making a really strong connection with Native American writers individually, but at that time I didn't see a visible community anywhere. I know they were there, but they weren't as visible as the Blacks or the Latinas or the lesbians or the queer guys. And then the other thing . . . I made a strong effort to pull together the spiritual voice, so I went out and interviewed Luisah Teish and tried to inject a little bit of the spiritual stuff in *This Bridge*, but that section really was never popular in the academy.

MAYLEI: *So do you remember when you first started hearing the notion of "third world women"? What did that mean to you?*

GLORIA: For me, it had to do with some of the political movement stuff coming out of [South and Central] America and Mexico. It had to do with the imperialistic ventures of the US to other countries and how third world women were even more oppressed than we were in this country but that we had, as Mexicans, as Latinas, blood in common even though we were from different [places], north of the border, south of the border. The difference was that in their own country they were legitimate, you know, as Mexicans, or *nicaragüenses*. They weren't second-class citizens in their country, with a second-class language, whereas Chicanas in a white-dominated country, we had a sense of being othered, so besides the fact that there was no way that I could compare our oppressions with theirs, because their oppressions were so much more radical—you know, starvation, war, disease—in this country our oppressions were psychological as well as physical but not to the extreme of theirs. We weren't fighting for our lives, we weren't getting disappeared, at least I don't think in great numbers. They had a sense of self that was very rooted in a nation or ethnicity. For Chicanos and Blacks and Native Americans on this side, that was denied to us, and our sense of self was always second-class. So, I was using the term interchangeably, but then when "women of color" came up, I dropped the other terms for those reasons that I mentioned.

MAYLEI: *We talked about women of color. What about radical women of color? "Radical," why was that an important adjective?*

GLORIA: There was a commitment. When I was in Austin I was reading the Radical Lesbian Manifesto, *Woman Identified Woman*, the *SCUM Manifesto*, and all these radical things.[10] I felt we were doing something radical because women of color did not have a visible presence or an articulated voice out there.

PART II

HOME-MAKING MOVIDAS

6 LA CAUSA DE LOS POBRES

ALICIA ESCALANTE'S LIVED EXPERIENCES OF POVERTY AND THE STRUGGLE FOR ECONOMIC JUSTICE

ROSIE C. BERMUDEZ

Alicia Escalante's advocacy on behalf of poor, single mothers in East Los Angeles and beyond began in her youth. As she came of age in Los Angeles she developed an early analysis of the interlocking systems of oppression based on race, class, and gender, what women of color activists would term "triple oppression" and, later, intersectionality.[1] As the daughter of a poor Chicana who lost custody of her children to an abusive ex-spouse, Escalante knew firsthand the plight of powerless women of color. In response to these and many other lived experiences, Escalante sought to better the circumstances of poor, single, Chicana, Mexican American, and Mexicana mothers through grassroots community organizing and advocacy at the local and national levels. For Escalante, being able to live a dignified life as a single mother receiving welfare entailed having adequate nutrition, clothing, a decent place and space to live, medical care for the family, and an honest job with a livable wage. It also meant being respected for the labor of raising children and caring for the elderly in the home and not being subjected to demeaning, racist, and sexist policies and practices, as she and many others had experienced continuously at the welfare offices.

At the heart of what Escalante and her supporters struggled toward was the right to economic justice, human dignity, and treatment with respect. As poor, single women of color they were and still are situated at the bottom of the social, political, and economic ladder within US society. Escalante's struggle for economic justice and human dignity articulated an activism and feminism rooted in the lived experience of poor women of color across, among, and within multiple constituencies and social movements. This little-known history forces us to rethink the gender, racial, and class politics of the social movements of the 1960s and 1970s and calls for space in these histories and in the history of the Chicano movement in particular. The history of Escalante and the East Los Angeles Welfare Rights Organization (ELAWRO) she would establish in 1967 as well as the broader vision they articulated also force us to reconsider the activism that took place in various social movements of the 1960s and 1970s. More specifically, it enables us to reconstruct what that activism looked like, who produced it, what issues participants battled, and from where it emerged. This reimagining and rearticulation is important in order to capture a more nuanced, complex, and accurate understanding of the legacy of these social movements for past, present, and future struggles for economic justice and human dignity. How Escalante and the ELAWRO's broader struggles emerged and the significance of those struggles is rooted in her early lived experience, which is where I begin.

One morning in the early 1940s, nine-year-old Alicia Lara, a resident of El Chamizal—a predominantly Spanish-speaking area of El Paso, Texas, lying directly across the Rio Grande from Juarez, Mexico—set out to follow through with a life-changing decision she had contemplated for some time. She decided to flee her father's household and reunite with her mother, Guadalupe, who had recently moved to Los Angeles after divorcing her husband, a violent alcoholic who had taken legal custody of her seven children, including Alicia, the second eldest. Throughout her young life, Escalante had witnessed her father and her uncles (her father's brothers) mistreat her mother. Indeed, for fifteen years Guadalupe suffered a difficult marriage that caused her great emotional pain. Unemployed and unable to prove that she could provide for her children, she lost custody of Alicia and her six siblings in the divorce. Her limited formal education and lack of skills or training as well as the rampant sexism and racism Mexican American women encountered in the workplace (the gains of World War II for people of color and women had yet to reveal themselves) and in other institutions in the early 1940s made it nearly impossible for her to feed seven mouths.

The absence of their mother devastated Escalante and her siblings, for they longed for Guadalupe's presence in the household. Before heading to Los Angeles, Guadalupe wrote to Escalante often, informing her of her decision to leave Texas. She reassured Escalante that she would send for her and her siblings as soon as she was settled. Escalante trusted her mother and waited patiently every day for the mail to arrive with news from her mother's whereabouts. After many days and weeks of waiting, she finally received the fateful letter informing her of her mother's circumstances, her work, and her contact information. To Escalante, the letter was like gold, and she held onto it tightly, using it to chart her own path to reunite with her beloved mother, a path that lay right around the corner.

Near Escalante's home in El Chamizal, freight trains frequently passed through swiftly, though at times they slowed and idled for a bit. One day, Escalante noticed the patterns of the trains, as she would often go down to the tracks to play, sit, think, or read her mother's letters, and she resolved to use them to find her mother in California. One morning Escalante packed a small bag and headed for the railroad tracks and soon enough came upon an idling freight train. She picked a car and jumped in but found herself nearly blinded, as it was unlit and pitch black. At that point, Escalante could not turn back. She had resolved to no longer sit idly by while her father and uncles verbally disrespected her mother in her absence for leaving Escalante's father. With determination, she felt her way through the darkness of the car and settled herself in a corner, attempting to make herself as comfortable as possible. She dozed off as the train began to gain momentum, and it was not long before she noticed that she was not alone. A transient startled her when he lit a small flame that illuminated his face. Fearful and untrusting, she tried to ignore him, but he was intrigued. When he asked if she was running away, she did not answer. When he later asked if she was hungry, again she did not answer. But when he threw half a sandwich in her direction, she reached out for it. She was hungry and ate it readily. As the train slowed down, she watched intently as the man readied himself to jump. Before he did so, he wished her good luck and warned her to be careful, and then he jumped off into the unknown.

Alone in the train car and relieved, Escalante dozed off. Suddenly, the train came to a stop and she found herself with flashlights in her face. Had she made it to California? How much time had passed since she had fallen asleep? She was not in California, she soon learned, but in Arizona. "Where are you going and where are your parents?" the police asked her. She told them she was going to reunite with her mother in California and that she was thirteen years old. The police knew otherwise, sensing she was a runaway and younger than she claimed. The police then proceeded to call her father at work. He told them that if she wanted to be with her mother, then she should go to California. Relieved, Escalante produced the letter with her mother's phone number and the police called Guadalupe and made arrangements to put Escalante on a bus to Los Angeles. Within a few hours, Escalante arrived in Los Angeles and was elated to finally reunite with her mother. Her determination had paid off. Escalante would never forget this early experience, as it would have a lasting impact on her life and in the development of her political consciousness as an activist and advocate for social justice for poor Mexican American and Chicana women in Los Angeles. This experience taught Escalante that if she felt that something was unjust, she had the power and the mental and physical ability to challenge the injustice and to create change.[2]

Years later, in 1967, after her own struggles with poverty, a conflicted marriage, and an unstable household, Escalante founded the East Los Angeles Welfare Rights Organization.[3] The organization—named for the local, grassroots nature of the group and its link to broader welfare rights organizing—advocated for the rights of welfare recipients and was specifically oriented toward obtaining social and economic justice for poor, single, Chicana mothers. As a woman of color on welfare, she also battled the stigma of being dependent on the government for assistance. Through it all, her experiences would give rise to a multisited activism and politics in the struggle for social and economic justice.[4] Central to her activism was the use of powerful speeches and published writings that asserted her beliefs and practices and spread awareness about poverty, living wages, and dignity. Her written and spoken words resonated with many people's experiences in the Chicana and Chicano community as well as in other historically impoverished, disenfranchised, and neglected communities, creating widespread support for Escalante and the ELAWRO's battles for social justice, economic justice, dignity, and respect.

While she is best known for her activism for Chicana welfare rights, Escalante did not limit her activism to welfare rights but also played a leading role in the Chicano movement—the Mexican American civil rights movement of the 1960s and 1970s—and as an advocate for women's rights within early Chicana feminism. Escalante's activism challenged accepted representations of who were the supposedly typical activists during that period. In her thirties and older than most Chicana activists of the 1960s and 1970s, she was a single mother of five children and an advocate for the basic rights of the poor (mostly women and children), an issue that seldom received attention in the Chicano movement.[5]

Escalante's life history provides an invaluable opportunity to gain a better understanding of the development of social and political consciousness among poor women of color in the 1960s and 1970s, a subject that continues to be relatively unknown but central to the activism of the period. Her accomplishments—namely, fighting for poor, disenfranchised Chicanas and other impoverished women of color through the ELAWRO—represents the continuity of a legacy of Mexicanas, Mexican American women, and Chicanas coming together to advocate collectively for social justice, civil rights, and human dignity. Through the ELAWRO, later also known as the Chicana Welfare Rights Organization (CWRO), Escalante forged a space where women could come together to hold each other and the larger Chicana and Chicano community accountable for the pursuit of their rights and at the same time hold local government officials and bureaucrats accountable to the poor communities they purported to represent. Through an examination of Escalante's history I seek to document and develop broader knowledge of the political activism and feminism she helped shape among impoverished women of color. Influenced by poor women's battles and the larger African American civil rights and, later, Black and Chicano power struggles, Escalante used her persistence and resilience to improve women's as well as entire families' living conditions in Chicana and Chicano communities.

CENTERING STORIES OF LIVED EXPERIENCE AND THE SIGNIFICANCE OF THEIR MEANING

When this project on Escalante and the ELAWRO began to unfold, I was an undergraduate student at the University of California, Los Angeles, taking a course on Chicana feminisms. For the class I read Escalante's article "Canto de Alicia," published in 1973 in the first Chicana feminist journal, *Encuentro Femenil*,[6] and I immediately became enthralled with this woman's story. Holding a copy of her essay in my hands, I found myself hanging onto every word she wrote, as I identified with her story, and reading it only furthered my resolve to explore her experiences. In searching for more answers, I came to find only traces of Escalante and her story in the narratives of the Chicano movement and welfare rights movement. I turned to Chicano movement archives at UCLA, the University of California, Santa Barbara, and the East Los Angeles public library and discovered a wealth of information about Escalante and her activism, but many questions still remained. I wanted to know the details the documents could not tell me about her battles and victories. I wondered what led this single Chicana mother on welfare to become such a determined and vital leader in the struggle for social and economic justice. What life experiences shaped her political consciousness that was centered on poor women's access to economic rights in order for them to sustain their families? These questions were only answered partially through the archive and in the master's thesis I later completed. Yet I knew Escalante's voice was missing. It was then I sought to find her and collect her oral history.

At the 2011 Mujeres Activas en Letras y Cambio Social (MALCS) Summer Institute in Los Angeles, I was invited to collaborate on an interview with Escalante through the Chicana por mi Raza Digital Memory Collective (CPMR), a project crucial to the recuperation and centering of histories that have been relegated to the margins, or "interstitial spaces," as historian Emma Pérez discusses.[7] It is often those histories on the margins that provide essential knowledge of the complexity of activists, activism, and struggles for social justice. The collaboration with CPMR not only opened the door for me to meet Escalante in early 2012 but also transformed me personally and intellectually, as it allowed me to witness the power of oral history. Following that initial experience, I interviewed Escalante over the course of several months, a process that proved generative, as every episode provided more and more of the threads that I needed to weave together a story that has been absent from narratives of the Chicano movement, Chicana feminisms, and the welfare rights movement. Her story is a crucial link among these social movement histories and brings to the center the challenges faced by poor, single, Chicana mothers on welfare. It is a story that disrupts romantic Chicano movement notions of "la familia," situates class and economic justice as Chicana feminist issues, and explodes the black-and-white binary of histories of the welfare rights movement.

Escalante's oral history is about her experiences of coming of age in the 1940s and 1950s and participating in activist work in the 1960s and 1970s, and it is about the multigenerational influences and storytelling among women in her family. Through the process of capturing Escalante's oral history I have been exposed to her own story as well as to the stories that have been shared with her by her mother, Guadalupe, and her *tía* Aurora. Escalante said, "Remember that I speak from oral knowledge" handed down by women like her mother, a theme that resonates within my own experiences and family history and has drawn me to her story.[8] As I have come to know Escalante, I have drawn many parallels between my life and Escalante's even though I was born fifty years later. In her mother, Guadalupe, I see the struggles of my own grandmother, Antonia, who endured a difficult marriage and was stripped of some of her children. In Escalante I also see the struggles of my mother, Amparo, who raised four children alone on welfare. We survived and thrived because of her determination and resilience, as did Escalante's children. These observations are testimony to the realities that poor, single mothers on welfare continue to face across the generations. Escalante's story of resilience and resourcefulness in the face of insurmountable odds is powerful and has the potential to change more lives than it already has. Arguably, her narrative transforms our understanding of the histories of Chicana feminisms, the Chicano movement, the welfare rights movement, and women's history.

LEARNING TO LIVE: DEVELOPING A DESIRE FOR SOCIAL JUSTICE, DIGNITY, AND RESPECT

Reunited with her mother at a young age, Escalante was overjoyed, but this joy was soon tempered by the harsh reality of living in poverty and by her mother's looming medical condition. Without much of an education and unskilled, her mother, Guadalupe, worked as a waitress and received meager wages, leading her to struggle to provide for herself and Escalante. After several years of waitressing, which required standing for long periods, Guadalupe developed a physical condition that made it extremely painful for her to stand on her feet. Her disability put the family in a grave situation, given that Guadalupe was the main provider. Faced with limited options, Guadalupe was advised by medical staff to go to the Los Angeles County Welfare Department to see if she could qualify for assistance because of her medical condition and inability to work. Escalante vividly recalled the experience of accompanying her mother to apply for the aid. She remembered the crowded waiting room and long hours of waiting before being called by the receptionist. Escalante was the one who produced the eligibility form since it was difficult for her mother to walk because of the pain in her legs and feet. In a gruff manner the receptionist remarked to Escalante, "She doesn't qualify, she's been working." Confused by the misunderstanding, Escalante explained her mother's situation. Unmoved, the reception retorted, "Well, can she come up here?" Escalante replied, "Her legs hurt." That seemed to produce little sympathy. When Guadalupe finally made her way to the receptionist, she was told, "I don't think you qualify."[9] Years later, Escalante recalled the pain of that exchange. She wrote in "Canto de Alicia" in 1973, "I remember feeling such anger at the Anglo woman. Her whole attitude towards my mother was one of hostility. I sensed prejudice; I sensed that she could have done something more than to give her tokens. And I hated her for stripping my mother of her pride, who was kind, good, struggling to survive."[10]

Following that experience at the welfare office, Guadalupe and Escalante returned to the general hospital where Guadalupe was first attended for a follow-up appointment only to receive worse news. Guadalupe would need to have surgery on her spine to stop the debilitating pain. A social worker from the hospital advised Guadalupe to send Escalante back to her father in El Paso, as she would likely be unable to care for her following surgery. After spending nearly three years in her mother's care, Escalante was sent to El Paso as her mother prepared for surgery. She recalled, "I was devastated in the sense that how was I going to leave her alone? She's going to have surgery."[11] Escalante had not seen her father or uncles since she left almost three years prior; she was now a preteen yet living a life beyond her years.

Upon her arrival she was treated coldly by her father, but Escalante only had one thing on her mind: how to get back to her mother. Escalante was able to return to California rather quickly, however, as she had secured a train ticket through an uncle who worked for the Southern Pacific Railroad. By the time she returned, her mother was in the care of her *tía*, recovering from surgery, which they soon learned had debilitated her even further. As her mother's health deteriorated, Escalante could not stand by and do nothing. Instead, she took it upon herself to get her mother to the Los Angeles General Hospital, the only place her mother could receive medical treatment because she was poor and did not have medical insurance. After examining Guadalupe, the doctors decided to reopen the incision, and they discovered a pair of scissors in her spine, which had led her to develop a severe infection. Stunned by the shoddy medical care, Guadalupe nevertheless recovered slowly. Yet the experience radically altered Escalante's understanding of social justice. She said, "It made me fully aware of the oppression that existed in that system. It left me with a scar in the sense that my mother never got assistance and that she had to endure what she had to endure. We went through some hard times."[12]

The shameful medical treatment Guadalupe received as well as the denial of welfare assistance are but two examples of the kind of institutional violence that poor women of color have experienced in history and continue to face in contemporary society.[13] Indeed, witnessing her mother's treatment at the hands of the very institutions that were meant to help women like her deeply affected Escalante and her consciousness of how the welfare and medical systems treated poor women of color. If Escalante had not advocated for her mother, what would have become of her? These experiences shaped Escalante's consciousness as a young woman struggling to assist her family. As they continued to scrape by, a fifteen-year-old Escalante decided to help her mother by finding a job assembling dolls in a factory in downtown Los Angeles, although this meant she had to drop out of school. Escalante worked for a while at the doll factory, but her employment was only temporary. She returned to school but attended sporadically because of the need to help sustain the household. Escalante's life seemed to improve when her mother remarried and her new husband sought to provide Guadalupe with economic independence by purchasing a hotdog stand she could manage. To make the business prosper, Escalante helped her mother after school.[14]

While working with her mother at the hotdog stand, seventeen-year-old Escalante met her future husband, Antonio Escalante Jr., who eventually turned her life upside down. After a short courtship, of which her mother did not approve, Escalante and Antonio were married in downtown Los Angeles in 1951 and moved to the Ramona Gardens housing project in East Los Angeles.[15] Her husband came from a respectable home, and both of his parents worked hard all their lives. Antonio, however, struggled with a drug addiction, making it hard to make ends meet. Escalante knew he used drugs but did not understand the extent of the disease or what it would mean for their marriage and future. A year after their marriage, in 1952, they had their first child, and despite her excitement for her family, life was anything but picture perfect. Antonio's battle with drugs led to his incarceration for extended periods, and though it strained the marriage, Alicia vowed to keep the family together and stand by her husband. To support the family, she provided child care in her neighborhood, ironed clothes, and sold Avon beauty products, but the work never provided enough means. Without an education, skills, or the resources for child care, Escalante found herself without recourse, much like her mother a decade earlier. By 1962, ten years into her marriage, Escalante was pregnant with her fifth child and essentially raising her children alone. Though her previous ill memories of the welfare department remained alive, her desperation compelled her to seek assistance from that same office again, but this time for her own household.[16]

Years later, reflecting on her early experiences, Escalante said the development of her politics and activism began with her advocacy on her mother's behalf: "I think that's where it begun. My ultimate goal was to please my mom because I saw her suffer and her hesitancy to question anyone. So I was always ready to advocate for her."[17] Guadalupe also served as an inspiration for Escalante to challenge and stand up against injustices that directly affected her family and the families of those also living in poverty. Despite all the suffering her mother endured during her own childhood and fifteen-year marriage, Guadalupe garnered the strength to escape those situations and create a life for herself and her daughter. Escalante took the life lessons to heart, and when she found herself in similar circumstances as her mother, she decided not to stand by and endure silently but instead to act on behalf of herself and her family.

CONNECTING POOR PEOPLE'S STRUGGLES: EVERYDAY LIFE STRUGGLES IN THE HOUSING PROJECT

Alicia Escalante put her awareness and consciousness of racial, class, and gender discrimination into practice beginning in the early 1960s while residing in a housing project. There, she learned how to be an advocate for herself, her family, and members of the community. As she recalled, the transformation was triggered by an exchange with a neighbor, an elderly woman who lived with her daughter. One afternoon the older woman approached Escalante, asking for her help with cashing her Social Security check. The elder woman's daughter was away at work and would not be home until late, and she needed the money right away. Her daughter, the elderly women explained, normally helped her because she did not know how to write and only signed with an X. Escalante explained that they could not carry out the transaction that day because they needed more time for travel, as the bank was far away. They then agreed to go the next day, after Escalante's children went to school.

The next morning, the elderly woman and Escalante walked quite a distance to the bank on Brooklyn Avenue and did so arm in arm. When they attempted to cash the check using her "X" mark, the teller looked baffled and explained they could not cash the check. Instead of accepting the teller's information, Escalante asked the teller to look into the records to see if the woman had cashed checks previously using the same approach but with her daughter present. Agreeable, the teller did so and even called the daughter to confirm the transaction. When all was cleared, the elderly woman received her payment and they walked home together feeling very accomplished. For Escalante, this experience was particularly significant because it taught her, once again, that she could make a difference in someone's life by advocating for them, as she had with her and her mother's situations. Escalante realized that the skills she had developed through her experiences could be utilized to advocate for others. This event, though seemingly insignificant, culminated in what Escalante recognized as her first real organizing effort on behalf of herself and her community.[18]

Living in the Ramona Gardens housing project was not an ideal situation for Escalante, but like the other families in the units she had little choice. Living on public assistance and raising children as a single mother, she struggled to stretch the meager funds she was allotted by the welfare system. Every dime, nickel, and penny counted, and it meant a world of difference if any funds were squandered. When Escalante was faced with a situation that threatened her family's and neighbors' ability to survive, she spoke out and challenged the injustices head on. Such was the situation she encountered with a small store down the street from the Ramona Gardens public housing complex. She knew the store well, as she often patronized it and sent her elder children there to buy things they needed. On one occasion Escalante sent her daughter to buy some items with strict instructions on how much to spend, given their dire economic situation. When her daughter returned from the store with inaccurate change, she knew something was not right. With daughter in tow, Escalante walked back to the store and approached the owner, inquiring about the incorrect change. The owner quickly accused Escalante's daughter of dropping or misplacing the change and followed with an explanation that the prices had recently increased on that particular item. Incensed, Escalante challenged him and informed him he had gouged the price. She also accused him of raising the prices at the beginning of the month when those on public assistance received their checks. Finally, she told him that if he did not give her the correct change, she would rally her neighbors and demonstrate publicly in front of his store. Unconvinced, he asked her why she wanted to create problems. In response she said, "You haven't seen nothing yet."[19]

With purpose, Escalante organized her neighbors in the housing projects and soon had a small group of mothers protesting outside of the store, discouraging shoppers. A relatively compact demonstration, it nevertheless had impact: the storeowner stopped inflating his prices at the beginning of the month. And though she never received the change that was due to her, Escalante gained much more from that incident. She realized that in order to pursue social justice and empowerment you had to be committed to your cause and "stick to your guns." This may have been a seemingly small success; Escalante could have just been content with creating this change, but this experience served as a catalyst for changing her approach to her life and that of many others. Taken together, her life experiences encouraged her to speak out against injustice and to stand up for what she thought was right. This was just the beginning for Escalante, for a few years later she would take her activism to a broader, political level.[20]

MAKING DESIRE A REALITY: THE ELAWRO

By the mid-1960s, Escalante faced her most difficult struggle yet. That struggle centered on fighting the threatened cutbacks to the Medi-Cal program on which her family and many other poor people in California depended for medical treatment. With the support of her family's physician, Dr. Carlow, and the community, Escalante founded the East Los Angeles Welfare Rights Organization in 1967 with the purpose of advocating for the community by creating awareness about the rights of welfare recipients and providing support to Chicana and Mexicana mothers on welfare. The daily business of the organization was conducted out of an office that was staffed by members of the organization and countless volunteers, many of them university students. Escalante and the organization challenged the status quo of the welfare system by providing informational services to recipients, representation during fair hearings (meetings to appeal decisions made by the welfare department), and direct engagement with the local and state bureaucracy to ensure that recipients' rights were respected and upheld. Escalante and the ELAWRO also advocated for the translation of welfare forms from English to Spanish, more local community welfare offices, and recipient involvement in the hiring and training of social workers and administrative staff. Additionally it organized against policies and legislation that directly violated recipients' rights or challenged their livelihoods.[21]

To Escalante, welfare rights were not only important to welfare recipients but also to the entire Chicana and Chicano community in East Los Angeles and across the state and country more broadly. Equally important to Escalante was creating awareness about the plight of poor, single mothers on welfare, a cause she viewed as central to the Chicano movement and women's movement and to the national debate over poverty and access.[22] At that moment the United States was fighting two wars, one in Vietnam and one at home against poverty. However, one war proved to be much more important to those in Washington, DC, and the nation's poor continued to be ignored and, in the process, exploited by the economically powerful. Escalante found herself immersed in multiple struggles at once, and like many other Chicanas of that era, she did not elect to work with one movement or separate her identity along an axis of race, gender, and class.[23]

As a result of her commitments, Escalante became personally involved in the struggles of the Chicano movement. She actively supported the student protestors during the East Los Angeles high school "blowouts" who were challenging the historical educational inequities that existed in Los Angeles high schools in 1968. Following the blowouts she participated in the sit-in at the Los Angeles School Board to reinstate Sal Castro to his teaching position at Lincoln High School.[24] She also participated in the Chicana and Chicano anti-war movement and attended three Chicano moratoriums; at the first one, in December 1969, she declared, "I'd rather have my sons die for La Raza and La Causa than in Vietnam."[25] She also participated in the second Chicano moratorium, on February 28, 1970, known as the March in the Rain, and the infamous August 29, 1970, Chicano moratorium, the largest Chicana/o anti-war protest, in which three people, among them the *Los Angeles Times* journalist Rúben Salazar, were killed.[26] Escalante participated in the Poor People's Campaign in Washington, DC, and she supported the cause of Católicos por La Raza and the Denver Crusade for Justice.[27] It was important to Escalante to be active in these struggles and to represent Chicana mothers on welfare as part of the Chicano movement. It is also significant to acknowledge that all of Escalante's five children, the oldest of whom was born in 1952 and the youngest in 1962, fought in the social justice struggles alongside their mother.[28]

By the early 1970s Escalante and the East Los Angeles Welfare Rights Organization had made a name for themselves and were well known throughout Los Angeles. Who could have imagined that a young girl from El Chamizal would become a prominent and respected activist leader? Escalante, however, made her voice heard by advocating and spreading awareness in Los Angeles and across the nation through her speeches and writings. Escalante recalled, "As the organization grew, my writings soon became a platform for speeches. Before I knew it I was being invited to speak all over the place."[29] Although Escalante did not complete her high school education, she was a confident writer. Her mother, Guadalupe, had instilled that confidence in Escalante when she was young. Although her mother could read and write English, a feat few Mexican American women of her generation achieved, Escalante explained that her mother lacked the confidence to write, so Escalante would write for her.

> She was always a little hesitant to do a little writing, not because she didn't know how—she was bilingual in both Spanish and English—but she didn't have the

self-esteem to write. . . . I would write the letters for her and she was so proud of my writing, whether it was to my aunt or if it was in reference to an application or a business of some kind. So she had that pride in me, and I think that also helped to motivate me, that here was something that I can work on because I am capable of it. If she believes in me I believe in myself.[30]

Her mother's encouragement went a long way, as Escalante wrote consistently throughout her time as an activist. She published articles about her experiences as an activist during the blowouts and the Poor People's Campaign and when she traveled in general.[31] Escalante placed special importance on writing, as she knew that she could reach a wider audience than through speaking alone. She said, "Well, basically, writing was one way to express myself and to get the opportunity to express for others that wouldn't write or didn't write or didn't have time to write. I've always liked writing, and so basically that was one way that I could reach more people."[32]

As a result of publishing and running ads about the organization in *La Raza* newspaper and later in *La Raza Magazine* she did indeed reach a wider audience, as *La Raza* was affiliated with the Chicano Press Association, an organization that circulated information about Chicano movement activities throughout the United States. Each publication that was a member of the Chicano Press Association would reprint selected articles in their own regional movement publications.[33] Escalante would also frequently write letters to the editor and publish articles in the *Eastside Sun*, a local newspaper in East Los Angeles, where her words were read by large audiences. Writing was such an effective method to create awareness that Escalante and the organization eventually attempted to publish an organizational newspaper. Though they released only one issue of *La Causa de Los Pobres* in Spanish and English in 1970, the effort deserves to be acknowledged and recognized for its advocacy on behalf of poor women of color and their families. The dedication of the newspaper read,

This newspaper is dedicated to all Chicano Welfare Rights Organizations. Our purpose is to bring you (our readers) especially welfare recipients and the poor any and all information, as possible, in regards to the welfare system. The laws, legislation, rules, rights, and regulations of it. The how's, the do's, don'ts, and the messes of it. And to keep you informed of what Chicano Welfare Rights are doing about it. How you can join it, fight it, live with it, or die of it. We call it, "La Causa de Los Pobres."

Not discouraged, Escalante continued to write and use her writings as an important organizing tool, especially with her fight against the US Talmadge Amendment, which was initially passed in December 1971. The amendment, introduced by Georgia Senator Herman Talmadge, required welfare recipients who were deemed capable of working to register with the Human Resources Development

Department as a condition of eligibility for welfare benefits. The aim of the Talmadge Amendment was to reduce the welfare rolls by providing employment training and placing people in jobs. While this sounded like an effective plan, the amendment was marred with problems that Escalante and the ELAWRO wanted the authorities to address and correct. They especially opposed the extra layers of bureaucracy that the amendment imposed and the ineffective and insufficient nature of job training for nonexistent jobs. The amendment also lacked provisions for transportation and child care. How were welfare recipients who were barely surviving able to go to the Human Resources Development Department to register or to find child care while they received training? The amendment raised another issue, too, about what the government considered real "work." Clearly, the government and society did not view raising children as work; rather, it remained invisible labor.

Escalante's battle did not go unnoticed. Other Chicana activists picked up on Escalante's struggle with the injustices of the Talmadge Amendment. In *Encuentro Femenil*, Anna NietoGomez wrote an article, "Madres por justicia," in which she outlined Escalante's and the CWRO's battle with the Talmadge Amendment. NietoGomez's article identified Escalante and the CWRO's supporters, including the San Francisco Third World Women's Group, La Raza Churchmen, the National Council of Churches, the National Welfare Rights Organization, the 1973 National Women's Political Caucus, and the staff of *Ms.* magazine.[34] Longtime Los Angeles Chicana activist Francisca Flores, editor of *Regeneración*, also wrote about Escalante's work. Flores's piece on Escalante and the CWRO was published in *Regeneración* and in the second volume of *Encuentro Femenil*, which also included a response piece by Escalante to Flores's essay.[35] Escalante's writing further outlined the growing support that the CWRO had received in response to opposition to the Talmadge Amendment, and she listed alternatives that would help people on welfare receive adequate training and meaningful employment. Following this exchange of ideas between Flores and Escalante, the organization that Flores cofounded, Comisión Femenil Mexicana Nacional, continued to support Escalante's and the CWRO's efforts to challenge the amendment; the Comisión Femenil proved a powerful ally in the battle for poor, single, Chicana mothers and the larger Chicana and Chicano community.

ECONOMIC JUSTICE, CHICANA FEMINISM, AND FAMILIA

During her activist years in the 1960s and 1970s Escalante identified as a Chicana, but she did not identify as a Chicana feminist. This is critical to acknowledge and understand, as during the heyday of the Chicano movement many female activists and leaders faced disciplining practices initiated by Chicano activists who labeled Chicanas who were doing "feminist" work as traitorous and divisive to the *movimiento*. Although Escalante did not adopt a Chicana feminist identity during the 1960s and 1970s, I argue that Escalante's history of coming of age and activism reflects a Chicana feminist consciousness that is rooted in her own and others' lived experiences. Her experiences and those of many other Chicanas living in poverty have served as a grassroots source of a feminist consciousness that has gone unrecognized. For Escalante and the women with whom she organized, Chicana feminism was a practice, a mode of survival, a strategy to challenge the oppressive policies of the welfare system and legislation such as the Talmadge Amendment.[36] Central to the argument against the Talmadge Amendment was that it, like the welfare system, did nothing to end the vicious cycle of poverty. Instead, it forced women on welfare to find work, even if that work was low-wage and dead-end, and failed to recognize the real labor involved with raising children. "Raising a family, caring for one's home, husband and children is a very real job in itself," Escalante argued and continued to argue.[37] Moreover, she insisted, the government has no place in dictating what constitutes work: "We are firm in our position that women should have the right to choose what their roles as mothers, housewives, or whatever is to be."[38]

Critical to Escalante's activism is creating awareness of the challenges faced by poor, single, Chicana mothers on welfare. During the Chicano movement, idealized and romantic notions of *la familia* abounded in the rhetoric and writings of the movement and served as the core of the unifying ideology of Chicano cultural nationalism. The ideal family was a hierarchical family unit, a heterosexual couple with children, the father at the head and everyone else below him. Escalante's experiences challenged this notion of family. She explained that family is "a beautiful concept but it's not always a reality, especially in issues of poverty or welfare systems that have not changed much, or have changed only when necessary."[39] In more recent interviews with Escalante about her past struggles, she recalled that many of the women who lived in the projects and organized shared similar experiences: "I saw it in a lot of families. It's sad to say the usual circumstances were not just poverty, it was that the father did not take responsibility, or abandoned them."[40] For Escalante and many other women in her community, family was constituted by mothers and their children. Ultimately this shared experience brought these women together in community to organize. Escalante's advocacy work on behalf of poor, Chicana, single mothers on welfare went beyond creating awareness to creating empowerment, and it encouraged single moms to never give up. Through collective action Escalante and members of the organization forged new meanings of *la familia* and of Chicana feminism that served to empower Mexican, Mexican American, and Chicana women.

CONCLUSION

Throughout her childhood and into adulthood, Escalante witnessed many injustices that stirred her passion for fighting for social justice. As a young girl, she witnessed her father's maltreatment of her mother, the institutional violence of local institutions that were supposed to help the poor, and the desperation of dire poverty. These experiences did not beat her down. Rather, they shaped her into a resilient woman with a keen desire for human dignity. Because she observed how her mother was denied justice, dignity, and respect, she would not allow this for herself or for others in similar situations any longer. The roots of her desire for justice emerged at an early age, and she acted on that desire by questioning and resisting what she knew was wrong. As a young girl, she often asked her mother why the men in the family had to be served first at the dinner table. Later, when she assisted her ailing mother at the hospital, she asked the doctors why her mother had not improved despite her recent surgery. Later, as an advocate in her community, she organized her neighbors to stand in front of the corner store and demand change. Through her mother's encouragement, support, and need, Escalante put her heart, thoughts, and action into writing, an act that not only had important implications for spreading awareness of the plight of poor, single mothers on welfare but also led to the forging of a collective struggle for women's rights.

Escalante's activism on behalf of poor women, single Chicana mothers, the Chicano community, and humanity has had a deep and wide impact on many people's lives, including my own, and more importantly, on history. Escalante's history is important more broadly for we, as a people, are still struggling against many of the injustices that she fought against and we must continue the fight. Escalante wrote, "The main thing is that I am a human being. I am a mother. I want to be treated with equality, with dignity, with respect. And this is a thing all people have the right to have."[41]

7 WOMEN WHO MAKE THEIR OWN WORLDS

THE LIFE AND WORK OF ESTER HERNÁNDEZ

MAYLEI BLACKWELL

Intimate. Feminist. Bold. Political. Irreverent. Sacred. Erotic. Unapologetic. Ester Hernández's work represents the feminine in larger-than-life form, from the humble street vendor to Our Lady of Guadalupe, rendered with the same dedication. In honor of the transformative artwork produced by women in the Chicano movement era, this essay features the work of Chicana artist Ester Hernández.[1] Her story is an important one to tell, not only to document one of the most recognizable and iconic Chicana *artistas*, but to understand her unique view of making art, a view that changed how Chicanas were represented in the world, giving them a new template of action and a brave new way of being.[2] The idea of a project documenting the life and art of Ester Hernández came about where much intellectual and artistic collaboration is done: at a bar, over tequila. Ester had come to my book presentation in the Bay Area in 2012, and we attended a poetry reading later that evening together. Afterward, we found ourselves at a local bar and she said to me, "But, you know? They only tell the stories of the good girls." This seemed provocatively like a challenge and an invitation. So I said, "Oh, yeah? Like what?" Ester responded, "Well . . . [*long dramatic pause*] like how the early Chicano art movement was influenced by our experimentation with LSD." She looked up at me under her arched eyebrow, checking to make sure she had caught my attention—one bad girl to another. She had.

After interviewing scores of women from the Chicano movement era, I am immediately moved by Ester Hernández's story. Art in the Chicano movement was used to raise consciousness within the community and society at large and was also a tool for teaching history to those with little access to formal education. Art imaged and imagined the new world that artists, along with activists in a mobilized community of resistance, were making possible. Chicano muralism was born from the Mexican mural tradition, creating a sense of historical continuity that linked early resistance to colonization and conquest to the struggle for independence, to the Mexican Revolution, to the contemporary Chicano condition.[3] Often challenging the epic narratives of mural art and the focus on what Hernández called the "grandeur of the Aztec past," Chicana artists and muralists called attention to the urgencies of "the right now" and the intimacies of power, migration, sexuality, and labor. Deeply devotional to the feminine divine in both the sacred and mundane forms, Hernández's art honors the labor of women and the creativity of other female artists and raises consciousness aeound ecological issues, environmental racism, and human rights violations in the United States and abroad.

This meditation on the life, art, and activism of Ester Hernández centers her passion for using art to turn dichotomies on their heads. It draws on a method of collaborative artistic *testimonio*—a hybrid form that, rather than relying on the art critic to interpret in isolation, produces a theory and analysis of art and aesthetic practice through a dialogue between the artist and the critic who share interpretive authority. Hernández's *testimonio* compelled me to approach this project by blending visual culture analysis and oral history, by recognizing that she narrated her life history through visual storytelling. This life history told through art is organized by a series of works produced over a roughly twenty-five-year period, between 1976 and 2010. Each piece of art, some famous, others less known, is a node within the arc of a lifelong visual story that Hernández has been telling through her art and life. In this way, each work of art guides us like a star shining brightly in the deep blue of the night sky she has so brilliantly rendered in *Mis madres*. As we move from star to star, what is revealed is a larger constellation of multiple movements, influences, techniques, conceptual innovations, and passions. By using the work of art as the narrative frame and window into a life both narrated and lived through art, Hernández's *obra* represents and theorizes the everyday, interlocking oppressions of race, poverty, gender, and sexuality.

The story within and beyond the frame is how Chicana artists came into their skills and talents in the politically charged context of the Chicano movement, honing their own individual craft while engaging in both individual and collective art-making practice. Yet, this is not a single-lens story. What also unfolds is the powerful story of how Chicana lesbians participated in the movement and in the multiple insurgencies of women of color organizing through their art and their activism.[4] While this essay keeps Chicana art in the *movimiento* as a central frame, Hernández should also be understood in relation to feminist and lesbian art history. As Chicana feminist art scholar Guisela Latorre argues, "Chicana feminist aesthetics emerge from an interstitial and bordered space wedged somewhere between feminist epistemologies and Chicano nationalism, among other discourses, refusing to stake allegiances to any one ideological camp."[5] While no one frame—Chicana, woman, artist, lesbian, mother—could offer a holistic story of Ester Hernández, her multiprismed art gives us a window into the constellation of her life and the politics, philosophies, and artistic praxis produced by that complexity.

CALIFORNIA SPECIAL: THE INHERITANCE

An artist of Yaqui and Chicano descent, Hernández was born to a farmworker family in Dinuba, California, in 1944 as one of six siblings. Her aesthetic—particularly her sense of color, movement, and texture—took shape as a child in the fields as she observed how the heat waves recast the visual field of the agricultural landscape and how the movement of the sunlight under the tree where the kids were left as their parents worked transformed the deep colors of the plants, the earth, and the sky with the changing light. *California Special—The Inheritance* (2005, color plate 1) is a self-portrait of Hernández as a child. It portrays a small girl in a watermelon-print dress sitting on top of burlap sacks of enriched flour, holding a small pre-Hispanic doll while looking out of the frame thoughtfully. She is surrounded by other sacks of flour, some stacked three high, each with a different design. The composition is created by symbols of rural female domesticity—large sacks of flour—replacing more typical backgrounds of domestic portraiture. The use of vibrant color in the artistic treatment of vernacular objects is intimately intertwined with Hernández's experience growing up as a farmworker. Hernández describes how as a child she learned to see color, light, and shadow in the agricultural fields of California.

> In those early days, there were no child care centers, so when everybody went to the fields [to work], *everybody* went. Nobody stayed behind, so I was a baby when I was first out in the fields. My mother was pregnant working, and the minute she could go back to work, we were all out there. Sometimes we were just put out in the shade, [and] as you got older you got responsibilities like watching the water and keeping the food out of the way of insects and out of the sun, things like that, you know. It just changed as you got older. I just remember when I was taken out there I could start manipulating everything around me like the rocks, the sand, drawing in the sand, getting leaves—like in the grape fields—and cutting them and getting some juice from the grapes, doing all of these little designs on my skin. Aside from working with these raw materials, because you are out there totally surrounded by the sun, like super-hot. The colors were like . . . the closest that I can say is they are like psychedelic in the real heat, so hot everything is kind of vibrating. I just remember being very much affected by color and becoming aware of color and just watching the colors change during the course of the day . . . and watching shadows grow and change. Things like that always moved me.[6]

Hernández's self-portrait as a child demonstrates how the public/private split does not hold for most immigrant and working-class women of color. While the painting gestures toward a form of sentimental art, that of child portraiture, it troubles the assumed private/public split in which the domain of children (the private or the home) is not conceived of as a domain of capital and paid labor. The story of this portrait illustrates the collapse of the public/private as well as the paid labor/reproductive labor divide. It also richly illustrates the ingenuity, creativity, and care of *campesina* (farmworker) moms and families. When I asked at what age she began working the fields as a child, Hernández explained,

> When you were little and you could barely walk, usually they would put you on the cotton sack and drag you through the rows, which was fun. So you would be there with the butterflies and the flowers and the plants. Then you start to walk better or then usually they would start putting you a little bit ahead of them in the fields, just a little bit 'cause they would have to keep an eye on you because they probably couldn't see you if you went too far when the cotton was high and ready to be picked. Then they would put you a little ahead of them and show you how to start picking the fluffy part, 'cause it has like a really sharp part—that holds the cotton—so that could hurt you. So they would show you how to pull it out and you worked ahead of your parents or whoever, your sister, what have you, and you would make little piles of cotton. [When the adults would catch up] they would praise you like you are fabulous—"y que linda niña"—'cause you are helping your family, so you're beautiful. "We love you." Then you would get a little bit bigger, then you graduated, which was a pretty big deal. They would make a little sack for you made out of the sacks like you see now for the beans or flour, like the fifty- or hundred-pound sack. They would make a little strap for you, but not really big so you would fill that.[7]

While the flour sacks in the self-portrait have significance in terms of the historical documentation of how farmworker children learned to work in the 1940s and 1950s, they also signal a mode of domesticity in which materials from the laboring world were repurposed from their use in the domestic space. Hernández recalled how these memories came back to her and what inspired her to do the painting.

> One time when I went to Fresno or out Tulare County, I stopped in the grocery store. I was in the aisle looking for Virgen de Guadalupe *veladoras* and I saw sacks of flour with patterns on them and I got really emotional. I was the youngest girl, so they would put me on the sacks to see how the color looked on me in order to make a dress, or curtains. It's just amazing how resourceful people are and making life beautiful out of nothing.

In the painting, Hernández is wearing the watermelon-print dress to acknowledge the inheritance of the strength and resourcefulness of farmworker families. In this way the self-portrait makes visible the creative labors of rural Mexicana and Chicana women who create curtains or children's clothes out of flour sacks and is a tribute to their artistry, creativity, and what Tomás Ybarra-Frausto has called "rasquachismo," making art by making do with what is around in the social environment. While *California Special* honors the inheritance of the creativity, ingenuity, and grit of *campesina* women, it is also a visual acknowledgment of the cultures that shaped Hernández and her community, which she honors through the different designs that appear on the stacked sacks of flour. The orange sacks with butterflies represent her own Mexican indigenous culture and the creative arts that she has inherited. The graphic on the burgundy sacks represents the Monache and Yokut, the indigenous people of California whose lands she grew up on and who were her friends she would visit in the foothills. The rocking horse represents the dominant American culture. The red design brings to life the Japanese culture that, as Hernández explained, has been

> seriously an important community in my life. From my Japanese friends, our neighbors, who worked the fields with us and first taught me about Japanese art and paper. They were relocated in the barrio after the internment camps. I didn't know until fifty years [later] that many of my friends were born in the camps. I found out at our high school reunion, and I couldn't stop crying. The culture has been so influential in my life. My son lives there now and is married to a Japanese woman, so I have been to Japan sixteen times. For that culture I used the *sakura*, or a cherry blossom.[8]

In the painting, the little girl sits on the sacks of flour and holds a pre-Columbian doll, which Hernández uses to visibilize her indigenous cultural roots, a central cultural and visual referent in her life and work.[9]

Hernández's mother and family have been involved in farmworker labor struggles since the 1930 cotton strikes in the Corcoran, California:

> My family participated in the strike and like many, many other farm workers, they were surrounded by all kinds of sheriffs and police. [Her mom] claimed it was like being in a prison camp because apparently they were surrounded and unable to leave for a few days. They wanted to get a well-deserved raise for their brutally hard work. When I was a teenager we no longer picked much cotton because the farmers started using cotton-picking machines, which probably made it easier for them than dealing with real people! It made our lives much harder because we counted on that money to get through the winter.[10]

In relation to the awakening of her political consciousness, Hernández vividly recalls the first United Farm Workers (UFW) march from Delano to Sacramento in 1965. The march was part of the campaign to bring national attention to the grape boycott, but it was also an organizing tactic to educate and mobilize workers in each town the UFW passed through. While hundreds of farmworkers would march all day in the hot sun with emerging leaders like Dolores Huerta and César Chávez, organizers were sent ahead to gather workers for Catholic Mass in the evening and to lead organizing sessions informing the workers about *la causa de los campesinos*. Hernández recalled that as a teenager she sensed the electricity as the crowds gathered to cheer or join the marchers as well as the felt sense of fear as police lined the streets. While many experienced violence, she said, "We weren't afraid. We were proud and this was the first time we stood tall." Despite the intimidation, Hernández remembered this life-changing event with fondness because her father was the first to join the farmworker union in Dinuba. Indeed, the ranks of the UFW swelled as the march moved from town to town and marchers were housed and fed by farmworkers who were stretched to feed themselves and their own families. Yet, the sense of solidarity and unity inspired people to join and change the course of history.

Ester Hernández's art visualizes the dignity and solidarity she learned by witnessing and participating in the arduous work of farm labor. It also makes visible, with almost spiritual reverence, the creativity and the beauty farmworker women found in the land, in everyday domestic materials, and in each other, despite hardship, pain, and exploitation. Her experience of learning to see the alchemy of light and color and the movement created by waves of heat can be seen in her vibrant use of color and movement in many of her pieces. Some examples are the night sky of *The Cosmic Cruise*, in the garments in her portraits of Lydia Mendoza, and in nature in *If This Is Death, I Like It*.

LIBERTAD

Like many artists of the 1960s and 1970s, Ester Hernández was motivated by the material living conditions she witnessed around her and the desire to create a more just world. She marshaled her talents for social justice and was enlisted into the Chicano movement. Hernández was formed as an artist in the movement, lending her artistic skills to the farmworker struggle by making signs, banners, and art. She eventually married a UFW solidarity worker, and they "did the hippy thing," moving up to the mountains to live off the grid in the early 1970s. After a few years, she then moved to the San Francisco Bay Area with her young son and attended classes at Grove Street College on the Oakland-Berkeley border. Hernández recalled, it was "a super activist school where I first met Malaquias Montoya and a lot of other artist community members of color."[11] Later she attended Laney Community College and was active in "la escuelita," an alternative school set up by activists. The kids and moms would march together and build community in the hotbed of activism that was Oakland at that time. It was the epicenter of the Black Panthers, and Hernández described Oakland as a wild and wonderful mix of "the Gray Panthers, the Chicano movement, the free speech movement up in Berkeley, the Muslims, and AIM [American Indian Movement]."[12]

In 1973, Ester Hernández was featured in *Mujeres de Aztlán: Third World Women's Art* at La Galeria de la Raza, an exhibition also featuring works by Joyce Ajuna, Beverly Sanchez-Padilla, Graciela Carrillo, Patricia Rodríguez, Irene Pérez, Mía Galaviz, Sara Ortiz, Ana Montano, and Natalia Rivas.[13] There she met other artists who began painting together and would become known as Las Mujeres Muralistas. They started with Consuelo Méndez, Graciela Carillo, Patricia Rodriguez, and Irene Pérez, who created a first mural, and later added Hernández, Miriam Olivo, Ruth Rodríguez, and Susan Cervántez.[14] This community-based art-making practice taught Hernández as much about technique as it did about the importance of mentoring and sharing community stories that helped women artists grow and develop. Hernández worked on *Para el mercado* at Pacos Tacos to help the local restaurant attract business when the first McDonald's was built down the block in 1974. Hernández also collaborated on the mural entitled *Latino-américa* on Mission between 25th and 26th Streets by painting a panel.[15] *Latino-américa*, at 20 by 76 feet, was the first large-scale outdoor mural commissioned by Mission Model Cities.[16] Hernández's panel echoed back to her beginnings, as it featured a mother and child working in the grape fields. Unlike the artists of the Mexican muralist tradition (in which Chicano muralism was rooted) whose aesthetic centered on the rural romanticism of the fields and populist representations of the worker-peasant based on revolutionary realism, Hernández drew on her own lived experience.[17]

It was during this period that Hernández began attending college at the University of California, Berkeley, and got involved with Movimiento Estudiantil Chicano de Aztlán (MEChA) and the farmworkers union support activities on campus.[18] She recalled, "Originally I started out studying anthropology and sociology and had to shift it around to have the main focus be art and take Chicano Studies on the side. I took a printmaking class because the teacher was hip to the Chicano movement, instead of teaching the Renaissance and the dinosaurs."[19] *Libertad* (1976, color plate 2) came about in response to the 1976 bicentennial of the American Revolution, which was celebrated as the birthday of the United States.[20] Reflecting on this piece, Hernández stated, "My feeling was that this is still native lands." The etching shows an artist carving a Mayan warrior goddess out of the stone that once made up the Statue of Liberty, standing on a base that reads "Aztlán." Set against the New York skyline with a long ladder propped half way up the structure, the artist stands on the outstretched hand of the goddess, with a powerful kinetic energy embodied by the back swing of a hammer in her hand as she chisels away at lady liberty, a European import, to reveal a Mayan stela of an indigenous warrior. That artist, Hernández explained, was "me carving my new life and new spirit." The Mayan stela, originally a male warrior, was carved by the artist into a woman warrior by giving her "*chichis* and all." The direct action represented by Hernández's artist suggests that underneath the European overlay of the United States is a deep and profound presence of indigenous peoples whose indigenous land and culture are roots rising up. Hernández felt that "with time [the United States] will become brown again. . . . So, [that was] my celebration of the bicentennial."[21] Edward McCaughan argues that Hernández's work in *Libertad* is an example of how artists "envisioned and performed a new model of citizenship that demystified patriotic national symbols" in the youth rebellion of the 1960s.[22] While the "new visions of citizenship were often compromised by the movements' internal contradictions" around race, class, gender, colonialism, and sexuality, Hernández negotiated those fault lines by reworking the visual codes of American nationhood and negotiating the gendered contradictions of Chicano nationalism.[23]

In fact, Hernández was a Chicano movement artist, but critically she was key in using the visual vocabulary of *el movimiento* to make interventions on behalf of women, reworking or liberating movement iconography to reimagine Chicanas. Latorre argues that *Libertad* as well as "Yolanda López's pastel drawings (1978) that depicted herself, her mother, and her grandmother in the role of the Virgin of Guadalupe were examples of early Chicana art that placed women at the center of discourses on liberation and decolonization."[24] *Libertad* reworked Chicano visual codes of *indigenismo* to make a claim during the bicentennial about the US settler nation on indigenous land, as it simultaneously called attention to the power of women to reimage that relationship by prominently featuring the female sculptor.[25] Finally, *Libertad* signaled what would become a signature motif of connecting, honoring, and calling upon the female divine of the Americas to intercede on behalf of victims of oppression during urgent times.

LA VIRGEN DE GUADALUPE DEFENDIENDO LOS DERECHOS DE LOS XICAN@S

While Chicana feminist artists have (re)imagined the Virgin de Guadalupe many times over, Hernández's 1976 etching *La Virgen de Guadalupe defendiendo los derechos de los Xican@s* (color plate 3) was one of the first to reimage the Virgin de Guadalupe.[26] Hernández's piece began a rich artistic tradition of Chicana artists, including Yolanda López, Santa Barraza, and Alma López, who have reworked this icon to image alternative forms of female agency in what Amalia Mesa-Bains has called the "transfigurative liberation of the icon."[27]

La Virgen de Guadalupe depicts Guadalupe with traditional rays of light framing her and the angel upholding her on a crescent moon. Yet, in this image, the Virgin dons a karate *gi*, martial arts attire, and her blessed mantle of stars hangs like a boxer's robe as she delivers a powerful karate (roundhouse) kick. The sense of movement and power springs from her kick that jolts the traditional notion of protection out of the frame or halo created by the rays of light that emanate from the iconic Virgen de Guadalupe image. As banners of the Virgen de Guadalupe were carried on the long marches and pilgrimages of the UFW, this Virgin in action reflects the spiritual power and female strength of the patron saint of the poor and of women who were mobilized into action by the cause for justice.

Hernández's etching honors not only the spiritual power of those seeking intercession, but the hard work the Virgin of Guadalupe has undertaken for social justice, by transforming the passive stance of her traditional representation (perched precariously on a half moon, eyes cast downward, hands in prayer) into the kinetic form of an action figure defending the rights of "Xican@s."[28]

According to Hernández, *La Virgen de Guadalupe defendiendo los derechos de los Xican@s* was created as a result of a class she was taking.

> This was an etching class. I had to learn to do aquatint, which was a more grainier way of printing and etching into with waxes to get this very beautiful texture. . . . I had been wanting to do something for a while. I had already drawn several images of the Virgin sort of building up to doing this. I had already started because I wanted to do something to honor my grandmother. She had died a few years earlier and she was a very, very strong, strong woman. When she died, like most Chicanas who had their memorials, they had the little cards with the Virgen de Guadalupe, and I just remember looking at that and thinking, "Oh my God. This is part of who she is, but she is also a very strong and dynamic woman." So that kind of stayed with me and wouldn't go away. . . . At that time I was also taking karate because the Chicanas, well, all of us were working on being *chingonas*. Self-empowerment and all that. I wasn't real good at karate, but I really loved the outfit. It was a women's self-defense class. At that point I was getting so much more involved with the *mujeres* and the Chicana feminists in the *movimiento*, so it just kind of came to me that it was a rallying cry for women to get involved, to kick ass, and to take care of business. To become strong. To pull that energy together that we have as *mujeres*. It all got all mixed in with my grandmother, the *mujeres*, the *movimiento*, and all that came together.[29]

Hernández remembered that at the University of California, Berkeley,

> a group of Chicana writers and poets were putting together an anthology of Chicana literature and they needed a cover. I believe they used the Virgin that I printed in the same class as *Libertad*. Then they did a little calendar and they landed up using the *Virgen* and *Libertad* so they [those images] were out there probably before the prints were even dry. They were circulating all over the place. They were taking it into the schools and universities so it got around really, really fast. It was amazing because, you know, I didn't know it was going to happen. I just did it *a la brava*.

Both images were widely seen as part of the vibrant Chicana print communities created through the broad circulation of the political news of the day, art, poetry, history, and conference reports in newspapers and magazines across regions, classes, and sectors of the Chicano movement.[30] In doing so, activists forged a Chicana counterpublic and new forms of Chicana feminism emerged by linking their struggles to each other, to Mexican feminist foremothers, and to third world women revolutionaries challenging the *machista* view that would label them as *agringadas* (whitewashed) or Malinches (traitors). As much as the work of social change was political, it was also cultural, and the work of creating new visual discourses was key to creating a Chicana subjectivity.

THE ART OF SOCIAL PROTEST: *SUN MAD* AND *LOS DESAPARECIDOS*

One of the most iconic images in Hernández's *obra*, *Sun Mad* (1981, color plate 4), blends the struggle for labor rights and environmental justice with feminist principles into a brave social commentary. It calls attention to the use of dangerous and toxic pesticides on an industrial scale without concern for the health risks of exposure for farmworkers and ignoring the gendered impact on women's health and reproduction. It further sheds light on the shameful history of spraying pesticides on farmworkers while they were working in the fields or downwind. The contamination of the land and aquifers produced large-scale cancer clusters in the San Joaquin Valley disproportionately impacting agricultural workers. Spoofing the classic idealization of the female figure bearing fruit on sunny California agricultural labels, *Sun Mad* rescripts the popular raisin label as a smiling, bonnet-clad skeleton maiden holding a basket of grapes "unnaturally grown with insecticides, miticides, herbicides, fungicides." Hernández draws on the visual history of Mexican artist José Guadalupe Posada's use of the *calaca* in satirical broadsides exposing social contradictions that ranged from the corruption of the Porfirio Díaz regime to the excesses of the bourgeoisie in the early twentieth century. Blending an artistic genealogy of popular art for social justice, Hernández grounds social commentary with lived experience.[31] Artist and Chicano movement activist Celia Herrera Rodríguez critically puts *Sun Mad* in conversation with a broader body of women of color art, specifically Betye Saar's 1972 *The Liberation of Aunt Jemima*, to consider how they "reappropriate icons created by racist america and reconfigure them for us anew. *Sun Mad* is not the 'Indian Maid' looking back at us in artificial pose, nor the pleasant peasant girl offering us her bounty. She is La Muerte, that intimate and bitter relative whom farm workers have come to know through pesticide poisoning in the fields of the central valle of California."[32] Indeed, the image came about on a 1979 trip Hernández made home to Dinuba. She explained,

> When I got to the tiny little house, my mom [was] boiling water in the middle of the day, which I found strange. She told me that they had shut down the wells because they had discovered chemicals in the water, so they warned people [that] they had to boil it [before they drank it]. Back then, so many people in my family were dying of cancer. After I left, I just couldn't stop thinking about how all of us [farmworkers] were totally enveloped in chemicals and probably poisoned [by]

drinking the water and bathing in it. It wouldn't let me go. It was torturous. On another trip to see my mom, I saw a Sun Maid logo posted on the end of [a] field because all the growers post the label they grow for, and I had an "aha" moment. I saw I could draw on Posada and bring it together with what was going on in the San Joaquin Valley. It came to me, "I am going to unmask the innocent young woman and let people really know what is going on there [by] changing the name to Sun Mad." . . . Everyone told me not to do it, that I would be sued, but a Chicano lawyer told me I could [do] it, and it was about First Amendment right[s].[33]

Hernández made the print initially for an auction at La Peña Cultural Center in Berkeley. In addition to donating art for the cause, or multiple causes, as it were, she would periodically sell prints to earn money for "papers and pens." She laughs as she tells me, "I couldn't give it away even in auction" when it debuted. Later she exhibited at one of the annual Day of the Dead shows, and it circulated widely among the farmworker, environmental, and Chicana art circles. She has also donated many prints to the UFW for fund-raising. The image has been all over the world, but "unfortunately, it is still relevant today," Hernández told me. One of the costs of her political art and social commentary is that it has been largely censored in the San Joaquin Valley.

In the 1980s Hernández, like other Chicana artists and writers such as Yreina Cervantes, Juana Alicia, Ana Castillo, and Helena Maria Viramontes, was moved to use her art to bring awareness and solidarity to the people of Central America who were suffering a massive human rights crisis at the hands of US-backed authoritarian regimes. Hernández called attention to the disappearances and political repression during the Guatemalan dirty war in *Tejido de los desaparecidos* (1984, color plate 5), a powerful black-and-white screen print patterned on traditional Mayan weaving. Looking more closely, the viewer notices that interwoven in the traditional pattern are small helicopters, *calacas* (skeletons), and *calaveras* (skulls). Thus the piece draws together traditional Mayan art forms that weave histories of place into textiles, with the history of low-intensity warfare in the highlands of Guatemala that resulted in the murder of approximately 200,000 Mayans during the civil war that took place between 1960 and 1996. Most were killed in organized campaigns of counterinsurgency and systematically exterminated in 1981–1983. The Guatemalan army and paramilitaries justified their genocidal violence by claiming that they could not tell the difference between the civilian community members and the guerrilla resistance fighters. To discourage communities from supporting or providing aid to the guerrillas, they engaged in a low-intensity and psychological warfare that included disappearances, torture, and mass murder of whole villages. So many Mayan villages were sites of massacres that indigenous intellectuals began to call the scale of violence a genocide to underscore that the mass murder of thousands upon thousands of people was a colonial legacy of attempted extermination. Hernández also honors Mayan women's experiences of gendered violence and war, which ranged from rape to torture to gendered mutilation of their bodies. Woven into the visual design, male and female skeletons are centered horizontally among trees that were also destroyed during the war. Upon closer inspection, the woman figure has a tiny *calavera* in her womb, representing the generations extinguished by the murder of whole communities. The image further bears witness to the specific forms of torture and violence indigenous women endured as pregnant women's bodies were often found with the fetuses cut out. She included the trees to visually represent her belief that "whatever happens to the people happens to the land, and whatever happens land happens to the people. During the massacres, whole villages and crops were being burned down."[34]

The original screen print, produced in 1984, was based on a trip Hernández had taken with friends to Guatemala.

> I had gone to Guatemala in the early '80s. When we were traveling around visiting the country, there was several times that we were stopped by the military who would board the bus armed with machine guns and make a search. It was scary because we were way up in the highlands of Guatemala. It really bothered me but I didn't quite know how to explain it until a speaker came to talk to us about the disappearances and violence in Guatemala in our Pan Indian North and South organization. It was extremely shocking to learn that we walked right into it and were able to come out of it. I kept thinking about it. Because I was broke as a student at the time, I remembered that all I could afford to bring home were these beautiful rebozos. I went home and I really, really tried to focus on what the message was by surrounding myself with the rebozos. I stayed up all night and they started talking to me. Each one had patterns unique to their pueblos [peoples, villages] or marriage status. I put myself in the place of all those weavers and I thought if I was in their place, I would weave the story of what was happening around me. I put in the helicopters and skulls. If everything was destroyed, there might be a remnant of the fabric that remains to tell the story and be a witness to the death.[35]

Indeed, other Latin American women sewed tapestries known as *arpilleras* to get the message out about the violence and mass disappearances under the military authoritarian regime in Chile.[36] This kind of witnessing was key for the Central American solidarity movement being organized in the United States against military aid and the training of Latin American military in the techniques of low-intensity warfare in the United States at a training center formerly known as the School of the Americas.[37] Tapestries not only provided witness to genocide, they also were a tool for building consciousness about where US taxpayer money was going and to what end. In the early 1990s, Hernández painted *Tejido de los desaparecidos* directly on the wall as an ephemeral mural at the San Francisco Art Institute as part of an exhibition critiquing art as a commodity. Hernández said that undertaking those dimensions—8 by 16 feet—was such arduous and intricate work that it felt like she was paying her dues to her female ancestors for not continuing to weave and embroider. Amalia Mesa-Bains saw the show and invited Hernández to create a mobile version of *Tejido de los desaparecidos* on canvas to travel with the *Art of the Other México* exhibition of the Mexican Fine Arts Center Museum in Chicago in 1993.

Years later Hernández updated the story for an exhibition in 2008 by producing a multimedia installation entitled *Tejido de los desaparecidos—Installation II* (color plate 6) featuring the screen print on canvas with a large-scale altar in front. The altar was a circle of sand "representing time" outlined with marigolds with additional marigolds in a vase in the middle with a white candle in each of the cardinal corners. For the exhibition at the Mission Cultural Center in San Francisco, Hernández incorporated the Guatemalan tradition of flying kites with messages to the spirits that have crossed over fastened to the kite tail. She created a kite, 30 by 30 inches, out of handmade Japanese paper that she had dyed red on one side and imprinted with the design of the weaving in red on black paper on the bottom side. The kite hung from the ceiling above the altar. Hernández wanted to honor the people who were still looking for their disappeared loved ones, so the entire tail of the kite is inscribed with a letter from a mother to her disappeared daughter. Because the same forms of state violence are still afflicting indigenous communities, most recently with the disappearance of forty-seven students from the rural teachers school in Ayotzinapa, Guerrero, Mexico, in September 2014, Hernández launched another installation for the Day of the Dead 2016 at the San Francisco Symphony with Lila Downs in concert.

MIS MADRES AND OTHER CHINGONAS

The art of Ester Hernández is dedicated to and inspired greatly by the strength of women. While there are many references to the divine mother in Hernández's *obra*, there is even more attention to the strength of incarnate women living on the earth. Throughout the arc of her work, Hernández has spent a lifetime studying Chicana and Mexicana immigrant women, who are largely invisible figures in traditional art. Hernández has shifted the representation of those women who have endured countless hardships and continue to embody resilience, smarts, and a "Don't mess with me" attitude. In short, one of the beloved objects of art in Hernández's oeuvre are *chingonas*. *Mis madres* (1986, color plate 7) features a wise or elder woman cast in silver and blue—as if washed with the light of the moon—holding the earth. The piece was developed from a photo of Hernández's grandmother,

> Tomasa Camacho Medina, who was an Indian of the mountains of Guanajuato. A real free spirit. I adored her because she was outspoken and full of life. She kept it real. She worked for decades in the canneries, so these are the type of ladies who taught me to stand up. At her service at the church in Selma, [California],

I saw the Virgen de Guadalupe, but the image didn't show that, like all of those *campesinas* who carry their weight in cotton or fruit on the shoulders all day long, they are so strong. She could kill a chicken with one hand. My grandmother had eleven kids. She, my mother, and my *tias* worked their whole lives in *los files*, in packing houses, [and] some worked as domestics. We didn't ask to be tough, life made us tough. Right about the time of the Apollo mission, I found an old picture of her. All those pictures coming back from Apollo made me think of those nighttime skies of the valley with the Guadalupanas with a canopy of stars under the indigo sky. This image reminds me that her spirit and the physical part of the earth . . . it's all connected. That's our ancestry . . . as all the cosmos. In the end, we are just stardust.[38]

Mis madres continues the devotional gaze Hernández developed to visualize the labor, strength, and care of Chicana and Mexicana women represented here in the grandmother, wrapped in a rebozo, holding the earth with gentleness and ease. In addition to the grandmother, the other mother is the earth, referencing not only the global shift in consciousness that images of Earth from space heralded but more ancient indigenous cosmologies that understand the interrelatedness of humans to the earth as the mother, a living being on whose life and health we depend.

Hernández's grandmother, as the first in her generation to make her own money and gain the small amount of female autonomy that financial independence gave her, taught her daughters grit and strength that were then passed down to Hernández. The 1997 mixed-media installation *Immigrant Woman's Dress* (color plate 8) was also inspired by Hernández's beloved grandmother Tomasa for a Day of the Dead exhibition. Hernández began the installation as a way to honor the ingenuity and art of survival of her female ancestors in 1997 at the SPARC (Social and Political Art Resource Center) exhibition in Venice, California. During the revolution, Hernández's grandfather had a carpentry school in Mexico, and when the soldiers came around, they wanted her grandmother and their land. Her grandparents fled when Hernández's mother was just a few months old. On the run, they hid precious things in the hems of their clothes. Like many who were displaced by the turbulence of the Mexican Revolution, Tomasa did not believe in banks. She would tell people that she had hidden all her money away, but when she died, they didn't find one penny. Members of the family even dug up the yard looking for where she could have buried it. One night sitting all together, the family was reminiscing about how Tomasa was always sewing, how everything was handsewn, from the clothes to the blankets to the curtains. It was then that it dawned on them and they began to look closely and found the money she had sewn in the seams, which totaled more than $16,000. For sixty-five years she had been hiding coins and dollar bills in the hems of things.

Over time, Hernández's grandmother became obsessed with hiding treasures in the hems of everything—just in case. The dress in the installation, made of silk organza, hangs on a hanger, and through the fabric one can see vintage coins Hernández created with the image of the Virgen de Guadalupe and Coyolxuaqui, Aztec goddess of the moon, on them. These feminine deities of protection and strength are sewn into the hems of the dress layers, sleeve cuffs, collar, and up the middle where buttons might be. In the installation, a basket sits next to the dress with a rebozo, imprinted with Coyolxauqui and Guadalupe, another protection used to keep warm or carry babies. In the pouches next to the rebozo are the other treasures migrant women carried, a beaded representation of golden corn and brown chile, that they could plant in the fields at any point as a means of survival, a built-in cultural defense system and economic safety net. The piece honors *abuela* Tomasa and all those women who survived using their creativity, tenacity, and ingenuity.

TODAS SOMOS GUADALUPE: *VIRGEN DE LAS CALLES* AND *WANTED*

Two other pieces that honor the labor of migrant women and continue the tradition of seeing Guadalupe within each of us are the 2001 *Virgen de las calles* (color plate 9) and the 2010 *Wanted* (color plate 10). In addition to the narrative pieces that visually chronicle the story of generations of strong women in Hernández's family, her body of work includes studies of individual figures like a neighborhood street vendor, Jesusa Rodriguez, in *Virgen de las calles* that document the hidden worlds operating in plain sight where migrant women create livelihoods on street corners selling fruit, tamales, or flowers. *Virgen de las calles* is a large, powerful image of a *vendedora de flores* (flower seller) standing just right of center clad in blue jeans, Nikes, a red and green rebozo covering her head, and a red sweatshirt that reads "USA." Her roses stand in a repurposed bucket that formerly held laundry detergent, with the label "Future" in front suggesting the future she labors for or perhaps a glimpse into the future of the United States. The woman stands with feet planted firmly, hands at her side, staring out at the viewer. Her gaze is direct rather than defiant, as if saying, "I am here," a brave stance in a context of increasing criminalization and xenophobic public policies and discourses on migrants and street vendors. The image illustrates the dignity of a woman who creates economic opportunity where there is none and documents the innovation and hustle of street vendors who generate millions of dollars in the informal economies of large American cities. Yet, many of the migrants who sell flowers, fruit, corn, ice cream, snow cones, and artisanal foods such as tamales and *champurado* (chocolate-based atole) are targeted and harassed in the street by police. Hernández's work continues Frank Romero's 1996 *The Arrest of the Paleteros* (The arrest of the popsicle sellers), which depicts street vendors being arrested in the Echo Park neighborhood of Los Angeles. Romero's piece visually satirizes the imbalance of power with three cop cars and numerous police officers with guns drawn surrounding the street vendors and their children, who all have their hands held up high. Both works of art call attention to the irony that the police would spend their time arresting vendors and confiscating their means of livelihood rather than fighting the crime that results from the lack of the economic opportunities their work creates or ensuring safety in a neighborhood with high rates of actual crime and poverty.

When I asked Hernández what inspired her to draw Jesusa Rodriguez, an immigrant woman from Puebla, Mexico, she said,

> It was a time when I was hearing and meeting more and more indigenous women from deeper into [southern] Mexico and all the people coming from Oaxaca. I was always touched by hearing their stories, their strength, resilience, and their ability to remake themselves through their work and their creativity. In my neighborhood [La Misión] at 24th [Street] and Byrant, I was always buying *flores* from a woman who was *pura indígena*, so we began talking and I asked her where she is from. I wanted to [do a piece] honoring immigrant women, so I decided to ask if she would model for me. We took some time to get to know each other, you know, to make sure I am not the *migra* and so she would feel comfortable to pose for me and allow me to take pictures of her. Things started to evolve. It was during that time Sandra Cisneros came to my house and wanted to buy the piece.[39]

Hernández wanted to capture the spirit and strength of all the migrant women doing "whatever you have to do for your family to survive and thrive" and "honoring the *mujeres* migrating themselves or with their families. [Those who are] just being powerful in their ability to move on. They are tough and beautiful. I want to capture their spirit and energy and take something of that inside of me. That's the real reason my work has all the *mujeres* . . . to surround me and remind me because they give me strength. I look for women who have made their own world."

When I asked if the juxtaposition of "virgin" and "mujer de la calle" (woman of the street) was a commentary on the virgin/whore dichotomy in Mexican and many other cultures, Hernández remarked, "I have a red and green rebozo that I asked Jesusa to model, and the image played on the idea of the Virgin and the rebozo . . . on the duality within the Mexican culture, which is also created by the tension of colors [between the Mexican rebozo and the American sweatshirt]. Sandra [Cisneros] was the one who named her *Virgen de las calles*." Returning to this eternal symbol, one that is repeated in much of Hernández's oeuvre, we talked about the ways she had worked the Virgencita into pieces directly and indirectly and in tattoos she has designed for friends or embroidery designs for her family. Hernández reflects further, "Todas somos la Virgen de Guadalupe. . . . She is our mother and she is our children. It is part of the trajectory of honoring the *mujer*, and it goes back to the Virgin. [Her family taught her] all work should be respected. We were farmworkers, and the powers that be looked down on us. My family really emphasized that we had honor and dignity for the work we do."[40]

In 2010, in response to the anti-immigrant politics of the state of Arizona, Hernández created a screen-printed *Wanted* poster featuring the Virgen de Guadalupe. *Wanted* is a powerful visual commentary on Arizona's xenophobic mix of home-brewed racism and post-9/11 state terror in which immigrants were further criminalized as terrorists. It shows a mug shot of a brown, indigenous women wearing a green mantel of silver stars. The text reads, "Should be considered powerful and dangerous. Born December 12, 1531, in Tepeyac, Tenochitlan/Mexico, standing 5' at 100 lbs, she goes by the alias Guadalupe, Reina de las Americas, Virgencita, Nuestra Madre, Tonantzin, Lupe, Lupita. Race: Amer-Indian. Nationality: American." The poster's satire on the Virgen's criminal record announces, "For over 160 years, La Virgen de Guadalupe has accompanied countless men, women and children illegally into the United States. She has given limitless aid and comfort to unidentified suspects at the time of their deaths, especially in the desert areas near the US/Mexico border." Caution, the poster warns, "she has an unexplainable, possibly dangerous light emanating from her body which could contain explosive material."

The Virgen de Guadalupe and the impulse to honor the goddess within every woman has been a lifelong motif in Hernández's work. In her 1990 *La Ofrenda*, Hernández offers a rose to the Virgin tattooed on the back of her female lover who sports a punk hair style.[41] *La Ofrenda*, the cover art for the first edition of Carla Trujillo's *Chicana Lesbianas: The Girls Our Mothers Warned Us About* (1991) had to be removed from the second edition due to the death threats Hernández received.[42] Hernández's profound connection to the Virgin was inherited from the Guadalupanos on her mother's side as well as from her father and his father and grandfather before that, forming a long, unbroken line of devotion and reverence. This Guadalupano legacy has a rich history. Hernández was raised in the tradition of reverence for the Virgin of Guadalupe as her father, a Mexican Yaqui farmworker, was a Guadalupano and part of a dance society dedicated to the veneration of the Virgin Mother known as *los matachines*. He was also a wood carver who created statues of *santos* and the Virgin out of wood. When I asked Hernández if hate mail and death threats have ever stopped her from continuing to create alternative images of the Virgen de Guadalupe that represent the strength of women, she tells me simply, "Hell no." When we go deeper, she refers back to those formative nights and the syncretism of indigenous Mexican cultures as, indeed, the poster reads that the suspect speaks Nahuatl, Yaqui, Purépecha, Maya, and Spanish. Hernández reflected,

[In] my growing up in the countryside as a child, there was no Catholic Church, so what I experienced was in the barrio of a small farming community. We would gather under the open air. Women would provide the prayers and discussion of being connected to something bigger than myself. In 1950s, then there was a little Catholic church. It was very, very different because the priest was from Ireland and the Mass was in Latin. It was very class-conscious. The rich sat in the front and the poorer people sat in the back, so I never had a super-strong connection to the Catholic Church, as such. The relationship with the Virgencita was also part of my own imagination growing up. What I took from all of that spirituality was we are God and we are the Virgin of Guadalupe. As a child, I learned I could make up gods and *santos* in my head, and that gave me freedom to join them as part of my own experiences. My dad was also part of a Yaqui tradition extremely devoted to Tonantzin. When he was a boy the late 1920s, he was brought up in the Matachin society, which is a syncretic tradition. According to family legend, my great-grandfather and grandfather were also part of the Matachin society around the turn of the century there at the Sagrado Corazón de Jesús Church in the Segundo Barrio of El Paso. The Catholic Church had her in their hands, but we understood her to be an Indian. She was a native woman like us. She is our mother. Without doubt.[43]

In contrast to patriarchal religions that reduce the power of the female divine as disembodied, unearthly, and chaste, Hernández honors the family lineage by locating that power within the earth, as our mother, and within ourselves. Visualizing how that sacredness can be embodied in our own bodies, in our desires, and in our partners is the powerful commentary of *La Ofrenda*, which asks how we honor ourselves and each other. Hernández insists on being seen holistically and not having one aspect of her identity or life, such as her sexuality, separated from the rest of who she is, from her farmworker and rural background, her indigenous and migrant roots, from her race, culture, her passion for art and *artistas*, or her social and political commitments to ecological balance, human rights, and social justice. Yet, her work has, without a doubt, visualized what is often erased within the Chicano, feminist, and even lesbian art canons—the lesbian erotic and the sensuality of Chicana lesbian working-class desire as exemplified in Hernández's *La troquera*. McCaughan has observed that "Hernández's truck driver and the Guadalupe-tattooed woman of her *La Ofrenda* refuse to let sexual longing stand in the way of belonging. They refuse to be excluded from their class, their community, their movement. They seem determined, like Anzaldúa (1987, 22), 'to stand and claim [their] space.'"[44]

MADRINAS DE ARTE Y OTRAS DIOSAS

In honoring the strength of women workers, migrants, ancestors, and deities, Hernández has also focused her artistic eye on the power of other Chicana/Mexicana artists, namely Lydia Mendoza, legendary Tejana conjunto musician, and Astrid Hadad, the Lebanese Mexican lesbian cabaret singer and performance artist. In *Lydia Mendoza, Ciudad Juárez, México, 1937* (1987, color plate 11), a young Mendoza cradles her guitar, strumming it as she looks out at the viewer with an intense stare. Cast in dramatic earth tones with a blue background, a bright red blouse, red lipstick, a rust-colored skirt, and a guitar washed in ochre, the screen print captures the intensity of the artist and the mastery of her form. While the work honors this legend of Tejano and conjunto music, it also reflects the close and beloved relationship between the two artists, as Hernández often cared for Mendoza in her later years, relating to her as her artistic *madrina* (godmother).

> My work is about the *mujeres*. It is to honor the work of *mujeres*. In the barrio where I am from, music is the lifeblood. Lydia was in Fresno and I called her. I don't know what it was that resonated, but I brought her tamales, queso, cassettes of music mixes I made for her. She was there for an artist residency of some kind, but they had put her in the student dorms and she was totally isolated. When I came she was so happy and played the music and in that way we became close friends. When she came to California she would stay at my house, and after awhile I became her northern California agent. This was around 1979 or 1980, when [the film] *Chulas fronteras* had just come out. She loved how I would float around her, and she got a kick out of me being *media* [half] Chicana hippy. She was a huge supporter of my art, and we talked many nights about what it meant for women to sacrifice for their art because [in her time] they didn't want women out in the world singing in cantinas. She taught me that the talent was a gift from God. It was something to be honored and shared. She talked to me about the importance of finding a partner who respected the work. She was a great model for me. She was a woman who did what she wanted. She shared her hard-learned lessons of life through stories she would share. For example, she would tell me, "A decent woman doesn't start drinking beer until noon." As she got on in years, her arthritis became very bad and I would find remedies for her as she continued to see *curanderas*. She was one of my favorite models. I took thousands of photos of her. They are in my archive at Stanford, and I've been told I have the largest Lydia Mendoza archives in the world built out of my love for her and the gifts she would bring me. . . . I was Lydia Mendoza's biggest fan. I was totally devoted to her. When I was with her, I felt I was with a goddess. I love music and I loved her singing. I dedicated all my attention to her because of our age. I felt we were passing in time and space . . . it was all about her. When she would visit she shared all these images and photos with me. This photo was taken in 1937. I did that [silkscreen] image 1987 after fifty years.[45]

Mendoza's music provided an early soundscape creating a Tejana, borderlands femininity that was at once rooted in place and culture and challenged patriarchal assumptions.[46]

While the portraits of Mendoza and Hadad are based on the power of female friendships and the community of artists they created together, filled with admiration, mentorship, recognition, and fandom, Hernández's works of art are also the forms of devotion and dedication that I referred to at the opening of this chapter. These sound and visual representations form circuits of affect, affection, desire, and devotion across borders, forming women's transborder public cultures and queer counterpublics.[47] Sound studies scholars have written about how systems of meaning are created by music, and performance scholars have shown us that the economies of affect and desire are central to how cultural forms circulate and through which circuits they travel.[48] Sound and visual production are technologies of representation and systems of meaning that transmit those forms of devotion and love through expressive cultures of Greater Mexico.

In *Astrid—La Diosa Peligrosa* (2007, color plate 12), Hernández continues this tradition of honoring powerful female artists. The image features the performance artist and cabaret singer with a microphone in her left hand and a smoking gun in her right, as she seems to be reaching down into the depths of her soul to channel it all into her song. Hadad's dress, as many of her signature costumes that outrageously invoke Mexican nationalism in an over-the-top fashion, features stone Aztec feathered serpents jetting out of the hips with hearts, hands, and skeletons covering the skirt and a full flounce of maguey protruding behind her. Hernández discusses Astrid Hadad as a woman who

> falls in line in the long line of strong women. She had performed at the Chicago Museum and saw one of my pieces and so she called me up when she got to San Francisco and we just hit it off. She became my favorite model after Lydia passed. She is a Lebanese Mexicana ranchera singer who makes fun of the stereotypes of Mexican women. The more I got to know her, the more I felt inspired to make things better by using my art. I really have a lot of respect for her because it can be dangerous in Mexico for women who openly criticize violence against women and women being subservient. She is one of the *guerrillas*.[49]

In this sense, Hernández, with her own artwork, is visually creating an alternative genealogy of Chicana/Mexicana *chingona* femininities that embody creativity, strength, gender rebellion, and a wide array of liberated sexualities and erotic possibilities which are present but rarely represented in the visual cultures of Greater Mexico. I asked about one of Hernández's most iconic images, a red *tacón* (high heel) with a spur on it, which provocatively fuses a Mexican symbol of masculine command and control with the red high heel, a symbol of women's sexuality, erotic power, and oppression. Hernández explains,

> Well, Astrid is a lesbian. It is kind of who she is but not all of her. I personally have never totally been butch or femme. I have that in-between, that dual nature, and all woman have all of that inside. There are other artists like Laura Aguilar who have focused on that [lesbian] world completely. I am not a purist. I'm just a real free spirit, honey. I've been burned by everyone. . . . I follow what Dolores Huerta told me way back in the 1970s. She told me it was important that Chicanas make images of women because there is so few images of women out there so we need to counteract the media's representation [of] woman as something to be pitied or feared. I want to represent the complexity. I don't know if people will see that I am

a lesbian. I know they will see my color first. They may not know me, but I work holistically as Chicana lesbian feminist artist.[50]

That refusal to be separated and the insistence on being whole is how Hernández's art queers Chicano art and browns and adds a working-class twist to the feminist and lesbian canons. As late as the 1990s, "lesbian art" was still imagined/curated/exhibited as art that was primarily white. Hernández's self-declared promiscuous point of view informs her aesthetic strategies and her philosophies of life and art. Hernández was among the earliest visible Chicana lesbian artists, along with muralist Judy Baca and photographer Laura Aguilar, whose art challenged the perceptions of what lesbian art is, particularly when viewed from a white frame.[51]

Oftentimes when studying the Chicano movement, certain forms of political agency (marches, protests, boycotts, certain leadership styles, and certain organizational forms) are viewed as the ultimate site of resistance, when poetry, song, or visual art more effectively express alternative points of view and imagine different futures.[52] While arguably Hernández's work emerged from and contributes to several social movements, historians tend to see art and cultural production as epiphenomenal to the movement (something that is inspired by it but plays only a supportive role). Yet, art can mobilize. It can shift one's worldview. Without dogma, it can create new paradigms and unleash the power to create new worlds. In the world of Ester Hernández's art, the strength, power, and resilience of women, workers, queers, and the marginalized shine through. Through her art, a wide and wonderful range of representations creates new horizons of possibility for Mexicanas and Chicanas. In this world, Chicanas are workers, lovers, migrants, goddesses, performers, *luchadoras* for farmworker justice, businesswomen, survivors, witnesses in solidarity, and ecological warriors protected by spiritual mothers and guardians. In this world created by art, made "from the heart and gut" of an artist, Chicanas are free.

8

FEMINISTA FREQUENCIES

CHICANA RADIO ACTIVISM IN THE PACIFIC NORTHWEST

MONICA DE LA TORRE

With Rosa's efforts, there was a balancing of the staff at KDNA. We had as many men as well as women. It all comes about from the efforts to reach and empower women from our community. Besides being subjected to poverty and the farmworker experience, women were also delegated a third citizen status. Women could not go to school. There was a machismo factor. There were many issues confronting women, and how do you address it? Radio. Radio became the instrument.

—RICARDO GARCÍA, 2014

We were fortunate enough that the news director was a woman, the station manager was a woman, and the main producer was a woman. We decided that it was important to have a woman's program addressing women's issues, that focused on music by women, and that's what we did on the show Mujer. *We covered all aspects of a woman's life and focused it on Latinas and in particular farmworker women. We opened the mic to women to come in and be interviewed. Women were really a part of Radio KDNA in those early days and still are.*

—ROSA RAMÓN, 2012

Sitting on top of a yellow pickup truck, founders and volunteers of Radio KDNA—the nation's first full-time noncommercial Spanish-language radio station—proudly point up to the radio tower they are constructing, realizing their dream of bringing community media to the Yakima Valley (figure 8.1). Their gaze directly engages the viewer, inviting us to bear witness to past, present, and future histories of struggle and activism in the region. The fields in the background serve as a visual marker of the socioeconomic conditions of the valley, which flourished as a result of low-wage migrant Mexican and Tejana/o labor.[1] The radio tower was built on Ahtanum Ridge, on land belonging to the Yakama Nation, signaling a coalition between Chicanas/os and the Yakamas.[2] Lastly, the people depicted in the image demonstrate that both men and women

FIGURE 8.1. KDNA founders and volunteers building the radio tower on Ahtanum Ridge, 1978–1979. © Rosa Ramón.

participated in Pacific Northwest Chicana/o activism, with women playing a central role in the founding and day-to-day activity of Radio KDNA.

KDNA officially went live on the air on December 19, 1979, crystalizing work that began in the mid-1970s during the Chicano movement. Prior to receiving the designated call letters "KDNA" in 1979, the radio station was often referred to as "Cadena" (chain or link in Spanish) in primary sources. The activism and work that created Radio KDNA must be understood as an integral component of Chicano movement activity in the Pacific Northwest. Indeed, Radio KDNA was part of a larger network of Chicano media activism in the 1970s, the Chicano media movement, which scholar and media activist Francisco J. Lewels documents as beginning alongside farmworker organizing.[3] Community radio producers and farmworkers harnessed the airwaves as a dialogic community-building space where the Yakima Valley's emergent Chicana/o community could tune in to KDNA to get the latest news on *Noticias Radio Cadena*, search for job openings on *Oportunidades de trabajo*, groove to Spanish tunes on *Caravana musical*, or learn about HIV/AIDS within migrant farmworker communities on the *radionovela Tres hombres sin fronteras* (Three men without borders). A tool for community building and social justice work, noncommercial community radio served as a cultural force for Chicano movement activists in rural central and eastern Washington and a way to communicate with and mobilize local migrant farmworkers through culturally relevant Spanish-language broadcasts.

I pivot the lens to community radio in a rural region of the Pacific Northwest and to Chicanas as early adopters and innovators of community radio platforms to provide an alternative understanding of Chicano movement practices beyond the Southwest urban paradigm, revealing the central role Chicanas played in movement projects. As illustrated in the opening quotes of this essay,[4] Radio KDNA's model of community radio production cultivated a leadership style I term "Chicana radio activism," a concept I advance in order to identify and explore a gender consciousness in Chicano movement activism in the Pacific Northwest during the mid- to late 1970s. While working-class women of Mexican descent may not be the first population we think of when we consider the deployment of feminist tactics in radio, at Radio KDNA Chicanas on community airwaves altered the soundscape of public broadcasting by incorporating Chicana radio activist tactics designed to reach women farmworkers. Radio KDNA was cofounded by Ricardo Garcia and Rosa Ramón, along with radio producers Julio César Guerrero and Daniel Roble. As leaders of noncommercial radio broadcast stations, their model of community-based production included training women as producers and technical staff, programming for Chicanas including farmworkers, segments of the population that had not been addressed by mass media, and institutionalizing antisexist station policies. Through this mode of Chicana radio activism, a small yet influential number of Chicanas in leadership and production roles at KDNA had a significant impact on the fabric of community radio broadcasting.

Drawing from evidence derived from oral histories I conducted with Ramón and García as well as the archival record, I demonstrate how Radio KDNA's founding and day-to-day activities present a unique example of gender consciousness and burgeoning feminist radio practices that relied on Chicana feminist forms of grassroots leadership and were grounded in the founders' personal experiences. In her oral history, Rosa Ramón—the only woman among the four cofounders of KDNA, who served as the station manager from 1979 to 1984—offers an account of the station's activities that unearths its deeply rooted feminist practices. García and Ramón explain how they promoted a model of community radio as a site for the negotiation of gender roles and as a sonic space for a Chicana feminist consciousness to grow. Moreover, the archival record created by Chicana administrative staff, record keepers, and secretaries demonstrates that, far from insignificant, these support roles have been critical to the preservation of institutional histories. For example, while working as the station manager, Ramón preserved important documents—radio-tower blueprints, newspaper articles, photographs, board minutes, program guides—which now serve as an archive of Chicana/o community radio activism. Given the ephemeral nature of the audio archive in this early period of community radio—few recorded programs have survived because many tapes were recorded over when a station did not have the financial resources to purchase more reels or tapes—it is essential to draw from the archival record preserved by administrators like Rosa Ramón to understand the ways in which community radio stations like KDNA functioned as a key networking and organizing tool in the Pacific Northwest.

KDNA's legacy as the nation's first full-time Spanish-language noncommercial radio station as well as its community-based programming activated various nodes of sociopolitical engagement across the Yakima Valley, including labor organizing, health and educational reform, and women's activism. Building upon Spanish-language radio scholar Dolores Inés Casillas's argument that "rural areas and farmworker based communities were the foundation for Mexican and Chicano-led community radio," I zero in on Chicanas' grassroots leadership style at KDNA.[5] By geographically centering the Pacific Northwest as a crucial site of activism based in community radio production and framing Chicanas as early adopters and innovators of community radio platforms, I enact a scholarly shift toward aural- and oral-based media movements that allows us to listen to Chicana feminist activism and thereby remix established Chicano movement narratives. The story of Radio KDNA calls us to listen to community radio as a mechanism that is networked and networking, a chain, a *cadena* connecting various aspects of the movement—labor, education, politics, and cultural production—to Chicana feminist activism throughout the nation yet still grounded by the urgent need to create a system of communication for migrant farmworkers in the Yakima Valley.[6]

Many civil rights activists saw access to media—radio, newspapers, and television—as an important front in the movement to achieve social equity. Maylei Blackwell offers critical insights about the importance of print culture to the development of Chicana feminism that are instructive to framing the political work of Chicana/o community radio. Blackwell argues,

> In the late 1960s and early 1970s Chicana feminists circulated their political ideas in Raza magazines, feminist circulars, manifestos, organizational newsletters, and political pamphlets. As a form of political pedagogy (Bhabba 1990), these print-mediated dialogues among women from different movement sectors and social locations created a space not only to formulate Chicana demands but to constitute new political, racial, and gender identities.[7]

The political pedagogy within movement print cultures offers evidence of a Chicano media movement that also reverberated throughout Chicana/o community radio stations. This Chicano media activism enacted important interventions in the establishment of spaces for Chicanas to create and access media, particularly through community radio. Yet, scholarship on this media movement tends to minimize the aural dimensions of this activism. Scholars amplifying sonic spaces of activism and resistance include Casillas and Gaye Theresa Johnson, who turn up the volume on radio as a site for space making and as an aural conduit to understanding larger structural, political, and socioeconomic issues pertaining to Latino communities.[8] Indeed, as Casillas astutely notes, "the political work of community-based radio outlets within rural Chicano areas complicates city- and visual-based accounts of the 'Chicano Media Movement.'"[9]

Moreover, as a sonic medium, the reach of community radio defies borders and has the power to transmit messages in ways that visual media cannot. For instance, KDNA's 20,000-watt radio tower atop Ahtanum Ridge had the capacity to reach across the fields of the Yakima Valley as far north as Wenatchee, Washington, and south into Oregon. Beginning in the mid-1970s, KDNA's radio waves mediated various components of activism in the Pacific Northwest, creating sonic spaces of solidarity that made radio an important technology in the Chicano movement.[10] Community radio, both as a format and within the structures that guide this form of media making, created a different register for community organizing throughout the 1960s and 1970s. This mode of media organizing is evident in the roots of KDNA's founding and its community radio model. Before I elaborate on the birth of KDNA, Ramón's and García's oral histories provide accounts that trace the migration of Tejana/o families from the Southwest to the Pacific Northwest, thereby creating the conditions for the emergence of a Chicana/o-controlled community radio station.

MIGRATIONS IN THE PACIFIC NORTHWEST

Radio KDNA's broadcasts sonically convened a Spanish-dominant audience that made the Pacific Northwest their home. The presence of Mexican and Chicana/o communities in the Pacific Northwest—Idaho, Oregon, and Washington—dates back as early as the 1800s. Mexicans and Chicana/os were drawn by jobs in the Pacific Northwest including cattle ranching, transportation, mining, and other activities pertaining to the development and settlement of the region.[11] During World War II, *braceros* and Chicano laborers from the Southwest were actively recruited to the Pacific Northwest due to labor shortages in the agricultural sector.[12] Irrigation projects in the Yakima Valley during this period also increased the viability and availability of land for the cultivation of nonmechanized crops like hops, asparagus, apples, and sugar beets. Mexican and Tejana/o migration to the Pacific Northwest increased after 1948 as the agricultural industry enlisted fewer Mexican *braceros* and turned to the recruitment of Mexican Americans from the Southwest. While growers relied on *braceros* to quell labor shortages during and after World War II, farmers preferred Chicano migrant families, many of whom followed the various migratory streams from Texas, Colorado, and Wyoming.[13] Historian Erasmo Gamboa explains, "It was not by chance that farmers sought Chicano laborers. These migrants, mostly families, had clear advantages over braceros. . . . They offered farmers the security of a stable labor force and freed them from the troublesome annual practice of contracting Mexican nationals."[14] Growers in the Pacific Northwest realized that the costs to recruit, transport, house, and feed *braceros*—even in the poor housing and working conditions they provided—could be dramatically lowered if they shifted from Mexican nationals to Mexican American migrant workers, and increasingly agri-businesses hired entire families of workers in order to sustain a more permanent and stable workforce.

Radio KDNA founders Rosa Ramón and Ricardo García are in many ways emblematic of this history of Chicana/o migration from the Southwest to the Pacific Northwest. Ramón recalls her family's migration, revealing the process by which many Mexican American and specifically Tejano families traveled from the Southwest to the Northwest in search of jobs, many ending up in the Yakima Valley to cultivate hops, apples, and asparagus, among other crops. Farmers and public entities strategically implemented advertising campaigns in Texas, California, and other states announcing the availability of work in Washington with ads running on Spanish-language radio programs and newspapers and posted in dance halls and stores.[15] Because of their lived experience as migrants, the founders of KDNA understood that radio was an accessible tool for farmworkers who had little access to other media. At the same time, they reworked this communication model by fostering dialectical media making, with producers as listeners and listeners as producers. With a growing population of Spanish-speaking communities resulting from an increased need for migrant labor in the region, KDNA used its Spanish-language radio platform to reflect the sociopolitical and cultural needs of this shifting demographic.

Both Ramón's and García's migratory narratives, family histories, and personal experiences influenced their work with various social justice movements in the Yakima Valley. Central to this activism was farmworker organizing, which was fashioned through a variety of grassroots organizations and student activist groups including the United Farm Workers Cooperative (UFW Co-op), Northwest Rural Opportunities (NRO), the Washington State Commission on Mexican American Affairs, United Mexican American Students (UMAS), and the Brown Berets.[16] In 1969, César Chávez visited Granger, Washington, where he spoke to approximately 800 Chicanas/os at a local school, and some of KDNA's founders were in attendance, which inspired their own farmworker organizing.[17] As this key shared experience suggests, farmworker activism in the Yakima Valley served as a driving force to the creation of Radio Cadena and the Northwest Chicano Radio Network (NCRN). The social conditions in the Northwest, including cold temperatures and the lack of a marked cultural and Spanish-speaking community, meant that the Pacific Northwest was very different from the Southwest.[18] That distinction, along with the lack of a commercial Spanish-language radio market like those prominent in the Southwest, provided the conditions for Chicano movement organizers in the Yakima Valley to embark on a journey to create Radio KDNA, which would later be known as *la voz del campesino* (the voice of the farmworker). The Chicano movement, community media activism, and the development of public radio all fused together at KDNA and sounded a call for social change in the Yakima Valley.

As the first Chicana community radio station manager in the United States, Rosa Ramón's experience offers an important point of entry in excavating a genealogy of Chicana radio broadcasters. Her insights into KDNA's efforts to make women central in programming and staffing point to the interventions she created within a community radio structure that was largely male-dominated. Because Ramón was aware of the gender inequity pervasive in radio, and in her community more broadly, she made a conscious effort to recruit women into positions of leadership. Her gender consciousness is tied to her experiences as a child migrant farmworker who harvested labor-intensive crops like asparagus alongside her parents and siblings. Her family traveled from Texas through Arizona and California before settling down in eastern Washington, where her family purchased a small farm in 1951. There was already a small community of Latinos, primarily Mexican Americans and Tejanos, who were moving to the Yakima Valley when Ramón's family arrived. "We grew up on a farm where we had animals," Ramón recalls. "We had horses, pigs, and chickens—and we grew our own vegetables and canned our own food because we were such a large family." She goes on, "That was how you supported a family of ten back then. You don't have a lot of money, but you do grow your own crops and can your own food and raise your own animals."[19]

Although the small community where Ramón grew up mostly comprised Tejano families, she experienced and witnessed racism and discrimination, especially at school, where she was reprimanded for speaking Spanish and mocked for eating tacos instead of bologna sandwiches. Ramón was only one of eight Latinas/os to graduate from Grandview High School. She recalls, "There were some experiences that were a little bit painful that you don't forget, like playing in the school ground and getting so excited that you start speaking Spanish and then having a teacher grab you by the arm and hit you with a book, telling you to stop speaking that gibberish because that's not the language that you should be speaking."[20]

Ramón's experiences are one example of the way institutional racism operated in the Yakima Valley. While Mexican American students may have predominated, they were economically and culturally relegated to a subordinate status. Furthermore, Ramón's postgraduation choices were limited due to financial constraints—her family could not economically support Rosa's collegiate aspirations. Ramón also faced employment discrimination. When she applied for an entry-level clerical job, she noticed her resume in the trash as she walked out the door. These early experiences of marginalization served as an impetus for Ramón to work in nonprofits that benefited her community, including Northwest Rural Opportunities, a community-based organization set up in 1968 to provide services to seasonal and migrant farmworkers in Washington state. In 1974, Ramón became assistant director of the Parent and Child Center that formed part of NRO's community social services programs. Ramón's experiences as a farmworker, her successful completion of high school, and her community organizing work proved invaluable to her practice of Chicana radio activism as KDNA's first station manager and as the first Chicana to ever hold such a position. As station manager, Ramón selected a team of producers, engineers, and staff who believed in KDNA's goal to create programming and content for the local community that was inclusive of women (*Mujer*) and children (*El Jardín de los Niños*). The programming schedule also shifted in the spring to begin at 4 a.m. on weekdays to accommodate farmworkers whose day started earlier during the farm labor season.

While she was at NRO, Ramón met Ricardo García, who was its director at the time. Like Ramón, García had gained insights from his life experiences that he applied to his work as an organizer and that aligned with Radio KDNA's goal of being *la voz del campesino*. Born in San Diego, Texas, Ricardo Romano García was raised by his mother after the early death of his father from tuberculosis when Ricardo was only two and a half years old. Relegated to what he describes as "second-class citizen status" after his father's death, which left his mother to care for him through low-wage labor, García witnessed the structural inequities and discrimination Tejanos were forced to contend with daily. His mother worked day and night for meager wages, which continued the cycle of poverty and food scarcity in their household. García recalls his gender consciousness stemming from his sensitivity to his mother and perhaps also based upon observing gender roles as a child:

> The whole root of it comes from sensitivity to my mother and aunts, who were brilliant women in their own way but never had a chance to develop. They didn't go to school. My grandmother also raised them after her husband Manuel Romano died from tuberculosis. My father died of tuberculosis. My grandmother had to raise a family of eight. They were picking cotton all over the area, and that was very hard work. They missed out unfairly. They also had husbands who drank and treated them harsh, to say the least. They were good men. They were providers, but they would go to San Diego to the cantinas and drink. It was a hard life for them. I was raised by women, and that's where my sensitivity comes from.[21]

What García refers to as "sensitivity" is an awareness of the intersectional conditions that created different challenges for Tejanas. García's early childhood experiences with poverty, gender inequality, and social injustice would no doubt prove influential to his community activism in the Pacific Northwest and in particular his strategic and intentional inclusion of women in Radio KDNA's founding and operations.

After graduating high school, Ricardo joined the army, a journey that took him to California, South Korea, Fort Lewis in Tacoma, Washington, and finally the Yakima Valley, where he settled down and became active in the Chicano movement. After training for a week in California with César Chávez, García worked with the United Farm Workers Organizing Committee in Washington with the goal of teaching farmworkers about their right to unionize to combat low wages and poor working conditions.[22] García served as the first executive director for the Washington State Commission on Mexican American Affairs, which was established in 1971 by Governor Daniel Evans to improve public policy development and access to government services for the Mexican American community. García served as executive director for the commission from 1971 to 1974. His tenure ended when the commission's board of directors felt that his Chicano farmworker activism was too radical and fired him. He then became director of NRO, where he met with directors of farmworker programs in Idaho and Oregon and was tasked with forming a radio station. During a presentation he gave at Western Washington University, García met two future KDNA cofounders, Daniel Roble and Julio César Guerrero, who had traveled to Washington from Michigan, where they had been training farmworkers to produce radio. Roble would serve as Cadena's project director and Guerrero as program manager and on-air talent.

Returning to the photo of the radio tower in the beginning of this essay, the images of the fields in the background highlight the spatial dimensions of Radio KDNA as a political project. In her incisive theorizing about sound and spatial entitlement in Los Angeles, Johnson argues, "Spatial entitlement is a way in which marginalized communities have created new collectivities based not just upon eviction and exclusion from physical places, but also new and imaginative uses of technology, creativity, and spaces."[23] The fields of the Yakima Valley, particularly the crops that demanded manual labor, altered the fabric of the Pacific Northwest in at least two ways: first, they created a channel and need for cheap labor, and many Tejana/o, Chicana/o, and later Mexican immigrant communities migrated to the Pacific Northwest. Second, the fields were ripe for a kind of media activism never before seen in the region or in the United States: a full-time Spanish-language educational community radio station that would alter the physical landscape and cultural soundscape of the Yakima Valley with a reverberation of activity and radio programming that reflected the needs and interests of Chicanas/os in the region.

Radio KDNA created a soundscape of the Chicano movement in the Yakima Valley through the voices of farmworkers that were carried over the airwaves across the fields through Spanish-language programming. Ultimately, this constituted a spatial entitlement that created a "critical sonic narrative" of the Chicano movement, which is why, as Johnson notes, radio is central to spatial entitlement in black and brown communities.[24] In the Pacific Northwest, spatial entitlement reverberated physically via the station's presence in the valley and aurally via KDNA's community radio airwaves that transmitted the community's narratives of struggle, activism, and change. Although farmworkers in the Yakima Valley experienced poverty and marginalization resulting from low wages, poor working conditions, and other structural inequities including exclusions from physical spaces, through KDNA, they creatively adopted radio technologies and claimed aural spaces that created communities of resistance. As such, the station and particularly its Chicana radio activism offer important insights into the media soundscapes of the Chicano movement.

THE BIRTH OF RADIO KDNA: TURNING UP THE VOLUME ON CHICANA/O COMMUNITY RADIO

The establishment of community-based radio stations like KDNA was fueled by national media reform trends as well as regional and national collaborations. The passage of the Public Broadcasting Act of 1967 marked a new phase in the national movement for media reform and created the conditions of possibility for Chicano community radio stations to emerge in the 1970s, including KDNA (1979), KBBF-FM (Santa Rosa, California [1973]), and Radio Bilingüe (Fresno, California [1980]), among other noncommercial radio stations.[25] KBBF, the nation's first bilingual noncommercial radio station (founded by Sonoma State University undergraduates and farmworkers), shared KDNA's goal of bringing communications technologies to farmworkers in the region, an aim that facilitated a dialogue among the stations. Indeed, when KDNA was in the process of starting up, its organizers turned to KBBF's founders and volunteers for advice.[26]

To begin the process of creating a Spanish-language radio station, Cadena's founders formed the Northwest Chicano Radio Network (NCRN). Organized and incorporated as a nonprofit entity in April 1976, NCRN planned to "gather, collect, and disseminate information and data on all affairs pertaining to this regional Chicano community to Spanish-speaking individuals and/or groups, organizations and programs in the Northwest via radio programming and media conferences."[27] NCRN was originally conceived as a tri-state radio initiative between Washington, Idaho, and Oregon. The NCRN self-designated title would be Radio Cadena, a chain or link, signaling how activists imagined radio technologies as a mechanism for linking Chicana/o organizers and farmworker communities across the three states. Unfortunately, the tri-state radio model did not materialize as planned, but Ramón, García, and the other founders moved forward with creating a radio station in the Yakima Valley. While Radio Cadena founders were preparing the application to the Federal Communications Commission for a licensing and construction permit, they also began broadcasting Spanish-language radio programming in Seattle at community radio station KRAB-FM through the use of the station's Subsidiary Communications Authorization signal.[28] At KRAB-FM, Cadena founders engineered a cutting-edge Spanish-language news production system whereby reporters from across the nation would call in and record news stories. Cadena producers would edit these stories and then feed them back to participating stations, which included commercial and noncommercial stations.[29] Known as the Spanish-Language News Network, this system aurally connected the Pacific Northwest to locations across the United States including California, Texas, Minneapolis, Michigan, Illinois, Colorado, and New Mexico.[30] Rosa Ramón explains, "We also started one of the first Spanish-language news networks. It was a very simple set-up: reel to reel and a telephone where news reporters from different radio stations throughout the country would call in and give us radio reports and then we would produce them into one concise segment and then feed them back to the radio stations."[31] KDNA later also shared programming with KBBF via the Spanish-Language News Network.[32] The Spanish-Language News Network facilitated a dialogue between Radio Cadena and Chicano movement activists across the country through shared news and programming.

As Radio Cadena was getting its application to the FCC, its staff actively engaged various community organizations across the Yakima Valley including NRO, Foundation for Chicano Education, and the Washington State Commission on Mexican American Affairs (now referred to as the Commission on Hispanic Affairs) that offered staff support and other resources to the burgeoning station. Prior to establishing the brick-and-mortar station in Granger, Radio Cadena worked with NRO to train ten farmworker youths in radio production in Lynden, Washington. Indeed, Cadena's founders and volunteers tapped into institutional resources and existing activist networks throughout Washington state.

Chicana/o activists, many of whom had been migrant farmworkers themselves, began to organize through various community-based organizations funded through President Lyndon B. Johnson's War on Poverty. The War on Poverty programs were a catalyst for many Yakima Valley Chicanas/os to get involved in political organizing and community-based organizations. Chicanas in Quincy, Washington, for instance, "benefited from the Great Society programs implemented by the Johnson administration in the 1960s. Programs such as the Migrant Day Care Center, the Quincy Community Center, the Grant County Community Action Council, and Northwest Rural Opportunities were all funded by the War on Poverty programs. . . . [Women] received valuable training and leadership experience during this time period."[33] Indeed, KDNA's women founders and volunteers, who already were active in social movement organizing, stepped into the roles of radio producer, station manager, news director, and producer and shaped a feminist consciousness at KDNA as they developed their own brand of on-air Chicana feminism. Chicana/o community broadcasters produced radio programs that sonically conveyed the advocacy work they performed in the community as farmworker organizers, child welfare advocates, and student activists. Chicanas at KDNA imagined the radical possibilities of community radio broadcasting by actively including women not only as listeners but as producers who created the conditions to produce *feminista* frequencies, which I turn to next.

FEMINISTA FREQUENCIES: SOWING THE SEEDS OF CHICANA RADIO ACTIVISM

In the 1970s, Chicana feminists utilized Chicana/o community radio stations as a platform for an emergent form of feminist media activism and community

FIGURE 8.2. KDNA *mujeres* Berenice Zuniga and Rosa Ramón. Copyright © Rosa Ramón.

building that I term "Chicana radio activism." A distinct model of organizing and leadership, the emergence of Chicana radio activism echoes Dionne Espinoza's observation about the development of women's leadership within the Texas La Raza Unida Party: "The fact that strong women were at the forefront early on influenced other women also to challenge the traditional gender division of labor."[34] Likewise, Chicana radio activists deployed radio technologies to transform the traditional gender division of labor in at least four ways. First, many Chicanas involved in the early days of Chicana/o community radio were founding members or were in leadership positions as station managers, news directors, announcers, and producers. Second, Chicana radio activists trained other women as radio producers, a practice that ensured that these technical skills would not be limited to specific individuals while guaranteeing women's involvement in the production process. Notably, this practice departed starkly from the norm in minority community radio as well as public broadcasting more generally, where most if not all of the chief engineers were male.[35] Indeed, Chicanas' entry into the male-dominated radio spaces was revolutionary not just for Chicana/o communities but also for noncommercial radio as a whole.[36] Within the day-to-day activities involved with running a community-based radio station, Chicana radio activists found ways to subvert gendered practices typical of radio stations by occupying roles usually gendered as male, such as producers, news directors, and station managers. Third, armed with the technical skills to create high-quality radio broadcasts, Chicana radio producers created programming specifically for women in their communities. And fourth, along with programming, they pushed for antisexist policies at the station, starting with the banning of sexist music from the airwaves. As a technology, radio provided a platform for women to develop a Chicana voice that was public in its reach but at the same time could be aired in the private sphere of the home or places of employment.

At Radio KDNA, Chicanas such as station manager Rosa Ramón, producer Estella Del Villar, and news director Berenice Zuniga attained formal leadership roles and harvested Chicana feminist radio activism throughout the Yakima Valley. Together, they produced the program *Mujer* (Woman), whose goal was to provide farmworker women with news stories, music, and informative pieces addressing their distinct subjectivities. *Mujer* aired twice a week, on Wednesday afternoons and Saturday mornings. "Everything in that program was about women, and it was the first time that anyone had ever heard a program like that, I'm sure," Ramón explains. "We covered all aspects of a woman's life and focused it on Latinas and in particular farmworker women. We did news stories, interviewed local women, we brought in music about social movements. We played music by Mercedes Sosa, and other Latina musicians and artists of the time. We did everything from interviews with directors of community programs to on-air cooking demonstrations."[37] This radio programming catered to a specific demographic—Chicana farmworkers—whose needs and interests reflected their unique positionality. Such programming gave women a space to discuss controversial topics like reproductive rights, abortion, and domestic violence and centered women within the radio production process by playing music by musicians like Mercedes Sosa and Lydia Mendoza, airing interviews with directors of community programs, and broadcasting on-air cooking demonstrations. This model of Chicana radio production echoed throughout the programming and day-to-day activity at KDNA, extending Chicana feminist activism and epistemologies to rural areas across the Pacific Northwest.

Chicana radio activism within Chicana/o-controlled community radio stations marks yet another node in the network of Chicana movement organizing.[38] Chicanas who stepped up to the microphone for the first time were not only hearing their own voices audibly broadcasted over public airwaves, they were announcing the arrival of a sonically distinct Chicana public sphere. KDNA producer Celia Prieto recounts the first time she was live on the air: "The very first time I did the news live, I was very, very nervous and after my news was over I came out and Rosa [Ramón] and Estella [Del Villar] were waiting for me at the door and they were applauding me, and that made me feel really good because I get a lot of support from them and I think that's what keeps me going."[39]

This community of Chicana radio producers was a source of support and sustenance for Prieto. At its core, Chicana radio activism was about creating a space for women to imagine themselves in roles they never thought possible while supporting each other as they carved spaces for themselves within public broadcasting. The feminist activism in community radio stations is of particular importance to Chicano movement historiography because it uncovers new evidence of Chicana grassroots leadership. Chicana radio activism was a political movement manifested through the act of producing aural cultural representations on the broadcast platforms Chicana radio producers helped create. Through an integration of feminist policies and woman-centered programming, Chicana broadcasters ruptured male-dominated media spaces. In this way, Chicana radio activists honed a feminist praxis that changed the soundscape of community radio, and in turn, producers as well as listeners often were inspired to change their living conditions—whether by leaving abusive relationships, seeking new career possibilities outside of low-wage farm labor, or attending institutions of higher education.

Women played an active role as content producers, a marked shift from the male producers working in public radio of this era. Resulting from the training of many women radio producers, Chicana radio activists were then able to create content unique to the Chicana experience. "The personal is political" took on aural dimensions and was carried out through the Chicana radio activism embedded in the soundwork of radio production.

RADIO KDNA AS LA VOZ DE LA CAMPESINA Y DEL CAMPESINO

My concept of Chicana radio activism excavates the strategies of women radio producers who worked in community radio stations to uncover important and sometimes unexpected sites of knowledge production. I focus on the involvement of Chicanas in 1970s community radio as a mode of Chicana radio activism to call attention to the consequences of rendering invisible the multifaceted work by Chicanas in community media. Little attention has been paid to Chicanas as active participants in the establishment of community radio stations in the Pacific Northwest and the United States more broadly. As an analytic, Chicana radio activism reveals the political processes and professional strategies deployed by Chicanas in community radio, making the act of creating radio—as founders, leaders, and producers of woman-centered programming—important to our understandings of feminist media production in the Pacific Northwest. Radio KDNA and the show *Mujer* were instrumental in centering women within radio broadcasting, suggesting a Chicana radio production praxis that represents a vital technological component of the Chicano movement era. These women producers and their audiences demonstrate the transformative power of community radio production and the role of women in a movement that often downplays their contributions. As we continue to examine Chicana activism in the Chicano movement by expanding and even rupturing the parameters of what constitutes activism, we find that when Chicanas helped build organizational structures, they became part of the structure and were able to influence its gender politics, divisions of labor, and gender consciousness.

The story of KDNA and the Chicana/o activists who saw the radical potential in radio compels scholars to conceive of new frameworks that listen to the sound migrations of Chicana/o media activism and the third spaces and technological tools of the Chicano movement not just in the Pacific Northwest but throughout the country. Aurally, Radio KDNA was the sounding board for issues confronting migrant Tejana/o and Chicana/o communities of the region. Spatially, the radio station served as a community center where Chicanas/os could turn for information, entertainment, and *convivencia*. The political work of KDNA as *la voz del campesino*—a hub for farmworker activism in the Yakima Valley—shifts our historical understanding of the Chicano movement to a site for media activism within a rural context beyond Aztlán. When remixed with other components of Chicana feminisms—like grassroots leadership and social justice activism—the sounds of Chicana radio activism constitute yet another track of resistance to historical narratives that seek to silence these Chicana *movidas*.

9 EXCAVATING THE CHICANO MOVEMENT

CHICANA FEMINISM, MOBILIZATION, AND LEADERSHIP AT EL CENTRO DE LA RAZA, 1972–1979

MICHAEL D. AGUIRRE

In early October 1972, members of a coalition took over an abandoned school in the Beacon Hill area of Seattle, later naming the site El Centro de la Raza (ECDLR).[1] The predominantly Chicana/o coalition intended to establish a multiservice center for the perpetuation of ethnic Mexican and Latina/o heritage for all Seattleites, with programs ranging from English language classes, a kitchen, a day care center, and an event center. During the initial months of the takeover, Chicano artist Daniel DeSiga painted a vivid mural on the main interior wall of the school. Titled *An Explosion of Chicano Creativity* (color plate 13), the mural depicted the faces of two large Mexica male warriors with the building's windows serving as their eyes. Aesthetically captivating, the windows let in ample amounts of sunlight, suggesting the warriors illuminated the *centro* and acted as its sentinels. On the lower left-center portion of the wall, DeSiga painted a woman's face that donned a golden eagle headdress. According to DeSiga, the woman and golden eagle were depicted because he wanted to "pay homage to women" who were involved in the takeover.[2]

The imposing visage of the Mexica warriors and the lower placement of the woman in eagle headdress reveal a more complex history of the *centro*, the larger Chicano movement, and the masculine-focused nationalism of Aztlán. The brush strokes of the 1972 mural effectively perform the dual function of Chicano politics and movement historiography that privilege Chicanos and minimize Chicana active participation in the founding of social service and community centers. The mural also hints at masculine structures of memory and history, what Vicki Ruiz has called a "hagiography of a pre-Columbian past" that leaves little space for counterhistories.[3] Moreover, cultural critic Shifra Goldman and Chicano scholar Tomás Ybarra-Frausto denote the primacy of movement art when they categorize the 1968–1975 phase as a "whole movement to recapture, at times romantically, a people's history and culture."[4] Yet, DeSiga understood his 1972 mural to be a work in progress, one he wished to revisit and finally call complete. Beyond aesthetics, DeSiga was aware of the power of the brush and the recording capability of paint, a power that he exercised once more, in 1997, at ECDLR.

Twenty-five years after he began working on the mural at El Centro de la Raza, Daniel DeSiga returned there in 1997 to finish his work. His completed mural expanded the original Chicana/o motifs to include a message of historical trajectories, cross-racial solidarity, and, most tellingly, women's labor.[5] The omnipotent warriors were transformed from symbols of virile masculinity to noble Mexica women with earrings, rose-colored lips, and rouged cheeks.[6] DeSiga's rationale for the regendering of the Mexica warriors was simple: "They [Chicanas] are the backbone of the *centro*."[7] Estela Ortega echoed DeSiga's statement by wryly commenting how the women's faces made sense because "El Centro was really a women's organization."[8] Graciela Gonzalez and Carmen Miranda likewise expressed pride in being physically memorialized on the main interior wall of the *centro*. For Gonzalez and Miranda, the women's faces were more than a touch-up, they were a visual testament to a fact that Gonzalez and Miranda knew since 1972: El Centro de la Raza functioned due to the stalwart volunteerism of numerous women.[9] The approval by Chicanas of the rouged cheeks, red lips, and jeweled earrings signaled pride in a politicized Chicana identity that multiplied Chicana/o visions of politics and aesthetics.[10] DeSiga's twenty-five-year visual documentation is emblematic of "retrofitted memory" by the artist and activists, where "social actors read the interstices, gaps, and silences of existing historical narratives in order to retrofit, rework, and refashion older narratives to create new historical openings, political possibilities, and genealogies of resistance."[11] *An Explosion of Chicano Creativity* thus presents a critical juncture between 1972 and 1997, where women's history at El Centro de la Raza can be excavated and written at the center of history rather than left in the margins of paint or letters.

A close reading of the mural and its gender politics demonstrates a matrix of femininity, sexism, and Chicana feminism in the mural and the *centro*. Indeed, the public display of the mural reflected Chicanas' challenge of the private/public dichotomy. Chicana activist politics at the *centro* were informed, in part, by their personal experiences with racist and sexist schools, jobs, organizations, and individuals. The processes of politicization that build from lived experiences, what I call "becoming Chicana," helped construct ECDLR as women took charge of numerous unpaid stations at the *centro* and served as leaders and mentors to other Chicanas from the *centro*'s beginnings.[12] Chicanas involved with the ECDLR point to the movement in its numerous manifestations as a catalyst toward new subjectivities in numerous spheres. Yet, Chicanas also broke from gendered expectations of the movement and became critical leaders and volunteers during the early years of El Centro de la Raza. The mural serves as an important lens to recover longer genealogies of Chicana leadership in Seattle and the Chicano movement. By listening to Chicanas, scholars can understand the spaces produced by Chicanas that worked within a multivalent civil rights project.

The acknowledged but unwritten history of Chicana politicization, activism, and leadership at El Centro de la Raza presents a unique nodal point from which we may begin to understand how Chicana activism worked within and beyond the Southwestern-focused Chicano movement. In order to unpack and address what I see as Chicana feminism at Seattle's El Centro de la Raza, I center on four core activists who lent their labor and leadership to the *centro*: Estela Ortega, Theresa Aragon, Carmen Miranda, and Graciela Gonzalez. How did these four women become Chicanas and Chicana activists? How were Chicanas a part of institution building? In what ways did becoming Chicana reconfigure gender relations within and beyond the movement? To address those questions I focus my analysis on these four Chicanas who were influential in establishing, directing, and staffing ECDLR during its period of fewest paid staff.[13] By weaving oral histories I conducted with archival materials from El Centro de Raza and the University of Washington, I argue that Chicanas' theory in the flesh informed the *centro*'s foundational philosophies and laid the groundwork for its ongoing work.[14] Focusing on Chicana praxis at ECDLR, I contend that Chicanas maneuvered between multiple sites of power, enacting a differential consciousness that challenged prescribed gender and political boundaries. I demonstrate how Chicana unpaid (volunteer) labor formed a major base of workers that kept the *centro*'s doors open and services operational despite a lack of funds and an unknown future in the city.

I build from existing historiography and regional archives on the movement in Seattle by critically reading archives (institutional and memory), analyzing Seattle from a perspective within the Chicano movement, and utilizing a more fluid conceptualization of Chicana activism and feminism to understand a community institution.[15] Two of the richest bodies of scholarship available on Chicanas/os in Seattle are Yolanda Alaniz and Megan Cornish's book, *Viva la Raza*, and essays and interviews featured in the Seattle Civil Rights and Labor History Project.[16] *Viva la Raza* presents a detailed gender and socialist analysis of Washington state history, as evident in its argument of UW Chicano studies staff worker Rosa Morales's suspension in 1977. The Seattle Civil Rights and Labor History Project's "Chicana/o Movement in Washington State" section painstakingly compiled numerous histories of Latinas/os in Seattle and Washington. More recently, Alan Eladio Gómez's dissertation provides a well-researched chapter on the establishment of ECDLR, debates with other ethnic Mexican organizations in the area and Seattle's city council, and the larger Third World coalitional politics in Seattle.[17] In this volume, Monica De La Torre expands and disrupts Chicana/o history in Washington state through her analysis of Radio KDNA and the politics of feminist sonic media making.

I move away from a university setting and self-identified radical feminist groups, allowing for a broader understanding of "multiple insurgencies" in under-researched spaces and places, locations where intersectionality took precedence over strict cultural nationalism of Aztlán and where Chicana activism pumped the lifeblood of a community institution.[18] Rather than passively accept the frail "women were central" refrain, I highlight how women volunteers and members at El Centro de la Raza were heavily responsible for the center's longevity through their commitment to racial and gender equity and how they ruptured subservient gender modalities. Through a narrative that puts Chicanas at the forefront of community institution building, I show how conceptions of politics include actors' daily struggles in the forging of a social movement. Chicanas at ECDLR were not just there, too. Along with other volunteers and allies, Chicanas *were* El Centro de la Raza through both their physical and philosophical masonry of the *centro*.

BECOMING CHICANA

Central to my argument is my conceptualization of becoming Chicana. Informed by the works of Chicana feminist theorists Cherríe Moraga, Gloria Anzaldúa, and Emma Pérez as well as Maylei Blackwell's multiple-insurgencies model, becoming Chicana underscores the making, adoption, and recrafting of the politicized identity "Chicana."[19] Becoming Chicana is grounded in Moraga's theory in the flesh, "a politic born out of necessity" that bridges racialized and gendered histories and illuminates the centrality of experience to political imaginings.[20] Becoming Chicana is also informed by Anzaldúa's theorization of *conocimiento*. As she defined it, *conocimiento* is "that aspect of consciousness urging you to act on the knowledge you gained."[21] That is, *conocimiento* is not just imagining a different world through new experiences or education but also participating in its creation with other peoples and groups. Emma Pérez stresses the connectivity between the past and the present, especially as it relates to the histories of racialized bodies.[22] My use of the verb "becoming" underscores the encounters and processes of political education and identity formation ranging from early experiences with racism and gender hierarchies to more contemporary events. While becoming Chicana highlights how "Chicana" is not an a priori identity or experience, it is not meant to suggest a teleological inevitability. Rather, I use the term "becoming" to point to how identities are both connected to past struggles against social injustices and formed in the interlinked webs of political, personal, and social dynamics in which mentors and friendships influenced Chicana activism and identity. While the women in this chapter expressed their social and political agency long before they self-identified as "Chicanas," it was the profound shift in political consciousness that made them invest in Chicana politics at certain junctures in their lives. Racialized and marginalized peoples do not have the luxury of erasing the past, nor do they necessarily want to forget their cultures of resistance.

The four women who are highlighted in this essay, Theresa Aragon, Carmen Miranda, Estela Ortega, and Graciela Gonzalez, arrived at ECDLR with their own histories that informed their praxis at the *centro*. Aragon moved to Seattle from New Mexico to attend Seattle University and then enrolled in UW's doctoral program in political science. Miranda, Gonzalez, and Ortega were originally from Texas and moved to Washington because of farm labor, a husband's new job, and involvement in ECLDR, respectively. Each Chicana encountered institutional racism in school and gendered expectations within the family. These varied experiences were built into the *centro*'s organizational philosophies and identity as Chicanas made the *centro* a community space that confronted issues of child care, leadership positions, and Chicana empowerment through mutual support. That is, becoming Chicana profoundly shaped the dimensions of the *centro*.

A shared thread among Theresa Aragon, Carmen Miranda, and Graciela Gonzalez were their early experiences with racism in elementary school that included segregation, assumptions of their language skills, and corporal punishment for speaking Spanish. In Las Vegas, New Mexico, Aragon's encounter with racism began in preschool at the local parochial school. Along with other "chicanitos," she was separated from white, English-speaking students and given clay to play with instead of instruction. Her mother later registered Aragon for classes in Albuquerque in second grade—Aragon belonged in first. Aragon convinced the nun at the Albuquerque school that she could read English because, coincidentally, the nun informally tested Aragon with the same book used at Aragon's preschool. Aragon memorized much of the book by listening to the teacher in Las Vegas read to the white students.[23] Miranda and her family were migrant farmworkers, moving from Texas to the Pacific Northwest. In Texas, she was corporally punished for speaking Spanish in the classroom, and in Moses Lake, Washington, her head was shaved for the presumption of having lice. A fieldworker from an early age, Miranda was also taunted by classmates and called racially derogatory names for going directly from field to class without showering in between.[24] Similarly, Graciela Gonzalez was assumed to have lice and was physically punished for speaking Spanish in the classroom in San Antonio, Texas.

Politicization for Graciela Gonzalez also took place outside school. Gonzalez was well acquainted with activism since she was a child. Her mother worked along with others in the 1938 pecan shellers' strike led by Emma Tenayuca in San Antonio, Texas. Interestingly, Gonzalez stated that her mother did not want to encourage Gonzalez to immerse herself in political and economic activism because of the personal and material toll exacted by the 1938 strike. And yet, her mother instilled in Gonzalez the power of fighting, especially as it related to retention of one's culture in racially myopic San Antonio, where speaking Spanish was a punishable offense. As Gonzalez said, "You never give up on your language, you never give up your culture. She [her mother] always told us to be proud of who we were." Along with teaching Gonzalez about the pecan shellers' strike and cultural pride, her mother removed her from school in the sixth grade to help take care of her siblings. The reality of material necessity outweighed Gonzalez's need of formal schooling, but she returned to it after her move to Washington.[25]

Originally from the Stafford area near Houston, Texas, Estela Ortega worked from an early age to contribute to her family's income, whether laboring in cotton fields or a cafeteria. One of her earliest cultural introductions to being Chicana occurred during her later teens when Ortega attended dances that showcased groups such as Little Joe and the Latinaires and Sunny and the Sunliners. Ortega was encouraged by others to visit Houston's Hermann Park on Sundays, and there she met politically minded people who were involved in numerous social activist groups. These cultural and political experiences galvanized Ortega's volunteerism for the United Farm Workers, Leonel Castillo's municipal political campaign, and the study groups she later joined. The Houston study groups interrogated numerous schools of philosophy and national liberation movements throughout the decolonizing world. It was these study groups that influenced Ortega to think that "the world could be a better place, but you had to work at it . . . day in and day out to make change." While in Houston, Ortega learned of a Chicana/o conference in El Paso. It was at this conference that she met Roberto Maestas, Juan José Bocanegra, and others from the Beacon Hill school takeover. Their initial meeting produced, at the very least, the sharing of contact information; a few weeks after the Beacon Hill school takeover, Ortega received a newspaper clipping and personal invitation from Maestas to visit the *centro*. Less than one month later, Ortega moved to Seattle, and in December 1972 she married Roberto Maestas.[26]

MIGRATING POLITICS

Migration from the Southwest to the Pacific Northwest and movement between the agricultural areas of eastern Washington and major cities in western Washington formed a facet of the state's Chicano movement. Collectively, the moves to Seattle by Miranda, Gonzalez, Ortega, and Aragon were embodied by a repertoire of experiences from which they drew to maneuver through different arenas including higher education, city politics, and family.[27] Their becoming Chicana was rooted in their early lives in the Southwest and continued throughout the establishment of the Beacon Hill school, future site of El Centro de la Raza.

Each of the migration narratives represented different waves and influences that, over time, pushed Seattle's Latina/o population to just over 10,000 residents by 1970 who increasingly demanded space in the city. During World War II, Mexican nationals were imported via the Bracero Program to satisfy wartime agricultural needs. In addition to siphoning racialized Mexican bodies into the fields, this guest-worker program introduced rising numbers of Mexican workers into eastern and central Washington's valleys, notably the Yakima Valley. The program was short-lived in Washington and ended in 1947, but by the 1960s, Keo Capestany of the Washington State Commission on Hispanic Affairs remarked that ethnic Mexicans increasingly took up residence in Seattle as farm labor became an insufficient occupation to maintain the lives of workers and their families.[28] Carmen Miranda and her family formed part of the larger migrant farmworker circuit that stretched between Texas, California, Idaho, and Washington. Born in the border town of Eagle Pass, Texas, Miranda was a migrant agricultural worker for the first twenty years of her life, then moved to Seattle in 1972.

Migration to Washington encompassed other social and economic factors as well. Aragon, Gonzalez, and Ortega migrated to Washington because of education opportunities, nonagricultural employment, and the Chicano movement, respectively. Aragon journeyed to Seattle from Las Vegas, New Mexico, in the early 1960s to attend Seattle University. Her academic excellence earned her scholarships to other universities, but financial constraints and her parents' insistence that Aragon attend a "good Catholic school" landed her in the Jesuit institution Seattle University.[29] In 1967, Gonzalez moved to Washington with her husband, who was set to begin a job at economic giant Boeing. Miranda settled with her parents in Moses Lake, Washington, in 1968. As previously mentioned, Ortega met Roberto Maestas and other leaders of El Centro de la Raza at a Chicano conference in El Paso in late October 1972. After two weeks, Ortega returned to Houston but only to arrange her personal affairs to permanently live in Seattle and take part in the development of El Centro de la Raza; the move occurred in November 1972.

The migrant connection between the Pacific Northwestern state of Washington and the Southwestern states of New Mexico and Texas forms part of the larger link between migration and politics. Closer examination of the Texas-Washington connection shows that Pierce County (including the city of Tacoma) received the majority of Texas migrants, followed by King County (including Seattle).[30] The more agricultural production areas of Yakima, Grant, and Walla Walla Counties received nearly 3,000 fewer migrants from Texas during this period than Pierce or King Counties. These migration patterns complicate the linearity of eastern-western Washington movement and reinforce arguments of ethnic Mexican urban migration patterns.[31]

All four narrators were from either New Mexico (Aragon) or Texas (Gonzalez, Ortega, Miranda), and each embodied particular experiences from their home states that they brought with them to Washington and continued to develop at El Centro de la Raza.[32] Aragon's early experience with education discrimination continued as she began her doctoral program in political science at the University of Washington. There was tension around her acceptance to the doctoral program and graduate stipend because she was a woman in academia, married, with children. Aragon battled the presumption in the Department of Political Science that she "would be a loss of their investment."[33] Nevertheless, Aragon was briefly appointed head of the Chicano studies program in 1971 and later vice provost of special programs at the University of Washington in 1971 while still a doctoral candidate and writing her dissertation. Aragon blended familial responsibilities, education administration, and scholarship with her involvement in the Chicano movement. Early and continual encounters with racism and sexism in education were the impetus for Aragon's actions for change.

Gonzalez first moved to Kent, Washington, in 1968 to be near the Boeing facility where her husband worked. With the lessons her mother taught her about education (especially its material consequences) and retention of cultural pride, Gonzalez soon enrolled and earned her general education diploma at Highline Community College in 1973. She later went on to earn her bachelor's degree at the Evergreen State College in Olympia in 1976. Gonzalez engaged with the Chicano movement and Third World coalitional politics at both Highline and Evergreen as she continued becoming Chicana in different spheres.[34]

Attending Highline was both a challenge and an opportunity for organizational politics for Gonzalez. She was a mother of three without the resources for day care, yet she managed to form a system of child care first with her classmates and later with the college's administration. Gonzalez and others petitioned and continuously demanded that Highline provide day care for students' children, and the administration listened. She was also active in Highline's Movimiento Estudiantil Chicano de Aztlán (MEChA) chapter and witnessed the racial and personal factionalism that ran through several organizations during the civil rights period.[35] Gonzalez effectively balanced numerous demands as she pursued her education while simultaneously pushing for day care and beginning her involvement with Chicana/o politics in MEChA. She refused to compartmentalize her life into fictitious public (education and activism) and private (motherhood and marital) worlds, instead using both as assets throughout her politicization of becoming Chicana.

During her time at Evergreen, Gonzalez joined the Third World Coalition and took a different view toward organizing. Working alongside other ethnic and racial groups at Evergreen, Gonzalez and the coalition were instrumental in getting a meeting space at the college, boycotting non–United Farm Workers lettuce, and making the coalition part of the faculty hiring process.[36] With the coalition, Gonzalez saw the effectiveness of cross-racial organizing in battling an established bureaucracy and advancing the concerns of marginalized peoples. As at Highline, Gonzalez was shaping Evergreen into an institution that was more responsive to the wants and needs of people of color. It was with the Third World Coalition that Gonzalez heard of a meeting where Roberto Maestas and others were going to discuss Chicana/o issues in Seattle.[37]

Prior to arriving in Seattle and El Centro de la Raza, Miranda settled with her parents in Moses Lake in 1968. She continued to work in the fields, mainly on top of harvesting machinery removing vines and rocks from collected potatoes. Miranda believed that her life was going to be dominated by field labor and household work. In effect, she normalized racism and confined gender scripts as a survival strategy. In 1972, this perception was exploded and reorganized into a kaleidoscope of life possibilities when she met Roberto Maestas, Estela Ortega, and Graciela Gonzalez, people she named as her mentors at El Centro de la Raza.

VOLUNTEER LABOR IN THE MAKING OF EL CENTRO DE LA RAZA

The creation of El Centro de la Raza depended heavily on the volunteer labor of activists as much as the larger civil rights movements, including the Chicano movement. There were forms of unremunerated labor that began even before activists took over the abandoned school in Beacon Hill, such as attending and planning meetings. During the takeover, numerous peoples volunteered to perform tasks that included building maintenance, meeting with city politicians, taking leadership positions, and fund-raising. Aragon, Miranda, Gonzalez, and Ortega represent a range of ways that Chicanas made ECDLR possible and the multiple struggles waged by the people of El Centro de la Raza during the movement.

Geographically distant from the Southwestern pulse of Aztlán, Seattle Chicanas/os closely followed events organized by their southern comrades, but they faced their own challenges within a white-dominated region undergoing an economic recession in the early 1970s.[38] Issues over the inability to exercise suffrage, the shortage of adequate housing and equal employment, the problem of language barriers in public services, and the unavailability of a community space were central to these groups. As early as 1968, the Mexican American Federation undertook a campaign to make "its people politically aware" and to encourage them to support issues that benefitted the entire ethnic Mexican community east and west of the Cascade Mountains.[39] Washington Chicana/o organizations also included the Chicano Education Association (CHE), the McNeil Island Mexican American Self Help group (MASH), MUJER, Las Chicanas, and Active Mexicanos. These groups' objectives ranged from education to prison reform to economic opportunities.

Within this civil rights milieu, members and supporters of El Centro de la Raza walked into the Beacon Hill school on October 11, 1972, under the pretense of inspecting the building for future use and began a precedence of volunteerism for the *centro*.[40] Theresa Aragon initiated a dialogue with the city months prior to the October 11 takeover of the school. She met with the superintendent of Seattle public schools in an effort to have the district lease the school to ECDLR for $1 per year. Aragon recalls, "They weren't using it," and early members of ECDLR planned to transform the unused space into a meaningful place where Chicanas/os could centralize social services and cultural practices outside of the University of Washington.

The impetus to occupy the school was the termination of the English as a Second Language (ESL) program at South Seattle Community College, which had its funding revoked in 1972 as part of the Nixon administration's scaling back of War on Poverty programs.[41] The ESL program taught more than language; it was also a program that educated students in need of social change, with language being one of many instruments to access jobs, education, and sociopolitical resources. Chicanas/os and their allies discussed potential strategies to pursue amid the closure of the ESL program. They met in members' basements and at the St. Peter Claver Center, which was administered by Asian American civil rights leader Bob Santos.[42] Influenced in large part by Native fishing struggles at Frank's Landing on the Nisqually River and the United Indians of All Tribes 1970 sit-in at Fort Lawton, Chicanas/os used a similar takeover technique to establish an ethnic Mexican-focused social services center and cultural space.[43] Chicanas/os also seized upon the site after Governor Dan Evans announced that abandoned civic buildings could be transferred to organizations that served the greater community.[44] After many discussions, meetings, and a sit-in in Mayor Wes Uhlman's office, the city leased the building to ECDLR, and the Seattle Model City Program subsequently agreed to provide $87,000 in start-up money for the *centro*.[45] This amount of funding was critical, yet the *centro* was estimated to cost $130,000 to become fully operational.[46]

While ECDLR volunteers painstakingly politicked at city hall, other members provided much of the unremunerated labor to keep the fledgling *centro*'s doors open. Economist Burton A. Weisbrod estimates that in 1980, more than 10 billion hours of volunteer labor was provided to US nonprofit organizations. Weisbrod also notes that the years 1974–1985 saw volunteer labor grow by 16 percent more than paid employees in tax-exempt organizations.[47] Roberto Maestas, Theresa Aragon, and Estela Ortega all note the centrality of unpaid labor at ECDLR. Ortega states that for the first seven years, volunteers ran the *centro* as the dominant labor force. Maestas recalls that one of the central issues facing the early *centro* was the ability to provide if not wages, at least child care, which was soon attained with the help of a nearby Methodist church. While acknowledging volunteer labor is an important step, in order to write Chicanas into history, as argued by Emma Pérez, the dimensions of Chicana activism demand further exploration.[48]

Soon after the occupation commenced on October 11, 1972, Seattle public schools transferred the building to the city government. The simultaneous strategy of occupying the school and lobbying public officials created two critical dialogues that engaged the city beyond the confines of either city hall or the school. Aragon used her position at UW to build awareness on campus, even getting students and faculty to do some general work at the Beacon Hill school. This effort assisted ECDLR in putting people inside the school and demonstrated to critics that different constituencies supported ECLDR.[49]

While pursuing the trail to city hall, Councilman John Miller and other officials agreed with Aragon on the need for a Chicana/o space. Aragon "toured all the little city halls," the various bureaucracies, as she spread the word about ECDLR and learned of different funding sources.[50] The politicking and takeover generated a lease, and Seattle Model Cities funding followed. The city pledged an extra $44,000, yet this money traveled much more slowly through the bureaucratic channels, finally reaching the *centro* in 1974.[51] Importantly, Aragon brought her administrative and writing skills from academia to the technical task of grant writing, a form of labor with major financial implications. Aragon continued to draft grant applications to various federal agencies, including Housing and Urban Development and Health, Education, and Welfare. Aragon's diplomatic work for the *centro* was a critical facet of building the community institution; she engaged politicians behind closed doors, participated in ECDLR meetings, and communicated Chicana/o concerns to groups that may not otherwise have heeded the call to establish a Chicana/o-focused community institution. Aragon, it should not be forgotten, was part of the fledgling *centro* while also a vice provost and doctoral candidate at UW and a mother.

Chicana leadership and political maneuvering at El Centro de la Raza must be traced to its first director, Gloria Rivera. Born in Yakima, Washington, and with a bachelor's degree from UW's College of Education, Rivera provided a strong example of leadership to other Chicanas through her service on the board of Active Mexicanos, a Seattle Chicana/o organization.[52] Rivera held numerous positions at ECDLR simultaneously, including director, accountant, and project coordinator.[53] While Rivera was director of ECDLR, she maintained a working relationship with Active Mexicanos despite each group's distinct philosophies and competition for limited city funds granted to ethnoracial and community organizations.[54] Rivera showed Chicanas that the federal government was not immune to challenges by the *centro*. In making arguments for "Spanish-speaking" groups' share of Manpower Revenue Sharing Funds, Rivera explained that the US Department of Labor's Service, Employment, Redevelopment program was unwilling to take a more local approach to its national program. Rivera was in effect pushing the federal government to uphold its policies of local needs.[55] Rivera's tenure at ECDLR ended by 1974, when Roberto Maestas took the position. Yet, Rivera demonstrated the multi-issue political activism that established dialogues with other community organizations and government agencies that allocated funds. More importantly, she presented Chicanas with a critical example of female leadership and involvement in the movement that belied the images in the *centro*'s 1972 mural.[56]

Upon her arrival in November 1972, Ortega soon engaged in volunteer work. Indeed, volunteer work kept the *centro*'s doors open and city eviction notices at bay. Most of the initial funds gained by the *centro* were for renovation and operating costs, not necessarily for funding staff positions. Ortega remarks that for at least the first seven years, "there was a lot of volunteering" due to a lack of funds and revenue. The city council continued its ambivalence about granting the *centro* more funds, and Roberto Maestas informed the city "that the Centro would attempt to continue its operation using existing volunteers and seeking alternative additional funds."[57] The *centro*'s funds were tied to city and federal programming, creating a situation in which the *centro* could afford approximately eight paid workers by 1975.[58] Indeed, into the early 1980s, the *centro* was still actively listing the federal Volunteers in Service to America (VISTA) program as one of its major sources of funds.[59] Regardless of the operating budget, Ortega was a custodian and secretary, and along with Tina Maestas, daughter of Roberto Maestas, Ortega opened a bookstore.[60] Volunteer labor ensured that these positions were created and staffed.

Volunteerism and institution building were two sides of the same coin for Gonzalez. She was part fund-raiser and part on-site volunteer during and following the October 1972 takeover. She juggled her classes at Evergreen, organized benefit lunches on the Olympia campus, and traveled back to Seattle to be a custodian and security guard at the *centro*.[61] Upon the conferral of her bachelor's degree, Gonzalez worked for the League of United Latin American Citizens (LULAC) while still volunteering for the *centro*'s ESL program. Gonzalez says volunteering for the ESL classes was significant and that "it became part of me." Through this personalization of the flagship ESL program, Gonzalez continued her dedication to social justice and revealed the extent to which her political identity was also her personal identity. The school, for Gonzalez, represented part of a larger goal to offer necessary services to Latinas/os in Seattle. Indeed, Gonzalez received her first paid position at El Centro in 1985.[62]

Chicanas also maneuvered and managed relationships while being activists, mothers, and partners. Gonzalez's becoming Chicana caused friction between her and her husband. While he was also involved in the movement and ECDLR, Gonzalez's husband expressed displeasure when her activism altered established home routines. Gonzalez managed these issues in two ways: she took her children with her to movement events, and she counseled her husband.[63] Whether it was at school or while being a security guard at the *centro*, Gonzalez integrated her politics with motherhood and vice versa. Gonzalez, similar to Ortega, attributed her continuous involvement in the movement, ECDLR, and her family to being a mother. That is, Gonzalez understood motherhood to be an asset in terms of multitasking and delegation, qualities essential for a stable family and an unyielding social justice mission.[64] By taking her children with her, Gonzalez was able to limit the amount of time spent away from her family. Defying prescribed gender roles entailed conflict when male privilege was undermined. Gonzalez's husband criticized her for attending meetings, which she countered through the application of straightforward logic to expose the flaw in his argument. Gonzalez's husband was also involved in the movement and the *centro*, and Gonzalez pointed out that his activism also took him away from the family. Gonzalez poignantly expressed how she helped her husband as she continually became Chicana. Gonzalez asked him, "Why are you feeling insecure? Why are you feeling threatened? Let's talk about it because I'm still going to do it [political action], whether you feel this way or not, I'm going to do it because I feel this is right for us." Not wanting to choose between marriage or activism, Gonzalez advised her husband through the process of becoming Chicana, helping him come to terms with alterations in gender relations that civil rights participation potentially catalyzed.[65] Gonzalez's use of "for us" in her response illuminates how she viewed her political engagements as bound to her personal and familial welfare. Such collective ideas also show the personal and societal gains of politicized gender identities, as the undoing of strictly enforced patriarchal systems created a space for alternative visions of society and family.

Gonzalez's refusal to dichotomize her activism and personal life formed a central component of Chicanas' intersecting struggles at ECDLR. This included multiple-insurgencies feminism, cross-racial solidarity, and Third Worldism. Early support for ECDLR was not limited to Chicanas/os and included Native Americans, blacks, whites, and East Asians. Indeed, ECDLR focused much more on cross-racial unity and Third Worldism than on questions of cultural national- ism or Aztlán.[66] When she first arrived at the Beacon Hill school in October 1972, Ortega was fond of the spruces, hemlocks, and Douglas firs, but she expressed much more admiration for the "sense of unity and welcoming by the people that were participating in the occupation," including Native Americans and African Americans.[67] This multiracial coalition also lobbied alongside Chicanas/os in city hall, demonstrated in part by black leader Larry Gossett's arrest by the Seattle police for his participation in a Chicana/o-led sit-in at city hall.[68] Seattle's low nonwhite population figures and interactions with the liberal state were part of the motivation and sustained willingness to work with other racial groups. In 1970, the city was home to approximately 77,000 people of color, including 10,000 Latinas/os who could be categorized as white by the US Census. Nonwhites were 14.5 percent of Seattle's total population, making the city slightly over 85 percent white.[69] According to Keo Capestany of the Washington State Commission on Hispanic Affairs, Chicanas/os also faced a problem of invisibility due to a lack of an ethnic Mexican or Latina/o neighborhood in the city. Third world coalitional politics in Seattle presented a philosophical and activist united front that coun- tered invisibility in an overwhelmingly white city while supporting the claims to space of other people of color.[70]

Chicana feminism at ECDLR named patriarchy and sexism as systems of oppression alongside racism, economic inequality, and US foreign policy. During seminars (open-floor meetings at ECDLR), Roberto Maestas and other members discussed global and local events. Ortega notes that sexism was debated at the insistence of Chicanas at the *centro* and Maestas as well. Indeed, Ortega, Maestas, and others encouraged Chicanas to broadcast their voices and have participants listen to Chicanas.[71] The opening of this speaking and listening space was critical to connect local events with global developments. The seminars were utilized by Chicanas to argue that systems of oppression and control including race, gen- der, class, and empire were interrelated. Chicanas were instrumental in shaping seminar discussions and prevented one analytic—whether race, gender, class, or Third Worldism—from taking precedence over other strategies and visions to combat oppressions. The insistence on intersectional and Third World frame- works reflected the histories and experiences of Ortega, Gonzalez, Miranda, and Aragon.

Estela Ortega's, Theresa Aragon's, and Graciela Gonzalez's Chicana political actions were demonstrative of nonseparatist feminism. None of the narrators expressed a sense of solidarity or identification with feminism, especially second-wave white feminism.[72] To identify as a feminist could be interpreted as being a turncoat, a Malinche, or as somebody who failed to uphold the virtues of the Chicano *familia*.[73] While each Chicana was involved in El Centro de la Raza when it hosted a Chicana conference in 1974, Ortega recalls how "the *centro* was actually criticized by the white women's movement because we specifically weren't highlighting 'women's issues,'" where such issues were understood as those impacting women only. Regarding the same conference, Gonzalez notes how some men felt unfairly excluded and seemingly could not understand the purpose for a Chicana conference.[74] Similarly, Aragon states, "The [white] women's movement was going . . . but that doesn't have anything to do with us. They were in some other world as far as we were concerned." Aragon goes on to say, "We had so far to go, and our issues were so much more immediate."[75] There was a disconnection between the proclamations broadcast by second-wave feminism as it reached Chicanas, whose interests were not confined to women but for whom gender inequality was one of several analytics in a nonsingular social and political landscape.

Between 1976 and 1977, the intersectional philosophy of Chicanas and El Centro de la Raza was codified in its "12 Principles" and the first issue of its newsletter, *Recobrando*, respectively. In 1976, ECDLR drafted and agreed on the underlying goals and mission of the *centro*.[76] The first five principles focused on redistribution of knowledge and services; elimination of institutional racism, sexism, and ageism; workers' rights; recapturing ethnic Mexican culture "without falling into ethnocentrism"; and cross-racial solidarity. Collectively, the first five principles were a multifaceted project that fused different political goals within one overarching organizational philosophy. The seventh principle stated a "struggle against all forms of racism, sexism, individualism, ageism, and violence in our work and our community center." This principle was a measure of the dialogues created by Chicanas at the *centro* as it focused on the day-to-day realities of work at the *centro* where Chicanas were a crucial arm of the labor force. The 1977 inaugural issue of ECDLR's newsletter, *Recobrando*, commemorated International Women's Day, and an editor forcefully argues, "The task then is one of educating all people to the fact that only through complete annihilation of institutionalized sexism and racism can we begin to totally uproot discrimination once and for all. We as women must not permit sexism or any other destructive weapon of this society to keep us from taking an active role in the struggles for the betterment of all people." The anonymous author furthers the analysis, stating that "the real cause of oppression [is] an inhumane society based on maximum profit."[77] Balancing numerous political projects remained complex, with or without the twelve principles adopted by ECDLR. Yet the balance exercised by Aragon, Ortega, Miranda, and Gonzalez demonstrated the powerful and revolutionary weaving of becoming Chicana within an organization to advance an intersectional politics that was expansive in its naming and recognition of multiple oppressions.

CONCLUSION

Chicana activism operated and shaped numerous facets of El Centro de la Raza, where becoming Chicana was profoundly critical for individual politicization and day-to-day operations. Becoming Chicana was a process that encompassed personal histories that predated ECDLR and was crucial to the foundational philosophies of the *centro*. It entailed a large measure of unacknowledged and unpaid labor for building a community institution, labor that was visually symbolized in Daniel DeSiga's 1997 repainting of the central mural. It was political labor that Chicanas believed in, labor that was an expression of their zeal for the movement and the dismantling of inequality with Latinas/os and other communities. Chicanas restructured parts of their lives and those of their families to interlace spheres into one another rather than segregate them into false divisions. Chicanas at El Centro de la Raza may inspire readers in rethinking not only whether to listen to this history, but also how to focus our archival lenses and guide epistemologies.

10 THE SPACE IN BETWEEN
EXPLORING THE DEVELOPMENT OF CHICANA FEMINIST THOUGHT IN CENTRAL TEXAS

BRENDA SENDEJO

This would be a place where we could make it a non-profit, but also a printing enterprise, a publishing enterprise . . . where we could encourage women to do more research and where women could work in the community and at the university. In the movement we had a lot of examples of things, organizations that were more flexible, that could work in the community and work in the university, and that's what we wanted: a space in between.

—MARTHA COTERA, 2014

It is clear that Chicanas must continue to research and document the realities of their experience. Until Chicanas begin to document and publish these realities from a Chicana perspective, historians will continue to ignore the contribution of Chicanas and other social scientists will continue to distort the image of la mujer Chicana. . . . *The Chicana Research and Learning Center intends to continue to research and document the Chicana experience and invites* nuestras hermanas y hermanos *to join us in this task.*

—EVEY CHAPA, *LA MUJER CHICANA*

A number of years ago my path intersected with that of a Chicana spiritual activist.[1] This chance encounter impacted me so profoundly that it came to inspire my current life's work. The journey from then to now has fulfilled me immensely. Along the way I have met numerous Chicana activists and intellectuals who shared their lives, wisdom, and knowledge with me so that I could more deeply understand the complex and dynamic relations between spirituality, gender, race, and feminism. These *feministas* and their unwavering commitments to justice facilitated my own feminist development, broadened my scholarly knowledge, shaped my teaching of Chicana feminisms, and deepened my understandings of my own South Texas upbringing. In this essay I explore such Chicana feminist *conocimientos*—the production and transmission of knowledge that is put into practice in the service of justice—by way of a pivotal enterprise in the development of Chicana feminist thought and Chicana studies: the Chicana Research and Learning Center (CRLC) in Austin.[2]

I was introduced to the CRLC by its cofounder, the feminist intellectual and activist Martha P. Cotera,[3] who played a pivotal role in creating Chicana studies. I conducted oral histories with Cotera and poured over materials from the CRLC and Cotera archives in my quest to study the center. Much to my surprise, over the course of my research I learned that Cotera's work with the CRLC and that of others actually set the stage for me to enter the field of Chicana studies and to teach a course on Chicanas at the University of Texas at Austin during graduate school. A serendipitous discovery in the archives involving the course, Cotera, and Gloria E. Anzaldúa would provide a glimpse into a genealogy of Chicana knowledge and research that was previously unknown to me. What I found revealed an interconnected web of historical moments and feminist moves involving the exchange of knowledge passed on through generations of Chicanas that is generative and fluid and persists today, as evidenced in the making of this very essay and anthology.

The impact and imprint of the CRLC is significant; it played a critical role in contributing to the production of Chicana feminist thought through its focus on scholarship and curricula by and about Chicanas in the United States. The center facilitated Chicana feminist thinking and theorizing that manifested in countless cultural productions—scholarly, spiritual, literary, artistic, and other—during the early 1970s and in the decades to follow. I examine this development of Chicana feminist thought that inspired such cultural productions and the conditions under which it emerged in the organizing strategies of Chicanas in the Central Texas region in the 1970s, particularly in Austin, a key site for Chicana feminist organizing. Informed by and at times in conjunction with universities, community-based groups, and political organizing efforts such as Mujeres por La Raza Unida (the women's caucus of La Raza Unida Party), and the University of Texas, the CRLC laid the groundwork for a specific genealogy of feminist and political thought that helped to shape Chicana feminist praxis in Central Texas and thereby influenced the work of future generations of scholars and community activists around the nation, including myself.[4]

During the Chicana/o *movimiento*, the CRLC served as a vital space, as Cotera states, "in between" academia and community. The purpose of the CRLC was to "seek and identify problems faced by the minority community and Hispanic women, in particular, in an effort to develop and demonstrate innovative and/ or alternative methods to deal with these problems."[5] Such problems included underemployment, poverty, and barriers to education.[6] The center actively promoted Chicana leadership development and assisted women in overcoming educational and social constraints. Incorporated as a nonprofit in 1973, the CRLC actively engaged in extensive publishing projects, grassroots training, and advocacy that involved compiling and conducting research on the development of women from 1974 to 1999.[7] The CRLC enacted a Chicana feminist praxis in its conception, administration, and mission. It was the first research and service project in the nation founded and run by and for Mexican American women.

It operated with the assistance of a small staff and board composed of women and numerous volunteers, including Chicana/o students from UT.[8]

CRLC founders and volunteers worked to create a space where early secondary sources on Chicana history could be researched, utilized, and disseminated—not just within universities but also in the community.[9] As I will elaborate upon further, this process of producing and transmitting knowledge was collaborative in that CRLC cofounders Martha Cotera and Evey Chapa drew from their own academic knowledge and shared it with university classes and in various community settings.[10] They also used curricula developed by Austin educators and other research by local organizations on women as well as information compiled by Chicana feminists around the country.

The CRLC worked dialogically to produce knowledge through collaborating with school districts, libraries, numerous universities, local newspapers, youth programs, churches, women's networks, male and female writers, activists, and other groups and individuals. Cotera, Chapa, and CRLC staff compiled a database consisting of bibliographies and other information on Hispanic women and made these resources available widely through the CRLC's Multicultural Women's Database and Information Services in Austin. The CRLC circulated information to dozens of schools and universities, community organizations, and other entities at their request. The database included "biographies and a wide diversity of statistical factual and historical information for the use of educators, research organizations and grass roots institutions. Focus of the database is women of color, but the service also includes other ethic and racial groups of women in the United States."[11]

CRLC staff presented free communication and assertiveness workshops to groups such as the Lone-Star Girl Scout Council Minority Girls Program, Mexican American Business and Professional Women of Austin, and the Stay in School Program for Hispanic Girls at Austin Independent School District. Information requested was also used in education curriculum guides, textbooks, community trainings, and movie productions. Requests for bibliographic material on Hispanic women came from entities such as the Bay Area Bilingual Education League, Maryland's Radio Project on Immigrant Women, Oakland's Campesina Curriculum and Training program, and KUT radio's *Mexican American Experience* program. Cotera gave dozens of class lectures and speeches at universities including St. Edward's, Texas Women's University, Texas Tech, and UT El Paso and at colleges in Colorado, California, Arizona, and elsewhere. She spoke at library studies, Chicana/o, and civil rights symposiums as well as at the Texas Women's Political Caucus and US Commission for Civil Rights in Baltimore. Cotera also would give hundreds of community presentations at area high schools, middle schools, churches, and libraries. Her community-building efforts were as prolific as her scholarship, which is vast.

The CRLC interwove theory and practice into and between what are typically understood as Chicano movement initiatives, exemplifying the Chicana *movidas* discussed by the editors in their introduction to this volume. Through their collaborative research and learning model, the CRLC played a critical role in the development of Chicana feminism and the creation of Chicana and Chicano studies. As active participants in the Chicana feminist movement and La Raza Unida Party (RUP), Cotera and Chapa recognized the need to document and disseminate information on women. The CRLC implemented this model through research and the sharing of resources that epitomized its work. Providing access to information and establishing connections with groups and organizations as opposed to individualist models of organizing is emblematic of a genealogy of Chicana feminist praxis that disrupts the chronology and dominant narrative of the Chicano *movimiento* and historiographies that omit Chicana intellectual contributions of the mid- to late 1970s, thereby rendering such work invisible. The CRLC model also challenges feminist movement narratives that erase women of color feminist roots, minimize their lived experiences, and position their contributions to feminism and feminist thought as tangential and/or nonexistent in first- and second-wave feminist historiographies. The work of the CRLC also shows that women-of-color feminist resistance is distinct from other forms of feminist resistance in its emphasis on praxis. The centrality of collaboration is key to this praxis within women of color feminist knowledge production. It can be seen in the different models of organizing, as in the numerous connections the CRLC forged with the community and university and between the CRLC and scholars like Cotera, Chapa, and Gloria Anzaldúa. This particular form of theorizing and praxis challenges static categories such as second- and third-wave feminism by underscoring the fluidity of Chicana feminist thought production and its commitment to societal change. Furthermore, it emphasizes a differential consciousness,[12] which transcends a solely oppositional stance by connecting feminist theories to the very material struggles they aim to examine and transform. This "theory in the flesh" is evident in work that characterizes many Chicana and other women of color feminist expressions and experiences, including the CRLC.[13]

While some argue that the *movimiento* ended in the 1970s, I view the CRLC as a generative political project in the subsequent continuation of the *movimiento*. The knowledge produced by and with the center and its directors has been utilized, theorized, and elaborated upon in subsequent decades.[14] This includes influences upon the generation of scholars following Cotera and Chapa, such as cultural theorist Gloria E. Anzaldúa, Nez Perce and Tejana scholar and poet Inés Hernández-Ávila (previously Inés Tovar) and Chicana writer Carmen Tafolla. The work of Cotera, Chapa, and the CRLC extended beyond the Chicana and Chicano movements in time frame and scope. These Chicana intellectuals contributed to both movements and later drew on organizing strategies they honed as movement participants to establish a historical legacy of collaborative feminist thought and praxis that continues today.[15]

A BRIDGE BETWEEN THE ACADEMY AND THE COMMUNITY: THE CHICANA RESEARCH AND LEARNING CENTER

During the period of the Chicano movement and in subsequent years, Texas Chicanas—like their peers in other states and at times in conjunction with them—produced literary and cultural works that documented their material circumstances as gendered, racialized, queer, and poor women. These materials contributed to the proliferation of Chicana feminist thought and culture in a web of interconnected actors and activists, organizations and initiatives that explored, constituted, and questioned "feminism." Examining this web reveals the relations between the Chicano and Chicana feminist movements, the CRLC, a bourgeoning field of Chicana studies, and a Chicana feminist genealogy of which Chapa and Cotera are part. Indeed, Cotera and Chapa drew on their backgrounds in education as well as their organizing experience as active participants in the Chicana feminist movement and RUP in their work of writing and compiling histories and producing curricula on Mexican American women. Both were committed to using knowledge in the service of raising awareness and improving the material conditions of Chicana/o communities. Hence, their approach was to bring together the CRLC and institutions such as universities. Cotera's reflection underscores the space they sought to create and the fluid nature of these partnerships: "As we merged with mainstream institutions. . . . Sometimes it's difficult to figure out where the community ends and the university begins."[16] According to Cotera, there was a sense of urgency that spurred this process of collaborative knowledge production:

> [The CRLC] was a way of resolving an issue that we felt was going to take a long time to be resolved at and by the university [of Texas]. What we were doing was— the organic part—taking information that was developed and being developed and putting it into a research model . . . [in] developing a research database of information that could be accessed by the community as needed but also by the university in order to speed up its development of Chicana and Chicano studies.[17]

The fluidity of the Chicana feminist praxis of which Cotera speaks is evident in the CRLC's dual purpose of conducting research that contributed to Chicana/o studies and employing such research in training programs on Chicana-based issues. Cotera recalls that they set out to "gather materials that would support the research we were doing in feminist studies and supply information to others."[18] To this effect, Cotera would compile substantial amounts of historical information on the history of Chicanas. She and Chapa published not just academic works but booklets on the study of Chicanas that they distributed in information packets to community groups.[19] The packets and pamphlets were important in that they were easy and quick ways to distribute information to a wider audience with a shorter production period than academic publications, enabling more efficient efforts toward politicizing and raising the consciousness of their target audience. The democratization of knowledge is another important contribution of early Chicana feminists.[20]

Cotera's and Chapa's efforts to gather materials and make them accessible resonated in college classrooms as well. Early courses on Chicanas at UT and elsewhere drew from writings by Cotera, Chapa, and others. The CRLC engaged in knowledge production as a political project, aligning with similar Chicana feminist efforts within and beyond university settings across the nation to raise awareness of gender inequality and sexism.[21] They and other Chicanas were at the forefront in producing writings that "chronicled struggles for social justice,"[22] largely in print materials such as the periodicals *Encuentro Femenil*, *Tejidos*, *Hijas de Cuauhtémoc*, *Regeneración*, and *Caracol*. While Chicanas had not yet made it into the publishing spaces of their white female or Chicano male counterparts, these sources made it possible for their voices to be heard and messages disseminated.[23] The importance of these early works is evidenced by the fact that they continue to be invoked by Chicana feminist scholars thirty-five years later.[24] These are the kinds of works included in the CRLC's repository of sources, which shows that Chicanas were producing feminist writings that spoke to the issues of the times and doing so, to a large extent, nationwide. They also represented the connections between Chicanas on a national scale, as with California-based Chicana feminist Anna NietoGomez and Martha Cotera, who reference each other's works in their early writings. Cotera articulates the strategic cross-referencing between her and NietoGomez as a Chicana feminist praxis.

> We were close . . . you know, in spirit. And we invited her to write a lot for Texas journals because it gave us a way to compare and a way for our guys . . . and our community . . . to feel that we were mainstream in the movement. And California was always seen as very progressive, as a model for progress, and it put us in that league. And we could justify our attitudes and our intellectual position when we would have them in our journals as well. It was good for us to have.[25]

Cotera notes that the CRLC was inspired by the work of feminists in California such as Anna NietoGomez and others.[26] Print materials developed and disseminated by Chicanas in California proved valuable to Tejana feminists, and they in return drew on the materials created by Cotera and the CRLC—another illustration of the collaborative model of women of color and Chicana feminist thought.[27]

Cotera understood the importance of documenting history so that it could be accessed by community members and researchers. She says the CRLC "emerged from the interaction with all the feminist writing that was going on nationally. There was an informal network. However, a lot of our writing was done through Chicano magazines—ephemeral because they were not being collected seriously, and it was very vulnerable to disappearing."[28]

"THE SPACE IN BETWEEN": AN EMBLEM OF CHICANA FEMINIST PRAXIS

The Chicana Research and Learning Center undertook a form of knowledge production and provided access to resources and trainings that together constituted Chicana feminist praxis and the "space in between" of which Cotera speaks. Such initiatives positioned Austin as a key site for numerous Chicano movement activities and initiatives, including Chicana feminist organizing and the infusing of feminist thought into practice, which was, in part, due to the CRLC. When Chicanas entered universities for the first time and learned new theories, histories, and concepts, many activists did not just use the knowledge for their own gain; they used it in the service of others to help improve the living and working conditions of Chicanas/os and their families and communities. This intersectionality of knowledge, academic and community-based, suggests that theories not only emerge from the material realities of Chicana lives but are then put into practice, a characteristic of Chicana feminism since its earliest inception. To this effect Cotera and others at CRLC demonstrated their commitment to the liberation of all women—sexual, social, economic, political—all of which were women's issues. Cotera states that as a feminist project, the CRLC aimed to

> recruit and politicize large numbers of women to work on them [issues] (on intergenerational basis); and we needed for all communities of all races and ethnicities to be politicized on women's issues. We especially wanted educational institutions to be politicized and responsive, which is why CRLC focused on developing information on women of all ethnicities and races, and why we focused on sharing them with educators and community organizations focused on education.[29]

This reflection points to the inclusive nature of Chicana feminism. Trainings and outreach efforts often provided space for all women, and those directed toward serving Hispanic women were noted as benefiting "the Hispanic female population (Cuban, Puerto Rican, Mexican American, Central and South American, Spanish and other women of Caribbean descent)."[30] To that effect neither Chicana feminism nor its praxis was then or is now homogeneous,[31] just as Chicanas, of course, possess various political, gender, spiritual, and feminist beliefs. While the CRLC was clearly a Chicana feminist enterprise, organizing also took place within various other initiatives and groups throughout the *movimiento* in Austin. They influenced Chicana feminists and women who disidentify with feminists (whom Anna NietoGomez conceptualizes as "loyalists")[32] involved in groups at UT and in the larger Austin community, including the Mexican American Youth Organization (MAYO), La Raza Unida Party, Chicanos Artistas Sirviendo a Aztlán (CASA), Teatro Chicano de Austin,[33] and *danza conchera* groups such as Xinachtli,[34] all of which had members who were connected in one way or another to the CRLC and/or Chapa and Cotera. This heterogeneity informed organizing efforts of that period and laid the groundwork for Chicana feminist formations that would follow in subsequent decades—in healing and women's groups, in the academy through mentoring and activist pedagogies and research, in spiritual practices, in community organizing, and in documentation and collection of Chicana histories. The efforts mark a continuity of feminist praxis that was not developed solely for academic purposes and as such is a continuation of the mission of the CRLC. Such praxis was employed for feminist consciousness raising and political activism that helped garner more rights and resources for women and greater attention to their needs and the needs of their families and communities.

In addition to developing and circulating Chicana/Mexicana intellectual histories, the CRLC identified and addressed Chicana educational, reproductive health, and economic needs and provided various job-training workshops. More than 500 women would participate in trainings and workshops offered by the CRLC. These included *concientización y desarollo de la mujer* (consciousness raising and development for women) and Chicana-organized bilingual, bicultural demonstration projects.[35] Programs also included human resource trainings to help equip women to address the multiple oppressions they faced relating to race, gender, and class and Chicana assertiveness. An especially noteworthy program that highlighted intercultural communication was the program Doña Doormat No Está Aquí, an original model developed through the use of secondary research that outlined values and communication styles specific to Chicanas/os.[36] Women were trained to recognize the difference between Anglo and Chicana styles so they could be more effective communicators within their families, at work, and in the community. They emphasized the need for appropriate bilingual and bicultural education models and for programs that considered socialization patterns of Chicanas, such as stereotypes around the confusion of social condition with "culture." The center was also a repository for information on Chicana political activities, conferences, and various statewide efforts. All of these social action efforts resulted in CRLC's connection to the US Civil Rights Commission and the Texas Manpower Commission as well as support by the Women's Educational Equity Act Program of the US Department of Education. The CRLC served an important role during the War on Poverty era in its programming that addressed issues like poverty, unemployment, and low educational attainment.[37] Such instances of Chicana feminist activism undertaken by the CRLC illuminate the intersections of the Chicano movement, Chicana feminism, and the development of Chicana studies.

IMPACT OF THE CRLC ON THE DEVELOPMENT OF CHICANA FEMINIST ACTIVISM IN TEXAS

To better understand the important transgenerational linkages between the work of the Chicana Research and Learning Center and contemporary Chicana feminist praxis, we must first excavate the context of production that shaped the aims of the center as well as its political investments. That a community research project like the CRLC emerged in Austin is no surprise, given that it is a university town that drew Chicana/o students from all over Texas. Mexican Americans entered universities en masse from the late 1960s to the mid-1970s. In Texas, they were drawn to the UT Austin campus because of its status as the state's flagship university. Chapa's connections as a student and Cotera's connections as a librarian poised the CRLC to influence the production and dissemination of knowledge at UT Austin during this formative period, impacting the consciousness of many first-generation Chicana and Chicano college students.[38] For example, students learned about the history of the colonization of the Americas and of Mexican American indigenous heritage. Through the source material of the CRLC students came to know the pantheon of goddesses in Nahua culture, including the earth goddess, Tonantzin, a lineage Cotera details extensively in her widely cited work *Diosa y Hembra: The History and Heritage of Chicanas in the US.*[39] These materials, coupled with students' personal experiences, resulted in a heightened sense of self-awareness and self-worth that would fuel the student movement and Chicana feminist movement. Cotera's contributions and legacy in particular are vast.

Through her leadership and legacy Cotera has helped to maintain the structural, intellectual, and feminist integrity of Chicana feminism over the decades. About the emergence of Chicana studies, Cynthia Orozco, in the foreword to Acosta and Winegarten's volume *Las Tejanas: 300 Years of History*, notes Cotera's influence and that of *Diosa y Hembra* as "the first survey of Chicana history. Cotera's pioneering work inspired the few Tejanas at Texas colleges and universities with the awareness that we had a past specific to ethnicity, race, religion and gender."[40] Indeed, Cotera has made countless contributions to and helped establish Chicana feminism and Chicana/o studies through her research, writings, political activism, speeches, panels, conference presentations, archival work, curriculum development, and mentorship of numerous Chicana and Chicano graduate students in her more than fifty years of feminist theorizing and practice. In addition to participating in the feminist and education reform initiatives of the *movimiento*, Cotera helped to open Juárez-Lincoln University—a Chicano university—in Austin. She has been active in local and statewide politics and community activism and has continued her work as a scholar, archivist, and feminist historian. She was a founding member of numerous organizations and was instrumental in creating the Mexican American Library program of the Benson Latin American Collection at UT Austin and the Mexican American Cultural Center in Austin.

While Cotera was the first to document the history of Chicanas in print with the notable *Diosa y Hembra*, her repertoire of works also includes numerous essays and bibliographies that even preceded (and likely informed) this foundational text and speaks to her pioneering work in the fields of Chicano and Chicana studies. Those works were intended to provide resources not only for scholars in the growing field of Chicana/o studies but also for wider audiences, particularly in the public schools such as those in Austin and Crystal City, Texas.

Her works include the reference document "Annotated List of the Chicano in History and the Social Sciences," published in 1973.[41] In that same year she produced "Educator's Guide to Chicano Resources."[42] The arduous tasks of researching and compiling information for these early works were but a few of Martha Cotera's numerous contributions to feminist thinking and studies.

One of Cotera's better-known works and an important contribution to Chicana studies and the study of Chicana feminism is *The Chicana Feminist* (1977). This collection of Cotera's essays and speeches addressed various concerns of Chicanas in Texas at the time and includes works from as early as 1972, including her essay "Feminism as We See It." This compilation reflects her thinking and observations of feminism in the context of the Chicana/o movements and documents feminism as a part of the history and heritage of Chicanas. The book was a vital component of the Tejana feminist movement, laying the groundwork and activist history that would inspire Tejanas in the Chicana feminist movement. As Acosta and Winegarten state, because Cotera was writing while engaging in political activism and feminist causes, her writings reflect what was occurring and how she experienced those events as they occurred.[43] Her work offers us a rich repository of the history of Tejana social justice and civil rights history and of women's participation in and contributions to Chicana feminist thought and praxis.

Cotera's influence has continued in her work as a writer, community activist, grassroots organizer, and researcher.[44] Her support of Chicana studies and students—including younger generations of feminist scholars such as myself to produce Chicana feminist works—has extended to spending countless hours sharing her life story and immense knowledge. Cotera's role in creating Chicana studies, producing and circulating Chicana feminist writings, and contributing to the development of future Chicana feminists cannot be overemphasized. In fact, any history of the Chicana movement or Chicana studies in Texas is incomplete without a mention of Cotera and her numerous and vital contributions.

RESEARCH AND CURRICULUM DEVELOPMENT AS CHICANA FEMINIST PRAXIS

In response to what they believed to be a lack of published resources on Chicanas, Martha Cotera and Evey Chapa produced a large volume of writings on the history and heritage of Chicanas and their involvement in Chicano movement politics. The works served as an early foundation for the emergence of Chicana feminist thought. A central effort of the CRLC was the extensive volume *La Mujer Chicana: An Annotated Bibliography*, which was compiled by Cotera and edited by Chapa. The bibliography illustrated this formative period in which Chicanas built a body of writings about their own experiences in the form of speeches and magazine and journal essays in Texas and California, among other places. Chapa cites *La Mujer Chicana* as the first attempt by Chicanas to "compile information in a comprehensive manner for classroom use." She goes on to state that "such a work is essential in the effort to produce a solid research base and hence a positive step towards documenting the Chicana experience."[45] *La Mujer Chicana* came about as a response to a lack of sources on and to stereotypical representations of Chicanas, to address a void "concerning Chicanas and to rectify the stereotypes developed about Chicanas."[46]

Both Chapa and Cotera produced nationally recognized bibliographies of Mexican American women's writings and important works on Chicana participation in the political realm during the Chicano movement. Cotera herself produced more than 100 works on Chicana feminism. Cotera's immense influence was evident not only in the breadth of the histories she uncovered and recovered through engaging with the historical work of Mexican scholars and offering groundbreaking analyses on Chicana feminist heritage but also in the fact that her works—particularly *Diosa y Hembra*—are regularly cited in contemporary Chicana feminist scholarship.

The CRLC publishing component produced a number of works provided at-cost to grassroots organizations and educators. These include *La Mujer Chicana* (1976), *Multicultural Women's Sourcebook: Materials Guide for Use in Women's Studies and Bilingual Multicultural Programs* (1982),[47] Las Fundadoras slide and tape kit on Hispanic women's history (1983), and materials for the assertiveness and communications skills program Doña Doormat No Está Aquí (1984).[48] The CRLC supported and contributed to these important feminist initiatives, which developing scholars at nearby UT would make use of.

As the CRLC's major publication effort, *La Mujer Chicana* is an example of Chicana feminist initiatives that are crucial to an understanding of how feminist thought developed during this period and in Texas. The importance of sources like the bibliography is that they shed light on the social positions of Chicanas and the political terrain of the period as it pertained to women. The extensive 320-source annotated bibliography was compiled and edited with the assistance of CRLC staff and volunteers. It is the result of an information and literature survey conducted by the CRLC in an effort to examine research conducted on the realities of Chicanas shortly following the Chicano movement and the development of the Chicana feminist movement. The bibliography was produced in response to a large number of requests made to the CRLC for information about Chicanas and in response to Chicanas working to establish themselves in women's studies and Chicano studies programs on campuses nationwide. As Chapa states in the introduction, the intent behind *La Mujer Chicana* was twofold: "to provide information sources to those who are interested in reading about or researching *la mujer Chicana*, and to serve as a classroom guide for those who are involved in Chicana Studies."[49] The bibliography provides detailed information on what works were being produced, by whom, and in what formats and what issues and topics they discussed. Chapa writes that the majority of the publications fall under the category of periodicals and "represent a major portion of the documentation which has been produced by Chicanas concerning Chicanas." She states that the journal entries represent the earliest efforts to focus on the issues of Chicanas in a concentrated manner, with the survey indicating that such activities began in 1971.[50]

The largest subject area in the bibliography is "Chicana Feminism y El Movimiento," indicative of the popularity of the subject by Chicana researchers and writers on the topic, which was of particular relevance at that time. Chapa writes that most entries in that section are articles that appeared in Chicana or Chicano publications. She goes on to state that those sources that were collected for inclusion in the bibliography focus on Chicana activism and that some of the major problems Chicanas faced dealt with stereotypes perpetuated by Anglos and misunderstandings on the part of Chicanos. Several sources distinguish the Chicana movement from the women's liberation movement and indicate a need for men and women to work together in the common struggle against oppression.

La Mujer Chicana comprised sections that represented relevant Chicana issues and, importantly, solutions to problems faced by Chicanas. The section titled "Education" documents challenges within education.[51] The "History" section includes sources predating the 1960s and is, interestingly, limited in terms of materials on Chicanas. This supports Cotera's and Chapa's contention of the need for Chicana studies and the importance of their work. "Labor/Employment" addresses themes of Chicana involvement in boycotts and strikes and the challenges in obtaining employment equality. "La Cultura" addresses Chicanas' involvement in literature. "La Familia" includes a substantial number of studies on Mexican American family issues that were conducted by Anglo researchers. Chapa notes that Chicana and Chicano researchers were in the process of challenging "stereotypic and ethnocentric perspectives being utilized by many researchers in their studies of *la familia Chicana*."[52] Other sections include "Machismo," "Politics," "Welfare," "Religion," and "Social Issues" such as "Prison" and "Sex-Role Stereotyping." Another important inclusion in the annotated bibliography is a section called "Third World Women." This is yet another indication of the CRLC's efforts to reach across racial and ethnic experiences, as was the *Multicultural Women's Sourcebook*. Chapa concedes that *La Mujer Chicana* was limited by the survey's emphasis on Chicanas. Nevertheless, Chapa acknowledges that Latinas and Mexicanas share similar roots with Chicanas and therefore are included throughout the bibliography rather than in the "Third World Women" section. Chapa states that until Chicanas write their own histories and document their own lived realities, the image of *la mujer* Chicana would continue to be distorted.[53]

Elaborating on the earlier point around urgency, Cotera's statement that she and collaborators "were desperate to document" Chicana feminist thought and initiatives illustrates also the desire to do so as they were developing on the ground, before the history of all of the conferences and other important events that were happening were lost.[54] This was one of the main inspirations behind

Cotera's writing of *Diosa y Hembra*.[55] According to Cotera, the center emphasized the creation of secondary sources that would document the history of Chicanas: "One of our purposes for the center was resources, and that's why we did secondary resources primarily, was because it was taking too long to build up the archive at the Benson [Collection at UT]. . . . We wanted it for people like Inés Tovar who were working on their PhDs."[56] Here Cotera references the goal of the center to support Chicana academics seeking their doctorates, such as Hernández-Ávila, who would also teach the Chicana course and go on to be a professor of Native American studies.[57]

THE GENEALOGY OF CHICANA STUDIES IN TEXAS: THE CRLC AND THE CHICANA COURSE

Chicana feminist organizing from the 1970s through the 1990s often went hand in hand with the production of writings, research, and curricula that articulated, analyzed, and made known the material circumstances of Chicana life. Such realities included subjugation but also agency and resistance, as seen through cultural productions such as print materials by Chicanas that would serve as the foundation of Chicana feminist thought. Not surprisingly, the CRLC's *La Mujer Chicana* annotated bibliography cites the development of Chicana studies as "one of the most viable solutions" to the problems Chicanas were facing in the area of education, such as a lack of materials and courses on Chicanas and Chicana representation in colleges and universities.[58] In "Getting Started in Chicana Studies" (1986) Cynthia Orozco observes, "For the most part, writings by and about Chicanas arose in the context of community struggles and/or the institution of Chicano Studies. Both the Chicano movement and the Chicana movement stimulated Chicana writings and much of this writing was connected to the institutions of Chicano Studies."[59] She asserts that Chicana writings were not published by (white) women's presses but rather Chicano presses and organizations and that such writings appeared in "newspapers, newsletters, pamphlets, and small press publications."[60] Cotera's and Chapa's urgency to get materials out quickly is understood in context of Orozco's sentiment that most Chicana writings would exist in Chicano libraries on or off campus and never make it to mainstream college and university libraries, which showed little interest in Mexican Americans.[61] Orozco states that the bibliography created by the CRLC was one of the best three bibliographies put out in 1976 and the only from Texas. She also links the production of Chicana academic writings to the number of Chicana and Latina PhDs, which were scarce at that time.[62] A proliferation of Chicana writings exists today thanks to an increase in Chicanas and Latinas earning PhDs.

During her time as CRLC executive director, Evey Chapa studied education in graduate school at UT. There she taught the first course on Chicanas during the spring of 1975, forging the connection between academia and community that was at the core of the CRLC's mission. Chapa, in her roles at UT, and Cotera, as a bibliographer for the Benson Collection at the time, were instrumental in garnering community support for the inclusion of the course on Chicanas. Given that *La Mujer Chicana* was produced the year after Chapa first taught the Mujer Chicana course at UT Austin in 1975, it is likely that Chapa's development of the course coincided with the production and publication of the bibliography compiled by Cotera and edited by Chapa and that the two mutually informed one another in some way(s).

Another Chicana doctoral student, Gloria Anzaldúa, would follow Chapa in teaching the course two years later, in the spring of 1977, while pursuing her doctoral degree in literature.[63] Anzaldúa was inspired to begin work on the groundbreaking anthology *This Bridge Called My Back: Writings by Radical Women of Color* as a result of having a lack of sources from which to draw in order to teach her course on Chicanas at UT Austin.[64] The immense influence Anzaldúa would come to have on Chicana studies and Chicana feminism led me to consider connections between her experience in preparing the curriculum for the Chicana course and her future work.

As noted by María Cotera, *This Bridge* is often mistakenly cited as the first work of women of color theory and practice; thus it erases the foundational work of scholar activists like Cotera, Chapa, and NietoGomez that preceded its publication.[65] This brings me back to the discovery in the archives that connects the CRLC to the creation of Chicana studies and provides evidence of intersectional feminism among Chicanas that predates *This Bridge*.

Anzaldúa's course files are housed in her archives at the Benson, the same place Cotera worked in helping to build the Mexican American Library Program during her time with the CRLC. Anzaldúa's files indicate that she drew from many of the materials gathered by the CRLC from the print culture of Chicana feminists of that era for her course readings.[66] A section of Anzaldúa's course syllabus titled "La Chicana Feminista and the Women's Liberation Movement" included works by Chicanas including Anna NietoGomez, Enriqueta Longeaux y Vásquez, and another activist intellectual of particular relevance to this essay, Martha Cotera.

As I examined the archives, the connections between the CRLC, Cotera, and Anzaldúa became surprisingly clear. The archives indicate that Anzaldúa taught the course as Ethnic Studies 375 (ETS 375) for the Center for Mexican American Studies in spring 1977. At that time it was titled La Chicana in America. The course description read, "An exploration into the aspects of being mujer via a three fold approach: social-political-historical, psychological-philosophical, and aesthetic; some questions considered: the Chicana's roles in the Chicano movement; the feminist movement; the Chicana's involvement in literature, drama and art; the Chicana's delineation by religion, film, journalism, and radio."[67] I was stunned to see that her course syllabus notes an early reading assignment: "Cotera-Diosa y Hembra—p. 1–54." Anzaldúa drew on Cotera's writings in her class. Cotera's *Diosa y Hembra* was published in May prior to that spring. It is one of only a handful of works by Chicanas that Anzaldúa included in her syllabus, likely due to the lack of availability of such sources.[68] But it signaled Anzaldúa's recognition of the importance of *Diosa y Hembra* as the first real history of Chicanas in the United States. In fact, her lecture notes also indicate an influence by Cotera: "Feminism—as a very dynamic aspect of the Chicana heritage, & not foreign to her nature. According to Marta Cotera 'the Mexicana has a long and wonderful history of Mexicano Feminism which is not Anglo inspired, imposed or oriented'—Lots of heroines, activists, armed rebels, adelitas—that Chicanas can

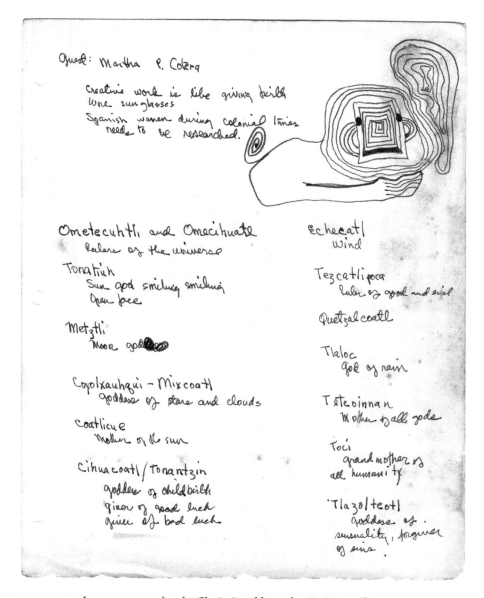

FIGURE 10.1. Lecture notes taken by Gloria Anzaldúa in her La Mujer Chicana course, 1977. "Guest: Martha P. Cotera" by Gloria E. Anzaldúa. Courtesy of Gloria E. Anzaldúa Literary Trust.

emulate."[69] The inclusion of *Diosa y Hembra* in Anzaldúa's syllabus suggests that Chicana feminist thought being produced outside the academy was circulated in the classroom. Another inclusion in the archives is a document titled "Cotera Lecture," notes handwritten by Anzaldúa (figure 10.1). Anzaldúa's notes are from a visit Cotera paid to Anzaldúa's class.[70] They include short descriptions of deities from the Aztec pantheon, including "Coyolxauhqui-Mixcoatl, goddess of the stars and clouds," "Coatlique, Mother of the Sun," and "Cihuacoatl/Tonantzin, Goddess of childbirth, giver of good luck, giver of bad luck," among other notations.[71] These notes provocatively suggest that Anzaldúa's attention to female deities in *Borderlands/La Frontera* may well have been influenced by Cotera's work.

These exchanges between Chapa, Anzaldúa, and Cotera, and by extension the CRLC, are indicative of the linkages and collaboration that characterize the genealogy of Chicana feminist praxis. This genealogy also includes the work of the CRLC in making available resources such as scholarship on Chicanas to the UT Austin Center for Mexican American Studies by way of PhD students who taught the course on Chicanas such as Chapa and Anzaldúa. Through the CRLC, Cotera and Chapa made available works that addressed race, class, and gender to feminists like Anzaldúa, who would come to expand feminist thought by theorizing lesbian and multicultural women's experiences. However, these linkages reverberate beyond Anzaldúa, as illustrated by my own experience teaching the course in 2007 and 2008.

When I taught the course some thirty years after it was offered by Chapa, Hernández Ávila, and Anzaldúa, it was called La Chicana: Ethnicity and Gender. However, this historical legacy was unknown to me until I made the connections in the archives. Unlike my predecessors, but in many ways *because* of them, I am fortunate to have rich sources on Chicana history, theory, and praxis readily available to me; central among them are foundational works by Anzaldúa and Cotera. Their work not only informs my own thinking and writing on the decolonial and liberatory potential of spiritual activism but has in many ways enabled its very existence. The genealogy reverberates with my students, the next generation profoundly impacted by Chicana feminism—a continuity that is testament to the potency and generative character of Chicana feminist thought.

The Chicana course at UT Austin offers an intriguing glance into the process by which foundational research produced by Chicana feminists outside the academy was incorporated into the newly forming field of Chicana studies. This community-university connection demonstrates how feminist thinking that was being inserted into the classroom would intersect and interweave with influential Chicana feminist works to come. Cotera and Chapa also worked with Carmen Tafolla, who was getting her PhD in bilingual and foreign education in 1981, and a leading feminist activist in the *movimiento*, Inés Hernández-Ávila, who held a tenure-track position at UT as assistant professor in Mexican American studies, American studies, and English.[72] As Cotera recalls, the center provided curricular materials to whoever would be teaching the course at the time: "We maintained secondary materials that people could use, including Inés and students. We were a big resource for students."[73] Instructors like Hernández-Ávila would borrow material for content, then develop their curricula and circulate it to students. This is yet another demonstration of the center's importance in the development of Chicana studies in Texas and beyond.

In addition to understanding the vulnerability of source materials and the necessity of documenting Chicana histories, Cotera shared with Anzaldúa an interest in examining the experiences of other women of color in relation to Chicana experiences. Cotera explored these experiences in *Multicultural Women's Sourcebook*, a bibliography, resource, and research tool she edited with Nella Cunningham. This important early resource was developed for public libraries and schools—specifically for bilingual educators—as a resource for bilingual and multicultural programs. It was also intended as a resource for feminists of color so that they could readily access the materials across ethnic and racial borders that Chicanas were reading and incorporating into their essays in comparative studies. According to Cotera, Chicanas wanted to encourage feminist reading across ethnic and racial lines in order to promote collaboration. Cotera drew most of the materials from her personal library and made them available to CRLC users, lending them or providing copies to local women of color to use in order to encourage them to enter ethnic and feminist studies locally. This is another testament to Cotera's importance to the history of Chicana feminism and emergence of Chicana studies.[74]

Anzaldúa's Chicana course materials contained works by other women of color, such as "Why Women's Liberation is Important to Black Women" by Maxine Williams and "Abolitionist" by Sojourner Truth.[75] Anzaldúa's interest in attending to the experiences of Chicanas in relation to the oppressions of other women of color was evident early on and came to inform the work that would be a catalyst for her to write *This Bridge Called My Back: Writings by Radical Women of Color*. The Mujer Chicana course marks a historical trajectory in which Anzaldúa and Cotera meet, resulting in an exchange of knowledge and collaborative thinking, theorizing, and practice.

CONCLUSION

The Chicana Research and Learning Center is an early and significant model of a feminist research and advocacy center that produced, circulated, and deployed Chicana feminist thought in practice. Chicana feminist thought continues to be circulated and employed in theorizing, activism, and advocacy. Today, social justice efforts are present in numerous arenas including education, policy reform, grassroots community initiatives, environmental justice, feminist history projects and pedagogies, and, as my own work shows, spiritual activism.[76] I have documented how Chicana feminism manifests in the contemporary work of women at the Alma de Mujer Center for Social Change, a prime example of the continuation of feminist thinking and, equally important, praxis.[77] Former Raza Unida Party chairperson María Elena Martínez has served on the women's council of Alma de Mujer Center for Social Change and conducted work with women of her generation and younger women around spiritual healing, leadership building, mentoring, and programs for youth.[78] In terms of feminist history, Martha Cotera has remained prolific in her writing and public speaking engagements and in working with future generations of Chicana scholars and activists in numerous settings, including the project Chicana por mi Raza Digital Memory Collective conceived of and directed by her daughter, María Cotera. Chicana por mi Raza seeks to create a digital archive documenting Chicana feminist praxis in its early years. María Cotera, a former CRLC staff member, remains committed to making Chicana history known and accessible, continuing the legacy of her mother.[79] She has said Chicana por mi Raza is an extension of her work at CRLC, a testament to the generative nature of the center's knowledge production.[80]

Since I met Martha Cotera in 2005 she has continued to impact my research, teaching, and feminist development. Some thirty years after her visit to Anzaldúa's La Mujer Chicana course, she graciously accepted an invitation to visit mine. Since then she has spoken to dozens of my students, spent countless hours illuminating Chicana/Tejana feminist histories with her wisdom and life stories, and contributed to the Latina History Project that I codirect at Southwestern University.[81] Another unexpected thread in the web I have presented in this essay comes in the form of a recent revelation that Cotera took part in an exhibit on Tejanas at Southwestern University in 1993, long before my arrival there, during the period when she worked with the CRLC. The exhibit included Martha's portrait taken in the CRLC period, which continues to be displayed today. Through her archival holdings and in-person meetings and class lectures, she has had an impact on the next generation of college students by sharing her *conocimientos* and her generosity of spirit.

In the 1970s, the Chicana Research and Learning Center played a critical role in the formation of an interconnected web of feminist thinking, writing, and praxis that helped to shape Chicana feminist thought in Central Texas and that would come to influence the work of future generations of scholars and community activists in Texas and beyond. I maintain that the CRLC and its work, the scholarship and activism of Martha P. Cotera, the trajectory of the Mujer Chicana course, and development of Chicana studies in Central Texas are all interrelated parts of a complex and compelling genealogy and feminist legacy that deserve recognition. This legacy provides us with a model of social justice that inhabits a space in between where research and scholarship are employed to promote social change. It is a model that encourages the melding of community and academics, collaboration, and the utilization of feminist thought and praxis to increase rights and resources for our communities, families, and future generations.

11 VISIONS OF UTOPIA WHILE LIVING IN OCCUPIED AZTLÁN

OSA HIDALGO DE LA RIVA AND
MAYLEI BLACKWELL

OSA: I was born Teresa Ann Hidalgo.[1] Now it is Dr. Osa Bear, or Osa T. Hidalgo de la Riva. My mom renamed me Royal Eagle Bear because when I was traveling once in Berlin, I kept having nightmares about war and my mom sent her magic. When I came out to my younger sister, Liz, I was fifteen and she was eleven. Her response was, "So what, I've *been* gay!" I thought, "Probably so, since she has five planets in Scorpio." I don't like getting into the whole debate about whether you are born gay, lesbian, transgender, or bisexual, or if it is just past lives, or the power of evolution. There is an underground story of sexuality within the Chicano movement that is important to tell because it has been omitted. I hope my story contributes to undoing that erasure.

My aunt Sally being gay was a good role model. Then, when my mom came out much later, it was really cool, but she came out at a different time, like in the eighties. I learned a lot from my aunt Sally who was actively gay in the 1950s. From both of them, I get those two different languages and culturally and historically specific representations of how Chicana *lesbianas* were, even if it was primarily through my family. I always say my family is matrilineal because the power of the energy runs through the women or the female part of the family. With the de la Rivas, this is really strong and there is a lot of lesbian presence. I don't like the word "matriarchy" even though matriarchal is more accepted. It makes me think of a more dominant system and it reminds me of patriarchy. I use "matrilineal" because matriarchy seems like merely the opposite of patriarchy, but I am describing a completely different situation. For me, matrilineal is having the energy running through or the decision making centered within the women.

I know my aunt Sally is butch-identified. She told me that in her day, before the second wave of feminism in the seventies, "butches were butches and femmes were femmes." There was not much confusion about the roles. While this may seem sexist or simplistic, she thought that with second-wave feminism the roles got confusing or washed out and diluted, and that is why people couldn't stay together that long. Before that, people had their roles and that is why they stayed together longer.

Now, I think because people are having children more and more in *lesbiana* relationships, I think they are lasting longer overall with more marriages with children. But for a while, there in the sixties and seventies, it was just more open. Not that there weren't relations and children like that, but I think what my aunt was saying is that they literally had like forty- or fifty-year relationships. It was a different world. In her day, it was illegal to be gay. She got persecuted for being gay. She got strip-searched in a way that was a form of rape by the police. She definitely participated in the queer clubs as a dark-skinned, Chicana *lesbiana*, and she didn't use the word "lesbian" that much or "homosexual." She told me about the word "homophile"—that she preferred the word "homophile." She did the same things [as we do now]: go listen to music and dance at parties, but they used to have lesbian brawls all the time. In Stockton, there was a lesbian bar by the port and she and her buddies would go there after they played baseball. They would go with their girlfriends. So many sailors and military guys would go have drinks there as well, and they would start hitting on the women but the butches wouldn't have it. Almost all fights at the time were with the guys because they thought that they could just come in and take some of the femmes and start flirting with them and all of that.

She also told me stories about the San Francisco scene and celebrities who were gay and would go to the clubs on the down low. She used to tell me all about the women's clubs back then, but it was hidden and they had codes to get in the club. The Daughters of Bilitis were predominantly white, and she told me that lesbian women had their own organizations but they were not as known as the gay men's organizations and clubs. But she is old-school. She bought a house in Dublin [California] because she always worked full-time as a teacher. My mom had just had the twins, and even though I had already been gay I came out to my mom. She took me to aunt Sally's house who said, "Mija, if it was up to me, I would not want you to be gay because it is such a hard lifestyle." I remember she told me, "Don't ever, ever put in writing that you are gay." That was way back in the late sixties, and ever since then I wanted to be a filmmaker and tell everyone I was gay. Even in Morelia [where she has lived for many decades], they have asked Aunt Sally to publicly read, when she published her own book of poetry, prose, and photographs entitled *Lágrimas y Cadenas/Chains and Tears*.[2] She is connected with a lot of the different generations of gay folk. It's cool because my mom was gay too and she came out in her own way in the eighties. My mom came back from Mexico, and women were asking if she was dating anyone. It was weird because basically they were asking me on the side if she was available. It was so funny. Liz and I were looking at each other like we were the grandparents who felt that Lola [their mom] really had to calm down, but she was happy and free. It was good to see the different generations since Liz and I had our coming-out in the seventies, before our mom. We definitely have a matrilineal, lesbian, feminist, *mujerista*, multigenerational spectrum.

MAYLEI: *What was it like when you came out?*

OSA: When I came out, it was traumatic for my mom because at that time she was a single mom in Southside Stockton. She worked in the canneries and she still did art and her political work, but it was difficult because I was the oldest. I was always such a model kid because I was involved in politics, in school, and I was getting good grades. I helped with the family. I was a good girl and all of a sudden I started missing school and cutting classes, lying and doing a few things. What happened was that I was coming out and I would want to go see my girlfriend. It was hard. I went to the library in Stockton—now it's called the César Chávez Library—and read all the things I could about homosexuality because nobody really talked about it. It was a big taboo.

When I came out to my mom, I wrote her this long, poetic letter about all the people that were gay in history, telling her that I was in love and that people should be celebrating that I am in love. I ran away. She thought that I was on drugs or something, so we ended up at the police station in Stockton. It was a challenge coming out as a teenager when you are in Stockton.

I ran away because my mom didn't know what was going on, and she had just had the twins or was pregnant with the twins. She was going through her own difficulties being a single mom with five kids on welfare. It was hard for her and she didn't know what was going on. They called my dad, so all of us, we went down there. My dad was really cool and my mom said, "If that is what you want to do, if this is really the issue, then I accept it." She was cool with it and she even let me move in with my partner. My dad said, "Well okay, let's go have some pizza." Right now there is an epidemic with our youth and teen suicides. I think I was really fortunate to have my aunt Sally and my parents. Of course, my sister Liz, she is my cosmic twin. Even though she is four years younger, she is so wise she feels like an older sister.

MAYLEI: *It seemed like there were sexual subcultures in the Chicano movement that are not well documented.*

OSA: Back in our day, the lesbian thing was in full practice in the seventies with the Whoremonia Society that Liz and I founded. The Whoremonia Society was a secret society encouraging women to explore their own sexuality and bodies through female-to-female free love. I can't really say more because it was secret, so I can't talk about it or else it won't be secret. To this day, Liz and I still argue over who was president. Well, now all of these words around gender and sexuality have changed their meanings, like how we now think of gender with the trans movement, but at that time, it was simple. In Southside Stockton in the seventies, we were young, free, and gay. Being with women was on the forefronts of our minds . . . a lot. We went to school at Cal State University, Long Beach in LA, so we continued to have encounters with women who were straight and some that were gay. Mainly, you have to realize it was during the sexual revolution, you know? The early seventies and all of that, so there was a lot of sexual openness at that time.

MAYLEI: *Were you an activist/artist when you were young?*

OSA: We all did our own thing. My sister Liz and I had our own newspaper called *Mama Sappho Press*.[3] Really, it was more like what people came to call "zines." From 1973 to 1975, we would make it in Long Beach, literally in a little closet. We had subscriptions from about 250 people in California and even all the way to Texas, where some Latino library ordered a regular subscription. We were inspired by what Lorna Dee [Cervantes] did with Mango Press. We ran our own paper made of articles, community *chisme*, comics, a calendar, and advertisements from various Stockton community members, businesses that supported us like our gay friend who had a flower shop or the colleges, so we got different little ads. We ran these advertisements and that allowed us to go back and forth from Long Beach to Stockton. We took them around the community, building up our subscriptions base so that at one point we had 250 folks that subscribed to *Mama Sappho Press*. We did that for a few years, going back and forth across the state on our motorcycles, delivering the paper. We didn't want to publish in a patriarchal press, so we made our own. Then we took the show on the road.

MAYLEI: *What was the motivation for the press?*

OSA: All I can say is, we grew up on a patriarchal planet where the dominant religions are patriarchal, Hollywood, the press . . . everything. This was before *This Bridge Called My Back* came out [in 1981], so we never wanted to publish or fall under patriarchal systems, even in publishing.[4] The queer situation in Stockton was so radically different than say LA, I mean it was totally the opposite. We had more of a rural situation and in LA you had an urban situation. I think that the idea was to be more inclusive of whoever wanted to be in this little gay rag. It allowed us to be ourselves, and since in many spaces we were discriminated against, often our work was separate. We were involved in the women's circles, and that was white and middle class. The Raza organizations were male-centric, heterosexist and sometimes we experienced homophobia from our straight Chicana sisters. The gay liberation movement was primarily white. My mom took the twins to La Escuelita de La Raza, a bilingual preschool and community *centro* in Long Beach. At Long Beach State, we were involved and influenced by strong Women's Studies and Chicano Studies Departments.

My mom was in the Art and Chicano Studies Departments and she was producing a lot of art. She met artists Leo Limon, John Valadez, Yreina Cervantes, Pete Ruiz, Linda Vallejo, members of Tierra then, and so my mom opened up her home and began running the Centro de Arte in East Long Beach. All the young artists mentioned above, and then some, actually, a lot of local, national, and international artists came through the Centro de Arte over the years. Liz and I were both working on our degrees in psychology and the Psychology Department was in the same area as [the] women's studies program, but the problem was that all the women's studies faculty were primarily white. We would ask, "What about the Chicanas and the women of color?" and they said, "If you are interested in that you have to go organize that yourself." They were being separatist. Trying to bridge two worlds together, Liz, my mom, and I started the Mextiza Colectiva, and we worked out of the Centro de Arte that my mom started in her home. That was the first time I met Sylvia Morales, since she came to the Centro. Anna NietoGomez came by too. Lots of activists, artists, musicians, UFW farmworker organizers, and so on visited the Centro de Arte; many even spent the night while travelling through. Director Lola Dela-Riva was very generous with her home and *familia*.[5] René Yañez and different directors from the first statewide coalition of Chicano art centers, the Concilio de Arte Popular, would come and go. From the Mextiza Colectiva, Liz also did her own collections of poetry. She wrote her first collection when she was about sixteen years old called *Phoenix* and later, *Primitive and Proud*. In fact, that is where I would get the title for my later film. Liz wrote her book through the Mextiza Colectiva and I edited *Women's Poetry*, an anthology based at Long Beach State. My mom did the cover art and design.

So we did *Mama Sappho* from '73 through '75. It was a little homemade publication—eight and a half by eleven inches—and we folded it in half. It was really grassroots. For the typography, we used rub-on letters at that time. We had the Mextiza Colectiva probably between 1973 through the early eighties because the twins were really small. The Colectiva hosted discussion groups and organized a Chicana *lesbiana* poetry tour in 1976. It was during the Bicentennial, so Liz and I went with a couple of the other women. We went to some of the first battered-women's shelters, women's bookstores and cafes. We set out across the country with a packed itinerary. We went in my little Dodge Colt station wagon, which had all these murals on it including a pre-Columbian goddess painted on the door whose hair went all the way back to the tail light. Four of us took that car on tour and we got invited all over the country, so we were going to drive to Florida, New York, Boston, and all over Texas and the Southwest. In the end, we couldn't drive the entire tour. We did make it to Albuquerque, Santa Fe, Denver, Boulder, Phoenix, Tucson, Santa Cruz, and Berkeley. Basically, we performed all across the golden states of Aztlán. The Chicana *lesbiana* poetry tour was sponsored and produced by the Mextiza Colectiva. Liz and I read our *lesbiana flor y canto* poetry, and that was before *This Bridge Called My Back*, so it was nice to see when *This Bridge* came out because it was like, "Wow! This is right up our alley!"

MAYLEI: *Were you active in the Chicano movement?*

OSA: Well, we were all active, as a family. My brother Louis did Chicano murals and he was always painting. When we organized events like a poetry reading or a Chicano art show, we would always have family and a large mix of people. Our community crossed many boundaries. For some events, the audience would be more Chicano and straight. At others, it would be maybe more white women or lesbians of color, but we would still have a mix of family and friends coming together. At that time, I think it was important to bring everyone together. I had a poem at that time, I don't remember the title, but what was important to me was to consciously want to read my *lesbiana* gay stuff to the Chicano groups, and I would read my pieces about being a dark brown woman to the white women's and gay groups, so I would always mix it up to make them feel a little uncomfortable. I felt that all those communities, identities, and sensibilities and *culturas* were part of me, so I didn't mind being in your face about it at that time.

I remember that feeling of a Chicano renaissance. I remember a lot of the artists painting, musicians making *música*, dancers, *teatro*, healers, lovers, writers, photographers, and so on surging with the creative spirit, doing their thing, especially at my mom's Centro de Arte. She offered her home base truly as all of our home. *Mí casa es su casa.* I was always traveling, coming here and going all over the planet and returning to Long Beach. But the community was a beautiful blend of the radicals, community leaders, and even the Chicano power guys that believed in violence. They believed, like warriors, that you have to fight fire with fire. They are the Aztec warriors, ancient power and pulse. Maybe another natural reason why it was easy for me to feel the matrilinear vibrations of *las olmecas*.

MAYLEI: *What was it like to be a lesbian around the Chicano movement?*

OSA: My family teases that I think everyone is gay. I think because Liz and I were with so many women that were straight it has always made me think that given an opportunity, people can just be sexual, you know? This is my own theory. I think that for straight women the dynamics are different since it is a straight world. They can go experiment or have an experience with another female because they know they can go back and get married and have children and live a traditional life without any repercussions. On the other hand, the women, and this is where it's really—you know, this is the first time I am coming out with this. . . . Anyway, I am coming out with my own identity and my own experiences, but that is why I have avoided mainstream media involvement. I am sixty-one. I'm going to be sixty-two this year. I know things have changed a lot, but there are so many straight Latina or Chicana women that I was sexual with. I would never, even until this day, if I see them at a conference or school or anywhere, whether they were married or whatever, out them because I respect their identity and however they want to identify. But, I know back in the day either we slept together, or we cuddled, or we kissed, or we made out, or we had sex, you know, one time, two times, three times, *o más*. I never felt that because I slept with a woman that I would have to ask her to change her identity. I was openly *lesbiana* and gay, and a lot of women at that time wanted to experiment or they felt safe with me or Liz, or both. Our pride and energy of being open *lesbianas* created a synergy, and women expressed their attraction to us. It was the era of free love and for us, it was the era of free Chicana *lesbiana* love. Two-spirited sexuality *y más*. This was way back in the day, so it was all good, you know. Now someone like me would be one of the first to be targeted. I am a visible outsider as the out, dark-skinned *lesbiana*. We are who we are. *Qué viva!*

MAYLEI: *What does that mean to you? To be an out, dark-skinned lesbian for your life, your political work, and your art?*

OSA: I think that it is so much a part of me that it is hard to know anything different, even in the films I made. That is how *mujerista* moviemaking happened because you see the white, male, straight hero so many times over and over, even if the majority of the context of the story was set in the neighborhood of people of color, or lesbians, or women. It's still so many white male heroes. That is why I thought it was important to put together my *mujerista* moviemaking theory and praxis. In needing to finish my dissertation, I was able to work with Sylvia Morales and Lourdes Portillo. I was able to interview them and to immerse myself in their work. I always say they are the *veterana* filmmakers because they were the first generation. They both produced their main first films in 1979. Chon Noriega says it's mainly because the schools at the time included affirmative action and they were able to go to college and do their art. So both make their first two pieces through schools, Otis for Lourdes and Sylvia at UCLA with their master's degree. As I studied their work, I interpreted their work from a queer Chicana lens.

MAYLEI: *When did you start making your own films?*

OSA: The filmmaking for me evolved because my mom, Lola Dela-Riva, was doing art with farmworker children at migrant camps in the sixties and being an artist and going to art camps. Because she was a teacher in the sixties, I was always surrounded by art in the house growing up. She had her little space where she had her art area and we were always encouraged to be artists, but I wanted to be an architect. I wanted to be a mathematician when I first arrived to Long

Beach. Anyway, growing up, there were always artists around the house. My mom recorded musicians and took us to a few concerts even though we were on welfare. Even though she was a single mom with five kids, we were still encouraged to be around art and be creative, so I and all my siblings always drew. I started writing poetry when I was seven. It was like my first language. I say that because I still don't speak Spanish too well, nor English, and I lived in Germany for nearly a year and can't speak German either. Some folks are natural at spoken languages, like my sister Liz. She learned conversational Chinese at twelve years young, was one of the first Chicana *lesbiana* mainframe computer programmers for IBM, learning many computer languages, and so on.[6] But poetry came out of me and music. I played the guitar since I was four, when my aunt Sally give me a little guitar. She had a whole lot of queer Hawaiian friends like in the late fifties and sixties when I was baby, and she would come to Stockton and get me and take me to meet her friends in the city where she was studying to be [a] teacher at the then San Francisco State College. I would sing, sing, sing at four and five and six years old. I remember growing up always listening to the ukulele. I remember them singing beautiful harmony. I loved that.

I think that film followed my writing. I remember when I was seven my mom busted me when I was supposed to be in bed sleeping. This was in Southside Stockton. I was under the covers with a little flashlight. I just felt compelled to write about nature and love. "The bright yellow full moon is shining so bright down upon me / The surrounding trees are saying good night, sleep tight." So I was writing that when my mom came in and saw the flashlight under the blankets and she said, "What are you doing?" I said, "I'm writing a poem." So poetry has always been my best friend since I was a kid. I have cases and cases and cases and cases of poetry. That is one thing: I have tons of journals and just like this oral history, it is kind of hard to let everything out. I am finally letting out my first book of poetry, mainly written in the seventies, with Korima Press, working with publisher Lorenzo Herrera y Lozano.[7]

Film encompasses the writing, the storytelling, the music, the sound, you know? All of it! It is the closest thing to being alive and allowing our imagination to create our past, present, and future worlds and universes. One thing that we didn't talk about, because we are talking specifically about [the] sixties, seventies, and eighties, is that a lot of my time is spent thinking about the future and the ancient past, like the Olmec. I feel for sure that I was there. I feel close to them ever since I read about them. I write to create my vision of utopia. I think that it is good to critique our here and now, but you do have to have an idea of a better world or a more perfect world even though it is still in the realm of fantasy. Of course, you don't want to stay in fantasyland all the time, but it allows me to play with this idea of science fiction.

This whole thing about cancer is like science fiction. I have been thinking about this connection a lot lately. I have this whole way, a parallel universe of sorts, of understanding why cancers have come through my body. I had my first bout with malignant cancer in my thyroid when I was fifteen. The doctor told me that there was a one in 10,000 chance that someone that young, fifteen or sixteen, would get that type of cancer. Seven years later they removed something from my breast, along with lymph nodes under my armpit. Over the years I had biopsies several times because they thought I had melanoma. At the USC Norris Cancer Center they monitored and removed a node from the back of my neck. A year later I had to have a total hysterectomy. Then, at sixty years old, I had malignant cancer again in my kidney. Shortly thereafter they took my gallbladder and then the appendix. They wanted to cut me open again within this two-year period, but I got very proactive by going to acupuncture weekly, taking supplements, and going to support groups. Working on my mind-body-spirit. Now they found another nodule, another node they are going to deal with probably next month and then possibly something still with my throat area. It is funny because that is the chakra of communication, the throat chakra—so I think that doing music, doing poetry, is all part of healing. I tell people that the cancer thing has been a science-fiction experiential narrative the way that I understand, feel, and interpret it.

I think it is cosmic. Some of it is karma. Some of it is symbolic for different things at different times in my life. So I say this cancer stuff is science fiction because even today in Western medicine, they don't know about cancer. They don't even really care too much because a lot of women are dealing with cancer. I won't go into all of that, but even in the hospitals, the health care system, the environment, and our stress levels, I think that a lot of it is on us, obviously, to heal and to understand our journeys that way. I think this is in part why I call it science fiction because they don't really know about the healing and the therapies that well. They don't even know about cancer that much yet. I'd rather just do it my own way and, you know, we are all going to die at some point and I am lucky that I have lived this long. I give thanks every day. I go in the morning, I go say a little prayer by the ocean to give thanks I am alive. I live near the ocean. At night I try to always say good night at sunset to the sun, hello to the moon, and give thanks for the day, for my beautiful *familia* and friends. So in my own way, I have my own spirituality and religion.

I wonder if one-third of my life has been spent on the here and now and one-third on the past and one-third on the future. What if the brain's hemispheres are divided as such—one half is in the here and now and the other half is split into the past and future? And then there is the un-time, non-time of both hemispheres, as well as their various combinations? Do you know what I mean? I don't even know how to do the math map of it, but I know that a large part of my creativity is what you can call the logic of fantasy, imagination, creativity, or dreams, whatever that other way of thinking and feeling is. It is hard to quantify quality. Measuring the delta, mythopoetic realities . . . Audre Lorde's work on the "uses of the erotic" touches this logic.[8]

So, the Olmec, I don't know why, and I know some people might cry heresy, but I am very connected with the Olmec. I have read everything I could about them. I visited where their temples are and where they have mounds in Veracruz. Studying the calendar, they say the Aztecs were the more recent culture, or we can say the Chicanos are the most recent. I see it as a continuum in that we are all related, like cuzins. The Aztecs, Toltec before them, Zapotecs before them, the Mayan before them, and then the mother *cultura, las olmecas*. The Olmec are the ones that came up with the concept of zero. For example, you cannot have the pyramids made until you know about zero. The advancement of science and mathematics depends on this concept and the Olmecs had this information. Some people say they are from Africa. Others say that they are Chinese or Asian. Other people say that they are indigenous to las Américas. And maybe it was all the above or none of the above. I do believe that they could communicate off the planet because so much of the cosmos or universe are imprinted or written in these architectures. I could go on and on. I am fascinated and that is why I was inspired to make the animated film *Mujería: The Olmeca Rap*.[9]

At the time, I was a poet, you know, I had about three minutes to do my thesis at San Francisco State University. We had this media collective, FOCUS [Film-makers of Color Us], of all film graduate students of color at San Francisco State University. We got a $5,000 grant and we split it ten ways so we all got $500 each. It allowed me to do the project. A friend who is a musician came over to my house in East Oakland and saw the little animations that I was doing of the Olmec. I made them into females because I always say the actual stone monolithic heads don't have any body or genitalia and they found thousands of little brown clay female figurines buried around the giant stone Olmec heads, so I figured there is at least a 51 percent chance that they could be female, right? As I've mentioned, the Olmeca connection to me is in essence matrilineal. After extensive study at Harvard, in museums all across Europe, in archival work, and with a few leading archaeologists, I believe the early Mesoamericanists have it wrong because their worldviews were patriarchal, so their interpretations of many ancient cultures are misinterpretations. Or maybe just in my imagination, or mythopoetic imaginary and cosmic worldview, the Olmecas, to me, represent the mighty suprafemale. Along with the concept of zero, with all the binaries, with the gods of duality, all this comes together and almost vanishes into infinity with the Olmec.

Their culture is said to have disappeared, so nobody has any real evidence and the big question for archaeologists has been, where did the Olmecs vanish to? Personally, I think they are still around. I think their energy is still around. Maybe even from outside, or inside of the planet . . . but I will stop there. The thing about *The Olmeca Rap* was that the film equipment at San Francisco State was so broken down. It was from the 1950s. They were building a whole new building when I was a graduate student there and they were transitioning into the digital world. But we had this old analog equipment that was all outdated. The animation stand where all the master's students were doing their thesis was broken, so every-body's film came back and it was jumping, glitched, you know? Like maybe you have somebody walking in the original footage but it came out jumping up and down because the machine was dilapidated and everyone freaked out because film is so expensive.

When I saw the animated Olmeca heads footage that I had spent so much time drawing and shooting frame by frame and they were jumping up and down, I said, "Oh, they could be dancing heads and have a little rap." So I put lipstick on them, shades, a little bling, and all that stuff. I didn't have time to rework it all because it would take a long time to remake all that movement with cell-by-cell animation. My friend Rita Lackey was getting ready at my place to go to a singing gig that evening. I was working on my animation cells and she looks at the characters and says, "Hey, they look like rappers!" We started laughing, "Oh yeah, a blast from the past." Then she left for her gig. That is when I wrote *The Olmeca Rap*, "The Olmeca Rappers with the blast from the past, are here to rock our world, are here to rock us at last. The Olmeca Rappers, ancient women with color, ancient Indian stones, are here to rock our world, are here to rock our bones!" And with those lyrics it turned into a three-minute music video.

This little film, made on broken-down equipment, went across the United States, all through Europe, to Canada, Mexico, and to South America. The premiere showing was at the Kabuki Theater so the heads were like life-size. It was so exciting, it was too real. It was . . . oh my goddess, almost spiritual. They were coming out again, not larger than life, but nearly actual size! Then Mario Barrera from UC Berkeley was teaching Chicano studies and it was the first time that I was invited to go speak about *The Olmeca Rap*. Another coincidence was that the class I visited, Ethnicity and Race in the US, was the class he created, but when he retired, I began to teach that class for about five years every spring and every summer from 2008 to 2013 at UC Berkeley.

Next, our company Royal Eagle Bear Productions, comprised of *familia* and friends mainly, Mama Lola Dela-Riva codirector and art director, and I did *Mujería: Primitive and Proud*.[10] The idea was to have the *Mujería* trilogy based on the story that Little Eagle Bear gets accidentally lost from the ancient Olmeca women's meditation circle. During meditation her healing crystal gets too hot and she drops it. In reaching down to find her crystal her third eye light beam leaves the center of the circle of the meditating women and gets crossed with an electromagnetic TV antenna wave from 1954. She gets transported across time and space and ends up in Stockton as a Chicana newborn. The ancient Olmecas realize what happened to Little Eagle Bear, that she got lost by mistake across 3,000 years and 3,000 miles, *más o menos*, and they call upon their woman warrior goddess Xicantzín to find and return lost Eagle Bear to their meditation circle. *Artista* activist *veterana* Dorinda Moreno helped name the Chicana goddess character Xicantzín that my mom, Lola Dela-Riva, designed. She had originally drawn her for this woman's calendar in Santa Cruz, a moon calendar. My mom was showing Dorinda Moreno the character and Dorinda said, "I think her name is Xicantzín." We used her as the ancient warrior goddess to find Eagle Bear and send her back to the meditation circle. That is the real feature-length movie idea but since we never had money, we did *The Olmeca Rap* to introduce the characters. Elizabeth "Betita" Martínez even put drawings of the Olmeca Rappers in her book *500 Years of Chicana Women's History*.[11] Without film critics like Chon Noriega and Rosa Linda Fregoso, I don't think *The Olmeca Rap* would have received so much attention and play. Chon Noriega took it over to the Whitney Museum in New York to be screened early on and listed it in his popular essay "The Aztlán Film Institute's Top 100 List."[12]

At that time, I had been in Europe. I was in London actually the first time I saw *This Bridge Called My Back*. I saw the book over there so it must have been the early eighties. It must have been around '81 or '82 or something. Cherríe and Gloria asked me to submit something in *This Bridge*. Gloria had wanted me to write something about my experiences with white women in the women's movement. At that time, I was doing my poetry. I was finishing my master's program in poetry at San Francisco State U, but at that time it was difficult to commit to outing racism within the women's movement.

At the time I was just consumed with other issues. I remember I went to Berlin after I finished my first master of arts degree and returned home to Stockton for a year where I worked in a maximum-security prison with Raza. Upon my return to the United States, we started doing *Me and Mr. Mauri: Turning Poison into Medicine* because all of my friends were dying of SIDA/AIDS.[13] I had gone to Europe before the wall came down and when I came back AIDS had been going on for a while. I think I started working on *Me and Mr. Mauri: Turning Poison into Medicine* somewhere around '85.

MAYLEI: *What was it like to see so many gay friends in the community get sick?*

OSA: I took off to Europe and when I came back that is what blew my mind. This thing . . . AIDS had all the beautiful young Latino friends and friends of friends sick and dying! All the young people that I knew. Since I had just been to Germany, it reminded me kind of what Hitler had done. I know there are conspiracy theories but I thought it was too strange to have a disease so targeted that hit only certain populations. Coming from Germany, it felt like history was repeating itself.

MAYLEI: *So, you started making the film?*

OSA: Well, I became friends with this young guy Mauricio Delgado from Nicaragua. Like all the other young Latinos, really cute, real sex-positive and everything, smart, and active politically. We just hit it off and became really good buddies. We met at Chili's house [Diana Felix, known in the community as DJ Chili D].[14] I was helping her paint her house one time; well, I helped her paint several times here and there over the years. I met Mauricio and then we became friends. I began to interview him and continue to document his life. He didn't mind. At the time, I used to do a lot of massage and bodywork and he would ask if I would give him massages so I would. I witnessed his strong healthy body become so frail. It was hard for us all and for those of us left behind. It is still difficult to deal with all of this contemporary genocide.

So this documentary was really nontraditional. We took the film rough cuts to the first Latino AIDS organizations and healers that were responding best they could. Some people were shocked. "Oh my god you're touching them without gloves" or "You were touching them with those rings on," but they liked it and wanted me to show them how to do the body work. So, I was being called to go and do what I could do. To touch them in their process of dying and to love them as *familia* while they were still alive. You know how they say the lesbians were really the caregivers early on and in the middle of the crisis? I feel as if I didn't really have time to stop and ponder the situation. Everyone was being affected before our eyes, hearts, and memory. Then our other friend Francisco Xavier Zamora got sick. Then John Juarez, one of the cofounders of AGUILAS.[15] Then Liz had many, many gay men friends who died. Her good friend Chente Villanzuela. Then Rodrigo Reyes. Then our friend Margarita Benitez. We were really close and I even pierced her son's ear when he was a kid. I still love them all. Other people started hearing that I was documenting people at that time. I would just grab whatever camera and I would ask people, "Do you have five dollars so I could buy a tape?" So, it was really ghetto, guerrilla filmmaking but I knew that time was short so I was just trying to capture their last words, and people had so much to say. In fact, people started requesting I take their video testimony. Rodrigo told Chili D, "I want you to bring Osa over to my house." He and my mom were close friends and used to party and hang out in San Francisco a lot together back in the day. Rodrigo Reyes, Juan Pablo Gutierrez, and Francisco X. Alarcón wrote one of the first gay Latino men's book together, an anthology of *poesía*. Rodrigo Reyes and Chili D cofounded the first gay Latino AIDS *centro* in San Francisco, Community United Response against SIDA [CURAS], to respond specifically to the needs of Latinos with SIDA/AIDS. Do you know we marched all together back in the day with GALA [Gay Latino Alliance]? I rode a motorcycle way, way back in the day during SF Gay Pride—it had to be in the seventies. GALA was a gay Latino organization that had all mixture of men and women and different types of Latinos. Rodrigo started it first and then Chili came from San Jose to join. Then my friend Debbie Huerta, I think she changed her name to Xihauanel, although I am not sure how it is spelled, whose father was a bodyguard of César Chávez, grew up around the movement as well. So, one time she took me to GALA and told everyone that I was a Chicana *lesbiana* poet, I did a poetry reading with them, and then they passed around the hat. It was one of the meetings that they had in Chili's house; it was a big group.

All those were amazing times and with all that I went on to get a BA in psychology, community clinical psychology, at Long Beach State. They had one of the few BA programs where you could actually go work in the community, so we worked at the Martin Luther King Jr. Community Center there in Longo [Long Beach] there, was the African American community center. Then we worked with Casa Orizaba and that is where we worked with Yvette Flores. She was a graduate student when we were still undergrads. I worked on a double minor in women's studies and in industrial arts because I wanted to be an architect. From there I went to UC Santa Cruz for the first time in 1976 or '77, where I worked with Professor Art Pearl in the Education Department. I did my teaching credential coursework for multicultural K-12, and my internship at Santa Cruz High School. I worked in the prison at that time as well, teaching Nancy Shaw's Women in Revolutionary Struggle [course at UC Santa Cruz] at the women's prison in Santa Rita, and I worked at Terminal Island and CIW [Correctional Institution for Women]. I taught creative writing and brought in musicians and guest speakers.

In the early eighties I returned to UC Santa Cruz to start a PhD in the history of consciousness. I was able to sit on a student-faculty committee to hire Angela Y. Davis. It was her first time to teach in the UC system since Reagan fired her from UCLA back in the day. In 1987 I got the boot from his. con., so I took off for a while. MALDEF [Mexican American Legal Defense and Education Fund] got involved, and a class-action suit was being considered. Many domestic Latinos, the majority of whom are Chicanos, were being admitted into the PhD program, but few were actually graduating, or they were taking a very long time to do so. I couldn't physically or emotionally handle such an extended battle at the time. Anytime something wild like that happened in my life, I'd take off. That time, I went to Mexico and I lived there for a while, traveled, realized the importance of independent scholarship and the meaning of community scholarship. I was given a second master's degree for my time in his. con., one of the few ever awarded. Over the years I have been so extremely grateful to witness the powerful impact Professor Angela Y. Davis has had on diversifying the program, student body, and matriculation of graduate women of color with the university at large.

MAYLEI: *So, you went to the Lesbian Feminist Encuentro in 1987?*

OSA: I went to four *encuentros* in one year. I went to Cocina de Imagenes, the Latina women's film festival in Mexico City in 1987.[16] I got to meet all these women filmmakers, then there was the huge international Feminista Encuentro in Taxco, and there was the Lesbiana Encuentro in Cuernavaca, I believe. After that, some of the organizers and some of the Latinas from South and Central America, the Caribe, and from the United States stayed around Mexico City. One place women stayed at was with this woman Amparo Jimenez's house in Coyoacán. I stayed there for a week, and that is when I met tatiana de la tierra. We hung around for a while with a lot of the other women from South America and all over. That experience was yet another *encuentro* that I called the fourth *encuentro*.

MAYLEI: *What was it like to be a Chicana lesbian and go to Mexico and meet filmmakers and feminist and lesbian activists?*

OSA: Well, there were several things. Of course, there were the contradictions that some of us Chicanas or Latinas from the United States do not speak Spanish or didn't speak Spanish well. While this was read as a marker of privilege, we were low-income or poor and many of us had even darker skin than those who spoke Spanish. I found some of the women from South America, Mexico, or Central America, mainly South America, were light-skinned and affluent. So, that was the first time I kind of tripped because they were not even middle class, they were well-to-do, you know? They were trying to criticize us for being *gringas* because we didn't speak Spanish. I was like, "That is still a European language, you know?" and they were being all uppity calling us *gringas*. I would be like, "They don't get it but it's okay." At that time, I was doing my own thing and I got close to a lot, a lot, a lot of women. I felt like we were having our own *encuentro*, with our own language, being able to communicate. Without words, we loved each other, you know?

MAYLEI: *Without words? What are you trying to tell me, Osa?*

OSA: Well, you know, it was sexual healing, sexual revolution, communication, and not just intellectual. You can just intellectualize your world away, and they did so much verbal fighting. My god, women were crying and fighting. They had two different camps in the Latina *lesbiana* delegation and you could tell from body language and all the fighting. It was so dramatic. The fighting was about politics, what was the right way to lead the world and what were the right politics for women to have. It just got so gruesome. I was so saddened and shocked I would just go out on the swing and I would start making out with somebody or somebody would start making out with me. I would sit out there and it was really beautiful. One time I remember they were fighting so bad and they had come to a standstill. Maria Cora just started singing a song in Spanish and it was so profound because I was in the room there. I would still try to sit in as many meetings as I possibly could until I couldn't take it anymore because it just seemed so counterproductive and just like the male stuff, fighting for power. Maria Cora was so profound. Her singing calmed everybody down and helped them to take it to another level with music. Like the sound, I had to experience things in a different way, through touching, feeling, and seeing the *mujerista* vibe. So, I pierced a lot of women's ears. A lot of women would trust me for some reason. People were asking me to do their ears, so I did a lot of piercings. I didn't want to be in front of the camera a lot. People were taking pictures and stuff, but I think that tatiana de la tierra took a picture of me on the grass and she told me she had it on her altar for a long time. I still kept contact with many women from many countries afterwards. I think over the years people maybe knew that I was there or remembered me but I didn't really talk a lot. I definitely did not. Another example was the National Women's Studies Association in Atlanta one year. Again, I didn't do the politics like that. I wasn't a fighter. I would do poetry or pierce ears or give massages. I would have fun and interact easier in nonverbal ways. So they asked me to speak. One time they worked really hard and had these points they wanted to submit to the general assembly. The women of color and lesbians of color wanted to submit their statement they had drafted up to this educational *encuentro* in Atlanta. The group I cared about most asked me if I would read it out loud to the large plenary. I was shocked and proud because finally I got to do something that they wanted and meant. I read it and I think that is on tape somewhere. So, at *encuentros*, I was always kind of there but not in the traditional way. Even in Mujerio, the San Francisco Bay Area organization for Latina *lesbianas*, I was always there with the camera, playing my guitar, painting signs, banners or whatever, always doing poetry, but I would never lead the meetings or seldom argue during meetings, caucuses, or breakout sessions.

MAYLEI: *So all these experiences brought you to the Mujerista aesthetic?*

OSA: So, that is how I came to the utopian concept of the *mujerista* aesthetic. I think you have to deal with the movements, *movimientos*, not just Chicano, but women's movements and gay liberation. You have to have the vision of what the better world you want would look like. You can't just criticize and say this world sucks, and this system sucks, and this racism sucks. You have to have at least a concept of what that better world would be. Imagine a better world and visualize how to make it happen. Like drawing up blueprints. I think that's where aesthetics comes in. What is beautiful and what is love—that's the *mujerista* moviemaking part in theory and praxis. I developed seven principles, and that is what gave me the momentum, the focus to do my dissertation. No matter if I was around film if it was Women Make Movies, as a company, the women of color filmmakers, like the film festivals, the one in Santa Cruz where I was able to participate as a speaker or filmmaker or participant in the majority of all [of] them. If it wasn't for these organized events I wouldn't have been able to meet all the people internationally and nationally and locally, so I felt blessed to have had these experiences.

MAYLEI: *I think that is where we met. At the Women of Color Film and Video Festival in Santa Cruz?*[17]

OSA: Yes, that is what I think. We didn't really get to talk a lot at UC Santa Cruz, but we were both going to Mexico and we made plans to talk over there. In Mexico, we met at a café and that was the first time we had time to talk and to get to know each other. So, the *mujerista* aesthetic was inspired by Alice Walker's womanism. There are seven elements but they are not in hierarchical order. Number one, the Mujerista filmmaker loves herself unconditionally and often radically. She is [a] woman-identified woman whether she has experienced emotional or physical intimacy with another woman. The Alice Walker definition says, "A woman who loves herself loves other women sexually and/or nonsexually."

Number two is getting the job done, willfully, using nonconventional methods, those outside of the traditional Hollywood studio system. It is the successful production and aim towards the liberation of self and others. It focused on making access to technology by any means necessary, its ideology informs its praxis, its praxis or methodology is informed by a responsible set of personal politics, this is always in flux, changing and transforming with the changing times. Number three: Mujerista movies are educational but in a nontraditional sense, not indoctrinating or subordinating all people to a WASP patriarchal mindset and hegemony. Rather, they offer transformational experience about people, events, issues, and point of view usually not dealt with, underrepresented, and misrepresented in mainstream media. Fourth, Mujerista filmmakers are activist in nature and reclaim our stories from a women-of-color and children-of-color POV. Fifth, *familia* is inclusive of all peoples, ages, religions, colors, abilities, classes, genders, and sexualities. Six is teaching others and including our communities in the production process as crew members. Seven, taking risks, being outlaws to create change and transformations for healthy beings. These principles talk about having a healthier world and that is why I think filmmaking has that responsibility. We don't do art just for art's sake. You just can't be talking about it, you actually have to make it. You are an activist in that way. The thing about the hero in Hollywood movies, that is the visual narrative dominating the planet with the same white male heterosexual hero. Mujerista moviemaking centers other types of protagonists and characters. Another principle is that we even make the films with our own crew members. To be sure, not only within the story or the narrative or the movie itself, but also in the making of it, that you become inclusive and intercultural with your crew members so the production process also serves an educational purpose. Those are the things that I feel are really vital in doing our work. Art is the vanguard of the revolution. The artist or cultural movement was a major part of Chicano movement with the murals and the *teatro*, the poetry, and all of it.

Being working class and dark skinned, being in my own body and being an out *lesbiana*, I was never closeted whether I worked in a men's maximum-security prison or USC; I always told people that I am gay. It is almost like it is part of my name because I want people to deal with that up front even if their religion does not agree with it. Sometimes the young Chicanas would get embarrassed but it would give them an opening. Even at UC Davis, I was just visiting there a few months ago. It is so sweet. When I came out, after class several students came to tell me their own thing, you know how it is with the students. Students would regularly come out to me. You hear all these things, like "I have always thought I was gay" or "My family is against this but I never really got to meet somebody," I mean that is still going on. I feel like, oh my god, they are getting degrees and going out into the world, they are the next generation of workers and they can't even deal with it still or even talk about it. Not just my sexuality, let alone their sexuality.

So, I don't know how I jumped to that, cuzin. But in the process of this interview, I realize that the presidential election was ripped off. What is passing as good is evil, and what is being sold to all as evil is really good. Those were the ancient prophesies of many tribes. Like-minded conscious folk will gravitate towards each other, and we will have once again the ability and responsibility to make correct choices, decisions to love ourselves, each other, our planet, and beyond. We still have a long way to go . . . and of course, of course, *Sí se puede*!

PART III

MOVIDAS OF CROSSING

12 FORGING A BROWN-BLACK MOVEMENT

CHICANA AND AFRICAN AMERICAN WOMEN ORGANIZING FOR WELFARE RIGHTS IN LOS ANGELES

ALEJANDRA MARCHEVSKY

O n June 30, 1966, more than 100 women and children marched to the County Hall of Administrators in downtown Los Angeles to denounce "a system that keeps us on welfare."[1] The protestors represented a cross-section of families who received public assistance: white public housing tenants, Mexican American mothers, and ANC Mothers Anonymous, a black women's group from Watts. Marching in solidarity with these families were striking case-workers from the Social Workers Union Local 535 of the Service Employees International Union. Demonstrators sought to expose rampant problems in the Aid to Families with Dependent Children (AFDC) program, which was overseen locally by the Board of Los Angeles County Supervisors. Vivian Romero, a Chicana mother of five, told Supervisor Kenneth Hahn, "We are demanding for our sake and yours too a decent job-training program. We don't want to stay on welfare. We want off." African American recipient Elizabeth Jackson asserted, "We want our children to be proud and hold their head up. The way it is, being on welfare is something to be ashamed of." Recipients testified that AFDC payments were inadequate, unemployed mothers needed quality jobs and child care, and fathers were forced to "go out the back door" so their children could qualify for aid.[2] Yet the board ignored their grievances. Throughout the next decade, poor women of color mobilized across Los Angeles County to challenge the injustices of the welfare system and demand structural change.

As poor people marched in Los Angeles in June 1966, so did others as far away as Baltimore and New York City. This was the first "national day of action for welfare rights," led by the Washington, DC–based Poverty/Rights Action Center, the precursor to the National Welfare Rights Organization (NWRO).[3] From its founding in 1967 until its demise in 1975, NWRO unified welfare rights organizations (WROs) from coast to coast in the fight for an adequate income and dignity for families on public assistance. With a membership of 25,000 recipients at its peak—the majority African American women, with whites, Native Americans, Puerto Ricans, and Mexican Americans participating in smaller numbers— NWRO led the largest interracial movement of poor people in US history.

The 1966 march in Los Angeles was organized by the nascent Los Angeles County Welfare Rights Organization (LAWRO).[4] A multiracial coalition of neighborhood-based AFDC recipient groups, LAWRO grew out of collaborative efforts in the late 1950s by Mexican American and African American women in South LA to demand fair treatment from the Department of Social Services. As LAWRO's president Catherine Jermany recalled, "We were loud. We were out there. And basically we wanted to be inclusive. We wanted a bunch of little groups that could attack the biggest offices of the welfare department."[5] Although people of many backgrounds participated in LAWRO, its principal leaders and rank-and-file activists were Chicanas and African American women who found common cause as poor mothers of color struggling for dignity and security within a hostile welfare system. As they drew connections between the AFDC system, economic exploitation of nonwhite communities, and sexual control of women of color, black and Chicana welfare rights activists insisted that public assistance should enable, not undermine, their autonomy and self-determination.

This chapter examines the welfare rights movement in greater Los Angeles in the 1960s and 1970s, focusing on Chicana leadership and coalition building with African American women. Overlooked in accounts of the movement (which focus on black and white women's organizing in the Northeast and Midwest), Chicanas were important leaders and activists in this struggle. Chicanas were involved at the outset of the movement and by the early 1970s had formed many WROs across Los Angeles County. The largest and most visible of these groups was the East Los Angeles Welfare Rights Organization started by AFDC recipient and mother of five Alicia Escalante in 1967 and later renamed the Chicana Welfare Rights Organization. Though less well documented, other Chicana mothers like Consuelo Campos and Alice Silvas organized WROs in the Harbor area and Orange County, respectively.

The history of LA's welfare rights movement thus centers Chicanas as targets of racialized patriarchal state violence, powerful thinkers and actors who resisted these conditions, and coalition builders who crafted a class-centered women of color politics. Chicana leaders collaborated with black women—especially Catherine Jermany and Johnnie Tillmon (both who also played prominent roles in the NWRO)—to build an alliance of recipient groups that could speak with one voice to Los Angeles County welfare officials. The salience and endurance of this local brown-black coalition is especially notable because Chicanas were marginalized within the black-led NWRO. The organization's board of directors included only one Latino/a at any given time, and Escalante broke ties with NWRO in 1968 because its leadership refused to address the rights of Spanish-speaking people in the organization's platform.[6] Where there was tension at the national level, historical evidence from Los Angeles shows that local black women leaders neither embraced nor opposed Chicana demands for culturally responsive social services. Chicana-led WROs organized separately from black groups on this issue, with support from Chicano movement organizations, and by the mid-1970s successfully pressured Los Angeles County to provide Spanish-language materials and hire Mexican American caseworkers. Chicanas thus expanded the discourse of welfare rights to include cultural citizenship and to have their language, customs, and identity represented and empowered within the public sphere.[7]

This history disrupts the historiography of the Chicano movement and the civil rights era more generally. Classic texts on twentieth-century Mexican American history are silent on the subject of public assistance—despite an abundance of primary sources that show sustained community organizing around the issue and the fact that movement organizations like the Brown Berets and Crusade for Justice included welfare rights in their political discourse after 1968.[8] Welfare rights did not fit organically into the record of the Chicano movement that was crafted by historians in the 1980s and 1990s. These narratives framed economic justice around land rights and farmworker struggles, pivoting the figure of the displaced male patriarch demanding land or living wages to support his family. Doubly stigmatized for lacking a male partner and depending on the "white man" (government), the Chicana welfare recipient seemed to clash with movement themes of a unified Chicano family and racial self-determination. Movement historiography associated barrio politics with youthful, countercultural rebellion, thronged by (male) masses of students, former gang members, and Vietnam draft resisters. In this imagined activist crowd, it was hard to spot the extremely poor and often middle-age women who led and participated in welfare rights struggles.[9] Yet when we look at archival sources, Chicana welfare activism is ubiquitous. Movement newspapers like *La Raza*, *Regeneración*, and *Encuentro Femenil* frequently covered welfare rights, and Chicano/a student organizations held panels on poverty and welfare. If we cannot see Chicana welfare rights activism from our historical vantage point, it is because the crafted picture of the movement hides it in plain sight.[10]

Scholars like Vicki Ruiz, Maylei Blackwell, Virginia Espino, and Rosie Bermudez have recuperated the history of the Chicana Welfare Rights Organization and its role in the development of Chicana feminism.[11] However, this scholarship has not moved beyond a racially bounded discussion, stuck in what some have termed a "silo approach" to civil rights history where each ethnic group has a separate story.[12] Claims to a unique cultural history and concerns that Chicano/a struggles not be cast as derivative of the black civil rights movement have resulted in a downplaying of influence, exchange, and cooperation between the Chicano/a and African American freedom struggles.[13] Thus, existing accounts of Chicana welfare rights activism do not examine in any depth how brown and black women forged a common social movement.

The silo mentality similarly hampers the historiography of the welfare rights movement. Historical accounts of the NWRO and related local struggles employ a black-white binary focused on dynamics between black welfare mothers and white middle-class organizers, and between black and white poor women. This black-white frame sidelines the historical experiences of Mexican American and Puerto Rican AFDC recipients and their contributions to the welfare rights movement, occluding our understanding of the ways that black and brown poor women interacted and sometimes united around poverty, motherhood, and welfare.[14]

The LA welfare rights movement challenges our view of antiracist radicalism in the 1960s, a period that historians associate with competition between African American and Mexican American groups for political prominence and limited state resources. Declension narratives cast conflict between blacks and Latinos as a "tragedy" of the civil rights era. The rise of cultural nationalism and identity politics are blamed for failed efforts at black-brown coalition, and the flagging progress of antiracist movements by the mid-1970s.[15] Yet Los Angeles tells a more complicated story. There was indisputable competition between the city's black and Mexican American politicians and some civil rights organizations over War on Poverty funds—competition that was expressed by some players in racial terms and trumpeted by the mainstream press as evidence that African Americans and Mexican Americans could not get along. Yet if we focus on grassroots organizing led by poor women of color, we see different cultural identities and political priorities existing alongside sustained cross-racial cooperation and solidarity.

Cross-racial collaboration did not prevent women leaders from embracing culturally specific identities, discourses, and organizing tactics. WROs reflected and advanced cultural nationalist projects that were gaining traction in black and Chicano communities in greater Los Angeles during the 1960s and 1970s. Escalante, for instance, had close ties to the militant Brown Berets and worked on myriad issues, from protesting the Vietnam War to fighting police brutality. Demands for welfare services in Spanish and the hiring of Mexican American caseworkers resonated with Chicano/a demands for cultural autonomy and pride. Similarly, African American welfare rights leaders were formed by and helped to shape black power politics in Los Angeles. At times, divergent racial identities and political priorities produced conflict between Chicana and African American activists. Yet, racial autonomy and cultural nationalism within the local movement existed simultaneously with—not in opposition to—a cross-racial alliance of poor Chicana and black mothers. Racial autonomy did not obstruct cross-racial collaboration among local activists; rather, I argue, it enabled solidarity. Though experienced through different cultural lenses, black and Chicana activists shared similar commitments to racial self-pride and conceptions of freedom that included women of color's sexual and economic autonomy.[16] Intersectional politics and a shared quest for poor women of color's self-determination bridged differences between Chicana and African American women and sustained the black-brown coalition for welfare rights.

RACE AND WELFARE IN CALIFORNIA

The welfare rights movement in Los Angeles emerged from the changing demographic and political landscape of welfare in California during the 1950s and 1960s. Growth of the state's nonwhite population, along with policy changes under Governor Pat Brown that made it easier to qualify for aid, led to growing numbers of African American and Mexican American recipients. Between 1950 and 1958, black families increased from 24 percent to 32 percent of the caseload and Mexican Americans from 17 percent to 22.5 percent. By 1960, for the first time in state history, families headed by women of color comprised the majority of those enrolled in Aid to Needy Children (ANC, California's name for AFDC until 1965). The "coloring" of public assistance was met by a racist backlash against families of color, cuts to welfare budgets, and punitive disciplinary measures to control the behavior of poor mothers. These changes also laid the groundwork for women of color in Los Angeles to organize for an adequate income, full access to social services, and an end to degrading welfare policies.

In postwar Los Angeles, growing caseloads followed economic downturn as the poverty rate grew 4.7 times faster than the population.[17] Black and Mexican workers who had migrated to Southern California during the wartime boom were devastated by postwar deindustrialization, as rubber, steel, and aircraft manufacturing downsized and moved out of central LA. Between 1963 and 1964 alone, twenty-eight industrial firms left South LA and East LA, respectively home to the majority of black and Mexican workers.[18] A 1965 study reported that more than half of area residents hovered around the poverty line, and it highlighted the extreme economic instability faced by women of color: "Female workers, whether Negro or Mexican are extremely low paid"; "4/5 of all Black women don't have a car, which hampers their job search," and 62 percent of all unemployed women were heads of households, including 30 percent of all unemployed Mexican American women who were either separated or divorced. Despite strong need, 84 percent of women did not receive unemployment benefits, and less than 28 percent received public assistance, leading researchers to conclude that "it is clear that government financial assistance does not go to a majority of unemployed persons."[19]

Caseloads ballooned in LA but did not keep pace with the poverty rate, as eligible families were deterred from accessing welfare. The stigma attached to welfare and an arduous application process led to underparticipation in the AFDC program. Los Angeles County caseworkers (the vast majority white) faced pressure from supervisors to weed out "fraud" and keep costs low. This led to systematic disentitlement as eligible applicants were denied aid or given the minimum allowable benefits. Reflecting societal views of Mexicans as peons and undeserving foreigners, Chicanas were often denied assistance and told by caseworkers to get a job as a maid or kitchen helper.[20] An editorial written by Escalante protested the pervasive disentitlement faced by Chicanas who sought public assistance:

> 1. Mrs. Ramirez goes into the [welfare] department with an emergency. Her daughter is very ill. She is badly in need of a medical card. She waits an amount of six hours, only to be told that she is to be given another appointment and told to come back. 2. Mrs. Esperanza Jaramillo goes into the department to apply for food stamps. She has gone eight times and has not been helped.[21]

African American women similarly complained of being deferred, denied, and underpaid by Los Angeles County caseworkers.[22] Systematic deferral and discrimination blocked women of color from accessing the social services they were entitled to by law.

Mothers receiving welfare also were denied constitutional protections. With no expectation to privacy rights, they were compelled to answer caseworkers' intrusive questions about their sexuality and personal behavior; denied reproductive choice, they were pressured to undergo sterilization or give up their babies for adoption; and in a system where most decisions rested with individual caseworkers, there was no balance of power or due process. As Chicana activist Anna NietoGomez recalls, the welfare office was "hostile to the 23rd power. . . . All your decisions were questioned. Why did you have sex? What did you feed your children? You were treated like in *The Scarlet Letter*."[23] Dale Clinton, a black welfare recipient from Long Beach, echoed this sentiment in a letter to President Johnson describing her caseworker's control over all domains of her life, questioning whether "I sold my citizenship so I could eat and pay rent."[24] For Escalante, the experience of being a welfare recipient was "more than the oppression of being treated like a second-class citizen, [it was] like you were not even of this country."[25] For poor women of color, the welfare system dramatized the unjust disciplinary power of the state and their precarious citizenship in US society.

Despite California's image as a generous welfare state, its maximum AFDC grant allowances did not keep up with inflation and consistently fell below federal standards. As the *Los Angeles Sentinel* editorialized, "Twenty-six states provide 100 percent of the basic needs for a family of four. . . . The Golden State provides only 91 percent of what a family of four needs to survive."[26] Recipients in the Bay Area and Los Angeles reported going hungry because they used AFDC food allowances to pay for rent. Mothers slept on sofas while children were crowded two to three to a bed, and families lived with dangerous, leaky gas stoves and broken refrigerators.[27] *Los Angeles Times* reporter Rúben Salazar documented the precarity commonly experienced by Chicana recipients through a profile of Margarita Sanchez, who lived with her ten children in a "mice-infested house with boarded up windows . . . torn-up floors, and a non-working toilet."[28] While this was all that Sanchez could afford with her $90 monthly housing allotment, the Probation Department cited the family's "unfit home" and removed the children to foster care. Recipients were stuck in a double-bind: welfare trapped them in unhealthful living conditions, yet public officials blamed them for these conditions, alleging that they were irresponsible mothers who deserved to be closely watched by social workers or lose custody of their children.

California conservatives—backed by powerful agribusiness, which saw welfare as undercutting its cheap labor supply—attacked AFDC as too costly and recipients as immoral freeloaders.[29] Whereas Southern politicians derided black recipients as "broodmares," California's antiwelfare discourse exemplified what scholar Ian Haney Lopez calls "dog whistle politics," a coded set of meanings that are publicly understood as racial without speaking openly about race.[30] A 1961 report by California's Senate Committee on Labor and Welfare, for instance, highlighted the rising number of nonwhite recipients followed by the racialized assertion that "the program reflects and magnifies the crime, deceit, irresponsibility, and immorality [in] some segments of our society."[31] A 1967 report by the Department of Mental Hygiene portrayed white recipients as psychologically damaged individuals in contrast to recipients of color, who were assigned a collective cultural pathology.[32] The report profiled one Mexican American family as follows: "Both parents were reared in Mexico, were illiterate and neither spoke English. . . . The family 'lived like pigs' and caseworker efforts to improve home management and living standards were markedly ineffective."[33] The report similarly cast African Americans as animalistic and resistant to progress. Dog-whistle racism drove California's war on welfare, as white politicians and voters ignored the structural forces that trapped black and Mexican American families in poverty, while they demanded that mothers of color assume moral and financial responsibility.

Beginning in the late 1950s and intensifying after Ronald Reagan's 1967 election to governor, California restricted welfare eligibility and cut benefits. The state began requiring parents to accept employment when available, and it barred pregnant women from receiving aid.[34] Counties initiated forced work programs for recipients and conducted midnight raids of homes of unmarried mothers suspected of having illicit relations with men. Warrantless searches of recipients' homes were so common that the NAACP's California chapter and the Community Service Organization united in 1965 to lobby Governor Pat Brown to stop midnight raids, arguing that African Americans and Mexican Americans were disproportionately targeted for these unconstitutional searches.[35] Governor Reagan later slashed public medical benefits for the poor, called for draconian audits of county welfare rolls, and refused to implement federally mandated increases in AFDC benefit levels.

Welfare recipients fought back. Like civil rights battles around education and voting rights, this fight was over public entitlements and constitutional rights that were legally endowed to people of color yet routinely withheld by the state. Early welfare rights organizing in South Los Angeles involved both interracial and intraracial organizing, as Mexican American and African American poor women together and separately began studying welfare policy to understand their rights, helping other women apply for aid and file appeals, and pressuring welfare officials to fire caseworkers known to have high denial rates.

A MOVEMENT RISES IN SOUTH LA

LA's welfare rights movement began with black and brown women working together. Though little is known about the Welfare Action and Community Organization (WACO), records show that it formed in 1957 or 1958 and involved African American and Mexican American women in South LA.[36] WACO's interracial membership reflected the mixed population of South LA in the 1950s, when African Americans were the majority (68 percent) and Mexican Americans composed a sizeable minority (over 18 percent) of area residents.[37] Cooperation between the two groups had been encouraged in the 1950s by the Los Angeles Federation of Settlements and Neighborhood Centers and Catholic Youth Services, including the latter's Watts Community House, which was dedicated to "bettering the relationship between Negroes and Mexican Americans" and ran an Interracial Mother's Group.[38] WACO thus followed from earlier projects in South LA to unite low-income Chicana and black women around common social problems.

WACO originally came together to pressure the Department of Social Services to fire a notorious caseworker in the South LA district office. The group began studying welfare statutes and teaching "know your rights" workshops at community centers in South LA. Dorothy Moore, a black welfare recipient who founded the group, explained, "The workers don't bother in many cases to explain the laws on the book."[39] Catherine Jermany joined WACO as a young, black, single mother who had been active in the Southern Christian Leadership Conference and wanted to see structural change in the welfare system. As she recalled, "[by only] changing one worker you could get someone equally as bad. The whole philosophy of the department had to be changed."[40] She continued, "Part of our work is giving welfare recipients the self-confidence to stand up to the county social workers as equals instead of doing whatever they say, like dogs."[41] Insisting that poor women were experts in all aspects of their lives, WACO's brown and black members demanded a voice in welfare policy.

So did the African American women in Watts who started ANC Mothers Anonymous in 1961. The group's leader was Johnnie Tillmon, a divorced mother of five from Arkansas who had labored most her life in sharecropping and commercial laundries. When Tillmon became ill and unable to work, she applied for public assistance and was outraged to discover how caseworkers mistreated recipients. With her neighbors in the Nickerson Gardens public housing project, she started ANC Mothers "to provide information, legislative and service action for the welfare recipients of Watts" and "to obtain decent jobs with adequate pay for those who can work, and to obtain an adequate income for those who cannot work."[42] The group also provided a social outlet for poor, black mothers, who shared child care and went on family trips to the beach and ball games. By the mid-1960s, ANC Mothers had moved out of Tillmon's home to an office on Central Avenue and had a core membership of fifteen to twenty black women who lived in four South LA housing projects.

Recipient-led organizing spread across Los Angeles in the latter half of the decade as poor women of color were inspired by broader civil rights struggles to challenge the social structures and ideologies that oppressed them. In February 1967, the NWRO-affiliated Poverty Research/Action Center counted twelve welfare rights groups in the Los Angeles area, with nearly half based in South LA. Reflecting the increasingly black character of this area as whites, Mexican Americans, and Japanese Americans moved out in the postwar era, most welfare rights organizations in South LA after 1965 were organized by black women. Demographic shifts during this period also transformed East LA from one of the most diverse working-class neighborhoods in the nation to a Chicano barrio, when by the mid-1960s over 90 percent of residents were of Mexican descent and nearly one-third were poor. Similar to the experience of African Americans in South LA, racial segregation and the growth of Chicano/a civil rights organizations in East LA in the 1950s and early 1960s laid the groundwork for Chicana organizing around poverty and welfare in the subsequent decade. Black women and Chicanas thus primarily worked in separate and parallel organizations that coordinated their message and tactics through a countywide coalition of welfare rights groups.

NAPP AND BLACK-BROWN CONFLICT AND COOPERATION AFTER 1965

A critical force in the spread of welfare rights organizing in black and brown communities was the Neighborhood Adult Participation Program (NAPP), the city's only War on Poverty program for adults (rather than youth), which ran "neighborhood outposts" in fifteen "poverty areas" that spanned South LA, the northeast San Fernando Valley, greater East LA, and the Harbor area. Initiated in 1965 and directed by black social worker Opal P. Jones, NAPP ran "neighborhood outposts" that employed African American and Mexican American residents to organize around community needs, from public services and installing street lights to adult literacy classes. Among these was NAPP's Boyle Heights Outpost, directed by Bob Gandera (whom Escalante married in 1974), which successfully forced Los Angeles County to open the first food stamp office in East LA in 1969.[43] Reflecting Jones's skepticism that "poverty experts" like social workers and social scientists knew what was best for the poor, NAPP ran "social welfare groups" in each of its outposts where recipients were trained and paid as "neighborhood aides."[44]

Because NAPP's outposts were named for the neighborhoods where they were located, many welfare rights groups assumed place-based names like San Pedro WRO or Venice WRO when they split from NAPP and developed their own governance and funding structures. Along with the Legal Aid Foundation, another War on Poverty program, NAPP provided critical training and resources to WROs and helped facilitate relations between the different neighborhood-based groups. These networks were critical to the development of the black-brown regional coalition for welfare rights.

NAPP's history illustrates the complexity of relations between African Americans and Mexican Americans in civil rights–era Los Angeles. The agency emerged from a political alliance between the city's black and Chicano civil rights leaders to wrest control over federal War on Poverty funding from conservative Mayor Sam Yorty. Yet from its inception, NAPP was encircled by competition for funding, as Mexican American leaders like Congressman Edward Roybal accused city and federal officials of a "Negroes first" approach that shortchanged Chicanas/os. East LA leaders complained that the majority of NAPP outposts were in South LA, with only three outposts in predominantly Mexican American areas, and that its executive board had not one Spanish-speaking representative. There was also conflict between Jones and Joe Maldonado, Chicano head of the Economic and Youth Opportunities Agency (EYOA), whom Jones publicly accused of serving the city's political bosses rather than poor residents. Tensions exploded in October 1966 when Jones fired Gabriel Yánez, East LA field director, angering many of the program's Mexican American staff, drawing ire from East LA leaders, and leading to Chicano/a pickets of NAPP offices.[45]

The conflict captured the attention of the mainstream press, as the *Los Angeles Times* ran more articles on black-brown fighting inside NAPP than it had previously on the program's accomplishments. Though blacks and Chicana/os continued to work together in NAPP until it closed in 1976, the program's troubles in the late 1960s sealed an enduring public myth of black versus brown conflict—one that has been endorsed by recent historical accounts of the city's War on Poverty.[46] Yet, the answer to the question of whether African Americans and Chicanas/os cooperated in LA's antipoverty struggles depends on where we look. If we turn our lens from political fights over limited state funding and flashpoints of racial conflict to an examination of grassroots organizing through NAPP, a vibrant black-brown coalition among the city's poor women comes clearly into view.

Nothing better exemplifies this cross-racial solidarity than the Los Angeles County WRO, which was directed by Jermany with the help of Chicana organizer Vivian Romero, both welfare recipients who had worked for NAPP as neighborhood aides. These women organized a Welfare Action Coalition (WAC) that engaged more than thirty welfare rights groups from across Los Angeles County to work together on common issues and goals. By the late 1960s, WAC representatives (including Jermany, Escalante, Tillmon, and Campos) met regularly with Department of Social Services Director Ellis Murphy to discuss their concerns and negotiate changes to county welfare policy. WAC organized countywide campaigns and mobilized mass public demonstrations that brought black and brown poor women and their children onto the streets and into government buildings to demand welfare justice. One early campaign in October 1966 called for $3 million in funding for child care and transportation costs for recipients participating in work training projects. About two dozen recipients picketed county supervisors' offices demanding that women who wanted to work be fully supported in their efforts. "Welfare recipients want off the welfare rolls," announced Romero. "We want to be self-supporting and productive." Later that afternoon, the board voted against the women's proposal.[47]

In November, following the death of a baby who was not able to get medical services because she was not listed on her mother's county medical identification card, LAWRO again called on recipients from across the county to picket supervisors' offices. This time protestors prevailed, as the department agreed to improve its card-processing system.[48] The coalition's demands became increasingly radical and their posture confrontational. In 1969, for instance, LAWRO called for all recipients to stage a rent strike by paying only the portion of their welfare grant allotted to rent. As protestor Maria Garcia announced, "I'm allowed $85 rent for housing . . . and my landlord wants $195 per month. He will have to get the other $119 from Reagan or Kenneth Hahn. I'm not going to pay the rest and no one is going to make me." While the rent strike never materialized, LAWRO's organizing got the attention of the state Department of Social Welfare and sparked a special hearing on the issue.[49] That same year, LAWRO threatened legal action if supervisors did not implement a recent federal increase in AFDC grants. More than 200 black and Chicana mothers stormed the supervisors' meeting carrying placards that read, "Raise our Money or We'll Raise Hell."[50]

THE EAST LOS ANGELES WELFARE RIGHTS ORGANIZATION

In a 1984 interview, Tillmon recalled meeting Escalante in 1967 to help her set up the East LA WRO.[51] While Escalante did not recollect this meeting, she has expressed that "the NWRO inspired me to organize our neighbors and friends in the barrio who were also affected by the cutbacks, but who were unaware of their rights as recipients."[52] Escalante met local welfare rights organizers in the summer of 1967, when she and her five children were receiving AFDC and living in the Ramona Gardens housing project in Boyle Heights. Governor Reagan had just slashed $210 million from Medi-Cal (California's Medicaid program) and implemented new coverage rules that eliminated all but emergency surgery, cut most dental care and all eyeglasses, and established an eight-day limit on private hospital care.[53] Progressive labor and antipoverty organizations in LA mobilized through the Committee to Save Medi-Cal, cochaired by Clarence Littlejohn, an African American doctor and president of the Urban League, and Ukrainian-born Molly Piontkowski, head of the Committee for the Rights for the Disabled.[54]

Angered by the cutbacks because her family relied on Medi-Cal for their health care, Escalante took the bus downtown on October 24 to join more than 250 demonstrators in denouncing Reagan's attack on the poor. The protest caught the attention of *Jet* magazine, which reported that "the lame, blind, [and] poor" had marched for three hours carrying placards that read, "Even Poor Children Have the Right to See a Dentist."[55] Escalante began attending campaign meetings and recalled that at one, "they asked if anyone was here to represent East LA and I was the only one who raised my hand."[56]

Escalante volunteered for the campaign and recruited other welfare mothers like Carmen Ceniza and her sister Irene Villalobos to distribute flyers about the Medi-Cal cuts in front of supermarkets, schools, and clinics in Boyle Heights. The cuts hit a nerve in East LA, where 23.6 percent of households fell below the federal poverty level.[57] The state of community health was dire. Los Angeles County General Hospital was one of only two area hospitals that served families on public assistance; at the other, the private White Memorial Hospital, fewer than 2 percent of patients received AFDC. A 1965 study found that General Hospital was severely impacted—with 3,151 hospital beds for almost 100,000 patients and an average waiting time of five to eight hours for emergency care. No East LA hospital offered services in Spanish or ambulance service.[58] Another study concluded that "Spanish-speaking patients [are] treated like second-class citizens" by white hospital administrators who viewed communication with them as "a nuisance."[59] The hospital was notorious for forcing sterilization on pregnant patients who did not speak English or received welfare. For these reasons, the Medi-Cal program was a lifeline for East LA residents, as it gave them access to quality care from private doctors and hospitals.

In November 1967, Escalante organized a meeting for welfare recipients at the All Nations Community Center. As she recalled, "I was still concerned that there were not enough people that were reached. And when I got there, I was shocked. Standing room only!"[60] More than seventy-five people attended and signed letters addressed to Governor Reagan that read, "Nosotros los recipientes de welfare, mi esposo, hijos, y yo protestamos el recorte de Medi-Cal; mi esposo está enfermo y sin atención médica no podrá restableserse" (We, the recipients of welfare, my husband, children and myself, protest the Medi-Cal cuts; my husband is sick, and without medical care he will not be able to get back on his feet). The letter's focus on a disabled father reflected the prevalence of poverty among two-parent Mexican American families, in which many men worked in the agricultural and informal sectors where injuries were common yet not covered by worker's compensation laws. As *La Raza* reported, Escalante "spoke of the need to organize a strong Welfare Rights Organization in the East Side," and "those present agreed to join and to pay 25 cents a month to contribute to the expenses of the organization and to hold classes in how to get the full benefits of present Welfare Programs."[61] While a few men joined the group, the organization was primarily run by and for women—a fact reflected in its later name change to the Chicana Welfare Rights Organization. CWRO volunteers ran workshops on welfare policies, helped individuals apply for aid and file grievances against the welfare department, and translated government forms for Spanish speakers. Escalante organized an Eastside Welfare Coalition, which unified community-based groups like the Brown Berets, Social Action Latinos for Unity Development (SALUD), and Chicana Service Action Center to demand improved services at the Department of Social Services Belvedere district office.

While advocating for the East LA community, Escalante also worked tirelessly for changes in welfare policy at the county, state, and federal levels. By 1969, she had emerged as a leader of the countywide welfare rights movement and frequently collaborated with Jermany and Tillmon in planning campaigns and negotiating with county welfare officials. In December of that year, the three leaders worked together on a campaign to protest the slashing of funds for food, appliances, furniture, and other household items (labeled "special needs"). On December 10, they led a multiracial delegation of fifty recipients to the supervisors' offices. When the supervisors failed to correct the problem, organizers returned with more than 300 recipients, who shut down the board meeting with loud clapping and chanting.[62] Public protests like these transformed black and brown welfare recipients from desperate supplicants to empowered citizens and shifted shame from poor mothers of color to the public officials who failed to uphold justice.

CHICANAS AND INTERRACIAL ORGANIZING IN THE HARBOR AREA

Chicana recipients were also leaders in the interracial struggle for welfare rights that rocked the LA–Long Beach Harbor area. Though little biographical information is available about activists in this part of Los Angeles, newspaper accounts document extensive organizing in Harbor communities and militant leadership by Mexican American women. Unlike most of LA in the late 1960s, where blacks and Mexican Americans often lived far apart from each other, Harbor cities had integrated poor neighborhoods, and blacks and Mexicans were served by the same social services district office in Long Beach; by many accounts, it was the most unfriendly and inefficient welfare office in the county. While some Harbor area WROs were integrated, Chicana recipients also formed groups that held meetings in Spanish, like the Hawaiian Gardens WRO led by Pat Meldez. Most of these WROs were affiliated with the NWRO, which drew them into common action campaigns. In 1969, Harbor groups rolled out an NWRO campaign to apply in mass for special grants in a strategic effort to overwhelm welfare bureaucracies with client demand and force officials to make reforms. Frustrated with the Department of Social Services' slow response to their applications, white, black, and Chicana WRO activists piled their worn-out bedding, furniture, and broken appliances at the entrance to the welfare department to drive home the urgency of their family's needs.[63] Jean Rasmussen, head of the Long Beach WRO, asked, "Would [department director] Pat Murphy like his ten children sleeping on couches or eating spoiled food?"[64] Conflict between Harbor activists and Paul Lowrey, the department's Long Beach District director, escalated in September 1970, as women demanded back-to-school clothing allowances for their children. Rosemarie Negron, Chicana leader of the Harbor Hills WRO, joined thirty other mothers in chanting "We want school clothes now" as the group took over Lowrey's office and refused to let him leave during their five-hour sit-in.[65] The protest attracted public attention to the desperation and militancy of welfare recipients and ultimately pressured the department to improve services in its Long Beach office.

Mass public demonstrations like these created a multiracial public space for poor women, encouraging black and Chicana recipients to forge a common language of welfare rights based on their parallel experiences of racial, class, and gender oppression. Cross-racial unity, however, did not supplant microlocal organizing based on each group's ethnic identity and particular community needs. Rather, WROs organized together and separately at the same time, fostering brown and black cultural autonomy simultaneously with mutual respect and solidarity.

"KEEPING WITH OUR CULTURE" WHILE FIGHTING FOR "POOR PEOPLE OF ALL RACES"

Though Escalante credits the NWRO for inspiring her jump into activism, the CWRO operated separately from the national organization. As she explained in a 1974 speech,

> The Chicano Movement also greatly influenced the ELAWRO in the late '60s. We chose to place more emphasis on the special needs and problems of the Raza communities. It was for this reason that a break was made from the national organization. Though basically the same goals [as the NWRO] were kept, the operation of the Chicana Welfare Rights Organization has been more in keeping with our culture and tradition.[66]

The CWRO's decision to break from the NWRO followed from Escalante's frustration when her proposal to include Spanish-language services among key demands of welfare rights was rejected at a NWRO convention in 1968.[67] While the NWRO's predominantly black leadership viewed language rights as a marginal issue, Chicana activists saw it as fundamental. Without the provision of social services in Spanish, Chicana leaders in LA argued, Mexican Americans could not fully access their citizenship rights. Across Los Angeles, Chicana-led WROs campaigned for the Department of Social Services to hire Spanish-speaking social workers and make of all its forms and services available in Spanish.

In April 1969, Chicana members of the Hawaiian Gardens WRO met with the department's assistant director, Leonard Panish, to voice their concerns about the "less than adequate" services provided by the Long Beach office, where an estimated 75 percent of recipients were Mexican American. One organizer told Panish, "Many of the women here can barely say yes or no [in English]. And yet none of the caseworkers speak Spanish—why?"[68] The women demanded that Panish assign a full-time Spanish-speaking social worker for the 300–400 Mexican American recipients who lived in the community. East LA activists went even further, demanding that the department recruit and promote Mexican American social workers who shared their clients' cultural background and values (not Anglo social workers who spoke Spanish). When the director refused to negotiate this issue, Escalante accused him of "insulting the entire East LA community."[69] CWRO members, the Brown Berets, and other community activists picketed outside Murphy's home for several days until he agreed with meet with her group. By 1974, Chicana activists had succeeded in pressuring the Department of Social Services to print its forms in Spanish and to open new welfare offices in East LA and the Harbor area that were staffed by Mexican Americans.[70]

The CWRO's close ties to the Brown Berets reflected Escalante's embracing of the youth organization's ideologies of Chicano/a self-determination, self-defense, and liberation. Two of Escalante's teenage children were Berets, and group members frequently hung out at her home and provided security against public brutality for mothers and their children at welfare rights protests, giving the CWRO a revolutionary public image and cache in the Chicano movement.[71] Reflecting her admiration of the Crusade for Justice's Corky Gonzalez, Escalante conceived of the CWRO's nonhierarchical structure as "familia," run by a volunteer staff of welfare mothers and their children, Chicana students from Cal State LA and Cal State Long Beach, and other community supporters. Convinced that private foundation and government funding would enable their political autonomy (a view shared by ANC Mothers), CWRO members cooked and sold tamales and menudo and Escalante earned money from speaking engagements across the nation. Escalante and other CWRO members wrote bilingual articles on welfare rights for *La Raza* and frequented the militant newspaper's office, where movement activists gathered to discuss Mexican and Mexican American history alongside the revolutionary theories of Mao and Che Guevara.[72] Movement critiques of racism and capitalism informed the CWRO's analysis of the welfare system, as a writer described in *La Raza*: "It is no accident that the streets of East LA and Watts are lousy . . . that the police are vicious to chicanos and black people, but not to Whites. . . . They are the results of a way of thinking that says that money and economic power is more important than human rights."[73]

The CWRO's position on welfare rights often was filtered through movement discourse of racial autonomy and cultural preservation. The CWRO led a national campaign against the 1974 Talmadge Amendment, which required all welfare recipients with children over age six to find employment. In a statement on behalf of the CWRO protesting the bill, one of the group's members, Anna NietoGomez, argued,

> If the Chicana is forced to put her children into educational centers which have dramatically failed her people, her children may become drop outs at a much earlier age. The child's life can be surrounded by not only racist, monolingual, monocultural institutions, but the child can also have to contend with the stigma and harassment encountered from the educational institutions towards people on welfare.[74]

Viewing welfare rights as one strand in a broader Chicana/o struggle for economic and racial justice, the CWRO and Escalante were active on many fronts: protesting the Vietnam War, supporting youth organizing for educational justice, challenging the Catholic Church, and fighting the forced sterilization of Chicana mothers by public health officials.[75]

Racial pride and a radically expansive political praxis similarly characterized LA's black welfare rights leaders. Premilla Nadasen argues that Tillmon had a "distinctive Black Power politics [that] placed black women at the center" and that was rooted in "a deep sense of independence, autonomy, and self-pride."[76] Tillmon advocated for community control of public institutions and was part of a broad-based struggle that included militant organizations like the Black Panthers that called for the construction of a public hospital in South LA that would be run by a community board that would "have a voice in the decision-making process."[77] Tillmon opposed the use of violence but supported physical confrontation tactics like sit-ins and threats of violence; she defended welfare mothers' right to "do whatever becomes necessary" to attain justice for their families.[78] Jermany was a member of Maulana Karenga's US organization, which advocated armed self-defense and black nationhood founded in pan-African cultural traditions. She co-chaired the LA Black Congress, which included more than twenty African American organizations to achieve "operational unity" in the city's black freedom movement.[79] Jermany often called for racial solidarity to build support for the welfare rights movement, such as in a speech to the Association of Black Social Workers encouraging them to "Think Black" and "Talk Black."[80]

Racial pride and cultural nationalism did not prevent these activists from working closely together through the mid-1970s. Escalante remembered that working with Jermany challenged both of them to be open to cross-cultural exploration. At first, she explained, they quibbled about meeting over soul food versus Mexican food, but then "Catherine discovered that she loved tacos and I loved soul."[81] The movement in Los Angeles, however, was not always an interracial paradise. Some black residents viewed Chicano/as with suspicion, perhaps reflecting an awareness that at certain historical moments, Mexican Americans had encountered comparatively fewer racial bars to employment and housing than African Americans had in the city. Escalante recounted that a black protestor at a welfare rights rally told her that she was not welcome because she was white. As the startled Escalante started to explain that Chicanos are not European and are also targets of structural racism, Jermany intervened to defend Escalante from her interlocutor: "She's with us and she's a sister."[82] Their sisterhood sprang not from society's hierarchical constructions of difference but from Jermany's and Escalante's intersectional understanding of poverty and their shared political convictions and commitments. They frequently called for "a coalition of welfare recipients of all ethnic backgrounds,"[83] emphasizing how all poor people lost when the government slashed social services to fund the war or when women were forced to choose between public aid and their right to bear as many children as they desired. Their similar experiences as racialized mothers and welfare recipients laid the groundwork for a radical sisterhood that was enriched by their antiracist, feminist, and class-centered politics.

This intersectionality emanated throughout these women's philosophies of welfare rights. In a stinging article published in *La Raza* in 1968, Escalante provocatively asked, "Are Welfare Recipients Human?" She elaborated:

> Notice to all welfare clients: You are not taxpayers; you don't support yourselves. You don't take good care of your kids; they are hungry, dirty, not clothed properly. . . . You are no good; you should be sterilized, your children put in homes; you should be forced to go to work; you should be ashamed of yourselves for living.

Jermany expressed a similarly layered analysis of poverty when she interrupted a supervisors' meeting with a group of 200 recipients carrying placards that read, "Mommy, I Want Some Milk." She lambasted rich, white, male politicians who tried to control poor women's lives: "Reagan and all these other people . . . making $1 a minute say you don't need your money . . . Ladies, do we want our money NOW?"[84] Similar views of poor women of color's autonomy over their bodies and finances were echoed in Tillmon's observation: "We know how easily the lobby for birth control can be perverted into a weapon against poor women. . . . Birth control is a right, not an obligation. A personal decision, not a condition of a welfare check."[85] In different words, LA's welfare rights leaders conceived a radical feminist of color framework that illuminated and challenged intersecting forms of sexism, racism, and class inequality.

RETHINKING IDENTITY POLITICS AND BLACK-BROWN COALITION

Black and Chicana activists in LA connected welfare rights to the historical exploitation of nonwhite workers and control over women's bodies and argued that public assistance should facilitate, not undermine, poor women's independence. This history shows how we can write more expansive accounts of grassroots black power and brown power movements that center women's economic justice struggles and break beyond racially siloed frames. Just as the story of the black and Chicano freedom movements are incomplete without welfare rights, so is the history of black power without Chicana/o activism or of brown power without African American activism. These were mutually informed struggles that intersected in substantive and long-lasting ways—not merely in rhetoric or in short-lived flashpoints of solidarity, as is often portrayed. Recent scholarship has documented other black-brown coalitions that thrived in this era, from Chicago's "original rainbow coalition,"[86] to multiracial coalitions of working women fighting for equal employment opportunity in the early 1970s.[87]

I offer a counterpoint here to pervasive pessimism about black and brown relations in the past and present, where "identity politics" (especially strains that emphasize intraracial solidarity) is cast as the enemy of progressive coalition and effective organizing by the Left. The LA story documented here proves otherwise; identity politics existed alongside and helped to foster coalition politics in the countywide welfare rights movement. In her 1991 treatise on intersectionality, African American feminist scholar Kimberlé Crenshaw argues that an identity politics that recognizes intragroup and intergroup differences based on gender, race, class, and sexuality can foster political solidarity: "Through an awareness of intersectionality, we can better acknowledge and ground the differences among us and negotiate the means by which these differences will find expression in constructing group politics."[88] For the African American and Chicana leaders of LA's welfare rights movement, their intersectional praxes as poor *and* women *and* nonwhite erected a bridge, not border, between them. The movement's decentered structure allowed small groups to organize at the microlocal level through culturally specific frameworks and issues that spoke to Chicana and black women's specific identities and experiences while laying an inclusive framework for self-love and self-determination for all poor people.

13 "TU REATA ES MI ESPADA"

ELIZABETH SUTHERLAND'S
CHICANA FORMATION

ANNEMARIE PEREZ

Took Tessa and her friend Valerie to see the Beatles' A Hard Day's Night *in New York. When it was over, we all got up without a word and RAN out of the theatre and across Second Ave . . . running running up three blocks to the car which we jumped into and I started it in a sec and drove sixty miles an hour straight to the Doubleday store on 5th Avenue which is open until midnight,* Yeah Yeah Yeah.

—ELIZABETH MARTÍNEZ, "YEAH, YEAH, YEAH"

The above passage, written in 1964, is an excerpt from Elizabeth "Betita" Martínez's personal journal, parts of which were published in a 2013 special issue of *Social Justice* dedicated to Martínez.[1] I open with it because it so well reflects Martínez's spirit, her youthfulness, voice, and ability to be caught up in wonder and joy. With all that was going on and that she was a part of in the United States in 1964, she was able to celebrate Beatlemania's mad, exuberant cultural moment with her daughter. Later, writing a review of the film for *New Republic*, she adopted a more detached, journalistic voice. In her review, written with more distance and less breathless excitement than her journal entry, Martínez compares the Beatles' film performance with the recently deceased Marilyn Monroe's singing of "Happy Birthday" to John Kennedy, in the process mentioning issues of class, communism, and the "moral beauty" of the Mississippi summer project.[2] Trying to capture something of this moment, I screened the film, imagining Martinez, her daughter, and her daughter's friend in what must have been a wildly enthusiastic New York theater. Watching *A Hard Day's Night*, I found I was looking at the way the Beatles, as depicted in the film, move with ease throughout British society, the film's and their environment's powerful center, while somehow remaining apart from the social groups they contacted, occupying a central yet liminal position. That liminal position, the powerful center somehow apart from their environment, observer rather than participant, offered me a way of reading Martínez in her writings as Elizabeth Sutherland. Likewise, the two voices, the energetic one in her journal and her critical and intellectual review for the *New Republic*, illustrate the way that in writing as Sutherland, her "Betita" voice changes and is sublimated into journalistic detachment. While both voices are clearly hers, it is notable that the journal entry captures the moment and energy of *A Hard Day's Night* best.

A difficulty with writing about someone whose life is as rich and whose work is as prolific as Elizabeth Sutherland/Elizabeth "Betita" Martínez's is knowing where and when to start. I have been fascinated with Martínez's career writing as Elizabeth Sutherland since I first discovered the open secret that the Elizabeth Sutherland who contributed to the women's liberation anthology *Sisterhood Is Powerful* is that book's second Chicana contributor. Too, I identify with her Chicana story, the mixed daughter of an Anglo mother and Mexican father, growing up in middle-class childhood surrounded by suburban whiteness, with the Mexican community as something expressed only within my family, never my neighborhood. Her East Coast, middle-class background is not what readers might expect of a 1960s and 1970s Chicano movement activist.

Martínez's production as an author, editor, and activist spans more than fifty years and intersects with multiple movements and causes—basically all Left causes of the United States in the late twentieth and early twenty-first centuries. She supported the Cuban revolution, the civil rights movement, women's liberation, socialism, and the Chicano movement, all the way to working for immigration rights and a living wage in the early 2010s. Her first professional publication credit was in 1960, her latest, 2013.[3] Martínez's writing across the decades is crisp, honest, and always revolutionary, always concerned with social justice, always connecting causes and movements. My focus here is on her work and publications not as Elizabeth "Betita" Martínez—works familiar to anyone in Chicana/o studies—but as Elizabeth "Liz" Sutherland, spanning the years 1960–1968. The name Sutherland was not simply a pen name for Martínez, a mistake I made in my earlier work on her, but an identity she worked—and to an extent lived—under. This was so much the case that many people who knew her during her 1960s work on the civil rights movement didn't know her as Martínez and didn't know she was Chicana/Latina.[4] Martínez's creation and assumption of this Sutherland self, and the ways in which it informed her experience in the civil rights movement and her accounts of the Cuban revolution, are the focus of this chapter. This adds to the scholarship demonstrating that the Chicano movement, rather than being simply nationalistic, was for activists and writers like Martínez part of a transnational revolution.

The year of Martínez's journal entry, 1964, was the year on which so much that happened in the turbulent, change-filled decade of the 1960s would turn. The United States was in the midst of social, political, and cultural change. Toward the end of the previous year, President Kennedy was assassinated, causing shockwaves throughout the US political and social landscape. In February 1964 two momentous events happened in the United States: the 1964 Civil Rights Act passed in the House of Representatives, and the Beatles made their first appearance on *The Ed Sullivan Show*. Both events marked seismic shifts in youth culture as issues of race and civil rights fomented on university campuses. That June began what would come to be called Freedom Summer, a time when, as part of the Student Nonviolent Coordinating Committee (SNCC), African American and white activists—mostly northern college students—risked their safety in the Summer Freedom Project, going south to Mississippi to establish Freedom schools, register voters, desegregate lunch counters and in other ways promote the cause of civil rights. As the nation collectively watched and followed the young people working on Freedom Summer in the press, they saw the brutality of Jim Crow racism and the evolution of national opinion on civil rights for all Americans. At the same time, in August 1964, further stoking the fires of Beatlemania, the film *A Hard Day's Night* made its New York premiere, providing the summer's soundtrack. Both events, led and influenced by the period's youth culture, are marked in the writings of Elizabeth Sutherland.

FORMATION

Though Elizabeth "Betita" Martínez/Elizabeth Sutherland was part of a generation and a class that second-wave feminist Betty Friedan claimed was "taught to pity the neurotic unfeminine, unhappy women who wanted to be poets or physicists or presidents,"[5] Martínez's life had (like Friedan's) actually taken a different path—not that of the middle-class marriage that a woman of her suburban class and elite liberal arts education would be expected to take. From her interviews it is clear that Martínez, like her mother, always intended to have a career and from an early age had longed to make a difference in the world. Likewise, her early life is not the expected narrative of the majority of 1960s and 1970s Chicana activists who came from working-class backgrounds or majority–Mexican American communities. Hers is a story of growing up on the East Coast and having access to a privileged education and potential assimilation to the US middle class. Both as a woman and as a Chicana her life challenged patterns of expected narratives and paths.

Born in 1925 to a Mexican immigrant father and Anglo mother, Martínez was always "Betita," the nickname given to her by her family. She grew up as an only child, her mother a high school Spanish teacher, her father working first at the Mexican consulate and then as a Spanish literature professor at Georgetown University. The family lived in the Washington, DC, segregated, whites-only Chevy Chase suburb. While they were not wealthy, her childhood was decidedly comfortable middle class,[6] but with clear and unspoken racial differences that unsettle her easy accounts of tennis games and children's parties.[7]

Discussing her work in the civil rights movement, Martínez recalled childhood experiences of racism and segregation, of a time when she and her dark-skinned father were sent to the back of a public bus, and when the girl next door was not allowed to play with her or come to her parties because Martínez was Mexican. At the same time, her parents gently told her it was not appropriate for her to eat in the kitchen with their black housekeeper.[8] Because she was not black in a region that saw race through a black-white lens, she moved in a default middle-class white world, albeit with a difference, marked by her being asked at school if she was Hawaiian. During World War II, 1942–1946, she attended Swarthmore College, a Quaker school interested in social justice, and was the school's first Chicana student. During her years there, writing for the student paper and graduating with honors and bachelor's degrees in history and Spanish, she was the only nonwhite student. In a 2006 interview with Loretta Ross, Martínez discussed being deeply affected by both the horror of the Nazi Holocaust and the United States' bombing of Hiroshima and Nagasaki and wanting to make a difference in the world. Upon graduation, these inhuman events and the large-scale loss of life influenced her decision to work at the newly created United Nations, with the mission of helping to bring about world peace.[9] She secured a job using her college connections and worked for the UN in various capacities and for different delegations, including India and African nations, on issues of colonialism and decolonization, from 1946 to 1954. Again because of her Swarthmore connections, she entered into the New York literary milieu while also becoming involved in various leftist causes.[10] In 1957 she left her work at the United Nations and began to work in photography and publishing under the name Elizabeth Sutherland.

The name "Liz Sutherland" was Martínez's creation, with "Liz," an Anglo and more adult version of her first name replacing the childhood Spanish diminutive "Betita," and "Sutherland" drawn from her Anglo mother's middle name. Her taking a last name from her mother may seem an odd anticipation of what would become the women's liberation movement's feminist practice of taking one's mother's name and rejecting the patriarchy of the father's surname; however, that was not Martínez's reason for making the change. There are a number of possible reasons for her adopting a new name and her seeming rejection of "Martínez," most of which have been given and expanded upon by Martínez herself across several interviews and in her later writings. Among the reasons she has enumerated are that she was attracted by Sutherland's "literary ring," especially as she moved into the Anglo-centric worlds of journalism and publishing. She did not, after all, take her mother's maiden name, instead opting for the Anglo-literary "Sutherland." Writers adopt pen names for a variety of reasons; for Martínez, "Sutherland" cloaked her Mexican American identity, allowing her to disguise her minority status in a way that she was unable to do with respect to her skin color. Additionally, this was the 1950s and 1960s East Coast, where race was defined as a black/white binary. That Martínez was concerned about being identified and judged (or prejudged) as a Mexican American, about not having an opportunity to have her writing considered, seems clear. Years later, answering the question of why she had adopted "Sutherland," Martínez wrote rhetorically, "Who would publish someone named Martínez then?"[11] By writing this, she points out that in the 1950s and 1960s the name "Martínez" brought her ability to write at all into question. Describing her work in the period, Tony Platt writes, commenting on Martínez's indigenous features, "As a woman who looked clearly 'Mexican' Elizabeth Sutherland had to work trebly hard to be noticed and taken seriously by New York's white, male literati."[12] As a member of Fair Play for Cuba and a socialist woman working in what were overwhelmingly male-dominated fields, her Latina name and Chicana identity were, perhaps, one intersecting oppression too many. Ultimately, the question is not why she adopted "Sutherland," but why, after successfully working and writing as Sutherland for most of a decade, she returned to Martínez.

In the years since the 1960s, Chicano studies and specifically Chicana feminism have emerged as theoretical fields, crossing and interconnecting disciplines. Karen Mary Davalos outlines six themes of Chicana feminist writing and praxis, identifying among them "not seeking legitimacy,"[13] or, in Edén Torres's title, *Chicana without Apology*.[14] As Elizabeth Sutherland, Martínez sought and found what can be read as middle-class legitimacy through publications in mainstream magazines and as an editor for Simon and Schuster. When she abandoned this identity, she sought (and achieved) a different sort of legitimacy within the Chicano movement and also reclaimed her identity as "Betita," a private name, in the public sphere of the Chicano movement, foreshadowing work by writers as politically different from her as Richard Rodriguez, who argued that Spanish and Chicano identity represented part of his private sphere. As a Chicana activist, Martínez consciously made this identity part of her public self.

WRITING AS ELIZABETH SUTHERLAND

By 1964, Sutherland had worked in publishing as a journalist and editor for several years, putting out books and articles on various leftist causes for several mainstream publications. As a mark of the uniqueness of Sutherland's career at this time, we might consider how Betty Friedan, discussing the literary landscape of 1963, wrote of the limitations placed on women in publishing: "A woman researcher on *Time* magazine, for instance, cannot, no matter what her ability, aspire to be a writer; the unwritten law makes the men writers and editors, the women researchers."[15] Yet by 1963, the same year *The Feminine Mystique* was published, thirty-eight-year-old Sutherland was both an editor for the publisher Simon and Schuster and writing political and arts journalism for *Horizons*, *New Republic*, *The Nation*, *Film Quarterly*, *Village Voice*, and the British newspaper *The Guardian*, among other publications.[16] She socialized with James Baldwin and the Russian poet Yevgeny Yevtushenko. Likewise, by 1963 she was also heavily involved with Friends of the Student Nonviolent Coordinating Committee, working on fund-raising and volunteer coordination, and a supporter of the Fair Play for Cuba Committee. Civil rights in the United States and postrevolutionary Cuba were the two causes at the center of Sutherland's work for the rest of the decade. Her most significant work as a writer and editor would focus on these topics.

Sutherland's relationship with Cuba and the Cuban Revolution began during her time in New York publishing. She belonged to Fair Play for Cuba, which supported the Cuban Revolution and deplored what they saw as unfair sanctions and aggression toward the newly formed Castro-led government. Sutherland's feelings about Cuba were deeply connected to her political idealism. Her friend and biographer Tony Platt, looking back on her life, wrote that her 1961 trip to Cuba for the National Congress of Cuban Writers and Artists was a "turning point" for Sutherland.[17] Yet her interest in and work with Cuba had begun earlier. Sutherland went to Cuba for the first time in 1959,[18] three months after Batista's overthrow; she was invested in revolutionary Cuba and Castro from the beginning. The Cuban Revolution (1953–1959) and its project of building the first socialist state in the Americas inspired and energized her. In later life, planting her flag in support of the revolution, Martínez wrote that "when Cuba declared itself socialist, so did I."[19]

She traveled to Cuba in 1961 (the year Castro declared Cuba communist and the United States sponsored the failed Bay of Pigs invasion) to document the social, political, and cultural impact of the revolution for *The Guardian*. The two-part series on Castro that Sutherland produced as a result of her experiences made her loyalties clear.[20] In this work, she revealed her interest, no doubt cultivated by her time working for the United Nations, in the global struggle of the poor and her sympathy for and belief in socialism and its potential to lift up the underclass. Martínez's socialism, though influenced by her studies of Marxism, was inspired by 1950s and 1960s land revolutions against colonialism. Her *Guardian* articles offered a counterpoint to prevailing US anti-Castro rhetoric, which was coming from both of the country's main political parties. Sutherland's writing was in near-total sympathy with the aims of the Cuban Revolution, demonstrating what was for her a lifelong position against capitalism and imperialism, especially US imperialism. She blamed Cuba's problems of the time on a combination of a "classic colonial pattern" of underdevelopment,[21] one being addressed by the creation of Soviet-style farm collectives,[22] and shortages created by the US boycott. She even defended the "630 executions reported since Batista's overthrow," pointing out how the "henchmen of the US-supported Batista regime" were responsible for the brutal deaths of "some twenty thousand."[23]

Sutherland's articles also focused on Cuban life outside of Havana (and therefore away from the city's elites and former elites), the success of the nationwide literacy drive, and the improvements in the lives of the campesinos in Cuba's rural areas.[24] Her articles read as statements of clear-eyed support for Cuba, the revolution, and Castro. That same year, drawing on her experiences in Cuba as well as her work as assistant to the director of photography for the Museum of Modern Art in New York, she published a study of postrevolution film in Cuba for the scholarly journal *Film Quarterly*.[25]

Sutherland's work on Cuban cinema for *Film Quarterly* reveals more than her sympathy for Castro and the Cuban Revolution. In the article, while detailing the state of Cuban cinema, Sutherland demonstrates her familiarity with Cuban film pre- and postrevolution as well as an understanding of socialist and communist films from around the world. She discusses how prerevolutionary Cuban cinema was influenced largely by the United States and Mexico, connections reflected in the period's Cuban productions.[26] Sutherland then describes the new film industry in Cuba, pointing out that at this point, it was only three years old and the first nationalized film industry in the Americas. She describes it as being "like the revolution . . . filled with youth, excitement and self-confidence."[27]

The image of Cuba as a youthful socialist endeavor infuses all of her writings about the island and its people over the next decade. She also examines films made in and about Cuba since the revolution as the island tried to come to terms with its identity, a mixture of its prerevolution island playground culture and the battles it fought (and was fighting) for its self-determination. Demonstrating its transgenre nature, the article is a hybrid combination of academic film studies, journalism on the evolution of Cuba, and propaganda. Among the parts of the article that read like propaganda are her descriptions of the facilities available to filmmakers—"a huge new 'film city' is being completed, worthy of Cecil B. DeMille"—that evoke Hollywood in its golden age, as well as her discussion of the Cuban amenities in equally gushing terms.[28] This aside, the article is well-researched, demonstrating Sutherland's background in photography and her wide understanding of socialist film, an interest she continues and expands in her discussion of Cuban film in her 1969 study of Cuban society and culture, *The Youngest Revolution: A Personal Report on Cuba*.[29]

A significant part of the *Film Quarterly* article "Cinema of Revolution: 90 Miles from Home" is Sutherland's discussion of the early work by director Tomás Gutiérrez Alea; later in his long career, he would direct *Strawberry and Chocolate*, the first Cuban film to be nominated for an Academy Award (1993). Highlighting Alea's "use of newsreel footage to produce an ideologically effective film,"[30] Sutherland references the realism that characterized the era's communist films. However, while ideology is important, it is not Sutherland's overwhelming concern. She distinguishes Cuban film from Soviet film, focusing on the Cuban cinema's "Latin" quality. Most of Sutherland's article is a detailed and thoughtful exploration of Cuban film in which she notes the country's uniqueness as a "socialist state, but . . . also (1) a Latin country and (2) much influenced by the United States."[31] Pointing out their hybrid history and visual influences, she effectively contrasts the Cuban films' human scale with the "Russian-style grandeur of Soviet cinema."[32] Given the influence of the USSR on Cuba, due to the island's financial dependence, this distinction is notable. In this article, her enthusiasm is tempered, in a way that would mark all her writings on Cuban art and culture, with discussion of problems encountered by films made outside of the official Cuban industry. She recounts how one film, *P.M.*, an exploration of Cuban nightlife, had been refused commercial booking by the Cuban government, a situation she hopes will change as the revolution "grows more secure and mature."[33] The tension between artistic freedom, human rights, and ideology is one that recurs in all of Sutherland's writings, but those on Cuba in particular.

LETTERS FROM A US REVOLUTION

According to Sutherland, when she was in Cuba the people she met saw the US civil rights movement as the start of a class and race revolution in the United States. She was involved in the civil rights movement as a Friend of SNCC from its early period and began publishing work about the organization in January 1964. In her *Nation* article "Mandate from History," she introduces readers to the organization, even offering that the name is pronounced "SNICK." She gives an account of the 1963 meeting of SNCC at Howard University and reports, in part, on Bayard Rustin's idea that rather than going into poor black communities, white northerners should go into poor white communities and organize there, in pursuit of what Sutherland calls "a true social revolution in America."[34] As in her work about Cuba, revolution, resistance to the hegemony of the United States, and a critique of capitalism are ever-present in her civil rights writing. In the *Nation* article, Sutherland writes against SNCC's recent popular depiction in a *Life* magazine article by Theodore White that had "asserted that SNCC is an extremist organization."[35] Sutherland's article is an undeniably sympathetic piece of journalism, yet in contrast to what would become Chicana feminist writing's tradition of autobiography,[36] and the budding movement of New Journalism, Sutherland did not reveal her own involvement with SNCC or locate herself within the movement, maintaining the somewhat distanced voice of the traditional journalist rather than embracing the "gonzo" journalism of the (largely) white Left.

The book *Letters from Mississippi*, edited by Sutherland in 1965 and reissued under the name Elizabeth Martínez in 2007 with additional material,[37] is a document that traces the collective journey of 152 volunteers, most of them white, who were students at northern universities, using excerpts from their letters to construct a narrative of their experiences working in Mississippi's black communities in the summer of 1964.[38] It is a masterful book, assembled from hundreds of letters that were painstakingly contextualized and reassembled to craft a coherent story of experiences that were both dangerous and transformative. The book is a mixture of idealism and tension, recounting the risks, successes, and limitations of the project. It begins with the tension felt between the white and black volunteers as the whites, "searching their minds and hearts," were confronted by their own savior complexes and an understanding of the dangers they would face in the South.[39]

The collection anticipates the collage editing style Martínez would employ for both the newspaper *El Grito del Norte* and the history book *500 Years of*

Chicano History in Pictures.[40] *Letters from Mississippi* is at times harrowing, as these snippets tell of threats, shootings, burnings, and deaths. One especially striking moment in a letter headed only "Moss Point, Monday, July 6" tells of a girl being shot in the chest, in church, while singing "We Shall Overcome."[41] The snippets of letters are linked by Sutherland's text, which she separates from the letters through the use of italics, reminding readers of the summer's news events or explaining background information about the letters. Read with fifty years' distance, the book holds up well as a rich and understandable history of the moment, losing little of its urgency. The 2007 edition offers a new preface by Julian Bond and adds writings from the Freedom Schools, introduced with a letter from Langston Hughes to their students. The Freedom School writings were by students, largely children, expressing longings for equality, for swimming pools, for an end to violence, and an awareness of the fragility of their own lives. Still in print and classroom use, the collection is considered one of the strongest documents of the period.

The publication of *Letters from Mississippi*, along with her 1964 editing, uncredited,[42] of the civil rights photodocumentary book *The Movement*,[43] marked Sutherland's move from journalist and editor to full-time civil rights activist. Among other leadership responsibilities, she directed the New York City SNCC office, handling much of the group's fund-raising and providing support for SNCC people deployed in Mississippi. In producing both books, Sutherland used not only her writing but also her editorial skills to tell compelling stories—visually in the case of *The Movement*—and without evidence of egotism. *The Movement* juxtaposes images of black and white Southern rural life with images of hooded Klan members and lynchings; the discordant images are tied together with text by poet and playwright Lorraine Hansberry. To tell this disturbing history, Sutherland used the techniques she developed through her work in photography as well as her considerable skills as an editor and visual storyteller. It is a powerful document, one Angela Davis recalls "assuaged [her] sense of grief" at not being part of the 1963 struggles in person.[44] *The Movement* is a beautiful book, using a combination of visual images and poetic text to impart a powerful message and, like *Letters from Mississippi*, does not feel dated, but rather offers a door into this urgent historical moment.

1967—LEFT WITH NO PLACE TO BE

As important as SNCC (and Cuba) clearly were to Sutherland, neither entirely gave her the space to be Elizabeth or Betita Martínez. While she identified with the goals and aims—and with the "Latin-ness"—of the Cuban Revolution, at one point writing in her journal that "every now and then" she would feel "this is my country. . . . I am home,"[45] she was not Cuban, not from the island, however much she might visit, work for, and support the revolution. SNCC, too, had her devotion as she fought in the United States for civil rights and economic justice, as she used the diplomatic and social skills she had developed during her work for the UN to run the important New York office and participate in the organization's leadership.

Like the Washington, DC, suburb where Sutherland grew up, however, as SNCC evolved there wasn't a space for her Latina self (or that of Maria Varela, also on the SNCC staff) to be seen in the black and white terms of SNCC's politics. Although in 1967 she wrote a paper for the SNCC Atlanta headquarters, "Black, White, and Tan," trying to find words to connect brown and black struggles,[46] by 1968 Liz Sutherland was identified as white by a movement that existed in a black/white binary. SNCC's black leadership would eventually decide it should be a black organization. The binary affected Sutherland's own writing and, seemingly, her ability to locate herself within it. In a 1967 article she wrote for *Mademoiselle*, "Because He Was Black and I Was White: Six Young Women Discuss Their Various Experiences in the Civil-Rights Movement," the title alone anticipates the article's not having a place for someone who looks like her.[47] The article opens with notes from the author, again in a detached journalistic voice but nonetheless tinged with regret:

> It is no news by now that an era of the '60s has drawn to a close—that period that saw a small but significant number of young white men and women work alongside black Americans in their struggle for freedom. Many liberal whites see this passing as a sad thing, and regret the replacement of "black and white together, we shall overcome" by calls for blacks to organize in the Negro community, whites in the white community.[48]

In this frank and groundbreaking discussion of sex, resentments, and interracial relationships in the civil rights movement, constructed out of a series of interviews and conversations with and between women in the movement, as the author Sutherland only appears as the recording or mediating voice, seemingly without any contribution of her own to make. There is an intersectionality to the article where Sutherland quotes one of her interviewees saying something they all agreed on: "You can't talk about race without talking about sex. You can't talk about the position of women without talking about men. And you can't talk about any of these things without looking at the whole society."[49] Ultimately, despite her hope that "this new period might also prove to be the beginning of honesty in race relations,"[50] she was excluded by many in SNCC, where she had been part of the leadership for most of the decade.[51]

The pain of her exclusion and the sense of not belonging, which Platt's biographical article also recounts, come across in the title of Sutherland's autobiographical essay for the 2010 collection *Hands on the Freedom Plow*—"Neither Black nor White in a Black-White World." Having left behind her father's name, Martínez, and adopted "Sutherland" so she could work and write in the white world of publishing, she was also exiled from a movement to which she had dedicated herself for most of the decade, because she was not black. Discussing post-1965 US literature, Martha E. Sánchez writes of a triangle of "interculturalism" created by the connections between Puerto Rican, African American, and Chicano cultures,[52] something Sutherland tried to do in the essay "Black, White, and Tan" ("tan" being how Sutherland Martínez attempted to name her position).

However, struggle as she might, by 1967, whether as "Sutherland" or "Sutherland Martínez," as she signed one of her last official papers for SNCC, there was no place for her in the SNCC organization. On the other hand, in the year that followed, she felt alienated by the overwhelming whiteness of the New York women's liberation movement and the New York Radical Women's Collective, where she briefly tried to pour her energies, writing in its journal *Notes from the First Year* the satirically toned essay "Women of the World Unite—We Have Nothing to Lose but Our Men."[53] In a later interview she recounted her profound alienation with the New York women's movement the night of Martin Luther King Jr.'s assassination. The group was meeting as usual, but no one but Sutherland was interested in talking about MLK's assassination.[54] It was then, she said, she decided the women's movement was racist, something she continued to write about, including in the essay "Listen Up, Anglo Sisters" from her 1998 collection *De Colores Means All of Us*.[55]

CUBAN REVOLUTION

When recounting her 1961 trip in an interview, Martínez said that her reaction to revolutionary Cuba was that "this is what the new world could be like."[56] Her idealism about Cuba was maintained through multiple trips throughout the 1960s, including one in 1968 when she took a leadership delegation from SNCC that included Stokely Carmichael/Kwame Ture, George Ware, and Julius Lester. This moment brought together the two struggles that had meant the most to her for much of the decade.

Cuba, in some ways more complex even than her SNCC work and writings, serves as a frame for Martínez's Sutherland years and publications. Her earliest professional journalism about Cuba focused on accounts of cinema and the impact of revolution on the island. By 1961, her trips to Cuba, her involvement in Fair Play, and her sympathetic accounts of Castro and the Cuban Revolution brought her to the attention of the FBI and resulted in a subpoena by the House Un-American Activities (HUAC) subcommittee, an experience she wrote somewhat ironically about for the *National Guardian*.[57] The article is intensely personal, a discussion of her experiences before the committee and how the members' badgering made her feel "afraid" and ultimately "dirty."[58] Unlike her writing on SNCC, in this account she makes use of her personal experiences to criticize HUAC and US policy toward travel to Cuba. In doing so she anticipates the Chicana feminist location of self in the text, as opposed to the abstract observer journalist.

Just as her earliest publications as Sutherland were about Cuba, likewise, among her last publications as Sutherland, in 1969, was her study on Cuba, the book *The Youngest Revolution: A Personal Report on Cuba*. The book, written as a series of accounts of the Cuban people Sutherland interacted with on the island, is both informative of the culture and politics on Cuba—the ways in which the revolution was succeeding and the ways it was not—and deeply personal, something that distinguishes it from most of her more journalistic writings. She writes at one point, in response to a reading of Marx and Fanon and how race and class revolution intersect on the island, "I have been, and in many ways still am, deeply colonized by Western literature, by North American and European culture," offering an examination of her own intellectual biases.[59] Through it all, the reader has a sense of Sutherland's hopes for Cuba, of the island's potential. Speaking through one of the "six voices" with which she opens the book, Sutherland writes that "the Cuban Revolution is the only one worth watching right now except for China—and Cuba is even more interesting than China because the population is more racially mixed."[60] Her writing on Cuba and postrevolutionary Cuban society is intensely intersectional, constantly looking at issues of race and gender in light of the changes in the class structure of the country, yet reading problems like machismo as relics of "petty bourgeois values . . . underdevelopment and colonization."[61] Still more remarkable is her criticism of the revolutionary state's repressive treatment of homosexuality. Her position was progressive for the time, especially when one considers the heteromasculinist bent of the civil rights movement, in lauding the Cuban publication of José Lezama Lima's "Joycean novel of homosexual experience" as a triumph.[62]

In her writings and interviews about Cuba, Sutherland's intersectional feminism and civil rights work becomes layered with a location of her self. She closely examines the contradictions between Latino traditions of masculinity and the declared gender/sexual equality of the communist revolution. Though Spanish isn't often mentioned in her work, her fluency in Spanish and therefore her connection to her Latina identity was a source of insecurity. Barbara Dane, a jazz singer and musician, recounts how, during her 1966 tour of Cuba, Martínez translated her comments and lyrics on the fly from English to Spanish before an audience of thousands.[63] There is much about Dane's account that resonates with the Chicana/o experience of language, as her identity as "Sutherland" slips into "Martínez," her Latina linguist heritage made visible. According to Dane, Martínez described her Spanish after the fact as "pretty shaky,"[64] due to her being raised and educated in the United States rather than Mexico, where her family spent her childhood summers, or another Spanish-speaking country. This insecurity about her Spanish fluency, even in the face of the success of her impromptu translation, touches on issues of authenticity and anticipates the tensions about English versus Spanish that often arose within the Chicano movement. Likewise, in trying to make Cuban politics understandable to her readers and in the process connect the civil rights movement to the Cuban Revolution, Martínez forges connections between key figures from each movement, describing Castro as "like the late Malcolm X" in his desire to educate himself and his people.[65]

Sutherland examined gender in Cuba through a variety of lenses, from the machismo of a teenage boy who felt he had to pay for ice cream, to the freely available child care that she saw as changing the lives of the nation's women, allowing them to work outside the home. But I find the most interesting expression of feminism in her reporting on the discussion between Cuban women about whether they should wear miniskirts. This was a telling issue about Cuba and reflected Sutherland's personal style. In the accounts found in the special issue of *Social Justice* on Martínez, several mention her as looking fashionable or dressing well. Mike Davis describes her, at a New York protest, as "dressed to the nines,"[66] while Jean Wiley describes her fashion sense as "bold," saying Martínez was the first person she ever saw in a miniskirt.[67] During her time in Cuba Martínez noticed what women were wearing, quoting some who said the miniskirt was not in keeping with the revolution but then wryly pointing out that one of the same women had started wearing a miniskirt several months later.[68] Miniskirts in Cuba represented women's ownership of their femininity and sexuality. The focus on the miniskirt, to which Sutherland returns several times in *The Youngest Revolution*, and whether it was revolutionary and/or transgressive, was in 1969 a battle being fought, along with the freedom to wear pantsuits, in US schools and workplaces.[69] By discussing whether women in Cuba were wearing miniskirts, Sutherland was writing against the characterization of socialist and communist societies as without individuality, color, and fashion. Sutherland's feminism and socialism were colorful and bold.

Issues of race, Cuba, its revolution, and all its contradictions loomed large for Sutherland. They spoke to her beliefs in the potential perfection of society as well as reflecting the work she was doing as part of the US civil rights movement. Their conjunction demonstrates the intersectional and international perspectives characterizing Martínez's writings on oppression. Because of this intersectionality it is important to not see the two areas of interest—the Cuban revolution and the civil rights movement—as separate when discussing Martínez's work and writings. Throughout the decade she visited Cuba, inspired by the potential of the revolution, bringing with her people from SNCC and the Black Power movements. Stokely Carmichael's trip to Cuba in the summer of 1967 reflected SNCC's connection to the Cuban Revolution and the idea of a transnational vision of the global South against imperialism, sexism, capitalism, and racism, highlighting the way African American activists saw Cuba as a model for defying the US government.[70] Likewise, Cubans, according to Sutherland, were discussing how the civil rights movement could be the basis for a socialist revolution in the United States. Through the accounts of these conversations, she made clear that she too looked for a revolutionary transformation of the United States, an ideal she continued to support, believe in, and work toward, even as social movements she was part of exploded and imploded.

ELIZABETH SUTHERLAND MARTÍNEZ—
YOUR WHIP IS MY SWORD

For the activist and writer Liz Sutherland to become Elizabeth "Betita" Martínez, there was a convergence of a different transnational history, going back to the Treaty of Guadalupe Hidalgo. Into the Chicano movement, Sutherland brought her UN experience of researching postcolonialism in Africa and South Asia, her childhood experiences of family summers spent in Mexico, and her experiences in postrevolution Cuba, all of which necessarily refracted through her work in the civil rights movement. In 1966, when she was still writing as Sutherland, Martínez covered the Delano, California, grape strike for the *Village Voice*, highlighting connections between the southern civil rights movement and the new farmworkers movement. In her article she introduces César Chávez and Dolores Huerta to her East Coast readers, likening their leadership within the farmworkers union to the arrival of Fannie Lou Hammer to the grassroots movement in the South.[71] She doesn't identify herself as Mexican American (the term "Chicano" isn't mentioned), but she points out that the image of the "lazy sombrero wearing Mexican" had "received its death blow."[72] However, it wasn't until 1968 that she would join the Chicano movement, and not in California but in New Mexico, connecting not with the United Farm Workers (UFW) but the Tierra Amarilla land rights movement. On the advice of her friend John "Tito" Gerassi she visited New Mexico with the thought of possibly founding a newspaper there in support of Reies López Tijerina and the New Mexican land struggle, which in some ways connected with her interest in revolutionary Cuba's peasant struggle for land rights.

Writing about her arrival in Española, New Mexico, and the way its landscape and community moved her, Martínez said a voice told her, "You can be Martínez here. It feels like home."[73] She stayed in New Mexico for eight years, writing, editing, and publishing as Elizabeth Martínez the bilingual monthly newspaper *El Grito del Norte*, which became a significant publication and made Española an activist hub for the Chicano movement in New Mexico. Moving from writing and publishing in mainstream East Coast publications of the Left to writing and editing a tiny regional newspaper in a remote corner of the Southwest, Martínez left behind middle-class and bohemian life among New York City literati. From the perspective of her middle-class upbringing and education, she moved herself from the center to the margins, no longer seeking legitimacy but rather using her editorial skills to foster writing by what became the El Grito collective. In doing so, she created a center of a different sort, a location in the Chicano movement and Aztlán, bringing with her a strong race and feminist consciousness as well as a sense of the Chicano movement as part of an international people's revolution.

It is tempting to look at Martínez's Chicano activism as shaped and formed mainly by her experiences in SNCC and with the Black Power movement, and these were, in fact, important parts of her political and cultural identity. However, as her writings demonstrate, her political identity—how she became "Betita"—was formed earlier and from a much wider set of experiences, including her work on and in Cuba. The experiences of international struggle and travel are ones she would encourage other leaders in first the civil rights movement and then the Chicano movement to have. Yet it was ultimately the feeling of not belonging in either place, neither in the blackness of the Black Power movement nor in the whiteness of the women's movement, that left her longing to find a place, to locate herself, in New Mexico, an Aztlán where she seemingly had no roots, no history, finding a homeplace in the Chicano collective and ultimately writing that history herself. Her final publication as Sutherland—or, rather, as Elizabeth Sutherland Martínez (and also her last for a mainstream press)—was for the 1974 book *Viva La Raza! The Struggle of the Mexican-American People*, which she coauthored with Enriqueta Vásquez.[74] In it, she writes not in the detached journalist voice, or even the first-person singular she employed in *The Youngest Revolution*. *Viva La Raza* is narrated in the first-person plural. As Chicanas, she and her coauthor were writing as part of a "we" about "our history."

The use of "we" and an authoritative voice in *Viva La Raza* is complex. On the one hand, it is a telling of Chicanos' history in the United States, but it is a history that, despite being exhaustively indexed, was written without citations or references, without referring to any authority outside the text, except to cite the names of the Raza, such as César Chávez. This structure, which devalues or silences Anglo scholarly authority while asserting Vásquez's and Martínez's own, frames the text as history that has always been known and one the readers either believe or not, writing against the mainstream structure of a historical text. Martínez and Vásquez inhabit authority in writing, for example, a new history about the California gold rush: "Another big source of new wealth for the Anglos was mining and here again they learned everything from the people whose lands they had invaded. . . . Our people had learned a great deal about mining techniques. In fact, gold itself was discovered in California six years before the big rush—by a Mexican herdsman named Francisco Lopez."[75] This style continues throughout the book. The "they" and "other" are "Anglos," whom readers are told are greedy, "gold-crazy gringos" that in one week "lynched and murdered dozens of our people."[76] The "we" are the authors, and "our people" in *Viva La Raza* are Native Americans, Chicanos, and Mexicans.

Viva La Raza connects Mexican American histories across the region, so the many struggles seem to have a single narrative, one of heroics and exploitation. The second half of the book, following a chapter on how mainstream US culture "brainwashed" Mexican Americans (whom they call "raza") into wanting to be white, calls on them to reject that construction and identify as Chicanos,[77] pulling together diverse movements and geographies. It links Tijerina—whose full name (like SNCC's a decade earlier) is carefully spelled out phonetically, underlining his importance while at the same time clearly writing for an English-only audience—and the land struggle in New Mexico with Chávez and Dolores Huerta and the farmworkers in California, Rodolfo "Corky" Gonzales and Colorado's Crusade for Justice, followed by a chapter on La Raza Unida Party and the building of

Aztlán. After unifying raza and calling on them to identify as Chicano and refuse to serve in Vietnam, the authors urge Chicanos to reject the United States and its capitalism, connecting the Chicano struggle and the fight for civil rights to struggles in "America, Asia, Africa and even Europe." This transnational identification and resistance to US political and cultural hegemony is one that characterizes Sutherland Martínez's writing throughout her fifty-plus-year career.

The "whip" becomes a guiding metaphor of the last chapter of *Viva La Raza*. The "you" addressed is clearly an Anglo US audience that is "only a progressive machine who doesn't dare to be human . . . a whip around humanity, a whip around the world."[78] The authors set themselves and the Chicano movement against this oppressive, colonial whip of war and conquest. Yet the image used to fight the imperialist whip is not one of SNCC's peaceful, nonviolent legacy. Instead, the authors call for the sword. As Martínez and Vásquez, writing as Longeaux y Vásquez, close the book, they declare that they have remade the master's tool, "*tu riata es mi espada—your whip is my sword*," transforming the oppressor's power into their own. That line is followed by "Raza" three times, echoing across the book's last line.[79] In this text, Sutherland, now Sutherland Martínez, is not reporting in a journalistic voice on the struggle, as was the case with her earlier writings on SNCC and the Cuban Revolution. Instead, she places herself in the struggle, claiming the history, the struggle, and the identity of a Chicana.

COLOR PLATE 1. Ester Hernández, *California Special—The Inheritance* (2005, acrylic on canvas, 5' x 4'). © Ester Hernández.

COLOR PLATE 2. Ester Hernández, *Libertad* (1976, etching, 15" x 12"). © Ester Hernández.

COLOR PLATE 3. Ester Hernández, *La Virgen de Guadalupe defendiendo los derechos de los Xican@s* (1976, etching/aquatint, 16" x 14"). © Ester Hernández.

COLOR PLATE 4. Ester Hernández, *Sun Mad* (1981, screen print, 26" x 20"). © Ester Hernández.

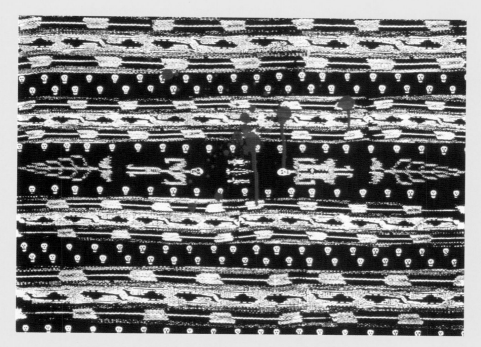

COLOR PLATE 5. Ester Hernández, *Tejido de los desaparecidos* (1984, screen print, 22" x 17").
© Ester Hernández.

COLOR PLATE 6. Ester Hernández, *Tejido de los desaparecidos—Installation II* (2008).
© Ester Hernández.

COLOR PLATE 7. Ester Hernández,
Mis madres (1986, screen print, 30" x 22").
© Ester Hernández.

COLOR PLATE 8. Ester Hernández,
Immigrant Woman's Dress
(1997, mixed-media installation).
© Ester Hernández.

COLOR PLATE 9. Ester Hernández, *Virgen de
las calles* (2001, pastel on paper, 44" x 30").
© Ester Hernández.

WANTED

TERRORIST

LA VIRGEN DE GUADALUPE

ALIAS: Guadalupe, Reina de las Americas, Virgencita, Nuestra Madre, Tonantzin, Lupe, Lupita

DESCRIPTION:

Date of Birth: 12/12/1531
Place of Birth: Tepeyac, Tenochtitlan/Mexico
Height: 5'
Weight: 100 lbs.

Build: Medium
Hair: Black
Eyes: Dark Brown
Complexion: Dark Brown

Scars and Marks: Unknown
Languages: Nahuatl, Zapotec, Yaqui, Purépucha,
  Maya and Spanish
Race: Amer-Indian
Nationality: American

SHOULD BE CONSIDERED POWERFUL AND DANGEROUS

OCCUPATION: Cult Leader, Human Trafficking, Terrorist.

REMARKS: La Virgen de Guadalupe always covers her head with a star patterned shawl and wears long rose patterned dresses. She is accompanied by a young child (possibly drugged) who wears wings and pretends he is flying.

CRIMINAL RECORD: For over 160 years, La Virgen de Guadalupe has accompanied countless men, women and children illegally into the USA. She has given limitless aid and comfort to unidentified suspects at the time of their death, especially in the desert areas near the U. S./Mexico border.

CAUTION: She has an unexplainable, possibly dangerous light emanating from her body which could contain explosive material. She is known to have a large loyal fanatic cult following.

REWARD: The State of Arizona is offering of up to $500,000 for any information leading directly to the apprehension and conviction of La Virgen de Guadalupe.

IF YOU HAVE INFORMATION CONCERNING THIS PERSON, PLEASE CONTACT THE ARIZONA STATE RANGERS OR YOUR LOCAL IMMIGRATION AND CUSTOMS ENFORCEMENT (ICE) OFFICE.

© 2010 Ester Hernandez

Janet Killemall
Janet Killemall, President of Arizona

COLOR PLATE 10. Ester Hernández, *Wanted* (2010, screen print, 30 ³⁄₁₆" x 22").
© Ester Hernández.

COLOR PLATE 11. Ester Hernández, *Lydia Mendoza, Ciudad Juárez, México, 1937* (1987, screen print, 22" x 30"). © Ester Hernández.

COLOR PLATE 12. Ester Hernández, *Astrid—La Diosa Peligrosa* (2007, pastel on paper, 40" x 30").
© Ester Hernández.

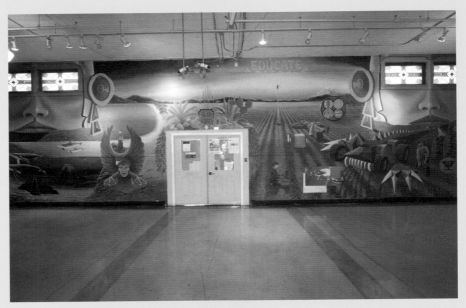

COLOR PLATE 13. Daniel DeSiga, *An Explosion of Chicano Creativity,* El Centro de la Raza mural, 1972/1997. Courtesy of Daniel DeSiga.

14 "LA RAZA EN CANADA"

SAN DIEGO CHICANA ACTIVISTS, THE INDOCHINESE WOMEN'S CONFERENCE OF 1971, AND THIRD WORLD WOMANISM

DIONNE ESPINOZA

In April 1971, Felicitas Nuñez, a Chicana student organizer at San Diego State College, attended the Indochinese Women's Conference in Vancouver, Canada, as part of a contingent of Chicanas from San Diego.[1] Initiated by the Voice of Women and Women Strike for Peace, the conference invited representatives from the women's liberation movement (which was majority white) and Third World women in the United States (Chicanas, African Americans, Asian Americans, and American Indians, separate and in collectives) to attend the conference, at which they would meet with six Indochinese women over three to four days as part of the antiwar effort. A little over a month after returning from the conference, Nuñez completed "La Raza en Canada," a twelve-page report in which she offered an account of her conference participation from her initial decision to attend as part of a Chicana contingent from San Diego to the experience at the conference over three days in Vancouver and summary reflections.[2]

Nuñez's report offers a rare glimpse into the dynamics of the international conference from a Chicana lens that contributes to our understanding of the historical, political, and cultural moment and its relationship to Chicana political cultures in the movement era. Among its themes, the report documents Chicana antiwar consciousness and Chicana engagement with the women's liberation movement and anti-imperialism in a global frame. In this respect, Nuñez's report offers a first-person perspective on the flourishing Third World solidarity concepts of the moment and Chicana engagement with these ideas at a grassroots level related to the antiwar movement and prior to the more top-down institutionalized approaches of the UN world conferences on women.[3] Nuñez's report also speaks to the organized Chicana activist presence in San Diego during the Chicano movement and the willingness of a group of Chicanas to travel long distances and across a national border to engage in solidarity work. The report and related materials take us on a journey through the challenge of building solidarity, for it also notes the tensions between a Chicana identity politics based in the Chicano movement and a more internationalist and Third World solidarity–based politics. It also documents how these tensions were reconciled at the conference through dialogue among women of different racial and ethnic communities and in relation to the larger struggle against the war and imperialism, culminating in a praxis of Third World womanism.

For a Chicana researcher of the herstory of Chicana feminism, coming across a document in the archives such as Nuñez's report opens up an incredible space for understanding the depth, layers, and forms of Chicana activism in the 1970s. The report became especially meaningful because I had been in conversation with Chicana activists in San Diego for another research project on Chicana student activism. This connection made it possible for me to learn more from three of the Chicana activists who attended the conference about what this kind of international engagement meant to them.[4] Chicana activism has been considered primarily in relation to either the women's liberation movement or to Chicano nationalist identity politics with less consideration of coalition, solidarity work, and internationalist exchanges such as attendance at the Vancouver conference.[5] In this essay I consider Nuñez's report and narratives of travel to the conference by other participants, not only to add to the few accounts of Chicana participation in practices of international solidarity but also to share how, as María Cotera has stated in relation to the Chicana por mi Raza project of recovering Chicana archives, I would argue that this research similarly "opens up a space for the reunification of old networks and the creation of new cross-generational communities of inquiry."[6] This act of recovery reminds us of the continuity between these forgotten solidarities of the past and present-day efforts to forge transnational connections, and reconnects generations to each other through storytelling and *testimonio*.

THE VANCOUVER CONFERENCE AND "LAS DIEZ DE SAN DIEGO"

The Indochinese Women's Conference took place in Vancouver, British Columbia, April 1–6, 1971. The conference featured a delegation of six women from the Indochinese region (two each from North Vietnam, South Vietnam, and Laos) to engage in dialogue with North American women. Organized against the backdrop of the US military intervention in Vietnam's civil war, the conference goal was to bring women together to learn about the US involvement in the war and its effects on the people of Vietnam, to discuss issues of peace and understanding, and, ultimately, to unite and to mobilize against the war and against imperialism.[7]

It was the first of two conferences held in Canada that April, with the other conference to be held in Toronto. Women across North America were called to attend the conferences, which were organized primarily by the established peace movements Voice of Women and Women Strike for Peace. In planning the conference, they wanted to make an effort to include the more contemporary women's liberation movement and Third World women.[8]

Word about the conference arrived in San Diego, according to Nuñez's report, through "members of the Womens' Liberation," with the understanding that "the Indochinese women asked that the oppressed minorities be included in order to accomplish their goals and make all aware of their self determination."[9] In the first two pages, Nuñez's report describes challenges she faced working with the local women's liberation groups in San Diego around identifying Chicana delegates to the Vancouver conference. Nuñez reports that when she attempted to work with the local representatives of the women's liberation movement, described as middle-class women who had funding to support conference attendance, the power dynamics were evident and problematic. Nuñez admits that the group she was involved in, Las Chicanas, did procrastinate in selecting delegates and that this played a role in the process, but she also states that they were put off by the sense of limitations imposed on how many could go to the conference due to limited lodging, which contributed to a sense of tokenism. After processing this as a group, she reports, "we decided to take as many Chicanas who could attend and take the responsibility of worrying for ourselves and what to do if there was no lod[g]ing available or room in the conference for all of us."[10]

Listed on the back page of her report as "Las Diez de San Diego" are the names of ten Chicanas who took the trip, among them five from San Diego State College (SDSC), three from the University of California, San Diego, one from San Diego City College, and one from Memorial Junior High.[11] These institutions reflected the networks that had developed through the regional MEChA Central (a gathering of Movimiento Estudiantil Chicano de Aztlán chapters from regional universities, colleges, and high schools) and the subsequent creation of a space that brought together Chicanas from local colleges and universities as "Las Chicanas." The development of Las Chicanas within San Diego is an important regional formation in the herstoriography of Chicana feminism. Due to their experiences of gender inequality within the campus MEChA, a group of Chicanas active in SDSC MEChA began to meet informally as "Las Chicanas" in order to think through ways of ensuring that their voices as women would be heard within MEChA.[12] Influenced by the Denver Youth Conferences of 1969 and 1970 as well as by the growing women's movement and empowered through their activism in the Chicano movement at SDSC and in the community, they were among the founding groups of the Chicana feminist movement. In fact, in addition to the Vancouver conference, the SDSC Las Chicanas group also traveled to the first National Chicana Conference in Houston, Texas, in late May 1971. Las Chicanas Central included the women not only from San Diego State College and UC San Diego but also from local high schools such as Hoover High School and Las Adelitas, a group that was based at Memorial Junior High School in Barrio Logan.[13]

The author of the report and key organizer of the effort, Felicitas Nuñez, was born and raised in the Imperial Valley city of Brawley, California. Nuñez had applied and been accepted to San Diego State College in 1968 and was among the pioneering cohorts admitted after student activism called for more recruitment of students of color. She quickly moved up the activist ranks through her dedicated work at the Barrio Station in San Ysidro and in supportive services for Chicana/o students. She was elected president of MEChA at SDSC and was a founding member of Las Chicanas and the codirector and cofounder of Teatro Chicana.

In addition to the five SDSC participants, there was one person listed as a student at San Diego City College. Teresa Oyos, who was studying art and Chicano studies at the time, was a single parent, originally from Poway, California. She was on her own journey of learning about the Chicano movement, Chicano studies, women's liberation, and women's studies and had been spending time in the San Diego movement and at San Diego State College, where she met other Chicana activists. Her roommate at the time, Silvia Romero, also one of Las Diez, was an active leader in the Las Chicanas and Teatro Chicana groups at SDSC. It may have been through this connection that Oyos became part of the circle of activist *mujeres* and decided to attend the conference.[14] She later wrote a poem, "Las Chingonas," in the collective memoir *Teatro Chicana* about her involvement in the Chicano movement that features lines about attending the conference: "We traveled all the way up the breathtaking West Coast to Vancouver, Canada . . . / Felicitas sang La Llorona while we ate whole wheat tortillas in the back of the van . . . / Hijole . . . so many wonderful women were at the Third World women's conference."[15]

The three participants from UCSD were staff member Betty Bane, faculty member Gracia Molina de Pick, and graduate student Martha Salinas. Gracia Molina de Pick in particular was credited by Nuñez as a key mobilizer of the local Chicana contingent due to her links to the women's liberation movement.[16] Mentioned by many San Diego Chicana activists I have interviewed, Molina de Pick is a noted Chicana feminist leader who supported, hosted, and mentored Chicana students in San Diego. She encouraged Chicanas to participate in major movement conferences such as the Denver Youth Conference that she also attended. Through her participation in conferences such as the National Women's Political Caucus in Houston in 1973 and the International Women's Year Conference in Mexico in 1975, she represented a cohort of Chicana mentors and leaders who ensured the involvement of Chicanas in the leadership of the women's movement (a fact that needs further note in mainstream women's movement narratives as well as within Chicana feminist studies).

In addition to Molina de Pick, UCSD graduate student Martha Salinas had chosen to attend. Martha Salinas was originally from Texas and had enrolled at UCSD as an undergraduate and received her bachelor's in French literature. In the interview, Salinas recalled that she had participated in the MEChA Central and that through it they learned about Las Chicanas. She emphasized that UCSD had a very different political culture from some of the other institutions in the area. For one thing, it had a very small cohort of Black and Chicano students, so the Black Student Union (BSU) and MEChA "worked closely to bring more minorities in the university," invoking a Third World coalition.[17] Salinas also was active in regional antiwar efforts that had involved organizing to march in the Chicano Moratorium against the War in Vietnam on August 29, 1970. This, she stated, was a primary motivation for her interest in the conference, to organize against the war. At this time, many Chicanas were less invested in the women's movement due to its middle-class and majority-white composition and lack of attention to issues of class that affected Chicanas. However, when they thought they heard that the Indochinese women "wanted women of color there" "maybe the conference was going to be a little bit different than just your traditional women's conference."[18]

Chicanas definitely had significant motivation to be part of this organizing effort. As shared in memoirs, interviews, poetry, and other documents, many Chicanas had experienced the effects of the war in their own families, as their brothers went off to war and, in some cases, did not return.[19] In her memoir in *Teatro Chicana*, Peggy Garcia writes, "I had such mixed feelings about our country's involvement in this seemingly unjust war. The Garcia family had lost a 21-year-old member and our pain was still deep."[20] In the videotaped interview, Nuñez read this section by Garcia to emphasize the war's effect on families. Nuñez also had a brother serving in Vietnam at that time, and she found herself questioning the war, at times putting her into conflict with family members.

With their motivation and interest, ten Chicanas prepared to embark on their journey to Vancouver, but as Nuñez writes in her report, they did have to face some opposition to their decision to go to the conference from the established leaders of the Chicano and women's liberation movements in San Diego. Nuñez writes, "Our elders made us feel irresponsible for not staying to help with the work at home and discouraged us because it was so far and dangerous."[21] In an interview Nuñez clarifies that the "elders" were those who were reticent about their participation in an international conference when it was more important in their view to stay and work with the community in San Diego.[22] The contingent also faced critique from "a member of the womens' liberation because of the action we took."[23] This member, according to Nuñez's report, called them "anarchists" for not following their process and terms. In defiance of these critiques, Las Diez started off to Vancouver on their road trip with gas money, a van, and "sleeping bags and food." Two members left ahead of time in another van, and Gracia Molina de Pick flew to the conference.

ARE WE CHICANAS OR THIRD WORLD WOMEN FIRST?

Framing the San Diego Chicana contingent's travel to the conference within the context of Chicana articulations of global solidarity in print as well as the antiwar movement and shifting political cultures of the race/ethnicity-based movements of the period reveals how their exchange with Indochinese women in Vancouver and with other women of color became an important site of reflection on cross-national, cross-cultural, and cross-racial dialogues—including tensions and moments of unity. Conferences have often been key flashpoints for the working out of simmering debates and conflicts in social movements as well as for their motivational gathering of energies that sustain and mobilize movements.[24] During the Chicano movement era, when activists did not have cell phones, the internet, or even fax machines, conferences served as central moments in the consolidation of political platforms, ideologies, and shared languages that primarily traveled with the activists, who took ideas with them to their home bases or other conferences or to other spaces they visited, as well as through the independent print media of these movements, which is why movement periodicals and other ephemera in the archives are crucial for projects of historical recovery.

On the first day they arrived, Nuñez recalls that they attended sessions about the war in Vietnam that featured films about US intervention and the horrible impact of the weapons of war that were used, such as napalm. What also impressed the participants was the presence of the Indochinese women and their words, that is, the face-to-face dialogue. Martha Salinas and Felicitas Nuñez both underscore the "strength and dignity" of the women who did not express any negative feelings toward them. As Salinas stated, "I got such a tremendous lesson in internationalism because . . . not just one of them but a number of them repeated that they knew how to separate the American people from the American government. They were not at war with the American people."[25] Felicitas Nuñez also had a chance to attend a dinner with the Indochinese women and to meet Phan Min Hien, one of the Vietnamese women, with whom she felt a strong connection despite their different languages and cultures. Indeed, as scholar Natalie Havlin has argued, these moments of affective description and face-to-face conversations may be the real foundation of revolution.[26] At the conference they met other Chicana antiwar activists such as Lea Ybarra from the Bay Area, who with her colleague Nina Genera had founded a Chicano draft counseling project.[27]

Chicana attendance at the Indochinese Women's Conference brought them into an international space of dialogue with other women about issues of race, peace, and imperialism. It also raised the question of Chicana collective identity in relation to a Third World collective identity that was becoming more prominent as a movement construct. As she narrates the activities of the conference, Nuñez tracks in her report the tensions of negotiating between a Chicana collective identity and a Third World collective identity, given the conference emphasis on Third World women as a group. While philosophies of nationalism and self-determination that derived from international anticolonialist movements generally appealed to movement activists in the racial/ethnic movements, in some corners there were still tensions between nationalism and internationalism in the political culture. In this respect, the Vancouver conference actually became a site in which diverse groups, some already engaged with the Third World concept and some less so, worked through a process of creating a Third World women's perspective.[28]

Entering the space of the conference, Las Diez came into contact with the meanings of "the Third World" as defined by conference organizers, although it is unclear who was defining the term, presumably other Third World women. It was suggested that Chicanas had to "intermix with the other races in order to comply with the revolutionary Third World concept."[29] They were not encouraged to meet or to lodge as a separate Chicana group. Nonetheless, Nuñez and others continued to feel that there was a need for Chicanas to have some space for their own self-definition: "A few of us felt that because we intended to relate to our Third World sisters it was necessary that as Chicanas we must know what was our common identity and goals. This way our Third World sisters would relate to us as a whole and not as individuals."[30]

Although Nuñez raised the importance of Chicana collective identity, she and Peggy Garcia both documented incidents of tension at the conference among Chicana delegates when Chicanas from the Bay Area confronted a member of Las Diez because her "bourgeois" clothing (a fur coat) was not sufficiently "revolutionary" and possibly because she had accidently leaned against a sign at the conference and caused it to fall. Nuñez diffused the potentially explosive moment by explaining that everyone "had a right to be here to learn and that all kinds of people can be of help who are willing to fight for a cause."[31] As suggested by a reference to the large contingent of women of color from the Bay Area who attended the conference, there was already a strong coalitional identity among women of color, a hallmark of the political culture there, where the Third World Liberation Front student strike at San Francisco State University and UC Berkeley in 1968 had been influential in building cross-racial ties of solidarity.

One of the activities at the conference that helped to build a sense of connection between Chicanas from different regions was the preparation of cultural presentations. San Diego's Teatro Chicana performed at the cultural workshop along with a group from the Bay Area. Their presentations included singing and skits about the Chicano Moratorium of August 29 as well as about the farmworker movement. According to Nuñez, presenting together forged strong connections with Chicanas from the Bay Area at the conference, including ties that she has maintained since then. The tensions they encountered initially and the project of presenting together also showed her the differences in political cultures of different campuses and regions. With this observation, she began to be more aware of the limits of cultural nationalism that had shaped the Chicano student movement at San Diego State College, but she also maintained the importance of a collective identity as Chicanas and Chicanos while participating in a shared understanding of Third World womanism.

FIGURE 14.1. San Diego Chicanas at the Vancouver conference, 1971. Courtesy of
Martha Salinas.

In reports I consulted, it is unclear exactly how many women attended and how
many of the total attendees were Third World women. Historian Judy Tzu-Chun
Wu estimates that there were about 1,000 total attendees at the conference.[32]
Anthropologist Kathleen Gough Aberle estimates that there were 600 women
attendees, of whom "Third World delegates, who numbered about 300, came from
Black, Chicano, Asian, and Native American and Canadian groups."[33] Another
account of the number of women of color attendees is presented in *El Grito del
Norte* newspaper by Donna (no last name given), who describes her "travel with
a group of about 120 Third World women from the San Francisco Bay area—the
single largest group."[34] She sketches a picture of this group of participants:

> Most of the sisters had never been to a conference before. Some were older
> women in their 50's and 60's, who went along with their daughters. We spent
> all three days up there—two full days rapping with the sisters from Indo-China.
> They made presentations, then we gave some on our Third World history. The one
> on Hawaii was really fine. What a similarity with New Mexico and Puerto Rico![35]

As recounted by Wu, in the early stages of organizing for the conferences there had been issues around how to include women of color. Initially women members of the Black Panthers and the Third World Women's Alliance had been invited to a planning meeting, but later, Wu describes, the East Coast organizers realized that they had misstepped by trying to decide which Third World women should be invited.[36] The dynamics of West Coast conference organizing are less clear, although Wu notes that there was a Los Angeles contingent of women of color (with Pat Sumi, a local activist who had traveled to Vietnam as a key leader) and that women of color on the West Coast had been instrumental in calling for a separate day of meetings with the Indochinese women.[37] In some accounts by Chicanas and other women of color who participated, they understood that the Indochinese women had themselves called for a separate conference day with US and Canadian Third World women.[38]

While it is not clear who initiated the invitation, one full day of the conference was devoted to a meeting between the Third World women and the Indochinese women's delegation. Although it had already been planned to have a day centered on Third World women, a flashpoint of debate occurred around whether to allow white women to attend the conference day as observers. Apparently this question was left up to the Third World–identified participants to decide. Nuñez reports, "The general consensus was that we wanted no observers but a few individuals were insistent that it was wrong to retain our racist attitude and this was not revolutionary." She makes the point that for her the issue was not racism, "but for the first time being able to know ourselves as Third World people and not restricted from vocalizing our anger against white injustice."[39] Other comments on that debate were shared in a brief article, "Chicanas Attend Vancouver Conference," published after the conference in the San Diego Chicano movement newspaper La Verdad. The author, not named, documents a number of arguments that arose in the debate. For example, "Another point brought up was that we should let the anglo women observe so that they could learn." In contrast to this and other views supporting the idea that white women should be allowed to observe was an opposing argument: "Self determination was brought up in that just as women had decided this would be a womens conference, third world women should be able to say that the sessions would be for third world women."[40] In the end, the session was restricted to Third World women.

Yet another site of tension, according to "Chicanas Attend Vancouver Conference," was that for the Chicanas from San Diego, there were still questions about how to resolve the identity politics and cultural specificity of Chicanas within "the third world concept."

> At the conference there was a group of Chicanas who expressed the feeling that they wanted the Chicanas to get together as a group to talk about the conference, to get to know each other, or just to bring our feelings and ideas. Another group of Chicanas were entirely against this. They argued that this went against the

concept of the third world. The meeting was attempted but it did not succeed. From this experience we began to ask ourselves "What exactly is the third world concept" and knowing that we are both Chicanas and third world women, when are we third world women first and when are we Chicanas first?"[41]

Similar to the question of whether one identifies as a Chicano first or a woman first, a question that resonated in the movement of the time, the posing of the dichotomy and its use in the conference seemed to center on a question of what was most revolutionary—as we now know, both/and constructions are probably the most revolutionary and also make visible the intersectionality of struggles and identities. That these reflections emerged speaks to the deep critical analysis among Chicana activists about the ways in which they invoked collective identities in different contexts and with respect to specific projects of solidarity and activism.

While the article in *La Verdad* leaves open the question "When are we third world women first and when are we Chicanas first?" at the conference there was a successful process of coming together as Third World women. As Wu has noted, "The political category itself was in the process of being constructed" at this time, and the conference served as a space to propose those meanings.[42] A centerpiece of the dialogues with the Indochinese women on that day was the writing and subsequent reading of the "Third World Statement of Solidarity." Nuñez and Salinas share that forging a collective statement was a long, intense, and complex process. Nuñez recalls, "We had to practice patience and respect for everyone because everyone wanted to say something."[43] The process may have been facilitated from the outset because the day featured presentations in which each group narrated its specific experience of colonialism, dispossession, and subjugation. As Nuñez writes, "In speech after speech the Historical Presentations made by our Hawaiian, Black, Native American, Indian, Puerto Ricana, Chicana, Philipina, and Indochinese, we saw how the same tactics used to conquer, betray and humiliate us as a people were repeated with others."[44] The act of sharing their different stories and seeing the threads of similarity in the same tactics set a foundation for Third World solidarity among the different groups.

After extensive dialogue, the group presented the "Third World Statement of Solidarity." In the personal copy that she shared with me, Nuñez included copies of two photographs that captured this moment in the conference. The first image, captioned "Reading of the statement of solidarity," was a photograph of different groups' representatives sitting at a panel table, and the second, captioned "applause," was a photograph taken after the statement had been read, with the representatives standing up. A key point in the statement was the naming of a "common enemy" as "United States imperialism," along with a clear declaration of the positionality of women of color living in the United States: "As we struggle here in the heart of the imperialist, racist beast, we look constantly to our comrades in Vietnam, Laos and Cambodia for revolutionary inspiration." Also noting struggles in Latin America and Africa, the statement continues, "To all of you we give our pledge that we will fulfill our duty, that we will build and intensify our struggle to smash imperialism from within."[45] Although it took a couple of days to clarify what held them together as a group, the "Third World Statement of Solidarity" demonstrated the possibility of being part of a Third World coalition while also being Chicana, Black, Hawaiian, Native American, Filipina, Puerto Rican, and Indochinese. Overall, Nuñez concludes that the experience crystalized for the Chicana group from San Diego the capacity to see themselves in relation to and solidarity with other Chicanas, Third World people, and "our white sisters": "We learned to act as a group from San Diego, to all other Chicanas, to unite as Third World people and to be grateful towards our white sisters who made this possible. We took the responsibility of freedom and allowed ourselves to grow. We came back with a pledge to do or die."[46]

CHICANAS AND THIRD WORLD WOMANISM

Amrita Basu, a scholar of global women's movements, has observed, "What better illustration of the productive interplay between global and local feminism is there than debates in which women ultimately define feminism by refusing to associate it with dominant values or groups." She goes on to state that various groups that locate themselves outside of dominant Western feminism have "relocated feminism amid marginalized or subordinated groups."[47] In her work, Chela Sandoval has applied the term "US third world feminism" to organizing practices and to the self-reference by women of color in the United States as "third world women" in the 1970s. Sandoval cites 1971 (the year of the Vancouver conference, coincidentally) as the beginning of grassroots organizations among "US third world feminists":

> A great number of their newsletters, pamphlets, and books were produced by underground publishers from 1971 to 1974, including separate works by Janice Mirikitani (1973) and Francis Beale (1971) both entitled, *Third World Women*, which were meant to affirm and develop the revolutionary kind of shared sisterhood/citizenship insistently emerging in the corridors and backrooms where US feminists of color congregated.[48]

For US women of color, as exemplified in the organization Third World Women's Alliance, this self-reference, a term of coalition and solidarity, enabled them to create their own agendas and grassroots solidarities that I am calling "Third World womanism."[49]

There are various considerations as to why the Third World concept made sense for Chicanas who had been living through and bearing witness to major social and anticolonial movements of the twentieth century. For one, as many women of color activists participated in movements based on their own racial/ethnic groups such as the Black Power, Chicano, and American Indian movements, the movements were framed as nationalist struggles of racial/ethnic self-determination even as they were also arguing for the "revolution within a revolution" based on gender that challenged male dominance in these movements. Because the movements were understood as nationalist struggles for self-determination as a group in the United States, they could therefore be viewed as closer to the experiences of women in other countries who were involved in anticolonial and nationalist struggles of self-determination.[50] Philosopher Ranjoo Seodu Herr has written that for women in colonized countries, struggles for self-determination are understood as intertwined with the improvement of their lives. In other words, calls for women's rights are inextricable from the struggle for national sovereignty.[51] These perspectives are heavily contested by scholars who have critiqued nationalism as inherently patriarchal, but here my point is to consider the reasons that nationalism as a name for self-determination served as a useful frame for thinking through difference and solidarity among racial/ethnic groups in the United States in the 1960s and '70s.

In the two years after the Vancouver conference, writings by Chicanas documented their understanding of themselves within the context of global solidarity as Third World women. In framing this context Chicanas were aware of the power differentials and, in fact, often underscored the differences between their experiences as Chicanas in the United States and those of women in anticolonial struggles in countries such as Vietnam. Rather than emphasize a simplistic identity politics of sameness that would erase differences of economic, cultural, and sociopolitical context, in most cases they engaged a politics of affiliation and connection that recognized differential privilege as well as their diverse and specific histories.[52]

An example of the articulation of solidarity can be found in *El Grito del Norte* newspaper, applauded for its internationalist perspective and reporting on worldwide anticolonial struggles. As editor of *El Grito del Norte*, Elizabeth "Betita" Martínez was instrumental in making the connection between Chicanas and Third World women (along with her colleague Enriqueta Vásquez, who also put forward a Third World feminist perspective). The newspaper framed rural land struggles in New Mexico and abroad as challenges to US imperialism and internal colonialism and invoked a local-global imaginary. An example of this framing is the "Special Section" on "La Chicana" published as an insert in the June 1971 issue. The editorial introduction to the section, "Viva La Chicana and All Brave Women of the Causa" (written by Elizabeth Martínez but uncredited in the newspaper), describes the "revolutionary Chicana" from Mexican revolutionary history to present-day rural women in northern New Mexico. Martinez then outlines a narrative trajectory as follows: "This section begins with historical articles about La Chicana in Mexico's struggle for independence and liberation. It ends with our hermanas in other parts of America, Asia, Africa—because we have common bonds." These bonds are identified as a common oppression by the "US system that exploits people all over the world, especially non-white people." The editorial then describes specific oppression of women: "We are directly subjugated to every kind of oppression, from the day-to-day denials of the US welfare system to rape, torture, and murder in Latin America, Africa, Asia." Finally, the editor states, "We should learn about our sisters around the world because someday we shall together form a force that nothing can stop."[53]

While offering a powerful statement of global sisterhood and the need to link and learn about others' struggles, Martinez articulates a local-global dynamic that moves from the day-to-day systemic violence women experience in the United States to physical violence in other countries in a way that may suggest a conflation of forms of violence. However, given the time, when there were reports of torture under cruel dictatorships in Latin America and Africa and war in Asia and her reference to "the US system that exploits people all over the world," Martinez's nod to the relative degrees of violence may also be an acknowledgement that these other countries are more vulnerable to US influence and intervention that also included support for or a refusal to criticize dictatorial governments on the part of the United States. Indeed, her link suggests a relationship between the two that on one hand suggests a horizontal affiliation between women's struggles but challenges an easy horizontalism by noting the degrees of violence as a continuum that has a direct relation to the "US system."

Another example of the internationalist perspective can be found in the landmark 1973 anthology *La mujer: En pie de lucha ¡Y la hora es ya!*, which heralded a Latin American and Chicana-based Third World womanism in a multiracial and international collection of writings by and about women from Mexico, Cuba, and Brazil. The collection, edited and published by Bay Area activist Dorinda Moreno, also included work by and about Chicanas, black women, American Indian women, and even some men (in a section entitled "Machismo").[54] The volume—not often recognized as an early precursor to the later *"tercermundista* stance" of writers like Cherríe Moraga—firmly locates Chicanas within an international scope of activism and thought by women. Indeed, *La mujer: En pie de lucha* may be one of the most forthright representations of Chicanas as advocates of and "braided within," to quote feminist scholar Elora Halim Chowdhury, a Third World feminist or womanist, and what we now might call transnational, perspective in the 1970s.[55]

CONCLUSION

While I am considering the travel of Las Diez de San Diego as a powerful moment in Third World womanism and antiwar activism by Chicanas, at the time their travel to the international conference resonated in the local Chicano movement in ways that seemed to bring Chicana activists who attended back to the realities of their regional movement experience. An account of the conference published in the local newspaper *La Verdad*, "Chicanas Attend Vancouver Conference," reminds us that despite their participation in creating a powerful space of solidarity with multiple struggles and groups, "Some of us Chicanas who went to the conference have been asked why we went to a white women's thing. Well, if the Vancouver Conference had been a white women's thing we would have gone to learn from the experiences and to make it a Chicano thing because the War in Viet Nam is affecting Chicano people too."[56] The writer responds to the questioning of their motives and commitment to the movement by refusing to take the "feminist baiting"; instead the writer argues that it did not matter who organized the conference given the issues and then challenges the implication that Chicanas did not have a strong sense of their own commitments to a collective by asserting that any knowledge gathered would be considered in relation to the Chicano community. The author continues, "We have also been asked why it was a women's conference since men and women could join together to end the war." In response, the writer states, "This conference was mainly a political experience for women" and calls for women to have political space for themselves. Indeed, Chicanas from San Diego next organized to travel to the Conferencia de Mujeres por La Raza in Houston in May 1971, and they continued to meet in the region through 1973.

By seeking to rebuild the context and listening to the Chicana voice on the Vancouver conference, I hope to restore a sense of the rich multiplicities and presences of a time and to remobilize conversations about topics such as transnational solidarity that can guide us forward in a continuing context of global dynamics of conflict and power among nation-states. By recovering these stories of solidarity work in the past and the story of Las Diez, we also see how women of all backgrounds have resisted war by crossing borders to learn each other's stories. The report, interviews, and additional sources I consulted point to models in the past that are relevant for current struggles, such as the need to be thoughtful about process, to observe and to reflect on the histories of struggle, and to commit to solidarity. The very act of participating in the conference as Chicanas and of experiencing a different context for thinking about Chicana identity within the Third World woman concept contributed to theories of solidarity that I argue are foundational and formative in Chicana feminist thought. Indeed, as Judy Tzu-Chun Wu has written, the conference itself was a site for Third World women to solidify their identity. They had to "develop relationships, determine mutual goals, and provide support for one another."[57] Additionally, Chicana participation contributed to their ongoing Chicana feminist organizing in San Diego by creating stronger bonds among those at different campuses in the area as well as creating bonds with Chicanas in other communities such as the Bay Area, bonds that continue to this day.

Finally, it is important to acknowledge the cross-generational dialogue developed through "doing research" and working with activists to document their testimonies of activism and community his/her/our stories. When I mentioned to Nuñez that I had found her report, she sent me a copy of the report with photos that were captioned. As I continued to develop this essay, I asked her if she might be open to talking about the report, and she then encouraged others who had been to the conference to respond if they were open to being interviewed (snowball sampling). She also organized a videotaped interviewing session with her and Martha Salinas that we hope will be part of a documentary or other set of presentations reactivating conversations about Chicana antiwar activism and global solidarity, past as well as present and future, to be shared with new audiences. For all of these interviews, the kitchen table became the chosen space for the conversation, placing us in the classic space of *plática* for women. I felt especially blessed to sit there with them and to hear their stories, filled with emotion, laughter, tears, and a shared appreciation for the powerful spirit of Chicana activism.

15 MARÍA JIMÉNEZ

REFLEXIONES ON TRAVERSING MULTIPLE FRONTERAS IN THE SOUTH

SAMANTHA RODRIGUEZ AND STALINA
EMMANUELLE VILLARREAL

Chicana/o movement historiography underscores the thoughts and actions of male leaders and has largely obscured the critical role that *mujeres* like María Jiménez played in advancing *la causa* and expanding the frames of racial justice.[1] As a feminist and activist, Jiménez was a vital source of empowerment for Texas Chicanas developing a gendered critique of protest struggles. She was also highly revered by her male counterparts for her keen analyses and ability to maneuver around institutional barriers. In her own right, Jiménez was a potent leader of the social movements of the 1960s and 1970s.[2] Based on her *testimonio* and employing a collaborative method, this essay highlights the ways Jiménez navigated structural and cultural racism, sexism, and classism. For Jiménez, it was not enough to pursue racial equality and subscribe to narrow conceptions of liberation. As a Texas Chicana, a migrant, a woman, and someone who was intimately aware of poverty, Jiménez was at the forefront of broader social justice struggles during the *movimiento*. Her forms of consciousness and movement-building practices foreshadow what fellow Texas Chicana Gloria Anzaldúa would theorize as *mestiza* consciousness almost two decades later.

¡*Oute*! The Spanglish word for "out" is the first word that María de los Ángeles Jiménez Flores spoke before the age of one, during a baseball game on the radio. Baseball has long been regarded as a thinker's game, and even at such a young age, a strategist emerged who took the role of a referee or umpire, calling out what is wrong or out of bounds. Like her mother, Elva Flores Guerra de Jiménez, who learned to maneuver around patriarchal spaces in order to obtain a measure of freedom, María Jiménez Flores negotiated male-dominated power structures:

From my mother, what I learned was how to deal with absolute power because she would figure out what to do in order to gain the objectives which Papá said we could not do. . . . I remember that she would organize us clandestinely: "No le digan a tu papá [Don't tell your father], but we are going to do this." So, from her I learned how to deal with that type of absolute power.[3]

Jiménez Flores recalls that she informally started mobilizing at the age of three when she adamantly protested against the preferential treatment of her newborn brother. As Jiménez Flores was learning to resist gender barriers, she became acutely aware of class inequality. In her early childhood in Castaños, Coahuila, Mexico, she often overheard her middle-class relatives "making disparaging comments against the very poor."[4] She also witnessed the stark material differences among the classes: the impoverished lived on dirt floors, the working class walked on cement floors, and the elites had the privilege of mosaic floors. Beyond her observations, conversations about labor organizing "were a standard" in her household as her father narrated his experiences with his miners' union every evening.[5] These early exposures to economic politics fostered Jiménez Flores's commitment to tackling class inequality.

Jiménez Flores's political genealogy encompasses encounters with oppression on both sides of the border. With her family, María Jiménez Flores crossed *la frontera* into Texas on May 9, 1957, at the age of six, when she legally became María Jiménez. Her initial experiences familiarized her with state-sponsored segregation and discriminatory practices in the Jim Crow South:

I remember seeing for the first time on the buses were African Americans in the back and white people in the front. I remember I had never seen an African American. I remember asking my father why that was and he said, "Well, they have to by law sit in the back." I also remember that . . . on the way to Houston there were certain little towns like Schulenberg and others where we were not permitted to eat in certain restaurants.[6]

Throughout her formative years in Houston, Jiménez was permitted to swim at the white-only Mason Park "on the day they cleaned it."[7] Jiménez's stark encounters with de jure and de facto segregation in the Jim Crow South served as a foundational layer to her political maturation.

Through her familial, cultural, and structural experiences, Jiménez mastered the art of navigating multiple terrains and outmaneuvering systems of power in order to achieve broad freedom. Her calculated moves were rooted in plurality. While Jiménez did not have the language to describe the intersectional *mestiza* consciousness that Gloria Anzaldúa would put forth in the late 1980s, she served as a prototype for activism centered on multifaceted and inclusive visions of liberation. Indeed, her transnational life history and border crossings in the spheres of class, race, and gender led her to resist all forms of rigidity. Her foundational encounters with racial discrimination allowed her to view social justice through a multi-issue prism and fueled her interest in class-oriented approaches to equality. Gloria Anzaldúa describes the borderlands as not just a physical boundary but also a mental and cultural space that activates a fluid consciousness. It is a *mestiza* consciousness in which "energy comes from continual creative motion that keeps breaking down the unitary aspect of each new paradigm."[8] This *mestiza* consciousness acts as a malleable portal for cultivating tolerance and freedom pathways that disrupt "all oppressive traditions of all cultures."[9] During her early activism, Jiménez traversed multiple *fronteras* as an emerging orator, coalition builder, and astute strategist. Drawing upon Anzaldúa's notion of the borderlands and the porous nature of *mestiza* consciousness, this essay charts how Jiménez became a grassroots actor for ethnic self-determination, cross-racial justice, and feminist liberation. Centering on Jiménez's *testimonio* and the weight of her *palabras* in speaking back to hegemonic forces, we reveal the multiple ways she sought to destabilize intersectional oppression in the Jim Crow South.[10]

CLAIMING THE POWER OF PALABRAS

In 1967, María Jiménez joined the debate team at Milby High School in Houston and honed her verbal power to dismantle structural and cultural oppression. Jiménez refined her skills at the time by transcending masculinist forms of speaking—the "bombastic" oratory style that "is culturally accepted."[11] She confronted sexism, classism, and racism by learning how to weave concrete analysis and storytelling into a formidable rhetorical strategy. This cross-genre style is emblematic of Jiménez's ability to surpass boundaries. It was during these teenage years in the segregated environment of Houston—where Chicanas/os were still grappling with limited educational and occupational opportunities—that Jiménez would utilize familial and institutional experiences to forge a social justice voice reflective of her multilayered identity.[12]

Jiménez initially crafted her oratorical style through her introduction to Mexican feminist poetry and grassroots acts of resistance:

> From my mother's family, with my grandfather, I was . . . exposed to a lot of other things that I think other people were not because my grandfather taught us poetry. . . . He opened his books to us. From a very early age, I would open books of la Revolución [in Mexico] and would look at all the *soldaderas*, and of course, everyone talked about Sor Juana Inés [de la Cruz] as part of the poetry. So, I was very familiar with strong women figures in Mexican history.[13]

As a forthright poet who was a nun in colonial Mexico, Sor Juana Inés de la Cruz boldly asserted protofeminist campaigns in the spheres of education and culture that Jiménez readily latched onto.[14] Jiménez's back-and-forth migration across the borderlands enriched and reaffirmed her contention that feminist acts of resistance are deeply rooted in the Mexican culture. Indeed, Jiménez would later rely upon her knowledge of Mexican history when combating male efforts to silence gender activism in the *movimiento* in the early 1970s.[15]

Alongside poetic political commentary, Jiménez developed her argumentative style through the narrative traditions of her father's lineage. Her paternal relatives invoked rhetorical devices that combined imagery with situational irony: "From [an] early age, I would hear my father and his side of the family express cynicisms regarding the role of the Catholic Church. Apparently, my great-grandfather Bruno Jiménez would criticize his churchgoing daughters, reminding them that while the pope wore sandals of gold, children were dying of hunger in Mexico."[16] Her great-grandfather utilized the visualization of opulence in contrast to the dire conditions of the poor in order to make his point memorable and clear. During Jiménez's rhetorical formation, she bridged symbolism and context to scrutinize the fallacy of arguments.[17]

While Jiménez was at Milby High School, she encountered institutional racism that shaped the ways she navigated her Mexican American identity and how she would use her words to address the plight of Chicanas/os:

> Specific school experiences would reinforce my rejection to these stereotypes and attempts to enforce them as a way of life. Clearly, the threat to be expelled from school for speaking Spanish created an insecurity. . . . My parents would pronounce that our Mexicanness could not be forgotten and forbade the speaking of English at home and adherence to behaviors appropriate for Mexican families. In that sense, the experience of being caught in two worlds pushed me to excel in both and to often make strict differentiations between them. It was the basis for later understanding the ideology driving the Chicano identity and the duality of cultures competing in our sense of belonging.[18]

The denial of language exacerbated the subjugation and the superimposed indignity of the Jim Crow South.[19] However, Jiménez's familial exposure to analytical storytellers encouraged adamant resistance. Her *palabras* were largely inspired by her mother, who "overcame all obstacles—language, segregation, poor neighborhoods—and made it work for her and her goals."[20] Jiménez developed her oratory technique by fusing Mexican and American discourses to disrupt silencing mechanisms. Jiménez's ephemeral experience at church provided a space to cultivate her activist voice and enhance her *mestiza* consciousness. While the Catholic Youth Organization at the Immaculate Heart of Mary offered her exposure to the class-oriented social justice cause of the farmworkers, she detested sermons that condemned women.[21] Accordingly, Jiménez forged a "plural" sensibility.[22] Multiple prejudices prompted Jiménez to take a proactive role against oppression.

Jiménez explored *fronteras* of social justice that shaped her crossing of intesectionality. In the 1960s, as a member of the Milby High School debate team, Jiménez crystalized her critical voice by fusing her on-the-ground protest experiences with theoretical political readings:

> In the debate team, my experience with support for the farmworkers and the various struggles for civil rights and equality that loomed in magazines and newspapers began to shape an understanding within me of the need for the confrontation of injustice with unified struggle. The oratory I recited in contests in my final year in high school dealt with the socioeconomic conditions of Mexican Americans and the need to forge movements of struggle like those already emerging with César Chávez and Reies López Tijerina. The *coraje* (fury) that had boiled inward year after year began to make sense only in the construction of an organized response—like the ones that had been part of the history of the Mexican people shared by my grandfather [and] my father's union struggles and the struggles for what was right many times explained by my aunts and cousins when we went to visit in Mexico.[23]

Jiménez further solidified her *mestiza* conceptualization when she established rationality as a foundation in her move toward justice and against xenophobia and racism in the segregated South. She and her debate partner, Brenda Culverhouse,

> won the girls state championship in debate. . . . I started to address the issue of the inequalities of Mexican Americans in oratory contests, and I learned there that we either won or lost. . . . We went to little towns like Goliad and tournaments like that where it was obvious that because I was Mexican . . . we lost those debates. The judges were prejudiced. So, very early, there's always this concept of exclusion and at some point, I got the right to go to [these] mock state legislatures that they do in high school, but I was not allowed to proceed because I was not a US citizen.[24]

Beyond racial and national-origin exclusion, Jiménez understood in this formative stage that the rejection of Mexican cultural norms furthered her minority status: "In order to win you do have to conform in many ways to the community norms and standards, and in some ways I was devious from those standards."[25] She was the only Latina on the debate team, and her sense of identity was further complicated by her immigrant experience as a Generation 1.5 student in the borderlands.

> My immigrant identity was firmly fixed. . . . Most importantly, the constant border crossing [with family] taught us how to survive Border Patrol questioning and when returning to Mexico, how to deal with corrupt customs agents on the Mexican side. No other experience of our foreignness would be more explicit than when I was denied to participate in a mock legislature for lack of US citizenship.

Eventually I would file for that right on my eighteenth birthday, encouraged by my debate coach, who was outraged at the opportunities that had been denied to me despite my qualifications.[26]

On another occasion, a debate judge broke his confidentiality and remarked, "How can we let that Mexican girl win?"[27] This institutional rejection informed Jiménez's commitment to justice. Beyond ethnic discrimination, her gender factored in her exclusion. Judges would opt to have male debaters instead of Jiménez and her Anglo female debate partner.[28] Jiménez's experiences with stark gender discrimination were not relegated to the outside world—cultural expectations also limited her opportunities as a woman: "I was getting scholarships and winning debates because my partner and I were debate champions of the state of Texas. We were being offered scholarships like to the University of Texas and elsewhere. My father would not permit it because I just could not go because I was female."[29]

Jiménez's intersectional identity forced her to face the sexism, racism, and xenophobia she encountered in school and in her community. Her layered politics strengthened Jiménez's approaches to social justice. She entertained the opponent's typical response and utilized her multiple understandings to counter with an unexpected rebuttal. Jiménez destabilized the flow of masculine arguments by drawing on marginalized voices and expressing a plural style. For Jiménez, communication facilitated her roles as a believer and an actor in social justice in diverse spaces. Her form of communication would prove vital when fighting for ethnic studies and student rights while she worked toward a degree in political science at the University of Houston.

ETHNIC AND GENDER COALITION BUILDING AT THE UNIVERSITY OF HOUSTON

During the late 1960s and early 1970s, María Jiménez and fellow Chicana/o activists in the University of Houston Mexican American Youth Organization (UH MAYO) sought to establish ethnic studies and transform higher education.[30] Beyond playing a central role in the formation of a Center for Mexican American Studies, Jiménez became the first Mexican American and female Student Government Association (SGA) president. While navigating the frontiers of academia, Jiménez acted as a bridge for uniting Chicanas/os, feminists, African Americans, international students, and Anglo radicals around the cause for university accountability, particularly in the areas of access and support services. Activating a "pluralistic mode," Jiménez set out on a mission to incorporate class and gender issues within the larger fight for a culturally relevant and inclusive education.[31]

For Jiménez and Texas Chicanas/os engaged in activism on campus and in the community, MAYO was the principal radical organization for cultivating a cultural, political, and gender consciousness. Formed in 1967 at Saint Mary's University in San Antonio, MAYO gleaned confrontational politics from the teachings of Saul Alinsky and the Black Power movement. MAYO meticulously studied Alinsky's *Reveille for Radicals* as well as the successful direct-action tactics that the Student Nonviolent Coordinating Committee (SNCC) and the Black Panther Party deployed.[32] Their knowledge of Alinsky's and the Black Power movement's proven methods led MAYO to contend that marches, protests, boycotts, and mass assemblies rather than resolutions, petitions, or letters to officials would solve their socioeconomic problems and further their quest for ethnic self-determination.[33]

Jiménez's introduction to UH MAYO came by way of her direct participation in the farmworkers struggle through the Young Democrats.

> I joined the Young Democrats because there was no MAYO [at the time]. It was LOMAS [League of Mexican American Students] and I thought it was just more of a social organization as opposed to a political organization. . . . There I met some of the people that I would later work with in MAYO and La Raza Unida Party—Daniel Bustamante and Arturo Eureste. The value for me there was that in the Young Democrats . . . the United Farm Workers came in to organize the grape and lettuce boycott, and it was through those contacts that I became part of the first committee that worked directly with César Chávez in organizing the boycott here in Houston.[34]

Dissatisfied with its electoral focus and the little regard Chicana/o issues were given, Jiménez left the Young Democrats and joined UH MAYO when LOMAS made the conversion in 1969. While she concentrated her activism in ethnic self-determination projects, she was dedicated to breaking down racial barriers and forging alliances with radical students.

While *mujeres* were largely relegated to supportive positions in MAYO chapters throughout the state, Jiménez's verbal prowess, keen observations, and ability to skillfully navigate institutional and interethnic *fronteras* elevated her status to that of a respected leader of UH MAYO. She maintained her influential role by refusing to become romantically involved with fellow Chicano activists. For Jiménez, dating movement men would threaten her position in the *movimiento*. She regularly witnessed how women lost their decision-making authority once they became engaged in relationships with male leaders. Jiménez recognized that in the eyes of her generation, "women could only be held high if you were a virgin or wife."[35] Accordingly, she rested on the perception of being an unattainable virgin in order to intervene in hypermasculine protest spaces. She would use her position of power to deconstruct the sexist contours of the Chicana/o movement.[36] As Jiménez fought for gender equality, she cultivated relationships with African Americans, socialists, international students, and Anglo feminists on campus, bridging the Chicana/o struggle for educational reform to broader fights for ethnic, class, and gender liberation.

In the late 1960s and early 1970s, Jiménez worked with UH MAYO members Cynthia Pérez, Jaime de la Isla, Inés Hernández Tovar, Mario Garza, and others to establish the University of Houston Center for Mexican American Studies.[37] She wrote parts of the Chicana/o studies proposal, coordinated with the administration, and lobbied the state legislature for ethnic studies funding.[38] As a bridge, Jiménez facilitated relations among UH MAYO and Afro-Americans for Black Liberation (AABL) as well as the Black Student Union. She recognized that solidifying relations among Chicanas/os and African American students on campus was mutually beneficial in that both groups were invested in ethnic studies centers that would address their particular needs and generate critical analyses of their communities.

> I think that we had a working relationship [with some AABL members]. I mean there was, . . . but they were further ahead, in terms of the Black studies program. So we kind of just defended each other's space. . . . We also negotiated, you know, particularly with the students' funds that created the ethnic studies department within the student association to continue working on speakers and so forth.[39]

Beyond supporting the activities of Afro-Americans for Black Liberation and the Black Student Union, Jiménez played an instrumental role in the University Information Program and the Student Opportunity Services, black and brown student recruitment and retention projects.[40]

Jiménez ran as the first ethnic Mexican and female Student Government Association president at UH in 1971.[41] She had received strong support from the Black Student Union, women's liberation, Young Socialist Alliance, Young Democrats, and International Student Organization. For Jiménez, leadership roles were more about advancing social equality than personal gratification. This communal style of organizing was reflective of her efforts to dismantle exclusionary paradigms: "In the Latino community . . . there is a leadership style that people look for. . . . I call it the male characteristic dominant leadership. . . . Women don't fit. . . . I see my role as a social movement builder as opposed [to] . . . as an organizer . . . [or] as opposed to the individual traditional male-dominant leadership style."[42] Her SGA platform targeted ethnic, working-class, and female enrollment by proposing free day care for children of all married students, open admissions, a night-student information center for students who could only attend classes in the evening, and student control of all student service fees.[43] Further, she advocated for reproductive rights—free contraceptives, a female gynecologist, and free abortion counseling.[44] The inclusion of gender issues in Jiménez's platform reflected her persistent dedication to tackling institutional and interethnic sexist *fronteras*:

> In those years, I would eventually shed all pretenses of the cultural concept of womanhood. I fought along feminists at the university to get the Women's

Studies program and child care for students started, and I took the first course on Women's History. I participated in events that fought for reproductive rights. I remember a national mock trial of anti-abortion rights held at UH and that I was asked to serve as one of four judges; we would find the anti-abortion laws unconstitutional and [sought to] protect a woman's right to decide whether or not to continue a pregnancy. It was clear to me that many women died in childbirth or abortions performed in unsafe conditions. I fought for a woman's right to decide what to do with her own body and imposed motherhood.[45]

Despite the looming repercussions from her male colleagues, Jiménez boldly championed women's ability to carve spaces in higher education. She contended that Chicanas' educational opportunities were crippled by the cultural expectation to be submissive housewives, a system that tracked them into vocational courses, and mass media that depicted marriage as a blissful affair. Jiménez wrote in 1971,

> *La cultura mejicana* subjects a Chicana to no greater expectation than that of being a housewife. . . . [By] stressing male superiority, her family discourages her ambitions and imposes a lack of confidence. . . . The Anglo education system simply reinforces her attitudes towards educational advancement. Like the Chicano, the Chicana is alienated by discrimination, language, difficulties, irrelevant subjects, and bad teachers. Her interests in education further diminishes and ill-trained, narrow minded counselors quickly channel her into "practical" occupations such as secretarial jobs. . . . Countless television programs and movies describe the bliss and happiness of married life. . . . For *La Raza*, the small number of Chicanas in colleges is detrimental to *La Causa* [because] development of future generations is in the hands of Chicanas.[46]

At the University of Houston, Jiménez was a trailblazer in the formation of cross-ethnic and gender alliances. Her cross-pollinating, bridging efforts expanded the frames of Chicana/o self-determination and pushed academia to be more responsive to the needs of ethnic, female, and poor students. For Jiménez, the Chicana/o movement "was a nationalist response to a concrete situation."[47] That is, Texas Chicana/o activism in the 1970s stemmed from stark experiences with racism and disfranchisement in the Jim Crow South. While Jiménez was committed to ethnic liberation, her transnational identity and staunch class awareness facilitated a more elastic view of Chicana/o nationalism. She understood that she could not, in Anzaldúa's words, "hold concepts or ideas in rigid boundaries."[48] Jiménez explains,

> I was a Mexican immigrant as opposed to many of my colleagues who were second- or third-generation Mexican Americans. I had a very distinct identity, and also the farmworker fight was like a broader fight because with the farmworkers

you dealt with economic inequality, and you dealt with union organizing and how the capitalist system worked. . . . So that experience I think helped me always to have a broader perspective of the Chicano movement as sort of a step toward equality but not necessarily the end in itself. . . . Because I was . . . Mexican and Chicana, I fought for that first. I mean I had to fight for that because that was my community. But I'm also a woman, so I had to fight for that. . . . But also the whole issue of income inequality would fit with poor whites and blacks.[49]

Jiménez would continue this fluid and uniting fight for equal rights as she entered the fray of electoral politics through La Raza Unida Party.

LA RAZA UNIDA PARTY: UNITED FOR CHICANA/O, AFRICAN AMERICAN, AND POOR PEOPLE'S JUSTICE

An outgrowth of MAYO, the Raza Unida Party (RUP) emerged in 1970 as a third party committed to the economic, social, and political self-determination of Chicanas/os. Witnessing the lack of policies directed toward Chicanas/os in both the Democratic and Republican Parties, Chicanas/os established RUP as a political alternative that recognized the "the existence of culturally distinct peoples," advocated for the "equal representation of all peoples," and sought to implement programs "relevant to individual communities."[50] While organizers touted the *partido* as the only alternative for Chicanas/os and concentrated its political campaigning in the ethnic Mexican areas of South Texas in the early years, they repackaged its platform as they sought statewide growth and influence. Its broad-based appeal made strategic sense for garnering votes in urban areas such as Houston where there were significant African American communities. In 1974, María Jiménez ran under the RUP ticket for state representative, drawing upon the bridging activism she nourished as a student leader in the *movimiento*. Her involvement in electoral politics not only represented the intervention of *mujeres* in the borderlands of RUP but also advanced interethnic, class, and gender solidarity in the 1970s.

By the early 1970s, Texas Chicanas had spent years managing the daily functions of RUP. They thoroughly studied the election code, coordinated campaigns, secured office spaces, and put together meetings. The Texas Election Code included an "opaque set of rules that had to be followed in order to ensure the party's legitimacy in the campaign and at the polls."[51] Indeed, *mujeres* in RUP had to become experts on the electoral process. Beyond electoral procedures, women contended with a *partido* that was male-driven and often relegated them to secretarial roles.[52] As Chicana historian Dionne Espinoza has argued, however, RUP women gained precinct and county leadership positions by laying "the framework of the party bureaucracy and doing the hard work of organizing campaigns and mobilizing voters on the ground."[53] Through their interventions, Chicanas successfully incorporated the Equal Rights Amendment and equal rights for women, whether they be "working mothers, career women, or housewives," in the Texas RUP platform.[54]

Chicana activists also carved out spaces for female leadership and political opportunities in the *partido* through the creation of Mujeres por La Raza, a woman's caucus that regularly held conferences in an effort to recruit women into the political process and generate party candidates. Jiménez along with Alma Canales, Martha Cotera, and Orelia Hisbrook Cole bravely navigated the male-dominated terrain of electoral politics to represent the collective community issues of Chicanas/os. For Jiménez, the choice to become a candidate was largely due to her confidence in what RUP offered the political process: "I was asked to be a candidate for state representative. I was an unwilling candidate [because] I really did not like electoral politics, but I believed in La Raza Unida, which was community involvement and the willingness to channel that community involvement into an independent political process."[55]

In her 1974 bid for state representative in the 87th District, Jiménez collaborated with African American community leaders she met through her fluid political organizing at UH. Her cross-cultural movement building not only was necessary for garnering significant votes in a multiethnic large city but also reflected Jiménez's commitment to comprehensive self-determination. By the time Jiménez ran under the RUP ticket, the *partido* had made appeals to African Americans in an effort to achieve state and national viability. In 1972, RUP declared that the "Democrats take for granted that the Black vote will always be there. They always howler that the 'minorities have it bad,' but no Blacks are ever consulted on a mass level, or involved in policy making." The RUP further stated that the "United People's Party known as La Raza Unida Party" was familiar with the "problems that confront Black people every day."[56]

The year Jiménez ran as a political candidate she solidified the United People's Party by recruiting African Americans as party members and working to have Amiri Baraka—secretary general of the National Black Political Assembly—as a keynote speaker at the state convention in Houston.

We started talking to [African Americans] about this possibility so that they would become our partner in the African American areas of the district, primarily the Fifth and Third Ward[s] in Houston. They did not take our word just because they knew us—they actually had a delegation go down to Crystal City . . . and observed what had happened there and the results, and once they came back they made the decision to join us. So we worked with them on knocking on doors in the African American areas of the district. The second Raza Unida Party convention, which took place in Houston, they actually had a keynote speaker there and they were present. So I think it's the only place where African Americans actually were present in the state convention and were part of the program.[57]

Jiménez bridged Chicana/o and African American activists, including Deloyd Parker, Ester King, and Omowali Lithuli, to canvass Houston's historic African American neighborhoods of the Fifth Ward and Third Ward. As she block-walked with Lithuli, Jiménez explained the purpose of the *partido* and presented her platform that spoke to the Black and Brown issues of equal access to higher education, proper and affordable health care, penal reform, inner-city pollution, and the right for workers to organize for better conditions and livable wages:[58]

> I remember going with Omowali and we said—when we were knocking on doors— "We are representing the Raza Unida Party." We had to immediately translate—it is the People's United Party and this is why we are doing this. It would take a long time to explain to people why it was an independent movement. To a certain extent, it fit in with our concept of educating the community . . . developing a conscious decision. One of the homes that I remember visiting in the African American community with Omowali was a very dilapidated house. I remember this elderly African American man coming out and there were holes in the floor. He talked about how he was on Social Security and at that time, I think he was [getting] forty-five dollars a month . . . it was seeing the tremendous impact of social systems not just for Latinas/os, but for African Americans as well.[59]

After generating a potent cross-ethnic campaign, Jiménez ended her RUP candidacy with roughly 17 percent of the vote.[60] While she did not win her bid for state representative, her electoral race bolstered black and brown alliances that would prove critical for future political endeavors.[61] For Jiménez, engaging in the electoral process was less about winning than it was a vehicle for dismantling traditional political machines and fusing ethnic spheres into a collective consciousness.

> I think we were all very focused on the building of the community power, as opposed to winning the position. I think in that sense, the door-to-door contact with people was really what we were looking for and . . . that we would be left with a series of contacts at the community base that would allow us to build independent political processes from there. . . . I think that one of the African American leaders, Omowali Lithuli, basically stated it best: We developed a working unity. It was a unity based on concrete working rather than like most coalitions sitting and developing programs. . . . For me, the trust that we had in each other in terms of the players involved in both the African American community and ourselves has continued over the years, in the sense that when we see each other, when we call upon each other to participate here and there, we do [it] without questions . . . because we had that experience in Raza Unida.[62]

Jiménez's campaign also illustrated the possibility of female governance. It signaled to women that they could meaningfully run for political positions on the RUP ticket. Her engagement in electoral politics was the culmination of her interventions as a Chicana in the borderlands of student activism. Lastly, Jiménez's race advanced RUP's mission to force the Democrats and Republicans to be responsive to the Chicana/o electorate. Her political campaign leaflet asserted,

I am convinced that Raza Unida is the only party where the Mexican people of this state have a voice. The Democratic Party in Texas has never heard the Mexican American. . . . The Mexican American people need to have a voice in government to push for solutions to . . . overall discrimination against the disadvantaged. Raza Unida is that voice. I choose to run on behalf of the Raza Unida Party because it is the voice of the people.[63]

OCCUPYING SPACES IN THE BORDERLANDS AS A COMMUNITY BUILDER

By 1975, María Jiménez was living in Sinaloa, Mexico, and married to a leftist national. She would use her time in Mexico to accelerate her intervention in the *frontera* as a community builder:

I remember that I felt that I could not abandon the Chicana/o movement but advanced ideologically to understand the root causes of inequality. . . . A lot of people said, well, you ran off like any other woman following your man, but the reality was that I could not find a Mexicano in the circles we were in who believed in women's rights and did not impose societal norms of what a woman should be. . . . [The] time in Mexico [allowed] me to grow . . . and understand particularly questions of relationships between the theory of social movement and the practice of social movements.[64]

Just as Gloria Anzaldúa argued that the borderlands are "in a constant state of transition," Jiménez crossed *la frontera* to learn how to transform racist, classist, and sexist barriers into zones of liberation.[65] Throughout the late 1960s and early 1970s, Jiménez's familiarity with border crossing emboldened her to disrupt the obstacles placed before her and advocate for the rights of Chicanas/os as well as people of color and marginalized populations in the segregated South more broadly.

Jiménez did not use leadership positions to implement her own agenda or to amass political capital but rather to serve as a facilitator for collective empowerment. In this way, her grassroots protests employed a layered sensibility of being a migrant, a Texas Chicana, and an impoverished woman who rooted her activism in the legacy of Mexican feminism. As a Mexican woman, Jiménez expanded the politics of economic marginalization to encompass racial and gender equality.

She furthered her bridging work when she returned to the United States in 1985 after spending a decade "as community organizer of economic development projects in agricultural communities" of Yucatan, Mexico, where she engaged in leftist independent unions and sought to "give voice to women."[66] Once back in the States, Jiménez quickly became engrossed in the immigrant rights struggle— a logical extension to her human rights and social justice work in Latin America. Her former RUP *compañera* Sandra Spector introduced her to the American

Friends Service Committee, a Quaker civil rights organization. It opened an office in Houston so that Jiménez could mount an aggressive sixteen-year immigrant rights campaign and have familial support for her children.[67] After becoming a leader in the movement to document how US immigration laws violate Latina/o human rights along the border, she facilitated the 2003 Immigrant Workers Freedom Ride by forging relations with African American civil rights activists to address the plight of migrants.[68] In 2005, Jiménez started working for the Central American Resource Center. For Jiménez, Houston was "an exceptional place where the Central American and Mexican leadership didn't fight [each other but] . . . worked together focusing on immigrant rights issues."[69] Building on her cross-racial and cross-ethnic work on both sides of the *frontera*, Jiménez has dedicated years—in many organizations—to facilitating relations among Latinas/os, particularly bridging the shared struggles of Mexicans, Guatemalans, and El Salvadorans. Indeed, Jiménez has fostered a plural consciousness in all of the battles that she has engaged in from the time of her youth.

Jiménez's *testimonio* of the *movimiento* not only documents trauma in the borderlands but also serves as a statement against institutional and cultural forces that seek to render Chicanas invisible. Her *palabras* about the 1960s and 1970s provide critical blueprints for intersectional struggles. Beyond sharing her accounts, Jiménez guided this collaborative effort by reviewing all drafts, demonstrating how the process of storytelling can be inclusive and empowering for both the writers and the subject. Her fame is largely associated with immigrant rights, but her *testimonio* provides a context for that activist trajectory.

16 DE CAMPESINA A INTERNACIONALISTA

A JOURNEY OF ENCUENTROS Y DESENCUENTROS

OLGA TALAMANTE

While I consider myself a feminist and have been active in the LGBTQ movement for several years now, the origins of my political consciousness spring from the fields, the *campos* of the Santa Clara Valley, where I lived and worked before venturing out to the university. I remember one late afternoon in the summer of 1961, I watched as my father and other parents formed a line to get paid for the work we had done that week. As a family, we all worked for one of the *ranchero* families that owned the various prune orchards throughout the Santa Clara Valley. At that time, Gilroy, Morgan Hill, San Jose—what is now known as Silicon Valley—were towns surrounded by prune, apricot, cherries, peach, and walnut orchards and fields of row crops such as strawberries, tomatoes, cucumbers, and of course, garlic, as Gilroy came to be known as the Garlic Capital of the World.

We had moved that summer from Mexicali to Gilroy, arriving by a Greyhound bus that dropped us off on Highway 101 at the entrance of the labor camp where we were to live for the next eight years. I did not mind so much that the work was hard—getting up early, in the cold morning fogs, then working through the heat of the day until sundown—and the living conditions fairly rudimentary—no indoor plumbing, cold showers, one room for the whole family, and kerosene stove. But the treatment and the power relations experienced primarily by the parents really bothered me as a child. Instead of paying what the family had earned that week, in order to ensure that families would not leave before the harvest season was completed, the growers would decide how much each family would receive, based on the number of children. The rest of the payment was accumulated and given at the end of the season.

Although I was only eleven years old at the time, that system seemed unfair and patronizing to our hardworking families. Who were they to decide how much a family needed for the week? And it was particularly appalling to me when a family had to leave early because one of the sons got very sick and they wanted to take him back home near Fresno. They did not get their full pay. Additionally, because I worked as babysitter for one of the *rancheros'* kids, I could not help but make comparisons between their homes and ours. One advantage of this cross-class experience was that it made me ponder why their home had all the comforts and ours had so few. So when the farmworkers organizing efforts began, I was ready. As I arrived at UC Santa Cruz in 1969, I became part of the student volunteer core group that supported the United Farm Workers by going out to the fields to sign up workers, working the picket line at supermarkets that were carrying scab lettuce and grapes, organizing food and fund-raising drives, and participating in the various rallies and marches, such as the ones to Salinas and Delano.

At the university level, we were concerned with the lack of Latino faculty, staff, and students and formed various entities to try to address those, including, of course, MEChA (Movimiento Estudiantil Chicano de Aztlán). I was part of forming the first MEChA chapter at UC Santa Cruz. We pushed for more representation at all levels, sourcing possible staff and faculty candidates, demanding to be part of hiring committees, sitting in the chancellor's office, and in our best moments, forming coalitions with the other students of color and Anglo allies. At our worst moments, we fought among ourselves over our already too small piece of the pie, until we would regain our senses and come together to fight for the whole pie. At UC Santa Cruz I found some of the terminology that explained my observations, my feelings, my fears and expectations: Chicana consciousness, class rage, equality, fairness. I also was fortunate to meet a fellow student in one of the Latin American classes with whom I immediately connected and who was to become my lifelong friend, Ed McCaughan. Maybe it was because we were both from small, rural towns or because of that first tequila-fueled party where I tried to teach him to dance to *norteño* music, but we have been political comrades and accomplices in life ever since.

One of the groups we formed as Chicana women, Chicana Consciousness, was fairly short-lived but crucially important in my understanding of women's oppression and the dangers of "speaking bitterness."[1] Some of our Chicano male comrades were very disapproving and uneasy with the formation of this group. The university also provided me a path by which to explore my ancient roots and travel to Mexico, Central America, and eventually Argentina. Being a member of UCSC MEChA sparked my interest in the counterpart Mexican student movement of the 1960s, and I became part of the first forays of Chicano/Mexicano *encuentros*. Oh yeah, we also went to classes and studied and wrote our papers.

One of the classes that had a huge impact on me was a cultural anthropology class whose focus was the Maya Indigenous people of the Mexican highlands. The descendants of the ancient philosophers represented in the Popol Vuh were calling to me. A group of us classmates formed one of the first groups of Chicanos venturing to Mexico, the motherland, to connect with our contemporaries in the Mexican student movement, which had just suffered a huge blow with the 1968 massacre in Mexico City. They were suffering persecution and incarceration of many of their leaders. We also went to connect with the descendants of our ancient cultures, the Chamulas and Tzotziles of the Chiapas highlands. Little did we know then that the extreme poverty, racism, and exploitation we witnessed while on a field study program in San Cristóbal de las Casas would lead the indigenous peoples of that area to the formation of the Ejército Zapatista de Liberación Nacional (EZLN, Zapatista Army of National Liberation) twenty-three years later. When I heard about their uprising becoming public on January 1, 1994, I only pondered what had taken them so long.

While living in Chiapas and then in Mexico City with the theater group Los Mascarones, I became aware of new ways to explain certain realities. With this new understanding, I then understood the power relations I witnessed while in the Gilroy labor camp as class relations. The word for the imposition of economic policies by the superpowers on the developing world was "imperialism." I became aware of and inspired by the magnificent efforts by individuals and movements to organize and unite the oppressed. I met Argentinians who had been traveling throughout the continent, from Argentina all the way up to New York and back to Mexico, as they prepared to return to Argentina. They had a vision to do a documentary entitled "Struggles of the Peoples of the American Continent as One Struggle, as One People," which envisioned unity from Patagonia to the Canadian border. These experiences and connections strengthened my understanding of the international nature of our struggles, the similarities of our issues, and the origin of our problems—US imperialism and the class structures of our Latin American countries. While there was support for the international struggles around us such as the Cuban Revolution, the Vietnamese people's war, there was also a strong Chicano nationalism that demanded total and undivided loyalty.

In 1970, I applied to participate in the Venceremos Brigade, which was taking groups of volunteers to support the Cuban Revolution. The Brigade was formed as a coalition of young people attempting to show solidarity with the Cuban Revolution by working side by side with Cuban workers and challenging US policies toward Cuba, including the US embargo against Cuba. After the application and interview process was completed, I was accepted. I was nervous but excited to participate in what would have been the second brigade. Upon sharing the news of my acceptance with close friends and fellow Chicano activists, I was surprised by their reactions and their admonitions. Why was I going to fight other struggles when we had such a crucial struggle here as Chicanos? I was desperately needed here, so why would I abandon our struggle? Of course we had hugely important struggles taking place at that time, Chicano representation in higher education, the farmworker movement, the Chale con el Draft antiwar movement, and so on. Out of loyalty, some dosage of guilt, and succumbing to the ego stroking,

I declined and did not participate in the brigade. While I value the importance of the struggles we faced as Chicanos, I don't believe that a three-month trip to Cuba would have derailed our progress. Those reactions and sentiments eventually gave way to more internationalist perspectives, but there was certainly a current of thought among some key activists that espoused a nationalistic, keep-our-ranks-closed mentality. Surprisingly, one of the more "traditionalist" leaders of the Chicano movement, Corky Gonzales, was one of the most open and accepting of the need to build an internationalist approach to our work.

In their travels, the Argentinian comrades had documented various struggles and accumulated film, interviews, slides, and photographs that they planned to put together in a film. They were planning their return to Argentina by land in order to complete some of their documentation, revisit some of the activists they had interviewed, and eventually end up in Argentina. They asked if I wanted to come along. I answered, "Yes, indeed." This time around I was not going to pass up the opportunity to travel and see firsthand the realities and struggles of our peoples. We outfitted a station wagon and started our journey down the continent, from California through Mexico, Guatemala, El Salvador, Honduras, Nicaragua, and Costa Rica. We returned to Nicaragua to conduct some interviews, and upon our return to Costa Rica the Nicaraguan National Guard detained us. After a few days the Somoza dictatorship expelled us for our connection with supporters of the anti-Somoza movement.

Eventually, my friends flew back to Argentina to be part of the resurgent movement to replace the military dictatorship that had been in power for eighteen years with a democratically elected government. In March 1973, Héctor Campora was elected president of Argentina; one of his first acts was to declare amnesty for all political prisoners. Argentina was living a moment of political freedom after eighteen years of struggle against the military dictatorships. Former political prisoners and leftist activists were now being elected to public office; women, youth, and labor groups again mobilized to ensure mass participation in the new democratic process. Didn't I want to go and be part of that process? In August 1973 I boarded a plane to Argentina from Mexico City after having visited my good friends Ed McCaughan and Peter Baird, who were living in Mexico at the time doing research. Sure enough, Argentina was in political upheaval, with mass participation at all levels, political redefinitions, new alliances, old rivalries, and all this just within the Peronist movement.

Soon after my arrival in Azul, a city of 50,000 about 400 miles south of Buenos Aires, where my friends lived, I became involved in the Peronista Youth movement, the left wing of Peronism. I started attending the organizing meetings in the barrios, the political study groups, and the various marches and eventually became fully integrated as a community organizer of the barrio San Francisco on the outskirts of Azul, where the children would spot me coming and start yelling, "¡Ahi viene México!" (Here comes Mexico!). During the period from August 1973 to November 1974, I experienced what became one of the most transformative episodes in my life: being part of a national social movement that demanded social change and a new political economic model through the participation of mass organizations. Living that at the grassroots level, with the people of the barrio San Francisco, with the children on the soccer teams and the neighborhood organizations intent on building the first first-aid clinic in the barrio, I participated in a disciplined organization that demanded full personal commitment in the service of the revolution and in the process got a rare glimpse of a new society in the making.

The right-wing Peronist government of Isabel Perón declared a state of siege on November 6, 1974. Numerous arrests and some disappearances began to take place. As we were leaving a hastily called meeting on November 11, eleven of us were abducted by gun-welding plainclothes federal police agents. After four days in the basement of the local police station, enduring beatings and torture with electric shocks, we were transferred and officially registered at the local Azul prison. Since the military junta did not seize power until 1976, Isabel Perón's government was still officially an "elected" civilian government and some judicial steps were respected, such as official recognition of detained persons, a practice that was completely ignored with the "disappearance" of close to 30,000 people afterwards. After sixteen months, on March 28, 1976, due to a massive campaign waged by my family and friends through the Olga Talamante Defense Committee, I was released and deported to the United States. I spent almost two years focused on bringing attention to the situation in Argentina, working to cut off US military aid on the basis that the authoritarian regime was violating the human rights of the Argentine people. I advocated for the freedom of political prisoners, especially those comrades with whom I had worked and who remained in prison.

After a couple of years, I began to shift my focus to US issues and returned to the Bay Area from the East Coast and joined the Democratic Workers Party (DWP), which was part of the party-building movement of that time (the mid- and late seventies). The Bay Area–based DWP considered itself a Marxist-Leninist organization, with an anti-imperialist, antiracist ideology and a program that called on workers and progressives to fight for services and jobs and for civic engagement locally, while supporting revolutionary struggles in the Americas and abroad. In my six years as a militant in the DWP, I again experienced transformations in the social political scene as well as in my personal life. California Proposition 13, which reduced property tax rates on homes, businesses and farms by about 57 percent, thus reducing the public funds available for public services, whose effects we feel to this day, had just passed. We organized against contracting out (the privatization of public services) for services and jobs on the domestic front and in support of the revolutionary movements taking place in Central America. We organized a strong and impactful campaign against the US role in Nicaragua and in particular the US support of the Contras.

Upon our dissolution of the DWP in 1984, due to the disillusionment of a failed political program and increasingly extreme demands on the lives of its members, we all embarked on journeys to reconstruct our lives, some going back to their original professions, others starting new ones. I went back to one of my passions, the training and development of young people, and worked for an agency promoting the leadership development of students of color. In 2003 I began working for the Chicana Latina Foundation, where our mission is the empowerment of Latinas through their personal, professional, and educational advancement. Throughout these various stages of my political journeying, I was constantly struggling with balancing the evolution of my social/political consciousness with personal evolution, the loves in my life, the *encuentros y desencuentros*.

While going through the usual and familiar dating rituals in high school and in college, I was struggling with my feelings and attraction to women. Many in my generation learned how to either stuff those feelings deep down inside or to live parallel lives, maintaining the conventional rituals and patterns and living with secret affairs and clandestine romances. And even when living openly with a woman, as I did with my former partner of eighteen years, there was not a fully public disclosure. During the fifteen years that I worked at a career and leadership development agency, I lived openly with my partner, surrounded by my family and circle of friends, but was not professionally or publicly identified as lesbian, even though I was a volunteer with an LGBT Latino group in San Mateo County and had been part of the caretaking army of our brothers stricken with HIV-AIDS.

This absence of public identification was something I wanted to change. And then the opportunity presented itself. I was so honored when the National Center for Lesbian Rights (NCLR) asked me to join their board and later elected me as the board co-chair. I had also recently begun my position as executive director of the Chicana Latina Foundation, an organization formed in 1977 by Chicanas in northern California inspired by the early feminist organization Comisión Femenil Mexicana Nacional. So finally my public and personal personas were fully aligned. This was such a change from my earlier years as a Chicana activist, UFW support organizer, Argentinian political cadre, political prisoner, and party-building movement cadre, where my sexual orientation, while not fully closeted, was certainly on the very "discreet" side of things. Homophobia was ever so present in all of those instances. In all of those stages of my life/activism, there were certainly lesbians involved. Though none openly identified, it was very much an identity that informed our views and participation. Lesbians were certainly at the forefront of fighting male chauvinism, fighting for the inclusion and respect of working-class women, and advocating for women's right to education, health, and gender parity. Just because we were not openly lesbian did not mean that we did not apply a lesbian lens to our work and activism.

My decision to join the board of the NCLR was also largely influenced by the need I saw to bring a Latina consciousness to the work of LGBT organizations, which I am pleased to see has developed into some institutionalized organizational changes such as the confluence of immigration and LGBT rights. Conversely,

Latino rights organizations such as the Mexican American Legal Defense and Education Fund (MALDEF) have also taken part in helping advance LGBT rights. MALDEF filed friend-of-the-court briefs in favor of overturning California's Proposition 8, which eliminated the right of same-sex couples to marry, and is part of a coalition supporting the repeal of the Defense of Marriage Act (DOMA). MALDEF has worked to support passage of the Uniting American Families Act, which would allow gay and lesbian Americans to sponsor their foreign spouses for residency in the United States, and it was among the first organizations to stand with immigration equality in calling for the passage of LGBT-inclusive comprehensive immigration reform legislation.

I am encouraged by the *encuentros* I see taking place between some of the national Latino organizations and national LGBT organizations, with groups like MALDEF and the National Council of La Raza supporting the overturning of Proposition 8 (which was ruled unconstitutional by the California Supreme Court in 2010) and calling for passage of LGBT-inclusive comprehensive immigration reform legislation. At the National Center for Lesbian Rights annual event in 2012, I presented a courage award to several LGBT Dreamers whom NCLR supported in their application for Deferred Action for Childhood Arrivals.

I am also very encouraged by what I see in my work with the young Latinas who participate in our Chicana Latina Foundation (CLF) scholarship and leadership programs. We have created a space where queer students can be comfortable and be totally at ease. Even though the Chicana Latina Foundation is not a queer organization, we are very clear about the inclusion of and respect for our queer students. I continue my work with LGBT organizations as a board member of Horizons Foundation, the oldest LGBT foundation in the Bay Area. One way of summarizing this stage of my journey is by sharing my experience in 2013 as one of the community grand marshals of the San Francisco Gay Pride Parade. We organized a contingent of "undocuqueer" students and had several of the young artists and activists do the undocuqueer posters and banners advocating for immigration reform. Marching in the contingent were *veterana* Chicana artists like Ester Hernández and Viva Paredes, young undocuqueer artists like Julio Salgado, old comrades who had been part of the Olga Talamante Defense Committee, many of the Chicana Latina Foundation scholarship awardees, several of my nieces and one of my brothers, and my partner, Vola, riding down Market Street with me on the very cool lowrider convertible. At least for me, that came very close to bringing our movements together. As I have been on this journey across borders, across sexual identities, these are hopeful signs that we have grown and learned that we should be able to live fully in one movement as well as the other.

PART IV

MEMORY MOVIDAS

17 UNPACKING OUR MOTHERS' LIBRARIES

PRACTICES OF CHICANA MEMORY BEFORE AND AFTER THE DIGITAL TURN

MARÍA COTERA

Every passion borders on the chaotic, but the collector's passion borders on the chaos of memories.

—WALTER BENJAMIN, "UNPACKING MY LIBRARY"

Let's begin at the beginning—or at least one of them—and step into my mother's library. To the uninitiated, her sprawling collection appears to be a random and somewhat disheveled array of unpublished papers, speeches delivered years ago, old newspapers and magazines sorted into piles that make sense only to her internalized cataloguing system. Rolled up posters, leaflets, and slide carousels compete for space with diskettes and other remnants of technology long abandoned, giving the collection of materials a chaotic appearance that belies its internal order. More traditional media forms like books from the golden age of Spanish literature compete for space on her crowded bookshelves with now out-of-print classics from the Chicano movement era and feminist pamphlets written in the 1960s and 1970s, materials she accumulated after years of work as an activist librarian/archivist and on her many journeys—from her visits to antiquarian bookshops in Mexico and Spain, to her participation at radical conferences and workshops. Some of these materials clearly arrived to her library by US mail from places like Boulder, Colorado, Madison, Wisconsin, Washington, DC, and even Ypsilanti, Michigan, where I now live.

As I hope to make clear in this essay, my mother's sprawling personal archive is just one node in a stunningly rich constellation of largely unexplored collections that collectively *haunt* the official archive of both the women's movement and the Chicano movement, a constellation that offers its own disruptive vision of the past.[1] However haphazard and disorganized they may appear to the untrained eye, these collections, I argue, are something more than the detritus of a life in a struggle—they constitute the evidence of Chicana presence. Indeed, we might think of the collections amassed and carefully preserved by Chicanas like my mother as a kind of *composite text*, an as yet unwritten history of intellectual labor that offers scholars a glimpse into the conditions of articulation that brought us to the place we are now—a place in which we can write and speak about Chicana feminism in our classrooms, conferences, and books.

Collections like my mother's are not uncommon among the Chicanas with whom I have been conducting oral histories since 2009. In fact, they are a regular feature of their domestic space, much in the way that *altares* might have been for their mothers and grandmothers a generation before. More than simply archives, these collections suggest modes of critical documentation and memory that bridge multiple polarities. Constituted through both practice and theory, they are intensely personal but also invested in collective transformation. While they carefully document the past, they are also deeply engaged with the present and even the future. And while they represent the traces of a particular intellectual and political development, they are also an active and disruptive space of collective remembrance and identity formation. If my years of labor in the libraries, offices, and garages of Chicana feminists have taught me anything, it is that these practices of collecting and remembrance are a central feature of Chicana feminist thought, and yet they remain largely unexplored in the historiography of the social movement era.

Scholars of Chicana history have long observed how the relative invisibility of Chicanas in institutional archives has structured absences in our collective historical knowledge about the central role they have played in shaping various movement ideologies and practices.[2] As I have noted elsewhere, there can be little doubt that one's access to power determines one's presence in the archive, and one's presence in the archive actively shapes the kinds of histories that can be written, which, in turn, informs the system of valuation that structures the priorities that govern collecting and preservation in institutions. Those further away from the mechanisms of power—women, the working class, ethnic and sexual minorities—are rarely represented in institutional archives. Consequently, their lives and interventions are rarely the subject of historical meaning-making.[3] This absence is structured; it is neither accidental nor merely a reflection of the relative historical significance of certain events, people, and organizations.

In his magnificent meditation on the production of historical knowledge about Haiti, *Silencing the Past: Power and the Production of History*, Michel-Rolph Trouillot dissects the mechanics of erasure that construct the "silences" of history and shape the very questions we think to ask about historical events. He points out that "historical relevance" does not necessarily "proceed directly from the original impact of an event, or its mode of inscription, or even the continuity of that inscription," all of which are exceeded by the narrative desires that condition what we choose to remember (and forget).[4] For this reason, Trouillot sees historical relevance as a constructed aftereffect of the events of history and historical monographs, genealogies, canons, and monuments as sites of *active* knowledge production, not innocent or transparent reflections of the past. Given the asymmetries of power embedded in this process of active construction, Trouillot urges us to explore not only "the presences and absences embodied in sources (artifacts and bodies that turn event into fact)" but also the constitution of archives themselves, the "facts collected, thematized, and processed as documents and monuments."[5] The absences and presences of history, as Trouillot cogently observes, "are neither neutral or natural. They are created. As such they are not mere presences or absences, but mentions and silences of various kinds or degrees."[6]

Trouillot's observations about the silences of historiographic memory and the archive have broad implications for those of us who are actively building genealogies, canons, and historical narratives through our recuperative engagement with the past. While insisting that institutional archives do a better job of collecting and preserving the materials of the dispossessed and the marginalized remains a vital task, mere inclusion is not enough. We must also move beyond the demand for recognition and incorporation within the official archive (with its active silences) and, as Trouillot suggests, interrogate the very logics that shape our understanding of the past and its legitimate artifacts. In this essay I want to take up this thread of critique to think about how privileging some forms of intellectual production (texts) over others (collections)—and writing itself as the preeminent object and method of recuperation—renders an immense body of Chicana intellectual labor "absent." While this privileging of writing over other forms of praxis has helped us to construct a genealogy of texts that form the canon of Chicana feminism today, it also constricts both our understanding of the past and the practices through which we might recover that past, by shaping, as Trouillot might put it, the very frames through which we understand the "artifacts and bodies that turn event into fact."[7]

I will unfold this analysis by focusing on Chicana collecting as a *praxis of memory* that offers us a model to critically reframe the relationship between the past and the present. I argue that this critical reframing of the past in the present offers new objects of inquiry and new methods of analysis. In and through this examination of objects and methods, I want to follow Gloria Anzaldúa's lead and trouble the implicit divide between process (collecting) and analysis (interpretation/text) that structures knowledge production in the academy. I want us to think, in other words, about whether and under what conditions practice and theory might converge. This rethinking of the archive as a site of feminist praxis owes as much to my own experiences negotiating the demands of the academy as a practitioner of Chicana feminist memory as it does to the body of memory practices that I have encountered in my own praxis of collecting. In this essay I hope to make a positive case for a Chicana praxis of memory—what Anzaldúa, in another context, has termed "autohistoria-teoría"—as both an object that can be recovered and a still relevant methodology for contemporary practices of historical recuperation.[8]

CHICANA MEMORY PRAXIS

A praxis of collecting and re-collecting, of membering and re-membering, Chicana practices of memory involve an active *encuentro* with the past to create new knowledges that engage the present in critical ways. Neither memorializing nor overly wedded to an idealized notion of historical facticity, Chicana memory practice uses the past to theorize the present and to move its practitioners through what Anzaldúa has called the path to *conocimiento*. In her section of *Borderlands/La Frontera* entitled "*el camino de la mestiza/*The Mestiza Way," Anzaldúa describes this process of encounter and exchange between past and present as a synthesis of collection and interpretation that simultaneously recuperates and ruptures the past:

> Her first step is to take inventory. *Despojando, desgranando, quitando paja.* Just what did she inherit from her ancestors? This weight on her back—which is the baggage from the Indian mother, the baggage from the Spanish father, which the baggage from the Anglo?
>
> *Pero es difícil* differentiating between *lo heredado, lo adquirido, lo impuesto.* She puts history through a sieve, winnows out the lies, looks at the forces that we as a race, as women, have been a part of. *Luego bota lo que no vale, los desmientos, los desencuentros, el embrutecimiento. Aguarda el juicio, hondo y enraizado, de la gente antigua.* This step is a conscious rupture with all oppressive traditions of all cultures and religions. She communicates that rupture, documents the struggle. She reinterprets history and, using new symbols, she shapes new myths.[9]

This methodology of *autohistoria-teoría*—of putting "history through a sieve" that is both personal and political—is reflected in the ways that Chicanas in the 1970s collected, sifted through, and eventually reframed the material of history to suit their particular organizing needs. As noted in the introduction to this volume, early Chicana feminist writers often deployed—and also departed from—historiographic norms to construct politically salient visions of "La Chicana." Crafted from myth, historical data, and even personal experience, the impulse behind these technologies of *autohistoria-teoría* was not only documentary but also deeply political—their ultimate aim was to write Chicana voices into the developing movement script. While "mythopoetic" mixes of politics, history, and myth were undoubtedly a key feature of movement counterhistories (Rodolfo "Corky" Gonzales's poem "Yo soy Joaquín" being a key example), Chicana practices of memory also illuminated the contradictions of nationalist countermemory.[10]

For example, in her book *¡Chicana Power!* Maylei Blackwell describes how the early Chicana feminist organization Las Hijas de Cuauhtémoc "retrofitted" memory to rearticulate movement deployments of history and inscribe themselves into the Chicano revolutionary imaginary as historical agents. Blackwell defines "retrofitted memory" as a social practice of countermemory that involves simultaneously excavating and critiquing both the dominant historical record and counterhegemonic (but nevertheless deeply masculinist) articulations of history to illuminate the suppressed knowledges of multiply oppressed subjects. Through this process Chicanas crafted new visions of political subjectivity in and through narratives about the past.

Though Blackwell documents instances of this practice of remembering and identity construction throughout her book, it is in her discussion of the name of the organization at the center of her study, Las Hijas de Cuauhtémoc, that she provides perhaps the most illuminating example of the methodology of retrofitted memory. With its paternal reference to the Aztec prince who resisted the Spanish colonizers, the organization's name, at first glance, suggests the symbolic deployment of indigeneity that was such a central part of Chicana/o movement discourse. However, as Blackwell points out, the group had originally called themselves Las Chicanas de Aztlán. After 1971 they changed their name to Las Hijas de Cuauhtémoc, the name that they had chosen for their fledgling newspaper. Blackwell suggests that this name change was adopted as a result of the contradictions that women in the group experienced as they adopted an increasingly feminist position within the Chicana/o movement. Noting that the name emerged as a result of historical research that Anna NietoGomez conducted into an early feminist organization (also named Las Hijas de Cuauhtémoc) active during the Mexican Revolution, Blackwell suggests that the organization's name choice was not a form of reverence to the Chicano indigenous father (the Aztec prince Cuauhtémoc) but rather an homage to their Mexican revolutionary foremothers. Refusing the movement script that would have them act as *soldaderas*, supporters of their men in struggle—a script that was reinforced by Chicano male countermemories of the Mexican revolutionary period—Chicanas opted instead to reference a long tradition of independent Mexicana/Chicana revolutionary activism and thereby reinscribe women into the historical record as fully articulated political agents.

It is important to point out that Blackwell's analysis of the ways in which Chicanas deployed retrofitted memory to explore the gaps of accepted history and develop new historical and political imaginaries reflects her own investments as a scholar and a feminist of color. Indeed, one could argue that her project, like the one articulated in the conferences, essays, and interventions of the Chicanas she documents, deploys its own brand of retrofitted memory to investigate the "gaps, interstices, silences, and crevices" of history, the places where "possibilities lie for fracturing dominant narratives and creating spaces for new historical subjects to emerge."[11] Blackwell's exploration of Chicana memory praxis illuminates a method and theory of collecting, sifting, and remixing that was central to the articulation of Chicana feminism in the 1960s and 1970s, one that resulted in both the foundational texts and the sprawling collections that I seek to uncover in my digital memory project, Chicana por mi Raza: a project that enacts its own technology of *autohistoria-teoría*—of putting history through a sieve—retrofitting the archive as a site of praxis that nurtures not only the creation of permanent collections but also potential collectivities.

Can we think of collecting itself as a practice that is interpretive or theoretical? What genealogical connections can we draw between collections like the one in my mother's office, practices of retrofitted memory that redeploy history in the interests of advancing Chicana feminism, theoretical articulations of memory like Anzaldúa's *autohistoria-teoría*, and the work that I am doing to explore and uncover the meanings of these *sitios y lenguas* (sites and discourses) through a digital memory project?[12] All of these acts of Chicana remembrance suggest that memory itself is a key site of Chicana praxis and that the process of collecting, sifting, sharing, and creating spaces for the articulation of countermemory might be figured as a linkage point between the digital present and the analog past of Chicana feminist thought. To elaborate these connections, I will turn first to the politics of collecting in the present and to the Chicana por mi Raza Digital Memory Project, which in large part has been enabled by what is commonly referred to in humanities scholarship as "the digital turn." In my brief overview of the project, I hope to show how its digital format opens up new and exciting possibilities for our scholarship, our teaching, and our broader work as feminist practitioners even as the methodological and theoretical interventions the project deploys recall the technologies of memory that it seeks to uncover. In doing so, I want to open up a conversation about how critical memory is articulated and processed as a Chicana praxis in the present and the past and how we might chart a new genealogy of women of color theory that includes canonical texts like *Borderlands/La Frontera* and *This Bridge Called My Back*, as well as what Amy Sara Carroll has called its "paraliterary" articulations and practices, those modes of praxis that are not texts but are nevertheless still central to Chicana literary and intellectual formations.[13]

CHICANA POR MI RAZA

Initiated in 2009 in response to a gap in the existing scholarship concerning women of color feminisms, the Chicana por mi Raza Digital Memory Project was born from a desire to document the prehistory of texts like *This Bridge Called My Back* and *Borderlands/La Frontera* and thereby spur new scholarship, teaching, and cultural production about Chicana feminism in the 1960s and 1970s. My key collaborator on the project is Linda Garcia Merchant, an Afro-Chicana filmmaker whose mother, Ruth "Rhea" Mojica Hammer, worked closely with my own in various activist spaces. Our plan was to videotape life histories and scan personal collections of women like our mothers who had been active in multiple sites of struggle—racial and social justice as well as women's liberation. At first, we imagined the public face of our archive as an interactive timeline through which students and scholars could gain access to primary documents and oral histories, but soon the mass of materials and stories we uncovered exceeded the form we had initially imagined, and we began to think more expansively about the project and its possibilities.

In large part this shift was due to the catalytic effect that the process of collecting had on the students (mostly but not exclusively from the University of Michigan) who worked on the project as they sifted through the old newspapers, photos, and journals in the personal collections of the Chicanas we interviewed. I like to tell a story about our first trip to Austin, in which we interviewed women including my mother who were active in the Raza Unida Party. The students were so taken with my mother's archive that it was impossible to get them to take a break from reading and scanning so that they could enjoy Austin's famed nightlife. On our last night, they finally went out—and came back with tattoos inspired by the materials that they found in the archive. Our students had quite literally inscribed images from my mother's collection onto their flesh. Their tattoos were not exact replicas; rather, they had taken iconography from the past that spoke to them and reshaped it to signify their political engagements in the present.[14]

After similar experiences on subsequent trips, Linda and I began to think seriously about the pedagogical impact of the process of finding, sifting, organizing, and witnessing remnants of our forgotten past. A new vision of the Chicana archive began to take shape. Our conceptualization of the archive shifted from a static resource or repository where knowledge is stored and later retrieved to an active site of encounter with the past, a space that could not only generate new historical interpretations but also open the way for new forms of consciousness. In an Anzaldúan sense, we began to imagine the archive as both noun and verb, as a process of *encuentro* and a path to *conocimiento*.

Our initial idea of a timeline, with its linear logic and its implied developmental march to "where we are now" seemed to work against the very nature of the archive we were uncovering. Stored in living rooms, basements, attics, offices, and garages across the Southwest and Midwest, the archive includes letters, photographs, meeting notes and agendas, conference programs, out-of-print books, journals, newspapers, flyers, posters, buttons, and even audio recordings and filmstrips. Stockpiled under beds, on shelves, and in boxes tucked discreetly into the corners of closets—constituted in memory and in artifact—it collectively documents a vibrant counterpublic in which women worked to forge connections between their lives as gendered, classed, and racialized subjects across multiple registers of difference. As women recounted their experiences and shared their carefully archived collections with us, a distinct discursive landscape began to take shape. Foundational texts like Martha Cotera's *Diosa y Hembra* and *The Chicana Feminist*, bibliographies and curriculum guides, journals, and newspapers like *Encuentro Femenil* and *Las Hijas de Cuauhtémoc* popped up in multiple personal archives.

Women we interviewed from across the Southwest and Midwest routinely pointed each other out in photos pulled from other women's collections that we shared with them. They recalled being at the same conferences, rallies, and meetings and fighting the same kinds of battles in various sites. In some contexts they were challenging the masculinist symbolic order of dominant nationalisms that sought to incorporate women as helpmeets of revolution and in others, dominant forms of white, hegemonic feminism that all too often relegated them to the margins or treated them as second-order tokens. As Linda and I began to make our own connections across the stories and documents in our growing archive, we became both witnesses and participants in an emerging network of memory traces that collectively documented a vibrant counterpublic forged in the margins of multiple counterpublics, one that suggested the complex and shifting forms of political identification—and disidentification—that remain a central feature of women of color praxis today. We soon realized that while a historical timeline could indeed register moments of heightened productivity—such as the explosion of bibliographies, sourcebooks, and curriculum guides between 1970 and 1972—its linearity seemed to work against the diffuse yet networked nature of this Chicana counterpublic.

What I want to suggest in this tale of our travels through the Chicana archive is that as the process of collecting began to change our understanding of the nature of Chicana feminism and the stakes of our work, we were forced to reconsider the product-oriented ethos of the scholar-documentarian. For example, our timeline's focus on "event" and its framing of bits and pieces of the archive as evidence suggested an all-too-common script of academic knowledge production in which the authorized scholar—the only appropriate interpreter of evidence—deploys the raw material of the archive to produce her singular vision of what happened. It became clear to us that forcing this rhizomatic archive into a singular coherent narrative would inevitably smooth over its productive sprawl, its networked connectivities, and its disruptive contradictions, replacing old erasures with new ones.[15]

What we were collecting wasn't just bits and pieces of evidence of historical presence, but collections themselves, some small and carefully curated, some haphazard, some sprawling and wild, and others meticulously organized in rows of file cabinets and folders. Our developing archive was something more than a collection of documents—it was a collection of *collections* and *recollections*, a space where Chicana memory practices are both preserved and performed. As such, the Chicana por mi Raza archive's guiding rationale extended beyond the purely historiographic, inciting a series of theoretical and methodological questions about memory, knowledge production, and historical meaning-making. Is it possible to interrupt the erasures of the archive/knowledge system, to decolonize the archive? Can we challenge the power relations between scholars and their objects of study that all too often render silent the multitude of voices and articulations that cannot be contained in a single coherent narrative? Can we create an archive that responds to the radical potential of the memory practices it documents? Can an archive become a site/*sitio* of *encuentro* and *conocimiento* rather than simply a repository—a place where new ways of producing and exchanging knowledge are explored, where new modes of identity, affiliation, and memory are forged in the meeting place between present and past? These are the questions at the heart of our own Chicana praxis of memory.

CHICANA MEMORY PRAXIS AFTER THE DIGITAL TURN

There can be little doubt that the democratizing effects of the digital revolution have, to a certain extent, made these kinds of questions more central to the practice of history, at least in terms of reimagining the archive as a networked community of users, producers, curators, and contributors. Like the emergence of photography, which as Walter Benjamin famously noted democratized portraiture as a memorializing form, the emergent "technologies, standards, and approaches" of the Web 2.0 environment have created new modalities of information sharing and collaborative authorship that disrupt conventional notions of expertise and authority.[16] As such, they present a challenge to top-down models of knowledge production. Take, for example, the Digital Humanities Manifesto, written in 2008 (and revised in 2009), which envisions a digital praxis that can bridge the gap between building and interpreting a conceptualization that disrupts the standard division of labor between archivists and historians. Linking the concept of copyright to the ownership of knowledge, the manifesto calls for open-source content "without walls." Pushing against the individualist ethos of standard models of scholarly production, it celebrates "collaborative co-creation" and new "distributed" and "horizontal" models of knowledge-making that are process oriented, not product oriented. Recalling earlier challenges to the authority of dominant knowledge systems emerging from ethnic studies, women's studies, and queer theory, the Digital Humanities Manifesto challenges disciplinary power and proposes new objects of study and new modes of analysis.[17] It urges scholars to grab hold of the tools of new media to transform the nature of our scholarship and its publics; in effect, it incites us to use the master's tools to dismantle the master's house.[18]

This twenty-first-century manifesto hails a political genre that made multiple appearances throughout the twentieth century. Manifestos were a key feature of the movement years, as evidenced in the proliferation of plans, programs, and agendas for action of the late 1960s—from the Black Panthers' Ten-Point Program to the Thirteen-Point Program of the Young Lords Party, to the Plan de Aztlán. Anyone with even a glancing familiarity with the 1960s can also make the connection here between the utopian possibility envisioned in the digital media revolution and the ways in which the emergent technologies of the 1960s, like the mass-produced still camera, the mimeograph machine, 16 mm film, and magnetic tape challenged the authority of top-down knowledge systems and enabled their own kind of distributed and horizontal circuits of knowledge exchange through consciousness-raising sessions, the radical press, pirate radio stations, artist collectives, and alternative media sources like Third World Newsreel.[19] What I want to suggest in pointing out these multiple convergences between new media and old is that the Chicana por mi Raza Digital Memory Project—as a praxis of memory with roots in the 1960s and as an example of the current digital revolution in humanities scholarship—speaks to both of these historical moments, bringing them together in its efforts to document and its commitment to process, knowledge exchange, and distributed authority.

Since the project's inception in 2009, we have collected more than 100 oral histories with some of the leading voices in the development of Chicana feminism, including Anna NietoGomez, Lupe Anguiano, Dorinda Moreno, Gloria Arellanes, Yolanda Alaniz, Evey Chapa, Ruth "Rhea" Mojica Hammer, Cecilia Burciaga, Cherríe Moraga, Felicitas Nuñez, Elizabeth "Betita" Martínez, Celia Herrera Rodríguez, Inés Hernández-Ávila, and Martha Cotera. Linked to our oral history work is the effort to digitize materials in the personal collections of the women we interview. We have collected more than 7,000 digital objects, some of them books, magazines, and pamphlets. We have also established collaborative partnerships with libraries, research centers, community organizations, cyberinfrastructure specialists, scholars, and students to encourage research on Chicana feminism, increase public knowledge about the role Chicanas have played in social movement history, and develop and sustain the project and its goals. Community organizations and public history projects play an important role in achieving these goals, especially with respect to ensuring that historical knowledge and archival literacy are expanded to as broad a field as possible. Our ongoing partnership with the El Museo del Norte project in Detroit, which has resulted in several public exhibitions of materials collected in the Chicana por mi Raza archive, demonstrates how digital and analog formats can productively commingle.[20]

Central to the success of this network is the development of pedagogical tools—from full course designs to research projects and short assignments— that enable students in diverse classroom environments to add oral histories and documents to the archive, work with an existing collection, or produce scholarly or creative content for our public website, chicanapormiraza.org. While the CPMR archival repository is secured by a login (our donors hold copyrights to their digital content), our public website functions as a space where researchers, students, and the women themselves can share scholarly and creative curations of materials from the archive. This space is not without its boundaries and obligations; individuals wishing to access the online repository are asked join the Chicana por mi Raza Digital Memory Collective and to do something to enrich and sustain the collection. Whether their work involves producing a biographical curation or a short essay for our website, adding key descriptive information to a document in our repository, or simply correcting tags and other metadata, users of the archive are reminded that they are not mining a repository but rather joining a network structured by the exchange of knowledge and *conocimiento*. In other words, we envision the public website less as a resource than as a memory hub that brings the network in our repository to life, a place of *encuentro* between the present and the past where archived memories are remixed and remediated into new knowledge forms such as digital storytelling projects, curations, and interactive timelines.

One significant feature of the contemporary digital environment that allows for this type of creative remixing is that digital objects are essentially unfixed from any single narrative. The modularity and automation of data in digital media offer new "opportunities for combining old media objects into new configurations in fast and efficient ways that are user focused."[21] The recombinant memory practices enabled by new media can reveal affinities and networked connectivities in previously isolated collections. Indeed, a feature that distinguishes digital media from old media—and here the difference between text-based historiography and digital memory projects is perhaps most stark—is its productive and sometimes unpredictable variability. For example, in a recent curation, Ariel Kaplowitz, a student research intern on the project, was able to draw from multiple sources in our collection (secondary scholarly sources, firsthand narrative accounts, primary archival documents, and oral histories) to tell a fascinating story of Chicana involvement in two historic feminist conferences: the International Women's Year conference in Mexico City (1975) and the 1977 National Women's Conference in Houston, Texas (conceived as a follow-up to the first conference). By drawing from multiple memories and collections and remixing them, Ariel was able to trace a link between Chicana efforts to organize with third world women at the conference in Mexico City and their efforts to organize coalitions that ensured that their voices and agendas were part of the US Platform on Women developed at the follow-up conference in Houston two years later (figures 17.1 and 17.2).[22]

Ariel's digital curation makes critical connections between Chicana efforts to organize across multiple political arenas even as it reveals crucial links between international and national feminist politics.[23] Such curations of history deploy strategies of remixing and remediation that have become significant features of cultural production in the digital age. But while these new technologies of memory have been facilitated by the networked systems and content-management architecture of the digital turn, it would be a mistake to see them as entirely new forms of Chicana memory praxis.

Indeed, as our collections reveal, remixing has been a central *movida* of Chicana memory praxis since at least the 1970s. An act of collection and curation that involves the thoughtful assembly and reinterpretation of existing cultural objects to make them relevant to contemporary audiences, Chicana remixing suggests an active mode of critical memory that takes existing knowledge forms and reshapes them to derive new meanings. For a literary example of this Chicana remixing one need only return to Anzaldúa's elaboration of *mestiza* consciousness within the very form of her book *Borderlands/La Frontera* and its generative (re)mixture of poetry, prose, incantation, history, autobiography, and anthropology. The creative genre mixing evident in Anzaldúa's *autohistoria* can be thought of as a curation of sorts, one that has curative powers.

FIGURE 17.1. *La Raza* newspaper photo page of IWY in Mexico City, 1975. Martha Cotera Collection, Chicana por mi Raza Digital Memory Collective Archive.

FIGURE 17.2. Martha Cotera speaking at the IWY conference in Houston, 1977. Martha Cotera Collection, Chicana por mi Raza Digital Memory Collective Archive.

Even earlier we have the example of *La mujer: En pie de lucha*. Compiled by Dorinda Moreno and published by Espina del Norte Press in 1973, *La mujer* is a remixing of previously published position papers, essays, and poems collected from feminist writers and organizations from across the globe, brought together by Moreno's commitment to the idea that women had always been the base of revolutionary struggle. Finally, we have the editorial labors of Elizabeth "Betita" Martínez, who, along with Enriqueta Longeaux y Vásquez, managed to keep the presses rolling for New Mexico's *El Grito del Norte* newspaper from 1968 to 1973. Martínez, like Moreno and other Chicana journalists, did her fair share of culling through movement reporting brought to her attention through old-media networks like the Liberation News Service and the Chicano Press Association to offer a vision of feminist-nationalist liberation to the people through her creative cutting, pasting, annotating, editing, and writing. In the 1990s Martínez deployed these remixing strategies to put together her book *500 Years of Chicana Women's History*, a curation of photographic objects that she and other Chicanas had collected over years of radical journalism—a collection that looks an awful lot like an archive in print.[24]

Remix practices usually rely on strategies of remediation—the representation of old media in new-media forms. A historical convergence between old and new, remediation recuperates mediascapes of the past to speak to new contexts and new publics. Far from a break with the past, then, new-media ecologies rely heavily on content produced in old media.[25] Remediation was a common strategy of Chicana cultural production, which frequently deployed old-media sources from revolutionary prints to Mesoamerican pictographs in an effort to construct a usable past. There is perhaps no better example of this counterdiscursive Chicana memory practice than the multiple remediations of a slideshow Anna NietoGomez developed in the mid-1970s. Remediating and remixing old photographs, magazine articles, paintings, murals, and even Aztec codices, NietoGomez traced a heroic past that explored women's role in pre-Columbian society, their experiences of conquest and colonization, their participation in the 1810 struggle for Mexican independence, their involvement in the US labor strikes in 1872, their contributions to the 1910 Mexican Revolution, their laboring lives throughout the twentieth century, and their leadership in contemporary civil rights causes. Using murals, engravings, photography and even live performance (NietoGomez wrote a script to be read along with her slides), the slideshow demonstrated how women in Mexico and the United States are and always have been active participants in history and culture (figure 17.3).

NietoGomez took her slideshow/performance to college campuses and community centers, reaching a broad audience inside and outside the academy. As Chicana film scholar Rosa Linda Fregoso has noted, the slideshow represented "not just Nieto-Gomez's [*sic*] scholarly research, but the important role she played as one of the first critics of sexism in the Chicano power movement. Inscribed in NietoGomez's slideshow is a feminist counterdiscourse to cultural nationalism

ANNA NIETO-GOMEZ
SPEAKS ON
THE HISTORY OF THE CHICANA
a slide show documentary
3rd COLLEGE LOUNGE   6:30 pm   Thurs. Jan. 27th 1977

Sponsored by
the women of:
AASA
BSU
Feminist Coalition
Mujer and
Women Center

the first of a series of events leading up to International Women's Day

FIGURE 17.3. Flyer for Chicana slideshow. Martha Cotera Collection, Chicana por mi Raza Digital Memory Collective Archive.

which, however marginalized and suppressed, nonetheless emerges dialectically as a counterdiscourse to Chicano nationalisms struggle against dominant culture."[26] In 1977, Chicana filmmaker Sylvia Morales saw the slideshow in Los Angeles and was so impressed that she approached NietoGomez about making it into a film. Morales's groundbreaking 1979 documentary, *Chicana*, essentially remediates NietoGomez's slideshow and is widely acknowledged as the first and, until recently, only treatment of Chicana history in the documentary form (figure 17.4).

It is tempting to frame Morales's film as a Chicana response to *Yo soy Joaquín*, a short film made ten years earlier by Luis Valdez based on Corky Gonzales's

FIGURE 17.4. Poster for *Chicana*, a film written by Anna NietoGomez and directed by Sylvia Morales. Martha Cotera Collection, Chicana por mi Raza Digital Memory Collective Archive.

epic poem. However, Morales's documentary is not only a negative critique of the masculinist ideology of the Chicano movement; it is also a positive articulation of Chicana memory, produced collaboratively, and across genres, through the practice of critical remediation. These collaborative practices of memory and recuperation, of sifting and collecting, of historical meaning-making, of sharing and exchange, shaped Chicana feminist thought in its early years. While some of this work undoubtedly informed the books and essays that have made their way into our bibliographies and syllabi, those sources provide only the barest hint of the diverse memory ecologies of early Chicana feminism. The Chicana por mi Raza Digital Memory Project seeks to recuperate these technologies of memory even as it replicates them in its own digital praxis.

DISRUPTING THE DIGITAL TURN

It is only fitting to end this essay where it began, with something found in my mother's office, a document that troubles the implied temporal divide suggested by the "before" and "after" of my title. It is the trace of an earlier attempt to make new media serve the practice of Chicana memory: a data file entry from a project begun in the early years of the digital age. The project was a *Bio-Bibliographic Encyclopedia of Hispanic Women*, and it was the last major research project launched by the Chicana Research and Learning Center before the non-profit lost its funding in the Reagan years. The bio-bibliographic database project proposed to collect information on historically significant Hispanic women across the Americas and to organize that information in a searchable format utilizing the newest database technology. The project had reached 1,000 entries before it was finally abandoned; eventually its stored data would be lost to the inevitable tide of technology obsolescence. The images pictured in figures 17.5a and 17.5b are two pages from a bibliographic entry for Francisca Flores, publisher of *Regeneración*, a Chicano movement magazine. Flores's entry includes a photocopied cover of one issue of the magazine and a dot-matrix printout, filled out by hand with key biographical information. Once filed away in my mother's personal collection, these digital images are now our remediation of an earlier series of remediations, enabled by the standard technologies of two intertwined historical moments.

One could argue that this formerly lost digital artifact, uncovered in remediated form by our own digital recuperation, is a foreboding reminder of the fleeting nature of the archive in the information age. Might not our project end like my mother's, as an ephemeral trace of something much grander in scale, something that we can no longer capture for our scholarship? I see it differently, especially since (I am forced to admit) *I helped my mother create this archive* when I first started working with her at the Chicana Research and Learning Center as a twelve-year-old Chicana-in-the-making. For me, the document we scanned in my mother's office is something more than simply a dead letter in the box of

REGENERACION

STAFF FOR VOLUME II, NUMBER 3

Issue Editor: Francisca Flores

Editors: Harry Gamboa, Jr.
John Ortiz

Contributing Authors: Rebecca Arellano
Adolfo Quezada
Francisca Flores
Yolanda M. Nava
Guillermo Flores
Pilar Bravo M.
Anna Nieto-Gomez
Cecilia C-R Suarez
Sylvia Delgado
Diane Drollinger
Iona Weenusk
Gabriela Mistral
Mary Santillanes
Josephine Madrid
Kathy L. Valadez
Betty Campbell

Graphic Design / Art Staff: Gronk
Patsy Valdez
Willie Herron
Harry Gamboa, Jr.

Contributing Artists: Diane Gamboa
William Bejarano
Charles D. Almaraz

(ABOVE) FIGURE 17.5A. Photocopied page of *Regeneración*, Francisca Flores data file, *Bio-Bibliographic Encyclopedia of Hispanic Women*. Martha Cotera Collection, Chicana por mi Raza Digital Memory Collective Archive.

(RIGHT) FIGURE 17.5B. Data file form for *Regeneración*, Francisca Flores, *Bio-Bibliographic Encyclopedia of Hispanic Women*. Martha Cotera Collection, Chicana por mi Raza Digital Memory Collective Archive.

history; it is evidence of a praxis of intergenerational memory exchange that imagines new collectivities by linking the past, present, and future. More than simply an archival object, it is an invitation to explore the vast landscape that lies beyond the various books and essays that constitute our current genealogy and to excavate the uses of memory in the Chicana feminist archive through an act of critical *encuentro* with the past—a decolonizing praxis of *autohistoria-teoría* for the digital age.

18 REFOCUSING CHICANA INTERNATIONAL FEMINISM

PHOTOGRAPHS, POSTMEMORY, AND POLITICAL TRAUMA

MARISELA R. CHÁVEZ

In 1975, the United Nations sponsored the first-ever World Conference of the International Women's Year (IWY) in Mexico City. Although the name suggests one conference, there were in effect two gatherings that occurred simultaneously. The first was the official UN meeting, to which recognized nation-states sent official government delegations. For the United States, that meant a delegation of high-profile and politically well-connected individuals (not all of them women) appointed by the federal government. The second forum was the International Women's Year Tribune, an assembly for nongovernmental organizations (figures 18.1, 18.2, 18.3). Although there certainly was governmental influence as to the groups of women attending the tribune, this gathering was open to the public the world over. Women and men from across the globe found the conference important enough to travel to Mexico City.[1]

Chicanas from across the United States became part of this international public and traveled to Mexico City for the inaugural International Women's Year Conference. Many of the women attended the conference as an extension of their social justice activism within the Chicano movement. Some attended on their own, while others represented Chicana feminist organizations such as the Comisión Femenil Mexicana Nacional (National Mexican Women's Commission), which was headquartered in Los Angeles and had chapters nationwide, as well as more mainstream *movimiento* organizations such as La Raza Unida Party, the Chicano third party, which also had a national following.

For the women affiliated with the Los Angeles chapter of the Comisión Femenil

FIGURE 18.1. What appears to be the entrance to the International Women's Year Tribune, Mexico City, 1975. Nancy De Los Santos Collection, Chicana por mi Raza Digital Memory Collective Archive. Courtesy of Nancy De Los Santos Reza.

FIGURE 18.2. International Women's Year sign. Nancy De Los Santos Collection, Chicana por mi Raza Digital Memory Collective Archive. Courtesy of Nancy De Los Santos Reza.

FIGURE 18.3. Women at the International Women's Year Tribune speaking before an audience. Nancy De Los Santos Collection, Chicana por mi Raza Digital Memory Collective Archive. Courtesy of Nancy De Los Santos Reza.

Mexicana Nacional, the trip was important enough that their experience was to be video-recorded and photographed for the records of the organization as well as for a documentary. Corinne Sánchez, who attended the conference as a member of the Los Angeles chapter of the Comisión Femenil, remembered, "There was a video done. A woman got funded, an Anglo woman, and she got money from NBC [television network] and taped us from the time we left the United States to the time we got to Mexico."[2] But Sánchez did not remember the name of the woman directing the shoot. Connie Pardo, also from the Los Angeles group, recalled, "There was a film person—a woman and man I think that was filming us."[3] She remembered that the group members had signed a contract with the filmmakers but that they never received a copy of the recording. Neither Pardo nor Sánchez could recollect any other details about these recordings, and the videos or photographs of the group in Mexico City are not in the organization's archives. Although they may exist, the evidence of Chicana participation in the IWY that might usually be found in personal papers, video or sound recordings, and photographs is scarce.[4]

The documentation, then, and thus our knowledge of one of the first international experiences of Chicanas remain elusive. So it is not surprising that I first came to know about the IWY conference by accident, in the early 2000s as I was conducting research for my dissertation, which focused on the experiences of women in the Chicano movement in Los Angeles and the various formulations of feminism that arose from these experiences.[5] One of the first archives I visited was the Chicano Studies Research Library at the University of California, Los Angeles, where I found a collection called "Año Internacional de la Mujer Mexicana" (International Year of the Mexican Woman). Although I had researched a variety of Chicana/o periodicals from the 1960s and 1970s by the time I visited the UCLA archive, I could not recall prominent mention of this conference. Periodicals, or what Maylei Blackwell calls the "Chicana print community," served as the main communication hub for Chicana activists of the era, and this conference should have been highlighted extensively.[6] The Año Internacional de la Mujer Mexicana collection at UCLA was small, only two boxes, but it contained copies of the periodical *Xilonen*, the newspaper published by the IWY Tribune, vital evidence with the calendar of events and meetings for the tribune.[7]

As I dug deeper into the collection, I found that the collection centered on a group of Chicanas from UCLA who had traveled to the conference under that institution's auspices. Two letters in the collection named the participants, but further inquiries about these women yielded no answers. The collection was rich, however, in ephemera. There were pamphlets from women all over the world stating their positions on a variety of topics. In addition, I found position papers drafted at the conference itself. And there was more evidence of Chicana attendance, the most obvious of which was a pamphlet put together by Chicanas of La Raza Unida Party in Texas (figure 18.4).[8] But in terms of photographs, video, notes from participants, logs of events they attended, or even sections of the calendar circled to denote interest, the archive was silent.

Finding the Año Internacional de la Mujer Mexicana collection led me to ask about the IWY conference at various stages of my dissertation research. In one of the confluences of research I found that women involved in two of the organizations that I examined, the Comisión Femenil Mexicana Nacional and El Centro de Acción Social Autónomo–Hermandad General de Trabajadores (Autonomous Center for Social Action–General Brotherhood of Workers) had also traveled to IWY in Mexico City in 1975. Aside from their rich recollections of attending the conference and some ephemera of their own, the women I interviewed did not have any other documentation, such as photographs, from their time in Mexico City. In addition, the archives of both organizations were also silent on this conference.[9] For my dissertation I pieced together the experiences of California Chicanas at the International Women's Year Conference through oral history interviews, government documents, US and Mexican periodicals, and a variety of other sources, including the Año Internacional de la Mujer Mexicana collection at UCLA. What would have fleshed out the research was photographs, audio, or video of these women at the conference.

In the early 2000s, the topic of internationalism in the Chicano movement was in its infancy, and the topic of Chicana international travel and feminism was definitely not in the literature. One of the few people who had discussed the topic was a Chicana feminist whose work had historically taken an internationalist perspective, Elizabeth "Betita" Martínez. The few other sources I found

FIGURE 18.4. "La Mujer Chicana" pamphlet by Chicanas of La Raza Unida Party. Martha Cotera Collection, Chicana por mi Raza Digital Memory Collective Archive.

connecting Chicanas to any kind of internationalism were two articles in Alma García's 1997 anthology *Chicana Feminist Thought: The Basic Historical Writings*. At the time, the literature on IWY and the UN was primarily within the field of political science, and within that literature, Chicanas were absent. Subsequently, some literature has been published on Chicanas in the international realm that has also challenged the notion of the Chicano movement existing as an insular, purely nationalist movement.[10]

As happens with research, however, sources appear when you least expect them. The collection of photographs included in this essay reveals the unpredictable nature of the research process, especially in regard to Chicana history. Indeed, this photographic discovery illustrates the ways in which Chicana feminist history is recovered, recast, and reinterpreted. As Miroslava Chávez-García reminds us about the Chicana past, there is a "compelled creativity in finding and reading sources as well as crossing disciplinary boundaries to develop a more complete understanding of that history."[11] In conducting the oral history interviews for the Chicana por mi Raza Digital Memory Project, the researchers interviewed Nancy De Los Santos Reza, a writer, producer, and director well known for cowriting and coproducing the Cinemax/HBO documentary *The Bronze Screen: 100 Years of the Latino Image in Hollywood Cinema* (2002) and serving as associate producer on the feature films *My Family/Mi Familia* (1995)and *Selena* (1997).[12] In the process of conducting the interview, they found a collection of about thirty-five photographs that De Los Santos Reza took when she attended the International Women's Year Conference in Mexico City in 1975. She had kept the photographs over the decades in suitcases and finally in plastic containers. De Los Santos Reza attended the IWY conference as part of a delegation from Mujeres Latinas en Acción, an early Chicana/Latina feminist organization from Chicago. She was a student at Northeastern Illinois University, a member of the campus Chicano Student Union, and a client of Mujeres Latinas. At Northeastern Illinois, De Los Santos Reza joined the staff of the student Chicano newspaper, *Contra la Pared* (Against the wall) and subsequently inherited a camera from the newspaper's photographer when he moved on. As the staff photographer, De Los Santos Reza documented the activities of the Chicano Student Union as well as other events that related to the organization. She used the inherited camera from *Contra la Pared* to photograph the IWY proceedings in 1975.[13]

Yet even this photographic evidence is dodgy. De Los Santos Reza recalled using her camera to document the event itself, not necessarily the group of women who attended the conference. She appears in one photo with fellow Mujeres Latinas member Luz Prieto (figure 18.5). De Los Santos Reza included a self-portrait with the camera covering her face (figure 18.6). Beyond these identifications, De Los Santos Reza did not recall who is in the other photos or the specific contexts under which she snapped the photos, other than that they were taken at the 1975 conference. I asked myself, what good are photographs in which I can only identify at most four people? What scholarly value do photographs with such scanty

FIGURE 18.5. Luz Prieto (*far left*) and Nancy De Los Santos (*far right*). Nancy De Los Santos Collection, Chicana por mi Raza Digital Memory Collective Archive. Courtesy of Nancy De Los Santos Reza.

FIGURE 18.6. Nancy De Los Santos, self-portrait. Nancy De Los Santos Collection, Chicana por mi Raza Digital Memory Collective Archive. Courtesy of Nancy De Los Santos Reza.

FIGURE 18.7. Connie Pardo (*background, center left*). Nancy De Los Santos Collection, Chicana por mi Raza Digital Memory Collective Archive. Courtesy of Nancy De Los Santos Reza.

FIGURE 18.8. Gracia Molina de Pick (*center*). Nancy De Los Santos Collection, Chicana por mi Raza Digital Memory Collective Archive. Courtesy of Nancy De Los Santos Reza.

information have for our work as Chicana historians? The photographs, however, reminded me that the search for Chicana history and specifically Chicana feminist history requires us to listen to silences and to make meaning of what others may call meaningless, like photographs stored in a box or in someone's photo album, images that give credence to our remembrances of an event but do not give us much more.[14]

The collection of photographs here, taken by someone who attended the conference from Chicago, partly provides a conclusion to the video and audio that never surfaced of the Los Angeles women. Without knowing it, De Los Santos Reza captured one of the Los Angeles women and another from San Diego in her photographic documentation. Connie Pardo, who traveled to Mexico City as a member of the Comisión Femenil Mexicana Nacional and the Chicana Service Action Center (both organizations in Los Angeles), appears in figure 18.7. Gracia Molina de Pick, who was active in Chicana feminist circles throughout California but most notably in Los Angeles and San Diego, appears in figure 18.8. While there are a number of other women featured in the photos, I have not been able to identify them. In this scenario, then, we have limited archival evidence of Chicana participation at the first international women's conference sponsored by the United Nations: oral history interviews that provide women's recollections of attending the conference, articles written by Chicanas who were present, and a collection of photographs taken by a Chicana and found almost forty years after the conference, most of which cannot be identified.

In thinking of how to read these newly discovered photographs of an event I had written about, I turned to the work of feminist theorist and memory scholar Marianne Hirsh. In "Surviving Images: Holocaust Photography and the Work of Postmemory" and *The Generation of Postmemory: Writing and Visual Culture after the Holocaust*, Hirsch studies iconic photographs of the Holocaust and explores the meaning of the ways in which certain photographs of this era come to "iconically and emblematically" represent the entire experience. She defines "postmemory" as "the response of the second generation to the trauma of the first."[15] For Hirsch, postmemory is related to photographs because of their prevalence and their importance to those who did not experience the Holocaust firsthand. For them, the iconic and emblematic photographs allow a "mostly helpful vehicle of working through a traumatic past."[16] While the trauma of genocide in no way compares to the experiences of Chicanas in the Chicano movement, Hirsch's insistence on the relation between trauma, photographs, and memory is useful for understanding the powerful and sometimes traumatic experiences of women's memories of the Chicano movement.

For Hirsch, postmemory is about how "postmemorial viewers [of the photographs] attempt to live with, and at the same time to reenvision and redirect, the mortifying gaze of these surviving images."[17] Postmemory in Hirsch's case relies on the overabundance of photographs, the overabundance of evidence of a particular historical event, however horrifying. Postmemory also relates to trauma and the canonization of this trauma through photographs. Utilizing Hirsch's idea of postmemory, the lack of evidence, the fuzziness of memory, and the trauma, both political and cultural, what I would call the trauma of erasure, elicits a Chicana postmemory of the movement and even for Chicanas today. Whereas the Holocaust is traumatic for those who directly experienced it and their future generations due to the repetitive effect of photographs and their ability to visually recall the experience of genocide, for Chicanas it is the *lack* of evidence of their experiences of international feminism that is the driving force of historical trauma. For Chicanas, when photographs do not exist or are forgotten or put away, or when the same set of photographs comes to represent the totality of Chicana experiences in the movement, it is the trauma of erasure, not the trauma of overremembrance, that structures postmemory.

Images and other materials that emerge over time, owing to the complexity of finding and interpreting historical sources, that show Chicana participation in historically complex and multifaceted ways come to serve as the objects to be worked through in a process of Chicana regenerative memory. Finding Nancy De Los Santos Reza's photographs stands as an example of the circuitous and sometimes fortuitous ways in which we research and write history, especially Chicana history. As Hirsch reminds us, "Oral or written testimony, like photography, leaves a trace, but, unlike writing, the photograph of the footprint is the index par excellence, pointing to the presence, the having-been-there, of the past."[18] Photographs seem to provide us with a perceived absoluteness that an event occurred, that a person attended a conference, for example, and that trace provides a connection between the past and present, however imperfect.[19] De Los Santos Reza's photographs provide the trace of Chicanas and their international feminist experiences. On the one hand, these photographs regenerate a sense of erasure among *movimiento* women because their emergence highlights the scarcity of archival sources and the reminder of the erasure of women's participation. On the other hand, the photographs regenerate an alternative herstory because they are "new" primary sources, available for study, analysis, and interpretation. For Chicana history, these photographs that were in suitcases and are now having their debut allow us to refocus on the complex nature of the ways in which Chicanas are represented and concealed in both the past and the present and to continue the project of developing a new image and new memory for the future.

19 LA MARIPOSA DE ORO
THE JOURNEY OF AN ADVOCATE

ELENA GUTIÉRREZ AND VIRGINIA MARTÍNEZ

This *testimonio* of Virginia Martínez draws from three oral history interviews conducted by Elena Gutiérrez in 2015–2016 for Chicana Chicago and the Chicana por mi Raza Digital Memory Project.

I was born on the last day of 1949, joining the baby boomer generation. My family was living on 25th and Wentworth near Chinatown in Chicago. I was the youngest of six, the two oldest being my half-brothers, who were in the army when I was born. My father, Manuel Martínez, was one of the original unaccompanied minors, fourteen years old when he walked across the Mexico-United States border by himself, into Texas. He was immediately contracted to go to California to pick crops. Like many Mexicans during that period, he came north to flee the revolution. His mother was afraid that he'd be forced into the war by *federales* or Pancho Villa, both of whom periodically visited their village near Torreon, Coahuila, to recruit men and boys. My grandmother pleaded with him to leave the country. He eventually rode the rails to Chicago, where he worked at the steel mills. He was injured on the job and was permanently crippled. He was widowed with two young boys when he met my mother, Juanita Rodríguez. They married and after the work injury, they moved to Mexico for a year. However, they had to return when the money ran out.

My mom, Juanita Rodríguez Martínez, came to Chicago when my grandmother was divorced and hitchhiked from Waco, Texas, with my mother and aunt. On the way, they slept wherever they could. Sometimes they would ask farm families for permission to sleep in the barn. At one point, I know that one of those families gave my mother shoes because hers were worn out. My grand-mother said, "Well, you need to give her something back, give her your doll." My mother was heartbroken to give away the only thing that she had, her doll.

After arriving in Chicago, my mother was put in a Catholic orphanage for a period of time because my grandmother couldn't support her daughters. Growing up in poverty stayed with my mother her whole life. She raised the family's six children on my father's low wages from a printing company. When I was in elementary school my mother went to work as a nurse's aide and then on an assembly line. My parents were hardworking and strict. We weren't allowed to go outside to play except right in front of the house. We weren't allowed to go to our girlfriends' houses and they weren't allowed to come to ours. I now know that part of the overprotection came out of a history of sexual abuse in our family. My mother was intent on protecting her daughters, though as it turned out, she failed. Early on I knew that girls weren't safe and that you couldn't trust anybody.

On the other hand, my mom loved museums and zoos, so we grew up in the cultural life of the city. Because of my father's injuries at the steel mills, he couldn't drive—my mom did. Sometimes she would drop him off at work on the afternoon shift and then we'd go to 12th Street Beach, walk around and look at the boats, or to the museums. She also bought us books to encourage all of us to do well in school. We were expected to go to school every day and get good grades. We were sometimes spared chores so that we could study. My mom never finished high school but expected us to. My dad only finished sixth grade. Both were bilingual, my father helping my mom with Spanish and my mom helping my father with English. I refused to speak Spanish—unless I had to—because we lived in an Italian community and I wanted to fit in. But I became fully bilingual later.

During my childhood, my family lived in an Italian area just south of Chinatown. We referred to it as Chinatown, though Chinese residences and businesses ended the block before ours. I loved the neighborhood, and we lived in the basement of an Italian family's house. The dividing line for African Americans was Wentworth, starting a few blocks south of our street. So the public school I attended served a diverse student body. Additionally, African American special education students came in from the housing projects east of our community. The African American students had to walk past the all-white Catholic school a block away. Periodically, African American students were chased, and on at least one occasion, I exited our school to see white teens being held by police outside of our school. They had come with chains ready to beat up black students. Blacks were not allowed to walk down our block or attend certain events. Even though I was young, I knew that the Chinese kept to themselves, the Italians ran everything, and African Americans were not allowed to live past Wentworth. There were a few Mexican families who rented apartments in Italian- and Chinese-owned buildings. I went to public school because by that time my mother had given up on trying to get us into Catholic schools. My older brothers had already been denied enrollment. The first two brothers were refused entry because they were

Mexican. My mom was told there was no space for the second two in another school, although she didn't believe that.

When I was twelve years old and about to enter eighth grade, the city decided to build an expressway through our neighborhood. Our block, along with a strip of others, was torn down and everybody had to move. The Italians moved to Bridgeport, which was the mayor's neighborhood. I really wanted to go there. My brother Danny also wanted to go that way. My sister was fourteen and the only one who wanted to live in Pilsen, because she knew a guy there. My parents decided it was time to purchase our own home. We couldn't afford anything in Bridgeport where most everyone else was moving, so we went to Pilsen. At the same time that we moved, Mexicans were being displaced by the building of the University of Illinois at Chicago (UIC), originally known as Circle Campus, and those families also found new homes in Pilsen. I knew the proposed UIC area of the city because we would go there on Sundays to the Maxwell Street Market and to visit my godparents, who lived on Taylor and Newberry. We also sometimes went to St. Francis of Assisi, which had become a Mexican church holding mass in Spanish. I was always intrigued by that community, with its mixture of Jewish, Italian, Greek, African American, and Mexican shops, businesses, and residents. It was one of the most diverse and exciting areas of the city.

A teacher in eighth grade told me after getting the results back from standardized tests that I could be anything I wanted to be. I didn't know what that could be and knew that we were being labeled as "inner city students," who didn't get to go on field trips or have access to other kinds of resources. I finished eighth grade at my old school and then went straight to Harrison High School. First-year students from Pilsen were supposed to go to Froebel branch before going to Harrison, but my records were sent directly. It meant that I started high school without my neighbors. I was already disconnected from my peers, having stayed at my old school. I felt somewhat out of place, which became a common feeling over the course of my life. I was in honors classes, which meant that for most of the day I was with the same students for all four years. Once I started going out with a guy from another neighborhood I was further isolated from teens in my immediate neighborhood. There were a lot of gangs and my boyfriend was from a gang in a different neighborhood, plus my parents were still strict, so I had a limited social life. The girls in my boyfriend's neighborhood didn't like me because I was going out with one of "their" guys and he wouldn't let the guys swear in front of me.

Harrison High School still had a substantial white student population. The cafeteria was self-segregated with Latinos and Whites on one side and Black students on the other. It was the tumultuous sixties and many of my neighbors were being drafted to fight in Vietnam. Some would not return. When my history teacher assigned us to speak with someone who had been in a war, I talked to my oldest brother, Tony, who had been in Korea when I was born. It was the first and only time I ever saw him cry. That interview had a huge impact on me. I had already been against the war, which not only seemed unwinnable but was taking a disproportionate number of young men from our community, including my next-door neighbor Joe. I had been angry with him and when he told me he had been drafted, I told him I hoped he would grow up. I never answered his mail from Vietnam, and when he was killed in action, I knew his family was angry with me. I learned from that experience not to hold grudges, especially about little stuff, because you never know if you will see the person again. It was very disturbing to have my last words be said in anger. Okay, so I don't always adhere to that rule, but I try.

There was also escalating violence on our streets as gangs became more aggressive. In my senior year I felt an increase in gun violence when a new gang entered the scene. Even one of my honors classmates was a victim a year after graduation. He had been in a gang and quit but was gunned down on the way home from a Motown concert. Members of another gang recognized him, though he protested that he was no longer affiliated. The death of Martin Luther King Jr. in 1968, a year after I graduated, led to a walkout by African American students and subsequent riots that left the West Side of Chicago in shambles. Pilsen was protected by the very same gangs that fought each other but were now stationed at the viaducts that divided Black from Brown. I felt that the war and the deaths of Martin Luther King Jr., President Kennedy, and Bobby Kennedy along with everyday problems of life in Pilsen cast a dark shadow over everything and everyone.

I did well in high school and graduated in the top 20 out of 400. When my name appeared in the school newspaper, someone said, "I didn't know you were smart." A counselor told me about minority scholarships to Cornell. I had no idea where that was and just said, "I'm not going to college, I'm getting married." There weren't any real examples or role models or encouragement for Latino students. So I didn't apply to any colleges.

One day my typing teacher assigned me to gather information about a secretarial program she had heard about at Loop College (now Harold Washington), part of the City Colleges of Chicago. While there, I ended up applying. I tested well and they said they would love to have me. I asked if I could work at the same time, and they said yes. I would go to school in the morning and work in the afternoon. That's how I entered City College. I was so unsure of myself that I took an English class in the summer just to make sure I could do it. I had so little faith in myself. Perhaps that's because in high school we had been told by a history teacher that we would never be able to compete against students from the North Shore. She did, however, point to the creativity I'd shown by creating a teepee, using my typewriter, on the cover of my paper on the Trail of Tears. I believe she was trying to encourage us to strive harder, but those words had a lasting impact on me. I always felt unprepared for higher education and took extra steps to make sure that I would be able to do the work. Now this is advice I give to students. When opportunities become available, you need to be ready and able to walk through that door. I always wanted to make extra-sure I did well.

Two years later I graduated with an associate of arts degree in secretarial business and started working at an insurance company. The Pilsen neighborhood was becoming more and more Mexican, more crowded, with increasing problems and violence. So all of this stuff is going on and I'm just working as a secretary in an office. Most of the time I transcribed from tapes. I'd use headphones and sit there typing everything my boss was saying. I kept thinking, "The world is going to fall in around me and I'm just going to sit here with these things in my ears, typing, and not knowing that the world has ended."

By chance, one of the attorneys at the insurance company one day asked me if I spoke Spanish, and I said yes. He mentioned a couple of friends who had a law office in Pilsen, and I said, "I live in Pilsen." He said, "Well they're looking for somebody as a secretary on Saturdays. Do you want a second job?" I said, "Yes, absolutely!" I was really not doing a lot, just spending my money on clothes. So I said, "Sure, I'll go talk to them." I ended up working for Reyes and Lopez, Attorneys at Law. Their office was right across the street from Nuevo Leon and a couple of blocks away from my house. It just so happened that these two law-yers had started the Mexican American Lawyers Association, MALA. And on the North Side, Puerto Ricans had started another organization called the Latin American Bar Association. The attorneys would take me to meetings after work, and I learned about Latino lawyers' professional culture. I knew all fifteen Latino lawyers in the state at that point. I was exposed to other types of food and how meetings were run. About the same time, I read a book, *La Raza: The Mexican Americans*, by Stan Steiner. I read it and other books about the Chicano move-ment and kept thinking, "OK, people are doing stuff in other places. I need to be doing something." Being in Pilsen and seeing those kinds of problems, reading other books about the Chicano movement, and just trying to understand more, I decided I was going to go back to school. So I quit my full-time job and kept my part-time job at the law office. I went to UIC.

When I entered and declared my major in sociology, I became familiar with the term "social stratification," the academic term for the segregation and inequality I had known as a child. I think I was drawn to sociology because I was trying to understand what was going on. The question I had always wondered about was Why were we separate? Although I was in and out of the Organization of Latin American Students (OLAS) because I was always working or going to school or both most of the time, I would periodically be involved in their activities. Some-times when we were participating in the grape boycott, we would picket some of the local supermarkets. I remember attending a Chicano conference in St. Paul, but I did not go to the big conference in Denver that many of the activists attended. I didn't meet but did hear about leaders like Reies López Tijerina and Corky Gonzales. It was a time of great expectation that change could be made. Upon graduating with honors, I planned to go to Jane Addams School of Social Work. When I told one of my bosses at the law firm that I wanted to be a social worker, he said, "Become a lawyer! We need more bilingual lawyers!" I already knew this well. During the time that I worked at the law office I saw a lot of the things that were going on to disenfranchise Latinos. For example, a real estate broker was reselling the same buildings to Mexican families on contract as opposed to conventional mortgages. If people failed to make a payment, he could just take the house back and didn't have to go through foreclosure like banks usually do. He was reselling the same property over and over again to Mexican families that he knew couldn't afford it. Other people came to the office having signed contracts that they didn't understand for used cars. At that point there wasn't a law in Illinois requiring contracts to be translated. People were signing and cosigning contracts, not knowing what they were agreeing to because they couldn't read English.

My parents were not very supportive of the law school idea and hadn't even encouraged me to go to college. They had retired to Texas by this time. Both had wanted all their children to graduate from high school, and we all did—but that was as far as it went. They didn't push any of us to go to college, and I'm the only one who actually got a degree. The girls weren't working in a factory, like my mom had. That was a big accomplishment. When I told my mother I was going to law school, she said, "Why, those lawyers treat you well." And I said, "Mom, I'm working on the wrong side of the desk." I was putting all the documents together for real estate closings, and then the lawyers would go to the closings and get paid. I was the one doing all the work! I knew I could do this.

Another thing that happened around the same time was that I ended up going to the Chicana conference in Houston in 1971. I, along with Christina Vital, went on behalf of OLAS. Professionally, the most important thing that happened there was that I heard Vilma Martínez and Graciela Olivarez speak. Vilma was president and general counsel of the Mexican American Legal Defense and Educational Fund (MALDEF). Graciela, also an attorney, was on the board. They both talked about MALDEF and all of the cases they litigated to protect the rights of Chicanos and Mexican Americans. They also talked about Chicana rights, which is a topic that was, and is, very important to me. After they spoke I raised my hand and said, "But what about the Midwest? What are you doing in the Midwest?" They told me they didn't have an office there, but they encouraged me to go to law school. Graciela had been the first woman to graduate from Notre Dame law school, even without having gotten a bachelor's degree. She came from a very humble beginning. She was clearly a very smart, very committed woman. Vilma had gone to Columbia University and urged me to apply to the law school there. And those two women made an impression on me and in my decision to become a lawyer. I had never dreamed that I would end up not only as an attorney but working for MALDEF.

In 1972, I applied to and attended DePaul University College of Law on a full scholarship. For the first time, about a third of the incoming class were women. We also had fifteen Latino students, which was also the number of Latino attorneys in the entire state. There was a large number of African American students compared to previous classes as well. The school changed overnight, and there was a lot of adjustment at the law school. There were very few minorities and women in the profession at that point. I joined the Women's Law Caucus and we'd meet with the dean and say, "You can't say 'reasonable man.' It's not the reasonable man, it's the reasonable person." Or we would complain that a professor was disrespecting women. We also had to complain that there were not enough stalls in women's restrooms. They weren't used to that many female law students. We would periodically take over the men's room, with a woman standing guard outside. We started doing feminist projects in our classes. I worked with another student to write a welfare rights pamphlet. We also started the Latino Law Student Association (LLSA), the first one in any of the law schools in Illinois. When Ray Figueroa first proposed the idea, I was a little skeptical. I had known Ray at UIC, and he was more radical than I was. But we came together and created the group with the idea of encouraging more Latino admissions and supporting each other. I became the first president. We were able to recommend Latino students for admission and eventually started a scholarship fund. DePaul's LLSA helped start similar organizations in other schools. We also had parties and, along with a close group of friends that I made, helped in making law school fun. I still attend LLSA events and am sometimes referred to as Mama LLSA. I am often approached by students interested in attending law school, and I try to provide information and contacts that will make the road a little easier. I had help not only from my former employers Manuel Reyes and Honoratus Lopez but also from two others I met through them. Cook County Judge David Cerda, who would later become a justice of the Illinois Appellate Court, encouraged me to go to law school. Cesar Velarde worked at Reyes and Lopez as a law student. Cesar graduated the year I entered DePaul, so he gave me his locker and books.

When I graduated from DePaul in 1975 I already had a job with the Legal Assistance Foundation in its Pilsen office. I was one of the first two Latinas licensed to practice law in Illinois. My classmate Viola Armijo Rouse was the other, and we remain close friends. During that first year as an attorney, I was asked by a community activist, Juan Velasquez, if I would join the board of directors of Centro de la Causa. It was a logical step from my student activities with OLAS and LLSA. Because I was a community resident and an attorney, they thought I would be a good board member. That was the start of a lifelong commitment to volunteering. I have served on many boards over the years, from the American Civil Liberties Union (ACLU) to Centro de la Causa, the Latino Institute, and the Latin American Bar Association. I still serve on the board of directors of Gads Hill Center, whose mission is to create opportunities for children and their families to build better lives through education, access to resources, and community engagement. Gads Hill Center started a mental health program a few years ago that I was very supportive of, having always seen the need for mental health services throughout the city. While Gads Hill's main office is in Pilsen, it provides services throughout the south and southwest sides of the city. I sometimes became an officer but never secretary. I always voiced my position that women should not be placed in the position of secretary. We should be in positions of leadership as president and vice president.

Shortly after graduating from law school, I again ran into Vilma Martínez at a conference. I said, "Now there are over 350,000 Latinos in Chicago and what are you doing?" At that point she invited me apply to the intern/extern program at MALDEF's national office. The purpose was for me to learn about civil rights issues and become their Midwest contact. I did apply, and this would be the start of a relationship between MALDEF and the Midwest. In fact, MALA and Judge Cerda had contacted MALDEF several times to discuss the possibilities of opening a Chicago office, starting when Mario Obledo was president of MALDEF. Judge Cerda also communicated with Vilma in 1974, scheduling a meeting when she was traveling and had a layover in Chicago's O'Hare Airport. I moved to San Francisco for a year, the only time I have ever lived outside of the Chicago area. Judge Cerda commented that I might not come back. I assured him I had no intention of staying in California. I'm a Chicagoan, although I actually live in Oak Park now, just west of Chicago.

During the time I was in San Francisco on the intern/extern program, I worked with MALDEF attorneys on cases involving voting rights, education, prison conditions and other civil rights issues. I was also asked if I wanted to go to Washington, DC, to attend the first White House meeting on domestic violence, in 1977. There were women from all over the country talking about issues facing battered women. Although I was not that involved with the issue of domestic violence in Chicago at that point, I had been meeting with a group of women in San Francisco who were working on domestic violence, especially among army wives. At that DC meeting a decision was reached that there should be some kind of national group to deal with this issue, so I became one of the incorporators of the National Coalition against Domestic Violence. I didn't have much participation in advocacy efforts until I returned to Chicago.

When I returned to Chicago in the fall of 1977, I opened my own law practice with assistance from MALDEF. I was a solo practitioner sharing space with four male attorneys, one of whom had been my professor in law school. It happened we were two floors up from the new Legal Assistance Foundation Battered Women's Project, run by my friend and former classmate Candace Wayne. As a result, we ended up working on issues together, and I represented clients who were being referred from the Pilsen neighborhood by Mujeres Latinas en Acción and sometimes by local priests. I did a lot of those cases for a while and sometimes got assigned to represent kids. It was very difficult for me emotionally. I learned how difficult and dangerous it was for women to leave abusive situations. Abusers isolate their victims from friends and family and convince them they are not worth better treatment. Some of my clients decided to leave once their children were old enough to intervene to try to protect their moms. The women knew that their children were now in danger, and as mothers they would take steps to protect themselves as well as their children. Although my father drank a lot, I never saw him raise his hand to my mother. I learned from my mother that he tried to hit her once during the year they lived in Mexico. She looked at him and said, "If you ever hit me I will leave." So he never tried again. But I knew I could have become a victim of abuse myself. Part of the cycle of violence is that the abuser apologizes and promises to never do it again, and then something happens to set off the violence again. I had in fact been struck by a boyfriend who blamed being drunk for pushing me to the ground. I forgave him because he promised not to do it again, but we eventually broke up over his cheating.

When MALDEF finally came to Chicago it was in 1979 with its census outreach project, focused on encouraging our communities to fill out US Census forms. The goal was to ensure that Latinos would be counted and more adequately represented. MALDEF rented a space in the shared office where I had my practice and began the census project with one staff person. Although she worked directly with the national office, I became friends with the project staff person, Eva Vera, the first staff person Mario Moreno had left when he passed the bar and became an attorney. Eva was the single mom of a three-month-old baby. I learned a lot about the challenges facing single mothers through her.

MALDEF opened its Chicago office in 1980, and I became the first regional counsel. I was responsible for managing the office, supervising the staff, and protecting the rights of Latinos in the entire eleven-state Midwest region. Obviously, we focused most of our attention in Chicago since it had the largest population and we had limited resources. We joined other community efforts around redistricting issues. We kept telling public officials, "Over the years you've seen our community grow and whenever you redistrict city wards, you divide our community." I was still living in Pilsen and the division between the 1st Ward and the 25th Ward was along Ashland Avenue—right in the middle of the community. And the same thing happened with the state districts—on the North Side as well as the South Side of Chicago, the Latino community was divided among various state representative districts. With that division, we didn't have the number of votes necessary to elect representatives of our choice. We went to the state hearings and the city council and we said, "If you do this again, we will sue." Latinos had never sued, and I guess they didn't really think that we would. There were no Latinos in either the city council or in the legislature in Springfield to speak up for us. So we sued. And there I was, along with staff attorney Ray Romero, in court against some of the best attorneys in the city and state. They represented the Democratic Party, the city council, mayor, and legislature. We also asked the Puerto Rican Legal Defense and Education Fund (PRDELF, now known as Latino Justice) from New York to come in, and they were represented by Juan Cartagena (later president and general counsel). At that point I had not done many trials, and never a federal trial. There we were, new kids on the block. Fortunately, we had support from others because African Americans and Republicans had sued and the cases were consolidated. There were three sets of attorneys, three sets of plaintiffs. I felt like we had been thrown into the deep end of the pool and I can't swim.

Although there were plenty of lawyers on these cases, I was the only woman who was a lead in the case. I was the only woman who got to do openings and closings. On the city case, we had a judge who never really understood the case. One of our witnesses said, "Hispanic is not a race." On the census, they can identify as Black, White, or Other, and 8,000 Hispanics in Chicago had checked "Black." The judge thought this was the key to the case. He was going to be able to resolve the whole case if we could find the Black Latinos. He started asking all of our witnesses, "Where do the Black Latinos live?" And we were all like, what? He finally gave up after a while. When the trial ended after three months and an hourlong closing argument by me on behalf of the Latinos, he said, "If all of the members of your community have the same charm and gentleness that you do, Ms. Martinez, I do not think there would be a whole lot of problems in having coalitions with other groups." You could hear jaws drop in the courtroom. We had in fact created coalitions that were working on this case together. We had worked with African Americans to come up with a map that recognized the rights of both groups. He never understood that this case was about our voting rights being denied by the white power structure. Not to mention that no one had ever called me gentle.

We filed the cases in '81 and it went over to Christmas '82. We won both cases. The decisions were appealed after I left MALDEF and eventually resulted in the first Latino-majority wards and legislative districts in the city of Chicago. As a result, we elected the first Latino aldermen in current times (there was a Hispanic in the 1920s) and Latino state representatives and senators. The aldermen ended up playing a key role in terms of supporting Mayor Harold Washington. So it was a historic event not only for Latinos but for the entire city because it helped balance power so that Mayor Washington could end what was called "Beirut on the Lake." Battles that became known as "the Council Wars" occurred when Harold Washington became mayor and white aldermen were able to prevent him from passing anything in the city council. He did not have enough votes to promote his agenda. Newly elected Latino aldermen changed the balance of power, siding with Mayor Washington on many issues.

In the middle of the second redistricting case, I realized I didn't really like litigation. I resigned my position but stayed on the case until it was completed at the district court level. The appeal would be handled by my successor, Ray Romero. At the same time that these cases put me into the center of local media attention, I felt very isolated. I once wrote a poem about that and how difficult it was to be a Chicana attorney at a time when there were very few. People hadn't seen a Latina attorney before. Even a client of mine asked if I was a real lawyer. There were high expectations of me especially when I was at MALDEF. It is sometimes very lonely to be in those positions with the difficulties of the day-to-day work and the pressure of everyone's expectations. And then the insecurities, "I've never done this before, how am I going to make it." Sleep-deprived, I wondered, "How am I going to get all of this done?" You've got to get support where you can find it, and many times that means from within yourself. I think that's something you learn with age. When you're young it's much harder to do that, to go inside for that support. You just have to figure out how to find it and have confidence. I would later return to MALDEF for a third time as legislative staff attorney in Chicago, from 2007 to 2011, doing policy work at a time when anti-immigrant ordinances were popping up throughout the country.

After taking a much-needed vacation and some time off, I found out I was pregnant. I was without a job and told the father he could be as involved with the baby as he wanted, or not. I went to Mario Aranda, executive director of the Latino Institute, and told him I needed a job. He said he felt like he was talking to a pregnant teenager. But I was a thirty-three-year-old attorney, unmarried and uninsured. He created a position as general counsel and director of advocacy for me. I was able to continue my work on policy issues affecting Latinos without the litigation or administrative responsibilities. We began a major effort to help Latino lawful permanent residents become citizens and therefore eligible to register to vote. While the numbers of Latinos in Chicago had continued to grow, we were still not the political force that we needed to be. MALDEF's redistricting work literally put us on the map, but we had a long way to go to realize our full political power.

On December 12, 1983, I gave birth to my son, Miguel Angel Martínez. I gave him my last name because I still was not sure where the father would be in our lives. I knew my son would always be with me and that I would never change my last name. I was proud to be a Martínez because I knew the strength and responsibility for which my father stood. I returned to work as a nursing mother, in an organization that supported families. We continued to develop the citizenship project, working with the United Neighborhood Organization (UNO) and churches throughout the city. When I would occasionally testify before the city council or other public bodies, my law degree and experience from MALDEF helped to make our voice stronger on behalf of the Latino Institute and Latinos in general.

In 1985, when the appeals were finally concluded on the city redistricting case, special elections were ordered. I was pregnant with my second child, Natalia. She was born on December 2, and a month later I decided to run for alderman in the Pilsen community where I had grown up and still lived. I was still unmarried, with two children and living with their father. I was attacked as being an unwed mother but also for being pro-choice. The anti-choice attacks were incredible, coming from a candidate who had been on the board of Planned Parenthood in another city. It was also strange that from that same camp came criticism of me for being an unmarried mother. So I thought okay, women are not supposed to get abortions and then you're criticizing me for keeping and raising my two children! Ironic but not unusual in politics, which can be a dirty business.

I lost, coming in third out of four. But I had a chance to raise issues of importance to families, including child care and early childhood education. The next year the regular elections were held, and I ran again against three Latino candidates.

At one point, my friend and campaign office manager, Sally Gonzalez, and I went to a press conference with the other candidates. Each of them had a known gang member by his side. I didn't know them, but Sally told me their names. I recognized one in particular from his reputation as a drug dealer who had spent time in jail. I wondered what I was doing getting involved in politics at all. But then women would tell me they were so glad that I ran because their daughters were watching. Just seeing me encouraged them to think about higher education and politics, so I stayed with it. I lost again, but Vilma Colon won on the North Side, becoming the only Latina to serve on the Chicago city council until 2015, when two Latinas won alderman races. Latinas have been much more successful in the state legislature, where a number serve in the Illinois House and Senate.

I then returned to the Latino Institute but left shortly thereafter. I worked for Voices for Illinois Children for a time, learning more about children's issues and the needs of families. Later, I became the executive director of Mujeres Latinas en Acción. Over the years I'd always had a connection with Mujeres. I had attended some of the early organizing meetings while I was in law school. At one point while they were still getting the organization off the ground, they asked me to teach a class offered in the community through the League of Women Voters to inform residents about government and political rights. It was given in the small storefront that was Mujeres' first office.

When Mujeres started there were a number of community organizations being created in Pilsen, but they weren't addressing women's issues. They weren't addressing the problems of women getting beaten up by their husbands or of young girls running away. Mujeres was started to try and address those issues because women in the community didn't have anywhere they could go for help. Mujeres filled that gap, and one of the first programs was for runaway youth. The programs were designed to work with parents and young girls to ensure that they could stay in their homes. They were getting the kind of counseling they needed. The parents also felt that they had someone to turn to for help in understanding their first-generation US-born children and US customs. Those were issues that I was very committed to, having represented some of Mujeres' clients in previous years.

There are many women who talk about how Mujeres saved their lives, about how Alicia Amador, who worked with youth, saved their lives. There's a funeral director who always talks about how she was in a gang at the time and ended up going to Alicia's program. It turned her life around. So we know that Mujeres has had a huge impact on women and children who have gone through their programs. Women have gone there for help because they are victims of domestic violence or sexual assault or need emergency assistance. I had wanted to be director of Mujeres because the organization fills a need, a desperate need in our community. I am a woman and a feminist. I have suffered sexual and physical abuse. The board originally questioned why a lawyer would want to be director. I said, "Why wouldn't you want a lawyer as executive director?" They interviewed me and I was able to get the job. That was the second time I had applied.

I was the executive director of the organization from 1992 to 1997. It was one of the most important jobs in my life. I would tell funders and other people all the time, "When I walk through the doors of Mujeres, I could be walking in as the executive director or I could be walking in as a client." All of us understand that we are who our clients are. We are women who have suffered at some point in our lives. Many of the staff had been victims of sexual assault, domestic violence, and economic distress, were new immigrants, or had experienced some other kind of impact on their lives that made them the same as the clients who walked through our doors. We didn't see ourselves as any better or any different. I've had some advantages in my life and people who have opened doors for me. I have been blessed. I do not ever forget that. People opened doors for me and I was allowed to go to college, I was allowed to go to law school, and I was able to do these things because somebody else was out there helping. So I'm not any different than any of the women or children who walk through those doors. Somebody needs to tell them that they have a future too.

Mujeres was able to start a sexual assault counseling program while I was there. Our Peace Program was a response to a funding call for programs to prevent juvenile delinquency. I said, "I don't know if we're going to get funded or not, and I might get fired over this, but I am not going to call these children potential juvenile delinquents." The program was funded even though I explained that we would call it the Peace Program because we saw our children as children with potential, not potential delinquents. The program continued with that name— the Peace program—for many years.

We started going to the Harrison Park field house for our International Women's Day luncheon. We would bring speakers, sometimes from out of town, and we would address different issues relevant to Latinas. We did educational programing to bring attention to issues of domestic violence and sexual assault but also economic health and social disparities between Latinas and other women. It was really about everyone understanding why we need to have these issues brought to the forefront, because those disparities exist. We were getting complaints that Latinas were always made to wash the floors in the domestic abuse shelters and not allowed, especially if they didn't speak English, in the other parts of the shelters. They were not allowed to eat at the same time or to do the same jobs as other residents. There was always a difference in the way Latinas were being treated, so it was our role to raise those issues. And it is why Mujeres is still needed now, because we are still facing some of those issues. For example, the women workers in restaurants who are being sexual assaulted or having inappropriate comments being made about them or being harassed by the male cooks. These things continue to take place.

One of the most life-changing experiences I had at Mujeres was when I went to the UN Conference on Women in Beijing in 1995. Norma Seledon, who was director of Mujeres' leadership program, and I were able to go for the entire three-week conference. We were able to see and hear women from around the world. They presented information about issues facing them in their countries and how they were being addressed. Workshops were only one way of presenting those issues. There was a quilt put together from pieces brought from all over the world. There were posters, dances, music, poetry, photographs, and many other methods of getting messages across. One of the most beautiful was a woman wearing a long, white kimono accompanied by drummers and others carrying posters explaining the plight of the comfort women. These were Chinese women who were forced by Japanese soldiers into sexual servitude during World War II. They were left physically and emotionally broken after the war, shunned by their communities, and many unable to have normal lives. They were seeking reparations for their injuries. The two most important lessons that I learned were that there is more than one way to tell your story and that you have to include young people in everything you do.

There had been a separate track for young women at the conference, and at one of the closing presentations, the young women said they should have been part of the full conference, not separated. It is a lesson that I have carried forward and surprise even my own children with the age range of my friends. I make sure that I always have friends who are in their early twenties to late eighties. Some of them are children of friends, others are young women I have mentored, and some are my dance friends. It helps me to understand the current environment as well as helping me to keep young.

I developed a reputation for speaking out. That meant that I was asked to join various boards and advocacy efforts. I once wrote a letter to Cardinal Bernadin in response to a message he had asked be read at all of the masses in Chicago. He spoke about the abuse of children by priests and the scandal that had shaken the Catholic Church. Cardinal Bernadin asked for compassion. I wrote and said that nowhere in his message had he mentioned that child sexual abuse was a crime. The result was that I was appointed to the first Professional Fitness Review Board that reviewed allegations of clerical misconduct and determined whether priests would be removed from parishes and contact with children. It was a very difficult task, especially because of my own abuse. The first day was especially hard, and when my boyfriend picked me up I said I needed to go walk around the rookery at the zoo before I could go home to my own children. I removed myself from consideration for a new term after the bishops came to see us on a case. I told the members of the board that I believed that the bishops were trying to influence us. Someone said, no, they just want to bring in information from parishioners who had signed a petition to bring the priest back. I said they are superiors to the three members who were priests. We had also not asked them to come in and never had the victims or families come before us. We relied on reports from investigators and psychiatric exams. Also, those parishioners had not protected the boys who were abused, and some had publicly said they didn't believe the boys. There was another time when one of the priests said, "I know him. He's a nice guy" about one of the alleged perpetrators. I told the board that abusers are not horrible, ugly men in trenchcoats. They are people who gain the trust of families and children. They are friendly and appear to be regular people. That priest never forgot what I said and mentioned it to me a few years later.

My next position after Mujeres was with the International Center for Health Leadership Development at UIC, a Kellogg Foundation–funded program. I was originally hired as associate director because of my long history of working with community-based organizations. Two years later when the director left, I became director. We worked with health professionals and advocates who came in for weeklong sessions over a two-year period, in an effort to increase their skills in collaboration. I was able to learn and teach a wide range of techniques, skills, and strategies to improve the health of communities through collaborative efforts. My experience at Mujeres had already taught me to be more collaborative in my management style, and this work was another step in the direction of becoming a collaborative leader. I thoroughly enjoyed my work but had to leave when funding ended.

The balancing of work, personal, and family life is very important to me, making sure that I have time for myself, making sure I have time for my family responsibilities, and working when I need to work. Women have told me, "You're my role model for balance." A lot had to do with being a divorced mother.

I have two children, Miguel and Natalia. I did marry their father and then was divorced when they were pretty young. Being a single mother means that you have to make sure that you are in control of your time. Time management is of utmost importance, though I wasn't always able to provide experiences that I would have liked for my children. I couldn't take them to all the activities they might have participated in, but I did make most performances and teacher meetings. I took them to museums and parks and on vacations, as my mother had done for me. They also spent time with adults, going to meetings and conferences with me. I took my daughter to a speaking event in Arizona when she was about four. The organizers were a little concerned because she would have to sit at a table with strangers while I was on the dais. When the luncheon was finished, they told me she had been having a conversation with the candidate for attorney general of the state. My son at about that same age was able to meet César Chávez during a stop he made in Chicago. I was a distance back, but some of my friends who were with Chávez pulled my son to the front. He got to shake hands and later would write about him for a school assignment.

For the most part, I have always tried to work nine to five. I do sometimes go to meetings or other events in the evenings. I might take work home with me, but I try to work during the day. I also think it's important to take a break, so I rarely eat my lunch at my desk. I go out and I might read something unrelated to work. I think it's important to refresh yourself and come back to work ready and able to concentrate.

One of the things that I have done, especially once my kids went to college, is that I love to dance. I dance three or four times a week, and I make sure I do that.

There will be friends of mine who say, "Oh, I wanna go dancing but I just don›t have time, I have too much work." You need to make time for yourself. So I do, and it's something that I talk to students about too. Yes, you're concerned about your career and making sure you get the right job and moving up, but you also have to always, always balance your life. Keep in contact with your body and with your spiritual side because that will help you do your job better. That will help you be a better parent and will help you be a better son or daughter to your own parents. I try to make sure that I'm not stressed out from work responsibilities, and I work that stress out dancing. This is much healthier than the drinking that I did earlier in my life.

When I turned fifty, I decided that I needed to have a big party. On my party invitation I drew a woman as a butterfly because I felt like it was a time of transition for me. Some young people think, "Oh, fifty, that's really old and you're ready for the rocking chair." NO! It is not like that at all. I knew it wasn't going to be. My fiftieth birthday was an opportunity to reflect back on my life, to bring together people who had been and were important to me. I also wanted to recognize those things that I had accomplished. I wanted to recognize the change occurring as something not to be ignored or worried about or dreaded. It is just another phase of life. I also held menopause parties for a few friends because no one ever prepares us for "the change." The parties were focused on honoring the woman and exchanging stories.

I always wanted to learn cake decorating, and when I saw the cake for my sixtieth birthday, I knew I had to do it. The cake was decorated by my daughter's friend with butterflies and flowers. I looked up cake-decorating classes and found one not far from me, in Spanish. My friend Norma also decided to take the class, and we went through all four levels. I have made cakes for friends and been totally surprised by the creative energy released by these projects. I also started making sock monkeys and other stuffed animals for friends. These creative activities are also a part of the balancing.

I have now entered the "mariposa de oro," phase of my life, the golden butterfly phase, when I turned sixty-five. Sixty-five used to be the age of retirement. I knew that was not going to be possible for me or for many who have had public-interest careers. But I also know that this age presents new opportunities as well as challenges. The golden butterfly represents my position as an elder and also a very active participant in society. I continue to work, to volunteer, to dance, and to create. Part of what I have not connected with sufficiently in the past few years is my spiritual life. So I'm going to do that and am starting now. I also know that within me there is another spark, and I will return to uncovering that gift.

I went to college and law school because I wanted to change things for my neighbors in Pilsen. I still do that, even though I don't live there any more. The work that I've done throughout my career has been for people in Pilsen and people like them—other Latinos, families, the poor, people of color, women. That has been the focus of my work throughout my career. I also talk to students any time

I am invited. I think it's my responsibility not only because I went to law school and college on full scholarships but because I think it's important. When I was in elementary school I think there might have been one Latino teacher, and there were no other Latino professionals that I saw. In high school, again—I think it was the Spanish teacher—one Latino teacher. There were no other Latino professionals that I knew. Until I went to work for attorneys Reyes and Lopez, I had never met Latino professionals. So it's my responsibility as a Latina professional to meet students who might benefit from my experience. It may help by talking to me, just seeing me, knowing that there are Latino and Latina attorneys. For law students, the model I represent is a career in public interest work.

I always tell students I became a lawyer by accident. I was always a good student, and when those windows of opportunity opened up, I was able to go through because I had the grades to do it. It is important to recognize when those opportunities are in front of you, and you need to be prepared to take advantage of them. Whatever level you are now, make sure that you're ready to do whatever you decide you want to do later. We all need to understand that all you need is within you already. You find the way to bring it out. That may mean an advanced degree, it may mean college, it may mean preparing in some other way. You could have a creative spark inside, some talent that you have. Bring it out. Whatever it is that is for you, it's already there. And age does not matter.

20 MY DELIBERATE PURSUIT OF FREEDOM

DEANNA ROMERO

This is a memoir about my deliberate pursuit of freedom. Let's take a ride with my free spirit through a journey that started about fifty years ago. There have been periods of time from my childhood to the present in which I deliberately set out to do the presumed impossible. My free-spirited nature has always guided me along to my deliberate pursuit of freedom. It was no accident that my spirit chose my parents, Theresa Montez and Richard Romero. They were my teachers early on and raised us during a time when liberation and self-determination were key elements to my upbringing. I was raised in the Chicano movement in Denver, Colorado. My parents were both totally committed to the cause and very passionate about creating a better place for their children.

I was taught at a young age about freedom: I remember a famous quote by Corky Gonzales, who was referred to as the *jefe* of the Chicano movement in Denver. He stated, "No man has the right to oppress people and all oppressed people have the right to revolution." That quote always stayed with me and even more so when my mother decided to stand up for women in the Chicano movement. She would remind them about how that quote includes women. As she would restate the quote, "No man has the right to oppress women and all oppressed women have the right to revolution."

My parents had an enormous love for their people and a passion for what they believed in. They were considered to be "Aunt Theresa and Uncle Rich" to all of the youth at our school, Escuela Tlatelolco, a freedom school developed in the Chicano movement. The Chicano movement in Denver decided that we needed our own school to educate the young people due to a 50 percent dropout rate and the discrimination that existed in the public education system. The public school system was failing our youth, so Escuela Tlatelolco was started in 1969. This is where I was taught about my history, which provided me with a sense of identity, pride, and self-dignity. My self-esteem and self-concept were sharpened and shaped by my experience learning the cultural historical story of my ancestors. Not only did we learn via word lessons, but also we experienced it through world lessons.

We grew up dancing Mexican *folklórico* dances from different regions of Mexico as well as *danza azteca*, which I am still able to dance today. We were taught Spanish and Nahuatl along with the history and culture of our ancestors. We were taught to do bead work as well as how to make moccasins and headbands. I was lucky. I was fortunate. I believed in making a difference for my people. I knew at a young age I would go on to college and become educated so I could return to my community to help out in some way, and that is exactly what I did. I was taught to always analyze information and not to just accept what is being said or taught as truth. "Read between the lines" is what my dad used to say.

And yet my father did not know how to read until he became an adult. Joining the Chicano movement motivated him to learn to read. Now he is a walking book of history and is well versed in his ability to speak about a variety of topics. As a child he was put in a corner because he spoke Spanish, which forced him to memorize books as if he could read them. That only lasted for a few years, so by the sixth grade he dropped out and was on the streets following his brother-in-law Corky Gonzales and my aunt (my dad's sister) Geraldine Gonzales around. My uncle Corky was a world-ranked professional boxer, and my dad was just a few years younger than his sister Geraldine. They came from a family of twelve, with my father being the youngest.

My grandmother Teresina Romero had my dad in her fifties. He was what you would call her change-of-life baby. I tease my dad today and tell him that is why he is so radical. My grandmother was half Apache—very strong and wise—and taught my dad what she could. She told him, "Richard, if they could do it we could do it." "They" referred to the white man. Not only could we do it but also we *had* to do it. My family helped build the Chicano movement, as many other families did, but my family was a very large family, and my grandmother supported the cause as well as all her daughters, who were right there with my Aunt Gerry creating the backbone of the movement. Grandma Teresina was quite elderly by the time my dad dropped out of school, so his older sisters raised him.

My dad became a spokesman in the Chicano movement and traveled with my uncle around the country. My uncle had him keep a record of all of the information that was delivered or received at different speaking engagements. My father's skill of memorization as a child paid off; he had a photographic memory, which came in handy. My father became well respected by the youth. He was really committed to the mission of the Chicano movement. He idolized my uncle Corky, who had been a role model to him since his youth. Unfortunately, my father had to make a decision to leave the Chicano movement, as he felt the mission had been lost by the leadership of the organization.

As for my mother, she was born with a heart of gold. She was a beautiful glow of light with a complexion like a baby's face. She was for sure put on earth for the children. Children are what she loved, and she gave of herself freely for any child in need. She was born to my grandmother, Francis Montez, who just recently made her journey to the spirit world at the ripe age of 105. My grandfather died when my mother was one year old.

My mother's work with children started as a teenager in a community center down the block from her home. She and my father married young. She was seventeen and my father was eighteen. My father had a lot of nieces and nephews. My mother always had children over to the house and would take good care of them by cooking and giving them quality time. All the children loved their aunt Theresa and have stories to tell of her singing in the kitchen and doing things to make them feel special. She continued to be involved with the care and education of children to the end of her life.

My grandmother Frances was given away at the age of twenty-seven to be married off to a man she hardly knew. She ended up raising five kids on her own after my grandfather José Alonias Montez died and she never remarried. She was a strong woman totally committed to her family and to God. And it is here where I really start to connect with my story about liberation. My grandmother was given away to be married, as if women were just objects in a trade exchange. Then there was my mother, who was one of those women in the Chicano movement who just accepted and lived as the majority of women did back in those days—they accepted their role as wives, which included accepting the infidelity of their husbands due to their bondage to the Catholic religion.

We grew up poor as far as material items but rich with love from both my parents. My mother and father sacrificed a lot to be part of the Chicano movement. They earned fifty dollars a week to support a family of seven. But one thing my mother was not going to sacrifice again was her self-respect. My father started an affair with a much younger woman when I was about ten years old. Women were attracted to the men who held status in the movement. To many men in that time it seemed a way to prove their manhood by having their mistresses. It was just what it was back in those days—men did what they did and most women put up with it.

But not this time. My mother said, *¡Ya basta!* Enough! And thus she gave birth to feminism within the Chicano movement in Denver. My mother, Theresa Romero, was the first to say "No more," and with that, she became a role model to young women in the movement. *Adelante mujer!* She was like a natural-born therapist, and women often sought her out when they were having trouble in their love relationships.

The women in my family were strong and determined—motivated by the love for their children. Now this is where my story and quest for freedom becomes more visible and deliberate. I started to see the generations of struggle that women in my family have had to endure and overcome. From my grandmother

Frances being given away for marriage to a stranger, to my mother saying *¡Ya basta!*, to myself saying "I love women," and to my daughter, Analicia, who is firmly grounded in the rights of humanity with her indigo spirit.

This is where my story begins. Although I was raised with the traditional mind-set of what relationships were all about, growing up with exposure to all this history I saw that I was going to do things my way. I was what you would call a tomboy. Yes, the skinny little long-haired Chicana who was tough was going to show them. Oh yeah, so you say the girls can't play? I will show you that I can play and I am better than some of the best male athletes. Football, basketball, kickball, boxing. I even dabbled in shooting marbles, but I was more interested in physically challenging activities. Yes, I did sports. I showed them and they wanted me on their teams eventually, and they learned to accept that girls could do it too, and so it is.

I took care of my younger brother, José Trinidad, or J. T., in my neighborhood. He always had friends who were older, and he was a little guy, so I had to watch over him and protect him. You know how boys like to fight and pick on the little ones. Well, my brother did not have to worry about that. My father always taught us if they mess with one of us, they mess with all of us. My brother's friends all knew if they messed with him they would have to deal with me. That was just a little too embarrassing for them, to have to let me show them what girls could do. I earned my respect in the neighborhood among the boys.

My childhood was filled with a lot of good memories. I was good at playing. I was very creative and had an imagination. I was quite entertaining and had leadership qualities at a young age. My best friend from second grade to graduation was Jon. This was a very atypical relationship for a boy and girl at the age of seven to spend so much time together. As we grew it was like we had a role reversal. He would hang out with the girls and I would go teach the boys that girls were equal to boys. Jon was always the best-dressed and one of the prettiest boys in school. He was very special to all of us. Everyone really loved Jon, and many of the girls had crushes on him. I was the athlete and he was the fashion designer. I knew I was different. I was just not your typical girl.

It is important to share that during this time, in the early 1980s, I became more and more aware of Chicano gay men because people close to me were coming out or were being understood as gay. One of them was my best friend. He was my dance partner in our Mexican folkloric dance group Ballet Chicano de Aztlán. The group was one of the cultural enrichment programs of the Crusade for Justice, a Mexican American social justice organization founded in 1965 in Denver. We would spend the night at each other's houses, as our parents were very close and our parents were okay with that. His mother was and is sort of like a mother figure to me. Her birthday and my mother's birthday are on the same day. Jon and I were dance partners who motivated each other and learned from each other. We both ended up graduating a year early. Since we were young, people would tease us and tell us we were going to get married. We tried to go steady once, but that just did not work out. We had a very special love for each other as friends.

When we graduated, a lot of things had changed and we went our separate ways. He finally decided to come out and to accept his sexuality as a gay Chicano male, which was something that was just not accepted in those days. For us, we saw a lack of acceptance in the Chicano movement and families, and that included his family initially. His family loved him regardless but did not do too well accepting his sexuality until later, and then they were there to support him when he was diagnosed with HIV/AIDS. Jon was like the heart to his family. He had so much love to give. He was the best son one could ask for, and he took care of his mother. As an uncle he was loved unconditionally.

One of my cousins, Enrique Montoya, was the director of our dance group and was the first Chicano to come out and announce his sexuality as a gay male. He also experienced an initial lack of acceptance in the Chicano movement including family members with the exception of my father. My dad loved his nephew, as he was very talented and intelligent. He was one of the first young people to get a college degree. He left the Crusade for Justice and took half the dance group with him to New York to make it big, and he did. He succeeded with his show called Cara Show, which represented four generations of Mexican history through dance ending with the pachuco dance style. Enrique was one of the first people we knew to become infected with HIV/AIDS. He moved back to Denver and was able to entertain our community with some fantastic shows shortly before he died. He did not die of HIV/AIDS. A policeman who ran a red light and did not have his siren or lights on crashed into Enrique's driver's side, T-boning his car. Enrique sustained major head trauma and was on life support until his family decided to disconnect and let him go to the spirit world.

Although I was beginning to feel and understand more about my attraction to women, I had met my husband and we had gotten married. This detoured me from exploring being with a woman, as I was resisting doing so based on being programmed to believe that it was wrong. My husband was about the only guy I was attracted to, and one thing led to another. It was not long before I became pregnant, and then of course the next thing was marriage. That was the traditional thing to do in my family. It all happened so fast that I had no idea what I had gotten myself into. At times I was unsure if this was the right path for me, but I followed the traditional norms as expected.

I had a beautiful son, Eliseo, five months later. I loved my son; he was beautiful and a special gift I accepted wholeheartedly. My son was about two years old when I went back to college to finish my prerequisites for the child health associate program, which was a physician's assistant program. I told myself that no matter what, I was going to finish my education. Marriage and children would not keep me from fulfilling my educational goals. I had my mother, who was very supportive of my continuing my education. And my son was a gift from God. We all adored him, and my mother had a special bond with him. She helped me a lot with him, and this allowed me to finish my prerequisites, and I was then accepted into the child health associate program at the University of Colorado Health Sciences Center.

Shortly after starting the CHAP program, my husband and I began to have problems, so it was helpful when my mother decided to open up her own day care center that would allow me a savings on day care and the peace of mind that I could have trust in my son's well-being. She was able to open her own day care because she had earned her degree in early childhood education from a nontraditional college during her involvement with Escuela Tlatelolco. My mother was the co-administrator of elementary education at Escuela Tlatelolco for several years. A program was being offered to some of the teachers and others who worked in the school for them to get their degrees. Their experience would apply to their credits for college and speed up the process to earn a degree. My mother did this program while working a full-time job at the school and part-time jobs while being a single parent to five children. At times she worked up to three jobs at a time. She was my biggest role model. My mother worked at the school and was totally dedicated to her work. She was an amazing organizer and really knew how to network. She was very resourceful and was good at getting donations to help keep the school going.

With my mom's help with child care, I started my first job with community health working for Denver Health at Mariposa Health Station, which was a small clinic in the west side of Denver, about a block from my grandmother Frances's home. This was a very convenient location to allow me to spend my lunches with my grandmother as I had done many times as an undergraduate student when I attended Metro State College, which was built just blocks from where my grandmother lived. This was one of the first communities to experience gentrification. The college was built right in a community and kept a block of the houses on campus as well as two churches.

I had a second child, a daughter, and stayed busy doing my community organizing with a youth group called the Tierra Amarilla Youth Brigades, which was founded in 1990. I was one of the original adults who were coming together to talk about the issues in our communities. We decided to focus on the youth. There was some land in Tierra Amarilla, New Mexico, that had been liberated through a land struggle. This was the first piece of land to be reclaimed by a Mexicano/Chicano community. We developed a curriculum and raised money to take youth from the inner city to raw, beautiful land in northern New Mexico. We taught them their history, from the seven tribes of the Americas to contemporary Mexicano/Chicano issues. We addressed the gang and drug issues along with gender issues. I was an adult organizer for about eight years.

One of our goals for the land was to build the first Mexican university, so we had different groups come and participate in the work brigades. Germans who fought fascism in Germany brought skilled carpenters to help. Spaniards, Basque people, and the New African Peoples Organization (NAPO) all came to be part of building the university in Tierra Amarilla. The New African Peoples Organization brought their youth group, called the Malcolm X Scouts, who were very disciplined and led by highly educated adults. This was a good mix for our youth—the love and bonding that took place replaced any racism with all the different groups that came to join the vision we had. The Tierra Amarilla Youth Brigades went on for fifteen years, but I stepped back after eight years. I felt I could be involved as a supporter as several of the original youths took over and became the leadership.

It was at this time my mother became very ill and was diagnosed with diabetes. Within one year, she became so ill as a result of diabetes that it seemed she'd had it for twenty years. She had several small strokes and chronic back pain that was not localized. I knew something else was wrong, but I was in denial. I finally was insistent that they do an ultrasound due to her back pain that they had diagnosed as arthritis. Sure enough, it was not arthritis but cancer. She had pancreatic cancer that had already spread to the liver, and she was given three to six months to live. We decided to go for quality over quantity, which meant that there would be no chemotherapy treatments. She was so brave and had so much courage.

Prior to her diagnosis of cancer my husband and I had decided to separate. After having arguments in regard to saying "If it were not for the kids" that we would break up, I decided it was time to end it. Seeing my mother become sick that year made me really take a look at the way I was living my life.

I was offered an opportunity to start up a pilot school-based clinic in an elementary school. After praying on it I was given a clear message that I would be able to help people and experience a lot of growth. My staff included a full-time mental health therapist, an outreach worker, and a medical assistant, and we teamed up with the school social worker and the nurse to build a team approach to offering a comprehensive health-delivery system to the students free of charge. We indeed were able to do some amazing work not only delivering health care but providing schoolwide health fairs and educational workshops for families. We were the second-busiest school-based clinic in Denver, after North High School. I was the site-based coordinator for six years and did the physician assistant work, dispensed meds, and even did nursing duties. In addition to supervising the Denver health staff I was responsible for playing an administrative role and making sure that we maintained a collaborative effort to provide quality, accessible services to our students. As long as I kept people on this page, that it was for the students, territorial battles were kept at a minimum. I basically performed the job of about four different roles.

I had no idea of the extent of personal growth that would come from making this career change. With my mother sick and my marriage on the rocks, this pretty much pushed me over the edge. I had to find out who Deanna really was. I decided to come out after finding myself strongly attracted to a professional woman at work and after meeting up with an old friend who brought me out of the closet.

The next thing was coming out to the family. My siblings had various responses including some resistance, and my dad had the most surprising and encouraging response. He told me that he was proud of me for doing what I believed in. I was conflicted about telling my mother since she was so sick. I thought maybe I would make her more ill or she would be too weak to handle it. One day we were sitting in the kitchen and she says, "What are you going to do?" when I told her about breaking up with my husband and getting a divorce. I could see her worry and her pain as if she were reliving her breakup with my father. She said, "You seem so happy," and I said, "Yes, Mom." I also told her, "You cannot base my breakup off of yours. Remember I am a product of you, and if you could do it I can do it. I have a good profession and I can support myself and my kids." She shifted at that point and she totally got it. I could see the relief in her face. I still could not come out and tell her about my sexuality yet.

Finally we were lying next to each other one day as she was resting and I said, "Mom, there is something I need to tell you," and she said, "What?" I said, "Well, you know I really love women." And she said, "Yes." I said, "I mean I want to have a love relationship with a woman." She said, "That is okay" and that she loved me no matter what. Boy, was that a big relief! I often wonder how I would feel now if I hadn't told her and if she had passed away without knowing. I realize that I needed to share this with her even though I knew that she loved me unconditionally.

That was my coming-out experience. It was really important for me to be able to let my family know that I was liberating myself from the traditional roles and expectations that are so prevalent in my cultural upbringing. I am so grateful to be living in these times, as I reflect on my grandmother's and mother's stories. Without their stories and struggles I would not be where I am today. My mother raised us to be so independent—especially her daughters as a result of her struggles, I am sure. She wanted us to be ready for whatever came our way in order to meet our goals.

Now I was ready to let her go and she was close to leaving. We both were starting new journeys in a way. And I was revisiting the path I once avoided but this time would pursue it without any fears. This new sense of freedom was very liberating and energizing at the same time. I was ready to meet a woman I could experience a deep sense of love with. I went on to have a meaningful relationship for seven and a half years with a beautiful woman, a year after my mother died in 1996. Our life paths eventually led us in different directions, but we allowed each other to move on, and I spread my wings and flew.

This is when I began to seek to strengthen my spirituality by exploring indigenous ways of praying. My first mentor in the world of alternative medicine was Gloria and her stepson, who is a spiritual shaman in Santa Fe. We had a good connection. I asked her stepson before I left Denver if I could study with him. He held sweat lodges every weekend and said I was welcome to go whenever I wanted. I would go up to Santa Fe on the weekends for sweat lodge, and sometimes I would go to Albuquerque or I would travel home to Denver. I wanted to learn the ways of praying from the indigenous part of me. I wanted to be connected with my ancestors. This was a phenomenal experience that has really given me a better connection to spirituality. I can relate to Mother Nature and what it feels like to respect our earth and all living things.

This was a major healing time in my life. I had been doing all this work over the years and doing a lot of writing and reading while in New Mexico. It was a time for solitude. For the first time in my life I was doing my thing solo, no kids, spouse, lovers, or family. I was enjoying all the new encounters I was making during this exploration of life.

My educational experiences throughout my life had been primarily through alternative realms of education. At Escuela Tlatelolco the grade levels were named after the tribes of Mesoamerican history—Olmeca, Maya, Tolteca, Teotihuacano, Zapoteca, Mixteca, and Nahuatlacas. We learned about the history of these tribes as we completed the year in that grade level. Upon graduation I went straight to college, although it was a challenging time because my brother had passed away and my mom was in mourning. I then went on to complete my bachelor's degree, then the physician's assistant program in 1990, and my master's in medical science a few years later. During my course of education as a physician's assistant I was introduced to alternative medicine when I wrote a paper on *curanderismo* to share the knowledge of healers from the Southwest and herbal medicine with my classmates. This form of medicine had not been integrated at all into the curriculum of health sciences. In order to address this void in my education I went out to meet Ana Vigil, a *curandera*, and she led me to other practitioners of alternative medicine including her niece, Gloria, who became one of my teachers, and Dolores, who furthered my knowledge of essential oils and encouraged me to take a course in bodywork practices such as neuroenergetic release (NER). I've also trained in self-development paths such as the Avatar courses that I call the "total mind detox." I am an Avatar Master/Wizard, which is what gives me the foundation and tools to be free of all indoctrination—I feel freedom completely from a place of "I am."

The combination of the knowledge of cleansing our bodies with the total mind detox has really been my way of living and teaching the healing strengths of tapping into energy medicine and being a facilitator of it by being part of people's transformation. I help people with my tools every day of my life, and I have gathered a pretty comprehensive set of tools. This is the high point for me out of all the knowledge I have gained in both worlds of medicine. Life is so full of possibilities, and there is so much to experience.

More recently, I went to the Pine Ridge Indian Reservation in South Dakota, where I was embraced and taken in by the community. It felt like home, and the lessons I learned were amazing, as this was the first time in my life that I ever lived completely alone. I never thought that the big-city girl could be the little-town lady. I connected with the land first, which connected me to the Mitakuye (relatives) of the Oglala *oyate* (which means "scatters their own nation" people). I shared my oils, helping to reconnect them to the earth's healing properties, as they have been bombarded with Indian Health Services healthcare as their only source of medical care besides their own traditional healers. The community was poverty-stricken due to acculturation and dependency, which led to the loss of traditional ways of healing and their replacement by the quick fix of short-term remedies and short-lived gratification. Just put a bandage on it, and take this pill while you are at it, so you do not have to feel or do what is necessary to balance your spiritual, physical, emotional, and mental states of being. It is like the oils sparked their olfactory systems to the memory of natural healing that is in their DNA. Among modeling examples of healthy ways of living, my health-nut ways touched those around me who to this day still remember and have made various adjustments to their diets with the understanding that food is medicine. I was able to use all my tools I had acquired over the years and just be me, without expectations or judgments. My truth to my life purpose was felt and received. I will always have a place in my heart for and connection to the Oglala *oyate*.

I returned home, where my daughter was preparing to give birth to her first child and my son had just been released from the prison system. I needed to return home to see my children and to be a grandmother and soon become recognized as an elder now in my community. I know and understand the importance of the role of grandparents and saw the effects of the lack of grandparents on the reservation due to the Oglala Lakota having the lowest life expectancy in the country. Their health status is yet another form of genocide of Native Americans, causing a breakdown in the family unit, with so many not making it to become elders who can pass on the traditions to the grandchildren. Needless to say, the birth of my grandchild called me back home.

This is the story of my deliberate pursuit of freedom. This is the path I will continue to walk and strive for every day. Now I am ready to celebrate freedom with my lifetime partner. Movement is in a forward direction with my goal to follow my drive to maintain a state of freedom and be in constant flight. I love life and consider myself a love warrior. I was put on this earth to be love and be a promoter of love. I love learning and exploring. I appreciate all the moments that life has to give. I live for the moment and in each moment I know that anything is possible and creates the next moments to come. This is what living is all about to me.

Without my experience in the movement and gaining an understanding of my ancestry's rich culture, I would not have gained the awareness of how to navigate through the maze of the traditional educational system. Learning how to succeed in academia was only one side; I later had to succeed on a spiritual level. Ultimately, I have to say that it was my mother who left an everlasting impression on the missing link of the Chicano movement—that is, the lack of spiritual connection in the *movimiento*. The Catholic Church was our people's indoctrinated religion that was forced on our indigenous ancestors by the Spaniards. This was something that the Chicano movement strayed away from due to the hypocrisy of the Church, although for my mom, Catholicism was an important touchstone. Therefore, my quest to grow in my spiritual connection came from my mother, although I chose instead to reconnect to spiritual practices of my indigenous blood, which led me to where I am in my spiritual journey. Tapping into the divine consciousness is where true success is achieved, through happiness and understanding that anything is possible.

21 MANIFESTO DE MEMORIA

(RE)LIVING THE MOVEMENT WITHOUT BLINKING

INÉS HERNÁNDEZ-ÁVILA

A veces soy como el rio
Llego cantando
Y sin que nadie lo sepa viday
Me voy llorando

—ATAHUALPA YUPANQUI, "PIEDRA Y CAMINO"

Twice in my life, once in Mexico and once in Venezuela, I've been told by individuals, "Me gusta como te manifiestas" (I like the way you manifest yourself). I am struck by that expression, those are the only two times in my life I've heard it, and I took it in as a profound validation, one that seems to connect with *conciencia*. It makes me think, in fact, of some black-and-white raw footage I saw of the demonstration at Tlatelolco Plaza on October 2, 1968. The footage did not show up close the actual massacre that happened that day, but I do remember seeing chaos break out in the film.[1] I recall the masses of students and supporters, in the streets, on tops of cars, in windows, everywhere, holding signs, banners, shouting, chanting. Two of the huge banners are engraved on my spirit: "Prohibido prohibir al pueblo!" and "Tu presencia es la manifestación de tu conciencia!" *Manifestar, manifiesto* imply an act of consciousness, intention, *compromiso*. My consciousness manifests itself in the way I am, with myself, with others.

The Chicano movement of the sixties and seventies (especially the latter) was pivotal in my formation as an activist, feminist, intellectual, poet, and cultural worker. This essay is a portion of my *auto-historia*, my *testimonio* about those movement years, and I want to address the following questions: How have Chicana feminists and activists developed their own theories and praxes as a result of their participation in multiple movement spaces, and how has that experience of multiplicity shaped the political subject of Chicana feminism? What are

FIGURE 21.1. Inés Hernández-Ávila in the fields. © Fred Garza.

some of the histories that have not been told about Chicana feminist organizing and leadership?

My own multiple movement spaces that definitely impacted my framings and praxes, include(d): MAYO; Raza Unida Party (and the Mujeres Caucus within the RUP); the student movement at the University of Houston to create Chicana/o studies; links with the American Indian movement; the Brown Berets; the United Farm Workers Union and the Texas Farm Workers Union; my participation in the Floricanto festivals in Austin and San Antonio; my membership in CASA, Chicanas/os Artistas Sirviendo a Aztlán, in Austin; my participation in *danza conchera* through the group Xinachtli in Texas and California; my position as assistant professor in Mexican American studies, American studies, and English at the University of Texas, Austin (1975–1978); my position as interim director of Ethnic Studies at then-named Texas A&I, Kingsville (1978–1979); and my membership in two *teatro* groups, albeit briefly, Teatro de los Barrios, San Antonio, and Teatro los Malqueridos, Kingsville.

In Texas I led solidarity movement events for some American Indian causes, and I felt deeply connected to elders I met through the White Roots of Peace touring group (emanating from the Akwesasne Mohawk Nation) that had visited different cities in the state and country, especially Phillip Deere, one of the main spiritual leaders of the American Indian Movement (AIM), whom I consider one of my life mentors. I visited his land several times, to attend his Youth and Elders gatherings, in Okemah, Oklahoma, and I brought him to Austin and San Antonio. When I moved to California in January 1982, I began to be connected to Native American ceremonial circles where I came to know other elders who would be immensely important to my spiritual path, such as Raymond Stone, the beloved Paiute elder that I knew as Grampa Raymond. I taught, lived, and served as a board member at the tribal college, D-Q University at Davis, California, in the early to mid-eighties, during the time when DQU was sued by the US Department of Education, and DQU sued back and reached a settlement that awarded the college deed to half of the acreage of the land.[2] At DQU in January 1982 I took part in the international tribunal that brought Ronald Reagan to trial for crimes against humanity; it was at this tribunal that I first met Rigoberta Menchú, who at a young age already had such an astounding presence. At DQU, a while afterwards, I met Paulo Freire and had some brief but fulfilling conversations with him and was on a panel with him; he wanted for himself my copy of *Pedagogy of the Oppressed* because of all the marginal notations I had made, in different colors of ink, that showed I had read the book again and again. I could not give up my copy to him, but I am deeply grateful for having met him. He signed my book, saying he would like to have known *Pedagogy* through my reading of it.

It was important to me to be involved with media during these times. In the early 1970s in Houston, I had a television program on Sunday mornings titled *¡Vámonos!* (as in "Let's get going with movement!"). The title came from a poem by Alurista that issued a call to arms: "Vámonos a hacer la lucha, vámonos a hacer la guerra, cultivando corazones, con amor y sabiduría." Unfortunately, I have no recordings of those shows, but I was proud of the openings I was making for coverage of the political awakenings in our community. In the late eighties I took part in two collectives that produced radio programming for KPFA in Berkeley—*Living on Indian Time* and *En Contacto Directo*. For ten years I had monthly segments of each program (as the producer and board operator for my segments), and again, I did my best to cover issues that mattered.

I was a single mother when I went back to graduate school at the University of Houston in 1971, with sons two and three years old. What I remember about those movement years is that children were not so welcome in movement circles at the time, so I recall and cherish those individuals who were kind and generous to my sons. During the seventies, I was in and out of relationships, one very positive one that was longer-lasting (five years) and others that were more short-lived. I spent some of those years as a clearly single woman, a whole being, which included my sexual being, and it was a time of "free love" and "We *mujeres* can do anything that a man can do." While Chicana feminist leadership and organizing in the public sphere did happen and it happened powerfully, in the private sphere, often women had hard times, some harder than others, for various reasons. These private stories, intimate narratives, will come out directly when they will, or they might appear creatively, in art, literature, theater.

On my father's side, I am Tejana through and through, which means I have a deeply rooted connection to the land where I was born, to the Texas/Mexican/indigenous earth, to *la cultura* Tejana. On my mother's side, I am Nimipu (Nez Perce) of Chief Joseph's band, which means I am of the band that ended up, through historical circumstance, on the Colville Reservation in northeastern Washington, not in Lapwai, Idaho, on the Nez Perce Reservation. I am enrolled Colville, but I am Nez Perce. Our original homelands are in the Wallowa Valley of Oregon. I grew up negotiating these identities; as a child, finding myself perplexed so often because of Mexican racism toward anything "Indian," my Indianness was something I kept to myself, intuiting that the topic would be troubling if I brought it up. Because of my gracious mom, I managed to navigate this subdued tension fairly smoothly. During the movement years, I felt respected for being both Tejana and Nez Perce; it was a wonderful feeling. It was afterward that I began to have to steel myself for the assaults on my person for being of both heritages. I have come to understand that this aggression has little to do with me but is the result of culturally racist programming that some (on both my "sides") refuse to surrender. From my parents and grandparents I learned the heartfelt, spirit-full meaning of dignity, self-respect, integrity, honesty, and courage. I owe my lucidity to my early upbringing, even though I came to test that lucidity through my movement experience(s). My foundational blueprint, then, is a fusion of what I learned from my own *familia en Tejas*, my family in Nespelem, Washington, and the *movimiento*, most of which was lived social, cultural, political experience, although, of course, I was also reading voraciously. From my childhood, I asked questions. I always wanted to pursue more, find more, uncover more.

As a child, I was privileged intellectually, the only daughter of my parents (no siblings), the first granddaughter of my grandfather's second marriage. My parents and grandparents raised me and all of my cousins with the mantra "Get an education." I was nurtured to excel in public school, and from kindergarten I was tracked by teachers into the "successful classes," where there were no other persons of color but me. Galveston was not yet integrated—there were separate schools for African American students. At Alamo Elementary, Lovenberg Junior High, and Ball High School, the Mexicans were tracked into either the "slower" classes (at the primary level) or the vocational education classes in junior high and high school. Not me. I was always in the top classes. I knew most of the white students from kindergarten through high school graduation. Two distinguished students who were in my cohort through high school were Albert Kauffman, who has long been a noted lawyer for MALDEF, and Elizabeth Jameson, feminist scholar in the Department of History at the University of Calgary. I have kept in touch with both of them, especially Betsy. Albert, Betsy, and I have talked about writing something together someday about our growing-up years.

My dad was a carpenter, from a line of *carpinteros*, and he was brilliant with math and science, so he was my tutor whenever I had questions. My mom was a housewife who took me faithfully to the library so that I could check out the seven-book maximum, especially in the summers. I remember one summer, probably between fifth and sixth grades, I read mythology from all over the world; between sixth and seventh, I read all of John Steinbeck. My mother was my literary muse and my first reader. Neither of my parents finished high school, but both of them encouraged my intellect, my artwork, my creativity. I was supremely fortunate because they loved each other and were faithful to each other, they both had a wonderful sense of humor, and they were just. My dad was a union man and someone who would help family, neighbors in need, friends, and the community in general at any time but especially when natural disasters like hurricanes struck. Both of them respected the earth and all the animal relations.

Did I notice discrimination when I was a kid? Yes. Did I know how to name it? Did I have the words? Not yet. But I never forgot what I saw. In elementary school I wondered why in fourth grade, "4 C" had all Mexican students, "4 B" had mostly white students and two Mexicans, and "4 A" had all whites. And me. I did notice, mostly in elementary school, that some students were troubled that I was different; they tried to mask it, but I felt it. As I progressed through junior high and high school, mostly other students liked me. I got along with my classmates, and many of my good friends were white; we used to get into silly competitions sometimes about who had the best grade on an exam or a paper. Throughout junior high and high school, I showed my *cariño* and solidarity with my *comunidad* by eating lunch at their tables, hanging out with them. I also deliriously loved *la música* Tejana, so as soon as I was old enough, the *bailes* were where I wanted to be on Saturday nights. There was a part of me that wondered if my white friends, as we got older, would want to socialize with me outside of classes and school events, but it was a tiny part, since I truly loved *bailes*.

I do remember some of my Mexicana friends telling me, "¡Ay, Inés cómo te gustan los libros!" I really was a nerd. I didn't have the looks, the figure, the audacity that many of my Mexicana schoolmates had (probably my white friends, too, but I didn't pay attention to their *cualidades*). In my social circles, I saw which girls were super-popular with the boys, and I was definitely not one of them, even though I yearned to know what that felt like. Everyone basically understood that I was dedicated to reading and studying. When I graduated, one of the Mexicano students told me he really wished me well because he knew I would do something with my life. I still remember that moment and his face and name.

My political consciousness was raised significantly in junior high when a white girlfriend challenged me to run for treasurer of the Student Council. Or rather, she accosted me and told me she knew I was running and she wanted me to know she was also going after that position. I kept telling her I had no idea what she was talking about, but she kept insisting so much that I finally said, "OK, I am running." She said, "I knew it!" But what she wasn't counting on (and what I hadn't quite realized) is that I had many of the white votes and a big number of the Mexicano votes, so I won! I don't know why, but she tried to beat me for the same position in high school, and history repeated itself. I won again. I learned something important then about coalitions, solidarity, and community building.

My experiences in the public school system in Galveston were riveting for me in many ways. I still remember things fairly clearly, and I go back to those experiences in my creative work. Even though I had started writing poetry in elementary school (very bad poetry), it was not until I became *concientizada en el movimiento* that my work began to really speak. My first real poem had to do with something that happened to me in sixth grade, at Alamo Elementary School, and I first read it in 1975 at the Festival Floricanto in Austin at a literary reading in the auditorium of Metz Elementary School. Alurista was the MC. As the writers went up to read their works, I started burning with something to say. I grabbed a piece of paper and began writing so fast I could hardly keep up with myself. When the open-mic segment of the evening started, I went up and read my poem, "Para Teresa"—it is still the best-known of my poems and has been reprinted countless times. I received room-filling applause when I finished, and Alurista walked up to me and said, "¿No que no?" The poem is dedicated to a girl who was a *pachuca* at Alamo Elementary. We didn't really know each other, but one day she and some of her buddies caught me alone in the girls' bathroom. They wouldn't let me out and she yelled at me,

> *que porqué me creía tan grande.*
> *What was I trying to do, you growled*
> *Show you up?*
> *Make the teacher like me, pet me,*
> *Tell me what a credit to my people I was?*
> *I was playing right into their hands, you challenged,*
> *And you would have none of it,*
> *I was to stop.* [3]

Teresa was smart and an awesome critical thinker. She saw the game that institutions play, what happens when some of us are singled out to succeed so that we can be manipulated into working against our very own people. Malcolm X's "house slave" versus "field slave," in a way. [4] At the moment that she challenged me, I wasn't thinking all of this. I answered her,

> *My fear salted with confusion*
> *Charged me to explain to you*
> *I did nothing for the teacher,*
> *I studied for my parents and for my grandparents*
> *Who cut out honor roll lists*
> *Whenever their nietos' names appeared*

For my shy mother who mastered her terror
To demand her place in mothers' clubs
For my carpenter father who helped me patiently with my math,
For my abuelos que me regalaron lapices en la Navidad
And for myself.

I told Teresa that we were both rebels, in different ways. I told her that our people were "good, honorable, brave / genuine, loyal, strong / And smart." I had to show them who we were, and "if I could do it, we all could." She let me go then, and in the poem, so many years later, I pay her my respects and ask her permission to call her *hermana*. What I didn't say in the poem but what was also a driving force for me was the fact that my paternal grandparents had both learned to speak and write perfect English; my Papá Sabas (my grandfather) taught citizenship classes and was a respected carpenter in Galveston; my Mamá Inés also claimed her space in mothers clubs, Mothers of the Marines (my father), Mothers of the Army (my twin uncles), Mothers of the Navy (my youngest uncle). My father and his siblings all returned from World War II; the family says my grandmother lost her eyesight in one eye because she cried and prayed so much. But in the poem, I do acknowledge what I always admired in *pachucas/os*, and in the *raza* living in the barrios who are likely to get pulled over by the police simply for "walking the wrong way." I admire(d) their fierce dignity, their rebellious head-held-high pride, no matter what was done to them, no matter what was said to them. I saw it even as a child.

From my protected vantage point (in comparison) I had to show the institution how capable I and, by extension, our community was. There was no way the teachers could get around my performance as a student. There was no way they could get around my grades and my popularity. Fanny Howe writes, in *Winter Sun*,

> People who are destabilized by historical forces are more intelligent than the secure ones who have got the formulas in place. The safety of received tastes and opinions, confirmed in furniture and inherited artworks, stops the true brain, the brain of the seeking blind. When people are uprooted and insecure, the tables are alive with the conversation of prophets—philosophy, music, literature, God. But when people are safe, the repetition of a formula goes around and around.[5]

I love this passage from Howe, and I think about it in relation to myself, Teresa, *la pachuca al alba*, and the rest of us. I also know that Galveston was a port of entry to many Jewish refugees of the Holocaust, so they too were uprooted and insecure, in their own way, and many of them were my friends. En fin, sabía como llevarme bién con la gente, como respetar. Again, this was something learned from my parents and grandparents.

Even though I was in all the advanced-placement classes and a straight-A honors student, even though I came in two-tenths of a point behind the valedictorian and one-tenth of a point behind the salutatorian, no counselor in high school ever encouraged me to go to college. I think I applied because my parents and grandparents trusted that this was my path. I graduated from high school in June 1965 and started college that fall at the University of Houston. However, I was already smitten with a young Mexicano, a roofer I had met in Houston, at a *baile*; my parents had taken me and one of my *primas* to a dance. I danced with this person all night, and when I started college, I began to get to know him better. He ended up becoming my first husband and the father to my two (and only) sons. I will not go into my life with him here—that is another story; suffice to say that I experienced times of unspeakable violence with him. I left him before my second son was born, and after he was born, we divorced.

APRIL 7, HIDDEN POEMS DAY

I woke up this morning to hear on NPR
today is a "Tribute to Hidden Poems Day"
the date is already a poem,
the birth day of the father of my sons,
who would know that we would come together
to bring two beings into the world
who would know that sometimes that is all that comes from a relationship
an all that is enormous and amazing
I give thanks always
APRIL 7, 2013

When I divorced, I was still in school, finishing a bachelor of arts in English. The significance of this part of my life is that when I got involved in social movements, I was a single mother. I remember that there were so few Mexicanos at the University of Houston we would make sure to at least nod at each other when we passed on the sidewalks. Finally, someone thought of organizing a group called LOMAS, League of Mexican American Students, which ended up being a forerunner to MAYO on that campus. The United Farm Workers were already going strong, so LOMAS addressed farmworker issues and issues on the campus. I went to some of the early meetings, but I could not really get involved. I had two very young sons, born in 1968 and 1969, and I was doing all I could to graduate.

I finished my degree in 1970, with the support of my parents, and started teaching high school. I loved the students but hated the rigid, doctrinaire nature of the public school system. By then I was keeping up with whatever was coming out regarding Chicanos and American Indians. I subscribed to the Quinto Sol publication *El Grito: A Journal of Mexican American Thought*, reading each volume completely. I loved *El Espejo: The Mirror*, an anthology of literature also published by Quinto Sol, and I still think Octavio Romano's creative writings are critically powerful; I appreciated Romano's early complicating of essentialist notions of Chicano culture.[6] Tomás Rivera's novel . . . *y no se lo tragó la tierra* blew me away, as did Rudy Anaya's novel *Bless Me, Ultima* (I cried from laughing so much at the Christmas scene the boys performed).[7] I later met both Rivera and Anaya and considered them cherished mentors. On the Indian side, I learned of the early activism, I was reading the American Indian newspaper *Akwesasne Notes*, published by the Mohawk Nation, and anything else I could find. I knew something huge was happening and I wanted to be a part of it. When I decided to go to graduate school, I was advised by one of the English Department faculty to pursue a Ford Foundation Doctoral Fellowship (which is what it was called back then), so I applied and I was successful.

In 1971 I returned to graduate school, to pursue a PhD in English, and I became involved in MAYO and Raza Unida Party as an activist and organizer. At the time, MAYO had several committees: Raza Unida Party, United Farm Workers support, Student Support Services for Chicano students, and Mexican American studies, among others. Many of the students on the University of Houston campus were activists and organizers on campus and in the community. Daniel Bustamante, María Jiménez, Eddy Canales, Eduardo Castillo, still known as "El Profe," Eskimo Rodriguez, Evangelina Vigil, Elliott Navarro, Sra. Zapata in the community, and more. María Jiménez was a brilliant, sophisticated young student, debate champion, well versed in Mexican history, culture, and politics as well as Mexican American issues. She was the archfeminist when the rest of us were just starting to grow our feminist wings. María is the person who introduced me to *la obra de Sor Juana Inés de la Cruz*, and María is the one who advised all the women organizers what *not* to do if we wanted the men to pay attention to us as thinkers, as intellectuals, as organizers: "Don't go to bed with them." Hmmm. She said this to us at a time when we were feeling our freedom; we were away from home, not bound by parental restrictions, everything in the air was about *mujeres* doing whatever they wanted, whenever, and with whomever they wanted. For her part, she didn't sleep with any of the men, and when she spoke, they were most reverent in their attention. Granted, she was an astute organizer and thinker, so that would have happened no matter what.

Being in the *movimiento* and being an engaged *mujer*, an activist, organizer, and sexual being, was difficult, maybe more so for some of us who were still hung up on the way relationships "were supposed to be," whatever that was, and for those of us who were not attached by wedlock, because it seemed to me that women who were married were off limits for harassment since they had their husbands to back them up (although these married women might have suffered their own kind of abuse in their marital relationships). Regarding our emerging feminism, what I noticed was that intellectually we were more than ready to espouse and vehemently defend women's rights, women's leadership, and women's participation and demand that women's issues be integrated into the political agendas of the movement. We were also ready to defend our sisters from abusive relationships. The untangling of old learned patterns of behavior in our own relationships was another matter. Patriarchy and misogyny showed their suffocating reach over and over again in daily life. We quickly learned that anything we did that appeared out of line with male-prescribed behavior could get us called all kinds of names, not the least of which were *puta, traicionera, cabrona, mala mujer.*

I wrote a poem to respond to these assaults, "Testimonio de Memoria: For all the mujeres de movimiento que saben de estas cosas,"[8] and it was published in 1992. In the poem I talk about my own feminist strategies for living through the judgment and derision, for staying connected to community and to the vision of a transformed pueblo. On-the-ground feminism was tough. I ask the *mujeres que saben de estas cosas* to remember with me.

> *Friendship, trust sisterhood*
> *Brotherhood tú sabes*
> *Carnalismo*
> *Were concepts remembered*
> *With each head throb*
> *Of the morning after cruda*
> *The waking up in strange rooms*
> *Where the ceiling and wallpaper*
> *Told you you hadn't been* there *before*
> *Looking at the figure smiling at you*
> *From the entrance to the room*
> *Or waking up with someone wrapped*
> *Around you*
> *Who had finally given up struggling*
> *To take off your dress*
> *That you had on over your body suit*
> *That you had on over your hose*
> *Some people could care less*
> *If you're conscious or not*
> *You know*

The sexual politics of the times were weird, a kind of super-crazy Nepantla. It's easy to point fingers, and sometimes they need to be pointed. I know there were sexual assaults, abuse, even rapes, that were never reported—nor did it occur to women to report them; it was an in-house *movimiento* kind of thing. A woman needing help with her car knowing that she would have to put out for the *compañero en la lucha* who helped her. A woman asking a *compañero* known to sell *mota* to bring her a joint and discovering that he assumed that what she really meant was that she wanted to have sex with him. A woman known for her strength and *coraje* being told by her *compañero* to not show him up, to stay more in the background, so that he would be the one with presence, all the while him puffing up with pride because she was *his* woman, and as his *camaradas* could see, he had her under control. Many, many stories.

I know that for many of us women, we were figuring out our feminism; we were determining what was wrong, what we wouldn't put up with, how we would respond. In "Testimonio de Memoria," I say that for me, my strategy was to arrive late at a party and sometimes sneak out early to avoid all the wrangling over hookups.

> if you told a sister that someone
> satisfied you, pués,
> she'd want some, too
> and the guys you thought were your bros
> asked if they could mess around with you
> and the husbands or boyfriends of your
> good friends wanted some, too
> . . . you saw the different levels of reality
> happening all at once at those times.

The poem covers a lot of territory, but in the end I say that I still show up for events, political, cultural, and otherwise, and I don't care if people call me *traicionera*.

> si no conformo
> Eso es
> No estoy conforme
> Así que cómo me puedo conformar?
> . . .
> y doy gracias que mi lengua es mía
> y es libre
> y grita
> y llora
> y canta
> y demanda
> y reclama
> > por la justicia verdadera
> > y la justiciera paz

Sadly, this poem still holds true, as I've heard from young Chicanas. They still get hit with "Are you down with the people?" (read: "the men"), and if you are, you won't say anything about sexual violence or abuse. I think if anything was difficult, sometimes devastatingly painful, during those times it was the sexual politics. It is hard to know that this hasn't changed (as I hear often from my young students). And yet, women and men worked together strategically and forcefully to call for the change(s) we wanted. As a member of MAYO, when I was a graduate student at the University of Houston, I helped to create Mexican American studies. We lobbied, occupied the chancellor's office, did what we had to, to achieve getting the program started and getting more services for Chicano students. Since I was a graduate student in the English Department, I could petition to teach a sophomore-level course on a topic of my choosing (I wish current PhD programs had this luxury). I petitioned to teach Chicano literature, and since I was a graduate student with a solid track record, it should have been a slam-dunk. But one of the faculty who was starting to claim a space for himself as a specialist in "ethnic literature" balked at my proposal. He asked to meet with me, and in our meeting, this professor who had never questioned my performance suddenly doubted my ability to use English properly, to my face. I reported him to the department, and he lost his position as graduate adviser, and I was awarded the course. The course filled when I taught it—all the student activists took the course, and then some. I had students like Cynthia Pérez, Luciano Salinas, Robert Perez, Anna Olivarez, and others in the class. We were energized with our victory and exhilarated to be studying the literature of our own community with each other.

In 1975, I took my first tenure-track appointment at UT Austin; I went there ABD. I continued with MAYO (as faculty sponsor), and what students there were! Roberto Calderón, David Rojas, and others, from Eagle Pass, Texas, as well as Edward Martinez, Benigna Rodriguez, so many others. Just as at the University of Houston, I might have been the one with more advanced degrees, but these students were also my teachers (I also wasn't so much older than them—in 1975, I was twenty-eight). We recommended books, music, to each other, had provocative discussions, talked about our hopes for the community. This was when I met and came to be *amigas del alma* with Gloria Anzaldúa and Yolanda Leyva. These are friendships *por vida y hasta más allá*, as with Gloria, who is one of my wondrous muses. In Austin, one of the most heartening revelations for me was the strong passion my *compañeras/os* had for cultural work and the arts (literature, visual art, performance) as legitimate and powerful forms of activism.

As a faculty member at the University of Texas, I remained active with the *partido*, as a local and statewide organizer, but I also came out as a poet, a creative writer, and a performer. I had started playing the guitar and often sang Latin American New Song movement songs (Violeta Parra's songs were favorites to me) along with my readings, or sometimes songs from the *movimiento*. I was an organizer of the San Antonio Festival Floricanto and a member of CASA, a collective of artists, writers, musicians that I believe numbered about twenty at our largest. We had an effective strategy for performing wherever we were invited. We figured out who could be at the event, and then we decided on a plan for our performance. Who would go first, who would follow, what songs we would sing, if there would be any kind of *teatro*, and where it would go. The real musicians (which I was not; I only knew a few chords with which to sing songs) would back up the ones who needed backing up. We usually made room for an open mic as well. As our finale, we often concluded with a song like "La media vuelta" that we knew the community would probably know, and we invited them to sing with us.

The CASA experience was intense and something I will not forget. We knew how to acknowledge each other and we worked hard. When I moved to California, one of the things I missed most, missed deeply, was the sense of a collective. It seemed to me in California, artists were much more individualistic. But then I was a diasporic Tejana; I don't know if that had anything to do with anything. In CASA some of the principles that guided us emerged from our readings of ancient Nahuatl philosophy, principally through very careful attention to Miguel León-Portilla's *Aztec Thought and Culture* (1990).[9] *In xochitl in cuicatl*, *flor-i-canto*, flower-and-song, was the Nahuatl *difrasismo* for poetry, for searching for truth in your heart. Many of us, in Texas, California, and other places, took to this concept and thus the Floricanto festivals burst forth, in California (1973), Austin (1975), San Antonio (1976), Albuquerque (1977), Tempe (1978), and then the Cantos al Pueblo took over, starting in the Midwest, going to the Fort McDowell Indian Reservation, then Corpus Christi (where virtuoso accordionist Esteban Jordán took part). These festivals brought artists, writers, and musicians together from all over the country; no one had their way paid. The on-site organizers were responsible for arranging lodging and meals for the participants and for setting up the reading and performance schedules on campuses and in the communities, at schools, senior citizen centers, cultural centers, wherever they were welcome. The impact was amazing; the spark that was struck in the communities was uplifting, energizing, inspirational for all ages. Art, music, poetry, *teatro*, all contributed to an immense recovery of our selves, a remembering of who we were and are, a healing, personal and collective, that gave us strength, courage, life force.

In Austin, CASA took off with the concept of *in xochitl in cuicatl*. We went into the public schools, grades K–12, and asked teachers to let us provide workshops about *floricanto* for their students—we did writing and art workshops with the students, and then we started getting invited by the teachers to give them workshops because they got it, they understood how nurturing creativity helped the whole child, the whole young person. At some point along the way, someone asked us why we hadn't applied to the Austin Arts Council to get funds to support our work. What a revelation! We did that and suddenly we were actually getting paid to do the workshops. We organized local Floricanto festivals where we highlighted and validated the work of the students in the schools. Juan Tejeda is the institutional memory of CASA; he was a meticulous record-keeper; he saved the flyers and other documentation of everything we did.

Tied to *floricanto*, of course, is the other important concept from the ancient Nahuatl philosophical tradition—*in ixtli in yollotl*, *cara-y-corazón*, face-and-heart, the term that describes their principle of education. True education was when the wise *tlamatinime*, the good teacher, nurtured the students so that their faces and hearts would emerge fully. This was what we needed to read, to have sink in to our *conciencias*; this is what our young people needed, not a violent institutional structure that would continuously dehumanize them, degrade them, belittle them, cause them to suffer, and push them out. Some say that the ancient

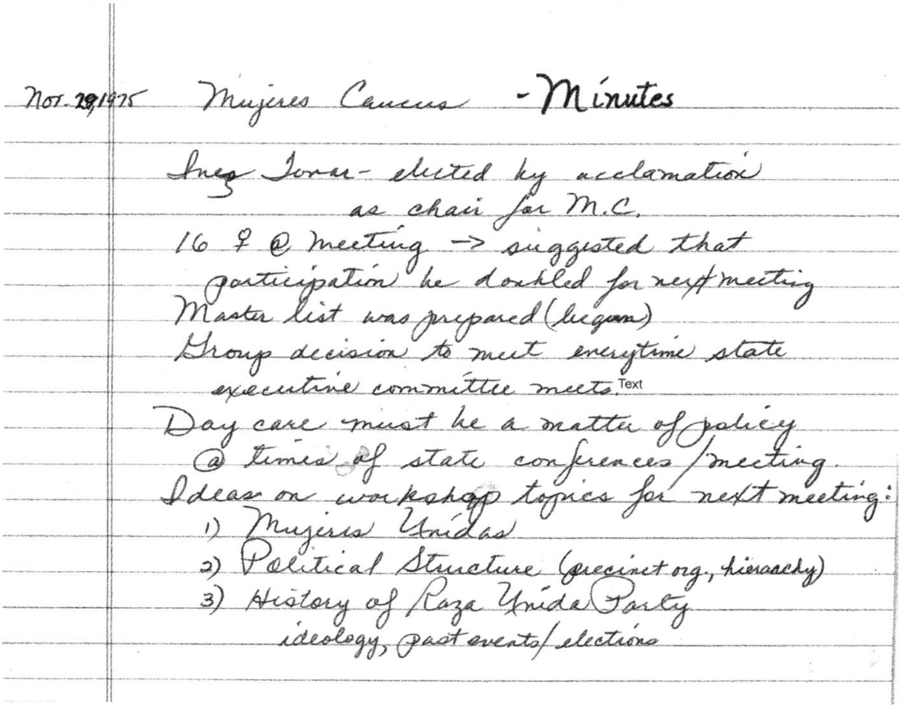

Nov. 29/1975   Mujeres Caucus   - Minutes

Ines Tovar - elected by acclamation
          as chair for M.C.
16 ♀ @ meeting → suggested that
    participation be doubled for next meeting
Master list was prepared (began)
Group decision to meet everytime state
    executive committee meets. Text
Day care must be a matter of policy
    @ times of state confrences / meeting.
Ideas on workshop topics for next meeting:
    1) Mujeres Unidas
    2) Political Structure (precinct org, hierarchy)
    3) History of Raza Unida Party
         ideology, past events / elections

FIGURE 21.2. Handwritten minutes, RUP Mujeres Caucus.

Nahuas were hierarchical in their societal structures, but what Chicanas/os did was to take this concept and democratize it, immediately. This was something we could use, this was something that made sense, and it came from what Pawnee legal scholar and Native rights activist Walter Echo-Hawk would call "indigenous wisdom traditions."[10] I have been writing about how this philosophy of education actually resonates with Paulo Freire's "education as the practice of liberation." Praxis: action and reflection. *In xochitl in cuicatl*: the path to truth that comes with reflection, deep reflection, in the heart. We were reading both of these texts and others back then, but I recently decided that I need to write about how I have brought the two together, because what matters to me most, then and now, is the link between creativity, autonomy (personal and collective), critical inquiry, and spirituality.

I think that the idea of *cara-y-corazón*, which for me is deeply related to personal and collective autonomy, manifested in the efforts of women organizers in the *partido*. We were intent on helping to bring forth the faces-and-hearts of the women in our *comunidad*. During my first year in Austin (1975) the women in Raza Unida created the Mujeres Caucus as a standing committee of the party. I was elected the first chairperson of that caucus, and we set about creating a plan of action to support the women in the *partido* and in the community. What spurred us is that José Ángel Gutiérrez and others had traveled in a delegation to

Cuba and returned, bringing us what they had learned. They came back wanting the formation of a national Federación de Mujeres, modeled on the one in Cuba. They intended to name two women who had not been so involved with us on the ground, so we decided to go an alternative route. We chose to create the Mujeres Caucus and to give it legitimacy in the party by making it a standing committee along with the other Texas Election Code–mandated committees. We had already insisted that each senatorial district have one man and one woman to represent the districts, so we were making good headway. It was inspiring to hear the community women talk about how they had worked to get their husbands to understand the urgency of their participation in the movement and the party. My lifelong friends from the RUP are Irma Mireles and Rosie Castro; I try to see them every time I'm in San Antonio. I recently reconnected with María Elena Martínez, and once in a while I see Martha Cotera, which brings me lots of joy, also. We keep going.

In the spring of 1976 my students and I organized a *mujeres* conference on the University of Texas campus, a gathering that bridged campus and community. Men as well as women participated in "La Mujer en la Comunidad: Ayer, Hoy, y Siempre." Santa Barraza produced our poster. We had sessions on professions, education, politics, social services, legal defense, civic organizations, Chicanas in universities, yerbas/health services, Chicana studies, organizing women's groups, and what I think of as the plenary, Concientización: The Role of the Chicana in Today's Community. The speakers on this panel were Ino Álvarez, Emilio Zamora, Raquel Orendain, David Riojas, Yolanda Santos, and Daniel Bustamante—not surprisingly, most of them Raza Unida Party members and organizers; I'm not sure if Raquel Orendain considered herself a *partido* member, but she was Antonio Orendain's wife and a veteran farmworker organizer and leader with the Texas Farm Workers Union. We thought it was important to have a balance of women and men on this panel and to have the selected men articulate their positions on the topic. Emilio could speak to the role of women in the 1910 Mexican Revolution and the role of women in Laredo, by way of the alternative newspaper *La Crónica* (of the Idar family, including Jovita Idar), and the nexus of the Mexicano community in Laredo with the Partido Liberal Mexicano organizing in Mexico by Sara Estela Ramirez. Some of the other women participants were also major organizers of the RUP: Irma Mireles, Juana Luera, María Elena Martínez, Carmen Zapata.

I received financial support from the Academic Development Funds of the University of Texas, Austin, and from a Modern Language Association grant to organize the conference and to produce a publication, again with my students, which I titled *HEMBRA: Hermanas en Movimiento Brotando Raíces de Aztlán*.[11] Carmen Lomas Garza designed the cover for the publication, which was done in journal format. *HEMBRA* includes poetry by Carmen Tafolla, Janis Palma Castroman, and others; fiction; art and a feature article on Santa Barraza's work; profiles on historical figures Sara Estela Ramirez and Emma Tenayuca; and brief notes on

Chicana activism. It also has articles on the 1959 International Ladies Garment Workers Union strike in San Antonio; the 1972 Farah strike in El Paso, San Antonio, and Victoria, Texas, and Las Cruces, New Mexico; the 1971 march in Pharr, Texas, to protest the shooting death of Alfonso Laredo Flores by local police; and the actions in 1975 by Texas Farm Workers Union women in support of a major strike in West Texas. I have an article in the journal titled "La mujer tejana en la política," in which I name many of the women organizers of Raza Unida. There is a full article on Virginia Muzquiz, a veteran RUP organizer from Crystal City, Texas, as well as an article by Martha Cotera on "Chicanas and Power" and an interview with TFW organizer María Salas titled "Campesina de Texas." I was sad that we were only able to produce one volume of *HEMBRA*, but we sent it out widely, and as a historical document, it is important.

I had and have a deeply immense respect for the Texas Farm Workers Union and for all the *gente* who made up the TFW, especially Antonio Orendain, Raquel Orendain, Jorge Zaragoza, and so many more. Their story has really not been told. Antonio was an amazing man, the "man in black," with his radio program, *La Voz del Campesino*, that reached into Mexico. I remember one march that we did in Laredo, or at least we ended up in Laredo at the border, where we distributed leaflets letting Mexicano workers know about the TFW. I know that the UFW won out in the end, and, of course, I support them, but there is still a part of me that feels that Tony Orendain and the others who were part of the TFW need to be recognized much more for what they did. In the early eighties when I was living and working at the tribal college, DQU in Davis, I was a site coordinator for a Youth and Elders Gathering that brought Native elders together with young people, so that the young ones could learn from them. I brought Antonio Orendain to that gathering as an elder from the Chicano, Mexicano community. I think he felt quite comfortable among all the Native elders.

In 1982 I had ended up in California, first in Fresno, then at Davis—for about two years at DQU and then at UC Davis, where I have been for about thirty years; I was a lecturer at UCD before I went on tenure track in 1989. My trajectory shifted from Texas to California for one major reason. While I was working with CASA and Raza Unida Party and the movement in general in the community, I was also teaching, serving my departments, and creating curricula at UT Austin. My appointment was in English, American studies, and Mexican American studies. I've said often it was like having three jealous lovers. I was never with any of them enough, but my favorite was, of course, Mexican American studies. I actually lost my position at Austin because I didn't finish my dissertation in the three years I was there. Yes, I was an activist, and besides teaching, my passion was the movement. I knew what we were doing, I could feel it, taste it; there would not be another time in my life quite like this one. At the same time, the faculty in Mexican American studies especially, since I spent most of my time with them, did not even think to protect me. I had no mentors to caution me to finish. I had no one, when those first three years were ending, to ask for a one-year extension

FIGURE 21.3. Texas Farm Workers march, Austin, 1977. "Inés—TFW March" © Fred Garza.

for me and the collegial protection from senior faculty that would have allowed me to write—it could have been that simple, I think. While I was on tenure track, I served on program committees, search committees, developed new courses, served as faculty sponsor to MAYO.

My major professor from the University of Houston, in a paternalistic gesture that spoke more to his not wanting one of his students to fail, got me a job offer at the University of Southern California, a lucrative offer including funding for my journal *HEMBRA*, but I said no. He was furious; he told me that if I accepted the position, I would graduate that summer (1978) and if I didn't, he didn't know if I would ever graduate. My children were in grade school; I was a single mother, juggling a triple appointment, and dedicated to the movement, to the women, to what we were creating. I could not see myself in Los Angeles with no family support. I lost my job at UT and floundered for several years, finally finishing my degree in 1984 after going back to the English Department and demanding my right to finish, and after changing my dissertation chair. It was a painful time. Yet, during those floundering years, I was at Texas A&I, where I learned and lived in El Valle, where I remained an activist and organizer—it was in Kingsville where I took part in Teatro los Malqueridos, where I got to know more of the Brown Berets, *los del valle*, including Pablillo, one of the Beret leaders.

I remember one time driving down to the border to pick up the elder Tlacaelel, who had come up from Mexico City with his group to visit, give talks, and support the Texas Farm Workers Union. Tlacaelel had first come to the United States as a member of the White Roots of Peace. After finishing the one-year position in Kingsville I returned to Austin, then Houston, and finally made my way to California, where I became active in Native ceremonial circles and with DQU. My formative years in Texas encompassed Galveston, Houston, Austin, San Antonio, and El Valle, and each of those cities that I visited through the movement, such as Odessa and El Paso. And Mexico! With Teatro de los Barrios of San Antonio, I traveled to Cuernavaca to perform at the Teatro los Mascarones site and at *huelga* sites, and I met a brilliant Catholic Marxist priest, José Luís Calvillo—he was one of the priests working under Bishop Sergio Mendez Arceo. With CASA I visited Albuquerque for Floricanto and the Fort McDowell reservation for Canto al Pueblo, where I met members of the American Indian movement and took part in life-changing ceremonies with them, including those of the Native American Church. It is hard to pinpoint one major site that influenced my formation, but if I had to, I would probably name the Austin-San Antonio connection, the reason being that it is during my time in these two cities where all the aspects of my intellectual, activist, cultural, creative, spiritual identity coalesced.

Speaking for myself, I did develop my own theories and praxes as a result of participating in multiple movement spaces, and I saw and lived this experience of multiplicity with my fused Mexicana, Tejana sensibility and my Native, indigenous sensibility. Hard as it might be for some to understand, within each drop of my blood, the blood of my Nez Perce lineage has united with the blood of my Tejana lineage. These life experiences had an impact on my own political subjectivity as a feminist. I appreciate(d) that during those movement years, everyone in Tejas knew that I was mixed-blood; I felt respected and acknowledged for who I am and for my on-the-ground work. I am grateful for the amazing critical and creative lessons I learned about collective action, organizing, praxis, solidarity.

I think what impacted me deeply, beyond or as well as the no-holds-barred, anything-goes sexual politics, was so often witnessing some version of *patrón/patrona* politics. I remember Guadalupe Youngblood, RUP organizer from Robstown and a leader of the *movimiento* in Texas, saying one time, "Si alguien se cree el líder, hay que cortarle las alas" (If someone thinks himself a leader, we need to cut his wings). It was a statement he made publicly, I don't remember where exactly, but he did not say this just to me personally. I was impressed because the context for his remark was the point that we needed to arrive collectively at decision making. Consensus. Critical consciousness. Freire reminds us to not become what we are fighting against, not to assume patterns of oppression that we detest. I relate Youngblood's comment to Freire's elaboration of praxis, action, and reflection, but praxis has to be achieved individually as well as collectively. And for us in the *movimiento*, it was and is work of the heart, and we are guided by our heartbeats. I wrote the following poem early on, in the seventies.

> *cuando palabras sobran*
> *las miradas hablan*
> *y el sonido del tambor*

nos llama a la defensa
de nuestra gente

when we are all ready I will be there
when we are all ready the guerra de casa will end
now our heartbeats
can be heard everywhere

mi mente corre por la montaña
ya mi alma canta una canción

The "guerra de casa" is a reference to the infighting, the power struggles and political machinations that are prone to emerge in social movements.

In a more recent essay, written at the invitation of Gloria Anzaldúa for *This Bridge We Call Home*, I wrote something similar but in particular reference to women gathering around a sacred fire to manifest, to bring about change:

> There is no need for words, there have already been many, many words. Powerful words, outraged words, liberating words. . . . Standing together, the women communicate their wishes, longings, and affirmations. . . . There is no First Speaker or Last Speaker: Standing with each other in a radiant circle of consciousness, each woman, at the same time, offers her palabra.[12]

What matters to me most is not the political articulation to bring about social change, although the words are centrally important. What matters to me is the action, the praxis. It's too easy to say the words. It's harder to live them. In terms of actions, one of my biggest life lessons from this experience is that anything is possible and nothing is impossible. It might sound cynical or even overly optimistic, but it is just true. Another of my early poems is short and to the point:

Pregunta sencilla
que culpa tengo yo
de creerte capaz
de cualquier cosa?

This *pregunta* is one I can ask of anyone, myself included.

What are some of the histories that have not been told about Chicana feminist organizing and leadership? The personal stories have not been told, and each woman's story contributes to Chicana feminist herstory. We were/are fighting for self-determination for our people, and we are part of the people. Autonomy. Autonomy is only achieved when each person realizes for herself what autonomy means, because when each of us realizes it, then we will be able to respect each other's right to autonomy. The deeper the internal dialogue, the heart-driven reflection, the closer we come to a profound collective *conciencia*. Self-determina-tion is not simply a political agenda or platform. It is learned and lived.

Another history that has not been told has to do with our mistakes, but perhaps those cannot be recorded publicly, or perhaps they need to emerge transformed in nuanced critical and creative actions. The information in my body tells me that I am whole but scarred, many scars, many lives, many wounds not healed; healer, make me whole, healer that I am, take hold of my life and nurse the cuts that have reached inside so deep I will think of them when I die. I know I am not alone. At the same time, I witness(ed) the radiance of heightened consciousness—I learn(ed) and play(ed) a part in lifting up the hearts of our people (as we would say among my mom's people). Would I have preferred to live another life? Would I have preferred to turn a blind eye to the *movimiento*? There is no way that I would trade that experience for anything. I went into it with my eyes wide open and my heart ready.

NOTES

INTRODUCTION

1. The epigraph is from Gloria Anzaldúa, *Making Face, Making Soul/Haciendo Caras: Creative and Critical Perspectives by Feminists of Color* (San Francisco: Spinsters/Aunt Lute, 1990), xxvii.

2. Chela Sandoval, *Methodology of the Oppressed* (Minneapolis: University of Minnesota Press, 2000), 182.

3. Maria Cotera, "'Invisibility Is an Unnatural Disaster': Feminist Archival Praxis after the Digital Turn," in "1970s Feminisms," ed. Lisa Disch, special issue, *South Atlantic Quarterly* 114, no. 4 (2015): 781–801.

4. Mapping movidas is a pedagogical strategy developed by Maylei Blackwell as a technique for teaching Chicana feminisms that we used to generate the framework for the first draft of our introduction. The classroom exercise of mapping movidas of Chicana feminism helps students visibilize the various analytic, political, and social practices enacted across temporal frames, disciplines, and contexts that form a repertoire of resistance that Chicanas have developed since the 1970s.

5. In the late 1960s and through the 1970s, Aztlán functioned as a spatial and ideological construct that illustrated the idea of Chicanos as a colonized population. Roughly corresponding to the territory ceded to the United States after 1848, as a spatial construct Aztlán reminded Chicanas and Chicanos that the territory of the Southwest was once their homeland despite their current marginalized status (while conveniently ignoring the indigenous populations that had lived in the region before Spanish and Mexican settlement). As an ideological construct, Aztlán created solidarity across differences of race, region, class, and gender by invoking a sense of nationhood and relatedness through the shared experience of deterritorialization and a renewed sense of belonging in the Southwest.

6. Cherríe Moraga and Gloria Anzaldúa, eds., *This Bridge Called My Back: Writings by Radical Women of Color* (Watertown, MA: Persephone Press, 1981); Gloria Anzaldúa, *Borderlands/La Frontera: The New Mestiza* (San Francisco: Aunt Lute, 1987).

7. Maylei Blackwell, *¡Chicana Power! Contested Histories of Feminism in the Chicano Movement* (Austin: University of Texas Press, 2011), 10.

8. One point of departure for this volume responds to the persistent absence of Chicana activist visibility in the early monographs of the Chicano movement that appeared in the 1990s. Books like Carlos Muñoz Jr.'s *Youth, Identity, Power: The Chicano Movement* (London: Verso, 1989), Ignacio García's *Chicanismo: The Forging of a Militant Ethos among Mexican Americans* (Tucson: University of Arizona, 1997), and Juan Gómez-Quiñones's *Chicano Politics: Reality and Promise* (Albuquerque: University of New Mexico, 1990) tended to focus on male leadership with, in some cases, a token mention of women. While there have been some attempts to identify patriarchal structures and attitudes in the movement such as Ernesto Chávez's *"¡Mi Raza Primero!" (My People First): The Chicano Movement in Los Angeles* (Berkeley: University of California Press, 2002) and more recent works such as David Montejano's *Quixote's Soldiers: A Local History of the Chicano Movement, 1966–1981* (Austin: University of Texas Press, 2010) and Lee Bebout's *Mythohistorical Interventions: The Chicano Movement and Its Legacies* (Minneapolis: University of Minnesota Press, 2011), which includes a chapter on Chicana feminists like Martha Cotera, such critique has taken place without a major rethinking of the movement based on an in-depth understanding of the meanings of Chicana activism and thought in the Chicano movement era.

9. Lorena Oropeza's *¡Raza Sí! ¡Guerra No! Chicano Protest and Patriotism during the Viet Nam War Era* (Berkeley: University of California Press, 2005) and more recently Mario García's edited collection *The Chicano Movement: Perspectives from the Twenty-First Century* (London: Routledge, 2014) and Marc Rodriguez's *The Tejano Diaspora: Mexican Americanism and Ethnic Politics in Texas and Wisconsin* (Chapel Hill: University of North Carolina Press, 2011) have brought attention to mobilizations and social spaces previously ignored in Chicano movement scholarship. Monographs like Gordon Mantler's *Power to the Poor: Black-Brown Coalition and the Fight for Economic Justice, 1960–1974* (Chapel Hill: University of North Carolina Press, 2013) and edited volumes like Brian Behnken's collection *The Struggle in Black and Brown: African American and Mexican American Relations during the Civil Rights Era* (Lincoln: University of Nebraska Press, 2012) have opened a productive space for talking about how multiple movement struggles intersected and converged.

10. This collection also owes much to the literature produced in recent years that focuses on women of color mobilizations in the 1960s and 1970s. Collections like *Want to Start a Revolution? Radical Women in the Black Freedom Struggle*, ed. Dayo Gore, Jeanne Theoharis, and Komozi Woodard (New York: New York University Press, 2009); single-author monographs like Kimberly Springer's *Living for the Revolution* (Durham, NC: Duke University Press, 2005) and Jennifer Nelson's *Women of Color in the Reproductive Rights Movement* (New York: New York University Press, 2003); and essays like Becky Thompson's "Multiracial Feminism: Recasting the Chronology of Second Wave Feminism," *Feminist Studies* 28, no. 2 (2002: 336–360), have expanded our understanding of both the strategies that women of color deployed to address their intersecting oppressions and the challenges that they faced as they moved across multiple movement spaces. Together, these new, intersectional accounts of women of color organizing during the 1960s and 1970s demonstrate the importance of looking to the interstices of mass mobilizations for fresh perspectives on the technologies of resistance that shaped social justice work then and now.

11. Alma M. García, "The Development of Chicana Feminist Discourse, 1970-1980," *Gender and Society* 3, no. 2 (1989): 217-238.

12. Alma M. García, ed., *Chicana Feminist Thought: The Basic Historical Writings* (London: Routledge, 1997).

13. Chela Sandoval, "US Third-World Feminism: The Theory and Method of Oppositional Consciousness in the Postmodern World," *Genders* 10 (1991): 1–24; Norma Alarcón, "The

Theoretical Subject(s) of *This Bridge Called My Back* and Anglo-American Feminism," in *Criticism in the Borderlands: Studies in Chicano Literature, Culture and Ideology*, ed. Héctor Calderón and José David Saldívar (Durham, NC: Duke University Press, 1991), 28-42; Dolores Delgado Bernal, "Grassroots Leadership Reconceptualized: Chicana Oral Histories and the 1968 East Los Angeles School Blowouts," *Frontiers: A Journal of Women Studies* 19, no. 2 (1998): 113–142; Yolanda Broyles-González, *Teatro Campesino: Theater in the Chicano Movement* (Austin: University of Texas Press, 1994).

14. Vicki Ruíz, *From Out of the Shadows: Mexican Women in Twentieth-Century America* (New York: Oxford University Press, 1998).

15. Marisela R. Chávez, "'We Lived and Breathed and Worked the Movement': Women in El Centro Acción Social Autónomo (CASA), 1975–1978," in *Las Obreras: Chicana Politics of Work and Family*, ed. Vicki L. Ruiz (UCLA Chicano Studies Research Center Publications, 2000), 83-105.

16. Dionne Espinoza, "Revolutionary Sisters": Women's Solidarity and Collective Identification among Chicana Brown Berets in East Los Angeles, 1967–1970," *Aztlán* 26, no. 1 (2001): 17-58.

17. Dionne Espinoza, "The Partido Belongs to Those Who Will Work for It": Chicana Organizing and Leadership in the Texas Raza Unida Party, 1970–1980," *Aztlán: A Journal of Chicano Studies* 36, no. 1 (2011): 191–210.

18. Delgado Bernal, "Grassroots Leadership Reconceptualized,"; Broyles-González, *El Teatro Campesino*.

19. Oropeza, *¡Raza Sí! ¡Guerra No!*, 104.

20. Maylei Blackwell, "Contested Histories: *Las hijas de Cuauhtémoc*, Chicana Feminisms, and Print Culture in the Chicano Movement, 1968–1975," in *Chicana Feminism: A Critical Reader*, ed. Gabriela F. Arredondo, Aida Hurtado, Norma Klahn, Olga Najera-Ramírez, and Patricia Zavella (Durham, NC: Duke University Press, 2003), 59–89.

21. Blackwell, *¡Chicana Power!*, 2.

22. Ibid., 38.

23. Sonia Alvarez discusses the amplification of the spaces and places where feminism is discussed in her article "Translating the Global Effects of Transnational Organizing on Local Feminist Discourses and Practices," *Meridians* 1, no. 1 (2000): 29–67.

24. Blackwell, *¡Chicana Power!*, 24.

25. Enriqueta Vásquez's writing in the aftermath of the Denver Youth Conference illustrates the complexities and contradictions of this historical turning point; Enriqueta Longeaux y Vásquez, *Enriqueta Vasquez and the Chicano Movement: Writings from El Grito del Norte*, ed. Lorena Oropeza and Dionne Espinoza (Houston: Arte Público, 2006), 111–137.

26. Lara Medina, *Las Hermanas: Chicana/Latina Religious-Political Activism in the U.S. Catholic Church* (Philadelphia: Temple University Press, 2004).

27. In this volume we capitalize "third world" only when referring to a specific social movement or organization. When used in more general contexts such as third world feminism and third world struggles or in general references to the third world, the term is lowercase.

28. For example, in her report on the 1981 NWSA Conference (reprinted in *Haciendo Caras*), Sandoval maps out the ways in which women of color negotiated their differences to intervene in a conference that was meant to address the problem of racism within the women's movement but that nevertheless enacted the very erasures, power plays, and deferrals that the conference was meant to address. The insights in this essay were later further elaborated in Sandoval's groundbreaking book *Methodology of the Oppressed*. Chela Sandoval, "Feminism and Racism: A Report on the 1981 National Women's Studies Association Conference," in *Making Face, Making Soul/Haciendo Caras: Creative and Critical Perspectives by Feminists of Color*, ed. Gloria Anzaldúa (San Francisco: Spinsters/Aunt Lute, 1990), 55–71.

29. In adopting "home-making" as a *movida* of Chicana praxis, we follow women of color theorists who have productively redeployed the term "home" for a political praxis of coalition-building. Feminists like Bernice Johnson Reagon, Chandra Mohanty, Biddy Martin, Gloria Anzaldúa, and Cherríe Moraga and the contributors to feminist of color anthologies like *Home Girls*, *This Bridge Called My Back*, and *This Bridge We Call Home* have redefined the meanings of "home" in an effort to make new spaces for feminism through coalition-building. In their own scholarly and artistic praxis, Chicana feminists have recuperated the domestic as a key site of cultural, political, and aesthetic meaning-making; Gloria E. Anzaldúa and AnaLouise Keating, eds., *This Bridge We Call Home: Radical Visions for Transformation* (New York: Routledge, 2002); Patricia Preciado Martin, *Songs My Mother Sang to Me: An Oral History of Mexican American Women* (University of Arizona Press, 1992); Amalia Mesa-Bains, "Domesticana: the Sensibility of Chicana Rasquache," *Aztlán: A Journal of Chicano Studies* 24, no. 2 (1999): 157–167; Chandra Talpade Mohanty (with Biddy Martin), "What's Home Got to Do with It," in Mohanty's *Feminism without Borders: Decolonizing Theory, Practicing Solidarity* (London: Duke University Press, 2003), 85–105; Moraga and Anzaldúa, *This Bridge Called My Back*; Barbara Smith, ed., *Home Girls: A Black Feminist Anthology* (New York: Kitchen Table: Women of Color Press, 1983); Bernice Johnson Reagon, "Coalition Politics: Turning the Next Century," in *Home Girls*, ed. Smith, 356–368.

30. Within La Raza Unida Party there were various names for the space that was created by Chicanas in the party based on their organizing projects, whether participating in the National Women's Political Caucus or within the RUP as the Chicana Caucus and more formally by the mid-1970s the Mujeres Caucus, as can be viewed in the archives. These are to be distinguished from Mujeres por/para La Raza Unida, the organizing project run by Martha Cotera and Evey Chapa roughly from 1970 to 1973 or 1974.

31. Eleanor Marx and Edward Aveling, *The Woman Question* (Leipzig, Germany: Verlag für die Frau, 1987).

32. Hilda Rodriguez, "Hilda Rodriguez," in *Teatro Chicana: A Collective Memoir and Selected Plays*, ed. Laura E. Garcia, Sandra M. Gutierrez, and Felicitas Nuñez (Austin: University of Texas Press, 2008), 93.

33. Anna NietoGomez, oral history interview, Irvine, CA, August 8, 2010, Chicana por mi Raza Digital Memory Collective; Boston Women's Health Book Collective, *Our Bodies, Ourselves* (New York: Simon and Schuster, 2011).

34. Dorinda Moreno, *La mujer es la tierra, la tierra da vida* (Berkeley, CA: Casa Editorial, 1975), 28.

35. Espinoza, "Revolutionary Sisters," 17–58.

36. Delgado Bernal, "Grassroots Leadership Reconceptualized."

37. The Women's Educational Equity Act (WEEA) was established in 1974 as an amendment (Title IV-A) to the Elementary and Secondary Education Act of 1965 to "promote educational equity for girls and women, including those who suffer multiple discrimination based on gender and on race, ethnicity, national origin, disability, or age, and to provide funds to help education agencies and institutions meet the requirements of Title IX of the Education Amendments of 1972." WEEA was an active funding source for publications and research on multicultural women from 1976 to 1986; Biennial Evaluation Report—FY 93-94: Women's Educational Equity, CFDA no. 84.083, https://www2.ed.gov/pubs/Biennial/125 .html (accessed July 20, 2016).

38. See Linda Burnham, "The Wellspring of Black Feminist Theory," Working Paper Series, no. 1 (Oakland, CA: Women of Color Resource Center, 2001); and Linda Burnham, introduction to *Time to Rise*, ed. Maylei Blackwell and Jung Hee Choi (Oakland, CA: Women of Color Resource Center, 2001), 7–16. See also Jaqui Alexander, *Pedagogies of Crossing:*

Meditations on Feminism, Sexual Politics, Memory, and the Sacred (Durham, NC: Duke University, 2005).

39. Sandoval, *Methodology of the Oppressed*, 139.

40. In Moraga and Anzaldúa, *This Bridge Called My Back*, 195.

41. Dorinda Moreno, *La mujer: En pie de lucha* (San Francisco: Espina del Norte, 1973).

42. Sandoval, *Methodology of the Oppressed*.

43. Martha Cotera, *Diosa y Hembra: The History and Heritage of Chicanas in the U.S.* (Austin: Information Systems Development, 1976).

44. *Chicana*, directed by Sylvia Morales, written by Anne NietoGomez, film (Hollywood, CA: Ruiz Productions, 1979).

45. Adelaida del Castillo, "Malintzín Tenépal: A Preliminary Look into a New Perspective," in *Essays on la Mujer*, ed. Rosaura Sánchez (Los Angeles: Chicano Studies Center Publications, UCLA, 1977), 124–149; Norma Alarcón, "Tradutora/Traditora: A Paradigmatic Figure of Chicana Feminism," in *Scattered Hegemonies: Postmodernity and Transnational Feminist Practices*, ed. Inderpal Grewal and Caren Kaplan (Minneapolis: University of Minnesota Press, 1994), 110–136; Anzaldúa, *Borderlands/La Frontera*; Cherríe Moraga, "Theory in the Flesh," introduction to *This Bridge Called My Back*.

46. Historian Vicki Ruiz cites Castro to articulate her understanding of Chicana leadership: "We have practiced a different kind of leadership, a leadership that empowers others, not a hierarchical kind of leadership"; in Vicki L. Ruiz, *From Out of the Shadows: Mexican Women in Twentieth-Century America* (New York: Oxford University Press, 1998), 100.

47. Cherríe Moraga, "Theory in the Flesh," introduction to *This Bridge Called My Back*, 23. See also Latina Feminist Group, ed., *Telling to Live: Latina Feminist Testimonios* (Durham, NC: Duke University Press, 2001). Latina Feminist Group members are Aurora Levins Morales, Patricia Zavella, Norma Alarcón, Ruth Behar, Luz del Alba Acevedo, Celia Alvarez, Rina Benmayor, Clara Lomas, Daisy Cocco de Filippis, Gloria Holguin Cuadraz, Licia Fiol-Matta, Yvette Gisele Flores-Ortiz, Mirtha F. Quintanales, Eliana Rivero, and Caridad Souza.

48. Horacio N. Roque Ramirez, "'That's My Place!': Negotiating Racial, Sexual, and Gender Politics in San Francisco's Gay Latino Alliance, 1975–1983," *Journal of the History of Sexuality* 12, no. 2 (2003): 224–258.

49. Sandoval, *Methodology of the Oppressed*, 64.

50. Chicana Chicago and Somos Latinas have contributed to an ongoing effort to write the history of Chicana and Latina activism in the Midwest through oral history accounts. See Leonard Ramírez, ed., *Chicanas of 18th Street: Narratives of a Movement from Latino Chicago* (Chicago: University of Illinois Press, 2011); Teresa Delgadillo, *Latina Lives in Milwaukee* (Chicago: University of Illinois Press, 2015).

51. For more on Nancy De Los Santos see the Chicana por mi Raza Digital Memory Collective website, http://chicanapormiraza.org/.

52. This research appeared in Marisela Chávez's article "Pilgrimage to the Homeland: California Chicanas and International Women's Year, Mexico City, 1975," in *Memories and Migrations: Mapping Boricua/Chicana Histories*, ed. Vicki Ruiz and John Chávez (Chicago: University of Illinois Press, 2008), 170–195.

CHAPTER 1

1. Felicia Pratto and Jim Sidanius, *Social Dominance* (Cambridge, England: Cambridge University Press, 2001), 37–38.

2. Bill Flores, "Elogio a Francisca Flores," in *TQS News: A Contemporary Newsletter of Eclectic Chicano Thought* 13, no. 3 (1996): 2–3.

3. "League of Mexican-American Women—Aims and Purposes," n.d., box 62, folder

2, Comisión Femenil Mexicana Nacional (CFMN) Archives, 1967–1997, California Ethnic and Multicultural (CEMA) Archives, Department of Special Collections, Davison Library, University of California, Santa Barbara (hereafter cited as CFMN Archives).

4. Joe Castorena, "In Memoriam: Francisca Flores: A Warrior for Our Times," speech given at the Los Angeles memorial service for Francisca Flores, May 1996, Los Angeles, in Anna NietoGomez private collection, Lakewood, CA (hereafter NietoGomez collection); Peter Dreier, "Henry Wallace, America's Forgotten Visionary," in *Truthout: Historical Analysis*, February 3, 2013, video, 6:55, http://truth-out.org/opinion/item/14297-henry-wallace-americas-forgotten-visionary.

5. Enrique M. Buelna, "Asociación Nacional México-Americana (ANMA) (1949–1954)," in *Latinas in the United States: A Historical Encyclopedia*, ed. Vicki L. Ruiz and Virginia Sanchez Korrol (Bloomington: Indiana University Press, 2006), 1:67.

6. Wendy Plotkin, "Community Service Organization (CSO) History Project," email, September 8, 1996, http://comm-org.wisc.edu/papers96/alinsky/cso.html.

7. Kenneth C. Burt, *The Search for a Civic Voice: California Latino Politics* (Claremont, CA: Regina Books, 2007), 179, 183.

8. Francisca Flores and Delfino Varela, eds., *Carta Editorial* 1, no. 6 (June 17, 1963): 1, box 53, CFMN Archives. Varela was an associate editor until January 1967. See Delfino Varela, "Bon Voyage," *Carta Editorial* 3, no. 24 (January 25, 1967): 1. Flores continued as sole editor and writer until the newsletter was incorporated into her Chicano magazine, *Regeneración*, in 1970.

9. Flores and Varela, "187th Anniversary of U.S. Independence," *Carta Editorial* 1, no. 7 (July 3, 1963): 1, box 53, CFMN Archives.

10. Flores and Varela, "Some Perspective on the Fight for Integration," *Carta Editorial* 1, no. 9 (August 6, 1963): 6, box 53, CFMN Archives.

11. Flores and Varela, "Women and Dogs Not Allowed," in *Carta Editorial* 1, no. 9 (August 6, 1963): 2, box 53, CFMN Archives.

12. Raul Morín, *Among the Valiant: Mexican-Americans in WW II and Korea* (Los Angeles: Borden, 1963).

13. Eddie Morín, interview by Anna NietoGomez, January 18, 2014, Los Angeles.

14. Juan Gómez Quiñones, *Chicano Politics: Reality and Promise, 1940–1990* (Albuquerque: University of New Mexico Press, 1990), 67.

15. Margaret Rose, "Gender and Civic Activism in the Mexican-American Barrios," in *Not June Cleaver: Women and Gender in Postwar America, 1940–1960*, ed. Joanne Meyerowitz (Philadelphia: Temple University Press, 1994), 182–193.

16. Linda M. Apodaca, *Mexican-American Women and Social Change: The Founding of the Community Service Organization in Los Angeles, an Oral History* (Tucson, AZ: Mexican-American Studies and Research Center, 1999), 7.

17. Manuel G. Gonzales, *Mexicanos: History of Mexicans in the United States*, 2nd ed. (Bloomington: Indiana University Press, 2009), 188.

18. Ramona Morín, "Democratic Women of East Los Angeles–Belvedere," press release, n.d.; "Democratic Women E.L.A.–Belvedere Present Annual Testimonial to Women Banquet Program, April 7, 1962," box 47, folder 5, CFMN Archives.

19. "YWCA History," n.d., YWCA, http://www.ywca.org/site/c.cuIRJ7NTKrLaG /b.7515891/k.C524/History.htm; "Ramona Morín Resume 1970," box 47, folder 5, CFMN Archives.

20. "Ramona Morín Resume 1970," CFMN Archives.

21. Cynthia E. Orozco, *No Mexicans, Women, or Dogs Allowed* (Austin: University of Texas Press, 2009): 202, 211; "The Women of LULAC," n.d., League of United Latin American Citizens, at http://lulac.org/about/history/women; Teresa Palomo Acosta, "American G.I.

Forum Women's Auxiliary," *Handbook of Texas Online*, modified June 15, 2010, http://www.tshaonline.org/handbook/online/articles/voa03.

22. "League of Mexican-American Women—Aims and Purposes," a historical narrative description handout, pp. 1-2; untitled description of the League and precursor of Comisión Femenil Mexicana Nacional; "Ramona Morín Resume 1970," CFMN Archives.

23. Congressman Edward Roybal, Western Union telegram to Dolores Huerta, May 6, 1966, box 47, folder 5, CFMN Archives.

24. "League of Mexican-American Women," a narrative history of the league, and "League of Mexican-American Women Aims and Purposes," box 62, folder 2, CFMN Archives.

25. Burt, *Search for a Civic Voice*, 187, 206–208.

26. "League of Mexican-American Women," box 62, folder 2, CFMN Archives.

27. "Democratic Women E.L.A.–Belvedere," banquet program.

28. Francisca Flores to East Los Angeles Belvedere Democratic Club members, February 1962, box 47, folder 4, CFMN Archives.

29. Ramona Morín, "Democratic Women of East Los Angeles–Belvedere."

30. "League of Mexican-American Women," box 62, folder 2, CFMN Archives; untitled summary of the history of the League and the precursor of Comisión Femenil Mexicana Nacional.

31. "League of Mexican-American Women Achievement Award," May 1966, box 47, folder 5, CFMR Archives.

32. Flores and Varela, "Women's Banquet," *Carta Editorial* 3, no. 13 (May 2, 1966): 1, box 53, folder 2, CFMN Archives.

33. Gary Pickard, "Mexican-American Women Form League with High Goals," *Arizona Republic*, March 20, 1966; "Fiesta en Xochimilco to Build Scholarships," *Arizona Daily Star*, August 17, 1969; "National Chicanas Conference July-August 1971," box 2, folder 37, Enriqueta Chavez Papers, 1955–2000, Special Collections and University Archives, San Diego State University; Francisca Flores, "Conference of Mexican Women in Houston—Un Remolino," *Regeneración* 1, no. 10, (1971): 2.

34. Ramona Morín, "Democratic Women of East Los Angeles–Belvedere"; "Democratic Women E.L.A.–Belvedere," banquet program.

35. Ibid.; Francisca Flores to East Los Angeles Belvedere Democratic Club members, February 1962, box 47, folder 4, CFMN Archives; "Pioneering Alumna Vaino Spencer Retires from the Bench," press release, October 2007, Southwestern School of Law, Los Angeles, http://www.swlaw.edu/news/overview/newsr.7fscslHpsi.

36. "In Memoriam: Lucille Beserra Roybal," UCLA Chicano Studies Research Center, http://www.chicano.ucla.edu/about/news/memoriam-lucille-beserra-roybal.

37. Leon J. Perales, "Mexican-American Women," *Carta Perales* 1, no. 2 (March 29, 1963): 6, box 53, CFMN Archives.

38. Eunice Valle, "A Proud Spanish Heritage Spawns Latin Music Center," in *Billboard: A Billboard Spotlight* (November 15, 1980): LA-24, http://www.americanradiohistory.com/Archive-Billboard/80s/1980/BB-1980–11–15.pdf; "Spanish Toasted by RCA Mexico," *Billboard* (December 16, 1967), 55. http://www.americanradiohistory.com/Archive-Billboard/60s/1967/Billboard%201967–12–16.pdf.

39. Perales, "Mexican-American Women"; Flores and Varela, "By the Way" and "Women and Dogs Not Allowed," *Carta Editorial* 1, no. 9 (August 6, 1963), 2, box 53, CFMN Archives; "Women on the Move: Graciela Olivarez, Keynote Speaker," in "1977 CSAC 5th Anniversary Banquet Program," box 54, folder 2, CFMN Archives.

40. Flores, "Attention Machos," *Carta Editorial* 1, no. 24 (May 7, 1964): 1; "Beauty, Grace, and Brains," *Carta Editorial*, 1, no. 18 (January 20, 1964): 3, box 53, CFMN Archives.

41. David B. Oppenheimer, "California's Anti-Discrimination Legislation, Proposition 14, and the Constitutional Protection of Minority Rights: The Fiftieth Anniversary of the

California Fair Employment and Housing Act," *Golden Gate University Law Review* 40, no. 2 (2010): 126, http://digitalcommons.law.ggu.edu/cgi/viewcontent.cgi?article=2010&context =ggulrev.

42. "Our Story," in "About Us," Colorado Latino Leadership, Advocacy, and Research Organization (CLLARO), accessed August 5, 2017, at http://www.larasa.org/.

43. Flores and Varela, "The League of Mexican-American Women," in *Carta Editorial* 2, no. 18 (March 18, 1965): 1, box 53, CFMN Archives.

44. Ibid.; Earl Siegel, "Health and Day Care of Migrant Workers," *Public Health Reports* 79, no. 10 (1964): 847.

45. Jan Cleere, "Building Bridges: Maria Luisa Legarra Urquides (1908–1994), in *Levi's and Lace*, by Jan Cleere (Tucson, AZ: Rio Nuevo, 2001), 113–115.

46. Flores and Varela, "Women's Banquet," *Carta Editorial* 3, no. 13 (May 2, 1966): 1, box 53, CFMN Archives.

47. "Dolores Huerta: Labor Movement Leader," Heroism Project, 1970s, http://www .heroism.org/class/1970/huerta.html; Margaret Rose, "Dolores Huerta," in *A Dolores Huerta Reader*, ed. Mario T. García (Albuquerque: University of New Mexico Press, 2008), 14–15; Burt, *Search for a Civic Voice*, 199.

48. Flores and Varela, "Attention Machos."

49. Lilia Aceves, interview by Virginia Espino, transcript 1, December, 11, 2008, Oral History Collection, Mexican American Civil Rights Pioneers: Historical Roots in an Activist Generation, Oral History Research, UCLA Library, http://oralhistory.library.ucla.edu/; Lilia Mercado Acuna Aceves, interview by Anna NietoGomez, September 27, 2013, Alhambra, CA.

50. Aceves, interview by NietoGomez; Flores and Varela, "Specific Programs Lead to Specific Gains," *Carta Editorial* 1, no. 17 (January 2, 1964): 2, box 53, CFMN Archives; Ruben Salazar, "Problems of Latins Seen Thing Apart; New Policy for U.S. Spanish-Speaking Students Urged," September 16, 1963, in *Border Correspondent: Selected Writings, 1955–1970*, by Ruben Salazar (Berkeley: University of California Press, 1998), 126–129; Anita Tijerina Revilla, introduction to *Marching Students*, ed. Margarita Berta-Ávila, Anita Tijerina Revilla, Julie Lopez Figueroa (Reno: University of Nevada Pres, 2011), 1.

51. Flores and Varela, "The Women Commissioners of the City of Los Angeles," *Carta Editorial* 2, no. 1 (May 28, 1964): 6.

52. Josephine Weiner, *The Story of WICS Women* (Alexandria, VA: Community Service, 1986), 25, 28, 33.

53. Flores and Varela, "Women Commissioners of the City of Los Angeles."

54. Weiner, *Story of WICS Women*.

55. Francisca Flores, "Women in Washington," *Carta Editorial* 4, no. 5 (May 26, 1967), 5, box 53, CFMN Archives; Acosta, "American G.I. Forum Women's Auxiliary."

56. Francisca Flores 1973 Vitae, box 40, folder 1, CFMN Archives; Ramona Morín Resume, CFMN Archives; Eddie Morín, interview by NietoGomez; Dominga G. Coronado, "Mexican American Problems and the Job Corps," in *The Mexican American: A New Focus on Opportunity; Testimony Presented at President Johnson's Cabinet Committee Hearings on Mexican American Affairs, El Paso, Texas, October 26–27, 1967* (Washington, DC: Interagency Committee on Mexican American Affairs, 1968), 177–178, http://files.eric.ed.gov/fulltext /ED032950.pdf.

57. Weiner, *Story of WICS Women*, 19-20; Henry Ramirez, "Ramirez Urges Spanish-Speaking Women to Pursue Policy-Making Positions," *Noticias de la Semana*, May 29, 1972, box 47, CFMN Archives.

58. "Mexican American National Issues Conference Steering Committee Members Selected on October 11, 1970," October 12, 1970, NietoGomez collection.

59. Flores and Varela, "Leadership Conference Has Big Potential," *Carta Editorial* 1, no.

13 (October 26, 1963): 1; "The Mexican American Adult Leadership Conference," *Carta Editorial* 3, no. 3 (September 23, 1965): 1; "The First Annual Conference," *Carta Editorial* 3, no. 6 (November 23, 1965): 5; Francisca Flores, "The Second Annual Convention," *Carta Editorial* 4, no. 5 (May 16, 1967): 1, box 53, CFMN Archives.

60. League of Mexican American Women, "Comisión Femenil, Women's Workshop Outline, Preliminary Ideas for Workshop Discussion," n.d.; Francisca Flores to Manuel Banda, September 25, 1970, NietoGomez collection.

61. Ann T. Keene, "Mink, Patsy," in *American National Biography Online*, updated October 2008, http://www.anb.org/articles/07/07–00812.html; "Shirley Chisholm Biography," Biography.com, http://www.biography.com/people/shirley-chisholm-9247015#personal-life -and-legacy.

62. Abby J. Cohen, "A Brief History of Federal Financing for Child Care in the United States," in "Financing Child Care," special issue, *Future of Children* 6, no. 2 (1996): 26–40.

63. Kirsten M. J. Thompson, "A Brief History of Birth Control in the U.S.," Our Bodies Our Selves, December 14, 2013, http://www.ourbodiesourselves.org/health-info/a-brief -history-of-birth-control/.

64. "Hershey Sees Female in the Draft" (California State University, Long Beach) *Forty-Niner*, February, 17, 1967, 4.

65. "Comisión Femenil, Women's Workshop Outline"; Flores to Banda, September 25, 1970, NietoGomez collection.

66. Anna NietoGomez, "Male Tokenism," *La Raza Newspaper*, December 1969, 5; Enriqueta Chavez, interview by Anna NietoGomez, January 27, 2012; "Resolutions from the Chicana Workshop," *La Verdad*, June 1970, 9.

67. Beatriz M. Pesquera and Denis A. Segura, "There Is No Going Back: Chicanas and Feminism," in *Chicana Feminist Thought: The Basic Historical Writings*, ed. Alma M. Garcia (London: Routledge, 1997), 298-299.

68. Flores to Banda, September 25, 1970, NietoGomez collection.

69. Bernice Rincon, "La Chicana, Her Role in the Past, and Her Search for a New Role in the Future," unpublished paper, NietoGomez collection. Part of Rincon's paper was published in *Regeneración* 1, no. 10 (1971): 15–18, box 59, folder 6, CFMN.

70. Ibid; Bernice Rincon, interview by Anna NietoGomez, November 4, 2013, Fresno, CA.

71. Arturo Cabrera, unpublished transcript of 1970 Chicana workshop at the first annual Mexican American National Issues Conference, Sacramento, CA, October 10, 1970, 5, NietoGomez collection; Feliciano Ribera, *A Mexican American Source Book* (Menlo Park, CA: Educational Consulting Associates, 1970).

72. Cabrera, transcript.

73. Ibid.

74. Ibid.

75. Ibid.

76. "Mexican American National Issues Conference, October 10, 1971 (1970), Sacramento, CA. Report on Workshop and Present Women's Activities," *Comisión Femenil Mexicana* 1, no. 1 (n.d.): 1.

77. "California," *Comisión Femenil Mexicana Report* 1, no. 5 [1971]: 1, box 54, folder 4, CFMN.

78. "Second Annual Comisión Workshop," 1, no. 6 [1971]: 1, box 54, folder 4, CFMN Archives; "A State Meeting of the Comisión Femenil Mexicana Took Place March 12, 1972," *Comisión Femenil Mexicana Report* 1, no. 7 (March 1972): 1, box 54, folder 4, CFMN Archives; Josephine Valdez Banda, CFMN recruitment letter, 1972, box 11, folder 5, CFMN Archives.

79. Gema Matsuda, "La Chicana Organizes: The CFMN in Perspective," *Regeneración* 2, no. 4 (1975): 25–27, box 59, folder 9, CFMN Archives; Francisca Flores, "Comisión Femenil

Mexicana Organizes in Los Angeles," CFM *Report* 2, no. 1 (1973): 3, box 54, folder 4, CFMN Archives; Diane Verdugo and Narcisa Espinoza, *La Comisión Femenil de Arizona Newsletter* 1, no. 1 (April 1972): 1, NietoGomez collection.

80. "Historical Documents: Resolution for a Women's Center," *Chicana Service Action Center Newsletter*, 1973, 2. Vera Carreon edited the newsletter.

81. Valdez Banda, CFMN recruitment letter, CFMN Archives; "Chicana Service and Action Center," CFM *Report* 1, no. 11 (1972): 1, box 54, folder 4, CFMN Archives.

82. Francisca Flores 1973 Vitae, CFMN Archives; Francisca Flores to Joseph Aguilar, July 1968, solicitation letter for donations for *Carta Editorial*, box 45, folder 8, CFMN Archives; Bill Flores, "Elogio a Francisca Flores."

83. CFMN minutes, June 19, 1972, box 1, folder 8, CFMN Archives; "80, Chicanas, on 3/72 . . . ," untitled report by an unnamed CFMN board member, n.d., box 38, folder 1, CFMN Archives; Flores, "Comisión Femenil Mexicana Organizes in Los Angeles," CFMN Archives.

84. Yolanda Nava to Carmen R. Maymi, director-designate, Women's Bureau, Department of Labor, August 2, 1973, box 38, folder 6, CFMN Archives.

85. "CFMN Annual Business Meeting," CFMN *Inc.*, booklet, 1975, box 11, folder 12, CFMN Archives; "1974—A Year of Action for the Chicana Center," CSAC *News*, 1, no. 8 (1975): 3; Ibert Phillips, "Events of January 30, 1975," February 15, 1975, box 39, folders 1 and 2, CFMN Archives; "Comisión Femenil Mexicana de Los Angeles," n.d., box 28, folder 19, CFMN Archives. The author was a member of the CSAC Board of Directors from 1974 to 1976 and present during these proceedings.

CHAPTER 2

1. Martha P. Cotera, "Feminism, the Chicana and Anglo Versions: A Historical Analysis," in *Chicana Feminist Thought: The Basic Historical Writings*, ed. Alma M. García (London: Routledge, 1997), 223–231.

2. Dionne Espinoza, "The Partido Belongs to Those Who Will Work for It: Chicana Organizing and Leadership in the Texas Raza Unida Party, 1970–1980," *Aztlán: A Journal of Chicano Studies* 36, no. 1 (2011): 198.

3. Martha P. Cotera, *Diosa y Hembra: The History and Heritage of Chicanas in the U.S.* (Austin: Information Systems Development, 1976), 168–173.

4. Martha P. Cotera, "Party Platform on Chicanas, 1972: La Raza Unida Party," in *Chicana Feminist Thought*, ed. Alma M. Garcia, 169.

5. Sonia R. Garcia and Marisela Márquez, "The Comisión Femenil: La Voz of a Chicana Organization," *Aztlán: A Journal of Chicano Studies* 36, no. 1 (2011): 161–162.

6. Cotera, "Feminism, the Chicana and Anglo Versions."

7. Linda Garcia Merchant, dir., *Las mujeres de la Caucus Chicana*, video (Voces Primeras, 2007).

8. Martha P. Cotera, *Chicana Feminist* (Austin: Information Systems Development, 1977), 17–20.

9. Cotera, *Diosa y Hembra*, 174–177; Garcia Merchant, *Las mujeres*.

10. Liz Carpenter was staff director and press secretary to Lady Bird Johnson; Ann Richards was governor of Texas, 1991–1995; Sarah Weddington is a Texas attorney who argued the case *Roe v. Wade* before the US Supreme Court, 1972–1973.

11. Chicana por mi Raza Digital Memory Collective, created by María Cotera and Linda Garcia Merchant, is a digital humanities project that provides content to correct the erasure of Chicana history. The CPMR team collects, digitizes, and displays archival materials and oral histories of Chicana feminist thought and praxis in the period 1960–1990. Since 2009, team members have recorded oral histories of fifty-two women and collected 5,500 archival items, 4,900 digital records, and 3,000 yet to digitize, at http://chicanapormiraza.org/.

12. Maylei Blackwell, *¡Chicana Power! Contested Histories of Feminism in the Chicano Movement* (Austin: University of Texas Press, 2011), 194–195.

13. "Presentation by Chicanas of La Raza Unida Party," in *Chicana Feminist Thought*, ed. Alma M. García, 180–181.

14. Yolanda M. López, "A Chicana's Look at the International Women's Year Conference," in *Chicana Feminist Thought*, ed. Alma M. García, 182.

15. In Texas, calls for delegations on national events were usually directed to the male leadership, and in this case, José Ángel Gutiérrez and other male leaders, not RUP feminist leaders, selected the RUP delegates who went to Mexico City. To the knowledge of the RUP Women's Caucus there was no follow-up action on the international conference except for those of us who organized the Chicana Advisory Committee for IWY. Lasting divisions on lack of transparency did affect our relations with Lupe Anguiano, one of RUP's chosen delegates to Mexico City.

16. National Commission on the Observance of International Women's Year, *The Spirit of Houston: The First National Women's Conference, an Official Report to the President, the Congress, and the People of the United States, March 1978* (Washington, DC: Government Printing Office, 1978), 10.

17. Ibid.

18. Diana Camacho to Pat Vasquez, letter of transmittal, and Diana Camacho, "Chicanas Change Course of Texas IWY," typewritten report to Vasquez for the Chicana Rights Project. The letter and report are found in box 9, Martha Cotera Papers, Nettie Lee Benson Latin American Collection, University of Texas, Austin (hereafter cited as Martha Cotera Papers).

19. Camacho, "Chicanas Change Course of Texas IWY," Martha Cotera Papers.

20. Cecilia Preciado Burciaga to Martha P. Cotera, March 18, 1977, International Women's Year 1977, box 9, folder 3, Martha Cotera Papers.

21. Quote from Chespirito (Shakespeare, aka Chapulin Colorado), a popular Mexican TV comic who saves the day through artfulness and ingenuity.

22. Claudia Stravato and Owanah Anderson, eds., *Texas Women's Meeting, Women at the Grass Roots: Growing toward Unity, June 24–26, 1977* (Austin: Texas IWY Coordinating Committee, 1977).

23. Ibid., iii.

24. Camacho, "Chicanas Change Course of Texas IWY," Martha Cotera Papers.

25. Olga Solíz to Martha P. Cotera, February 24, 1977, International Women's Year (IWY) 1977, box 9, folder 3, Martha Cotera Papers.

26. Minutes of the Texas IWY Executive Committee, March 25, 1977, box 9, folder 16, Martha Cotera Papers.

27. Memorandum, Chicana Advisory Committee for IWY Concerns, February 5, 1977, International Women's Year (IWY) 1977, box 9, folder 3, Martha Cotera Papers.

28. Ibid.

29. Ibid.

30. Camacho, "Chicanas Change Course of Texas IWY," Martha Cotera Papers.

31. Transmittal for proposal package to Sarah Weddington, February 5, 1977, International Women's Year (IWY) 1977, box 9, Martha Cotera Papers.

32. Proposal for Contract Services to Provide for Outreach and Programming for the Participation of Texas Chicanas at the IWY State Conference, February 18, 1977, box 9, folder 2, Martha Cotera Papers.

33. "The Radical Feminist Perspective at the Texas International Women's Year Conference," February 18, 1977, box 9, folder 2, Martha Cotera Papers.

34. Proposal for Participation of a Major Portion of Texas' Population of Women/United Campus Ministry of Austin, February 18, 1977, box 9, folder 2, Martha Cotera Papers.

35. Stravato and Anderson, *Texas Women's Meeting*, 12.

36. Minutes of the Texas IWY Executive Committee, March 25, 1977, Martha Cotera Papers.

37. Martha P. Cotera to Pat Vasquez, June 22, 1977, International Women's Year (IWY) 1977, box 9, folder 1, Martha Cotera Papers.

38. Martha P. Cotera to Owanah Anderson, Chair, Texas Coordinating Committee, IWY, May 19, 1977, box 9, folder 1, Martha Cotera Papers.

39. Cotera to Vasquez, June 22, 1977, Martha Cotera Papers.

40. Cotera to Anderson, May 19, 1977, Martha Cotera Papers.

41. Minutes of the Texas IWY Executive Committee, March 25, 1977, Martha Cotera Papers.

42. Stravato and Anderson, *Texas Women's Meeting*, 107.

43. Martha P. Cotera to Owanah Anderson, May 19, 1977, International Women's Year (IWY) 1977, box 9, folder 1, Martha Cotera Papers.

44. Stravato and Anderson, *Texas Women's Meeting*, 36.

45. Ibid., 39.

46. Ibid., 55.

47. Ibid., 53.

48. Ibid., 97.

49. Ibid., 63.

50. Ibid., 65.

51. Ibid., 68, 99.

52. Ibid., 69, 97.

53. Ibid., 70.

54. Ibid., 71.

55. Ibid, 73–74.

56. Ibid., 80.

57. Ibid., 41.

58. Ibid., 91.

59. Ibid., 25.

60. Camacho to Vasquez, letter of transmittal, Martha Cotera Papers.

61. Martha Smiley, conversation with Martha P. Cotera, July 1977, Austin.

62. National Commission, *Spirit of Houston*, 157.

63. Ibid., 158.

64. Ibid., 157.

65. Ibid., 156.

66. Ibid., 157.

67. Stravato and Anderson, *Texas Women's Meeting*, ii.

68. Ibid., iii.

69. Ibid., iii, 97.

70. Camacho, "Chicanas Change Course of Texas IWY," Martha Cotera Papers.

71. Cecilia P. Burciaga, "The 1977 National Women's Conference in Houston," in *Chicana Feminist Thought*, ed. Alma M. García, 184.

72. Blackwell, *¡Chicana Power!*, 189.

CHAPTER 3

1. Olga Villa, interview by Linda Garcia Merchant, Indianapolis, IN, 2006, for the Voces Primeras documentary *Las mujeres de la Caucus Chicana*, released in 2007. Garcia Merchant allowed me access to the original interview videos. I use the term "La Raza" as the Midwest Council of La Raza defines it—inclusive of those from Mexico, Puerto Rico, Cuba, and other Latin American countries—in "A Struggle for Self Determination," *Los Desarraigados* 1, no. 1 (November 1972), MS 2009.8., binder section 2, Julian Samora Library at the Institute for Latino Studies, University of Notre Dame (hereafter Samora Library).

2. Anna NietoGomez, "Empieza la revolución verdadera (1971)," in *Chicana Feminist Thought: The Basic Historical Writings*, ed. Alma M. Garcia (London: Routledge, 1997). This is mentioned in NietoGomez's poem "Empieza La Revolución Verdadera," translated title reads, "The Real Revolution Begins."

3. "Struggle for Self Determination," *Los Desarraigados*.

4. "100 Raza Women Attend Adelante Mujer Conference," *The Militant*, July 7, 1972, catalogued in Barbara Driscoll, "A Newspaper Documentary History of the Chicano Community of South Bend, Indiana," Ricardo Parra and Olga Villa Parra Papers, Samora Library (hereafter Parra Papers).

5. "El Plan Espiritual de Aztlán," the Spiritual Plan of Aztlán, was adopted in 1969 during the First National Chicano Liberation Youth Conference spearheaded by Rodolfo "Corky" Gonzales, a well-known Chicano activist. For more on nationalism and Aztlán see Laura Elisa Pérez, "El Desorden, Nationalism, and Chicana/o Aesthetics," in *Between Woman and Nation: Nationalisms, Transnational Feminism, and the State*, ed. Caren Kaplan, Norma Alarcón, and Minoo Moallem (Durham, NC: Duke University Press, 1999), 19. Within this work Pérez draws heavily on Benedict Anderson's *Imagined Communities* to highlight how this nationalism first took its form within the United States. The name "Aztlán" refers to the ancestral home of the Aztec Indians of Mexico, believed to be in the US Southwest.

6. Maylei Blackwell, *¡Chicana Power! Contested Histories of Feminism in the Chicano Movement* (Austin: University of Texas Press, 2011), 96–97.

7. Flores, quoted in Laura Perez, "El Desorden," 23.

8. Blackwell and others are claiming a place in the historiography of feminism and activism in the 1960s and 1970s book for Chicana and Latinas. Her work *¡Chicana Power!* focuses on the experiences of Anna NietoGomez, among other Southwestern Chicana women, particularly from Southern California and Texas, and their calls to action from the 1960s to 1980s.

9. The locations I chose to highlight reflect the amount of information I have for activities and activist sites in these locales generally.

10. Historian Lilia Fernández explores the feminism and founding of Mujeres Latinas en Acción in Chicago in her book *Brown in the Windy City: Mexicans and Puerto Ricans in Postwar Chicago* (Chicago: University of Chicago Press, 2012).

11. Rogelio Saenz, "The Changing Demography of Latinos in the Midwest," in Ruben O. Martinez, ed. *Latinos in the Midwest* (East Lansing: Michigan State University Press, 2011), 34.

12. Rogelio Saenz explains that, before 1970, the Census Bureau did not have a way to classify the population. Additionally, there was hardly any reference to the Midwest in the mainstream media. Saenz, "The Changing Demography of Latinos in the Midwest," 35. Gilberto Cárdenas sought to bring attention to the midwestern Latino population as a sociology graduate student at Notre Dame in the 1970s.

13. As Delia Fernández illustrates, this is especially true of the sugar beet industry in Michigan. Delia Fernández, "Becoming Latino: Mexican and Puerto Rican Community Formation in Grand Rapids, Michigan, 1926–1964," *Michigan Historical Review* 29, no. 1 (2013): 78.

14. Ricardo Parra, Victor Rios, and Armando Gutiérrez, "Chicano Organizations in the Midwest: Past, Present, and Possibilities," *Aztlán* 7, no. 2 (1978): 243.

15. Anne M. Santiago, "Life in the Industrial Heartland: A Profile of Latinos in the Midwest," *Institute Research Report*, no. 2 (May 1990): 11. A research associate at Michigan State University's Julian Samora Research Institute, Santiago wrote that the 1970 US Census defined Spanish speakers differently based on their region; Latinos in the Southwest were asked if they were "persons of Spanish language or Spanish surname," and in the Midwest, Latinos were identified on the basis of "Spanish language." Inconsistencies in the questions make comparisons difficult; p. 7.

16. Villa, interview by Garcia Merchant, January 27, 2006, part B.

17. Teresa Palomo Acosta, "La Raza Unida Party," in *Handbook of Texas Online* (Austin: Texas State Historical Association), modified March 25, 2016, http://www.tshaonline.org /handbook/online/articles/war01; Armando Navarro, *La Raza Unida Party: A Chicano Challenge to the U.S. Two-Party Dictatorship* (Philadelphia: Temple University Press 2000), iv.

18. Armando Navarro highlights that there were no similar catalysts for activism in the Midwest, asserting that the activism in the region stemmed from movements such as El Paso's La Raza Unida Conference in 1967 and the development of Chicano studies programs in the California University System. Navarro, *La Raza Unida Party*, iv.

19. Parra, Rios, and Gutiérrez, "Chicano Organizations in the Midwest," 240.

20. Ricardo Parra and Olga Villa Parra, "Serving Our Communities (1970–1980)," in *Moving beyond Borders: Julian Samora and the Establishment of Latino Studies*, ed. Alberto López Pulido, Barbara Driscoll de Alvarado, and Carmen Samora (Urbana: University of Illinois Press, 2009), 79.

21. Gilberto Cárdenas, interview by Leticia Wiggins, March 13, 2013, by phone; Olga Villa Parra, "Hispanic Women: Nurturing Tomorrow's Philanthropy," *New Directions for Philanthropic Fundraising* 24 (1999): 75–84.

22. Parra and Villa Parra, "Serving Our Communities," 80.

23. Ibid., 79.

24. Cárdenas, interview by Wiggins.

25. Villa, interview by Garcia Merchant, 2006, part B.

26. Pulido, Driscoll de Alvarado, and Samora, *Moving beyond Borders*, 79.

27. Vicki L. Ruiz, *Cannery Women, Cannery Lives: Mexican Women, Unionization, and the California Food Processing Industry, 1930–1950* (Albuquerque: University of New Mexico Press, 1992). Ruiz is one of the first Chicana/Latina historians to highlight the importance of women in establishing and maintaining community networks. This community building, she argues, provides the base for organizing around the interests of these ethnic communities.

28. Ricardo Parra to conference attendees, March 1972, detailing events of Mi Raza Primero conference, Midwest Council of La Raza Manuscripts CMCL 1/002 (Mi Raza Primero Conference 1972 folder), Midwest Council of La Raza Records, University of Notre Dame Archives (council records hereafter cited as CMCL and folder number).

29. "Struggle for Self-Determination," *Los Desarraigados* (Parra quote); Steven Nickeson, "Chicanos Unite in the Midwest," *Race Relations Reporter*, n.d., CMCL 1.001 (Miscellaneous Memos and Correspondence 1970–1976).

30. Steven Nickeson, "Women's Caucus—Resolutions," *Race Relations Reporter*, n.d., CMCL 1.001.

31. Ibid.

32. Ibid.

33. Jane Gonzalez resume, MSS 382, Juana and Jesse Gonzales Papers, José F. Treviño Chicano/Latino Activism Collections, Special Collections, MSU Libraries, Michigan State University, East Lansing.

34. Parra to conference attendees, March 1972, CMCL 1.001.

35. Benita Roth, *Separate Roads to Feminism: Black, Chicana, and White Feminist Movements in America's Second Wave* (Cambridge, England: Cambridge University Press, 2004), 145.

36. Epigraph, Maria Mangual, interview by Lilia Fernández, December 8, 2003, Chicago, transcript, p. 5; Olga Villa to "Miss La Plante," CMCL 3.002 (Olga Villa's Letter File re. Mujeres 1972–1975).

37. Mangual, interview by Fernández, transcript, p. 5. From this point on, I will use "Latina" to encompass both Chicana and Latina actors.

38. Villa, interview by Garcia Merchant, 2006, part C.

39. Martha Cotera, interview by Leticia Wiggins, May 12, 2015, Austin.

40. Ibid.

41. Olga Villa to Thomas Bergin, April 26, 1972, CMCL 3/002. This letter to Bergin is incredibly interesting, but with the second page missing, it is difficult to determine whether Villa completed her list of complaints.

42. Ibid.

43. Natalia Molina makes similar arguments in considering public health facilities in Los Angeles; *Fit to Be Citizens? Public Health and Race in Los Angeles, 1879–1939* (Berkeley: University of California Press, 2006).

44. List of 12 demands, box 1, Gilberto Cárdenas Papers, Samora Archives.

45. Leticia Wiggins, "Planting the 'Uprooted Ones': La Raza in the Midwest 1970–1979" (PhD diss., Ohio State University, 2016). I explore the relationship between the Catholic Church, Notre Dame, and the Midwest Council most directly in the fifth chapter of the dissertation, on page 181.

46. "100 Raza Women Attend Adelante Mujer Conference," *The Militant*. In her discussion of the organization of the first national Chicana conference in Houston (1971), Blackwell demonstrates the importance of such community connections, showing how women in the Magnolia Park area of Houston and their local YWCA branch secured a location for their conference. Blackwell, Chapter 5, *¡Chicana Power!*

47. These connections might imply an interesting relationship between South Bend Latinos and labor movements. Additionally, they complicate the idea of support from an elite private educational institution; "100 Raza Women Attend Adelante Mujer Conference," *The Militant*.

48. Villa, interview by Garcia Merchant, 2006, part C.

49. Villa, interview by Garcia Merchant, 2006, part A.

50. Ibid.

51. Ibid.

52. Ibid.

53. Ibid.

54. The Conferencia de las Mujeres in Houston is detailed most directly in Blackwell's work; see her *¡Chicana Power!*.

55. "Chicano Women Organize to Control Own Lives," *South Bend Tribune*, June 18, 1972, catalogued in Driscoll, "A Newspaper Documentary History of the Chicano Community of South Bend, Indiana," Parra Papers.

56. Nora Salas, "'We Are a Distinct People': Defending Difference in Schools through the Chicano Movement in Michigan, 1966–1980," in *The Chicano Movement: Perspectives from the Twenty-First Century*, ed. Mario T. García (New York: Routledge, 2014), 227. Salas reveals how bilingual and bicultural education, push-out rates, and the classification of Mexican children as retarded were major issues in Michigan at the time.

57. Ibid.

58. Salas, "We Are a Distinct People," 230.

59. Soriano quoted in Salas, "'We Are a Distinct People,'" 227. Here Jesse Soriano explains his role as the bilingual-education coordinator for Ann Arbor, Michigan. Salas also cites Soriano's work with James McClafferty described in the latter's article "Spanish Speakers of the Midwest: They Are Americans Too," *Foreign Language Annals* 2, no. 3 (March 1969): 322. Soriano's involvement with the MWCLR dates back to 1971; Minutes of Board of Directors, December 9, 1972, CMCL 1/021 (MWCLR Minutes 1972–1973). Jesse Soriano to L. G. Lopez, Lee's Summit, MO, April 1, 1976, formalizes Soriano's resignation from the MWCLR due to lack of time to commit to the organization; Correspondence 1976, CMCL 2/005.

60. Soriano quoted in Salas, "We Are a Distinct People," 231.

61. Villa, interview by Garcia Merchant, 2006, part A.

62. "100 Raza Women Attend Adelante Mujer Conference," Parra Papers. What these women were promoting is unclear; more oral histories need to flesh out this information, as their presence was merely evidenced by this newspaper article.

63. Ibid. It is unclear if the coalition representatives were Anglo or Hispanic women.

64. Villa, interview by Garcia Merchant, 2006, part B.

65. Ibid.

66. Ibid.

67. Villa, interview by Garcia Merchant, 2006, part C.

68. "Chicano Women Organize to Control Own Lives," *South Bend Tribune*.

69. Ibid.

70. Ibid.

71. Ibid.

72. Ibid.

73. Villa, interview by Garcia Merchant, 2006, part B.

74. Ibid.

75. Ibid.

76. "Chicano Women Organize to Control Own Lives," *South Bend Tribune*.

77. Fernández, *Brown in the Windy City*, 259.

78. "100 Raza Women Attend Adelante Mujer Conference," *The Militant*.

79. Villa, interview by Garcia Merchant, 2006, part D.

80. Domingo Rosas to MWCLR, August 1972, CMCL 3.002.

81. In my master's paper titled "Institutionalizing Activism, Deconstructing Borderlines: La Raza in the Midwest, 1970–1978" (Ohio State University, 2013), I explain further the potential meaning behind the title of the newsletter *Los Desarraigados*, which represented a population "uprooted" from their ancestral land and transplanted into an unfamiliar geographical place and setting.

82. Examples are found in the Samora Library in *Los Desarraigados*, 1970–1978, MS 2009.8, binder section 2.

83. Villa, interview by Garcia Merchant, 2006, part B.

84. Ibid.

85. Ibid.

86. Examples are filed in *Los Desarraigados*, 1970–1978, MS 2009.8, binder section 2, Samora Library.

87. Villa, interview by Garcia Merchant, 2006, part D.

88. Blackwell, *¡Chicana Power!*, 22.

89. Beverly Welsh, "Two for the Migrants: Even Marriage Won't Halt Their Social Dedication," *South Bend Tribune*, June 27, 1979.

90. Villa, interview by Garcia Merchant, 2006, part D.

91. Blackwell, *¡Chicana Power!*, 191.

92. Steven Nickeson, "Women's Caucus—Resolutions," *Race Relations Reporter*, n.d., CMCL 1.001.

CHAPTER 4

1. A note on usage: The Catholic Cursillo is a nationally recognized Catholic movement. I use the lowercase term "cursillo" to reflect an independent cursillo movement organized by my informants. Similarly, I use "Church," capitalized, to refer to the institutional Catholic Church and lowercase "church" to reflect a sociological usage.

2. See Rudy V. Busto, *King Tiger: The Religious Vision of Reies López Tijerina* (Albuquerque: University of New Mexico Press, 2005).

3. Religious studies scholar Rudy Busto notes that Chicano nationalist discourse "contained, suppressed, and even erased dissident and religious voices from its collective ethnic memory"; *King Tiger*, 4.

4. Ana Castillo, *Massacre of the Dreamers* (Albuquerque: University of New Mexico Press, 1994), 13.

5. See Cesar Chavez, "No More Cathedrals," in *An Organizer's Tale: Speeches*, ed. Ilan Stavans (New York: Penguin Books, 2008), 84–87.

6. For the most thorough treatment of clerical activism in the church, see Lara Medina, *Las Hermanas: Chicana/Latina Religious-Political Activism in the U.S. Catholic Church* (Philadelphia: Temple University Press, 2004), and Richard Martinez, *PADRES: The National Chicano Priest Movement* (Austin: University of Texas Press, 2005). Also see my own work on the Chicano Priests Organization in San Jose, in chapter 3 of Gallardo, "'I Never Left the Church': Redefining Chicana/o Catholic Religious Identities in San Jose, California" (PhD diss., Stanford University, 2012).

7. Ada María Isasi Díaz, *Mujerista Theology: A Theology for the Twenty-First Century* (Maryknoll, NY: Orbis, 1996); Anthony Stevens-Arroyo, *Prophets Denied Honor* (Maryknoll, NY: Orbis 1980). See also Gilbert Cadena's "Chicanos and the Catholic Church: Liberation Theology as a Form of Empowerment" (PhD diss., University of California, Riverside, 1987) and Ada María Isasi-Díaz and Yolanda Tarango, *Hispanic Women: Prophetic Voice in the Church* (San Francisco: Harper and Row, 1988).

8. For example, see Elisa Facio and Irene Lara, *Fleshing the Spirit: Spirituality and Activism in Chicana, Latina, and Indigenous Women's Lives* (Tucson: University of Arizona Press, 2014), and Brenda Sendejo, "The Cultural Production of Spiritual Activisms: Gender, Social Justice, and the Remaking of Religion in the Borderlands," *Chicana/Latina Studies* 12, no. 2 (2013): 59–109.

9. Castillo, *Massacre of the Dreamers*, 89.

10. Ibid., 90.

11. See Alberto López Pulido, "Nuestra Señora de Guadalupe: The Mexican Catholic Experience in San Diego," *Journal of San Diego History* 37, no. 4 (1991): 237–254; Milagros Peña, *Latina Activists across Borders* (Durham, NC: Duke University Press, 2007), 99; and Mary Pardo, *Mexican American Women Activists* (Philadelphia: Temple University Press, 1998).

12. I don't mean to be simplistic here. In many cases, progressive, white, Spanish-speaking priests made significant contributions to local communities, such as San Jose's Donald McDonnell, while imported Spanish or Latin American priests could be more authoritarian than local priests. But the low numbers of Latino clergy meant that for most Latina/o parishioners, Church authority figures were white and male.

13. Stephen J. Pitti, *The Devil in Silicon Valley: Northern California, Race and Mexican Americans* (Princeton, NJ: Princeton University Press, 2004), 180.

14. San Jose State University *Spartan Daily*, November 2, 1967, cited in Pitti, *Devil in Silicon Valley*, 180.

15. Elsewhere I explore the emergence of an unusual independent Catholic community out of the parish church, Our Lady of Guadalupe in San Jose, California, in the late 1970s. The Cursillo began in the San Francisco Bay Area in the mid-1960s and took root at Guadalupe by the early 1970s; Gallardo, "I Never Left the Church." Also see Kristy Nabhan-Warren, *The Cursillo Movement in America* (Chapel Hill: University of North Carolina Press, 2013).

16. Debra Campbell, *Graceful Exits: Catholic Women and the Art of Departure* (Bloomington: Indiana University Press, 2003), 199.

17. Anthony Soto, "The Cursillo Movement," in *The Inner Crusade: The Closed Retreat in the United States*, ed. Thomas C. Hennessy (Chicago: Loyola University Press, 1965).

18. See Gallardo, "I Never Left the Church."

19. R. Marie Griffith and Barbara Dianne Savage, introduction to *Women and Religion in the African Diaspora*, ed. Griffith and Savage (Baltimore, MD: Johns Hopkins University Press, 2006), xvii.

20. Jay P. Dolan, *The American Catholic Experience* (New York: Doubleday, 1985), 221.

21. Roberto R. Treviño, *The Church in the Barrio: Mexican American Ethno-Catholicism in Houston* (Chapel Hill: University of North Carolina Press, 2006), 4–5.

22. Maria Oropesa, interview by Susana L. Gallardo, March 3, 1995, San Jose, CA.

23. Maria O., interview by Anthony Soto, 1983, San Jose, CA, unpublished manuscript in author's possession.

24. Ibid.

25. Ibid.

26. Oropesa, interview by Gallardo, March 3, 1995, San Jose, CA.

27. Ibid.

28. Ibid. The Stanford-Binet Intelligence Quotient identifies 69 as "mild learning difficulty" and 90–109 as "normal." Maria remembered being told it meant "mildly retarded."

29. Ibid.

30. Maria Oropesa, interview by Susana L. Gallardo, June 1, 1995, San Jose, CA.

31. Ibid.

32. Ibid.

33. Ibid.

34. Ibid.

35. Ibid.

36. The Guadalupe parish pastor Anthony Soto often shared the work of the Catholic theologian Hans Kung, who wrote, "All Christians are taught and led and supported by the Spirit directly, without mediation, and they are all to live by the Spirit. The anointing is not just given to prophets and kings, but to the whole community, each individual being filled with the fullness of God. This means that all believers have direct access to God, allowing themselves to be a spiritual offering to God thus becoming holy in every action. All believers also are called to be preachers, not simply with words but with actions, not simply in the church building but in all of their lives"; Hans Kung, *The Church* (London: Burns and Oates, 1967).

37. To this day, Mexican American children assessed by the county Child Protective Services Division are significantly more likely to be taken from their families than are white children.

38. Oropesa, interview by Gallardo, March 3, 1995.

39. Untitled poem by Maria Oropesa, November 26, 1982, personal copy in the author's possession.

40. Jessie Garibaldi, interview by Susana L. Gallardo, July 19, 2011, San Jose, CA.

41. Ibid.

42. Ibid.

43. Ibid.

44. Ibid.

45. Attendance at Mass was historically low and remains so among Chicana/o and Latina/o Catholics. Clerics and Catholic researchers have long lamented this pattern as a "Mexican problem," which I argue is a shortsighted interpretation, given the prevalence of Catholic symbols and ideology throughout the culture. See Treviño, *Church in the Barrio*.

46. Phyllis Soto, interview by Susana L. Gallardo, July 28, 1992, San Jose, CA.

47. Phyllis Soto, interview by Susana L. Gallardo, July 8, 1992, San Jose, CA.

48. Ibid.

49. Phyllis Soto, "Know Yourself," typescript, June 1979, in the author's possession.

50. Gloria Anzaldúa, "Now Let Us Shift . . . The Path of Conocimiento . . . Inner Work, Public Acts," in AnaLouise Keating and Gloria Anzaldúa, *This Bridge We Call Home: Radical Visions for Transformation* (New York: Routledge, 2002), 572.

51. Amy Kesselman, interviewed in Alice Echols, *Daring to Be Bad: Radical Feminism in America 1967–1975* (Minneapolis: University of Minnesota Press, 1989), 83.

52. Linda Gonzales, interview by Susana L. Gallardo, October 14, 2011, San Jose, CA.

53. Phyllis Soto, "Baptism in a Chicano Catholic Faith Community: An Alternative Ceremony," undated copy in the author's possession.

54. Soto, interview by Gallardo, July 8, 1992.

CHAPTER 5

1. From the series of interviews, I selected and edited this passage for publication. I thank Audrey Silvestre for her many talents as a research assistant and Maria Cotera for editorial assistance. This interview is published with the permission of the Gloria E. Anzaldúa Literary Trust.

2. Rodolfo "Corky" Gonzales, *I Am Joaquin: An Epic Poem* (Santa Barbara, CA: La Causa, 1967); Alurista, the *nom de plume* of Chicano movement activist and poet Alberto Baltazar Urista Heredia. Alurista's poem became the preamble to the "Plan Espiritual de Aztlán" after he read his poetry at the 1969 Denver Youth Liberation Conference, where this statement was drafted.

3. Gloria Anzaldúa, *Borderlands/La Frontera: The New Mestiza* (San Francisco: Aunt Lute, 1987).

4. Anna NietoGomez, "La feminista," *Encuentro Femenil* 1, no. 2 (1974): 28-33; "La Chicana: Legacy of Suffering and Self-Denial," *Scene* 8, no. 1 (1975): 22-24.

5. See Estela Portillo-Trambley, "The Day of the Swallows," *El Grito* 7, no. 1 (1973): 5-47.

6. Anzaldúa, *Borderlands/ La Frontera*; Gloria Anzaldúa, ed., *Making Face, Making Soul / Haciendo Caras: Creative and Critical Perspectives by Feminists of Color* (San Francisco: Aunt Lute, 1990).

7. Gloria Anzaldúa, "La Prieta," in *This Bridge Called My Back: Writings By Radical Women of Color*, ed. Cherríe Moraga and Gloria E. Anzaldúa (Watertown, MA: Persephone Press, 1981); for more on Prieta stories see Anzaldúa's *Interviews/Entrevistas*, ed. AnaLouise Keating (New York: Routledge, 2000); and AnaLouise Keating, ed., *The Gloria Anzaldúa Reader* (Durham, NC: Duke University Press, 2009).

8. Gloria Anzaldúa, *Interviews/Entrevistas*, ed. Ana Louise Keating (New York: Routledge, 2000):53.

9. My thanks to AnaLouise Keating, who informed me that "EL Mundo Surdo" is spelled with an *s*, not *z*, according to the flyers advertising the events, and in a note in the archive Anzaldúa mentions spelling "zurdo" with an "s" in an homage to a South Tejas accent; Gloria Evangelina Anzaldúa Papers, University of Texas as Austin.

10. Radicalesbians, "*Women Identified Women*," in *Notes from the Third Year*, ed. Anne Koedt (New York: N.p., 1971); Valerie Solanas, *The Scum Manifesto* (New York: Olympia Press, 1968).

CHAPTER 6

1. See, for instance, Elizabeth "Betita" Martínez, "La Chicana," in *Chicana Feminist Thought: The Basic Historical Writings*, ed. Alma M. García (London: Routledge, 1997), 32; Angela Y. Davis, *Women, Race, and Class* (New York: Random House, 1981); Denise A.

Segura, "Chicanas and Triple Oppression in the Labor Force," in *Chicana Voices: Intersections of Class, Race, and Gender*, ed. Teresa Córdova (Austin: Center for Mexican American Studies, University of Texas, 1986), 47–65; Kimberlé Crenshaw, "Demarginalizing the Intersection of Race and Sex: A Black Feminist Critique of Antidiscrimination Doctrine, Feminist Theory, and Antiracist Politics," *University of Chicago Legal Forum* 1, no. 8 (1989); Patricia Hill Collins and Sirma Bilge, *Intersectionality* (Cambridge, England: Polity, 2016).

2. Alicia Escalante, interview by Maria E. Cotera, February 23 and 24, 2012, Sacramento, CA, Chicana por mi Raza Digital Memory Collective; Alicia Escalante, interview by Rosie Bermudez, October 31, 2012, by phone. All interviews conducted by the author included in this publication have received institutional approval: UCSB HSC ID 16–0472.

3. East Los Angeles Welfare Rights Organization was the name under which the organization was incorporated as it reflected the local, grassroots nature of the group as well as its link to the larger welfare rights organizing across the United States. The group was also known as the National Chicano Welfare Rights Organization, the Chicana Welfare Rights Organization, and La Causa de Los Pobres, the namesake of its newspaper. The shifting identities of the organization reflected the evolution of Escalante's and the organization's political consciousness and commitments from a local to a national vision.

4. For a detailed discussion of "the multsited emergence of women of color as a historical political formation," see Maylei Blackwell, *¡Chicana Power! Contested Histories of Feminism in the Chicano Movement* (Austin: University of Texas Press, 2011), 21.

5. It is important to note that while Escalante diverged from the "typical" depiction of a Chicano movement activist as a single mother in her thirties, she certainly was not alone. See the important work on the life and activism of Enriqueta Vásquez in Enriqueta Longeaux y Vásquez, *Enriqueta Vasquez and the Chicano Movement: Writings from* El Grito del Norte, ed. Lorena Oropeza and Dionne Espinoza (Houston: Arte Público, 2006).

6. Escalante, "Canto de Alicia," *Encuentro Femenil* 1, no. 1 (1973): 5-11.

7. Emma Pérez, *The Decolonial Imaginary: Writing Chicanas into History* (Bloomington: Indiana University Press, 1999).

8. Alicia Escalante, interview by Rosie Bermudez, October 5, 2014, Sacramento, CA.

9. Ibid.

10. Escalante, "Canto de Alicia," 5.

11. Escalante, interview by Bermudez, October 5, 2014.

12. Ibid.

13. Barbara Bair and Susan E. Cayleff, *Wings of Gauze: Women of Color and the Experience of Health and Illness* (Detroit: Wayne State University Press, 1993); Josephine A. V. Allen, "Poverty as a Form of Violence," *Journal of Human Behavior in the Social Environment* 4, no. 2/3 (2001): 45–59.

14. Alicia Escalante, interview by Rosie Bermudez, November 10, 2012, Sacramento, CA.

15. Escalante did not make clear in interviews why her mother disapproved of Antonio Escalante Jr., only that her mother had a sense that he was not the one for her; Escalante, interview by Cotera, February 23 and 24, 2012; Escalante, interview by Bermudez, November 10, 2012.

16. Escalante, interview by Bermudez, November 10, 2012.

17. Ibid.

18. Alicia Escalante, interview by Rosie Bermudez, January 24, 2014, Sacramento, CA; Escalante, interview by Bermudez, October 5, 2014.

19. Escalante, interview by Bermudez, January 24, 2014.

20. Ibid.

21. For a detailed account of Alicia Escalante's organizing with the ELAWRO and activism during the Chicano movement, see Rosie Bermudez, "Alicia Escalante: The Chicana

Welfare Rights Organization and the Chicano Movement," in *The Chicano Movement: Perspectives from the Twenty-First Century*, ed. Mario T. García (New York: Routledge, 2014). For an account of Escalante's early activism with African American women in Los Angeles see Alejandra Marchevsky's chapter in this anthology.

22. For recent histories of the Chicano movement see Juan Gómez-Quiñones and Irene Vásquez, *Making Aztlán: Ideology and Culture of the Chicana and Chicano Movement, 1966–1977* (Albuquerque: University of New Mexico Press, 2014); Mario T. García, *The Chicano Movement: Perspectives for the Twenty-First Century* (New York: Routledge, 2014); Maylei Blackwell, *¡Chicana Power!: Contested Histories of Feminism in the Chicano Movement* (Austin: University of Texas, 2011); Longeaux y Vásquez, *Enriqueta Vasquez and the Chicano Movement* (2006); Lorena Oropeza, *¡Raza Sí! ¡Guerra No! Chicano Protest and Patriotism during the Viet Nam War Era* (Berkeley: University of California Press, 2005); George Mariscal, *Brown-Eyed Children of the Sun: Lessons from the Chicano Movement, 1965–1975* (Albuquerque: University of New Mexico Press, 2005).

23. For histories on Chicana activism and feminism during this era see Blackwell, *¡Chicana Power!*; Longeaux y Vásquez, *Enriqueta Vasquez and the Chicano Movement*; Elizabeth Martínez, *500 Years of Chicana Women's History/500 Años de la Mujer Chicana* (New Brunswick, NJ: Rutgers University Press, 2008); Marisela R. Chávez, "'We Have a Long, Beautiful History': Chicana Feminist Trajectories and Legacies," In *No Permanent Waves: Recasting Histories of U.S. Feminism*, ed. Nancy A. Hewitt (New Brunswick, NJ: Rutgers University Press, 2010); Dolores Delgado Bernal, "Grassroots Leadership Reconceptualized: Chicana Oral Histories and the 1968 East Los Angeles School Blowouts," *Frontiers: A Journal of Women Studies* 19, no. 2 (1998): 113–142.

24. "Los 35 Arrested for Liberation," in "Chicanos Liberate Board of Education,"special issue, *La Raza*, October 15, 1968, n.p. For histories of the East Los Angeles high school blowouts see García and Castro, *Blowout! Sal Castro and the Struggle for Education Justice* (Chapel Hill: University of North Carolina Press, 2011); Bernal, "Grassroots Leadership Reconceptualized."

25. Escalante quoted in Oropeza, *¡Raza Si! ¡Guerra No!*, 141–142, from *People's World*, December 27, 1969.

26. "National Chicano Moratorium," *La Causa*, February 28, 1970, 12; Escalante, interview by Cotera, February 23 and 24, 2012. For more on Escalante's experience as an activist mother see Sylvia Morales, dir., *A Crushing Love: Chicanas, Motherhood, and Activism*, video, Women Make Movies, 2009.

27. Bermudez, "Alicia Escalante."

28. Escalante's children were present and participated in events such as the Poor People's Campaign in 1968 and the St. Basil's demonstration held on Christmas Eve in 1969.

29. Escalante, interviews by Bermudez, November 10, 2012, and October 5, 2014.

30. Escalante, interview by Bermudez, January 24, 2014.

31. Alicia Escalante, untitled report on the Poor People's Campaign, *La Raza*, May 11, 1968, 7; "Los 35 Arrested for Liberation," La Raza, October 15, 1968; Alicia Escalante, "Around the World to Expose Hunger in the U.S.A.," *La Raza* 2, no. 9 (1969): 12.

32. Escalante, interview by Bermudez, November 10, 2012.

33. For more on the Chicano Press Association, see Raul Ruiz, "The Chicanos and the Underground Press," *La Raza Magazine* 3, no. 1 (1977), 8–10; Blackwell, *¡Chicana Power!*, 138. For more on *La Raza* newspaper and *La Raza Magazine*, see Francisco Manuel Andrade, "The History of La Raza Newspaper and Magazine and Its Role in the Chicano Community from 1967–1977" (master's thesis, California State University, Fullerton, 1979).

34. Anna NietoGomez, "Madres por justicia," *Encuentro Femenil* 1, no. 1 (1973): 12–18.

35. Francisca Flores, "A Reaction to Discussions on the Talmadge Amendment to the

Social Security Act," *Regeneración* 2, no. 3 (1973): 16; Francisca Flores, "A Reaction to Discussions on the Talmadge Amendment to the Social Security Act," *Encuentro Femenil* 1, no. 2 (1974): 13–14; Alicia Escalante, "A Letter from the Chicana Welfare Rights Organization," *Encuentro Femenil* 1, no. 2 (1974): 15–19.

36. Although Escalante did not identify as a Chicana feminist during the 1960s and 1970s, in her reflections during our interviews she did acknowledge that her activism was feminist, and she articulated clear distinctions between the feminism of white women and the feminism that she practiced; Escalante, interview by Bermudez, January 24, 2014.

37. Escalante, "Letter from the Chicana Welfare Rights Organization," 17.

38. Ibid.

39. Escalante, interview by Bermudez, January 24, 2014.

40. Escalante, interview by Bermudez, October 5, 2014.

41. Escalante, "Canto de Alicia," 10.

CHAPTER 7

1. I am grateful to Ester Hernández for sharing her story with me over many conversations and oral history sessions. I thank her for opening her home and archives to me. My gratitude also goes to Audrey Silvestre for her research assistance and Cristina Serna and María Cotera for their helpful feedback on an earlier draft of this work.

2. For more on the work of Ester Hernández, see Laura E. Pérez, *Chicana Art: The Politics of Spiritual and Aesthetic Altarities* (Durham, NC: Duke University Press, 2007); Clara Román-Odio, *Sacred Iconographies in Chicana Cultural Production* (New York: Palgrave Macmillan, 2013); Edward McCaughan, *Art and Social Movements in Mexico and Aztlán* (Durham, NC: Duke University Press, 2012).

3. Shifra Goldman, "How, Why, Where, and When It All Happened: Chicano Murals of California," in *Signs from the Heart: California Chicano Murals*, ed. Eva Sperling Cockcroft and Holly Barnet-Sánchez (Albuquerque: University of New Mexico Press in association with the Social and Public Art Resource Center, 1993), 22-53; Alicia Gaspar de Alba, *Chicano Art Inside/Outside the Master's House: Cultural Politics and the CARA Exhibition* (Austin: University of Texas Press, 1998); Guisela Latorre, *Walls of Empowerment: Chicana/o Indigenist Murals of California* (Austin: University of Texas Press, 2008); Carlos Francisco Jackson, *Chicana and Chicano Art: ProtestArte* (Tucson: University of Arizona Press, 2009).

4. For a theory of multiple insurgencies of women of color organizing, see Maylei Blackwell, *¡Chicana Power! Contested Histories of Feminism in the Chicano Movement* (Austin: University of Texas Press, 2011).

5. Guisela Latorre, "Chicana Art and Scholarship on the Interstices of Our Disciplines," *Journal of Chicana/Latina Studies* 6, no. 2 (2007): 11.

6. Ester Hernández, interview by Maylei Blackwell, July 6, 2013.

7. Ibid.

8. Ester Hernández, interview by Maylei Blackwell, June 17, 2015.

9. Ibid.

10. Ester Hernández, correspondence with Maylei Blackwell, July 1, 2015. See Devra Weber's *Dark Sweat, White Gold: California Cotton, Farm Workers, and the New Deal, 1919–1939* (Berkeley: University of California Press, 1994).

11. Ester Hernández, interview by Maylei Blackwell, July 1, 2015.

12. Ester Hernández, interview by Maylei Blackwell, June 8, 2015.

13. For more on the exhibition, see Galeria de La Raza website, http://www.galeriadelaraza.org/eng/events/index.php?op=view&id=46.

14. Yolanda M. López, "Mujeres Muralistas," in *Encyclopedia of Latino Popular Culture*, ed. Cordelia Candelaria (Westport, CT: Greenwood, 2004), 569–570.

15. Patricia Rodriguez, "Mujeres Muralistas," in *Ten Years That Shook the City: San Francisco 1968–78*, ed. Chris Carlsson (San Francisco: City Lights Foundation, 2011) 81–91. See also videos, interviews, and photos at the Mujeres Muralistas website, http:// mujeresmuralistas.tumblr.com.

16. For histories of Mujeres Muralistas, see Gaspar de Alba, *Chicano Art Inside/Outside the Master's House*; Terezita Romo, "A Collective History: Las Mujeres Muralistas" in *Art, Women, California 1950–2000: Parallels and Intersections*, ed. Diana Burgess Fuller and Daniela Salvioni (Berkeley: University of California, 2002), 177–186; Latorre, *Walls of Empowerment*, 185–188.

17. See Latorre, *Walls of Empowerment*, chapter 1.

18. Hernández graduated in 1976 with a bachelor's in fine art; she immediately received a California Arts Council grant and worked under the mentorship of Luis Valdez, Ruth Asawa, and Noah Purifory.

19. Hernández, interview by Blackwell, July 6, 2013.

20. McCaughan, *Art and Social Movements*.

21. Hernández, interview by Blackwell, June 8, 2015.

22. McCaughan, *Art and Social Movements*, 35.

23. Ibid., 56.

24. Latorre, "Chicana Art and Scholarship," 11.

25. Others who have discussed *Libertad* include Gaspar de Alba in *Chicano Art Inside/ Outside the Master's House*, 141–143, and Pérez in *Chicana Art*, 268–269.

26. At the time of our interviews Hernández shared that she would use the term "Xican@s" if she were to reprint the etching, noting that she has always changed the name with the times to be more inclusive. Laura E. Pérez points to Patssi Valdez's rendition of the Virgen in the 1972 performance by Asco, an East Los Angeles Chicano art collective, of "The Walking Mural" as a first Chicana feminist reworking of the Virgen. Asco's performance engaged Chicano muralism of the day and critiqued the fixed stock of images by reimaging what happens when the mural figures get bored and walk off the wall and out of the frame; Pérez, *Chicana Art*, 267.

27. Amalia Mesa-Bains, "El Mundo Femenino: Chicana Artists of the Movement— A Commentary on Development and Production," in *Chicano Art: Resistance and Affirmation* (Los Angeles: Wright Art Gallery, UCLA, 1991), 131–140. Karen Mary Davalos, *Yolanda M. Lopez* (Los Angeles: UCLA Chicano Studies Research Center, 2008); Alicia Gaspar de Alba and Alma López, *Our Lady of Controversy: Alma Lopez's "Irreverent Apparition"* (Austin: University of Texas Press, 2011).

28. Irene Lara, "Tonanlupanisma: Re-Membering Tonantzin-Guadalupe in Chicana Visual Art," *Aztlán: A Jounal of Chicano Studies* 33, no. 2 (2008): 61–90; Román-Odio, *Sacred Iconographies*, 2013.

29. Hernandez interview, June 8, 2015.

30. Blackwell, *¡Chicana Power!*, chapter 4.

31. Amalia Mesa-Bains, *Ester Hernández*, Artist Monograph Series, no. 1 (San Francisco: Galeria de la Raza/Studio 24, 1988).

32. Celia Herrera Rodríguez, "A Sacred Thing That Takes Us Home (A Curatorial Statement)," in *This Bridge Called My Back: Writings by Radical Women of Color*, ed. Cherríe Moraga and Gloria E. Anzaldúa (Berkeley, CA: Third Woman Press, 2002), 279–287. My thanks to Cristina Serna for reminding me of this essay and important connection placing Hernández in conversation with the broader world of women of color artists.

33. Hernández, interview, July 6, 2013. For more information on the political context,

see Shifra Goldman and Tomás Ybarra-Frausto, "The Political and Social Contexts of Chicano Art," in *Chicano Art: Resistance and Affirmation*, ed. Richard Griswold del Castillo, Teresa McKenna, and Yvonne Yarbro-Bejarano (Los Angeles: Wight Art Gallery and University of California, 1991), 83–95.

34. Ester Hernández, interview by Maylei Blackwell, September 6, 2017.

35. Hernández, interview, July 6, 2013.

36. Marjorie Agosín, *Tapestries of Hope, Threads of Love: The Arpillera Movement in Chile*, 2nd ed. (New York: Rowman and Littlefield, 2007).

37. Because people of conscience and many Central American solidary activists began to target the School of the Americas by performing civil disobedience, the school relocated and changed its name to the Western Hemisphere Institute for Security Cooperation.

38. Hernández, interview, July 6, 2013.

39. Ester Hernández, interview by Maylei Blackwell, June 19, 2015.

40. Hernández, interview, July 6, 2013.

41. See Yvonne Yarbro-Bejarano, "The Lesbian Body in Latina Cultural Production," in *Entiendes? Queer Readings, Hispanic Writings*, ed. Paul Julian Smith and Emilie L. Bergmann (Durham, NC: Duke University Press, 1995), 181–197; Carla Trujillo, "La Virgen de Guadalupe and Her Reconstruction in Chicana Lesbian Desire," in *Living Chicana Theory*, ed. Carla Trujillo (Berkeley: Third Woman Press, 1998), 214–231.

42. Carla Trujillo, *Chicana Lesbians: The Girls Our Mothers Warned Us About* (Berkeley: Third Woman Press, 1991).

43. Hernández, interview, June 17, 2015.

44. McCaughan, *Art and Social Movements*, 100.

45. Hernández, interview, July 6, 2013.

46. Yolanda Broyles-González, *Lydia Mendoza's Life in Music/La Historia de Lydia Mendoza: Norteno Tejano Legacies* (New York: Oxford University Press, 2001). For a critical history of women in Tejano music, see Deborah R. Vargas, *Dissonant Divas: The Limits of La Onda* (Minneapolis: University of Minnesota Press, 2012).

47. This argument posits how sound and visual representations extend the notion of Chicana counterpublics constituted by Chicana print and visual cultures; Blackwell, *¡Chicana Power!*. See also Cristina Serna, *Deconstructing the Nation: Queer and Feminist Art in Mexican and Chicana/o Social Movements* (PhD diss., University of California, Santa Barbara, 2014) for her analysis of Chicana and Mexicana art creating a transborder counterpublic fraught with the creative conflicts of translation.

48. See, for example, Dolores Inés Casillas, *Sounds of Belonging: U.S. Spanish-Language Radio and Public Advocacy* (New York: New York University Press, 2014), and Laura G. Gutiérrez, *Performing Mexicanidad: Vendidas y Cabreteras on the Transnational Stage* (Austin: University of Texas, 2010).

49. Hernández, interview, June 19, 2015; for more on Astrid Hadad, see Gutiérrez, *Performing Mexicanidad*.

50. Hernández, interview, June 19, 2015.

51. See, for example, Harmony Hammond, *Lesbian Art in America: A Contemporary History* (New York: Rizzoli International, 2000). For more on Laura Aquilar, see Yvonne Yarbro-Bejarano, "Laying It Bare: The Queer/Colored Body in Photography by Laura Aguilar," in *Living Chicana Theory*, ed. Carla Trujillo (Berkeley, CA: Third Woman Press, 1998), 277–305; Luz Calvo, "Embodied at the Shrine of Cultural Disjuncture," in *Beyond the Frame: Women of Color and Visual Representation*, ed. Angela Y. Davis and Neferti X. Tadiar (New York: Palgrave, 2005): 207–218; and Rebecca Epstein, ed., *Laura Aguilar, Show and Tell* (Los Angeles: UCLA Chicano Research Center Press, 2017).

52. Robin D. G. Kelly, *Freedom Dreams: The Black Radical Imagination* (New York: Beacon, 2002).

CHAPTER 8

1. For more on the labor migration circuit from Texas and Mexico, see Erasmo Gamboa, *Mexican Labor and World War II: Braceros in the Pacific Northwest, 1942–1947* (Seattle: University of Washington Press, 2000); Antonia I. Castañeda, "'Que Se Pudieran Defender (So You Could Defend Yourselves)': Chicanas, Regional History, and National Discourses," *Frontiers: A Journal of Women Studies* 22, no. 3 (2001): 116-142; Jerry Garcia and Gilberto Garcia, eds., *Memory, Community, and Activism: Mexican Migration and Labor in the Pacific Northwest* (East Lansing: Michigan State University Press, 2005).

2. During my interview with Rosa Ramón, she discussed the process of obtaining a reasonable lease on land where the tower would be built; Rosa Ramón, interview by Monica de la Torre, March 9, 2012, Seattle. Ahtanum Ridge is on the Yakama Reservation, which was created when Yakama leaders were forced to sign the Treaty of 1855 that ceded 90 percent of Yakama homeland to the U.S. government. The Yakama Nation, comprised of descendants from fourteen distinct tribes and bands and who speak the Ichishkíin language, continue to resist settler-colonial violence through the recovery of traditional cultural practices. For more on Yakama cultural revitalization projects see Michelle M. Jacob, *Yakama Rising: Indigenous Cultural Revitalization, Activism, and Healing* (Tucson: University of Arizona Press, 2013).

3. Francisco Lewels, *The Uses of the Media by the Chicano Movement: A Study in Minority Access* (New York: Praeger, 1974).

4. Epigraphs: Ricardo García, interview by Monica De La Torre, April 11, 2014, Granger, WA; Rosa Ramón, interview by De La Torre, March 9, 2012.

5. Dolores Inés Casillas, *Sounds of Belonging: U.S. Spanish-Language Radio and Public Advocacy* (New York: New York University Press, 2014), 53.

6. For more on Chicana feminist activism in the Chicano movement see Dolores Delgado Bernal, "Grassroots Leadership Reconceptualized: Chicana Oral Histories and the 1968 East Los Angeles School Blowouts," *Frontiers: A Journal of Women Studies* 19, no. 2 (1998): 113–142; Maylei Blackwell, *¡Chicana Power! Contested Histories of Feminism in the Chicano Movement* (Austin: University of Texas Press, 2011); Dionne Espinoza, "'Revolutionary Sisters': Women's Solidarity and Collective Identification among Chicana Brown Berets in East Los Angeles, 1967-1970," *Aztlán: A Journal of Chicano Studies* 26, no. 1 (2001): 17-57; Alma M. García, *Chicana Feminist Thought : The Basic Historical Writings* (London: Routledge, 1997).

7. Maylei Blackwell, "Contested Histories: *Las Hijas de Cuauhtémoc*, Chicana Feminisms, and Print Culture in the Chicano Movement, 1968–1973," in *Chicana Feminisms: A Critical Reader*, ed. Gabriela F. Arredondo, Aida Hurtado, Norma Klahn, Olga Najera-Ramirez, and Patricia Zavella (Durham, NC: Duke University Press, 2003), 61.

8. Gaye Theresa Johnson, *Spaces of Conflict, Sounds of Solidarity: Music, Race, and Spatial Entitlement in Los Angeles* (Berkeley: University of California Press, 2013).

9. Casillas, *Sounds of Belonging*, 54.

10. Johnson, *Spaces of Conflict, Sounds of Solidarity*. A similar phenomenon occurred with the power of Chicana print culture, which intersected and connected various components of Chicana feminist activism, thereby creating what Maylei Blackwell calls a "Chicana counterpublic"; Blackwell, *Chicana Power!*.

11. Scholars have also documented the Spanish presence in the Pacific Northwest dating back to the mid-1700s, predating the Lewis and Clark expeditions to the region. For a more

nuanced account of the various periods of Mexican and Chicano migration to the Pacific Northwest, see Carlos S. Maldonado and Gilberto Garcia, *The Chicano Experience in the Northwest* (Dubuque, IA: Kendall/Hunt, 1995); Garcia and Garcia, *Memory, Community, and Activism*; Gamboa, *Mexican Labor and World War II*.

12. From 1942 to 1964, the Bracero Program brought millions of Mexican guest workers to labor primarily in agriculture through a bilateral agreement between the United States and Mexico.

13. Erasmo Gamboa, "Mexican Migration into Washington State: A History, 1940–1950," *Pacific Northwest Quarterly* 72, no. 3 (1981): 121–131.

14. Ibid., 127.

15. Ibid.

16. For a timeline on Chicano movement activism in the Pacific Northwest from 1960 to 1985, see Oscar Rosales Castañeda, "Timeline: Movimiento from 1960–1985," Seattle Civil Rights and Labor History Project, http://depts.washington.edu/civilr/mecha _timeline.htm.

17. Yolanda Alaniz and Megan Cornish, *Viva La Raza: A History of Chicano Identity and Resistance* (Seattle: Red Letter Press, 2008).

18. Gamboa, *Mexican Labor and World War II*, xix.

19. Ramón, interview by De La Torre, March 9, 2012.

20. Ibid.

21. García, interview by De La Torre, April 11, 2014.

22. Jean Guerrero, "KDNA Founder Plans an Active Retirement," *Yakima Herald-Republic*, June 28, 2009.

23. Johnson, *Spaces of Conflict, Sounds of Solidarity*, x.

24. Ibid.

25. The Public Broadcasting Act of 1967 was instrumental in creating a funding mechanism for community-based media via the Corporation for Public Broadcasting (CPB) as a public subsidy for the development and expansion of educational public broadcasting.

26. Rosa Ramón, interview by Monica De La Torre, April 11, 2014.

27. Northwest Chicano Radio Network Articles of Incorporation, April 27, 1976.

28. A subsidiary communications authorization (SCA) is a subcarrier on a radio station allowing the station to broadcast additional services on its signal. KRAB-FM was the fourth noncommercial station in the United States. For a rich online archive of KRAB's history see its website, http://krab.fm.

29. Susan Marionneaux, "KDNA Radio's Estella Del Villar Breaks Gender Barriers with a Strong Voice," *Yakima Herald-Republic*, June 22, 2000.

30. Ramón Chávez, "Emerging Media: A History and Analysis of Chicano Communication Efforts in Washington State" (master's thesis, University of Washington, 1979).

31. Ramón, interview by De La Torre, March 9, 2012.

32. María Martin, interview by Monica De La Torre, February 24, 2014, by phone.

33. Dora Sánchez Treviño, "A Chicana in Northern Aztlán: An Oral History of Dora Sánchez Treviño," interview by Jerry García, *Frontiers: A Journal of Women Studies* 19, no. 2 (1998): 46.

34. Dionne Espinoza, "The Partido Belongs to Those Who Will Work for It: Chicana Organizing and Leadership in the Texas Raza Unida Party, 1970–1980," *Aztlán: A Journal of Chicano Studies* 36, no. 1 (2011): 196.

35. The 1978 report found that only 11 percent of minority women had participated in technical training; US Task Force on Minorities in Public Broadcasting, *A Formula for Change: The Report of the Task Force on Minorities in Public Broadcasting* (Washington, DC: US Task Force on Minorities in Public Broadcasting, 1978). For its 1975 report, the Task Force

on Women in Public Broadcasting surveyed public broadcasting to assess the employment and representation of women in this medium; Caroline Isber and Muriel G. Cantor, *Report of the Task Force on Women in Public Broadcasting* (Washington, DC: Corporation for Public Broadcasting and US Task Force on Women in Public Broadcasting, 1975). Although the statistics in the report on women in broadcast predate KDNA's founding, they are indicative of the status of the field of public broadcasting, especially the potential challenges women faced in technical positions.

36. According to the 1975 report of the Task Force on Women in Public Broadcasting, employment statistics for the 1974 fiscal year showed that "women held slightly fewer than thirty percent of all jobs in public broadcasting. Most women employed in public broadcasting industries are found in low-level secretarial or clerical positions"; Muriel G. Cantor, "Women and Public Broadcasting," *Journal of Communication* 27, no. 1 (1977): 17.

37. Ramón, interview by De La Torre, March 9, 2012.

38. For more on the work of Chicana community radio broadcasters and their feminist radio praxis, refer to Monica De La Torre, "*Programas Sin Vergüenza* (Shameless Programs): Mapping Chicanas in Community Radio in the 1970s," *Women's Studies Quarterly WSQ: The 1970s* 43, no. 3–4 (2015): 175-190.

39. Prieto, *Women of Radio* KDNA program, 1984, recording in the author's possession, courtesy of Rosa Ramón.

CHAPTER 9

1. I am deeply indebted to Estela Ortega, Graciela Gonzalez, Carmen Miranda, Daniel DeSiga, and the staff at El Centro de la Raza. Our dialogues, oral histories, trust, humor, and time made this chapter possible. I am grateful for the guidance of James Gregory, Susan Glenn, Michelle Habell-Pallán, and Adam Warren in conceptualizing this chapter. I am thankful to Estela Ortega, Monica De La Torre, Ryan Archibald, and Kevin McKenna, who each read iterations of it at various stages. I am particularly thankful to Maylei Blackwell and Dionne Espinoza for their critical feedback and patience. I also appreciate comments from the two readers through the University of Texas Press. I am very appreciative to the archivists at El Centro de la Raza and Special Collections at the University of Washington Libraries who helped me locate vital documents of ECDLR and the Pacific Northwest.

2. Daniel DeSiga, interviews by Michael D. Aguirre, July 26–August 7, 2011, El Centro de la Raza, Seattle, Seattle Civil Rights and Labor History Project, University of Washington, http://depts.washington.edu/civilr/desiga_interview.htm. Throughout the essay, I refer to El Centro de la Raza as ECDLR and the *centro* (center), names that reflect archival materials, oral histories, and quotidian conversations.

3. Vicki L. Ruiz, *From Out of the Shadows: Mexican Women in Twentieth Century America* (New York: Oxford University Press, 1998), 106.

4. Shifra Goldman and Tomás Ybarra-Frausto, "The Political and Social Contexts of Chicano Art," in *Chicano Art: Resistance and Affirmation, 1965–1985*, ed. Richard Griswold del Castillo, Teresa McKenna, and Yvonne Yarbro-Bejarano (Los Angeles: Wight Art Gallery, University of California, Los Angeles, 1991), 84.

5. For DeSiga's explanation of the motifs in the mural from both the 1972 and 1997 phases, see DeSiga, interviews by Aguirre, July 26–August 7, 2011.

6. Daniel DeSiga, interview by Michael D. Aguirre, March 9, 2011, by phone.

7. DeSiga, interview by Aguirre, July 26, 2011.

8. Estela Ortega, interview by Michael D. Aguirre, August 26, 2011, El Centro de la Raza, Seattle, Seattle Civil Rights and Labor History Project, http://depts.washington.edu/civilr/ortega.htm.

9. The longtime director of El Centro de la Raza was Roberto Maestas. He was the public face, voice, and leader of the *centro*. Several workers at ECDLR and in the city respected his lifelong commitment to the *centro* and to Latinas/os in Seattle and Latin America. During the 1997 work, Maestas asked DeSiga to remove the red lips, and DeSiga conferred with Ortega. DeSiga smiled as he recalled that Ortega quickly and unequivocally said no; DeSiga, interviews by Aguirre, July 26–August 7, 2011.

10. Marisela R. Chávez, "Despierten Hermanas y Hermanos! Women, the Chicano Movement, and Chicana Femisnism in California, 1966–1981" (PhD diss., Stanford University, 2004), 120–121.

11. Maylei Blackwell, *¡Chicana Power! Contested Histories of Feminism in the Chicano Movement* (Austin: University of Texas Press, 2011), 102.

12. Dolores Delgado Bernal argues for the East Los Angeles school blowouts that a cooperative leadership paradigm like the one developed at ECDLR revealed organizational methods masked by an overreliance on static models of male leadership; "Grassroots Leadership Reconceptualized: Chicana Oral Histories and the 1968 East Los Angeles School Blowouts," *Frontiers: A Journal of Women Studies* 19, no. 2 (1998): 135–136.

13. Ortega, interview by Aguirre, August 26, 2011.

14. Cherríe Moraga, "Theory in the Flesh," in *This Bridge Called My Back: Writings by Radical Women of Color*, ed. Cherríe Moraga and Gloria Anzaldúa, 2nd ed. (New York: Kitchen Table: Women of Color Press, 1983), 23. For public activism and its influence on Chicanas' private lives, see Mary Pardo's essay "Creating Community: Mexican American Women in Eastside Los Angeles," in *Las Obreras: Chicana Politics of Work and Family*, ed. Vicki L. Ruiz (Los Angeles: UCLA Chicano Studies Research Center, 2000), 107–136; Mary Pardo, *Mexican American Activists: Identity and Resistance in Two Los Angeles Communities* (Philadelphia: Temple University Press, 1998); Maylei Blackwell, "Líderes Campesinas: Nepantla Strategies and Grassroots Organizing at the Intersection of Gender and Globalization," *Aztlán: A Journal of Chicano Studies* 35, no. 1 (2010), 13–47. For the possibilities and limits of oral history, see Blackwell, *¡Chicana Power!*, 9–11; Richard White, *Remembering Ahanagran: A History of Stories* (Seattle: University of Washington Press, 1998), 4.

15. There is a growing literature on ethnic Mexicans in the Pacific Northwest that pushes scholars to investigate the complexities of the region. Historian Erasmo Gamboa provides one of the earliest texts on the region in *Mexican Labor and World War II: Braceros in the Pacific Northwest, 1942–1947* (Seattle: University of Washington Press, 2000). Jerry Garcia, Gilberto Garcia, and Bruce Johansen also contribute to the regional literature, at different points highlighting the importance of the post-1960 Texas and New Mexico diaspora into the Pacific Northwest.

16. Yolanda Alaniz and Megan Cornish, *Viva la Raza: A History of Chicano Identity and Resistance*, foreword by Rodolfo Acuña, (Seattle: Red Letter Press, 2008). For Chicana/o oral histories and essays featured on the Seattle Civil Rights and Labor History Project, see the webpage at http://depts.washington.edu/civilr/mecha_intro.htm.

17. Alan Eladio Gómez, "'From Below and to the Left': Re-Imagining the Chicano Movement through the Circulation of Third World Struggles, 1970–1979" (PhD diss., University of Texas, Austin, 2006).

18. None of the narrators defined themselves as radical and/or as feminist, yet this is precisely why a multiple insurgency model is required, where feminism can encompass Chicana intersectional praxis. Although I interpret their histories as radical and their accomplishments as Chicana feminist, I also respect the narrators' identification of themselves and the *centro* from their oral histories and personal conversations.

19. For the multiple insurgencies model, see Blackwell, *¡Chicana Power!*, 25–27.

20. Moraga, "Theory in the Flesh," 23.

21. Gloria Anzaldúa, *Light in the Dark/Luz en Lo Oscuro: Rewriting Identity, Spirituality, Reality*, ed. AnaLouise Keating (Durham, NC: Duke University Press, 2015), 237n1. The seven stages of *conocimiento* encompass the moments of rupture from previous knowledge constructs (including family, gender, and religion) to activism; 121–156.

22. Emma Pérez, *The Decolonial Imaginary: Writing Chicanas into History* (Bloomington: Indiana University Press, 1999), 106–110.

23. Theresa Aragon, interview by Maria Quintana and Oscar Rosales-Castañeda, January 26, 2009, Evergreen State College, Olympia, WA, Seattle Civil Rights and Labor History Project, University of Washington, http://depts.washington.edu/civilr/aragon.htm. Aragon's entire oral history is being processed in Seattle Civil Rights and Labor History Project records.

24. Carmen Miranda, interview by Michael D. Aguirre, August 30, 2011, El Centro de la Raza, Seattle, Seattle Civil Rights and Labor History Project, University of Washington, http://depts.washington.edu/civilr/miranda_interview.htm.

25. Graciela Gonzalez, interview by Michael D. Aguirre, August 23, 2011, El Centro de la Raza, Seattle, Seattle Civil Rights and Labor History Project, University of Washington.

26. Ortega, interview by Aguirre, August 26, 2011; Steve Sanger, "Chicanos Wed in Chilly Ritual," *Seattle Post-Intelligencer*, December 11, 1972.

27. Echoing what James Gregory proposed in *The Southern Diaspora*, focusing on migration genealogy can illuminate how moving peoples are the "architects" of history rather than passive actors of a changing political economy; Gregory, *The Southern Diaspora: How the Great Migrations of Black and White Southerners Transformed America* (Chapel Hill: University of North Carolina Press, 2005), 9. For the role of the movement of peoples from the South and Texas to West Coast politics, also see Marc Simon Rodriguez, *The Tejano Diaspora: Mexican Americanism and Ethnic Politics in Texas and Wisconsin* (Chapel Hill: University of North Carolina Press, 2011).

28. Keo Capestany, in *Los Chicanos de Seattle*, dir. Jack Norman, film (KOMO-ABC News, Seattle, 1973). Capestany served as a member of the Washington State Commission on Hispanic Affairs from 1971 to 1977.

29. Aragon, interview by Quintana and Rosales-Castañeda.

30. US Census Bureau, "General Characteristics of Persons of Spanish Language for Areas and Places: 1970," General Social and Economic Characteristics, Washington, Table 96, pp. 49–229 (Washington, DC: Government Printing Office, 1973; US Census Bureau, "Residence in 1970 by Residence in 1965 of Migrants between State Economic Areas," Subject Reports: Migration between State Economic Areas: 1970, Table 4, p. 286. Pierce County received 5,594 migrants, and King County received 4,446 migrants. The table presents migration figures from Texas to Washington in 1970. Despite the notorious undercounting in the census, these figures do provide a larger context of Texas-Washington migration between 1965 and 1970. Unlike other patterns of urbanization across the southwestern states, the burgeoning Seattle Chicana/o population did not reside in an identifiable barrio.

31. Rodriguez, *Tejano Diaspora*, 8–9. Rodriguez theorizes the "Tejano diaspora" and its influence on the shaping of local politics, focusing on the Crystal City, Texas, and Milwaukee, Wisconsin, labor circuit.

32. Interestingly, Roberto Maestas was also from Las Vegas, New Mexico, though he and Aragon met in Seattle.

33. Aragon, interview by Quintana and Rosales-Castañeda.

34. Gonzalez, interview by Aguirre.

35. Ibid.

36. Ibid.

37. Ibid.

38. This is regionally marked by the Boeing Bust, a period when the company began a series of layoffs due to a decrease in federal contracts; "Jobless-Benefit Extensions Urged" and "Spokane Has Light Answer for Seattle," *Seattle Times*, June 10, 1971.

39. Minutes of Yakima MAF Meeting, November 23, 1968, box 7, folder 11, Tomás Ybarra-Frausto Papers, accession no. 4339–001, University of Washington Libraries.

40. "Chicanos Occupy Beacon School," *Seattle Post-Intelligencer*, October 12, 1972. Early archival material refer to this group as the Chicano Ad-Hoc Committee, but members soon changed its name to El Centro de la Raza. I refer to the group that took over the school as El Centro de la Raza for consistency and to avoid confusion.

41. Ortega, interview by Aguirre, August 26, 2011; Gonzalez, interview by Aguirre; Bob Santos, *Hum Bows, Not Hot Dogs! Memoirs of a Savvy Asian American Activist* (Seattle: International Examiner, 2002), 77–78.

42. Robert Gallegos, interview by Oscar Rosales-Castañeda, November 23, 2011, Seattle; Bob Santos, interview by Trevor Griffey and Michelle Goshorn, November 12, 2004, Seattle, Seattle Civil Rights and Labor History Project, University of Washington, http://depts .washington.edu/civilr/santos.htm.

43. Ortega, interview by Aguirre, August 26, 2011; Gonzalez, interview by Aguirre; Stephen H. Dunphy, "Seattle Chicano Leader Is a 'Practical Idealist,'" *Seattle Times*, December 31, 1972; Santos, *Hum Bows*, 56, 60.

44. Bruce Johansen and Roberto Maestas, *El Pueblo: The Gallegos Family's American Journey, 1503–1980* (New York: Monthly Review, 1983), 127; Raúl Homero Villa, *Barrio-Logos: Space and Place in Urban Chicano Literature and Culture* (Austin: University of Texas Press, 2000), 235.

45. Larry McCarten, "18 Cited after Uhlman Office Sit-in," *Seattle Post-Intelligencer*, April 6, 1973; Hilda Bryant, "Chilly Chicanos Wait It Out," *Seattle Post-Intelligencer*, October 20, 1972; 1977 Health, Education, and Welfare Research Grant Proposal, box 1C, folder 43, El Centro de La Raza Papers, University of Washington, Libraries, Special Collections, Seattle (hereafter ECDLR Papers). El Centro de la Raza Papers are currently housed at the *centro*. There are ongoing negotiations between the *centro* and Special Collections at the University of Washington for deposit and processing at UW. Future researchers may find that my citations do not correspond with a future finding aid from UW's Special Collections. Seattle Model City was the city's branch of Model Cities, a War on Poverty program meant to give communities direct control over renewal projects, spur job creation, foster small businesses, and provide social services.

46. Roberto Maestas to Councilman Tim Hill, May 2, 1974, box 2D, folder 2, ECDLR Papers.

47. Burton A. Weisbrod, *The Nonprofit Economy* (Cambridge, MA: Harvard University Press, 1988), 131–132.

48. Roberto Maestas, interview by Trevor Griffey, February 22, 2005, El Centro de la Raza, Seattle, Seattle Civil Rights and Labor History Project, University of Washington, http://depts.washington.edu/civilr/maestas.htm; Ortega, interview by Aguirre, August 26, 2011; Aragon, interview by Quintana and Rosales-Castañeda; Roberto Maestas to Bernard Salazar of the Seattle Model Cities Program, March 5, 1974, box 6, folder 15, Theresa Aragon de Shepro Papers, accession no. 2913-002, Special Collections, University of Washington Libraries, Seattle.

49. Aragon, interview by Quintana and Rosales-Castañeda.

50. Ibid. As Marisela Chávez demonstrates with the Comisión Femenil Mexicana in Los Angeles, access and knowledge of federal and municipal funds was one of the key factors in sustaining a social services organization; "Despierten Hemanas," 103.

51. City Council Resolution, Minutes of City Council Committee of the Whole, December 26, 1972, box 1C, folder 5; Approved Contract between SMCP and Northwest Rural Opportunities Inc., September 9, 1974, box 5C, folder 13; both documents in ECDLR Papers.

52. HEW Project Grant Proposal for El Centro de la Raza, prepared by Theresa Shepro, Juan Bocanegra, Luis Salinas, May 3, 1973, box 5C, folder 13, ECDLR Papers; Letter of Resignation from Gloria Rivera to Tomas Sandoval, October 15, 1973, box 1c, folder 14, ECDLR Papers. After the establishment of ECDLR, Rivera soon resigned from Active Mexicanos because that organization's leaders saw her involvement with ECLDR as a conflict of interest. Historian Alan Eladio Gómez documents the political and philosophical differences between ECLDR and Active Mexicanos; Gómez, "'From Below and to the Left,' 319–324.

53. HEW Project Grant Proposal for El Centro de la Raza, ECDLR Papers.

54. Gloria Rivera and Carlos Young to Walter Hundley, February 5, 1973, box 1c, folder 14, ECDLR Papers.

55. Gloria Rivera to the CMP [Comprehensive of Manpower Program] Executive Committee, June 20, 1973, box 2D, folder 9, ECDLR Papers.

56. Frances Martinez was a longtime volunteer and staff at the *centro*. Upon her passing in the early 1980s, a division of the *centro* was renamed after her. Further research may complicate the arguments in this chapter, but her activism and dedication no doubt motivated and impressed her colleagues, perhaps demonstrating how becoming Chicana altered the direction of the *centro*.

57. Seattle City Council Memorandum, Allan Barrie to Tim Hill, June 4, 1974, box 2D, folder 1, ECDLR Papers.

58. 1975 Proposal for Funding, box 2D, folder 1, ECDLR Papers.

59. Award application from E. K. and Lillian F. Bishop Foundation/Trust Division/Rainier National Bank (Seattle), circa 1983, box 1C, folder 17, ECDLR Papers. VISTA was a national volunteer program created by Lyndon Johnson.

60. Ortega, interview by Aguirre, August 26, 2011.

61. Gonzalez, interview by Aguirre. Marisela Chávez also notes how Chicanas "pulled security" at CASA; "Despierten Hermanas," 219.

62. Gonzalez, interview by Aguirre.

63. Ibid. Chicanas at CASA took their children with them to events and meetings if child care could not be found; Chávez, "Despierten Hermanas," 225.

64. Gonzalez, interview by Aguirre.

65. Ibid.

66. Gallegos, interview by Rosales-Castañeda.

67. Ibid.

68. Lou Corsaletti, "New Chicano Protest Staged at City Hall," *Seattle Times*, April 11, 1973.

69. US Census Bureau, "Age by Race and Sex, for Areas and Places: 1970," General Population Characteristics, Washington, Table 24, pp. 49–63 (Washington, DC: GPO, 1973).

70. Capestany, in *Los Chicanos de Seattle*, dir. Norman. For more on population figures and cross-racial solidarity in Seattle, see Joseph Madsen, "Bernie Whitebear and the Urban Indian Fight for Land and Justice" (Seattle Civil Rights and Labor History Project, 2013), http://depts.washington.edu/civilr/whitebear.htm; Santos, interview by Griffey and Goshorn; Maestas, interview by Griffey; Larry Gossett, interviews by Trevor Griffey and Brooke Clarke, March 16 and June 3, 2005, Seattle, Seattle Civil Rights and Labor History Project, http://depts.washington.edu/civilr/gossett.htm.

71. Estela Ortega, interview by Michael D. Aguirre, August 2, 2016, by phone.

72. As documented extensively by historians Maylei Blackwell, Marisela Chávez, and Emma Pérez, theorist Chela Sandoval, and Dionne Espinoza, the Combahee River Collective, Deborah King, and Kimberly Springer, self-identified women of color (as individuals and collectives) understood multiple oppressions as interrelated, and they combated gender, race, sexual, and class privilege within and through the same social movement; Blackwell, *¡Chicana Power!*; Pérez, *Decolonial Imaginary*; Sandoval, *Methodology of the Oppressed* (Minneapolis: University of Minnesota Press, 2000); Espinoza, "'The Partido Belongs to

Those Who Will Work for It': Chicana Organizing and Leadership in the Texas Raza Unida Party, 1970–1980," *Aztlán: A Journal of Chicano Studies* 36, no. 1 (2011): 191–210; Combahee River Collective, "A Black Feminist Statement," in *Still Brave: The Evolution of Black Women's Studies* (New York: Feminist Press at the City University of New York, 2009); Deborah J. King, "Multiple Jeopardy, Multiple Consciousness: The Context of a Black Feminist Ideology," in *Signs* 14, no. 1 (1988): 42–72.

73. Blackwell, *¡Chicana Power!*, 82–83; Cherríe Moraga, *Loving in the War Years: Lo Que Nunca Pasó por Sus Labios* (Boston: South End, 1983), 105–113.

74. Invitation to the Chicano Mobile Institute from the University of Washington's Office of Minority Affairs, Chicano Student Division [ca. early 1974], box 1C, folder 14, ECDLR Papers; Ortega, interview by Aguirre, August 26, 2011. Unfortunately, little material or memory exists of this conference beyond what is presented in this chapter.

75. Aragon, interview by Quintana and Rosales-Castañeda.

76. "The 12 Principles of El Centro de la Raza," Fall 1976, ECDLR, http://elcentrodelaraza.org/documents/Principles.pdf. ECDLR credits the drafting of the principles in part to the participation of Chilean exiles from Pinochet's regime.

77. "8 de Marzo: Dia Internacional de la Mujer," *Recobrando* 1, no. 1 (1977): 14. The article is archived in *Recobrando: Organo Oficial del Centro de la Raza* 1, nos. 1–15 (1977), Departamento de Comunicaciones del Centro de la Raza, HN 18.R43, Special Collections, University of Washington Libraries. My thanks go to Michael Castañeda for informing me of this rich record.

CHAPTER 10

The epigraphs are from Martha P. Cotera, interview by Brenda Sendejo, June 24, 2014, Austin, and Evey Chapa, preface to *La Mujer Chicana: An Annotated Bibliography*, ed. Chapa (Austin: Chicana Research and Learning Center, 1976), xiv.

1. Here I am referring to María Elena Martínez, former La Raza Unida Party chair and member of its women's caucus, Mujeres por la Raza Unida.

2. For most of its existence the CRLC was housed in the offices of Martha Cotera's consulting and publishing company, Information Systems Development. It was located in downtown Austin at 10th and Brazos until 1975, when they moved to 1100 E. 8th Street in Austin. Cotera provided free office space for the CRLC.

3. Nationally recognized scholar Martha P. Cotera was born in Chihuahua, Mexico, and immigrated to El Paso, Texas, with her mother in 1946. Raised in a family with a penchant for progressive politics, she would go on to a long career in political and community activism, including as a founding member of La Raza Unida Party. Cotera earned her bachelor's degree in English with a minor in history from the University of Texas at El Paso in 1962. She earned a master's degree in education from Antioch College in 1971. Cotera is nationally recognized as a feminist historian, independent scholar, and former archivist at the Nettie Lee Benson Latin American Collection at the University of Texas. She is national adviser for the Chicana por mi Raza Digital Memory Collective. She is a founding member of two dozen local, state, and national organizations advocating for women and families. She has received numerous honors and national, state, and local awards for scholarship, leadership, and civic activism from 1964 to the present. The information on her education is taken from Martha P. Cotera Resume, Chicana Research and Learning Center Records, 1972–1999, Nettie Lee Benson Latin American Collection, University of Texas Libraries, Austin (hereafter cited as Benson Collection); all other information is from the Latina History Project website, Southwestern University, http://latinahistoryproject.omeka.net.

4. In compiling data for this chapter, I drew on my previous works, including my

manuscript in progress on Chicana spiritual activism as a contemporary manifestation of Chicana feminist thought. I also relied on the Martha P. Cotera Papers, Gloria E. Anzaldúa Collection, and Chicana Research and Learning Center archives, all housed at the Benson Collection. I conducted two interviews in person with Martha P. Cotera and also rely on phone calls and email correspondence with her. I drew on personal reflections and interactions with early Chicana feminists who have contributed immensely to my research.

5. Chicana Research and Learning Center 1988–1989 Annual Report, Chicana Research and Learning Center Records, 1972–1999, Benson Collection.

6. Descriptive summary, Chicana Research and Learning Center Records, 1972–1999, Benson Collection.

7. Ibid. The CRLC was run as a nonprofit for two years, but its records date to 1999, indicating that its work persisted into the 1990s.

8. Teresa Palomo Acosta and Ruthe Winegarten, *Las Tejanas: 300 Years of History* (Austin: University of Texas Press, 2003), 247–248.

9. Several people worked at the CRLC, alternating between paid work when funds were available and volunteering on projects. Over a period of about fifteen years, staff members were Evey Chapa, Martha P. Cotera, Lydia Espinoza, María Eugenia Cotera, Nella Cunningham, Irene Dominguez, Mary Jo Galindo, and Teresa Rabago. Numerous individuals, including some men, served on the CRLC board over the years and as trainers and administrative staff; Martha P. Cotera, email to Brenda Sendejo, June 13, 2016. Others associated with the CRLC included Belinda Herrera (research director), Emilio Zamora (academic consultant), Aurelio Montemayor (trainer), Cecilia Preciado-Burciaga (consultant), and Juan Gómez-Quiñones (consultant); Concept paper, Chicana Research and Learning Center, September 1974, Chicana por mi Raza Digital Memory Collective.

10. Oliva Evey Chapa was born in Alice, Texas. She earned a bachelor's degree from UT Austin in education and secondary certifications in Spanish and history. She received a master of arts degree in teaching from Antioch Graduate School of Education and holds a PhD in education, specializing in bilingual education, Chicana studies, and community education. Chapa served as the first executive director of the Chicana Research and Learning Center in Austin, as a consultant for the Texas Institute for Educational Development and the Colorado Migrant Council, and as a research specialist and education writer at the Southwest Educational Development Laboratory, established in 1966 in Austin. In 2007 its name was changed to SEDL to reflect its expanded reach beyond the US Southwest. She has produced numerous publications on Chicanas, bilingual education, and issues related to racism and sexism. Chapa is a founding member of the Raza Unida Party women's caucus, Mujeres por La Raza (1973–1978). She helped write the party platform, which advocated for *la mujer*, *la familia*, and women's equality. Chapa bio information is from Elaine Hedges and Ingrid Wendt, eds., *In Her Own Image: Women Working in the Arts* (New York: Feminist Press at City University of New York, 1993); Vicki L. Ruiz and Virginia Sánchez Korrol, eds., *Latinas in the United States: Historical Encyclopedia* (Bloomington: Indiana University Press, 2006); M. P. Cotera, *Diosa y Hembra*.

11. Chicana Research and Learning Center 1988–1989 Annual Report, Benson Collection.

12. Chela Sandoval, *Methodology of the Oppressed* (Minneapolis: University of Minnesota Press, 2000).

13. Cherríe Moraga, "Theory in the Flesh," in *This Bridge Called My Back: Writings by Radical Women of Color*, ed. Cherríe Moraga and Gloria Anzaldúa (New York: Kitchen Table: Women of Color Press, 1983), 24.

14. *Diosa y Hembra* has been cited numerous times in published Chicana feminist works since its publication.

15. Martha P. Cotera, interview by Brenda Sendejo, June 24, 2014, Austin.

16. Ibid.

17. Martha P. Cotera, interview by Brenda Sendejo, June 3, 2016, Austin.

18. Martha P. Cotera, interview by Brenda Sendejo, June 12, 2014, by phone.

19. Administrative History, Chicana Research and Learning Center, Benson Collection web page, accessed May 2, 2016, http://www.lib.utexas.edu/taro/utlac/00373/lac-00373.html#adminlink.

20. I draw from María Cotera's discussion of the potential of digital archives to circulate otherwise silenced and underrepresented perspectives to wider audiences, thereby working to democratize access to knowledge. See María Cotera, "'Invisibility Is an Unnatural Disaster: Feminist Archival Praxis after the Digital Turn," special issue, ed. Lisa Disch, *South Atlantic Quarterly* 114, no. 4 (2015): 781–801.

21. See Maylei Blackwell's *¡Chicana Power! Contested Histories of Feminism in the Chicano Movement* (Austin: University of Texas Press, 2011) for her discussion of the activist print culture of the Latina feminist organization Hijas de Cuauhtémoc at Long Beach State University. Dionne Espinoza notes that a Chicana feminist movement was "capable of encompassing various levels of consciousness while incisively critical of women's subordination, [and] carried women forward in organizations such as Comisión Femenil Mexicana, Hijas de Cuauhtémoc, Mujeres por la Raza Unida, and Las Chicanas"; Espinoza, "'Revolutionary Sisters': Women's Solidarity and Collective Identification among Chicana Brown Berets in East Los Angeles, 1967–1970," *Aztlán: A Journal of Chicano Studies* 26, no. 1 (2001): 43. I wish to acknowledge Blackwell for her use of the phrase "knowledge production as a political project," which I borrow here; Maylei Blackwell to Brenda Sendejo, June 3, 2016, by phone.

22. Alma M. García, acknowledgments, *Chicana Feminist Thought: The Basic Historical Writings*, ed. García (London: Routledge, 1997), xiii.

23. According to Anzaldúa and Hernández-Ávila, the Chicano movement was important for some Chicana and Chicano writers in that it provided forums and support to share their work during a time when the mainstream press ignored the voices of marginalized communities. Chicanos/as and other groups were creating their own journals and circulating them along with magazines in which they felt they could express themselves in their bilingualism as a form of cultural expression; Anzaldúa and Tovar, "Chicanas and Literature," *Onda Latina*, hosted by Alejandro Saenz, Longhorn Radio, University of Texas, Austin, July 6, 1977.

24. Dionne Espinoza wrote on Enriqueta Vasquez in "Rethinking Cultural Nationalism and La Familia through Women's Communities: Enriqueta Vasquez and Chicana Feminist Thought," in *Enriqueta Vasquez and the Chicano Movement: Writings from El Grito del Norte*, by Enriqueta Longeaux y Vásquez, ed. Lorena Oropeza and Dionne Espinoza (Houston: Arte Público, 2006). Blackwell wrote extensively on NietoGomez in *¡Chicana Power!*. I wrote on Cotera; Sendejo, "The Cultural Production of Spiritual Activisms: Gender, Social Justice, and the Remaking of Religion in the Borderlands," *Chicana/Latina Studies* 12, no. 2 (2013): 59–109; and Sendejo, "'The Face of God Has Changed': Tejana Cultural Production and the Politics of Spirituality in the Borderlands" (PhD diss., University of Texas, Austin, 2011).

25. Cotera, interview by Sendejo, June 24, 2014.

26. Ibid.

27. See Blackwell's contribution to this discussion of the decentering of hegemonic narratives in *¡Chicana Power!*, important for its shared emphasis on the theorizing and praxis of Chicana activists of this period and the relations between the CRLC and Hijas de Cuauhtémoc, upon which I elaborate. Anzaldúa's Chicana course materials in the Benson Collection include writings by Anna NietoGomez, and Cotera cites NietoGomez broadly as well.

28. Cotera, interview by Sendejo, June 24, 2014.

29. Cotera, email to Sendejo, June 13, 2016.

30. Nature of the Proposal, Project Proposals Hispanic Database Women's Educational Equity Act 1985, Chicana Research and Learning Center, box 2, folder 34, Benson Collection.

31. See García, *Chicana Feminist Thought*. This compilation shows a wide range of experiences and positionalities of Chicana feminists.

32. Anna NietoGomez, "La Feminista," *Encuentro Femenil* 1, no. 2 (1974): 34–47.

33. Elizabeth C. Ramírez, "Mexican-American Theater," *Handbook of Texas Online* (Austin: Texas State Historical Association), accessed February 10, 2015. http://www.tshaonline.org/handbook/online/articles/kkmvs.

34. In her chapter 21 in this volume Inés Hernández-Ávila notes her involvement in Chicanos Artistas Sirviendo a Aztlán (CASA) and Xinachtli.

35. Teresa Palomo Acosta, "Chicana Research and Learning Center," *Handbook of Texas Online* (Austin: Texas State Historical Association), http://www.tshaonline.org/handbook/online/articles/spc01, accessed June 20, 2014.

36. The Doña Doormat Project was funded by the Women's Educational Equity Project and US Office of Education; Martha P. Cotera, email to Brenda Sendejo, October 31, 2014; Chicana Research and Learning Center, Administrative Records, Founding Proposal, 1973, box 1, folder 8, Chicana Research and Learning Center Records, 1972–1999, Benson Collection.

37. Acosta and Winegarten, *Las Tejanas*, 248; Cotera, interview, 2014.

38. UT Austin was the largest but not only university in Austin during this period. Chicanos also attended St. Edward's University and Juárez-Lincoln University, a Mexican American institution of higher learning, with which Cotera and Chapa were involved; María-Cristina García, "Juárez-Lincoln University," *Handbook of Texas Online* (Austin: Texas State Historical Association), http://www.tshaonline.org/handbook/online/articles/kcj03, accessed May 2, 2014.

39. M. P. Cotera, *Diosa y Hembra*.

40. Orozco, foreword to *Las Tejanas*, by Acosta and Winegarten, xi.

41. Martha P. Cotera, "Annotated List of the Chicano in History and the Social Sciences" (Clarksville, TX: Baker and Taylor, 1973); Capabilities, 1982, Martha P. Cotera Comprehensive Resume, Administrative Records, box 1, folder 5, Chicana Research and Learning Center Records, 1972–1999, Benson Collection.

42. "Educator's Guide to Chicano Resources" (Crystal City, TX: Committee for Rural Democracy, 1973).

43. Acosta and Winegarten, *Las Tejanas*, 235.

44. Sendejo, "Cultural Production of Spiritual Activisms."

45. Chapa, *La Mujer Chicana*, ix.

46. Ibid.

47. Martha P. Cotera and Nella Cunningham, eds., *Multicultural Women's Sourcebook: Materials Guide for Use in Women's Studies and Bilingual/Multicultural Programs* (Washington, DC: Women's Educational Equity Act Program, US Department of Education, 1982).

48. Chicana Research and Learning Center 1988–1989 Annual Report, Benson Collection.

49. Chapa, *La Mujer Chicana*, xi.

50. Ibid., xiii.

51. Ibid.

52. Ibid.

53. Ibid., xiv.

54. Cotera, interview by Sendejo, June 24, 2014.

55. Ibid.

56. Ibid.

57. Cotera cites Hernández-Ávila as a very important figure in early Chicana studies who acted as a key liaison between the university and community, helping to facilitate the dissemination of resources into the universities, in particular UT Austin.

58. Chapa, *La Mujer Chicana*, xiii.

59. Cynthia Orozco, "Getting Started in Chicana Studies" (n.p., 1986), 2–3.

60. Ibid., 3.

61. Ibid.

62. Ibid., 4.

63. Anzaldúa worked with a variety of political groups during this time, including MEChA, farmworker protests, feminist organizations, and consciousness-raising groups; Biographical sketch, Gloria Evangelina Anzaldúa Papers, Benson Collection (hereafter Anzaldúa Papers).

64. Ibid.; Cherríe Moraga and Gloria Anzaldúa, eds., *This Bridge Called My Back: Writings by Radical Women of Color* (New York: Kitchen Table: Women of Color Press, 1983).

65. María Cotera, "'Invisibility Is an Unnatural Disaster: Feminist Archival Praxis after the Digital Turn," special issue, ed. Lisa Disch, *South Atlantic Quarterly* 114, no. 4 (2015): 781–801.

66. See Maylei Blackwell's *¡Chicana Power!* for a substantive examination of print culture and its effects during the Chicana movement, such as its ability to mobilize and foster solidarity among Chicanas on a national level.

67. La Mujer Chicana course syllabus, box 228, folder 1, Anzaldúa Papers. Anzaldúa's course syllabus included the following topics: "History and Heritage of La Chicana," "Esthetics and La Chicana," "Psychological/Philosophical Concerns of La Chicana," "Cultural Concerns of La Chicana," "Archetypal/Mythological Views of La Chicana," "Linguistic Concerns," and "La Chicana and Mass Media." Part 1 comprised "Pre-Columbian, Colonization Period, Revolutionary Period, Early 1900s, Protesting 60s, Subliminal 70s, Today."

68. Cotera notes in the book's introduction that prior to *Diosa y Hembra* there was "no single source which can provide a profile on the Mexican American woman"; *Diosa y Hembra*, 1.

69. Anzaldúa's handwritten notes on Cotera, La Mujer Chicana, 1976–77, box 228, folder 1, Anzaldúa Papers.

70. Anzaldúa stated in an interview that Cotera was in fact a lecturer in Anzaldúa's Chicana course; Gloria Anzaldúa, interview by Maylei Blackwell, September 24, 1999, Santa Cruz, CA.

71. La Mujer Chicana course syllabus, box 228, folder 2, Anzaldúa Papers.

72. As Hernández-Ávila notes in chapter 21 in this volume, she was a PhD candidate at the University of Houston during the time she held her position at UT. She was an active member of MAYO, La Raza Unida Party, and the RUP women's caucus, Mujeres por La Raza Unida. She is a professor of Native American studies at UC Davis and a poet and cultural worker.

73. Cotera, interview by Sendejo, June 24, 2014.

74. Cotera and Cunningham, *Multicultural Women's Sourcebook*. This sourcebook was another important indication of Cotera's impact on future generations of feminists and Chicana studies. Its editors assert that sourcebook entries "belie statements that materials on ethnic women are not available in the United States"; iii.

75. La Mujer Chicana course materials, spring 1977, box 228, folder 2, Anzaldúa Papers.

76. Anzaldúa addressed the topic of spirituality immensely in her work. Her Chicana course materials suggest indications of her early theorizing of the concept of spiritual activism, in which spirituality can be used to garner the resources to do the inner work that enables one to make outer change in the world. See my application of Anzaldúa's spiritual activism in my ethnographic research on Tejana activists from the *movimiento* in Sendejo,

"Cultural Production of Spiritual Activisms." See Teresa Delgadillo's use of Anzaldúa's concept of spiritual *mestizaje* in literary analyses in *Spiritual Mestizaje: Religion, Gender, Race, and Nation in Contemporary Chicana Narrative* (Durham, NC: Duke University Press, 2011).

77. The name Alma de Mujer means "Soul of Woman." Alma, located in Austin, is the educational center of the Indigenous Women's Network (IWN), a national nonprofit organization established in 1985 by a group of prominent indigenous women activists. Alma is run by an intergenerational and ethnically diverse local women's council. Alma provides educational and training programs and resources including publications for the local Latina community and indigenous and nonindigenous peoples. Alma offers youth workshops and summer camps to help youth build self-esteem, community awareness, and leadership skills. Workshops and programs taught by local experts address issues around sustainable agriculture, composting, land mapping, pond and waterway care, and herbology; Mary Margaret Návar, former women's council member at Alma de Mujer, email to Brenda Sendejo, February 20, 2009; Indigenous Women, http://indigenouswomen.org.

78. See Alicia Elizabeth Enciso Litschi, "Con Alma: Dialogues in Decolonizing Counseling—Reciprocal Ethnographic Explorations in Indigenous Spaces for Community Healing" (PhD diss., University of Texas, 2014).

79. Chicana por mi Raza is a digital humanities project that employs feminist pedagogies and scholarship using digital media, making archives accessible to wider audiences. According to its website (http://chicanapormiraza.org/), "The Chicana por mi Raza Digital Memory Project and Archive was created under the supervision of professor María Cotera and Linda Garcia Merchant in collaboration with the Institute for Computing in Humanities Arts and Sciences at the University of Illinois Urbana Champaign."

80. María Cotera, "Practices of Chicana Memory: Before and after the 'Digital Turn,'" plenary paper presented at El Mundo Zurdo Conference, May 28, 2015, Austin.

81. The Latina History Project (LHP) at Southwestern University, codirected by Alison Kafer (feminist studies) and me (anthropology), is a faculty-student research and recovery project that aims to enhance undergraduate education, build an archive, and provide resources on Latina/o and Chicana/o history in Central Texas. While the project began with the goal of digitizing the 1993 "Rostros y Almas/Faces and Souls" exhibit on the contributions of local Tejanas, it has grown to encompass the broader mission of broadening understandings of Latina/o and Chicana/o history. The LHP does so through the collection of oral histories from past and present members of the Southwestern University community as well as activists including key figures in the Chicana/o movement in Texas such as María Elena Martínez, Yolanda Leyva, and Martha Cotera, who contributed oral histories to the project in 2015.

CHAPTER 11

Osa Hidalgo de la Riva would like to thank the editors of *Chicana Movidas*, as well as Audrey Silvestre and Marcus Woo, for their valuable assistance preparing the manuscript for publication. She also wishes to thank *maestras* Marsha Kinder, Angela Y. Davis, and Trinh T. Minh-ha for their mentorship. Finally, a big thank you to the de la Riva *familia*: Lola, Celia, Louis, Liz, twins Tim and Laura, Alie, and the next-generation Cuauhtémoc, Angela, Maya, and Mahina, with love *siempre*!

1. Maylei, Osa, and Lola met in the 1990s and have stayed friends ever since. Maylei worked on documenting Lola's history and interviewed her as part of that process. For this book, Maylei invited Osa to submit something from her dissertation on Chicana filmmakers Lourdes Portillo and Sylvia Morales, which she completed at the University of Southern California. After this book was submitted to the publisher, we learned that the outside readers seemed more interested in Osa's story and how she came to *mujerista*

moviemaking. So, after two decades of friendship, Maylei sat down in 2016 to conduct an oral history interview with Osa about her experiences in the Chicano movement era for this book. She wanted to make lesbiana cultures visible within the broader cultural and political movements of the time, and Osa had always told her great stories. They worked quickly to try to produce something during the revision process. Maylei conducted several interviews with Osa, and Audrey Silvestre transcribed them. Maylei edited the first draft of the interviews, and over several work sessions and follow-up interviews with Osa, they filled in gaps, added context, and clarified the story. This is one of Osa's first academic publications. Osa's original chapter was resubmitted for the book *Erotic Sovereignty at the Decolonial Crossroads*, edited by Raul Moarquech Ferrera-Blanquet and under review by Duke University Press.

2. Celia de la Riva Rubio, *Lágrimas y Cadenas*, bilingual ed. (Colectivo Artístico Morelia, 1994). This was a self-published collection.

3. In all of the research Osa did for her first master's thesis on Sappho, Gabriela Mistral, and Lillian Hellman, she discovered there was debate as to where Sappho originated. There are references that say she was darker-skinned and shorter and had a wider nose than most Greeks. Her belief is that Sappho was of Africana descent. Also, they found her ancient poetry on Egyptian tombs.

4. Cherríe Moraga and Gloria Anzaldúa, eds., *This Bridge Called My Back: Writings by Radical Women of Color* (Watertown, MA: Persephone Press, 1981).

5. Lola spells her last name Dela-Riva, and Osa spells her last name Hidalgo de la Riva.

6. Osa Hidalgo de la Riva, "Chicana Spectators and Media Makers" *Spectator* 26, no. 1 (2006): 7–12.

7. Osa Hidalgo de la Riva, *Mama Sappho: Poems con Sabor a Caló* (San Francisco: Korima, 2017).

8. Audre Lorde, "The Uses of the Erotic: The Erotic as Power" in *Sister/Outsider: Essays and Speeches* (Berkeley: Crossing Press, 1984): 53–59.

9. Osa Hidalgo de la Riva, dir., *Mujería, Part 1: The Olmeca Rap* (1990, Royal Eagle Bear Productions, 3 minutes).

10. Osa Hidalgo de la Riva and Lola Dela-Riva, dirs., *Mujería, Part 2: Primitive and Proud* (1992, Royal Eagle Bear Productions, 17 minutes).

11. Elizabeth "Betita" Martínez, *500 Years of Chicana Women's History/500 años de historia de las Chicanas* (New Brunswick, NJ: Rutgers University Press, 2008).

12. Chon Noriega, "Aztlán Film Institute's Top 100 List," *Aztlán: A Journal of Chicano Studies* 23, no. 2 (1998): 1–9.

13. Osa Hidalgo de la Riva and Lola Dela-Riva, dirs., *Me and Mr. Mauri: Turning Poison into Medicine* (2017, 60 min.)

14. Diane Felix (aka "Chili D"—her DJ persona) is a Chicana lesbiana community leader and DJ in San Francisco. From a farmworker family in Stockton, California, she became active with the United Farm Workers in high school. In the 1970s, she became one of the core members of Gay Latina/Latino Alliance (GALA). She cofounded Community United in Response to AIDS/SIDA (CURAS) in 1983, and then Projecto ContraSIDA por Vida (PCPV). Osa remembers, "We went to school together at St. George's Catholic Elementary School. We grew up in Southside Stockton and have remained *familia* ever since. It was cool meeting her again in the context of queer SF years later."

15. Founded in 1991, AGUILAS stands for Asamblea Gay Unida Impactando Latinos a Superarse, which translates to Assembly of United Gays Impacting Latinos toward Self-Empowerment.

16. Cocina de Imagenes in October 1987 was the first Latin American women's film festival and "marked the beginning of a historical moment for Latin American and Caribbean women cineastes." It was a gathering of more than seventy-five filmmakers and video

artists at various stages of their careers from more than twelve Latin American countries as well as the United States and Canada; Annette Kuhn and Susannah Radstone, eds. *The Women's Companion to International Film* (Berkeley: University of California Press, 1990), 90.

17. The Women of Color Film and Video Festival was founded by Margaret Daniel in the early 1990s. After the first two years, the Research Cluster for the Study of Women of Color in Conflict and Collaboration began to organize the festival, with several coordinators and scores of volunteers. Maylei was a co-curator and organizer for five years. Over its more than ten years, it featured hundreds of documentaries and narrative films, both shorts and feature-lengths, and brought dozens of film- and videomakers to UC Santa Cruz.

CHAPTER 12

I am deeply grateful to Alicia Escalante for sharing with me her deep knowledge and expertise as an organizer and movement leader through her oral history interview for this chapter. Heartfelt *gracias* to the late Joe Razo and David Novagrodsky for making time to do phone interviews about their recollections about LA's Chicano movement and welfare rights struggle, respectively. Thank you to historian Premilla Nadasen for generously sharing the recording of her phone interview with Catherine Jermany, to the editors of this volume—Dionne Espinoza, María Cotera, and Maylei Blackwell—for valuable feedback on my essay, and to Jeanne Theoharis for the countless conversations and readings of drafts that moved this project forward and made it fuller and sharper.

1. Jack Jones, "100 Recipients March against Welfare Setup," *Los Angeles Times*, July 1, 1966.

2. Ibid. For another account of this march, see Johnnie Tillmon, interviewed by Sherna Berger Gluck, February 3, 1984, California State University, Long Beach Oral History Collection.

3. Premilla Nadasen, *Welfare Warriors: The Welfare Rights Movement in the United States* (London: Routledge, 2004), 30.

4. Ibid.

5. Catherine Jermany, interview by Premilla Nadasen, October 11, 2003, by phone; the audio recording was shared with the author by Nadasen.

6. Maylei Blackwell, *¡Chicana Power! Contested Histories of Feminism in the Chicano Movement* (Austin: University of Texas Press, 2011); Rosie Bermudez, "Alicia Escalante: The Chicana Welfare Rights Organization and the Chicano Movement," in *The Chicano Movement: Perspectives from the Twenty-First Century*, ed. Mario T. García (London: Routledge, 2014), 96–116. Both texts briefly discuss the marginalization of Chicanas within the NWRO.

7. This concept of cultural citizenship comes from William Flores and Rina Benmayor, *Latino Cultural Citizenship: Claiming Identity, Space, and Rights* (Boston: Beacon, 1998).

8. Of the formative texts on twentieth-century Chicano/a history, only Rodolfo Acuña's *Occupied America: A History of Chicanos*, 6th ed. (London: Longman, 2006), acknowledges the East LA WRO in a subsection on women's activism that disappears and reappears in editions published after 1972.

9. For example, Ernesto Chávez, *"¡Mi Raza Primero!" (My People First): Nationalism, Identity, and Insurgency in the Chicano Movement in Los Angeles, 1966–1978* (Berkeley: University of California Press, 2002); Carlos J. Muñoz Jr., *Youth, Identity, Power* (London: Verso, 1989); and Arturo Rosales, *Chicano! The History of the Mexican American Civil Rights Movement* (Houston: Arte Público, 1996).

10. I borrow this idea of complicated civil rights histories being hidden in plain sight from Jeanne Theoharis, *The Rebellious Life of Mrs. Rosa Parks* (Boston: Beacon, 2013).

11. The only published work focused on the history of the CWRO is Bermudez's 2014 article "Alicia Escalante." Vicki Ruiz's *From Out of the Shadows: Mexican Women in*

Twentieth-Century America (New York: Oxford University Press, 1998) discusses Alicia Escalante and the CWRO, as does Virginia Espino's article "Women Sterilized as They Give Birth: Forced Sterilization and Chicana Resistance in the 1970s," in *Las Obreras: Chicana Politics of Work and Family*, ed. Vicki Ruiz (Los Angeles: Chicano Studies Research Center, 2000), 83–104, and Blackwell's *¡Chicana Power!*.

12. Stephanie Gilmore, ed., *Feminist Coalitions: Historical Perspectives on Second-Wave Feminism in the United States* (Champaign: University of Illinois Press, 2004).

13. Gordon Mantler, *Power to the Poor: Black-Brown Coalition and the Fight for Economic Justice, 1960–1974* (Chapel Hill: University of North Carolina Press, 2013). Mantler describes an "activist hierarchy" in the 1960s when African American organizations paternalistically cast themselves as more advanced than their Mexican American counterparts, leading the latter to adopt a separatist stance.

14. One exception is Eileen Boris and Jennifer Klein, *Caring for America: Home Health Care Workers in the Shadow of the Welfare State* (New York: Oxford University Press, 2012). The book briefly documents the multiracial organizing of the LAWRO. Felicia Kornbluh, *The Battle for Welfare Rights* (Philadelphia: University of Pennsylvania Press, 2007), acknowledges Mexican Americans—but no individual leaders—in her short section on California; she includes Puerto Ricans in a more detailed study of the movement in New York City, though it focuses on black women leaders. Premilla Nadasen includes the voices of Chicanas in the Midwest in "Welfare's a Green Problem: Cross-Race Coalitions in Welfare Rights Organizing," in *Feminist Coalitions: Historical Perspectives on Second-Wave Feminism in the United States*, ed. Stephanie Gilmore (Urbana: University of Illinois Press, 2004), 178–195.

15. Neil Foley, *Quest for Equality: The Failed Promise of Black-Brown Solidarity* (Cambridge, MA: Harvard University Press, 2010); Brian D. Benkhen, *Fighting Their Own Battles: Mexican Americans, African Americans, and the Struggle for Civil Rights in Texas* (Chapel Hill: University of North Carolina Press, 2011). Works on civil rights-era LA commonly bemoan the failure of a black-brown coalition that is partly blamed on cultural nationalist ideologies. See Laura Pulido's *Black, Brown, Yellow, and Left: Radical Activism in Los Angeles* (Berkeley: University of California Press, 2006) and Robert Bauman's *Race and the War on Poverty from Watts to East L.A.* (Norman: University of Oklahoma Press, 2008).

16. I build on Nadasen's theorizing of the tremendous synergy between the rhetorics of black power politics and welfare rights as welfare rights activists "laid the basis for a political analysis that combined race, class, gender, sexuality, and political and economic autonomy"; Nadasen, "'We Do Whatever Becomes Necessary': Johnnie Tillmon, Welfare Rights, and Black Power," in *Wanna Start a Revolution? Radical Women in the Black Freedom Struggle*, ed. Dayo Gore, Jeanne Theoharis, and Komozi Woodard (New York: New York University Press, 2009), 319.

17. "What Is It Really Like to Be Poor?" *Los Angeles Times*, September 9, 1968.

18. Josh Sides, *L.A. City Limits: African American Los Angeles from the Great Depression to the Present* (Berkeley: University of California Press, 2003), 180.

19. Institute of Industrial Relations, University of California, Los Angeles, *Hard-Core Unemployment and Poverty in Los Angeles* (Washington, DC: US Department of Commerce, 1965).

20. Miguel Garcia, interviews by Carlos Vasquez, February and May 1990, California State Archives, State Government Oral History Collection. As a caseworker employed by Los Angeles County in the mid-1960s, Garcia was outraged by the county's treatment of Mexican Americans. He and a Puerto Rican coworker started a group of Latino social workers called Social Action Latinos for Unity Development (SALUD) that worked closely with the CWRO to push for improvements in social services in East LA.

21. Alicia Escalante, "ELA Chicana Welfare Rights Report," *Eastside Sun*, November 1, 1973, 1.

22. Tillmon, interview by Gluck.

23. Anna NietoGomez, public comments, May 6, 2010, California State University, Los Angeles.

24. Jack Jones, "Letter Expresses Thanks: Mother Tells Johnson of Good in Poverty Project," *Los Angeles Times*, December 29, 1967.

25. Alicia Escalante, interview by Alejandra Marchevsky, September 3, 2009, Sacramento, CA.

26. "Welfare Recipients Want Realistic Rent Allotment," *Los Angeles Sentinel*, October 2, 1969. When the federal government raised AFDC grant allowances in the late 1960s and early 1970s, California welfare rights activists had to repeatedly sue to get Governor Ronald Reagan to implement the new standards.

27. American Civil Liberties Union of Southern California and Social Workers Union, Local 535, "Welfare: A Question of Equal Protection," pamphlet, Los Angeles, May 1968.

28. Rúben Salazar, "Needy Family of 11 Points up Problems in Welfare System," *Los Angeles Times*, May 25, 1969.

29. Ellen Reese, *Backlash against Welfare Mothers Past and Present* (Berkeley: University of California Press, 2005).

30. Ian Haney Lopez, *Dog Whistle Politics: How Coded Racial Meanings Have Reinvented Racism and Wrecked the Middle-Class* (New York: Oxford University Press, 2014).

31. California State Senate, *Aid to Needy Children Program: Report of the Senate Fact Finding Committee on Labor and Welfare* (Sacramento, CA: 1961), 23.

32. This was typical of racialized distinctions drawn between poor women in the postwar era; Rickie Solinger, *Beggars and Choosers: How the Politics of Choice Shapes Adoption, Abortion, and Welfare in the United States* (New York: Hill and Wang, 2002).

33. Helen Herrick, *Mental Health Problems of Public Assistance Clients* (Sacramento: California Department of Mental Hygiene, June 1967), 83.

34. Reese, *Backlash against Welfare Mothers*, 96.

35. Elizabeth H. Pleck, *Not Just Roommates: Cohabitation after the Sexual Revolution* (Chicago: University of Chicago Press, 2012), 53.

36. Jermany, interview by Nadasen.

37. Institute of Industrial Relations, UCLA, *Hard-Core Unemployment and Poverty in Los Angeles*.

38. Welfare Planning Council Los Angeles Region, "Settlements and Centers: Their History, Self Study, and Development," June 1954, box 1, NAPP Collection, USC Social Welfare Archive. For a description of the Watts Community House, see Andrew Knox, *Blazing an African American Trail* (Minneapolis: Mill City, 2008), 7.

39. In Jim Cleaver, "Welfare Administration: Blessing or Fraud?" *Los Angeles Sentinel*, July 3, 1969.

40. Ibid.

41. Jermany, interview by Nadasen.

42. Kazuyo Tsuchiya, "Contesting Citizenship: Race, Gender, and the Politics of Participation in the U.S. and Japanese Welfare States, 1962–1982" (PhD diss., University of California, San Diego, 2008), 194.

43. "Food Stamp Office Opens," *Eastside Sun*, June 16, 1969. Eastside Chicana activist Gloria Arellanes also worked as a NAPP aide before she joined the Brown Berets and opened El Barrio Free Clinic. Opal Jones's support of direct-action organizing and recruitment of young black and Chicano/a activists frequently put her at odds with the city's political establishment, including some council members who charged that she was "aiding and abetting militant individuals and groups"; "Poverty Units Accused of Aiding, Abetting Militants," *Los Angeles Times*, May 21, 1970.

44. Welfare Planning Council Los Angeles Region, "Settlements and Centers: Their

History, Self Study, and Development," June 1954, box 1, folders 3–4, Neighborhood Adult Participation Project Records, Collection no. 0488, California Social Welfare Archives, Special Collections, USC Libraries, University of Southern California. For an account of NAPP's work, see Kazuyo Tsuchiya, "Race, Class, and Gender in America's 'War on Poverty': The Case of Opal C. Jones in Los Angeles, 1964–68," *Japanese Journal of American Studies* 15 (2004): 213–233.

45. Correspondence re conflict between Hispanic/Latino and African American participants 1966, box 1, folder 5, Neighborhood Adult Participation Project Records, USC Libraries. Bauman's 2008 book, *Race and the War on Poverty*, provides an exhaustive account of racial conflict within NAPP.

46. Robert Bauman, "The Black Power and Chicano Movements in the Poverty Wars in Los Angeles," *Journal of Urban History* 33, no. 2 (2007): 277–295.

47. "Welfare Pickets Seek Return of Expense Money," *Los Angeles Times*, October 19, 1966.

48. *P/RAC Newsletter* #3, December 21, 1966, box 1, folder 3, Kristin Ockershauser Papers, Southern California Library for Social Studies Research.

49. "Welfare Recipients Want Realistic Rent Allotment," *Los Angeles Times*, October 2, 1969.

50. "200 Mothers Demand Increased Welfare, Win Supervisors' Aid," *Los Angeles Times*, July 1, 1969.

51. Tillmon, interview by Gluck.

52. Quoted in Blackwell, *¡Chicana Power!*, 147.

53. "Medi-Cal: Furor over Reagan Slash Grows," *Los Angeles Times*, September 17, 1967.

54. "Rebajas en medical," *La Raza*, December 25, 1967.

55. "Watts Lame, Blind, Poor Protest Cut in Medical Care," *Jet*, October 26, 1967, 16.

56. Escalante, interview by Marchevsky.

57. Harry Bernstein, "Poverty Areas Worsen in Prosperity," *Los Angeles Times*, October 4, 1966.

58. California State Department of Mental Hygiene, *Hospital Beds in the Poverty Areas of Los Angeles County*, Sacramento, CA: March 1965.

59. "East Los Angeles Health: A Community Report from a Project and Conferences on Health Problems and Priorities in East Los Angeles," 1970, Welfare Planning Council, Los Angeles Records, Social Welfare Archives, Special Collections, USC Libraries, University of Southern California.

60. Escalante, interview by Marchevsky.

61. "Welfare Rights Organization," *La Raza*, November 15, 1967, 45.

62. "Welfare Rights Unit Charges County Cuts Relief Funds," *Los Angeles Times*, December 10, 1969; "300 Welfare Clients Disrupt Board Meeting," *Los Angeles Times*, December 19, 1969.

63. Organizational Materials 1969, box 1, folder 5, Kristin Ockershauser Papers, 1965–1987, Collection no. MSS 082, Southern California Library for Social Studies and Research.

64. "Special Welfare Needs Issue Boils Up," *Long Beach Independent Press Telegram*, April 13, 1969.

65. "L.B. Welfare Mothers Imprison Director," *Long Beach Press Telegram*, September 4, 1970; "Welfare Recipients Arrested in Sit-In," *Long Beach Press Telegram*, September 11, 1970.

66. Cited in Bermudez, "Alicia Escalante," 99.

67. While the NWRO published a Spanish version of its newsletter, there was only one Latina representative on the executive committee between 1967 and 1975, and the issues relevant to Latino communities such as language rights and cultural discrimination within the welfare system were not taken up in national-level organizing and lobbying.

68. "Mothers Rap Services of Welfare Unit," *Los Angeles Times*, April 3, 1969.

69. "Mexican-American Community Groups Plan 'Neglect' Protest," *Los Angeles Times*, February 11, 1969.

70. Blackwell, ¡*Chicana Power!*, 149.

71. Escalante, interview by Marchevsky. Also, Alicia Escalante, interviewed by Antonio Valle Jr., East Los Angeles, November 13 and December 9, 1968, Mexican American History Collection, Center for Oral and Public History, California State University, Fullerton.

72. Joe Razo, interview by Alejandra Marchevsky, August 20, 2013, by phone.

73. b. n. estar, "Welfare Doesn't Help," *La Raza*, March 31, 1968, 2.

74. Anna NietoGomez, "Madres por justicia," *Encuentro Femenil* 1, no. 1 (1973): 17.

75. See Bermudez, "Alicia Escalante," for a thorough account of Escalante's multi-pronged activism.

76. Nadasen, "We Do Whatever Becomes Necessary," 334.

77. "Watts Finally Gets a Hospital," *Ebony*, November 1974, 124–147. See also Jenna Loyd, "Freedom's Body: Radical Health Activism in Los Angeles, 1963–1978" (PhD diss., University of California, Berkeley, 2005).

78. Nadasen, "We Do Whatever Becomes Necessary," 325.

79. Scott Brown, *Fighting for US: Maulana Karenga, the US Organization, and Black Cultural Nationalism* (New York: New York University Press, 2003), 83.

80. Nadasen, "Welfare's a Green Problem," 186.

81. Escalante, interview by Marchevsky.

82. Ibid.

83. This phrase comes from announcements for the East LA WRO that regularly appeared in *La Raza* newspaper in the late 1960s.

84. "200 Mothers Demand Increased Welfare, Win Supervisors' Aid," *Los Angeles Times*, July 1, 1969.

85. Nadasen, "We Do Whatever Becomes Necessary," 328.

86. Jakobi Williams, *From the Bullet to the Ballot: The Illinois Chapter of the Black Panther Party and Racial Coalition Politics in Chicago* (Chapel Hill: University of North Carolina Press, 2013).

87. Emily Zuckerman, "The Cooperative Origins of EEOC vs. Sears," in *Feminist Coalitions: Historical Perspectives on Second-Wave Feminism in the United States*, ed. Stephanie Gilmore (Urbana: University of Illinois Press, 2004), 225–251.

88. Kimberlé Crenshaw, "Mapping the Margins: Intersectionality, Identity Politics, and Violence against Women of Color," *Stanford Law Review* 43, no. 6 (1991): 1290.

CHAPTER 13

1. Elizabeth Martínez, "Yeah, Yeah, Yeah (1964)," *Social Justice* 39, no. 2–3 (2013): 55. Elizabeth (Betita) Sutherland Martínez published under variations on her names, including with and without the accented "Martínez," throughout her life. The publications discussed here are primarily ones she wrote under the name Elizabeth Sutherland. In 2013 the journal *Social Justice* did a special issue on Martínez titled "Elizabeth 'Betita' Sutherland Martínez: A Life in Struggle." The issue published original essays about Martínez by people who had known her throughout her civil rights work, reprints of articles and essays by Martínez, and, as is the case with "Yeah, Yeah, Yeah," writings from her journal.

2. Elizabeth Sutherland, "A Vote for the Sweet Parade," *New Republic*, October 10, 1964, 26–29.

3. Kathryn Blackmer Reyes, "Elizabeth Sutherland/Elizabeth 'Betita' Sutherland Martínez: Bibliography, 1960–2013," *Social Justice* 39, no. 2–3 (2013): 12–25.

4. Chude Pam Allen, "Always Connecting the Struggles," *Social Justice* 39, no. 2–3 (2013): 93.

5. Betty Friedan, *The Feminine Mystique: 50 Years* (New York: W. W. Norton, 2013), 2.

6. To a point—she comments in an interview that her parents were unable to afford braces for her teeth.

7. Elizabeth "Betita" Martínez, interview by Loretta Ross, March 3 and August 6, 2006, Atlanta, GA, and Oakland, CA, Voices of Feminism Oral History Project, pp. 2–4, Sophia Smith Collection, Smith College, https://www.smith.edu/libraries/libs/ssc/vof/transcripts /MartinezBetita.pdf.

8. Ibid., 2.

9. Ibid., 4.

10. Tony Platt, "The Heart Just Insists: In Struggle with Elizabeth 'Betita' Sutherland Martínez," *Social Justice* 39, no. 2–3 (2013): 29.

11. Elizabeth Martínez, "History Makes Us, We Make History," in *The Feminist Memoir Project: Voices from Women's Liberation*, ed. Rachel Blau DuPlessis and Ann Barr Snitow (New York: Three Rivers, 1998), 116.

12. Platt, "The Heart Just Insists," 31.

13. Karen Mary Davalos, "Sin Vergüenza: Chicana Feminist Theorizing," *Feminist Studies* 34, no. 1–2 (2008): 153–155.

14. Edén E. Torres, *Chicana without Apology: The New Chicana Cultural Studies* (New York: Routledge, 2003).

15. Friedan, *Feminine Mystique*, 216.

16. Sutherland's first publication credit was as one of two translators of Carlo Coccioli's novel *The White Stone* (New York: Simon and Schuster, 1960, written and published originally in French as *Le Blanc Caillou*), demonstrating her skills as a translator. Coccioli was an Italian novelist who lived and worked most of his adult life in Mexico. The novel, which Sutherland and Vera Bleuer translated into English from the original French, draws from socialist Albert Camus's philosophy and his questioning of religion to tell the story of a priest who both longs for God and freedom from him. *The White Stone* reflects the author's socialist sympathies, which Sutherland shared, as evidenced by her own writings. Elizabeth Sutherland's/Betita Martínez's commitment to social justice has manifested throughout her life, in part through her dedication to socialism not in pursuit of ideology but of social justice.

17. Platt, "The Heart Just Insists," 33.

18. It is unclear whether this trip was made as part of Martínez's work for the United Nations.

19. Elizabeth Sutherland Martínez, "Neither Black nor White in a Black-White World," in *Hands on the Freedom Plow: Personal Accounts by Women in SNCC*, ed. Faith S. Holsaert, Martha Prescod Norman Noonan, Judy Richardson, Betty Garman Robinson, Jean Smith Young, and Dorothy M. Zellner (Urbana: University of Illinois Press, 2010), 531–540.

20. Elizabeth Sutherland, "Cuban Faith in Castro," *The Guardian*, December 5, 1961, and "Castro's Work for the Peasants," *The Guardian*, December 6, 1961.

21. Sutherland, "Cuban Faith in Castro."

22. Sutherland, "Castro's Work for the Peasants."

23. Ibid.

24. Ibid.

25. Elizabeth Sutherland. "Cinema of Revolution: 90 Miles from Home," *Film Quarterly* 15, no. 2 (1961): 42–49.

26. Ibid., 42.

27. Ibid.

28. Ibid., 46.

29. Elizabeth Sutherland, *The Youngest Revolution: A Personal Report on Cuba* (New York: Dial, 1969).

30. Sutherland, "Cinema of Revolution," 43.

31. Ibid., 46.

32. Ibid., 47.

33. Ibid., 48.

34. Elizabeth Sutherland, "SNCC Takes Stock: Mandate from History," *The Nation*, January 6, 1964, 32.

35. Ibid., 30.

36. Davalos, "Sin Vergüenza."

37. Elizabeth Sutherland, ed., *Letters from Mississippi: Personal Reports from Volunteers in the Summer Freedom Project, 1964, to Their Parents and Friends* (New York: McGraw-Hill, 1965); reissued with new material as Elizabeth Martínez, ed., *Letters from Mississippi: Reports from Civil Rights Volunteers and Poetry of the 1964 Freedom Summer* (Brookline, MA: Zephyr, 2007).

38. Sutherland, *Letters from Mississippi* (1965).

39. Ibid., 27.

40. Elizabeth Sutherland Martínez, *500 Años del Pueblo Chicano: 500 Years of Chicano History in Pictures*, rev. ed. (Albuquerque, NM: SouthWest Organizing Project, 1991).

41. Ibid., 114.

42. Not only did Sutherland receive no credit for her work on the book, she arranged for the proceeds of its sale to go to SNCC.

43. Lorraine Hansberry, *The Movement: Documentary of a Struggle for Equality* (New York: Simon and Schuster, 1964).

44. Angela Davis, "Before I Knew Elizabeth Martínez," *Social Justice* 39, no. 2–3 (2013): 96.

45. Elizabeth Sutherland Martínez, "Every Now and Then (1966)," *Social Justice* 39, no. 2–3 (2013).

46. She discusses her unpublished SNCC paper "Black, White, and Tan" in her essay "Neither Black nor White in a Black-White World," written for the collection *Hands on the Freedom Plow*.

47. Elizabeth Sutherland Martínez, "Because He Was Black and I Was White: Six Young Women Discuss Their Various Experiences in the Civil-Rights Movement (1967)," *Social Justice* 39, no. 2–3 (2013): 61–74.

48. Ibid., 61.

49. Ibid.

50. Ibid.

51. Martínez, interview by Ross, 10.

52. Martha E. Sánchez, *"Shakin' Up" Race and Gender: Intercultural Connections in Puerto Rican, African American, and Chicano Narratives and Culture (1965–1995)* (Austin: University of Texas Press, 2005).

53. Elizabeth Sutherland Martínez, "Women of the World Unite—We Have Nothing to Lose but Our Men (1968)," *Social Justice* 39, no. 2–3 (2013).

54. Martínez, interview by Ross, 29.

55. Elizabeth Martínez, *De Colores Means All of Us: Latina Views for a Multi-Colored Century* (Cambridge, MA: South End, 1998), 182–189.

56. Martinez, interview by Ross, 11.

57. Elizabeth Sutherland Martínez, "A Day in the Committee Room" (1963), *Social Justice* 39, no. 2–3 (2013): 52–54.

58. Ibid., 53.

59. Sutherland, *Youngest Revolution*, 97.

60. Ibid., 19.

61. Ibid., 101.

62. Ibid., 23. She refers to Lezama Lima's 1967 novel *Paradiso*.

63. Barbara Dane, "Solidarity Forever," *Social Justice* 39, no. 2–3 (2013): 104–106.

64. Ibid., 105.

65. Sutherland, *Youngest Revolution*, 112.

66. Mike Davis, "Elizabeth Occupies Wall Street," *Social Justice* 39, no. 2–3 (2013): 86–87.

67. Wiley is quoted in Allen, "Always Connecting the Struggles," 93.

68. Sutherland, *Youngest Revolution*.

69. Betty Luther Hillman, "'The Clothes I Wear Help Me to Know My Own Power': The Politics of Gender Presentation in the Era of Women's Liberation," *Frontiers: A Journal of Women's Studies* 34, no. 2 (2013).

70. Sarah Seidman, "Tricontinental Route of Solidarity: Stokely Carmichael in Cuba," *Journal of Transnational American Studies* 4, no. 2 (2012): n.p.

71. Elizabeth Sutherland, "The Grapes of Wrath Begat a Movement," *Village Voice*, May 5, 1966.

72. Ibid., 7.

73. Sutherland Martínez, "Neither Black nor White," 536.

74. Elizabeth Sutherland Martínez and Enriqueta Longeaux y Vásquez, *Viva La Raza! The Struggle of the Mexican-American People* (Garden City, NY: Doubleday, 1974).

75. Ibid., 78–79.

76. Ibid., 85.

77. Ibid., 139–153.

78. Ibid., 339.

79. Ibid., 340.

CHAPTER 14

1. This essay is dedicated to Felicitas Nuñez, Teresa Oyos, Martha Salinas, and the other participants from San Diego, whom I hope to meet some day ("Las Diez"), and to the powerful Chicana activists I have been blessed to know. I am especially thankful to Felicitas for the intergenerational collaboration we have forged through this conversation.

2. Felicitas M. Nuñez, "La Raza en Canada, Vancouver Conference, April 2–4, 1971," May 26, 1971. Shared from the personal collection of Felicitas Nuñez. A copy of this report is located in the Enriqueta Chavez Collection, San Diego State University Special Collections. I am using this copy as my primary source because it has clearly paginated numbers. Nuñez shared her copy, which included photographs of the actual conference interspersed. I reference her document when I reference the photographs.

3. For an excellent account of Chicana participation in the United Nations–sponsored International Women's Year Conference in Mexico in 1975, see Marisela R. Chávez, "Pilgrimage to the Homeland: California Chicanas and International Women's Year, Mexico City, 1975," in *Memories and Migrations: Mapping Boricua and Chicana Histories*, ed. Vicki L. Ruiz and John R. Chávez, 170–195 (Chicago: University of Illinois Press, 2008).

4. Teresa Oyos, interview by Dionne Espinoza, September 23, 2016, San Diego, CA; Felicitas Nuñez and Martha Salinas, interview by Dionne Espinoza, November 4, 2016, San Diego, CA, videotaped by Jessica Cordova.

5. I note this kind of erasure in some of the editorial choices made for the landmark anthology *Chicana Feminist Thought*. Specifically, in some of the pieces reprinted from *El Grito del Norte*, key sentences and even paragraphs that addressed Chicana perspectives on the struggles of women in Third World countries or that offered nuanced analysis about coalition were edited out. Although there are essays relating to international conferences

that Chicanas attended elsewhere in the anthology (and the brief excerpt from *La Verdad* contained in that volume first raised my interest in finding out more about San Diego Chicana participation in the conference), it was especially problematic that *El Grito del Norte*, known for its Third World and internationalist lens, was recalibrated into the dominant understanding of the Chicano movement as a nationalist movement that did not engage other struggles. See Alma M. García, ed., *Chicana Feminist Thought: The Basic Historical Writings* (New York: Routledge, 1997), especially 80–81.

6. María Cotera, "'Invisibility Is an Unnatural Disaster': Feminist Archival Praxis after the Digital Turn," in "1970s Feminisms," ed. Lisa Disch, special issue, *South Atlantic Quarterly* 114, no. 4 (2015): 793.

7. The most comprehensive account of the Indochinese Women's Conferences in Vancouver and Toronto has been written by historian Judy Tzu-Chun Wu. She brilliantly explores the conference in relation to various strands of the women's movements and peace movements. See her *Radicals on the Road: Internationalism, Orientalism, and Feminism during the Vietnam War Era* (Ithaca, NY: Cornell University Press, 2013), especially part 3, "Journeys for Global Sisterhood." Her chapter on the conference offers a rich account and analysis. However, the section on Third World women's participation is not as fleshed out as her writing about the other major participants and organizers of the conference, specifically "Voice of Women," "Women Strike for Peace," and "Women's Liberation." In particular, Wu does not explore the differences among "Third World women" that were also in discussion at the conference or the specificity of Chicana participation.

8. Wu, *Radicals on the Road*, 220–221.

9. Nuñez, "La Raza en Canada," 1.

10. Ibid., 1. According to Wu, one context for the sense of exclusivity may have been that in these early planning stages, organizers were concerned about information sharing and invitations due to the oversight of antiwar activities by the United States, especially those relating to Canada, positioned as a "neutral" safe space for draft resisters and also for dialogues on peace and those involving North American interactions with the Indochinese. Regardless of the reasons, these various concerns gave the impression of exclusivity about who should attend; *Radicals on the Road*, 225–226. Wu does state that the quotas only applied to "new friends" of the women's liberation movement and that all women of color were invited to attend; 231–232.

11. The original report lists the participants as "Las Diez," which I understand as a reference to the group as all women. My thanks to Martha Salinas for clarifying that the USCD participants included a graduate student (herself), a staff member (Betty Bane), and instructor Gracia Molina de Pick; Martha Salinas, email to the author, February 23, 2017. Felicitas Nuñez also confirmed that one of the participants was a junior high school student.

12. The San Diego State College chapter had evolved from the Mexican American Youth Association (MAYA) to a period of listing both names, MAYA and MEChA, through 1969 (MAYA-MEChA) to simply MEChA by spring 1970.

13. My research on Chicana activists in SDSC MEChA and the formation of Las Chicanas is further discussed in a forthcoming manuscript on Chicana activism in Chicano movement organizations.

14. Oyos, interview by Dionne Espinoza.

15. Teresa Oyos, "Las Chingonas," in *Teatro Chicana: A Collective Memoir and Selected Plays*, ed. Laura E. Garcia, Sandra M. Gutierrez, and Felicitas Nuñez (Austin: University of Texas Press, 2008), 48. Oyos is a longtime and highly respected figure in San Diego LGBTQ his/herstory.

16. Nuñez and Salinas, interview by Espinoza.

17. Nuñez and Salinas, interview by Espinoza.

18. Ibid.

19. George Mariscal, ed., *Aztlán and Viet Nam: Chicano and Chicana Experiences of the War* (Berkeley: University of California Press, 1999).

20. Peggy Garcia, in *Teatro Chicana: A Collective Memoir and Selected Plays*, ed. Laura E. Garcia, Sandra M. Gutierrez, and Felicitas Nuñez (Austin: University of Texas Press, 2008), 21.

21. Nuñez, "La Raza en Canada," 3.

22. Nuñez and Salinas, interview by Espinoza.

23. Nuñez, "La Raza en Canada," 2.

24. See, for example, Maylei Blackwell's analysis of the Conferencia de Mujeres por la Raza in *¡Chicana Power! Contested Histories of Feminism in the Chicano Movement* (Austin: University of Texas Press, 2011), 160-191, and Marisela R. Chávez, "Pilgrimage to the Homeland," as well as Martha P. Cotera's first-person perspective in this volume (chapter 2) on the National Women's Conference in 1977 in Houston.

25. Nuñez and Salinas, interview by Espinoza.

26. For an interesting approach to thinking about internationalism in relation to affect and "Chicana revolutionary love," see Natalie Havlin, "'To Live a Humanity under the Skin': Revolutionary Love and Third World Praxis in 1970s Chicana Feminism," *Women's Studies Quarterly* 43, no. 3–4 (2015): 78–97.

27. On the draft counseling work of Lea Ybarra and Nina Genera, see Lorena Oropeza, *¡Raza Si! ¡Guerra No! Chicano Protest and Patriotism during the Viet Nam War Era* (Berkeley: University of California Press, 2005), 104–110. I also had the privilege of interviewing Nina Genera about her student activism and lifelong commitment to human rights in an interview with Genera and Maria Elena Ramirez that also touched on their attendance at the Vancouver conference; Nina Genera and Maria Elena Ramirez, interview by Dionne Espinoza, January 5, 2017, Hayward, CA.

28. For more on the currents of Third Worldism during this time within the student movements, see George Mariscal, who has written on student organizing for a Third World college at UCSD in his book *Brown-Eyed Children of the Sun: Lessons from the Chicano Movement, 1965–1975* (Albuquerque: University of New Mexico Press, 2005), especially chapter 6, "To Demand That the University Work for Our People," 210–246; also Gary Y. Okihiro, *Third World Studies: Theorizing Liberation* (Durham, NC: Duke University Press, 2016).

29. Nuñez, "La Raza en Canada," 2.

30. Ibid., 7.

31. Ibid., 5. The conflict is also recounted in the narrative of Peggy Garcia in *Teatro Chicana*, 21–22.

32. Wu, *Radicals on the Road*, 194.

33. Kathleen Gough Aberle, "An Indochinese Conference in Vancouver," *Bulletin of Concerned Asian Scholars* 3, no. 3–4 (1971): 2. Aberle's reference to "Canadian groups" may mean to reference indigenous peoples of Canada. Felicitas Nuñez shared that there was a significant representation of indigenous Canadians at the conference.

34. Donna, "The Enemy is Imperialism," in "La Chicana/El Grito del Norte," special section, *El Grito del Norte*, June 5, 1971, p. K.

35. Ibid.

36. Wu, *Radicals on the Road*, 223–224. Wu writes in the section "War at a Peace Conference" that later self-criticism by white women activists demonstrates that they realized that by deciding which groups were initially contacted and included—women members of the Black Panthers and Third World Women's Alliance—they may have already been setting the terms of who was appropriate to include rather than allowing Third World women/women of color to decide for themselves how they wanted to participate.

37. Wu, *Radicals on the Road*, 224.

38. The article "Chicanas Attend Vancouver Conference" states, "...it was brought up that it had been the decision of the Indochinese women to meet with us exclusively"; *La Verdad*, May 1971, 14. This understanding was also expressed in my interviews with Nuñez and Salinas.

39. Nuñez, "La Raza en Canada," 7.

40. "Chicanas Attend Vancouver Conference," *La Verdad*.

41. Ibid.

42. Wu, *Radicals on the Road*, 224.

43. Nuñez and Salinas, interview by Espinoza.

44. Nuñez, "La Raza en Canada," 8.

45. Ibid., 9.

46. Ibid., 15.

47. Amrita Basu, ed., *The Challenge of Local Feminisms: Women's Movement in Global Perspective* (Boulder, CO: Westview Press, 1995), 20.

48. Chela Sandoval, "Mestizaje as Method: Feminists-of-Color Challenge the Canon," in *Living Chicana Theory*, ed. Carla Trujillo (Berkeley, CA: Third Woman Press, 1989), 356.

49. On the Third World Women's Alliance see Stephen Ward, "The Third World Women's Alliance: Black Feminist Radicalism and Black Power Politics," in *The Black Power Movement: Rethinking the Civil Rights-Black Power Era*, ed. Peniel Joseph (New York and London: Routledge, 2006), 119–144; Maylei Blackwell, "Triple Jeopardy: The Third World Women's Alliance and the Transnational Roots of Women-of-Color Feminisms," in *Provocations: A Transnational Reader on the History of Feminist Thought*, eds. Susan Border, M. Cristina Alcalde, and Ellen Rosenman (Oakland: University of California Press, 2015), 280–287.

50. Chela Sandoval traces the genealogy of this movement as "generated out of the juxtaposition of anticolonial and antisexist U.S. histories that are often underestimated or misunderstood"; "Mestizaje as Method," 353–354. See also Ranjoo Seodu Herr's sharp discussion of the dynamic of Third World feminism as a call for specificity and perspective of Third World women in "Reclaiming Third World Feminism: Or Why Transnational Feminism Needs Third World Feminism," *Meridians: Feminism, Race, Transnationalism* 12, no. 1 (2014): 1–30.

51. Ranjoo Seodu Herr, "The Possibility of Nationalist Feminism," *Hypatia* 18, no. 3 (2003): 135–160. For a set of essays debating "feminist nationalism," see Lois West, ed., *Feminist Nationalism* (New York: Routledge, 1997). See also Herr, "Reclaiming Third World Feminism."

52. See Chandra Talpade Mohanty's chapter "Under Western Eyes Revisited" for reference to the "feminist solidarity model" that I would argue was constructed in the discourse of Chicana feminists through Third World womanism; Mohanty, *Feminism without Borders: Decolonizing Theory Practicing Solidarity* (London: Duke University Press, 2004), 221–251.

53. "Viva La Chicana and All Brave Women of the Causa," in "La Chicana/El Grito del Norte," special section, *El Grito del Norte*, June 1971, p. B.

54. Dorinda Moreno, ed., *La mujer: En pie de lucha ¡Y la hora es ya!* (Mexico City: Espina del Norte, 1973).

55. See Elora Halim Chowdhury, "Locating Global Feminisms Everywhere: Braiding US Women of Color and Transnational Feminisms," *Cultural Dynamics* 21, no. 1 (2009): 51–78.

56. "Chicanas Attend Vancouver Conference," *La Verdad*.

57. Wu, *Radicals on the Road*, 224.

CHAPTER 15

1. Carlos Muñoz Jr.'s *Youth, Identity, Power: The Chicano Movement* (London: Verso, 1989) is a pioneering text that locates Chicana/o student militancy within the larger political history of the 1960s. While his monograph was among the first in the field to assess Chicana/o

youth movements, it sets up a prevailing trend in the Chicana/o movement scholarship that highlights male leaders and is devoid of a gender lens of analysis. In particular, Muñoz posits that Chicanas challenged Chicano patriarchy by forming their own separate groups; thus, he does not address how Chicanas navigated male-driven terrains by becoming leaders and raising women's issues. Recent scholars have highlighted the heterogeneous nature of the Chicana/o struggle, addressing the anti-Vietnam War movement and ideological fault lines. While these works offer fresh and nuanced perspectives of the Chicana/o movement, they do not center on women's experiences of this protest era. See Muñoz Jr., *Youth, Identity, Power*; Ernesto Chávez, *"¡Mi Raza Primero!" (My People First): Nationalism, Identity, and Insurgency in the Chicano Movement in Los Angeles, 1966–1978* (Berkeley: University of California Press, 2002); and Lorena Oropeza, *¡Raza Sí! ¡Guerra No! Chicano Protest and Patriotism during the Viet Nam War Era* (Berkeley: University of California Press, 2005).

2. Yolanda Birdwell, interview by Samantha Rodriguez, February 12, 2014, Houston; Daniel Bustamante, interview by Samantha Rodriguez, May 20, 2014, Houston; Inés Hernández-Ávila, interview by Samantha Rodriguez, January 19, 2015, by phone; Louise Villejo, interview by Samantha Rodriguez, January, 9, 2015, Houston.

3. María de los Ángeles Jiménez, interview by María Cotera, August 31, 2012, El Paso, TX, Chicana por mi Raza Digital Memory Collective.

4. Ibid.

5. Ibid.

6. Ibid.

7. María Jiménez, interview by Samantha Rodriguez, February 6, 2014, Houston.

8. Gloria Anzaldúa, *Borderlands/La Frontera: The New Mestiza* (San Francisco: Spinsters/Aunt Lute, 1987), 80.

9. Ibid., 82.

10. Throughout the Americas, Latinas/os have utilized testimonials to challenge social and cultural systems of repression and to bear witness to their lived experiences. See Rina Benmayor, "Testimony, Action, Research, and Empowerment: Puerto Rican Women and Popular Education," in *Women's Words: The Feminist Practice of Oral History*, ed. Sherna Berger Gluck and Daphne Patai (New York: Routledge, 1991), 159–174; Aurora Chang, Vanessa Fonseca, Lilia Soto, and Dolores Saucedo Cardona, "Latina Faculty/Staff Testimonios on Scholarship Production," *Chicana/Latina Studies: The Journal of MALCS* 15, no. 2 (2016): 125–149; Graciela Di Marco, "The Mothers and Grandmothers of Plaza de Mayo Speak," in *Women's Activism in Latin America and the Caribbean: Engendering Social Justice, Democratizing Citizenship*, ed. Elizabeth Maier and Nathalie Lebon (New Brunswick, NJ: Rutgers University Press, 2010), 95–110.

11. Jiménez, interview by Cotera.

12. Arnoldo De León, *Ethnicity in the Sunbelt: Mexican Americans in Houston* (College Station: Texas A&M University Press, 2001); Thomas K. Kreneck, *Del Pueblo: A History of Houston's Hispanic Community* (College Station: Texas A&M University Press, 2012).

13. Jiménez, interview by Cotera.

14. During the 1960s and 1970s, Chicanas across the nation widely regarded Sor Juana Inés de la Cruz as one of the first feminists in the hemisphere due to her poetic and prose writings that confronted religious and social patriarchy. See Martha P. Cotera, *Diosa y Hembra: The History and Heritage of Chicanas in the U.S.* (Austin: Information Systems Development, 1976); Anna NietoGomez, "Chicana Feminism," in *Chicana Feminist Thought: The Basic Historical Writings*, ed. Alma M. García (New York: Routledge, 1997): 52–57; Alfredo Mirandé and Evangelina Enríquez, *La Chicana: The Mexican American Woman* (Chicago: University of Chicago Press, 1979).

15. María Jiménez, interview by Samantha Rodriguez, July 25, 2013, Houston, University of Houston Oral History Project.

16. Jiménez, interview by Rodriguez, February 6, 2014.

17. Jiménez, interview by Cotera.

18. Jiménez, interview by Rodriguez, February 6, 2014.

19. Jiménez, interview by Rodriguez, July 25, 2013.

20. Jiménez, interview by Rodriguez, February 6, 2014.

21. Ibid.

22. Anzaldúa, *Borderlands/La Frontera*, 79.

23. Jiménez, interview by Rodriguez, February 6, 2014.

24. Jiménez, interview by Cotera.

25. Ibid.

26. Ibid.

27. Ibid.

28. Jiménez, interview by Rodriguez, February 6, 2014.

29. Jiménez, interview by Rodriguez, July 25, 2013.

30. "Ethnic studies" is employed in this chapter to point out that Chicana/o studies was a part of a larger movement for ethnic-based teaching and research centers, such as African American studies. MAYO was a statewide organization most notable for bringing together students and barrio youth for the purpose of challenging the social, political, and economic domination of the Anglo power structure. In Houston, there were two MAYO chapters, one at the university level (UHMAYO) and one in the community (barrio MAYO); for more information on MAYO, see Armando Navarro, *Mexican American Youth Organization: Avant-Garde of the Chicano Movement in Texas* (Austin: University of Texas Press, 1995).

31. Anzaldúa, *Borderlands/La Frontera*, 79. Gloria Anzaldúa defines "the pluralistic mode" as merging all elements of one's identity. By balancing race, class, and gender in her university social justice endeavors, Maria Jiménez exhibited a pluralistic mode.

32. Navarro, *Mexican American Youth Organization*, 85–86; Saul Alinsky, *Reveille for Radicals* (New York: Vintage Books, 1989).

33. Mexican American Youth Organization, box 53, folder 4, José Ángel Gutiérrez Papers, Nettie Lee Benson Latin American Collection, University of Texas Libraries (hereafter Benson Collection).

34. Jiménez, interview by Rodriguez, February 6, 2014.

35. Ibid.

36. Ibid. During the 1970s, Chicana/o cultural nationalists pushed forth an idealized notion of the patriarchal Mexican family that rendered Chicanas as selfless, hardworking women whose mission was to preserve the culture and particularly the family; Alma M. García, "The Development of Chicana Feminist Discourse," *Gender and Society* 3, no. 2 (1989): 217–237.

37. Inés Hernández Tovar would later become Inés Hernández-Ávila.

38. "MAYO and the Mexican American Studies at UH in 1972," roundtable hosted by the Center for Mexican American Studies, October 3, 2012, Fall Speaker Series, University of Houston; Pedro Vasquez, "Maria Jimenez: Vice-President University of Houston Students," *Papel Chicano* 1, no. 8 (1971): 5.

39. Jiménez, interview by Rodriguez, July 25, 2013.

40. Vasquez, "Maria Jimenez."

41. María Jiménez was able to become the first female SGA president in part because she had worked out a deal with white liberal student groups. She ran with Steve Umoff, who agreed to be student body president for six months and then resign, allowing Jiménez to be the president for the remaining six months.

42. Jiménez, interview by Cotera.

43. Vasquez, "Maria Jimenez."

44. The free abortion counseling proposition was radical for its time since it predated the *Roe v. Wade* Supreme Court decision in 1973.

45. Jiménez, interview by Rodriguez, February 6, 2014.

46. Maria Jiménez, "Women Still Powerless," *Papel Chicano* 1, no. 4 (1971): 8.

47. Jiménez, interview by Rodriguez, February 6, 2014.

48. Anzaldúa, *Borderlands/La Frontera*, 79.

49. Jiménez, interview by Rodriguez, July 25, 2013.

50. "Why Raza Unida," box 1, folder 1, Raza Unida Party Records, Benson Collection.

51. Dionne Espinoza, "The Partido Belongs to Those Who Will Work for It: Chicana Organizing and Leadership in the Texas Raza Unida Party, 1970–1980," *Aztlán: A Journal of Chicano Studies* 36, no. 1 (2011): 198.

52. Muñoz, *Youth, Identity, Power* 116–117.

53. Espinoza, "The Partido Belongs to Those Who Will Work for It," 199.

54. La Mujer, box 1, folder 3, Raza Unida Party Records, 1969–1979, Benson Collection.

55. Jiménez, interview by Cotera.

56. United Peoples Party (Raza Unida), box 2, folder 4, Raza Unida Party Records, 1969–1979, Benson Collection.

57. Jiménez, interview by Cotera.

58. RUP state representative campaign leaflet, November 1974, María Jiménez personal papers, Houston.

59. Jiménez, interview by Rodriguez, February 6, 2014.

60. La Raza Unida Party Reunion Program Book, July 6–7, 2012, p. 30, http://www.larazaunidapartyreunion.org/La_Raza_Unida_Program_Book_2012.pdf.

61. Due to his work on the RUP campaign with María Jiménez, Omowali Luthuli would become involved in the Immigrant Rights Freedom Ride in 2003.

62. Jiménez, interview by Cotera.

63. RUP state representative campaign leaflet, María Jiménez personal papers.

64. Jiménez, interview by Cotera.

65. Anzaldúa, *Borderlands/La Frontera*, 3.

66. Jiménez, interview by Rodriguez, February 6, 2014.

67. During her tenure at the American Friends Service Committee, Jiménez helped bring together Latina/o, British, Sikh, Indian, and Pakistani immigrants to push for amnesty in 2000. She also supported the Zapatista uprising in Chiapas, Mexico, through the Houston Comité de Solidaridad con el Pueblo de Mexico (Houston Solidarity Committee for the People of Mexico) and the National Commission for Democracy in Mexico.

68. Jiménez, interview by Rodriguez, February 6, 2014.

69. Jiménez, interview by Cotera.

CHAPTER 16

1. "Speaking bitterness" was a consciousness-raising technique borrowed from women revolutionaries in the Chinese revolution. Used extensively in the women's liberation movement, this practice was a vehicle for raising consciousness about women's lived conditions of oppression.

CHAPTER 17

The epigraph is from Walter Benjamin, "Unpacking My Library: A Talk about Book Collecting," in Walter Benjamin, *Illuminations: Essays and Reflections*, ed. Hannah Arendt (New York: Shocken Books, 1968), 60.

1. The "haunting" nature of this archive bespeaks the relations of power underwriting "official" memories of the past and the methodologies that support them. As Avery Gordon has demonstrated in her masterful interdisciplinary critique of sociology, *Ghostly Matters*, traditional methodologies for uncovering the past are all too often haunted by the stories they cannot reveal. See *Ghostly Matters: Haunting and the Sociological Imagination*, 2nd ed. (Minneapolis: University of Minnesota Press, 2008).

2. Miroslava Chávez-García, "The Interdisciplinary Project of Chicana History: Looking Back, Moving Forward," *Pacific Historical Review* 82, no. 4 (2013): 542–565; Yolanda Chávez Leyva, "Listening to the Silences in Latina/Chicana Lesbian History," in *Living Chicana Theory*, ed. Carla Trujillo (Berkeley, CA: Third Woman Press, 1998), 429–434; Yolanda Retter Vargas, "Preservation of LGBT Theory: The One Archive," in *Pathways to Progress: Issues and Advances in Latino Librarianship*, ed. John L. Ayala and Salvador Guereña (Denver: Libraries Unlimited, 2011), 169–176; Maylei Blackwell, ¡*Chicana Power! Contested Histories of Feminism in the Chicano Movement* (Austin: University of Texas Press, 2011); María Cotera, "'Invisibility Is an Unnatural Disaster': Feminist Archival Praxis after the Digital Turn," in 1970s Feminisms Special Issue, *South Atlantic Quarterly* 114, no. 4 (2015): 781–801.

3. María Cotera, "Invisibility," 785.

4. Michel-Rolph Trouillot, *Silencing the Past: Power and the Production of History* (Boston: Beacon, 1995), 19.

5. Ibid., 48.

6. Ibid.

7. Ibid.

8. Gloria Anzaldúa, "now let us shift . . . the path of conocimiento . . . inner work, public acts," in *This Bridge We Call Home: Radical Visions for Transformation*, ed. Gloria Anzaldúa and AnaLouise Keating (New York: Routledge, 2002), 540-578.

9. Gloria Anzaldúa, *Borderlands/La Frontera: The New Mestiza* (San Francisco: Spinsters/Aunt Lute Books, 1987), 104.

10. For more on the "mythopoetics" of movement narratives, see Lee Bebout, *Mytho-historical Interventions: The Chicano Movement and Its Legacies* (Minneapolis: University of Minnesota Press, 2011).

11. Blackwell, ¡*Chicana Power!*, 2. These observations on Blackwell's analysis of the memory practices of Las Hijas de Cuauhtémoc first appeared in my review of her book in *Signs: Journal of Women in Culture and Society* 38, no. 3 (2013): 748–757.

12. I borrow here from historian Emma Pérez, who calls attention to the need for both new *sitios* (sites) and *lenguas* (discourses) to support the elaboration of Chicana lesbian theory. See Perez, "Irigaray's Female Symbolic in the Making of Chicana Lesbian Sitios y Lenguas (Sites and Discourses)," in *Living Chicana Theory*, ed. Carla Trujillo (Berkeley, CA: Third Woman Press, 1997) 87–101.

13. Amy Sara Carroll, "Lesbianism-Poetry/Poetry-Lesbianism," in *Cambridge Companion to Lesbian Literature* (New York: Cambridge University Press, 2015), 188–203.

14. For more on the pedagogical impact of the project and the many students who have been involved with it, see María Cotera, "Invisibility."

15. This observation in no way diminishes the important legacy of feminist historiographic interventions into the scholarship on the Chicano movement, a legacy that the editors outline in detail in the introduction to this volume. Important precedents to our attention to Chicana memory include the oral histories conducted by Chicanas themselves during the movement years as well as more recent works like *Chicanas in Charge: Texas Women in the Public Arena*, ed. José Ángel Gutiérrez, Michelle Melendez, and Sonia A. Noyola (New York: AltaMira Press, 2007); Leonard Ramirez's edited volume of oral history, *Chicanas of 18th Street: Narratives of a Movement from Latino Chicago* (Chicago: University of

Illinois Press, 2011); and Theresa Delgadillo's *Latina Lives in Milwaukee* (Chicago: University of Illinois Press, 2015).

16. Paul Arthur, "Saving Lives: Digital Biography and Life Writing," in *Save As, Digital Memories*, ed. Joanne Garde-Hansen, Andrew Hoskins, and Anna Reading (New York: Palgrave Macmillan, 2009), 49. For more on the impact of photography on the politics of representation see Walter Benjamin, "The Work of Art in the Age of Mechanical Reproduction," in his *Illuminations*, 219–254.

17. Jeremy Schnapp and Todd Presner, "Digital Humanities Manifesto 2.0," 2009, http://www.humanitiesblast.com/manifesto/Manifesto_V2.pdf.

18. Audre Lord, "The Master's Tools Will Never Dismantle the Master's House," in *Sister Outsider: Essays and Speeches* (Trumansburg, NY: Crossing Press, 1984), 110–113.

19. A major source of news and information on black, Chicano, Asian American and Indigenous struggles in the US and decolonial struggles worldwide, Third World Newsreel disseminated short documentaries to a networked community of activists across the United States. Bill Nichols, *Newsreel: Documentary Filmmaking on the American Left* (New York: Arno Press, 1977). In recent years, several monographs have emerged that explore the ways in which photography shaped the civil rights movement. In his essay "The Chicano/a Photographic: Art as Social Practice in the Chicano Movement," Colin Gunkel proposes that the analysis of Chicano photography move beyond a focus on the representational image itself to explore the circuits of production and exchange that enabled Chicana/o image making across a broad array of media; "The Chicano/a Photographic: Art as Social Practice in the Chicano Movement," *American Quarterly* 67, no. 2 (2015): 377–412. In a different context, Leigh Raiford points out how the technology of the "filmstrip" (a set of interconnected stills that could be played coupled with narration) was developed by women in SNCC, including Maria Varela, who later collaborated with Elizabeth "Betita" Martínez, as a key tool for popular education projects; *Imprisoned in a Luminous Glare: Photography and the African American Freedom Struggle* (Chapel Hill: University of North Carolina Press, 2011), 113–117.

20. In the spring of 2014, University of Michigan students under the direction of María Cotera and Hannah Smotrich at the Stamps School of Art and Design collaboratively curated a historical exhibition based on oral histories and archives that they collected in a class connected to the Chicana por mi Raza digital archive. The exhibition, entitled "Las Rebeldes: Stories of Strength and Struggle in Southeastern Michigan," was presented in partnership with El Museo del Norte in Detroit and is posted at the museum's website, http://www.elmuseodelnorte.org. In a follow-up community collaboration, this time with El Museo del Norte and the Walter P. Reuther Archive at Wayne State University, the project co-curated a traveling exhibit of photographs discovered in Nancy De Los Santos personal collection. The photographs, taken in the 1970s, document Chicano movement activities in the Midwest and Texas, as well as the activities of early Latina feminist formations in Chicago. De Los Santos's collection includes priceless photographs of Latina and Third World women's organizing at the International Women's Year conference in Mexico City in 1975, images that historian Marisela Chávez examines in her chapter in this volume.

21. Andrew Hoskins, introduction to *Save As, Digital Memories*, ed. Joanne Garde-Hansen, Andrew Hoskins, and Anna Reading (New York: Palgrave Macmillan, 2009), 15.

22. For an account of Chicana participation in the Mexico City conference, see Marisela R. Chávez, "Pilgrimage to the Homeland: California Chicanas and International Women's Year, Mexico City, 1975," in *Memories and Migrations: Mapping Boricua and Chicana Histories*, ed. Vicki L. Ruiz and John R. Chávez (Chicago: University of Illinois Press, 2008), 170–195.

23. Ariel Kaplowitz, "Texan Chicanas and International Women's Year: A Timeline," Historias, Chicana por mi Raza Digital Memory Collective.

24. Elizabeth "Betita" Martínez, *500 Years of Chicana Women's History/500 Años de la Mujer Chicana*, bilingual ed. (New Brunswick, NJ: Rutgers University Press, 2008).

25. Jay David Bolter and Richard Grusin, *Remediation: Understanding New Media*, rev. ed. (Cambridge, MA: MIT Press, 2000).

26. Rosa Linda Fregoso, *The Bronze Screen: Chicana and Chicano Film Culture* (Minneapolis: University of Minnesota Press, 1993), 16.

CHAPTER 18

1. For previous work on this conference, see Marisela R. Chávez, "Pilgrimage to the Homeland: Chicanas and International Women's Year, Mexico City, 1975," in *Memories and Migrations: Mapping Chicana and Boricua Histories*, ed. Vicki L. Ruiz and John R. Chávez (Chicago: University of Illinois Press, 2008), 170–195. Also see, for example, Yolanda M. López, "A Chicana's Look at the International Women's Year Conference," *Chicano Federation Newsletter* (San Diego, CA), August 1975, 2–4, reprinted in *Chicana Feminist Thought: The Basic Historical Writings*, ed. Alma M. García (London: Routledge, 1997), 181–183; Virginia R. Allan, Margaret E. Galey, and Mildred E. Persinger, "World Conference of International Women's Year," in *Women, Politics, and the United Nations*, ed. Anne Winslow (Westport, CT: Greenwood, 1995), 29–44; Jocelyn Olcott, "Cold War Conflicts and Cheap Cabaret: Performing Politics at the 1975 United Nations International Women's Year Conference in Mexico City," *Gender and History* 22, no. 3 (2010): 733–754.

2. Corinne Sánchez, interview by Marisela R. Chávez, April 4, 2002, Los Angeles. NBC has no record of the recordings.

3. Connie Pardo, interview by Marisela R. Chávez, March 29, 2002, Los Angeles.

4. Comisión Femenil Mexicana Nacional Records, CEMA 30, California Ethnic and Multicultural Archives, University of California, Santa Barbara; Comisión Femenil de Los Angeles Papers, 30, Chicano Studies Research Center, University of California, Los Angeles.

5. Marisela R. Chávez, "Despierten Hermanas y Hermanos!: Women, the Chicano Movement, and Chicana Feminisms in California, 1966–1981" (PhD diss., Stanford University, 2004).

6. Maylei Blackwell, *¡Chicana Power! Contested Histories of Feminism in the Chicano Movement* (Austin: University of Texas Press, 2011), chapter 4.

7. "Calendar," *Xilonen* (Mexico City, Mexico), June 20–July 1, 1975.

8. Chicanas of La Raza Unida Party, "International Women's Year Conference: La Mujer Chicana," June 23, 1975, Año Internacional de la Mujer Mexicana Collection, Chicano Studies Research Center, University of California, Los Angeles. While I first saw this pamphlet in the UCLA collection, the image here is from Martha P. Cotera's collection in the Chicana por mi Raza Archive.

9. Comisión Femenil Mexicana Nacional Records, El Centro de Acción Social Autónomo (CASA) Collection, M0325, Department of Special Collections, Stanford University.

10. See Elizabeth Martínez, *De Colores Means All of Us: Latina Views for a Multi-Colored Century* (Cambridge, MA: South End, 1998); George Mariscal, *Brown-Eyed Children of the Sun: Lessons from the Chicano Movement, 1965–1975* (Albuquerque: University of New Mexico Press, 2005); Lorena Oropeza, *¡Raza Sí! ¡Guerra No! Chicano Protest and Patriotism during the Viet Nam War Era* (Berkeley: University of California Press, 2005); Judy Tzu-Chun Wu, *Radicals on the Road: Internationalism, Orientalism, and Feminism during the Vietnam Era* (Ithaca, NY: Cornell University Press, 2013).

11. Miroslava Chávez-García, "The Interdisciplinary Project of Chicana History: Looking Back, Moving Forward," *Pacific Historical Review* 82, no. 4 (2013): 543.

12. Nancy De Los Santos Reza, interview by María Cotera, November 14, 2014, Los

Angeles. De Los Santos Reza has many other credits, including coproducing the documentary *Lalo Guerrero: The Original Chicano*, which aired on HBO, and a host of writing credits for shows such as *Resurrection Boulevard* (Showtime) and more recently the television show *Cristela* (ABC). See Nancy De Los Santos, "We Sit Down with Nancy De Los Santos, writer. Period," interview by Al Carlos Hernandez, *Herald de Paris*, November 22, 2009, http://www.heralddeparis.com/we-sit-down-with-nancy-de-los-santos-writer-period/; Elia Esparza, "Nancy De Los Santos: Writer Who Pushes the Envelope," *Latin Heat Entertainment*, April 30, 2015, http://www.latinheat.com/spotlight-news/nancy-de-los-santos-writer-who-pushes-the-envelope; Nancy De Los Santos, "Bio," email to author, June 11, 2015.

13. Nancy De Los Santos Reza, email to Marisela R. Chávez, May 21, 2015; Nancy De Los Santos Reza, conversation with Marisela R. Chávez, June 11, 2015, by phone.

14. See Yolanda Chávez Leyva, "Listening to the Silences in Latina/Chicana Lesbian History," in *Living Chicana Theory*, ed. Carla Trujillo (Berkeley, CA: Third Woman Press, 1998), 429–434.

15. Marianne Hirsch, "Surviving Images: Holocaust Photographs and the Work of Postmemory," *Yale Journal of Criticism* 14, no. 1 (2001): 8. See also Marianne Hirsch, *The Generation of Postmemory: Writing and Visual Culture after the Holocaust* (New York: Columbia University Press, 2012).

16. Hirsch, "Surviving Images," 9.

17. Ibid., 28.

18. Ibid., 14.

19. See, for example, Avery Gordon, *Ghostly Matters: Haunting and the Sociological Imagination* (Minneapolis: University of Minnesota Press, 2008).

CHAPTER 21

1. "Mexico's 1968 Massacre: What Really Happened?" *All Things Considered*, National Public Radio, December 1, 2008, http://www.npr.org/templates/story/story.php?storyId =97546687.

2. The tribal college, DQU, was started when Jack Forbes, David Risling Jr., and Sarah Hutchison signed a lease agreement with the federal government to use what had been government surplus property to start a school for Native and Chicano students. When they named the school Deganawidah-Quetzalcoatl University, they failed to ask permission of the Six Nations people, the Haudenosaunee, for the use of the word "Deganawidah," which is a reference to the one they call the Great Peacemaker. The Six Nations people asked the new college to not use the full name but rather the initial "D" instead. Thus, the college became known as DQU.

3. Inés Hernández-Ávila, "Para Teresa," in *Infinite Divisions: An Anthology of Chicana Literature*, ed. Tey Diana Rebodello and Eliana S. Rivero (Tucson: University of Arizona Press, 1993), 330–332.

4. Malcolm X, "Malcolm Describes the Difference between the 'House Negro' and the 'Field Negro,'" Michigan State University, East Lansing, January 23, 1963, Speeches and Interviews, "The Autobiography of Malcolm X" website, Columbia Center for New Media Teaching and Learning and Columbia University Center for Contemporary Black History, http://ccnmtl.columbia.edu/projects/mmt/mxp/speeches/mxa17.html.

5. Fanny Howe, The *Winter Sun: Notes on a Vocation* (Minneapolis, MN: Graywolf, 2009), 147.

6. Octavio Romano-V, ed., *El Espejo—The Mirror: Selected Mexican-American* Literature (Berkeley, CA: Quinto Sol, 1969).

7. Tomás Rivera, *. . . y no se lo tragó la tierra/. . . and the Earth Did Not Devour Him*, trans.

Evangelina Vigil-Piñon, 4th ed. (Houston: Arte Público, 2015); Rudolfo Anaya, *Bless Me Ultima* (New York: Warner Books, 1994).

8. Inés Hernández-Ávila, "Testimonio de Memoria: For all the mujeres de movimiento que saben de estas cosas," in *New Chicana/Chicano Writing*, ed. C. M. Tatum (Tucson: University of Arizona Press, 1992), 9–17.

9. Miguel León-Portilla, *Aztec Thought and Culture: A Study of the Ancient Nahuatl Mind*, rev. ed. (Norman: University of Oklahoma Press, 1990).

10. Walter Echo-Hawk, *In the Light of Justice: The Rise of Human Rights in Native America and the UN Declaration on the Rights of Indigenous Peoples* (Golden, CO: Fulcrum, 2013), 258.

11. We produced the journal *HEMBRA* in 1976 through the Center for Mexican American Studies at the University of Texas, Austin. My students and I edited the publication.

12. Inés Hernández-Ávila, "In the Presence of Spirit(s): A Meditation on the Politics of Solidarity and Transformation," in *This Bridge We Call Home: Radical Visions for Transformation*, ed. Gloria Anzaldúa and AnaLouise Keating (New York: Routledge, 2002), 533, 536.

CONTRIBUTORS

MICHAEL D. AGUIRRE is a doctoral candidate in the Department of History at the University of Washington, Seattle. His dissertation explores transborder labor organizing, class formations, and transnational capitalism in the Mexico-US borderlands. His research reveals the intersections of citizenship, migration, and economic change for peoples in the post-Bracero Program borderlands, especially workers in agriculture and industry on both sides of the border. His public scholarship bridges academia with broader audiences by working with and for the communities that inform his theorizations.

GLORIA E. ANZALDÚA (1942–2004) was a Chicana Tejana dyke cultural theorist, feminist philosopher, visionary, creative writer, and poet. She co-edited *This Bridge Called My Back: Writings by Radical Women of Color* (1981) with Cherríe Moraga and is best known for her semi-autobiographical book, *Borderlands/La Frontera: The New Mestiza (1987)*, which remains a classic in multiple fields including ethnic studies, gender studies, and cultural theory. She edited *Making Face, Making Soul/Haciendo Caras: Creative and Critical Perspectives by Women of Color* (1990) and co-edited *This Bridge We Call Home: Radical Visions for Transformation* (2002) with AnaLouise Keating. Anzaldúa was born and raised in the South Rio Grande Valley of Texas, where as a child she labored as a farmworker with her family. In addition to writing on feminism, the body, border culture, and language, her work and life was profoundly concerned with spirituality, which was the topic of her writing in the last ten years of her life and the subject of her dissertation in progress. Her book *Light In the Dark/Luz en lo Oscuro: Rewriting Identity, Spirituality, Reality* was published posthumously in 2015. Anzaldúa died in 2004 of diabetes complications. Despite her prominence as a creative writer, theorist and philosopher, she died without health insurance.

ROSIE CANO BERMUDEZ is a Chicana from Southeast Los Angeles and the first in her family to attain a higher education. Her journey through the academy began at East Los Angeles College. She is a doctoral candidate in the department of Chicana and Chicano studies at the University of California, Santa Barbara. Her dissertation, "Doing Dignity Work: Alicia Escalante and the East Los Angeles Welfare Rights Organization, 1967–1974," focuses on the human dignity struggles waged by single Chicana welfare mothers in East Los Angeles in the 1960s and 1970s at the confluence of multiple social movements. Her research interests are centered on the histories of Chicana and Mexican American women's activism, identity, and feminisms during the second half of the twentieth century in Los Angeles.

MAYLEI BLACKWELL is associate professor of Chicana and Chicano studies and gender studies and affiliated faculty in LGBT studies and American Indian studies at the University of California, Los Angeles. She is the author of the landmark book *¡Chicana Power! Contested Histories of Feminism in the Chicano Movement*. For the last two decades, she has accompanied indigenous women organizers in Mexico, feminist movement and sexual rights activists throughout Latin America, and more recently, and indigenous migrant women's activism in California. Her forthcoming book is entitled *Scales of Resistance: Indigenous Women's Transborder Organizing in Mexico and the U.S.* with Duke University Press. She co-directs the Mapping Indigenous LA Project (mila.ss.ucla.edu), a digital story-mapping project underway with indigenous communities of Los Angeles.

MARISELA R. CHÁVEZ is a Chicana historian and associate professor in the Department of Chicana and Chicano Studies at California State University, Dominguez Hills. She has published articles on Chicana feminist history in *Memories and Migrations: Mapping Boricua and Chicana Histories* (University of Illinois Press, 2008) and *No Permanent Waves: Recasting U.S. Feminist History* (Rutgers University Press, 2010). Her research focuses on Chicana and Mexican American women's activism in Los Angeles from the 1960s to 1980, oral history/herstory, and memory.

MARÍA COTERA holds a joint appointment in the Departments of Women's Studies and American Culture at the University of Michigan. Cotera's first book, *Native Speakers: Ella Deloria, Zora Neale Hurston, Jovita González, and the Poetics of Culture* (University of Texas Press, 2008) received the Gloria Anzaldúa book prize for 2009 from the National Women's Studies Association. She is director of the Chicana por mi Raza Digital Memory Project, an online interactive collection of oral histories and archives documenting Chicana Feminist praxis from 1960 to 1990.

MARTHA P. COTERA is a feminist historian, and since 1974, an adjunct professor at Austin Community College. She authored the groundbreaking feminist texts *Diosa y Hembra: History and Heritage of Chicanas in the US*, *The Chicana*

Feminist, and *Multicultural Women's Sourcebook*. Her writings also include more than 100 books, essays, articles, and book chapters on topics of activism, civil rights, feminism, and Latino history. She is a founding member of the National Women's Political Caucus, Texas Women's Political Caucus, Colegio Jacinto Treviño, Partido Raza Unida, and Mexican American Cultural Center in Austin.

MONICA DE LA TORRE is assistant professor of media and expressive culture in the School of Transborder Studies at Arizona State University. De La Torre's interdisciplinary research and teaching practices bridge Chicana feminist theory, Latina/o media studies, radio and sound studies, and women's and gender studies. A former community radio producer, De La Torre is working on a manuscript, "Feminista Frequencies: Chicana Radio Activism in Public Broadcasting," detailing the powerful story of Chicana farmworkers and activists turned community radio broadcasters beginning in the 1970s.

DIONNE ESPINOZA is professor of women's, gender, and sexuality studies in the Department of Liberal Studies at California State University, Los Angeles. Her teaching and research center on documenting, sharing, and analyzing Chicana and women of color herstories of activism, feminism, and leadership in movements for social justice. She coedited with Lorena Oropeza the award-winning anthology *Enriqueta Vasquez and the Chicano Movement: Writings from El Grito del Norte* (Arte Público, 2006). She is revising her monograph entitled *Bronze Womanhood: Chicana Activists in Chicano Movement Organizations in the Southwest*. She has developed and coordinated several community-engaged and public humanities efforts that document past and present Chicana activism in Southern California.

SUSANA L. GALLARDO is a lecturer in women, gender, and sexuality studies in the Department of Sociology and Interdisciplinary Social Sciences at San Jose State University. Born and raised in Southern California, she lives in San Jose with her partner, Ken, and ten-year-old daughter. This essay is based on ethnographic work conducted for her 2012 Stanford dissertation, "'I Never Left the Church': Redefining Chicana/o Catholic Religious Identities in San Jose, California." Her writings include "Theoretical Shifts in the Analysis of Latina Sexuality," with Ana M. Juarez and Stella Beatríz Kerl-McClain, in *Are All the Women Still White? Race, Shifts, and Critical Interventions in Feminist Studies*, edited by Janell Hobson (SUNY Press, 2016), and "'Tía María de la Maternity Leave': Reflections on Race, Class, and the Natural Birth Experience," in *Mothers' Lives in Academia*, edited by Mari Castaneda and Kirsten Isgro (Columbia University Press, 2013).

ELENA R. GUTIÉRREZ is associate professor in gender and women's studies and Latin American and Latino studies at the University of Illinois, Chicago. She researches and writes in the areas of Latinx reproductive politics, intersectional feminism and organizing, and Chicana/Latina studies. Her book publications include *Undivided Rights: Women of Color Organize for Reproductive Justice*, with Jael Silliman, Marlene Gerber Fried, and Loretta Ross (South End, 2004), and *Fertile Matters: The Politics of Mexican-Origin Women's Reproduction* (University of Texas Press, 2008). Gutiérrez curates the Reproductive Justice Virtual Library, an online research hub that connects organizers and academic scholarship. She also directs Chicana Chicago, a collaborative research project dedicated to documenting the activism, leadership, and contributions of Mexican-origin women to the city and its Latinx communities.

ESTER HERNÁNDEZ, born in the San Joaquin Valley of California to a Mexican/Yaqui farmworker family, is an internationally acclaimed San Francisco–based visual artist and graduate of the University of California, Berkeley. She is best known for her depiction of Native/Latina women through pastels, paintings, prints, and installations. She recently illustrated author Sandra Cisneros's book *Have You Seen Marie?*. She has had numerous solo and group shows throughout the United States and internationally. Her work is part of the Smithsonian's *Our America—The Latino Presence in American Art* exhibition, which has toured the United States. Her work is included in the permanent collections of the National Museum of American Art–Smithsonian, Institute of American Indian Arts in Santa Fe, San Francisco Museum of Modern Art, National Museum of Mexican Art in Chicago, and Museo Casa Estudio Diego Rivera y Frida Kahlo in Mexico City. Her artistic and personal archives are housed at Stanford University.

INÉS HERNÁNDEZ-ÁVILA is professor of Native American studies and a scholar, poet, and visual artist. She is Nez Perce, enrolled on the Colville Reservation, Washington, and Tejana. She is one of the six founders of the international Native American and Indigenous Studies Association. In 2008 she won an American Council of Learned Societies fellowship. In 2009 she received the Academic Senate Distinguished Teaching Award at the graduate and professional level. She codirected the University of California, Davis, Social Justice Initiative from 2013 to 2016. Her research focuses on the national movement of indigenous writers in Mexico, especially poets in Chiapas, and the influence of ancient Nahuatl philosophy on contemporary Chicana/indigenous creative expression. She has taught summer-abroad courses in Mexico City and San Cristobl de las Casas. She is coeditor, with Norma E. Cantú, of *Entre Guadalupe y Malinche: Tejanas in Literature and Art* (University of Texas Press, 2016).

OSA HIDALGO DE LA RIVA received her PhD from the University of Southern California's School of Cinematic Arts in the Critical Studies Division. She taught in the Ethnic Studies Department at the University of California, Berkeley, from 2008 to 2013 and received the Chancellor's Public Scholar Award in 2012. Her films *Mujería: The Olmeca Rap* (1990) and *Mujería: Primitive and Proud* (1992) were distributed by Women Make Movies. Her *Two Spirits: Native Lesbians and Gay Men* (1992) was distributed by Third World Newsreel. In 2007, her animation artwork *Las Olmecas* was included in *500 Years of Chicana Women's History*, edited by Elizabeth Martínez. She has lectured at numerous film festivals, seminars, community centers, and universities throughout California as well as nationally and in Mexico, Canada, and Europe.

ALEJANDRA MARCHEVSKY is director of Women's, Gender, and Sexuality Studies, professor of liberal studies, and affiliated faculty of Latin American studies at California State University, Los Angeles. She is coauthor, with Jeanne Theoharis, of *Not Working: Latina Immigrants, Low-Wage Jobs, and the Failure of Welfare Reform* (New York University Press, 2006). Her work has appeared in *The Nation*, *Boston Review*, *The Root*, *The Los Angeles Times*, the *Journal of American Studies*, and the *Journal of Sociology and Social Work*. She serves on the board of directors of CHIRLA, one of California's largest membership-based immigrant rights organizations.

In 1975 VIRGINIA MARTÍNEZ was one of the first Latinas to be licensed to practice law in Illinois. Virginia had the life-changing opportunity of participating in the 1995 UN Conference on Women in Beijing and is a frequent speaker on issues affecting Latinos, women, and children. Virginia has spent most of her career working in nonprofit organizations and has been a strong advocate for Latinos, women, children, and the poor. She was appointed to the Illinois Prisoner Review Board on March 8, 2017. She previously served as senior policy analyst for the Illinois Latino Family Commission, which advises the governor and legislators on issues that affect Latinos. She served as legislative staff attorney in the Midwest office of the Mexican American Legal Defense and Educational Fund (MALDEF). Earlier in her career she had opened the MALDEF Midwest office as its first regional counsel. Through that position, she was lead counsel in the historic redistricting cases of 1982 that created the first Latino Chicago wards and state legislative districts. She served as executive director of Mujeres Latinas en Acción from 1992 until 1997. She is the proud mother of Miguel and Natalia. Virginia is an avid dancer, a cake decorator, Reiki practitioner, and sporadic crafter.

ANNA NIETOGOMEZ was born in San Bernardino, California. She is a pioneering feminist activist, educator, editor, feminist speaker, poet, and writer. She was the publisher of one of the first Chicana feminist newspapers, *Hijas De Cuauhtémoc*, in 1971, and the first Chicana feminist journal, *Encuentro Feminil*, in 1973 and 1974. She is the author of a number of classic works of early Chicana feminism such as "La Feminista" and was among the first to teach Chicana studies, from 1972 to 1976, at California State University, Northridge, where she advocated through her publishing and pedagogy for Chicanas in higher education, addressed issues of women in prison, recognized Chicana community activists, and celebrated Chicana history. She was coeditor of one of the first Chicana studies curriculum guides. In 1977, she created and produced the "History of La Chicana" slide show, and she wrote the film script for *Chicana*, the first Chicana film, directed by Sylvia Morales in 1979. Throughout the 1970s, NietoGomez worked with many prominent Chicana leaders and organizations in Los Angeles, including Francisca Flores and the Chicana Service Action Center, Alicia Escalante and the Chicana East Los Angeles Welfare Rights Organization, and Carmen Duran and Las Mujeres Unidas in Van Nuys. She went on to obtain her master's in social work from the University of Southern California in 1981 and become a licensed clinical social worker for the California Department of Mental Health and for domestic violence counseling centers.

ANNEMARIE PEREZ is assistant professor of interdisciplinary studies at California State University, Dominguez Hills. Her specialty is Latina/o literature, with a focus on Chicana feminist writer-editors from 1965 to the present. Her interests include digital humanities and digital pedagogy work and their intersections and divisions within ethnic and cultural studies. She is working on a book on Chicana feminist editorship, using digital research to perform close readings across multiple editions and versions of articles and essays.

SAMANTHA M. RODRIGUEZ is professor of history at Houston Community College and a doctoral candidate in the Department of History at the University of Houston. Her research interests include relational social movement history, Chicana/o history, Chicana feminisms, African American history, borderlands, oral history, and U.S. South. Her dissertation relies heavily on oral histories to investigate the ways Texas Chicanas straddled a commitment to gender equality and ethnic self-determination within the broader matrix of the Chicana/o movement, the Black Power movement, and the women's liberation movement. She has served in public history initiatives including the TCU Civil Rights in Black and Brown Oral History Project. She also served as the 2014–2016 Chicana Caucus Co-Chair for the National Association for Chicana and Chicano Studies.

DEANNA ROMERO started her medicine journey as a child. In her family, she was the one who cared for the wounded or sick animals. She started massage at a young age to help her father, who had a herniated disk. With a lifelong desire to help people, she pursued a health professions career and soon found out the limitations of Western medicine. She became a physician's assistant in 1980, graduating from the University of Colorado Health Science Center Child Health Associate Program, and obtained a master's degree from the center. She has worked at the Pine Ridge Reservation Kyle Health Clinic in South Dakota, where she became an HIV specialist. She also has studied alternative medicine and *curanderismo*, neuromuscular massage, and therapy with essential oils. She resides in Denver and works for the community Salud Clinic. She is blessed with the love of her family and the arrival of her grandson, Orlando.

BRENDA SENDEJO is associate professor of anthropology and affiliate faculty in feminist studies and race and ethnicity studies at Southwestern University. Her work examines the history of Chicana feminism in Texas and contemporary manifestations of Chicana/Tejana feminist thought, such as the making of religious/spiritual traditions, histories, and identities in the Texas-Mexico borderlands. She developed two student-faculty collaborative oral history projects at Southwestern: the Latina History Project and Spirit Stories: Narratives of Social Justice and Spirituality. The projects bring undergraduate students together with Tejanas involved in social justice work since the 1960s and document Chicana feminist thought and praxis in Texas.

OLGA TALAMANTE became the first executive director of the Chicana Latina Foundation in January 2003. She is widely respected for her community activism and leadership in the Chicano, Latin American solidarity, LGBT, and progressive political movements. She gained national recognition in the 1970s as she participated in Argentina's political movement and as a result was tortured and held as political prisoner for sixteen months. Thanks to a national campaign, she was released and returned home in 1976. Some of her awards include Heroes and Heroines of the Latino Community from KQED-TV, the Diversity Award from *Hispanic Magazine*, the San Francisco Bay Girl Scout Council DAISY Award, and the Women Making History Award from the San Francisco Commission on the Status of Women. She was recognized as one of the most influential Hispanics in the Bay Area by the San Francisco Hispanic Chamber of Commerce and the *San Francisco Business Times*, awarded the Latino Heritage Community Award from the City of San Francisco, and most recently, given the Women Helping Women Ruby Award from the Soroptimist International of San Francisco.

STALINA EMMANUELLE VILLARREAL lives as a rhyming-slogan creative activist and is María Jiménez's daughter. Villarreal is a Generation 1.5 poet (Mexicana and Chicana), a translator, a sonic-improv collaborator, an instructor of English, a director of Mexican American/Latino studies at Houston Community College, and a doctoral student in creative writing at University of Houston. Her master of fine arts degree in writing is from California College of the Arts, and her bachelor's in studio art is from the University of Texas, Austin. She has published translations of poetry, including *Enigmas* by Sor Juana Inés de la Cruz (Señal: a project of Libros Antena Books, *BOMB*, and Ugly Duckling, 2015), and she translated *regiomontana* poet Minerva Reynosa's *Photograms of My Conceptual Heart, Absolutely Blind* (Cardboard House Press, 2016). Her visual poetry was part of the Antena Books exhibit during spring 2014 at University of Houston's Blaffer

Art Museum, where she displayed bilingualism, opaque queer erotica, interactive pinko materialism, and maximalism in four dimensions.

LETICIA WIGGINS earned her doctorate degree from the Ohio State University Department of History in 2016. Interested in the relationship between institutions, place, and activism, her dissertation focused on the Chicano movement (1970s–1980s) in the Midwest. The project serves as an intellectual history of the political ideas forming the basis of midwestern Latino/a activism within a unique regional and institutional context. Leticia has served as an editorial assistant for *Frontiers, A Journal of Women's Studies* and Ohio State's *Origins: Current Events in Historical Perspective*. She currently works to incorporate Latino stories into public media programming as a producer for the Emmy award-winning documentary series and community engagement project *Columbus Neighborhoods*.

INDEX